Irwin Allen's *Voyage to the Bottom of the Sea*:

The Authorized Biography of a Classic Sci-Fi Series

ALSO BY MARC CUSHMAN

Long Distance Voyagers: The Story of the Moody Blues
(in two volumes)
These Are the Voyages — Star Trek: TOS, Season One
These Are the Voyages — Star Trek: TOS, Season Two
These Are the Voyages — Star Trek: TOS, Season Three
Irwin Allen's Lost in Space: The Authorized Biography of a Classic Sci-Fi Series
(in three volumes)
I SPY: A History and Episode Guide of the Groundbreaking Television Series

Irwin Allen's *Voyage to the Bottom of the Sea*: The Authorized Biography of a Classic Sci-Fi Series

Volume 1

Marc Cushman

and Mark Alfred

Preface by Mark Phillips

Jacobs/Brown Press

Los Angeles and Frazier Park, California, and Clarksville, Tennessee.

LIBRARY OF CONGRESS CATALOGUING-IN-PUBLICATION DATA
Cushman, Marc
Irwin Allen's *Voyage to the Bottom of the Sea*: The Authorized Biography of a Classic Sci-Fi Series, Vol. 1
Marc Cushman and Mark Alfred; with foreword by Mark Phillips
Editorial team: Jim Alexander, Mike Clark, Mark Phillips, and Thomas C. Tucker
Publisher: Matthew Williams Brown
p.   cm.
Includes bibliographical reference and index

ISBN 978-0-9995078-2-7 (soft)
ISBN 978-0-9995078-3-4 (ebook)

First Edition – May 2018

Library of Congress Control Number: 2018941755
©2018 Marc Cushman. All rights reserved

Voyage to the Bottom of the Sea® and its characters and designs are © 20th Century-Fox Television and Legend Pictures, LLC, and licensed by Synthesis Entertainment. All rights reserved.
All photographs, script excerpts, artwork, contractual information, and transcripts taken from the Irwin Allen Archives are ©Legend Pictures, LLC, and used with permission, except where otherwise noted.
The Fantasy Worlds of Irwin Allen ® is a registered trademark of Synthesis Entertainment. All rights reserved.

This book is a work of journalism, protected under the First Amendment, with information presented under "fair usage" guidelines.

Queries regarding rights and permissions should be addressed to Jacobs Brown Press, P.O. Box 31152, Clarksville, TN 37040

No part of this book may be reproduced or transmitted in any form or by any means, electronic or mechanical, including photocopying or recording, or by any information storage and retrieval system, without permission in writing from the publisher.

Cover design: Zack Korn
Interior Design: Marc Cushman

First Edition softback manufactured in the United States of America

Jacobs/Brown Press
An imprint of Jacobs/Brown Media Group, LLC
Los Angeles and Frazier Park, California, and Clarksville, Tennessee
www.JacobsBrownMediaGroup.com

Marc Cushman says thank you:

To Irwin Allen

for daring to open the door for science fiction and fantasy on television; for winning the space race in TV; for opening eyes and minds everywhere.

To Kevin Burns

for supplying images, as well as information, interviews, and connections that made much of what follows possible.

To Mark Phillips and William Bailey

for their helpful and insightful contributions to this book.

* * *

Mark Alfred says thank you:

To those unafraid to look below the surface.

Acknowledgments

Beyond Kevin Burns, Mike Clark, Mark Phillips, Bill Cotter, and the late William Bailey, who contributed to this project with their research and interviews, the authors further appreciation to those who gave encouragement, guidance and support:

For their help during research in the Irwin Allen Papers Collection and *Voyage to the Bottom of the Sea* show files at the UCLA Performing Arts Library (since absorbed into the UCLA Special Collections Library), our gratitude to the staff.

To Ron Hamill for joining Marc Cushman in digging through the "Private" Irwin Allen Archives, archived by Legend Pictures; and to Derek Thielges of Legend Pictures / Synthesis Entertainment, for his invaluable aide.

For providing many of the Nielsen ratings for the original broadcasts of *Voyage to the Bottom of the Sea*, and other science-fiction series from that era, we are indebted to Kate Barnett at Nielsen Media Services, as well as Derek Thielges of Synthesis Entertainment.

A special "Thank You" to those who kindly granted interviews: Michael Allen, Roger C. Carmel, Angela Cartwright, Mike Clark, Paul Comi, Joe D'Agosta, Kevin Burns, James Darren, Barbara Eden, Harlan Ellison, David Hedison, Lew Hunter, Sean Kenney, Walter Koenig, Marta Kristen, Derek Lewis, Barbara "BarBra" Luna, Vitina Marcus, Steve Marlo, Bruce Mars, Don Marshall, Lee Meriwether, Lawrence Montaigne, Sean Morgan, Bill Mumy, Herman Rush, Malachi Throne, and Francine York.

Sadly, many of those who helped to make *Voyage to the Bottom of the Sea* possible are no longer with us. In an effort to include their voices in this work, we relied on hundreds of newspaper and magazine articles, as well as dozens of books. A full list of these sources can be found in the Bibliography, but we wish to give special mention here to the following books and their authors: *Irwin Allen Television Productions, 1964-1970*, by Jon Abbott; *Seaview: A 50th Anniversary Tribute to Voyage to the Bottom of the Sea,* by William E. Anchors, Jr. and Frederick Barr, with Lynne Holland; *Seaview: The Making of Voyage to the Bottom of the Sea,* by Tim Colliver; and *Science Fiction Television Series*, by Mark Phillips and Frank Garcia.

For those who have given their support and encouragement in other meaningful ways: James Alexander, Doug Diamond, Mike Makkreel, and, from Jacobs/Brown Media Group: Sondra Burrows, Andrew Johnson, Steven Kates, Susan Templeton, and Thomas C. Tucker.

TABLE OF CONTENTS

Foreword / Preface / Author's Note	xi
01: Introduction: Sci-Fi on the Screen … Before Irwin Allen	1
02: The Greatest Show on Earth	39
03: *Voyage* to the Box Office	135
04: From the Big Screen to the Small Tube	155
05: *Voyage* to Television: Premise and Pilot	169
06: Season One: ABC's Initial Order of 16	228
6-1: "Eleven Days to Zero"	228
6-2: "The Village of Guilt"	240
6-3: "The Mist of Silence"	255
6-4: "The City Beneath the Sea"	269
6-5: "Turn Back the Clock"	283
6-6: "Hail to the Chief"	297
6-7: "The Fear-Makers"	309
6-8: "Hot Line"	322
6-9: "The Sky Is Falling"	334
6-10: "The Price of Doom"	346
6-11: "Long Live the King"	358
6-12: "Submarine Sunk Here"	368
6-13: "The Magnus Beam"	378
6-14: "No Way Out"	393
6-15: "The Blizzard Makers"	405
6-16: "The Ghost of Moby Dick"	415
07: Fathoming Irwin Allen	326
08: Season One: ABC's Back Order of 16	436
8-17: "Doomsday"	436
8-18: "Mutiny"	447
8-19: "The Last Battle"	455
8-20: "The Invaders"	466
8-21: "The Indestructible Man"	474
8-22: "The Buccaneer"	481
8-23: "The Human Computer"	489
8-24: "The Saboteur"	496
8-25: "Cradle of the Deep"	506
8-26: "The Exile"	514
8-27: "The Amphibians"	525
8-28: "The Creature"	538
8-29: "The Enemies"	550
8-30: "The Secret of the Loch"	561
8-31: "The Condemned"	574

8-32: "The Traitor"	582
09: Wrapping Season One	592
APPENDIX A: The Composers of *Voyage*	602
APPENDIX B: Episode Quick Reference	610
Bibliography	620
Quote Index	630

Foreword

The night light was supposed to keep the robot away, but I knew the Indestructible Man was drawn to light. If it could tear the submarine Seaview's bulkheads apart, he could do a real number on my bedroom walls. It was this sense of exhilarating terror that first appealed to me about *Voyage to the Bottom of the Sea*. As a four-year-old during the 1964-65 season, I watched *Voyage* on Sunday afternoons on a Canadian channel. I vividly recall the rampaging plankton, Zar the merciless invader, the killer whale, and the expanding amoeba. I didn't frighten easily but there were two *Voyage* critters that really got to me – the robot of "Indestructible Man" and the two faceless monsters who cornered doomed crewman Peters in a later show, "Deadly Invasion."

I used to wear a sailor hat during our neighborhood toy gun battles and pretend I was a Seaview crewman. Yet, while I liked the *Voyage* regulars, I was too young to really form a bond with them. They were certainly heroic but rather undistinguished, which was OK. I recall Richard Basehart and David Hedison showing up in their black flight jackets on *The Mike Douglas Show* around 1966 and I couldn't have cared less; I went out to play. I also remember watching *The Bugs Bunny Show* and suddenly David Hedison popped up beside the rambunctious rabbit and urged kids to tune into *Voyage*! Captain Crane and Bugs Bunny? That dubious demographic may have explained why adults in my life didn't share my enthusiasm for the show.

When "Deadly Creature Below" aired on my uncle's TV in 1966, we were preparing to leave for dinner at the Hotel Vancouver. But after seeing the exciting Teaser, with the two-headed jellyfish attacking the diving bell, it was excruciating for me to have to leave and miss the show. Minutes after arriving at the prestigious hotel's dining room, we all heard the distant but familiar pings of the Seaview's sonar. With my urging, my puzzled grandfather took me into the lounge next door and there, playing on the big color TV set, was "Deadly Creature Below." Intently watching the show were many men and women, the trendy VIPs of Vancouver. Back at our table, my grandfather, who was a well-known Canadian politician himself, explained with astonishment what we had just seen – that these top business people were watching "Mark's show, the one about the submarine." My parents, uncle, and aunt could not believe it and they never forgot this incident. The guest villain of that episode was played by Nehemiah Persoff, who got a big kick out of this story when I told it to him years later.

Voyage ended its run on ABC in 1968 but I didn't notice. We had just moved to Creston, Canada and I figured such a remote mountain valley town didn't get the show. In spring 1970, a friend named Kenny had the bright idea of launching his Aurora Seaview model into a scum-covered pond. Bad move! He had a string attached to the sub, with a tiny Canadian flag glued to its hull. He gave the Seaview a push and into the water it went. It quickly rolled onto its side and sank. Kenny screamed and panicked, and he pulled sharply on the string, only for the sub to get caught on underwater debris. The string broke and Seaview was lost. We knew the pond was teeming with blood-sucking leeches and flesh-eating water beetles, so that scrubbed any salvage operations. Thirty years later, an Australian fan heard about this incident and emailed to ask me where the pond was? Did the pond still exist? Did I think the Seaview was still down here? He had researched a plane trip to Canada, and a car rental to drive to Creston but he needed instructions as to how to find the pond. I told him to belay this mission, that the pond had probably been paved over by developers years ago, and that ended that.

Voyage reruns were rare for me until 1977, when a major Seattle station ran all of the episodes. For the first time, I was able to evaluate the show from a more mature perspective. I appreciated the fine acting by the cast. Like James Cagney and Humphrey Bogart, the cast rose above thinly-drawn characters by projecting their own likeable personalities, thus making viewers care about them. The natural chemistry of the regulars provided true camaraderie. The lack of pretension in the stories and the superb special effects and model work were also great assets. I was surprised by how many good scripts there were in the first two years, although there were some bitter disappointments. The once terrifying Indestructible Man was now, sadly, a stumbling bucket of bolts. Episodes with budget-deprived invaders like the Shadowman or Heat Monster grew repetitious.

I recall my father watched several episodes with me in 1977 and he always caught episodes like "Wax Men" or "Return of Blackbeard." After watching "Terrible Toys," he said, "Why doesn't this show ever do any normal stories, like trying to break crush depth?" He couldn't understand why a state-of-the-art nuclear submarine was being menaced by a vindictive toy elephant. Months later, he happened to catch a b/w episode, "The Sky Is Falling," a thoughtful tale of Admiral Nelson establishing friendly relations with misunderstood aliens. As the episode ended, with a soaring affirmation of the alliance between humans and extraterrestrials, my father was deeply impressed. "That was a really good episode," he said. "What went wrong?" I was confused. "Nothing went wrong, Dad. Like you said, that was a really good episode." He replied, "Yes, I know. So what went wrong?"

Oh.

It did illustrate how *Voyage*, because of its inconsistent scripting and production values, attracted many slaps from a jaded media. A Seattle TV columnist sifted through the clutter of syndication in 1973 to declare that *Gilligan's Island*, *I Dream of Jeannie*, and *Voyage to the Bottom of the* Sea were the three worst series ever created in the history of television. To me, this kind of lazy analysis meant the critic had not done his homework.

However, not everyone had forgotten the show. An episode of *Baywatch* included a mention of the series and the query, "Hey, do you remember the one about the talking brain?" Mel Gibson performed a signature Seaview "rock 'n' roll" on *The Arsenio Hall Show*, and asked, "Do you remember *Voyage to the Bottom of the Sea*?" In 1981, the game show *Joker's Wild* featured a question about *Voyage* that was aced by a fashionable young lady contestant. In 1980, Merv Griffin called *Voyage* "a wonderful show," but maybe he had to, since David Hedison was his next guest. Comedian Tim Allen said *Voyage* was one of his favorite shows as a kid, "at least, until it got stupid." Ouch!

In her recent autobiography, Melissa Gilbert (Laura Ingalls on *Little House on the Prairie*) said that a highlight of doing her pioneer series was having Richard Basehart appear as a guest star. "He was a giant in my eyes for having starred as Admiral Nelson on *Voyage*," she said. David Duchovny once splashed around in a pool on Jay Leno's *Tonight Show*, to the accompaniment of Paul Sawtell's *Voyage* music theme. Even the Seaview once showed up as stock footage on a *Wonder Woman* episode – renamed Stingray, and was unceremoniously blown up by Lynda Carter.

When Bjo Trimble kidded Irwin Allen shows in a *Starlog* column in 1982, I wrote to her, outlining the many positive points of his productions. She wrote back a nice letter, conceding some things and suggesting I write for *Starlog*. Soon after, thanks to editor David McDonnell, I was fortunate enough to interview many of the writers, directors, and actors of *Voyage*. David Hedison was warm and funny; Allan Hunt (Riley) was super friendly (and what a memory he proved to have!); Terry Becker (Chief Sharkey) was candid and insightful; Del Monroe (Kowalski) was such a polite, genuine person, and Arch Whiting (Sparks) shared interesting reflections on fandom. Stuntman George Robotham was right when he told me, "The cast of *Voyage* were not only good actors but they were good people."

There were many off-the-record observations from various interviews over the years. One guest actor told me he was disturbed to see himself appear on *Voyage* as "stock footage" and he made sure Irwin Allen paid him for that. Costume designer-assistant to the producer Paul Zastupnevich, a very easy-going person, confided how he once stopped production of a *Voyage* episode because he was concerned a guest actor was not qualified to do a semi-stunt scene and, in the interest of safety, the man was replaced.

Several other people sent me unsolicited boxes of material, from rare production photos to unfilmed scripts like "The Abominable Seahorse." My best discovery was finding Ray Didsbury, who was not only Richard Basehart's stand-in but appeared in almost all of the 110 episodes, usually as "crewman Ray." He became a good friend and he gave me an amazing insider's view of making *Voyage* over the years. Some fans have stubbornly claimed that Didsbury did the main-title announcing for every episode, but Ray denied that. What he did do was 90% of the Seaview's intercom voices for the color episodes, usually as the damage-control voice.

Then there were the fans, in particular the late Mike Bailey. He was a radio DJ in Portland, Oregon, and had created a great *Voyage* website. This included rare photos, interviews, and Mike's own refreshing appraisal of a series he had grown up watching. We had a lot of fun reviewing all of the episodes for his website, offering contrasting opinions, such as for "Doomsday" and "Deadly Creature Below." Mike was a great friend with a terrific sense of humor. He was someone who had successfully pursued a career in broadcasting, raised a great family, and appreciated *Voyage*'s innocent yet durable charms. He would have loved this book, which, thanks to author Marc Cushman, is both entertaining and incredibly comprehensive. It's also fair and objective, a treatment *Voyage* has rarely received from the media. Marc's excellent research is an honor to a unique television series that is still playing around the world.

Mark Phillips,
January 2018

Preface

Was Irwin Allen a madman? Or did he lose sight of what his TV audiences wanted to see in his series? Was he just trying to please the networks? I often wondered these things.

Allen created fantastic and well-crafted television series in the 1960s, with *Voyage to the Bottom of the Sea*, *Lost in Space*, *The Time Tunnel*, and *Land of the Giants*. The first two were essential in opening the door for *Star Trek* and, therefore, many of the other non-anthology science-fiction series to follow. But *Voyage*'s third season and *Space*'s second season, both beginning in the fall of 1966, took a severe left turn, story-wise. They went from pseudo-adult sci-fi to kiddie fare; from semi-serious drama to silly monsters or, in the case of *Space*, out-and-out comedy. Allen's thinking was hard to fathom.

Surprisingly, there has been comparatively little information about Allen in books and genre magazines. And can one really trust what is found on the internet?

The books and fan websites which have appeared over the years present a sketchy, hazy and indistinct profile of the man. According to the spotty interviews available in these sources, many who worked for Allen during the 1960s described him as out-of-touch, egocentric, officious, loud, crass, cheap, volatile, meddling, controlling, infuriating, and downright impossible to work for. But how could he be all these things and yet gain the confidence of a major studio – 20th Century-Fox – and two American television networks – ABC and CBS? Would those institutions – managed by astute and successful entertainment executives – have entrusted four of the most daring and expensive prime-time television series of the 1960s to an out-of-control egomaniac?

It is curious and frustrating that a man of Irwin Allen's accomplishments, both in TV and on the big screen, has remained mostly unexplored … and unexplained. What *has* been written hardly provides any real insight into Allen's complex personality, or into the immense obstacles he faced in realizing his unprecedented television projects.

As the 1960s progressed, the dream of the conquest of space caught fire in the popular imagination, fueled by JFK's 1962 vow that the U.S. should reach the moon with a manned mission before the decade's end. At the same time, oceanographers, such as Rachel Carson in the 1950s and Jacques Cousteau in the 1960s, increased public interests in the exploration of Earth's "inner space." For that matter, so did "mind excursionists" like Timothy Leary. There were many frontiers awaiting exploration and exploitation on television. But could someone devise a salable approach and successfully present it to a network? And which of the three – ABC, CBS, or NBC – would be first to launch a weekly one-hour science-fiction series set in the future with a recurring cast? Such an undertaking would be the equivalent to making half a science-fiction movie per week.

While *The Twilight Zone* and *The Outer Limits* had proven there was an audience for TV sci-fi, that viewership had not been large enough to satisfy the networks. Quite simply, neither series had been a ratings winner. Further, as anthology shows, they faced a different and less demanding set of challenges than, say, a series like *Voyage to the Bottom of the Sea*. A serious "space" show – be it inner or outer space – with set characters, required an established format, costumes, and innovative sets, as well as costly and time-consuming miniature model work and/or photographic effects, *each and every week*. Surely only a madman, or somebody on a mission, would take on this kind of thing.

There were only two creator/producers who dared the challenge. Irwin Allen and Gene Roddenberry began their respective projects within months of one another.

Allen got a head start when his 1961 feature film, *Voyage to the Bottom of the Sea*, was retooled and proposed as a television series in August 1963. By April 1964, a pilot had been filmed and ABC had announced it was adding *Voyage* to its Fall schedule.

Meanwhile, Gene Roddenberry, coming off his cancelled series, *The Lieutenant*, had been imagining a second series – a science-fiction adventure called *Star Trek* – in March, 1964. By April – days before ABC made its announcement regarding *Voyage* – Roddenberry had Desilu Studios backing his project. *Star Trek* would eventually win the support of NBC, with the network co-financing the pilot film, "The Cage." It was made during late November and early December, 1964, two months after *Voyage* had premiered on ABC.

One can argue that Roddenberry drew from *Voyage*, changing a nuclear submarine into a warp-driven starship. Both shows had a nautical flavor, and both the Seaview and the Enterprise would alternate missions of scientific exploration with those of military might. What was important, to a network programmer's thinking, was that the immediate success of *Voyage to the Bottom of the Sea* proved there was indeed a mass audience beyond kids and "sci-fi kooks." This certainly factored into NBC's decision to order a second pilot for *Star Trek* – which went before the cameras in late July 1965.

By the time NBC had its second look at *Star Trek*, with "Where No Man Has Gone Before," *Lost in Space* was on the air and winning its Wednesday-night time slot for CBS. Irwin Allen had once again proved that a science-fiction series, even with expensive sets, time-consuming photographic effects, and recurring characters, could be produced for TV. And, for the second time in a row, he demonstrated that such a show could attract a large enough audience to satisfy Madison Avenue's advertising agencies. If not for the combined success of

Voyage to the Bottom of the Sea and *Lost in Space*, NBC might never have chosen to gamble in early 1966 by placing an initial order for 16 episodes of *Star Trek*.

Allen won the race, paving the road for much of what was to come, but he would never garner the respect awarded to Gene Roddenberry. The deck was stacked against Allen, since all of his series aired in the "Family Hour" and faced much greater restrictions as to the stories they could tell and the ways their characters could be portrayed. Allen then seemed to shoot himself in the foot, frustrating and mystifying a large segment of his audience when he altered the formats of his first two series. He seemed content to simply aim them towards undiscriminating children. Were the changes his idea, or were they forced on him by the TV networks?

A handful of books written for fans, *by* fans, have taken a loving look at *Voyage to the Bottom of the Sea* and *Lost in Space*, but many questions remained unanswered about both Allen and his formative sci-fi series. Worse, Allen's achievements have never fully been explored and acknowledged. We've tried to rectify these omissions, and solve the mysteries. Many answers can be found in this and a second volume in a two-book set covering *Voyage to the Bottom of the Sea*, and their sibling three-volume chronicle, *Irwin Allen's Lost in Space: The Authorized Biography of a Classic Sci-Fi Series*.

With these books, I believe that you will discover aspects of Irwin Allen's talent and vision that have not been previously explored … and maybe you will decide that there was a method to his madness after all.

Marc Cushman,
February 2018.

Author's Note

If you have read *Irwin Allen's Lost in Space: The Authorized Biography of a Classic Sci-Fi Series, Volume 1*, you may experience *déjà vu* when you encounter a pair of chapters in this book.

Chapter 1, "The Making of Irwin Allen – The Greatest Show on Earth," chronicles Allen's formative years and early career, setting the stage for the making of both the *Voyage to the Bottom of the Sea* 1961 feature film and its 1964 spin-off TV series. This chapter is a modified version of Chapter 1 in *Irwin Allen's Lost in Space: The Authorized Biography of a Classic Sci-Fi Series*, which is simply called "Irwin Allen." This information is vital in *any* narration of Allen's early career. Without this background, Allen's achievements lack their vital context.

As for the second instance of *déjà vu*, you will realize that this book's Chapter 8, "From Inner Space to Outer Space," duplicates material about the pilot of *Lost in Space* from Volume 1 of the book series devoted to that Irwin Allen project. Here we present an abridged version of that narrative, again necessary to appreciate Allen's audacity in juggling *two* such high-energy, demanding projects.

Lastly, regarding the TV ratings presented in this book:

A.C. Nielsen routinely prepared three different ratings reports each week during the 1960s. The first was a 12-City Trendix report, giving overnight ratings from the largest cities in the United States. A week later, Nielsen issued a 30-City survey report. A third report, with rural audience samplings included, was issued next, and identified as the "National Survey." There were also ratings surveys from Arbitron, *Variety*, and TvQ. Different reports of course give different numbers. The reports Irwin Allen chose to keep in his files were the 30-City Nielsen surveys. Those have been presented here, one for each episode.

1

Introduction: Sci-Fi on the Screen ... Before Irwin Allen

Judd Holdren and Larry Stewart in *Captain Video, Master of the Stratosphere*, the only movie serial based on a TV show – TV's first sci-fi series, *Captain Video and His Video Rangers*. (Columbia Pictures, 1951)

Of all the various media, television has routinely been the least hospitable to science fiction. It may not have been that way in 1967, the banner year for the genre on TV; there were nine series in prime time which fell in or around the sci-fi genre: *Voyage to the Bottom of the Sea*; *The Man from U.N.C.L.E.*; *The Invaders*; *Lost in Space*; *Batman*; *The Wild, Wild West*; *Star Trek*; *Get Smart*; and even *The Second Hundred Years*. *The Monkees* was also in prime time; despite being a pop-music sitcom, it featured a handful of episodes depicting mad-scientist types. You could argue that *Mission: Impossible* stretched its espionage format into borderline science fiction. When you add fantasy sitcoms like *Bewitched* and *I Dream of Jeannie*, the hybrid genre of "Fantastic TV" represented about 15% of the networks' programming. But this was not typical of most years. Jump back one decade to 1957; there was not one single science-fiction series in prime time. Jump ahead by two decades from 1967 and you'll find only two shows of this genre: the silly *Max Headroom* and the fledgling *Star Trek: The Next Generation*.

Yet science fiction had remained well-represented in print, and, except for a few "off years," in motion pictures. Irwin Allen loved to read and watch science fiction ... along with action/adventure.

In his early years, Allen was likely watching when Universal Studios had become a player in Hollywood, with its sci-fi-tinged horror films, commencing with 1931's *Frankenstein*, starring Boris Karloff. Costing $262,000 to make, *Frankenstein* earned back $12 million at the U.S. box office. *The Bride of Frankenstein* followed in 1935, turning a $400,000 cost into $2 million in revenue. Universal also made a tidy profit from its 1933 *The Invisible Man*, starring the mostly unseen Claude Rains. Paramount Pictures did well with *Dr. Jekyll and Mr. Hyde* in 1931, starring Fredric March in the dual role. The studio turned its production cost of $500,000 into a U.S. box-office take of $1.25 million. Fredric March's Oscar as Best Actor in *Jekyll and Hyde* was an added dividend. Another sci-fi motion-picture event from the decade was 1936's *Things to Come*, distributed by United Artists. Based on a book by H.G. Wells, it starred Raymond Massey, Ralph Richardson, and Cedric Hardwicke. The latter would work for Irwin Allen more than once. But where sci-fi really soared was in the movie serials – usually 20 minutes in length, in 12 to 15 chapters.

Jean Rogers and Buster Crabbe in *Flash Gordon*, the movies' first outer-space serial. (Universal Pictures, 1936)

The Vanishing Shadow, featuring invisibility rays and a robot, kicked it off in 1934 for Universal. But few serials were more fun than Universal's mighty *Flash Gordon*, starring Buster Crabbe, a two-time Olympic swimmer and 1932 Gold Medal winner. Presented in 13 chapters, with a budget of $27,700 each, *Flash* blasted off in 1936. Called "an unusually ambitious effort" by *Variety* at the time of its release, *Flash Gordon* was motion pictures' first action/adventure outer-space series. It was also one of the first serials designed to appeal to adults as well as children. The countless scantily-dressed Hollywood beauties – and even Buck in his short-shorts – provided eye-candy for ogling adults. Irwin Allen was 20 when *Flash Gordon* first hit the screen, and there can be little doubt that he was in the movie houses every weekend to catch the latest installment. Watch only the first four chapters of this first *Flash Gordon* serial and you'll see a stoic hero; action on top of action, speeding through the episodes at an exhilarating pace; shaven-headed Oriental-looking meanies (such as Ming the Merciless); hypnotism; interplanetary travel as well as voyages through inner space (underwater); ray guns; dragons walking upright (and looking very much like the one in *Lost in Space*'s "The Questing Beast"); crab men; aquamen (called "shark men" here); underwater fight sequences shot in a studio water tank (with the shark men, as well as with octopuses); a handy vessel called the "Hydro-Cycle," which is the spitting image of the "Flying Sub"; a giant octopus threatening the mini-sub; a city beneath the sea; an underwater chamber filling with water and threatening to drown our hero; the "space-o-graph" (video phone); and even lizards photographed to appear as giant dinosaurs, battling one another over which will get to eat Flash and Dale Arden (a sequence later emulated by Irwin Allen in *The Lost World*, and in the *Voyage* episode "Turn Back the Clock").

Also in 1936, while Universal focused on outer space, Republic Pictures turned towards inner space, with the 12-chapter serial *Underwater Kingdom*, starring Ray "Crash" Corrigan. You can't help but think that the future creator of *Voyage to the Bottom of the Sea* must have been watching.

Because of the success of *Flash Gordon*, Universal brought Buster Crabbe back for a sequel – 1938's *Flash Gordon's Trip to Mars* … in 15 chapters. In 1939, movie audiences got a third helping of Crabbe's journeys through the cosmos, this time as *Buck Rogers*, for a 12-chapter serial.

Above: Ray "Crash" Corrigan and C. Montague Shaw in lobby card for *Undersea Kingdom*.
(Republic Pictures, 1936)

There was also a sci-fi fiasco – the biggest genre bomb since Fritz Lang's 1927 epic *Metropolis* had bankrupted UFA, Germany's largest studio. The new giant misstep came in 1930, with Fox Film Corporation's *Just Imagine*, starring Maureen

3

O'Sullivan. If you will, just imagine a big-budget sci-fi-musical-comedy from that era. Not even the Marx Brothers could have rescued this one!

Hollywood blamed the genre for the film's failure, believing space operas could only work in the Saturday and Sunday daytime movie serials in which *Flash Gordon* and *Buck Rogers* thrived. For the evening audiences, along with song and dance, romance, adult drama, and either sophisticated or madcap comedy, horror movies instead of science fiction seemed the ticket. Some of these scare films, like *Frankenstein* and *The Invisible Man*, had a sprinkling of sci-fi, but there would be no more space adventures ... at least in feature films, for one very long decade.

Above: Maureen O'Sullivan and John Garrick feel a song coming on, in *Just Imagine*. (Fox Films Corporation, 1930)

To evaluate or understand what influenced and inspired Irwin Allen and his creations, we must know more about the media he experienced in his formative years.

Production of science-fiction movies and serials had gotten off to a promising start for the 1940s. There was more Buster Crabbe, with the 12-episode *Flash Gordon Conquers the Universe*. At the same time, Republic launched 15 chapters of *Mysterious Doctor Satan*, your run-of-the-mill mad scientist, with good-guy "The Copperhead" fighting on the side of truth and justice. Turning to feature films, Paramount had *Dr. Cyclops*; Universal served up Vincent Price as the new "now-you-see-him-now-you-don't fellow" in *The Invisible Man Returns*; and the studio exploited the gimmick even further with *The Invisible Woman*. For 1941, MGM released its own *Dr. Jekyll and Mr. Hyde*, with some of its biggest stars. Spencer Tracy played the title role(s), supported by no less than Ingrid Bergman and Lana Turner. It cost $1.2 million to make and earned back $2.3 million in its initial release. Despite this success, there were no other major science-fiction feature releases that year. The rest of the decade was even more anemic, with only movie serials representing the genre.

There was a reason for the slowdown, besides the money lost on *Just Imagine*. With the world at war, studios and movie patrons alike seemed more interested in either flag-waving, patriotic war films, or the outright escapism of comedy and fantasy. If there were going to be any mad scientists and megalomaniacal evildoers on the screen, let superheroes deal with them. This national mindset jump-started the superhero serials. They included *Batman* and *The Phantom* (both from Columbia, 1943); *The Masked Marvel* (Republic, 1943); *Captain America* (Republic, 1944); *Superman* (Columbia, 1948); and *Batman and Robin* (Columbia, 1949).

By the end of the 1940s, with so little science fiction on the movie screens, it might seem natural that the genre would find a home on the small screen. Not yet.

TV had been demonstrated at the 1933 Chicago World's Fair as a mere curiosity. It's estimated that in 1945 there were fewer than 10,000 TV sets in the United States. The primary reason was the economic strain of World War II, and various levels of rationing of common items, like gasoline, rubber, metal, food, and electronics. With the war's end in 1945, a period of affluence began … and birth rates in America shot up, starting the Baby Boomer generation. However, at the end of 1948, the total number of TV sets in the U.S. had risen to only about 38,000. They didn't come cheap: a new DuMont was around $500, for a 12-inch black-and-white screen. RCA and GE were charging over $300 for a mere 10 inches of monochrome picture. If you wanted something bigger, Admiral had a 16-inch screen to sell you … for a whopping $700. DuMont could put a 20-inch screen in your house … provided you could spare $2,500. That would be like shelling out $25,000 for a set in 2018.

The second hurdle in getting more Americans to buy TV sets was the lack of programming that was worth watching. Local TV productions were archaic in all ways, painfully stagnant and remarkably cheap-looking. And the networks, although with better production values, had very spotty schedules. It wasn't until the Fall of 1948 when the prime-time hours (7 to 11 p.m. Eastern Time) became somewhat filled with network offerings, driven mostly by America's first two TV networks, NBC and DuMont – both owned by companies which manufactured radio and TV sets. The nighttime schedule consisted of sporting events – especially ones which allowed easy camera coverage, such as boxing, wrestling, and roller derby; the man-at-a-desk news programs; a handful of live stage dramas, limited to a few stage sets; and panel shows, which Irwin Allen pioneered on TV (more about that later). Regardless of the bland fare, the increased broadcast content sparked television sales. By 1949, an average of 10,000 new TV sets were being sold each week.

As a result, for the second official TV season – 1949-50 – the caliber of TV programs improved. Now on NBC, live-from-New-York, were situation comedies, such as *The Aldrich Family* and *Life of Riley*; live hour-long dramas, like *Philco TV Playhouse* and *Texaco Star Theater*; and live puppet shows for the kids, namely *Kukla, Fran & Ollie*. For variety, CBS had Ed Sullivan's *Toast of the Town*, plus the pull-your-leg antics of *Candid Camera*. The great-great-granddaddy of today's *America's Got Talent* also premiered – a star-making vehicle called *Arthur Godfrey's Talent Scouts*. ABC countered with TV's first prime-time Western, *The Lone Ranger*, and three nights of *Roller Derby*. The smallest of the four networks – the only one without a radio network to provide a steady stream of crossover stars – was DuMont.

Since the manufacturing of TV sets was DuMont's lifeblood, it is not surprising that its network was early in going after the juvenile market. *Captain Video and His Video Rangers* premiered on June 27, 1949, on DuMont. Post Cereals and Skippy Peanut Butter picked up the tab, sponsoring *Captain Video* five nights a week (Monday-Friday, 7-7:30 p.m.), with a sixth weekly segment added on Saturday nights during the show's peak years. This 25-minute, super-cheap, broadcast-live series, was set in Earth's distant future. It presented the adventures of

Al Hodge and Don Hastings in *Captain Video and His Video Rangers*.
(DuMont Television Network, 1950)

Captain Video (played by jut-jawed Richard Coogan for two years, followed by the equally stolid Al Hodge). With him were his Video Rangers, who fought for truth and justice on behalf of the Interplanetary Alliance's Solar Council. They operated from their secret mountaintop headquarters, righting wrongs with ray guns (even though the show couldn't afford ray gun "beams"). Recurring adversaries included "I Tobor," which, when spelled backwards by the smarter kids, came out as "Robot 1." Other often-seen villains included Mook the Moon Man, Dr. Clysmok, Nargola (played by Ernest Borgnine before he became an Oscar-winning actor with *Marty*), and the "wily Oriental," Hing Foo Sung. So cheap was *Captain Video* that the weekly prop budget at first was only $25; cast members made more money from appearing at supermarket openings than from acting in the show. But that didn't stop this "first" from becoming an iconic event in American pop culture, for good reason – there were no sci-fi "space movies" released in the late 1940s, except for the serial *King of the Rocket Men*. This status, as TV's first sci-fi show, inspired a major story point in the October 1, 1955 episode of *The Honeymooners*. In "TV or Not TV," honorary Video Ranger Ed Norton drives Ralph Kramden nuts every weeknight at 7 p.m. by wearing a space helmet while watching *Captain Video* on the TV which the Kramdens and Nortons are supposedly "sharing."

Jackie Gleason and Art Carney spoof *Captain Video* on *The Honeymooners*.
(Columbia Broadcasting System, 1955)

So popular was *Captain Video* during its first year that ABC decided to get in on the "TV Space Race" too. With sponsorship from Peter Paul candy bars, the network turned to a sci-fi staple from the late 1930s – the Saturday-morning serial *Buck Rogers* – and restaged it for live Saturday-evening transmission. It began in April 1950, from 7 to 7:30 p.m., opposite the Saturday installment of *Captain Video*. Actor Kim Dibbs was the brand new *Buck Rogers*, protector of the universe, but few saw him. *Captain Video* already had a lock on the kids. For the Fall of 1950, ABC re-launched *Buck Rogers* on Tuesday nights from 8:30 to 9 p.m., with Robert Pastene in the title role). Adults, who controlled the TV dial at that hour, had little interest. This incarnation of *Buck Rogers* crash-landed after only four months.

Regardless of Rogers's fate, *Captain Video* was a TV sensation. This prompted some of Hollywood's motion-picture studios to consider offering sci-fi on the big screen once more. In 1950, Republic introduced the 12-part *Flying Disc Man from Mars*. On a slightly bigger scale, Lippert Pictures, one of the minors, released what was billed as "The screen's FIRST story of man's conquest of space!" It had been a close race to be "first," with the bigger Eagle-Lion Classics outfit readying a highly publicized space movie of its own, *Destination Moon* – promoted as being two years in the making! *Rocketship X-M* ("Expedition Moon"), on the other hand, was shot in only eleven days, and hurriedly premiered in New York City on May 26, 1950. Lloyd Bridges led the cast.

E.B. Radcliffe, longtime theater critic for *The Cincinnati Enquirer* was awestruck.

> ... Takeoff of five-story rocket ship, shots of events taking place in its interior when it changes from vertical to horizontal flight to gather speed for change of course to moon, and shots of ship interior with amazing assortment of gadgets are most interesting. ... A meteor bombardment of star dust is most exciting. ...

Moviegoers were eating it up. *The Brooklyn Daily Eagle* reported that *Rocketship X-M* was "getting off to a flying start with capacity audiences at every show." Louella Parsons wrote in her syndicated column: "*Rocketship X-M* did $19,000 business in less than a week at the Criterion in New York, which is wonderful for a movie which cost only $100,000 to make." It actually cost less – only $94,000.

Days later, *The Los Angeles Times* reported that a "ready-made audience awaits the science-fiction film, as packed houses and even waiting lines attested over the weekend at the astonished Orpheum, Hawaii, Forum, and Beverly Hills Music Hall." Moviegoers were rightfully starved for science fiction, and, when released across America weeks later, *Rocketship X-M* made *Variety*'s Top 10

National Boxoffice Survey list for three weeks, getting as high as No. 6. This kind of performance got Hollywood talking.

On June 24, 1950, nationally syndicated Hollywood columnist Jimmie Fiddler wrote:

> ... *Rocketship X-M*, made for peanuts as Hollywood budgets go, is a smash wherever it's shown, and it's a smash hit for the very obvious reason that it is something new and different in screen entertainment. Every foot of its film is a challenge to the imagination of those who see it.

"Harvey in Hollywood" predicted: "Look for a rash of science-fiction, rocket and man-on-the-moon pictures now that Lippert's *Rocketship X-M* is doing such great business at the box-office. Western actors may have to learn to point up when they say, 'They went that-a-way.'"

Just as *Voyage to the Bottom of the Sea* would open the door for *Lost in Space*, and *Star Trek*, this modest film deserves notice for its historical significance. It was the first space movie to be launched in post-World War II America, and all of Hollywood was watching. Another minor "first" for *X-M*: Its score, by classical composer Ferde Grofé, was the first science-fiction movie to feature the warblings of the Theremin.

Adding to the clamor was advance publicity for *Destination Moon*, which had been meticulously made by rising sci-fi "star producer" George Pal.

As an animator, Pal made a name for himself in the 1940s with the "Puppetoons" series, which won him an honorary Oscar in 1943 for "the development of novel methods and techniques in the production of short subjects." This success enabled Pal to make the 1950 fantasy-comedy, *The Great Rupert*, a feature-length film which combined animated squirrels with flesh and blood Hollywood actors, notably Jimmy Durante. Pal's next movie – only his second feature – was *Destination Moon*, released on June 27, 1950. It had been made for under $600,000, but went on to gross $1.3 million in the U.S., with a total worldwide box office of $5 million. The reviews were mostly positive.

Even the stuffy critics couldn't help but like this new spin of science fiction. Bosley Crowther, in *The New York Times*, conceded:

> ... [W]e've got to say this for Mr. Pal and his film: They make a lunar expedition a most intriguing and picturesque event. Even the solemn preparations for this unique exploratory trip, though the lesser phase of the adventure, are profoundly impressive to observe.... but, most of all, it is exciting to climb aboard the ship with those four men... to wiggle and squirm with them in agony as their silver tube roars into space, and to join in their general amazement at the various phenomena which occur. It is even a little amusing to watch the inevitable comic character float about in non-gravitational freedom when he becomes a "free orbit," whatever that means. And the emergency necessity for the scientists to go outside their ship (in their inter-space suits) to do repair work while the ship is in flight, cues quite a scene. ...

One small step for man, one giant leap for motion pictures: *Destination Moon*.
(George Pal Productions / Eagle-Lion Films, 1950)

(Nearly all of these space-travel highlights would show up later in "The Reluctant Stowaway," the premiere episode of Irwin Allen's *Lost in Space*.)

The icing on the cake was an Oscar for Best Special Effects, and a Hugo Award for Best Dramatic Presentation. More importantly, for fans of science fiction, the one-two punch of *Rocketship X-M* and *Destination Moon* successfully changed Hollywood's attitude about the genre, blazing the spaceways for what was to come.

It took television to prompt the return of science fiction to the big screen. As always, the influence became reciprocal.

The Fall of 1950 saw the number of TV sets in the U.S. up to 3,880,000, now in 9% of U.S. homes. NBC introduced the innovative comedy *Your Show of Shows*, starring Sid Caesar and Imogene Coca, plus suspense programs transmitted live, such as *Lights Out*, and music shows, like *Your Hit Parade*. On CBS, a singing cowboy rode the range into American's living rooms, on *The Gene Autry Show*. For the older crowd, there was *The Frank Sinatra Show*, as well as the first of the prestigious anthologies, *Studio One*, and, partly thanks to Irwin Allen's innovation, a slew of panel shows: *Beat the Clock*, *Truth or Consequences*, and *What's My Line?* ABC took a page from the comic books, with a "live" version *Dick Tracy* (sans the costly sci-fi gimmicks and props). The network also continued to do well with *The Lone Ranger* (a Top 10 rated series). Science fiction got a boost on television this year, too.

Tom Corbett, Space Cadet, inspired by Robert A. Heinlein's 1948 juvenile novel, *Space Cadet*, premiered October 2, 1950 on CBS. The show was created to cash in on the popularity of DuMont's *Captain Video*, and scheduled from 6:45 – 7 p.m., three times a week, right *before* the start time of *Video* (at 7 p.m.). It was only 15 minutes in length (minus commercial time), but, with the backing of CBS, *Tom Corbett* had more money to spend on its sets, props, blastoffs, sequins, and instances of weightlessness. The spaceship Polaris – and viewers occasionally got a look at the thing – flew on the network for three months, before the series moved to rival network ABC in January 1951. Once there, still in a 12-minute format, and still three nights a week, the series stayed space-bound for a year and a half (through September 1952). Future *Voyage to the*

Left to right: Frankie Thomas (Tom Corbett), Al Markim (Astro), and Jack Grimes (T.J. Thistle), in *Tom Corbett, Space Cadet*. (Rockhill Productions, 1950)

Bottom of the Sea guest star Jan Merlin ("No Way Out," "The X Factor," and "Death from the Past") was a regular on *Tom Corbett*, playing the wisecracking cadet Robert Manning ("Aw, go blow your jets!").

Space Patrol was the fourth series to take a trip into outer space on network TV. It had actually hit the air on March 9, 1950 as a Saturday-morning offering in the Los Angeles area, then received a pickup from the ABC network on December 30th. The show proved popular enough to make the move to "pre-prime time" on Saturday, June 9, 1951, programmed from 6 to 6:30 p.m. ABC used it as a lead in for DuMont's *Captain Video*.

Set in the 30th century A.D., *Space Patrol* starred real-life WWII flying hero Ed Kemmer, as Cmdr. Buzz Corey, the leader of the patrol. Of course, he had a young sidekick, Cadet Happy, who was given such wide-eyed exclamations as "Smokin' rockets,

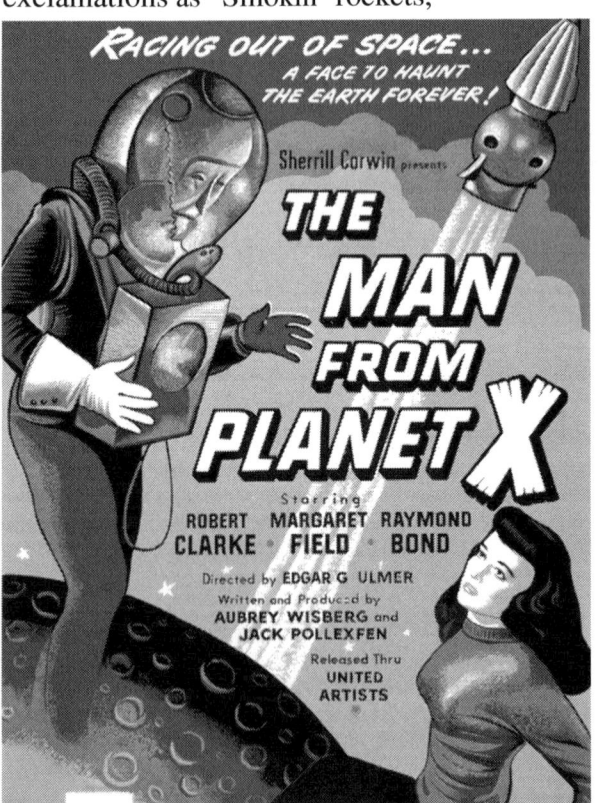

Clockwise: Ken Mayer, Ed Kemmer, Lyn Osborn, Virginia Hewitt, and Nina Bara, in *Space Patrol*.
(American Broadcasting Company, 1950)

Commander!" The patrol battled the villains of the cosmos on behalf of the United Planets of the Universe ... until ABC cancelled the flight following its June 1, 1952 airing.

Films took the lead in 1951 for science fiction, a year which brought several classics. Up first was *The Man from Planet X*, independently produced on a shoestring budget of $51,000, then picked up for distribution by United Artists. It earns its place in pop-culture history for being the third post-World War II sci-fi themed feature film ... and the first of these movies to make Earth the

12

target. Herb Rau reported in March 1951: "It's a switch from the usual plot in that, instead of having American scientists exploring space, a visitor from another planet lands upon this world."

The budget was modest, with a small cast, limited locations, and only one alien (and its rocket) in sight. But it grossed $1.2 million in its first year.

Many Hollywood producers wanted to get a piece of this action before the novelty wore off. Irwin Allen was one; he was starting to move away from the melodramas and comedies he had been producing up to this point, branching out into films exploring science, evolution, and, soon after, science fiction and fantasy.

No sooner had *The Man from Planet X* landed in the movie houses when, on April 6, 1951, RKO Radio Pictures released *The Thing from Another World*. It was produced by one of Hollywood's favored filmmakers – Howard Hawks – who had made numerous big hits, such as *Bringing Up Baby*, *His Girl Friday*, *Sergeant York* (for which Hawks received an Oscar nomination, as Best Director); *The Big Sleep*, and *Red River*. His latest, *The Thing*, cost $1.6 million, and, like most of Hawk's films, struck box-office gold. It grossed $4.2 million by year's end, making it the biggest money-maker of all the science fiction movies from 1951. It also garnered predominately positive notices. The tone of these reviews gives clear indication of just how big of a shot to the arm sci-fi was giving to the movies.

James Arness as *The Thing (from Another World)*. (RKO Radio Pictures, 1951)

E.B. Radcliffe, of *The Cincinnati Enquirer*, raved, "It's the most refreshing fun in movie watching I've had in I wouldn't know how long!"

The New York Times's Bosley Crowther wrote:

> Well, it arrived yesterday at the Criterion and it certainly is something. *The Thing*, as Howard Hawks calls his new movie, is quite a show, folks. Not since Dr. Frankenstein wrought his mechanical monster has the screen had such a good time dabbling in scientific-fiction. ...

Gene Handsaker, of the Associated Press, reported:

... Bullets can't harm him. Chop off his arm, and he grows a new one. He even starts to grow a new body on the severed arm! Fantastic, of course, but only the beginning …. The thing has no blood inside it, but it feasts on blood … [and] it can produce acres of offspring. …

Phillip K. Scheuer, of *The Los Angeles Times*, was giddy:

… The most delicious shudders are provided by a scene in the laboratory, after the head scientist has planted shreds of the Thing's arm (which has been torn off by sled dogs) and nurtured them with blood plasma. What do the shreds do but start sprouting a whole garden of new baby Things – Things that breathe and give off little crying sounds!

A few months later, on September 18, 1951, another major studio – this time 20th Century-Fox – entered the invasion-from-space game with *The Day the Earth Stood Still*, directed by Robert Wise (other Wise films: *West Side Story*, *The Sound of Music*, *The Sand Pebbles*, and *Star Trek: The Motion Picture*). Bernard Herrmann wrote the spine-tingling score, which was later used by Irwin Allen in the TV version of *Voyage to the Bottom of the Sea*, as well as *Lost in Space* and *The Time Tunnel*. Michael Rennie, the star of the movie, appeared for Allen in the feature *The Lost World*, and on TV's *The Time Tunnel* and *Lost in Space*.

Edwin Schallert, of *The Los Angeles Times*, noted that *The Day the Earth Stood Still* was "quite a picture. It's more than simply a thriller. It has a sociological and philosophical side, besides being vastly interesting and exciting."

Irwin Allen wasn't much interested in the sociology or philosophy; he was drawn to the excitement, and the chills induced by the Bernard Herrmann score, which he later sampled. Something else Allen likely paid attention to: *The Day the Earth Stood Still* cost under $1 million to make, and grossed nearly two million. It was the second biggest money-making sci-fi of the year, outgrossed by only *The Thing*. Also noteworthy, the film won the Golden Globe award as "Best Film Presentation," and was nominated for a second – for Herrmann's score.

Paramount Pictures had George Pal's second sci-fi feature film, *When Worlds Collide*, out on November 15, 1951. It featured several name players, including Richard Derr, Barbara Rush, and John Hoyt.

Donald Kirley, film critic for *The Baltimore Sun*, called *When Worlds Collide* "another excellent specimen of science fiction."

Helen Bower, of the *Detroit Free Press*, raved:

> There can be no doubt about George Pal's pre-eminence as a producer of science-fiction movies. ... Tidal waves flood the canyons of New York streets and surge over tropic islands. Torrents boil through mountain passes. Dead volcanoes come alive in bursts of fiery lava. Arctic ice cliffs fall into chill, surging seas. ...

Irwin Allen must have been envious, and eager to join the ranks of sci-fi filmmakers. In only a few years' time, we would see just about everything Bower described show up in *Voyage to the Bottom of the Sea*, both the film and the TV series, and other productions from Allen, such as *Dangerous Mission* and *The Lost World*.

Joe FitzGerald, of Nebraska's *The Lincoln Star*, was also awestruck by the effects, and their "spectacular demonstration of what can happen when the Earth crosses orbits with a star running amok." He enthused:

> ... One of the exciting themes under consideration is the possibility of human life surviving on another planet. The film states that it can be done, and shows a space ship filled with refugees from doomsday on Earth successfully making its way to another world.

Allen would do the same with *Lost in Space*.

Emulating the fleeing hordes of the film, moviegoers were running to their local movie houses. Edwin Schallert reported in the November 23rd edition of *The Los Angeles Times*:

> Evidently it takes a scientific thriller to prove that movies are still the favored entertainment of a large segment of the public. *When Worlds Collide* seems to be the picture especially to demonstrate this. Audiences flocked to see it yesterday at the Paramount Theater downtown and the Hawaii in Hollywood. Such lines as foregathered to wait a chance to view the film have seldom been seen in later days at any show house in the center of the city. The Paramount was packed for the evening screenings, and the Hawaii did equally notable business.

These were not just neighborhood theatres. The Hawaii in Hollywood had 1,106 seats; the Paramount was more than three times that size – the biggest in Los Angeles, with 3,600 seats. As Schallert reported, it was packed, screening after screening.

Irwin Allen saved newspaper clippings with statistics of this type, as he relentlessly researched popular trends and tracked box-office performances and TV ratings, not only for his own films and television programs, but for the stats concerning his competitors, as well. While he was stuck making smaller-budget contemporary pictures for RKO at this time, spectacles like *When Worlds Collide* were exactly the splashy movies Allen aspired to make.

The same week in which *When Wolds Collide* premiered, "poverty row" studio Monogram Pictures released *Flight to Mars*, depicting a trip to the forenamed planet by a group of four scientists and a newspaperman. No women were along for the ride this time, and it was a good thing: The Martians had plenty of alluring beauties of their own to tempt the Earthmen. *The Los Angeles Times* review noted:

> ... [I]f masculine viewers of the film believe what they see in the way of femme beauty on Mars, there's going to be a scramble even among scientists to find a way to the distant planet. Especially as the gals all wear tights, like fugitives from the Follies.

Capping the year for science fiction in the movie houses was Lippert Picture's November 23rd release of *Superman and the Mole Men*, introducing George Reeves as the Man of Steel – and actually shot by a TV unit, as an advance look at a new series being readied for television.

Beginning on the B-side of a double bill, *Superman and the Mole Men* toured the nation slowly over a 12-month period, gradually gaining stature and becoming the top half of the bill.

On the TV side, come August 3, 1951, ABC premiered a series to attract adult sci-fi fans: the 30-minute anthology *Tales of Tomorrow*, running from 9:30 to 10 pm, Fridays.

The Billboard, in its August 18, 1951 issue, opined:

> *Tales of Tomorrow* is a commendable attempt to integrate mystery and science fiction – aim being to produce a show with the former's fast pace and the latter's suspense. The idea has prolific possibilities audience-wise, since mystery fans are legion and science fiction devotees form the current wonder market of the publishing and movie industry.

Among the tales were "The Monsters"; "The Search for the Flying Saucer"; "The Crystal Egg," based on a story by H.G. Wells; and a two-part episode based on Jules Verne's *20,000 Leagues Under the Sea*. Guest stars included Lon Chaney, Jr. (playing the Frankenstein monster), Lee J. Cobb, Eva Gabor, Boris Karloff, Veronica Lake, and Leslie Nielsen. The show's budget was kept on the skinny side; many episodes were aired live from the East Coast, with kinescopes broadcast three hours later for the West Coast. Contrary to the predictions from the Hollywood trades, the series did not attract a mass audience. It alternated with other series, until its final episode on June 12, 1953.

For the 1951-52 TV season, there were now 10.3 million TV sets in the U.S., three times as many as one year earlier – and these sets could be found in 23.5% of American homes. Variety shows remained top of the heap, followed by situation comedies, panel shows, and stage dramas, shot by giraffe-size TV cameras which were barely mobile. *I Love Lucy* premiered in this season and jumped right into the Top 10. Even though it was perfect for a juvenile audience, it was mostly adults watching, since the show didn't air until after 9 p.m. The small fry still had *Kukla, Fran & Ollie*, *The Lone Ranger*, a new panel show called *Quiz Kids*, and, as the sole sci-fi offering, *Captain Video*, now down to five nights a week on DuMont. Despite its immense success the previous year, the genre was in short supply on the big screen, too. Republic had another serial in distribution, *Radar Men from the Moon*, and one about aliens who come to Earth – *Zombies of the Stratosphere*, with a very young Leonard Nimoy in a minor part. And Peter Graves starred in a low-budget movie handled by UA called *Red Planet Mars*.

The following year, for the 1952-53 TV season, there were 15,000,000 TV sets in America, now in 34% of U.S. homes. *I Love Lucy* hit No. 1, remaining there for the next several years. Adults were also gathering around the TV to watch *Dragnet*, No. 2 in the year-end ratings. Jack Webb's police show also won Emmy Awards a few years in a row as Outstanding Drama Series. *The Jackie Gleason Show*, with its "The Honeymooners" skits, was also hot, and more accessible for young viewers, as it aired Saturdays at 8 p.m. Meanwhile, sci-fi was about to take a big leap forward.

On September 19, 1952, syndicated to stations across America, *The Adventures of Superman* took to the air, the first sci-fi TV series shot on film. Cereal maker Kellogg's sponsored the show, which had begun filming in 1951. The series' first two seasons were shot in black-and-white, while Seasons Three through Six were filmed in color. *Adventures of Superman* was also TV's biggest budgeted sci-fi to date – with a stupendous (for its time) budget of $15,000 per episode. (That equates to $140,000 in 2018, just about enough to make an episode of a lower-end reality show.)

TV critic Gene Plotnik wrote in the November 1st issue of *The Billboard*:

> The popularity of "Superman" in the past 15 years is legendary. That the current litter of kids will flock to the new TV-film series is a better than good bet. The "superman" concept is a perennially attractive one for modern pre-adolescents, and the vidpic, which Kellogg is spotting in 52 markets, is as faithful to the original as you can get. First of all, George Reeves, former Mr. America, is the spitting image of the comic-strip drawing of Clark Kent-Superman. He has the same dark wavy hair and square face. And he's hefty enough to look as if he can bend those bars. Second, the opening of each segment uses the same copy that the old radio series made famous ("Faster than a speeding bullet ... it's a bird, a man," etc.), only here it's accompanied by visuals. And, finally, the scripts are based on the same thrillers used in the other media, which present Superman as the irrepressible champion of the common man.

The series immediately jumped into the Top 10 in nearly every market. In Pittsburg, it hit No. 10, with a 33.5% audience share; in Buffalo, *Superman* soared to No. 5, with a 32.9% share; in Denver it was No. 1, with 32.5%; in Charlotte, it landed at No. 7, with a 30.9 share; in Philadelphia, the Man of Steel was No. 1 on the day the show aired, carrying away 36.9% of the total viewing audience. So sudden was the success – faster than a speeding bullet – that George Reeves, as both Clark Kent and Superman, had the cover of *TV Guide*'s September 25, 1953 issue. The show was soon airing in 80 markets, including 25 ABC affiliates – making for a hybrid part-syndicated-part-network series. A year later it was on 130 stations across America; a year after that, in 167 markets.

Contrary to folklore, *The Adventures of Superman* was not cancelled in 1957 after six seasons. It merely suspended production, while continuing to air in prime time, repeating the episodes already filmed, and now on nearly 200 stations. Kellogg's had come to realize that the reruns drew as many viewers as the first-run episodes, so it declined to incur the cost of new productions until the market demanded it. By 1959, two seasons of new adventures were being planned when George Reeves tragically died, under circumstances which created a real-life Hollywood mystery … as yet unsolved.

George Reeves and Phyllis Coates in *Adventures of Superman*. (Motion Pictures for Television, 1952)

The Golden Era of 1950s big-screen sci-fi – usually in the form of B-films – kicked into gear in 1953. The year started with the February 4th premiere of 20th Century-Fox's *Invaders from Mars*. Its story of a 12-year-old protagonist (Jimmy Hunt) who encounters Martians certainly resonated with youngsters, as the young hero can't find any grown-up to take his story seriously. Its depiction of alien abductions and behavior-controlling implants may have inspired these concepts in pop culture and UFO circles. The critic for *The Los Angeles Times* was also intrigued by the story of the boy's parents, "captured by the invaders from Mars and controlled through radio gadgets installed in their brains." This idea also found its way into an episode of *Voyage to the Bottom of the Sea*.

Days later, on February 11th, United Artists released *The Magnetic Monster*, produced by Ivan Tors, and starring Richard Carlson. The new Dr. Frankenstein for the 1950s was the atomic scientist. The one in this movie creates, as John L. Scott of *The Los Angeles Times* phrased it in his review, "an all-consuming element that eats up energy from its surroundings and doubles in size every eleven hours." Perhaps there was no coincidence that Richard Carlson was cast as a Frankenstein type who experiments to enlarge the size of fish in "Village of Guilt" on *Voyage to the Bottom of the Sea*. The idea of a substance doubling in size every several hours was used to threaten the Seaview for the *Voyage* episode, "Cradle of the Deep."

A few weeks later, on February 28th, Paramount Pictures unleashed an invading army of Martians for H.G. Wells's *The War of the Worlds*. This was the third big science-fiction movie from producer George Pal, this time directed by Byron Haskins (who later played a part in getting both *The Outer Limits* and *Star Trek* off the ground). *Boxoffice* predicted: "Inasmuch as for some time the screen has been free of so-called space operas – of which so many were popular and profitable a few months back – there is every reason to predict that this will be one of the most widely discussed and generously patronized among upcoming features." *Variety* called *The War of the Worlds* "a socko science-fiction feature," saying, "The George Pal production tops by a wide margin his previous film ventures into the realm of space." *The Los Angeles Times* called the film "the finest of science-fiction thrillers." Paramount spent $2 million making *The War of the Worlds*, which starred Gene Barry. It made back $4,360,000 in U.S. rentals alone; more than double its cost and ranked as the second-biggest money-maker of all the sci-fi films in release during the year. And there were awards – an Oscar, for its Special Effects, and a Hugo, as Best Dramatic Presentation.

On April 7th, *It Came from Outer Space* showed up on Earth in movie houses. Directed by Jack Arnold (who would helm numerous iconic science-fiction films in the years to come), it was taken from a story treatment by Ray Bradbury. The Universal-International film, released in 3-D, starred Richard Carlson (again), and featured Barbara Rush, Charles Drake, and Russell Johnson (later the Professor from *Gilligan's Island*). The movie had an opening similar to the *The War of the Worlds*, with what is thought to be a meteor strike in the Arizona desert, but turns out to be a spaceship. A short time later, townspeople disappear, taken over by duplicates from space. This is the first use of the sci-fi doppelganger device, later to be used numerous times by Irwin Allen, and in films like *Invasion of the body-Snatchers*. Made for $800,000, *It Came from Outer Space* brought in $1.6 million at the box office. Barbara Rush won a Golden Globe for her acting here, as "Most Promising Newcomer, Female," and the film was nominated for a Hugo Award, as Best Dramatic Presentation.

The sci-fi films were coming fast and furious by summer. On June 17th, Warner Bros. released *The Beast from 20,000 Fathoms*, with a no-star cast but one hell of a monster. Fred Freiberger, later to produce one season each of *The Wild, Wild West*, *Star Trek*, and *Space: 1999*, wrote the script, whose beginning was inspired by Ray Bradbury's "The Fog Horn." As the movie had it, an experimental atomic blast in the Arctic region

It took a whole lot of stop-frame animation from Ray Harryhausen to create *The Beast from 20,000 Fathoms*. Here the Rhedosaurus threatens New York City, before terrorizing riders on a roller coaster. (Warner Bros., 1953)

was to blame for the "unfreezing" of the strange prehistoric reptile of the dinosaur family. *Boxoffice* said: "This highly exploitable thriller about a prehistoric monster has thrills and shocks to put even the famous 'King Kong' in the shade. … These scenes are startlingly realistic and will have many patrons screaming." *Variety* said, "The sight of the beast stalking through Gotham's downtown streets is awesome. Special credit should go to Ray Harryhausen for the socko technical effects, including the beast itself and the destruction of buildings as the monster causes a serious panic in lower Manhattan."

Made for $210,000, the film grossed $5 million, the top-grossing sci-fi film of 1954. It was also validated with a Hugo nomination, as Best Dramatic Presentation of the year. That award, as reported, went to *The War of the Worlds*.

There were also plenty of cheapies. On July 16th, Republic released the 12-episode serial *Commando Cody: Sky Marshal of the Universe*. The title tells you all you need to know about this one, except for one bit of sci-fi trivia: Cody and his deputy sky marshals had badges which doubled as communication devices – 30 years before *Star Trek: The Next Generation*.

The low-budget features included, on August 7th, Hammer Films' *Spaceways* (distributed in the U.S. by Lippert, starring Howard Duff). On September 3rd, Astor Pictures had *Cat-Women of Mars* and *Robot Monster* paired together (the latter made for $50,000 and grossing $1 million). One day later, Galaxy Pictures had *Project Moonbase*, with screenplay by sci-fi author Robert A. Heinlein.

Calling *Commando Cody: Sky Marshal of the Universe*: Aline Towne and Judd Holdren test their badge communicators. (Republic Pictures, 1953)

On September 30th, United Artists released another of 1953's bigger sci-fi attractions, *Donovan's Brain*, starring Lew Ayres. It was directed by Felix Feist (later to direct for *Voyage*).

For the 1953-54 TV season, with 20,400,000 boob tubes now in 44.7% of U.S. homes, ABC put *Sky King* in the air, and moved *The Adventures of Ozzie and Harriet* over from the radio; Wally Cox played *Mr. Peepers* on NBC, while Milton Berle got viewers to laugh until it hurt by putting on a dress. CBS found belly laughs with the *George Burns and Gracie Allen Show*, *Topper*, and *Our Miss Brooks*. DuMont, losing affiliates to the bigger three networks, was beginning to sputter out. Half its prime-time schedule went dark, and *Captain*

Video was cut to 15 minutes per night. Elsewhere on the video sci-fi front, CBS, with the support of Jell-O Instant Pudding, tried another juvenile space show, coming up with the 30-minute-long *Rod Brown of the Rocket Rangers*, for a 13-month run on Saturdays (April 18, 1953 to May 29, 1954). The series followed the adventures of the Rocket Rangers, operating from Omega Base, and traveling throughout the solar system in their nuclear-powered spaceship, the Beta. Rod Brown was played by none other than a young Cliff Robertson, with bespectacled comic relief, Wilbur "Wormsey" Wormser (Jack Weston). What set this one apart from the other serialized space shows is that most of its stories were "stand-alone" episodes. A lawsuit from the makers of *Tom Corbett* shortened Rod Brown's galactic journeys after 58 episodes.

A new *Flash Gordon* series was produced for the 1953-54 TV season and sold into syndication. Like *The Adventures of Superman*, the new *Flash Gordon* was shot on film, with three days spent making each episode, at a cost of $15,000 each. In the title role, Steve Holland faced danger as

Above: Cliff Robertson, in *Rod Brown of the Rocket Rangers*.
(Columbia Broadcasting System, 1953)
Below: Sally Mansfield and Richard Crane in *Rocky Jones, Space Ranger*.
(Roland Reed Productions)

an agent for the Galactic Bureau of Investigation, travelling the cosmos in his spaceship, the Sky Flash. This flight ended 39 episodes later.

On February 23, 1954, yet another 30-minute syndicated sci-fi series, filmed rather than beamed live from the East Coast, was sold into syndication. *Rocky Jones, Space Ranger*, played by Richard Crane, was a "space policeman" who patrolled the United Worlds of the Solar System. The 39th and final episode aired on November 16, 1954.

For 1954, and in the movie houses on January 14th, Richard Carlson and lovely Dawn Addams starred in Ivan Tors's *Riders to the Stars*, for United Artists. *Picturegoer* magazine in England set the scene:

Three young scientists, each in a jet-propelled rocket, make a journey into outer space to capture a meteor, cruising along at about 20,000 miles an hour. One scientist collides with his meteor; another panics and jumps overboard – to float in space for eternity. The third brings home the prize.

Variety called *Riders to the Stars* "intelligently handled," and *Boxoffice* said, "From every angle this is easily one of the best of the science-fiction films produced to date."

Next, premiering on January 23rd, Peter Graves was the star of RKO's *Killers from Space*. The reviews were mixed, at best. In February, Universal-International was first out with Jack Arnold's *Creature from the Black Lagoon*. It really wasn't a science fiction; just an old-fashioned monster movie, which brought in a tidy $1.3 million at the box office. Curvy Julia Adams's swim in the lagoon almost made viewers forget the rock-jawed hero, Richard Carlson. Staying with the water theme, in May 1954, was Lippert Pictures' *Monsters from the Ocean Floor*, the first sci-fi/horror movie from Roger Corman. Made for a very cheap $30,000, it grossed $850,000, and Corman was on his way. In the spring, Ivan Tors and UA thrilled audiences with a killer robot named *Gog* ... in 3-D, no less. In June, for the first big sci-fi release of the year, Warner Bros. had giant mutated ants invading cities in *Them!*, with James Whitmore and James Arness and a cast of thousands . . . of ants. It received an Oscar nomination for its radiated insects, and some good reviews – *The Los Angeles Times* called it "an ingenious thriller." Even more important, it racked up $2.2 million in U.S. rental fees. Mere days after the ants were set loose by Warner Bros., Republic Pictures unleashed *Tobor the Great*, starring Charles Drake ... but he didn't play Tobor; a stuntman was needed for that role. Here's a hint: Spell "Tobor" backwards and you'll get the joke – perhaps the screenwriters had been watching *Captain Video*! (Tobor, by the way, was designed and built by Robert Kinoshita, who also gave us Robby the Robot in *Forbidden Planet*, and the Class B-9-M-3 General Utility Non-Theorizing Environmental Control Robot. You know him as Dr. Smith's "bubble-headed booby" in *Lost in Space*.)

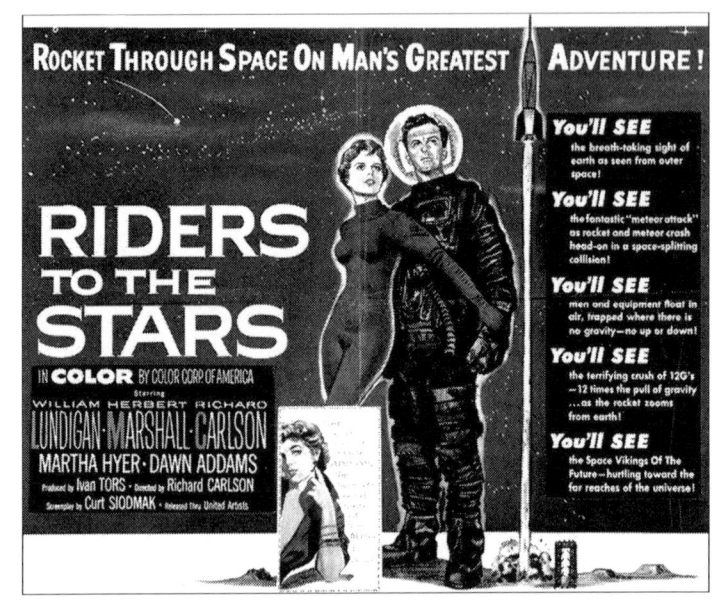

Starting November 7th, Republic sponsored an invasion of robots from the planet Venus, attacking Chicago in Allied Artists' *Target Earth*. The shots of the deserted city streets foreshadow "The Day the Earth Ended," an eerily effective third-season episode of *Voyage to the Bottom of the Sea*.

In time for Christmas, 1954, Walt Disney's production had Jules Verne's *20,000 Leagues Under the Sea* in movie houses, with Kirk Douglas, Peter Lorre, and, as Captain Nemo, James Mason. It cost $5 million to make and grossed over $28 million in U.S. release alone.

The same man who designed the *Lost in Space* robot for Irwin Allen built the title character of *Tobor the Great*.
(Republic Pictures, 1954)

For the 1954-55 TV season, *Disneyland* (later named *Walt Disney's Wonderful World of Color*) became a Top 10 contender. Children of all ages became hooked on such mini-series within the show as "Davy Crockett" and "Swamp Fox." Also on ABC, a new show for the kids: *The Adventures of Rin Tin Tin*. Another show about a heroic canine, *Lassie*, premiered on CBS. And the network put *Father Knows Best* on the air, but, curiously, at 10 p.m. on Sundays. DuMont, on its last legs, cut half its programming, and trimmed *Captain Video* down to 12 minutes per evening. There were now an estimated 26,000,000 TV sets in America, putting the new media into 55.7% of U.S. homes.

Nineteen Hundred and Fifty-Five was another banner year for science fiction in the movie houses. Director Jack Arnold and Universal-International got things going with *Revenge of the Creature*, featuring the return of the Gill Man from the Black Lagoon. It would bring the studio $1.1 million at the U.S. box office. In April, George Pal and Byron Haskins were back, with Paramount's *Conquest of Space*, in Technicolor. It earned a million bucks at the box offices. Also in April, British Lion Films had *Devil Girl from Mars* come to Earth to repopulate her race. The tight top and leatherette skirt worn by Patricia Laffan as Nyah, the Devil Girl, made many adolescent males ready to pack their bags. In June, Ed Wood Jr. had a movie in circulation – *Bride of the Atom*, starring Bela Lugosi as a mad scientist, with Tor Johnson as his mute, strong-arm man. Wood made it for $70,000. *Variety*, to nobody's surprise, labeled it "an amateurish effort which even the least discriminating audience will find dull."

Summer was better. U-I had a classier and more costly entry, *This Island Earth*. It starred Jeff Morrow and Rex Reason, with Faith Domergue (who had worked for and dated Irwin Allen in the late 1940s). It cost $800,000 and earned back $1.7 million. Columbia Pictures had *It Came from Beneath the Sea*, also starring Domergue, this time with Kenneth Tobey. Sounding like an episode from *Voyage to the Bottom of the Sea*, it involved "a new atom submarine," encountering a horrible marine monster under the Pacific waters. It cost $150,000 and netted $1.7 million. The studio also released *Creature with the Atom Brain*, starring Richard Denning. Roger Corman, beginning his relationship with American International Pictures, had *The Beast with 1,000,000 Eyes*.

Above: Patricia Laffan as Nyah, in *Devil Girl from Mars*. Was this the model for Francine York's Niolani in *Lost in Space*'s "The Colonists"?
(British Lions Films, 1954)
Below (L-R) Faith Domergue, Rex Reason, and Jeff Morrow, in *This Island Earth*.
(Universal-International Pictures, 1955)

It cost $33,000 (some sources say only $23,000). A-I had another Corman cheapie – *It Conquered the World*. In the fall, Universal had *Tarantula*, about a big spider (injected with a formula that makes it grow), and a big box office of $1.1 million in the U.S. With American Releasing Corporation, Corman brought out *Day the World Ended*, for a cost of $94,000, as part of a double bill with *The Phantom from 10,000 Leagues*.

TV couldn't match the scope of these sci-fi movies, even though many were considered B-films. For the 1955-56 season, CBS brought to America the British-made *The Adventures of Robin Hood*, an immediate hit, at No. 20 in the year-end Nielsens (and at the same position for the following year). The network also presented *Sgt. Preston of the Yukon*, perfect for the family hour, and, later in the night, billed as "the first adult western," *Gunsmoke*, forever rescuing James Arness from future roles in monster movies. *The Lone Ranger* was still going strong on ABC, as was *Topper, Disneyland*, and *The Adventures of Rin Tin Tin*. And a new one: *The Life and Legend of Wyatt Earp*, leading into Danny Thomas's *Make Room for Daddy*. NBC inherited *Father Knows Best* from CBS and wisely put it in an earlier time slot and continued to get the whole family together for Groucho Marx on *You Bet Your Life*.

After its final broadcast, a boxing match on August 6, 1956, DuMont went dark. Now there wasn't a single science-fiction show on TV. But one network's sign-off didn't mean television was losing its audience. There were now an estimated 30,700,000 TV sets in America, plugged into 64.5% of U.S. homes.

In the movie houses, 1956 started off with Allied Artists' *Invasion of the Body Snatchers*, costing $416,911, and grossing $3 million. In March, there was a dark sci-fi from Columbia Pictures, with George Orwell's *1984*. One week later, MGM did the genre right with the excellent *Forbidden Planet*, starring Walter Pidgeon, Leslie Nielsen, Warren Stevens, and Robby the Robot, all of whom went on to work for Irwin Allen. Anne Francis also starred. The studio spent a hefty $1.98 million, making back 2.76 million, and helping to inspire *Star Trek*. *Forbidden Planet* is also notable as the first movie with an entirely electronic score.

Anne Francis and Robby the Robot in *Forbidden Planet*. (Metro-Goldwyn-Mayer, 1956)

The studio did better – though in black-and-white – with *Earth vs. the Flying Saucers*, which memorably featured one alien ship crashing into the Capitol dome and another amputating the Washington Monument. The film grossed $1.25 million in the U.S., partly thanks to Ray Harryhausen's superb model work for the saucers. From 20th Century-Fox came another sci-fi A-picture, *On the Threshold of Space*, starring Guy Madison and Vivien Leith. The movie earned back its $1.5 million with its initial U.S. release. Universal-International was aiming lower, with Jeff Morrow and Rex Reason reunited for *The Creature Walks Among Us*, and another cheapie – *The Mole People*, starring John Agar and

Above: The classic *Earth vs. the Flying Saucers*. (Columbia Pictures Corporation, 1956)

Hugh Beaumont. A bit more of a tease was a film out of England: *Five Maidens of Outer Space*. A U.S./Japanese co-venture, *Godzilla, King of the Monsters!* featured Raymond Burr as the token American "star," cut into the original 1954 film. It cost $650,000 to make and earned $2 million in the U.S. alone. Allied Artists had Lon Chaney, Jr. as *The Indestructible Man*, and, to better returns, the classic *Invasion of the Body Snatchers*, starring Kevin McCarthy. The studio also released *World Without End*, in CinemaScope and Technicolor. After expenses of $417,000, the film earned back $3 million at the U.S. box office. Meanwhile, Roger Corman was back, and he had Peter Graves, in the American International Pictures release, *It Conquered the World*.

For the 1956-57 TV season, the networks continued to ignore science fiction. It was a pretty big snub, considering there were now an estimated 34,900,000 TV sets in 71.8% of American homes. And those homes were filled with kids, consumers primed to welcome the future.

For the young, NBC programmed *Tales of the 77th Bengal Lancers*, *Circus Boy* (with Micky Dolenz, later one of the Monkees), and the *Adventures of Sir Lancelot*. ABC, doing well with *The Lone Ranger*, *Rin Tin Tin*, and *Wyatt Earp*, premiered more Westerns: *Cheyenne*, *Broken Arrow,* and *The Adventures of Jim Bowie*. CBS gave America *The Phil Silvers Show* (aka "Sgt. Bilko"), *My Friend Flicka*, and people "loved that Bob" on *The Bob Cummings Show*.

There were too many science-fiction movies released in 1957 to mention them all. The genre was peaking. Some of the biggest were:

Universal-International had a mini-classic, *The Incredible Shrinking Man*, starring Grant Williams locked into a cycle of diminishing returns. It cost $750,000 and made $1.43 million at the U.S. box office;

Above: Grant Williams flees his doll house in *The Incredible Shrinking Man*.
(Universal International Pictures, 1957)
Below: The ultimate Volkswagen Beetle customization, in Roger Corman's *Attack of the Crab Monsters*. (Allied Artists, 1957)

Columbia Pictures journeyed *20 Million Miles to Earth*; and also set loose *The Giant Claw*, with Jeff Morrow as a jet pilot fighting a giant anti-matter bird in the sky (a scrawny critter considered one of the worst "special effects" ever);

American International Pictures released *The Amazing Colossal Man*, and *Invasion of the Saucer-Men*;

Allied Artists unleashed *Attack of the Crab Monsters*, from Roger Corman (with $1 million in U.S. rentals) – infamous for its monster made from a Volkswagen Beetle – and, on the double bill, another Corman film, *Not of This Earth*, costing $100,000 and sharing in that cool million in returns;

29

Republic Pictures' *Beginning of the End*, starring Peter Graves, this time against giant grasshoppers (a result of radiation exposure, of course);

Universal-International had *The Deadly Mantis*, with Craig Stevens (of TV's *Peter Gunn*) fighting the giant praying mantis; and

MGM released *The Invisible Boy*, with Richard Eyer (as "Timmie") and, from *Forbidden Planet*, that menacing Robby the Robot.

For the 1957-58 TV season, more eyes were trained toward the small screens. The estimates now said that 38,900,000 sets were plugged into 78.6% of U.S. homes. Of the Top 25 series, according to A.C. Nielsen, nine were westerns, with *Gunsmoke* leading the pack at No. 1. The other favorites were *Tales of Wells Fargo*, *The Life and Legend of Wyatt Earp*, *The Restless Gun*, *Cheyenne*, *Zane Grey Theater*, *Wagon Train*, and *Sugarfoot*. Families could come together for other top-rated shows that season, such as *The Danny Thomas Show*, *You Bet Your Life*, *Alfred Hitchcock Presents*, *The Red Skelton Show*, *Father Knows Best*, and *Lassie*. New to ABC, a prime-time version of *American Bandstand*, along with *The Real McCoys*, *Zorro*, and, from 7:30 to 8 p.m. on Fridays, *Leave It to Beaver*. But, again, not a single sci-fi property was seen on the networks.

Above: MGM marketed their new star, Robby the Robot, with child actor Richard Eyer, in *The Invisible Boy*. (M-G-M, 1957)

The science-fiction boom in movie houses and drive-in theaters continued into 1958. It was a stellar year, producing some wonderfully cheesy – and some not-so-cheesy – classics. Some of the top big-screen attractions in the genre included:

Allied Artists Pictures' *Attack of the 50 Foot Woman*, starring curvy Allison Hayes, in a 1950s-type bikini no less. The flick was made for $89,000 – enough young boys and their fathers rushed off to see it that it earned $480,000 in the U.S.; Paramount Pictures' *The Blob*, starring Steve McQueen. It was shot for $110,000 and quickly earned back $4 million. Also: *Queen of Outer Space*, with Zsa Zsa Gabor as the alien queen (re-using *Forbidden Planet* costumes); *The Space Children*, about a brain from outer space that can communicate telepathically with children; *I Married a Monster from Outer Space*, starring Gloria Talbott as the not-so-happy Earth bride; and American International's *The Brain Eaters*, starring Ed Nelson, and featuring Leonard Nimoy in the cast; Paramount Pictures' *The Colossus of New York*, in which Ross Martin's brain is transplanted into a frightening cyborg, with a touching scene in which the cyborg meets the man's unwitting daughter; 20th Century-Fox's *The Fly*, starring David "Al" Hedison, future co-star of *Voyage to the Bottom of the Sea*, and Vincent Price; RKO's *From the Earth to the Moon*, starring Joseph Cotton and George Sanders, the latter to guest-star in an episode of *Voyage*; and United Artists' infamous *It! The Terror from Beyond Space*, starring Marshall Thompson, about the first mission to Mars, and the monster that sneaks aboard the rocket ship before it blasts off for home – the movie that inspired *Alien*. On the down side, the costume worn by Ray "Crash" Corrigan as "It" was so ill-fitting that the actor's chin stuck out through the mask's open mouth!

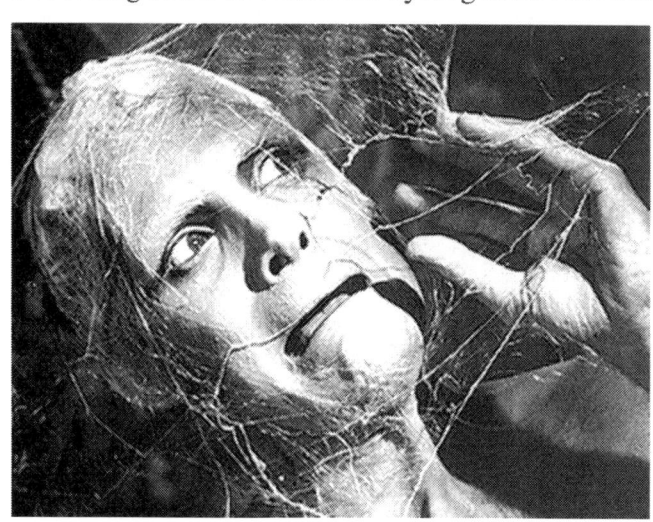

David "Al" Hedison in *The Fly*. (20th Century-Fox, 1958)

TV continued to steer clear of science fiction for the Fall of 1958. Westerns were much cheaper to make and seemed to appeal to the young just as well, or so the networks rationalized. New to NBC: *Bat Masterson*, *Restless Gun*, and a show that sounded like a Western but wasn't, *Peter Gunn*. New to CBS: *Trackdown*. New to ABC: *The Lawman*, *Colt .45*, and a non-western for hip teens: *77 Sunset Strip*. The reason for the continuing sagebrush stampede: Among newer shows to make A.C. Nielsen's Top 25 were *Have Gun – Will Travel*, *The Rifleman*, *Maverick*, *The Texan*, and *Wanted: Dead or Alive*, joining the staples *Gunsmoke* and *Wagon Train* (the No. 1 and No. 2 rated series, respectively). The audience was spreading like a prairie fire, too. Estimates said there were now 41,920,000 TV sets in operation, showing up in 83.2% of U.S. homes. The picture-tube invasion was in full swing.

What TV couldn't – or wouldn't – do, the movies were happy to provide. In 1959, 20th Century-Fox had one of the biggest, with Jules Verne's *Journey to the Center of the Earth*, starring James Mason and Pat Boone. It cost $3.44 million but returned $10 million in U.S. rentals alone. Fox also let loose *Return of the Fly*, with Vincent Price. United Artists aimed high with *On the Beach*, starring Gregory Peck, Ava Garner, Fred Astaire, and Anthony Perkins, in a story about a U.S. nuclear submarine in the months following World War III, sailing from Australia to an annihilated North America in response to an S.O.S. signal. This plot would

Vampira and Tor Johnson in *Plan 9 from Outer Space*. (Distributors Corp. of America, 1959)

have made one hell of an episode for *Voyage to the Bottom of the Sea* (though probably the *final* one!). Universal-International put out *4-D Man*, starring Robert Lansing and, later of *The Time Tunnel*, Lee Meriwether, and *Monster on the Campus*, with Troy Donahue and Whit Bissell (also later in *The Time Tunnel*). American International had *The Angry Red Planet*, starring Gerald Mohr, later to guest-star in numerous Irwin Allen TV shows, including *Voyage*; Allied Artists released *The Atomic Submarine*, foreshadowing *Voyage to the Bottom of the Sea*. MGM had Marshall Thompson as the *First Man into Space*; Columbia Pictures presented The Three Stooges in *Have Rocket – Will Travel*; Warner Brothers had their hands full with *Teenagers from Outer Space*; and Valiant Pictures distributed Ed Wood's wonderfully awful *Plan 9 from Outer Space*, with Bela Lugosi, Vampira, and Tor Johnson. In the words of the Amazing Criswell's introduction from *Plan 9*, "We are all interested in the future, for that is where you and I are going to spend the rest of our lives. And remember, my friend, future events such as these will affect you in the future."

New on TV in the Fall of 1959: *Dennis the Menace*; *Richard Diamond, Private Detective*; *The Rebel*; *Bronco*; *Laramie*; *The Donna Reed Show*; *Rawhide*; *The Many Loves of Dobie Gillis*; *Bonanza*, and a series starring David Hedison – *Five Fingers*. TV audiences continued to grow. There were, approximately, 43,950,000 TV sets, and they had infiltrated 85.9% of U.S. homes. And some of those people could finally watch science fiction in their homes, for the first time in years.

Ziv Television had been having great success in making half-hour TV series directly for the syndicated market, most notably *The Cisco Kid* (1950-56), starring Duncan Renaldo as TV's first Hispanic hero; *I Led 3 Lives* (1953-56), which starred Richard Carlson, later a *Voyage to the Bottom of the Sea* guest star, as a F.B.I. agent hunting Communists in America; *Highway Patrol* (1955-59), staring Broderick ("10-4") Crawford; and *Sea Hunt* (1958-61), starring Lloyd Bridges, who made a career in TV swimming around in a studio water tank before David Hedison and Richard Basehart. In 1959, Ziv tried its luck with a half-hour filmed sci-fi series made for CBS ... until the network decided to sell it into syndication. *World of Giants* starred Marshall Thompson (later of *Daktari*) as an American spy who, while on a covert operation, is accidentally shrunk to a height of six inches. Trying to make the best of a bad situation, he uses his small size to infiltrate places a standard-sized secret agent could not. Something tells us Irwin Allen may have liked this one – but if he blinked, he may have missed it. *World of Giants* only lasted 13 weeks.

Above: Below: A little Marshall Thomas has a big problem in *World of Giants*.
(Ziv Television Programs, 1959)
Below: Nancy Gates and William Lundigan in *Men into Space*. (Ziv Television Programs, 1959)

Ziv had another sci-fi series up its sleeve but waited until later in 1959 to get the support of a network – CBS – before attempting *Men into Space*, which was produced with the cooperation of the U.S. Army, Navy, and Air Force, as part of a joint American government effort to raise public awareness of the very real space race. The series starred

William Lundigan as Col. Edward McCauley and chronicled his adventures on a U.S. moon-base installation, a government space station, and in a rocket ship which took him to other planets within our solar system. The ambitious show, aimed more at adults than kids, was programmed just outside the family hour, on Wednesday nights, 8:30 to 9:30. Thirty-eight episodes were made before this particular space program was cancelled at the end of its one season (1959-60).

Days after the high-profile, government-endorsed *Men into Space* premiered on CBS, sci-fi got a legendary boost when the same network premiered *The Twilight Zone*. No one, however, including the network, thought it would amount to anything. The only reason the show made it onto the air is because of the man behind it.

Starting in 1952, Rod Serling had been one of the busiest writers in films and television, having had 85 of his scripts produced by 1959. Serling was not only prolific, but revered. His 1956 *Playhouse 90* episode, "Requiem for a Heavyweight," had won him an Emmy, a Writers Guild of America Award, and a Peabody Award. One year earlier, he'd won an Emmy for the *Kraft Television Theater* episode, "Patterns," and was nominated for "The Champion," which aired on *Climax!* In 1958, he won a third Emmy for the *Playhouse 90* presentation of "The Comedian." In 1959, he was nominated a fifth time for an Emmy, for another *Playhouse 90* – "A Town Has Turned to Dust." With these accolades, CBS had been pursuing Serling to create and host an anthology series of his own (and to write as many of its episodes as he possibly could). The show Serling chose to make, to the horror of CBS, was *The Twilight Zone*, which used sci-fi, fantasy, and downright weirdness to shake viewers up. The network reluctantly took the show but scheduled it between 10 and 10:30 p.m. on Friday nights – the "death slot."

Rod Serling, master of *The Twilight Zone*.
(Cayuga Productions / CBS, 1959)

So looked-down-upon was *The Twilight Zone* that Mike Wallace, interviewing Serling for CBS on September 22, 1959, just days before the series premiere, said, "[Y]ou've given up on writing anything important for television. Right?"

Wrong. During the five TV seasons in which *The Twilight Zone* was in production – racking up 156 episodes – Serling won two Emmys for scriptwriting and was nominated for another. He also won three Hugo Awards. The series garnered a third Emmy for its cinematography and was nominated during one season as "Outstanding Program in the Field of Drama." But it could never win in the area CBS most desired – the TV ratings race. The reason that *The Twilight Zone* lasted five seasons in its terrible Friday-night time period is that the network didn't expect *any* show to do well on that night, at that hour … and Serling's show was not only winning awards but bringing CBS a bit of prestige too.

With science fiction finally on television – and that included many of those 1950s monster pictures showing up on local TV stations – the movie studios started reducing the number of genre releases in 1960. Another factor in the cutback was that second-run science-fiction movies – especially those cheap monster flicks – could be booked into movie houses for weekend exhibition, keeping the latest crop of pre-teens content.

Rod Taylor in *The Time Machine*. (Metro-Goldwyn-Mayer, 1960)

Of the handful of new sci-fi movies made in 1960, 20th Century-Fox released Irwin Allen's *The Lost World*, which cost $1.5 million but made back $2.5 million at U.S. box offices. Metro-Goldwyn-Mayer had the top contender with George Pal's take on H.G. Wells's *The Time Machine*. It starred Rod Taylor and Yvette Mimieux, cost around $850,000 to make, and earned back $2.6 million in its first year. Columbia Pictures had *12 to the Moon*. American International Pictures released *Beyond the Time Barrier*. Roger Corman had a wonderful exploitation title, *The Last Woman on Earth*. And Paramount played it strictly for laughs when it released *Visit to a Small Planet*, starring Jerry Lewis. The film threw the arch, satirical intent of Gore Vidal's original play out like old dishwater. Still, its North American box-office take, $3.2 million, was nothing to laugh at.

Was the sci-fi boom over? Hollywood seemed to think so. The glut of monster films from the 1950s (and we didn't even mention the horror tales) had resulted in a backlash. Usually when things run their course on the big screen, they move to the small one. Despite *The Twilight Zone*, TV was still playing hard to get.

For 1960-61 on television, Westerns still ruled the roost, with *Gunsmoke*, *Wagon Train*, and *Have Gun – Will Travel* coming in at No. 1, 2 and 3, respectively. Right under them was a show geared for the whole family: *The Andy Griffith Show*. Also in the Top 25 shows as rated by A.C. Nielsen: *The Flintstones*, *The Many Loves of Dobie Gillis*, and *My Three Sons*. After the small ones went to bed, Mom and Dad could relax with something a bit less juvenile, such as *The Untouchables*, *The Jack Benny Show*, or *Perry Mason*. There were plenty of viewers to go around; the statistics reported that 87.1% of U.S. homes had at least one TV set.

By 1961, science-fiction filmmaking in America had ground almost to a stop. Only eight titles were released, and one of those had been filmed in 1958. MGM had a George Pal movie – *Atlantis, The Lost Continent*. Disney had *The Absent-Minded Professor*, with Fred MacMurray. And 20th Century-Fox had Irwin Allen's *Voyage to the Bottom of the Sea*. The movie was profitable, but didn't make as much on its initial release as Allen and Fox had hoped for, causing both to rethink making more big-budget science fiction movies for the big-screen.

Despite the drop-off of interest in Hollywood, some good science-fiction movies were being made outside of America. For instance, *Mysterious Island*, based on a Jules Verne story, with British money, was filmed in Spain and England, and distributed by Columbia.

With the 1961-62 television season, another Western had pushed its way toward the top. *Bonanza* was No. 2 in the ratings, sandwiched between *Wagon Train* and *Gunsmoke*. The family was gathering around the TV set (and most homes only had one) to enjoy *Hazel*, *Candid Camera*, and *Car 54, Where Are You?* And teenage girls were now stuck on Richard Chamberlain's *Dr. Kildare* and Vince Edwards's *Ben Casey*. The younger kids still had Barney Fife of *The Andy Griffith Show*, *Dennis the Menace*, *The Flintstones*, and a dog named *Lassie* among the Top 20 shows to enjoy each week. Also in for a long run on CBS: *Route 66* and *The Defenders*. It was reported that 88.8% of American homes had TV now. And that brought the number of TV sets to 47,200,000.

On the big screen in 1962, there were only a handful of science-fiction movies. *Journey to the 7th Planet*, from American International Pictures, starred John Agar. Also from AIP: *Panic in Year Zero!*, starring Ray Milland and Frankie Avalon. Disney made fun of it all, with *Moon Pilot*, starring Tom Tryon and Brian Keith.

For the 1962-63 TV season, *The Beverly Hillbillies* shot to the top of the ratings. A more sophisticated style of humor was offered in the Top 10 hit, *The Dick Van Dyke Show*. Science fiction got another boost on television in the Fall of 1962 when ABC premiered *The Jetsons*. It was geared for kids – it was a cartoon, after all – but adults enjoyed the show too. Regardless, it lasted just one season, with 24 half-hour episodes. On other channels, Lucy was back on Monday nights (after a divorce with Desi), in her own series, *The Lucy Show*.

Incidentally, by this time, an estimated 90% of U.S. homes had TV sets.

In 1963, Jerry Lewis, and Paramount Pictures, released *The Nutty Professor*. A classy, and somewhat frightening, sci-fi film from England called *The Damned* made its way to America. And there were more monster movies from Japan.

For the Fall of 1963, *The Fugitive* began his four-year run from the law, on ABC. A millionaire was solving crimes on *Burke's Law*. Gene Roddenberry's first series (as a producer) was on NBC. It was called *The Lieutenant* and starred Gary Lockwood and Robert Vaughn. World War II broke out on television with the excellent *Combat!*, trenching in for a five-season run (nearly four years longer than American soldiers actually fought in France and Germany). And, while *The Twilight Zone* was still out of sight for most Baby Boomers in

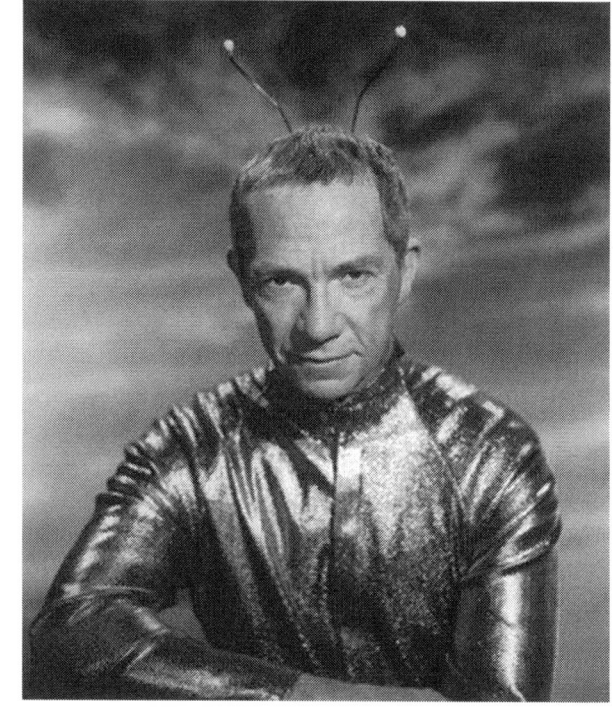

Ray Walston in *My Favorite Martian*.
(CBS Television Network, 1963)

its late prime-time slot, CBS put a show on the air for the kids – *My Favorite Martian*. More ambitious, and certainly more like what fans would call science fiction, was an ABC contender that year – *The Outer Limits*. This excellent anthology series – which was both film noir in look and a "monster-of-the-week" show – was impressive in all areas: scripting, music, cinematography, acting, and the monster costuming and make-up. Leslie Stevens, who had been a writer on *Playhouse 90*, and a writer and producer on *Stoney Burke*, created the show. He also wrote the pilot and several other episodes. Joseph Stefano, who had written the screenplay for Alfred Hitchcock's *Psycho* (1960), wrote and producered.

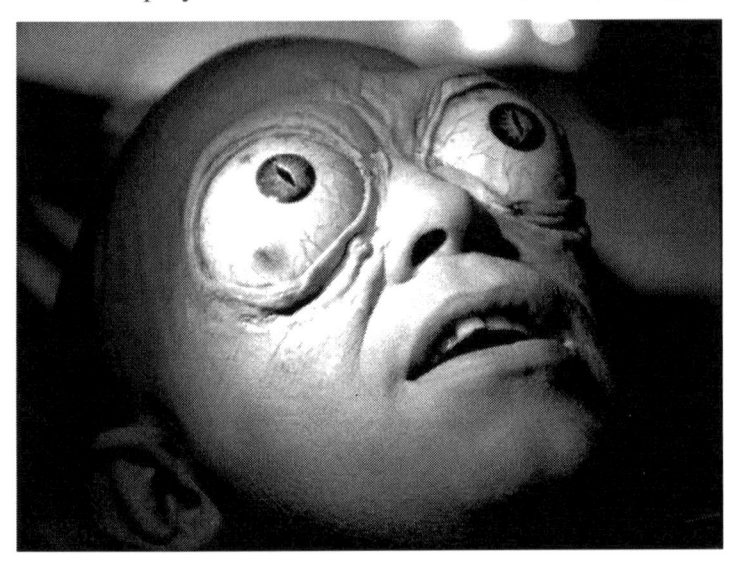

While you may have watched the series – either in first run, as we certainly did, or later – it wasn't a ratings hit. ABC considered it a "prestige show," and was reluctant to pull the plug on *The Outer Limits*. But a decision was made to move it from its Monday night, 7:30 to 8:30 p.m. time slot. And this opened a scheduling space for *Voyage to the Bottom of the Sea*.

Warren Oates, in "The Mutant," an episode of *The Outer Limits*.
(Daystar Productions / United Artists Television, 1963/1964)

We've now walked you through the history of science fiction on TV, prior to the fall of 1964. With the exception of *My Favorite Martian*, none of them had made it into Nielsen's Top 20. *The Twilight Zone* and *The Outer Limits* hadn't even made the Top 50. If science fiction – other than that seen in sitcoms – were to have a chance, it would need a premise which would attract a mass audience. Its creator would also have to overcome the networks' monumental mental block against the concept. Nobody believed that a well-mounted hour-long science-fiction series, with recurring characters and futuristic sets, could be made on budget and on schedule. The person to change their minds was about to return to television, taking TV sci-fi to new depths (literally) and new heights (figuratively).

2

The Greatest Show on Earth

Irwin Allen in his Warner Bros. office, 1979.
(Photo by Mike Clark)

In 1948, Irwin Allen was a brash thirty-three-year-old West Coast literary agent. He was also a talk-show host on radio and TV, a panel-show creator and host, and a syndicated Hollywood gossip columnist. But his true goal was to be a recognized creator in Hollywood. And since no studio would refuse admittance to an entertainment journalist, he intended to make as many contacts as possible, seeking a receptive ear for his ideas.

Ten years earlier, Allen had arrived in Los Angeles with no friends and no connections. He and his cousin Al Gail came into town, as the saying goes, with nothing but their dreams. But the previous decade had been a series of small steps toward breaching the walls of the insular community of studio decision-makers.

Allen worked tirelessly, often for twelve hours a day, every day. He denied himself many of the basics in life – including the pleasures and comforts of marriage and children. His time, energy, and focus were directed towards one goal – becoming a filmmaker in Hollywood. It had been his dream since childhood; no other future would do. For him, there was no looking back.

As far as most people were concerned, Allen was a man without a past. Nobody need know of his low-rent upbringing in the Bronx. He had reinvented his accent to emulate somebody from a ritzier part of the Northeast – Boston, perhaps. No one was to know that he barely made it into college, and that his higher learning came from community school, not a university (although he did briefly take some night classes at Columbia University). His knowledge mainly came from experience. And from books, for Allen was a ravenous reader. No one would know how the little, homely Jewish kid with Russian immigrant parents got kicked around back in New York, or upon his arrival in Hollywood. He provided himself with an entourage, for safety came in numbers. And he trusted no one more than Cousin Al.

Al Gail was raised in a more upscale neighborhood. Unlike his cousin Irwin, Gail had attended a proper university. He played a key role in Allen's success. And where Gail lacked restless, driving ambition, Allen had enough *chutzpah* for a dozen men. He was driven to succeed, bringing Gail along on a wild ride to the top. Failure was unimaginable.

Now, Irwin Allen passed through the doors of opportunity. He was about to assume the position of apprentice second-chair producer on a comedy feature film for RKO Radio Pictures. He'd achieved the spot because he held the screen option on a literary property the studio wanted to produce. More than that, he had maneuvered all the key elements into place to make this motion picture a reality.

Al Gail said, "One day he had a script that he liked, and he decided to see if he could package it – that is, get a director, a star, and backing from one of the studios." (AG-KB95)

Now that Allen had done all three, the next step toward his dream could be taken.

The working title was "It's Only Money," one far more suitable for the material than its eventual moniker. Humorist and journalist Leo Rosten was the writer. Allen was struck by the title – a phrase he would jokingly use throughout his later career as he planned multimillion-dollar "disaster films." He liked this quirky tale of a bank employee who bets on the horse races to win the money needed to marry his sweetheart, only to be suspected of embezzling when he starts showering his fiancée with presents purchased from his race-track winnings.

With *Hollywood Merry-Go-Round*, his radio show which featured industry news and movie insiders, Allen had become friendly with screenwriter Irving Cummings, Jr. Just as important to Allen, the writer's father was Irving Cummings, Sr., who had directed many of child star Shirley Temple's movies. The younger Cummings liked Leo Rosten's story. He agreed to partner with Allen to get it produced.

The first step for Allen and Cummings, Jr. was to create a buzz around Hollywood concerning the project. Allen booked Cummings, Jr. for the premiere broadcast of his KLAC-TV video version of *Hollywood Merry-Go-Round* to plug "It's Only Money."

Cummings, Sr. was watching the program that night, to see how his boy would do in the new medium of television. Senior was impressed, and it didn't take long for him to offer to come out of retirement to direct the proposed film. With his involvement, and that of Cummings, Jr., Allen went in search of financing and studio distribution.

Al Gail said, "That was in the era of [studio mogul] Howard Hughes. And Irwin liked Howard; Howard liked Irwin. They knew each other. And, he would occasionally see Howard at odd times and at strange places." (AG-KB95)

At one of these meetings, Hughes agreed to distribute the movie through RKO. As a boost for the film, he handed over his biggest studio asset – contract actress Jane Russell – for the top female role. In addition to Cummings, Sr. as director, RKO as distributor, and Russell as female lead, the package soon included Frank Sinatra and Groucho Marx. They had openings in their schedules, if production began between Thanksgiving and New Year's, when activity in Hollywood was generally low.

Syndicated entertainment columnist Hedda Hopper announced the deal on October 1st. She reported that "the picture will be made either by RKO or by an independent outfit which will release through that studio." That independent outfit was Westwood Productions – aka Cummings, Jr. and Allen.

"It's Only Money" was the only movie at RKO in production during November and December, 1948, and into January 1949. And it was the first to get a green light since Howard Hughes had taken control of the studio. It was only natural that Hughes wanted Jane Russell as the female lead. Russell, along with Faith

Irwin Allen's first film, as associate producer – the comedy *Double Dynamite*, starring Jane Russell, Frank Sinatra, and Groucho Marx.
(RKO Radio Pictures, 1952)

Domergue, had been signed as contract actresses to Hughes Tool Company, Inc., from the days before his studio acquisition.

41

When asked by entertainment columnist Sheilah Graham if she had picked this or any of her past roles for herself, Russell shot back, "None whatsoever! The first I heard about the Sinatra picture was when I read about it in the papers. But I can read the script and if I don't like it I can scream like hell … I suppose." (JR-IS48)

Melville Shavelson was hired to write the script. He was a future Oscar winner; a writer known for speedy screenwriting turnarounds. He had just completed the screenplay for the upcoming Bob Hope comedy, *Sorrowful Jones*. Meanwhile, songwriters Jule Styne and Sammy Cahn were commissioned to pen a comical title tune for Sinatra and Marx to sing, as well as a slower romantic one for Sinatra to croon to Russell.

Hollywood worked faster in those days, but neither Irving Cummings, Sr. nor his son had witnessed the type of drive displayed by Allen, the former Bronx salesman eager to plow into the picture business. The irony was, Allen wouldn't even receive a screen acknowledgement for this first production. His participation, as "co-producer," would go uncredited.

On November 22, 1948, principal photography began. With Allen in the front office, the production of "It's Only Money" raced by at the same clip with which it had sailed during its pre-production phase. The film finished three days ahead of schedule, on December 18th, after only twenty-six days of filming, and for $100,000 below its projected cost of $1 million. Howard Hughes was impressed. But then, just as quickly, the fast-moving production hit a brick wall.

Louis Berg, "Movie Editor" for the *Los Angeles Times*, for an August 13, 1950 article, gave some insight into Hughes's practice of putting actresses under contract without releasing their completed films. Berg wrote:

> Mr. Hughes is an independently wealthy man. And his investments do not have to pay off in a hurry – whether in oil, airplanes, real estate or movie stars. An oil well can wait, but some of his younger contract players get fidgety. A few bold ones have even invaded his office: "Mr. Hughes, I want to make a picture." Mr. Hughes is unfailingly courteous but rarely explicit. "Don't worry," he says absentmindedly, "we have plans for you."

"It's Only Money" was kept on the shelf for more than a year as Hughes prepared the release of *The Outlaw*, also starring Russell, and which he had made as an independent producer prior to buying controlling interest in RKO. After that, another year passed as Hughes waited for what he felt would be just the right moment to launch "It's Only Money." Even the movie's title was up for grabs.

The title Hughes eventually picked for "It's Only Money" was *Double Dynamite*, referencing Jane Russell's obvious feminine assets. The film was finally released in late 1951.

On November 7, 1951, a film critic for *Variety* called *Double Dynamite* "a lightweight hodgepodge," a "formula comedy with a slapdash air that doesn't build sufficiently on the laugh line to carry it through to more than just moderate success."

Variety's sister trade paper, *Daily Variety*, printed its assessment the same day, affirming that the film was "pretty static, lacking imagination as well as zip." The critic added, "Miss Russell, per usual, looks okay and part is no strain on her acting ability…. Marx is the picture's standout, dishing out his familiar line of patter for number of laughs."

For his review in the December 26th edition of Louisville, Kentucky's *The Courier-Journal*, Sam Moss was perhaps the first to say what was to become a refrain about Allen's work: "The picture nowhere makes an effort to be serious or teach a lesson. It's just something to while the time away."

The New York Times's critic, for the newspaper's December 26th edition, warned moviegoers:

> Even the most ardent devotees of Frank Sinatra, Jane Russell and Groucho Marx will find meager Christmas cheer in *Double Dynamite*…. Whatever that sizzling title is supposed to mean, this thin little comedy is strictly a used fire-cracker.

Others were a little kinder.

On February 4, 1952, Howard McClay of the *Los Angeles Daily News*, said:

> *Double Dynamite*, now at the RKO Pantages and [RKO] Hillcrest, is prevented from slipping into the category of ordinary film comedy by the sly buffoonery of capable Groucho Marx. His inimitable manner of tossing a line or

word into an otherwise dull tableau accounts for a great deal of the picture's yak value. And li'l ol' Frank Sinatra, who is held down to two songs, displays quite a knack himself in getting rid of some funny tag lines.

Also on February 4th, Dorothy Manners of the *Los Angeles Examiner* enthused:

> It's impossible to put Groucho Marx, Jane Russell and Frank Sinatra together and come up with anything but an entertaining film.

Alan Warwick, the key film critic for *Picturegoer*, slyly observed:

> [T]here are various theories as to why the latest Jane Russell film is called *Double Dynamite*. I can conclude only that it describes the performances of Frank Sinatra and Groucho Marx. They make a wonderful pair.

Perhaps because of a heavy ad campaign of $85,000 (which equates to nearly $800,000 in 2016), and the hype about the lead actress's attributes, the February 6, 1952 edition of *Variety* ranked the movie as the sixth top moneymaker over the New Year's holiday weekend. "Confounding the [critics] who did not expect it to fare so well," *Double Dynamite* had inched up to the Number 5 box office slot in January.

By this time, Allen's second film project, *Where Danger Lives*, had already been filmed and released – a production which seemed more suitable for a man who would later aim for nail-biting suspense, or at least relentless action and adventure.

***

In the March 8, 1949 edition of Texas's *Amarillo Daily News*, Leonard Lyons's syndicated column, "The Lyon's Den," reported that "Leo Rosten's newest original screen story is called 'A White Rose for Julie.' The studios now are bidding for it."

It was actually an unpublished novel, sent to the studios as a possible screen story.

You may recall that Leo Rosten wrote the story that Irwin Allen optioned and turned into "It's Only Money," which became the not-yet-released *Double Dynamite*. Allen and Cummings, Jr. were quick to take an interest in this new property from Rosten.

RKO won the bidding. The property was then offered to Westwood Productions, the company formed by Irving Cummings, Jr. and Irwin Allen. One of the stars Howard Hughes had in mind was, again, Jane Russell. The other was up-and-comer Robert Mitchum, for whom Hughes co-owned a contract. These announcements were made on May 6th, and April 20th, 1949, respectively.

"A White Rose for Julie" was an atypical tale from Rosten the humorist. "Rose" was a romantic crime drama about a young doctor who falls hard for a mysterious "dame," then learns that she has a husband – which leads to a fight, a death, and a run for the border. A different type of screenwriter would be needed for this project, and producer Irving Cummings, Jr. had someone in mind.

On May 27th, it was announced that Cummings, Jr. and Allen had hired playwright L. Arthur Ross to turn Leo Rosten's story into a screenplay. Ross had written B-movies for RKO, such as 1946's *Vacation in Reno* and *San Quentin*, and 1947's *Beat the Band*. His "White Rose for Julie" script, however, was deemed unacceptable and a second writer was engaged in July.

Charles Bennett was best known as the primary writer on seven popular films by Alfred Hitchcock (written *with* the two Hitchcocks – Alfred and his wife Alma). These cinematic landmarks included England's first talkie, *Blackmail*, and both versions of *The Man Who Knew Too Much* (1934 and 1956), as well as *The 39 Steps* and *Foreign Correspondent*, the latter of which brought Bennett an Academy Award nomination. Bennett's future would involve scripting numerous movies for Irwin Allen, including *The Lost World* and the big-screen version of *Voyage to the Bottom of the Sea*. However, at this time – the early 1950s – Bennett could not have imagined the relationship going that far.

Bennett's chance encounter with Allen was innocuous enough. He said, "I had been directing a lot of television for Hollywood in England. When I came back, Irving Cummings was going to produce a picture called *Where Danger Lives* with Robert Mitchum and Claude Rains, and I was asked to write it." (CB-SL93)

Bennett was also asked to appear on *The Irwin Allen Show*, as it was now called. On the same program was Vincent Price, with whom Allen would soon work in motion pictures, and Allen's film-making partner, Irving Cummings, Jr. While appearing on the program, Bennett was surprised to learn that the TV host would also be helping out with the production of the film. He later said dismissively, "Irwin Allen knew somebody who worked for Howard Hughes, and Hughes owned RKO, so it was somehow finagled into him being associate producer." (CB-SL93)

Bennett completed his own screenplay for "A White Rose for Julie" in early September, 1949. With script in hand, Cummings, Jr. and Allen began the search for the film's director.

Allen was burning his candle at both ends. He was hosting his radio show six days a week, and his TV show once a week; and he was sitting in on the editing of "It's Only Money" while casting "A White Rose for Julie." But this breakneck pace was just how Allen, the work-obsessed dreamer, wanted it.

The man Allen and Irving Cummings, Jr. eventually chose to direct was 45-year-old John Farrow, husband of actress Maureen O'Sullivan. Farrow had won the 1942 New York Film Critics Circle Award for the Brian Donlevy-William Bendix starrer, *Wake Island*.

Howard Hughes was firmly set on casting Robert Mitchum as the film's male lead. A Hughes contract player, Mitchum was being paid by the week whether he worked or not.

On January 6, 1950, *Daily Variety* announced that Jane Russell was out but that Hughes's other contract actress, Faith Domergue, would be the female lead, opposite Mitchum, and that the film would begin rolling the following day. Principal photography actually began on January 9th.

Faith Domergue was 25. Hughes had so fussed over every detail for his latest femme discovery that her previous film, *Vendetta*, had not yet been released. These types of delays kept Domergue from reaching her greatest success until after leaving RKO, and Hughes. She later became a leading lady in B-westerns for Universal opposite the likes of Audie Murphy and Jeff Chandler, and received first or second billing in the monster mashes *It Came from Beneath the Sea*, *This Island Earth*, and *The Atomic Man*.

Faith Domergue and Robert Mitchum in Irwin Allen's second film as associate producer: *Where Danger Lives*. (RKO Radio Pictures, 1950)

Robert Mitchum, 34, was cast as Dr. Jeff Cameron, the male lead of "A White Rose for Julie." He had received an Oscar nomination for his supporting role in 1945's *The Story of G.I. Joe*. He'd had the lead in RKO movies such as 1948's *Blood on the Moon* and 1949's *The Big Steel*.

Claude Rains was 52 when cast as Mr. Lannington. Rains had already received four Best Supporting Actor Oscar nominations – for 1939's *Mr. Smith Goes to Washington*, 1942's *Casablanca*, 1944's *Mr. Skeffington*, and 1946's *Notorious*.

Maureen O'Sullivan, 39, was cast as Nurse Julie Dawn. The wife of the film's director, O'Sullivan was best known for playing Jane opposite Johnny Weissmuller's Tarzan in six movies between 1932 and 1942.

Irwin Allen with Claude Rains and Robert Mitchum during the making of *Where Danger Lives*.
(RKO Radio Pictures, 1950)

On the January 26, 1950 episode of KLAC-TV's *Irwin Allen's House Party*, the host devoted his show to the production-crew unit from "A White Rose for Julie," as they discussed the movie and their craft. The artists and technicians who explained their work to the TV audience were Irving Cummings, Jr.; assistant director Sam Ruman; make-up artist Layne Britton; costumer Virginia Tutwiler; prop man George McGonigle; and director John Farrow. And, of course, co-producer Irwin Allen.

Meanwhile, principal photography for "A White Rose for Julie" continued into early March, wrapping on schedule, and within budget, after 40 days of filming. But before its release, mogul Hughes changed its title to *Where Danger Lives*, a name originally planned for the 1949 film released as *The Woman on Pier 13*.

In May, with the post-production for the film reaching completion, Irwin Allen resumed hosting his TV talk show, awaiting the release of *Where Danger Lives*. Its critical and box-office reception would endorse or deny his hoped-for future as a movie producer.

On June 16, 1950, after a tradeshow screening, the film critic for *Daily Variety* reported:

> As a vehicle to introduce Faith Domergue, *Where Danger Lives* is by no means sock [short for "socko"]. It is a rambling, confused feature that will lean heavily on the draw value of Robert Mitchum.... Both John Farrow's direction and the script by Charles Bennett shroud the melodrama with too much confusion and the pacing is uneven.... Production by Irving Cummings, Jr. and Irwin Allen emphasizes [melodrama] factors in the story, mounting it physically in keeping but falling short on realizing the best from the Leo Rosten original.

Sister trade *Variety* chimed in on June 21st, calling the film "just a fair mystery melodrama."

On November 17th, Lowell F. Redelings of the *Hollywood Citizen-News*, said:

> The news about RKO's *Where Danger Lives* at the Hillstreet and Pantages palaces of cinematic entertainment is no news at all – with one exception. Faith Domergue is the exception. She can act, for she has that "inner fire" that comes off the screen, without which no film player is more than a celluloid image. If she is unhappily burdened with a weakly-conceived role in this contrived melodrama, she accepts it for what it is – and just for the record: She does better by it than it deserves.

Less impressed with Domergue, *Time* magazine, from December 18, 1950, said:

> ... Actress Domergue smolders and storms like an overheated Theda Bara, gets some ludicrous lines to read (and gives them the delivery they warrant), builds up fast to an overpowering impression that she has done her best work in publicity stills.

On January 6, 1951, Jesse Zunser, of *Cue* magazine, wrote:

> There is no excuse for a picture as bad as this one. In all departments – writing, direction, performance – it just doesn't rate.

While some critics were harsh, the overall reviews were mixed. *Where Danger Lives,* like *Double Dynamite*, is an entertaining film. Constant discussions of Domergue contributed to male curiosity, and moviegoers of this simpler time fell for her smoldering wares. During the last week of November, 1950, *Where Danger Lives* was the sixth highest-grossing film across America.

Irwin Allen had survived his first two film productions, and unwittingly set a pattern for the future. His projects might not wow the critics, but they were solid draws for audiences eager for spectacle or sensation.

Allen had taken his gamble, and the future he'd worked so hard to realize lay before him. He was on the brink of bringing to life the rags-to-riches tales he had read and cherished as a child.

***

After his birth in New York City on June 12, 1916, for the first twenty-two years of his life, Allen's name was Irwin Grinovit. He was the youngest of four brothers – after Rubin, George, and Fred – born to a Russian Jewish immigrant who worked as a tailor. Allen's cousin, Al Gail, told interviewer Kevin Burns, "The era was, unfortunately, depression days – '30s and '40s – [but] we both grew up in what you would call normal middle-class families. Not poor – we always had something to eat. Not wealthy, of course, especially during the depression years. [There] was a lot of struggle – his father and my father – but, as kids, you didn't realize that times were tough. Everyone was in the same predicament." (AG-KB95)

The times were more difficult for the Grinovit family than cousin Al realized. Al Gail lived on Coney Island; Irwin Grinovit and his family lived in the Bronx.

Nephew Michael Allen disclosed, "They were typical of people who lived on the Lower East Side of New York at that time. His father was a relatively recent immigrant. English was clearly a second language. They had limited means. They lived in one of those tenement flats, and they took in boarders. My father [Rubin] eventually went to work as a window decorator. My uncle Fred was a piano cleaner. George was a superintendent – a janitor. They were all working men, not of means." (MA-AI15)

Irwin Grinovit, however, had bigger dreams than his older brothers. And when he achieved success, he never spoke of his early hardships, or the worries and insecurities he may have harbored. That time and place was merely an environment to escape.

Even Sheila Mathews Allen, his wife of seventeen years, admitted, "Irwin was a very private man, and I don't really know that much about his childhood. I think you learned more by talking to his cousin [Al Gail] than I ever knew…. But I know they weren't a well-to-do family. If anything, he had to think at an early age about what he was going to do, *and he did*. He followed his dream." (SM-KB95)

Michael Allen was not surprised to hear this. He observed, "Irwin was extremely conscious of not doing anything that he would have to hide. That mattered to him a lot, perhaps more than you might think. But this was part of the way he was brought up. My father [Irwin's brother Rubin] was much the same way. I would think my uncles George and Fred were probably the same way, as well. Irwin was private… so taking someone into his life didn't constitute an opening of conversations that would be uncomfortable. Quite the contrary, Irwin was very conscious of *not* doing anything ever that he would be uncomfortable about afterwards."

That included discussions of his poor background. Michael Allen continued, "Irwin used to say he didn't care as much about weeds as he did about flowers. That was his way of avoiding the issue. He really had no interest and didn't talk about his early childhood or his early adulthood; of his various family relationships, whether they were good, bad or indifferent, male or female. And the same with business associates. Those people he did business with – and raising money was a big part of that – were all very private, and he didn't transcend those rules. That was a conscious effort on his part. I can say my father was exactly the same way, and I can presume that my grandfather and grandmother [Irwin's parents] were. Assuredly that can be traced back to them being Russian/Jewish immigrants. Those were difficult times." (MA-AI15)

Al Gail said, "As the youngest of four boys, he pretty much had to make his own way, which he did. You know the phrase of 'pulling yourself up by your own bootstraps' – that was Irwin. Because he never had any help, from the very beginning to his eventual success. He did it all on his own." (AG-KB95)

Allen had chosen his own role models – people whose success and accomplishments inspired him. P.T. Barnum was one.

Entertainment legend Phineas Taylor Barnum (1810-1891) was an American showman who made a name for himself by promoting celebrated hoaxes and human curiosities through his P.T. Barnum's Grand Traveling Museum, Menagerie, Caravan & Hippodrome. Some thought it an interesting showcase, a strange mix of ragged and exotic oddities; others considered it a crude parade of freaks and monsters. Either way, it was a hit, a perpetual moneymaker.

Barnum was also a journalist, author, editor, and publisher. In his autobiography, he wrote: "I am a showman by profession ... and all the gilding shall make nothing else of me."

In 1919, after Barnum's death, his enterprise joined with James Anthony Bailey's Cooper and Bailey's Circus to become "The Greatest Show on Earth," The Ringling Brothers Barnum & Bailey's Circus, which remained a feature of pop culture until its final bow, in 2017.

As Barnum had done before him, Irwin Allen studied journalism. Al Gail had a sense early on about his cousin's inclinations: "Something literary, because in his high school days he wrote a column for the high school newspaper, [and] he did some freelance work on local newspapers. He was always interested in writing, advertising, publicity." (AG-KB95)

Allen escaped the Great Depression through his keen interest in books. Gail disclosed, "He was an avid reader. He read all the ones we all read in those days – Frank Merriwell, Nick Carter, Horatio Alger, Tom Swift – and we were both, of course, enamored by Richard Halliburton, the travel writer…. I think most of the reading in those days, when we weren't studying or going to school, or playing football or stoop ball, or roller-skating or bicycling, was adventure books, science books, science fiction – Jules Verne. I guess it was the excitement, the adventure, the creativity of the writers. And we always sought to emulate them if possible. We all wanted to be writers in those days, and many of us *became* writers."

Gail said of his cousin, "He'd come down on weekends, because he lived in the Bronx and I was on Coney Island. And we'd sit on the beach and we'd look at some of these tremendous ocean liners coming from Europe, coming into New York Harbor, and we'd say, 'Someday!', because then it was just a wild dream. Who could afford that kind of a luxury of traveling on the ocean steamer? But he said, 'Someday we'll make it, and we'll do all those things. You'll see.'"

Gail was a little older, and his first step in that dream of "someday" came earlier. He said, "I went to University of Alabama. Irwin wanted to go there, too, and I was hoping he'd be able to. But, unfortunately, as I say, with depression times, his family just couldn't afford it. So he went to night school. He went to Columbia." (AG-KB95)

Allen's nighttime studies at Columbia University included courses in advertising and journalism. He also took free community-college classes at City College of New York. During the day, and between classes, he earned money writing publicity material for nightclubs in Greenwich Village and on 52nd Street. Also – in true P.T. Barnum fashion – he worked as a barker at a carnival. When

Gail returned after four years of college, he found cousin Irwin working in a low-level position for an advertising agency.

Gail stressed, "Somehow, it seemed to be a dead end. There was really nothing happening. We had a cousin in Los Angeles, and one day we're sitting around and [Irwin] said, 'What the hell, let's go to California and see what's doing.' Within a week or so, we were on our way. We were hopeful to land something either in the movie industry or advertising, or one of the allied arts, and make our own way. We really had no specific target – just to get a job; start working and see where it goes from there." (AG-KB95)

Sheila Mathews Allen said, "He always wanted to be associated with the circus in some way. So, I guess when he came out here, he was running away to *join* the circus." (SMA-KB95)

According to Al Gail, it was on the trip to California that Irwin Grinovit decided to change his name. Gail said, "Grinovit was an old family name, and it was a difficult name. It was a harsh name, and people had trouble remembering it. So, when we came out here, we decided to change it to something that's more easily spoken and remembered, and we came up with 'Allen.' ... I said, 'Well, it's a good name, and easy to say, and easy to remember.' So, he liked it. He decided on *Irwin Allen*." (AG-KB95)

Nephew Michael Allen said, "He probably changed his name around 1936 or '37. He came to Boston to visit my father, and we lived on Allen Street in the West End of Boston. And he thought he would change his name to help him in his profession and he liked the sound of Allen." (MA-AI15)

In time, other family members also adopted this new surname.

Allen's father died shortly after his ambitious son left for Los Angeles. Michael Allen said, "My grandmother did not live very much longer, either. She passed away probably in the early 1940s." (MA-AI15)

It was actually earlier, in 1938, when Irwin Allen was twenty-two.

Allen and his cousin Al found jobs with a magazine called *Key*, which served as an entertainment directory and nightclub guide. Gail said of Allen, "He had a very agile mind. And he was a great salesman. So we came out and we started to work for a local entertainment magazine. We were always a team. He did what he did best and I did what I did best. I was basically a writer; he was a presenter, a talker, a salesman, and very creative on his own. He was also a writer. I wrote a column, and he sold advertising in the magazine, and did very well." (AG-KB95)

Almost compulsively driven to succeed, Allen ventured into other areas of media, first as an all-night disc jockey at local radio station KMTR, which was affiliated with the *Los Angeles Evening Herald* newspaper. A short while later he became a station announcer. Then, with uncanny speed, he had his own radio program – *Hollywood Merry-Go-Round* – a quarter-hour-long celebrity gossip show heard six nights a week at 9:45 p.m. The title gave a wink and a nod toward Drew Pearson's decade old syndicated column, "The Washington Merry-Go-Round," which, by this time, was also a radio program. For Irwin Allen's *Hollywood Merry-Go-Round*, cousin Al served as producer.

From 1940 through 1949, Allen made countless contacts throughout the industry by means of newsprint, radio, and video versions of his breathless showbiz reports. He also produced a column, "On the Set," for Hollywood Features Syndicates.

Irwin Allen's radio career began in Los Angeles as an all-night disc jockey and announcer for KMTR, circa 1939.

Allen worked tirelessly. He rose before the sun and toiled after it had set. And, like the sun, he never took a day off. This work ethic eventually brought success, but also bred harsh critics within Allen's own inner circle. Famed screenwriter Charles Bennett, who co-wrote many movies with the ambitious producer-director, would lie in wait until after Allen's death before venomously claiming that his former employer was *not* a writer. More so, Bennett claimed that Allen did *not* write at all, but would routinely take credit for other writers' work. This was an absurd statement, and Allen's "On the Set" column disproves it. The quality of his prose aside, Allen *did* write – daily. And he daydreamed daily, too.

Although his columns and broadcast shows were undeniably promotions for the industry, Allen tried to bring some fun and innovations.

In the fall of 1948, his *Hollywood Merry-Go-Round* radio program began broadcasting to a national audience. Even with this early incarnation of an Irwin Allen Production, high concepts and speed were emphasized over substance. The September 13, 1948 issue of *Daily Variety* reported:

> Allen corralled Hugh Herbert, Ellen Drew, George Tobias and Irving Cummings, Jr., for the initialer. An excellent opportunity for light banter and humor was missed by

adhering too closely to a somber "guessing game" script. Quartet were asked to identify stills, soundtracks from recent pictures, a mystery guest, and a personality by tracking him or her down through 20 questions. Allen raced through the telecast too rapidly, killing what interest could have been provoked.

Allen defended his grab bag of gimmicks and rapid-fire approach, saying, "It's not so easy to switch a radio show to television as it may appear. Listening is one thing, but watching me sit at a mike reading Hollywood news items doesn't add up to a good show…. Just because there's a picture star with me, it doesn't necessarily follow that people at home are going to glue their eyes to the receiver watching the star do *nothing*!" (IA-TV48)

Even though the results were mixed, Allen was justifiably proud. He later boasted, "I invented the panel show *and* the mystery guest!" (IA-DV64)

In May 1949, the video version of *Hollywood Merry-Go-Round* got the axe from Channel 13. But Allen received a stay of execution when he shifted to a new video series in August, *Irwin Allen's Hollywood Party*. The title was different, but this show used the same bag of tricks. The *Billboard* trade paper reviewed the new series on December 10, 1949:

Irwin Allen's *Hollywood Merry-Go-Round*, TV's first known panel show (KLAC-TV, circa late 1948).

... Irwin Allen's stanza has been a feature of KLAC-TV since the station's inception, the latest offering having undergone surgery to make it more palatable. The chief objection is that the show goes nowhere, lacking both cohesive continuity or good production.

At this time, Allen still had his 15-minute audio show on KLAC radio. But it was no longer the talk of the town. It was just … talk. With his thinly disguised Bronx accent, and his tendency for scripted banter over natural conversation, Allen was suddenly out of favor. To him, this fall from critical acceptance probably didn't matter. What he really wanted was to produce films.

Allen (center) with panel guests for one of his *Hollywood Merry-Go-Round* broadcasts (KLAC-TV, circa late 1940s).

***

In 1947, while still appearing regularly on radio and TV, Irwin Allen, the ambitious workaholic, branched out even further by becoming a Hollywood agent. The first step was a position as head of the Radio Department at the Orsatti Agency. A short while later, Allen began wearing a second hat at the talent agency – as a story editor.

Workaholic Allen still kept his other day job, as host of TV's *Hollywood Merry-Go-Round*, now called *The Irwin Allen Show* (KLAC-TV, 1950).

This position was what he was really after. As a story editor, his job entailed finding writers and, in particular, specific stories – books and scripts worthy of representation by the agency. For such an avid reader, this position was a natural for Allen. By May 1948, he resigned from the Orsatti Agency to open an office under his own name.

Now Allen was in a position to further his goal of becoming a motion-picture producer. To his thinking, the best way to accomplish this would be to find a hot property, option it, and go in search of a studio or other financial backers. After years of being a Hollywood columnist, and a radio and TV personality, there were few people in Tinseltown who would not take a phone call from Irwin Allen.

That first property, as described earlier, was "It's Only Money," by Leo Rosten, which became *Double Dynamite*. Although two and a half years passed before its release, Allen and Cummings, Jr. were able to get a second film into development with RKO – *Where Danger Lives*. Its release before *Double Dynamite* made it the first movie to hit the big screen that was co-produced by Irwin Allen.

For his third shot at being a big-time, big-screen producer, Allen turned back to comedy ... and Groucho Marx.

Hitting movie screens in 1952, a year and a half after *Where Danger Lives*, but only one month after Allen's first film, *Double Dynamite*, *A Girl in Every Port* was the third and final pairing of co-producers Irwin Allen and Irving Cummings, Jr. This time Allen moved up to first chair as producer.

Movie No. 3 for Irwin Allen, now as co-producer – *A Girl in Every Port*. **Pictured (L-R): William Bendix, Marie Wilson, and Groucho Marx.** (RKO Radio Pictures, 1952)

Allen had first become friendly with Groucho Marx during the production of *Double Dynamite*. In October, 1950, he began selling his pal on the property he was trying to package as his first as top producer. It was based on the humorous short story, "They Sell Sailors Elephants," by Frederick Hazlitt Brennan. (It was also identified in the trades as "They Sell Elephants to Sailors.") Feeling it would make a good vehicle for his new friend, Allen optioned the story for $20,000, which he later recouped from RKO.

Thirty days later, *Daily Variety* reported that Allen and Cummings, Jr. were "avidly awaiting Howard Hughes' okay" to announce Marie Wilson as the leading lady. William Bendix was confirmed as co-star, with Marx, and Chester Erskine was on board as director.

Marie Wilson was 33. The radio series she headlined, *My Friend Irma*, had been brought to the big screen in two movies which also starred Wilson (1949's *My Friend Irma* and 1950's *My Friend Irma Goes West*). It would soon jump to TV, too, with Wilson.

Bendix was 44, and had been nominated for an Oscar as Best Supporting Actor for 1942's *Wake Island*. He was a star at the time, having played the title roles for 1948's *The Babe Ruth Story* and 1949's *The Life of Riley*. *Riley* was later developed into a TV series, also starring Bendix.

Writer/director Chester Erskine was 46. He was from the stage, but had recently made the transition to film, writing, directing, and producing the 1947 hit *The Egg and I*, starring Claudette Colbert and Fred MacMurray.

Allen with (left-to-right) Groucho Marx, Marie Wilson, and William Bendix, during production of *A Girl in Every Port*. (RKO Radio Pictures, 1952)

The holdup was Marie Wilson. Hughes wasn't going to green-light a film that didn't prominently exploit one of his well-endowed studio contract starlets, or, in Wilson's case, a well-endowed actress he was contemplating putting under contract. It wasn't until June 1951 that Wilson was available, and film could start running through the camera.

It was too bad for Allen that he was cutting his teeth as a producer at a studio that had become an industry joke. RKO had been a great studio in its glory days, decades previously. Now, under millionaire Hughes, its reputation had become tarnished. Hughes liked to "discover" buxom starlets and place them under contract. Some he would keep out of sight for years as he fussed over them, like Faith Domergue. Other actresses were featured in films that sometimes sat on the shelf for years until Hughes felt that the time was right, like Jane Russell's *Double Dynamite*. Or, he might pick movie titles that were exploitative, with more to do with the measurements of the leading lady than the plot.

On May 7, 1951, shortly before the start of production, Marie Wilson teasingly complained to Hollywood syndicated correspondent Erskine Johnson that "Tight sweaters and shorts" was the wardrobe she was assigned for "They Sell Elephants to Sailors."

"It's Groucho's doing," she pouted. "When he worked with Jane Russell, she wore high-necked gowns all through the picture. Groucho told Howard Hughes that he didn't want to make that mistake with me." (MW-IR51)

By the third week of June, cameras were rolling. Covering the production for his *Los Angeles Daily News* column, Darr Smith wrote:

> You go to the set of the movie "They Sell Sailors Elephants" at RKO studios these days and you see acres of cleavage. It's a wonder they don't have a censor on hand, what with those car-hop uniforms.... We asked Marie Wilson, one of the more prominent young ladies around town, how she was getting away with it.
>
> "It IS rather gappy, isn't it?" she asked, answering a question with a question. "I don't know either. You ever see the picture *My Forbidden Past*? Well, this is 'My Forbidden Front!'"
>
> Just then a couple middle-aged sailors named Groucho Marx and William Bendix strolled over, verified our findings with sidelong looks, and sat down....
>
> Groucho [said], "This is a lousy title, this 'Sailors Sell Elephants,' or whatever it is. Why don't they call it 'Baby, It's Crowded in Here' or something like that? It's a perfect title. You got Russell on the next stage and you got Wilson here. Brother, you can hardly get into the commissary for lunch. On the other hand, come to think of it, who wants lunch?"

We asked Groucho, apropos of Russell, whatever happened to the picture he made at least two years ago with her and Frank Sinatra called "It's Only Money"? He said he didn't know except that RKO loves to get pictures out in a hurry so it can put them on the shelf.

Howard Hughes didn't put "They Sell Sailors Elephants" on the shelf – although he did change the title. *A Girl in Every Port* was in movie houses in time for the Christmas box-office boom.

On December 20, 1951, *Daily Variety* said:

> Basic yarn is a fragile framework on which to project the merry adventures of two gobs, Marx and Bendix, who become owners of a racehorse. Although lacking in explosive laughs, pic maintains a fairly steady humorous pace, mainly generated by Groucho's quick-triggered cracks and double-takes.

On the same day, the *Hollywood Reporter* echoed:

> Although *A Girl in Every Port* fails to generate the hysteria expected of a comedy in which Groucho Marx is the headliner, the Irwin Allen-Irving Cummings, Jr.

production shapes up as average laugh fare, able to fill the bill in secondary and family situations.

Kay Proctor, film critic for the *Los Angeles Examiner*, gave her opinion in the newspaper's March 22nd edition:

> If a potpourri is a spicy mixture, and hokum is exaggerated nonsense, I'd call *A Girl in Every Port* a potpourri of hokum. It's got gangsters, saboteurs, a society girl, and – s' help me! – a couple of horses in a Navy brig. It's also got Groucho Marx with his elevator eyebrows; William Bendix with his dumb-bunny routine; and Marie Wilson with her double-barreled charms properly emphasized.

Irwin Allen, who always read his reviews – and hired newspaper clipping services to keep him well supplied – was hungry to learn from each success, failure, or anything in between. The lesson was clear, reinforced by his own movie-going youth: Cast as many likable stars as possible.

One lesson not so palatable was that a production didn't always need "everything including the kitchen sink" thrown into the story.

Despite reviews that leaned from mixed to negative, business at the box office was surprisingly good. Syndicated columnist Jimmie Fidler, in the April 4th edition of Missouri's *Joplin Globe*, analyzed the curious situation:

> A few weeks ago, R-K-O put into general release a rather modest little picture entitled *A Girl in Every Port.* In view of the fact that it had been made as a small budget offering, and the further fact that it co-starred Groucho Marx and Marie Wilson, neither of whom was regarded as "hot" box office, the best the studio hoped for was a small margin of profit. Such pictures ordinarily are relegated to the lower spot on double bills.
>
> So what happened? Well, this modest little opus, to the complete astonishment of everyone in the R-K-O organization, proved to be a big money-maker. With little or no ballyhoo to help it along, it "packed 'em" in for two straight weeks at the New York Paramount – and it's been packing them in everywhere it's played.
>
> It's caused a lot of meditation at R-K-O – and the result of all that thinking is the conclusion that *A Girl in Every Port* owes its success to television. Its stars, Groucho Marx and Marie Wilson, may not be top-ranking personalities in

movie circles, but they're both favorites with the TV audiences. And it's been the TV fans, in the opinion of the studio bosses, who have been rushing the theaters to see them.

Irwin Allen took this lesson to heart: Once a star, always a star. In his big-budget disaster movies of the 1970s and '80s, he would always book two or three major movie stars, like Gene Hackman, Paul Newman, Steve McQueen, or Michael Caine. Then he would fill out the cast with "stars" who might be past their prime years at the box office, but whose names still registered with audiences. These faded luminaries were still able to warm people's hearts; their built-in TV familiarity might lure people away from home to follow their favorite small-screen personalities back to the big screen.

A Girl in Every Port took its time moving across the nation, playing in neighborhood movie houses. On the national scene, it never made the Top 10, having to settle for the fifteenth place, but it nonetheless earned back its costs a few times over. And, while Jimmie Fidler gave credit to TV, with Groucho Marx's hit *You Bet Your Life* and Marie Wilson's popular *My Friend Irma*, RKO credited producer Allen. With this success, he now had the opportunity to lose his co-producing partner, Cummings, Jr., and reach for the big brass ring on his own.

***

Irwin Allen wrapped up his KLAC-TV series in early 1951. Interest in the show had waned. He continued on KLAC radio with his 15-minute Hollywood report into early 1952, but discontinued that after *A Girl in Every Port* was released by RKO.

Allen was ready to put all his eggs into his own basket. He was risking much in turning away from the comfort

KLAC's *The Irwin Allen Show*, circa 1952. Allen is second from right. Among guests: Vincent Price (fourth from left) and, to Price's right, Don DeFore, who appeared in *A Girl in Every Port*.

zone of radio and TV to become a movie producer. All of his earlier efforts – the newspaper column, the literary agency, and broadcasting – had merely been stepping stones toward what he really wanted to do – direct, produce, and create.

Al Gail said, "We all had interest in films, obviously, where you'd go to the Saturday afternoon serials, and all the movies in the local houses. So he recognized the opportunity, and he *had* the ability. And he learned how to become a director, producer and a writer for films – *specialized writing* – all on his own, with no help from anyone above him. No nepotism involved anyplace." (AG-KB95)

Allen had become interested in science and oceanography. Soon after its 1951 publication, he read marine biologist Rachel Carson's *The Sea Around Us*, a wide-ranging panorama of sea life. It was Carson's second published book – the second of her "Sea Trilogy." Upon publication in the summer of 1951, this paean to ocean life garnered excellent reviews. It remained on *The New York Times* Best Seller List for an impressive eighty-six weeks, and won both the 1952 National Book Award for Nonfiction and a Burroughs Medal in nature writing. Allen became determined, even obsessed, to adapt it for the screen. Allen, the salesman who never accepted "no" for an answer, began a new phase in his own career by seeking the book's author.

National Book Award presentation, Hotel Commodore, New York City, 1952. Left to right: recipients Marianne Moore, James Jones, and Rachel Carson, with toastmaster James Mason Brown. (Associated Press)

Al Gail said of Allen's fascination regarding *The Sea Around Us*, "It was the project that somehow appealed to him, and he had a lot of trouble getting an okay from Rachel Carson, the writer. She didn't want to do anything in Hollywood with it. But he flew to New York, saw her in New York, with her agent and attorneys, and talked her into it, telling her pretty much what he had in mind. And she was satisfied he wouldn't desecrate it." (AG-KB95)

Allen's idea was to break the immense subject down into vignettes, combining new footage with that already filmed by various scientific researchers.

Allen told David Bombard, of the *Los Angeles Daily News*, "The best seller is one of the most beautifully written textbooks, and we wanted to bring it

Allen posing with assistant, reviewing film footage for *The Sea Around Us*, his first film as a solo producer, writer, and director. (RKO Radio Pictures, 1953)

to the screen, but how could we do it in reasonably theatrical terms? This was the big problem which confronted us." (IA-DN53)

Allen cited studio estimates of $4,500,000 to send a full production crew to various parts of the world to photograph the seventy-five categories of sea life described in Rachel Carson's book, and two-and-a-half years to do it. Of course, this kind of investment of time and money was out of the question for any studio, much less RKO, which had been in a decline for several years.

Instead, Allen got a list of forty people who'd helped Rachel Carson with her research. He immediately posted forty letters, asking them to assist his screen version.

Allen told Hollywood correspondent Aline Mosby, "I wrote to 2,341 institutions of oceanography and told them what we had in mind. I kept four secretaries busy for fourteen months, with 6,000 pieces of correspondence.

"About 75 percent of the movie was shot just for us, and the rest was scientific film these institutions had in their vaults. Some was 16mm film that had to be enlarged. The film was shot in every color process known, and some we hadn't heard of, so our laboratory had to fix it so the colors in the different sections matched."

Belying his reputation as a man with no sense of humor, Allen told Mosby, "This is the first time a textbook was made into a movie. I've got a hot script working on an algebra book, too." (IA-UP53)

David Bombard, for his *Los Angeles Daily News* article, revealed:

> Some [of the zoological institutes] did it for free, others released footage on a royalty basis, and some the studio bought outright. From the 2,341 sources came 1,620,000 feet of 16-mm colored film. In other terms, the footage represented some 300 hours of film which would require twelve 24-hour days to run. From this, some 5,552 feet were culled to make the documentary....

Philip K. Scheuer, writing in the October 30, 1952 edition of the *Los Angeles Times*, reported:

> ... Allen, a young producer (*A Girl in Every Port*) on the Gower St. lot, has been working on the Rachel Carson best-seller for more than a year. The feature-length documentary he has put together is said to reveal exciting aspects of marine life; whether it will match the profundity of Miss Carson's prose remains, of course, to be seen. ...

On November 30th, Oregon's *Eugene Register-Guard* carried this wire story from Hollywood:

> In order to qualify it for an Academy Award nomination, Irwin Allen has rushed completion of the feature length documentary in Technicolor, *The Sea Around Us*, to have it ready for a special December release. Allen, who wrote and produced the picturized version of the Rachel Carson best seller for RKO, has been working on the project for over a year.

The November 26th issue of *Variety* announced that Irwin Allen would world-premiere the movie in Washington under the sponsorship of the National Geographic Society. This would be followed by Hollywood trade screenings in late December.

By arranging these previews, Allen – who could never be accused of not dreaming big – was making sure *The Sea Around Us* would qualify for the 1953 Academy Awards. In addition, if the early screenings garnered positive reviews, he would have built up anticipation for the film's general release the following May.

After the screenings, the new year brought reviews which must have seemed like tardy Christmas presents. These reviews also reveal that, with *The Sea Around Us*, Allen was sowing seeds which later become the bumper crop known as *Voyage to the Bottom of the Sea*.

From the January 14, 1953 issue of *Daily Variety*:

> Footage used is from actual scientific expeditions and filmed marine studies, all edited to take up most of the categories covered in the book and arranged so as to hold the attention throughout. Subjects range from microscopic life, invisible to the naked eye, to the huge whale, largest of all mammals.... For thrills, picture shows a fight between an octopus and a shark; for chuckles

there are clips of the eye-brow raising professions of shark-walking and crab-herding.... Film's ending sounds an ominous note, observing that if all the ice and snow of the world's glacier areas should melt, the present level of the oceans would be raised 100 feet, covering most of the Earth.

On January 17th, *Boxoffice* trade magazine opined:

Writer-Producer Irwin Allen assembled an impressive collection of underwater and kindred film, most of it expertly photographed and all of it in high-quality Technicolor, and welded it with appropriate commentary. The result is an educational, engrossing and sometimes exciting morsel of film fare that will displease none and entertain most.

A two-page ad in the January 19, 1953 issue of *Daily Variety*, paid for by Allen, trumpeted the good notices:

The *Hollywood Reporter* called *The Sea Around Us*: "Thrilling... amazing spectacle... [an] unforgettable theatrical experience..."

Showman's Trade Review said: "Producer Irwin Allen... has achieved a near-miracle..."

The Film Daily said: "Gripping... definite Academy Award contender..."

Motion Picture Daily said: "May well be best documentary ever produced..."

Edwin Schallert of the *Los Angeles Times* said: "Bound to make audiences starry-eyed..."

The Los Angeles Independent said: "Undersea masterpiece... strong Academy contender..."

Joe Hyams of *The Los Angeles Citizen-News* said: "Must-seeing for everyone in the family..."

Boxoffice magazine said: "Engrossing... Impressive... Exciting..."

The Los Angeles Exhibitor said: "Superb entertainment... New prestige for motion pictures..."

Dick Williams of the *Los Angeles Mirror* said: "One of the unusual film features of the year... will snag Academy Award nomination..."

Beginning in late January, Allen embarked on a tour of fifteen key U.S. cities to promote *The Sea Around Us*. Hitting the road to plug a new movie was a task studios usually assigned to a film's stars, not its director. But this documentary had no stars – no air-breathing stars, anyway. It only made sense that the film's best promoter would be the man whose vision had brought it to the screen. And if plugging his movie involved a little self-promotion, he felt he had earned that, too. This was the time that Allen began a routine of meeting and schmoozing the major motion-picture exhibitors, smooth-talking them into booking his product, and even outlining ways they could better attract a mass audience to their theaters with his films. Allen showed himself a master of the promotional gimmick, with ideas often outside-of-the-box for the typical motion-picture Public Relations man.

Several weeks before the film was scheduled to be released, the greatest opportunity for advance promotion came.

The 25th Academy Awards ceremony was held on March 13, 1953, at the RKO Pantages Theatre in Hollywood, California. Irwin Allen was in attendance, dressed to the nines. He was hopeful, yet understandably nervous. His very first film as a solo producer, writer, and director had been nominated for Best Documentary of 1952. This nomination had brought Allen his first taste of artistic respect from the Hollywood community. The maker of lowbrow comedies and disposable melodramas, and his downward-trending studio, were suddenly receiving public praise from the show-business elite.

The film's victory was far from assured. The first hurdle to cross was the stigma associated with being the product of an exploitation film-maker and a once prestigious, now diminished studio. The second hurdle was the competition. *The Sea Around Us* was up against Dore Schary's *The Hoaxters*, a red-scare look at communism in the United States. It had been a hit with the public, and the conservative crowd was certainly pulling for this MGM production. It was narrated by an impressive stable of celebrities: Howard Keel, George Murphy, Walter Pidgeon, Barry Sullivan, Robert Taylor, and James Whitmore. Also vying for the esteemed award was Hall Bartlett's *Navajo*, the story of a Native American boy faced with cultural

Jean Hersholt presents Irwin Allen with his Oscar at the 25th Academy Awards ceremony held on March 19, 1953, at the RKO Pantages Theatre in Hollywood, California.

conflict when he rejects "the white man's school." Many among Hollywood's liberal crowd favored this one.

In spite of any politics at play, Irwin Allen went home that night the triumphant bearer of an Oscar, due to his own tenacity, drive, and hard work.

Nephew Michael Allen said, "Irwin understood the importance of that moment. That award changed the nature of his career dramatically." (MA-AI15)

After harvesting the 1953 Academy Award for Best Documentary, *The Sea Around Us* found an even wider reception. Interviewed by United Press immediately following his Oscar win, a jubilant Irwin Allen said, "Everyone said I was crazy when I announced that I was going to make a picture from Rachel Carson's best seller. But that book topped the best seller list for seventy weeks! How could I lose? I figured if people were that interested in fish and other marine life, they'd sure as shootin' want to see it on the screen." (IA-UP53-2)

This success inspired Allen's eagerness to use stock footage, which in years to come became a deficit whose practice brought him ridicule. For now, though, he had coined gold from others' celluloid. He said, "If we had shot this film from scratch, it would have cost us four-and-a-half-million dollars. This way, we brought it in for a little over $200,000." (IA-UP52-2)

Striking five hundred prints, RKO gave *The Sea Around Us* a deliberately slow release schedule for the duration of 1953.

After a second look, some film critics were less enamored with the movie. Philip K. Scheuer, on behalf of the *Los Angeles Times*, from July 3, 1953, wrote:

> A book like Rachel L. Carson's *The Sea Around Us* comes along once in a generation, if that generation is lucky. Comparable genius would be required to turn it into a film and the maker of the film now at the Fine Arts Theater would hardly lay claim to that distinction. What RKO's Irwin Allen has done is to take Miss Carson's title, which certainly allows a lot of leeway, and append to it a

hodgepodge of odd and interesting facts and theories about the sea around *him*.

Barbara Wolfe, writing in *The Indianapolis Star* on October 8th, astutely observed:

> Responsibility for the success of a film without actors most naturally falls on the narrative continuity, supplied in *The Sea Around Us* by Don Forbes and Theodore Von Eltz. With anything like a hackneyed travelogue commentary, the multi-colored scenes and sea life portraits would go to waste. Strangely enough, the narrative in this case travels farther imaginatively than do the photographic shots. The drama is lost when the cameras fail to follow up the lines of action so aptly described. The result is, at best, fragmentary glimpses of a world surrounded by water, the inhabitants of which demand further elucidation to sturdy landlubbers.

It turned out that one of the film's harshest critics was Rachel Carson herself. According to author Linda Lear in *Rachel Carson: Witness for Nature*, Allen had sent Carson the film script, which included the bridging narration which would link all the vignettes together, offer commentary, and even serve as comedy relief in many instances. Carson's response was not favorable.

In a letter to Shirley Collier, her film agent in Hollywood, Carson wrote:

> Frankly, I could not believe my first reading, and had to put it away and then sneak back to it the next day to see if it could possibly be as bad as I thought. But every reading sends my blood pressure higher.

Jeff Stafford, in an article for the internet site Movie Morlocks in 2011, wrote:

> Carson was shocked that instead of sticking to the atmosphere and basic concepts of her book and presenting the authoritative scientific knowledge of the ocean as she had, Allen's script was full of outmoded, unscientific concepts, presented in a distressingly amateurish manner. She particularly objected to the anthropomorphism of the language Allen used to describe ocean creatures and their relationships with each other.

Allen had also scripted many of the narrative passages in an attempt to inject playful humor, even giving human voice to many of the animals on display.

Illustrating Carson's dissatisfaction, her letter to Shirley Collier continued:

> [T]he practice of attributing human vices and virtues to the lower animals went out of fashion many years ago. It persists only at the level of certain Sunday Supplements.

While Carson's reservations were understandable, she missed an important point. Her book had been addressed primarily to the educated. Conversely, Allen's intent was to convey her message of conservation to a much larger audience, even if through a sensational presentation. The humanistic dialogue, and Allen's decision to arrange events into narrative vignettes, were necessary to engage a mass moviegoing audience. As any successful preacher knows, you have to get the audience into their seats before they will listen. It's regrettable that Carson didn't seem to appreciate that Allen's "Sunday Supplement" had won an Academy Award and brought the world's attention to her environmental concerns.

In later years, Allen was famous for stating that his intent was to produce entertainment, not "message" pictures. Still, at the beginning of his producing career, with *The Sea Around Us*, he helped spread an eerily prescient-sounding warning about possible climate change.

In Los Angeles, where *Variety* said it was "displaying surprising strength," *Sea* was rated as "socko" and settled in for a long eight-week stay at the Fine Arts Theater. A two-month run was a rare occurrence, even for a small house such as the Fine Arts, which seated only 631 people. The story was the same elsewhere. On Broadway, *The Sea Around Us* stayed at New York's 458-seat Trans-Lux at 60th Street for eight weeks. In Philadelphia (where it also was ranked "socko"), it held on for six weeks in a single theater. It rated "big" during its premiere engagement in San Francisco, perhaps because it was in the small 370-seat Stage Door. In Chicago, at the Surf Theatre, with its 685 seats, *Sea* rated "nice," and stayed for six weeks. In Portland, at the 400-seat Gould, it was classified as "very good."

Irwin Allen had gambled more than a year of his life in the making of a documentary, and that gamble paid off with Hollywood's most prestigious award. Few would remember the mixed reviews the film received upon its general release. Allen made sure that the Oscar nod remained the film's legacy.

***

Irwin Allen had a *Dangerous Mission* for William Bendix, Piper Laurie, Victor Mature, and Vincent Price. (RKO Radio Pictures, 1954)

Within weeks of winning his Oscar, Irwin Allen had already set up his next film with RKO. The prestige he'd gained allowed him to survive a massive shakeup at the studio during 1952. Howard Hughes, blaming "the infiltration by Reds" for the production shutdown and mass layoffs, had brought activity at the studio to a complete standstill. His Red-seeking axe slashed through all departments, cutting the number of employed from around 2,000 to an estimated 375 persons.

For its April 7, 1952 issue, Hughes told *Daily Variety*, "RKO will perfect a plan and a system of operation which will eliminate Red participation and still permit production at a steady and reasonable rate.... It is not too difficult to operate under these conditions, if a certain amount of compromise can be tolerated. However, I have decided that RKO will not compromise. ...

"Obviously, there is no point in screening people employed on a motion picture only to discover that the script we have purchased innocently enough was written five years ago by someone with a Communist front record or that the script was based on an original story or book which was written by a Red sympathizer. ... Ours is a story of a fight against Communist infiltration, the winning of that battle, and continuous vigilance to expose and flush out communism and communists wherever they may be found."

Allen took steps to ensure that the script for his next film had no roots in the soil of the Communist Party. The story came from author James Edmiston (who wrote the book *Home Again*, about the treatment of Japanese Americans during World War II), with a script by Horace McCoy (who had written 1942's *Gentleman Jim*), and a rewrite by W.R. Burnett (who had received an Academy Award nomination for 1942's *Wake Island*).

Daily Variety announced on May 14th that Horace McCoy was already busy writing the screenplay for "The Glacier Story" ... and had collapsed while working for Mr. Allen. Enter W.R. Burnett.

Two months later, the same trade announced that Robert Mitchum would be called back from his vacation to head north for location filming for "The Glacier Story."

On December 17th, *Daily Variety* reported that manpower problems continued to beset RKO in its efforts to get back into production. Only five producers were able to maintain their contracts – Edmund Grainger (best known for *Sands of Iwo Jima*), Harriet Parsons (*I Remember Mama*), Sam Wiesenthal (*Cry Danger*), Robert Sparks (the *Blondie* film series), and Irwin Allen. Days later, with the instability of RKO under Hughes escalating, sister trade weekly *Variety* reported that it appeared that "The Glacier Story" was off the schedule, and that Allen would instead be working with producers Sam Wiesenthal under executive producer Edmund Grainger on a film called "Second Chance," set for a mid-January start.

To serve as a mere co-producer under Grainger represented a step back for Allen. He would rather be a film's sole producer; his Oscar win had earned him that distinction, he felt. With this clear goal, and within a few months, Allen was back on "The Glacier Story." All systems were go for filming to begin in Montana at Glacier National Park in late July.

On July 17, 1953, *Daily Variety* reported a title change to "Rangers of the North." Mitchum was out. Vincent Price, however, was in – the first star to be signed. He would play the villain.

At forty-one, Price was just finding his niche playing sinister characters, as in 1946's *Dragonwyck* and 1953's *House of Wax*. "Rangers of the North" would be the start of a working friendship between Allen and Price, which would reunite them for 1957's *The Story of Mankind*, 1959's *The Big Circus*, and a 1967 episode of TV's *Voyage to the Bottom of the Sea*.

Within days, Victor Mature and William Bendix were added to the cast, followed days later by Piper Laurie.

Victor Mature was forty-two, and had been a silver-screen leading man since the end of World War II, with a standout role in John Ford's 1946 film, *My Darling Clementine*. He played the leads in 1947's *Kiss of Death* and Cecil B. DeMille's 1949 epic, *Samson & Delilah*, as well as other high-profile appearances, such as 1953's *The Robe*. He and Allen would have a friendly professional relationship also, and Mature would return to star in Allen's 1959 spectacle *The Big Circus*.

Piper Laurie would play Louise Graham, the damsel in distress. She was twenty-one, and had already had youthful top female roles in movies starring Donald O'Connor, Tony Curtis, and Rock Hudson.

William Bendix had worked for Allen in *A Girl in Every Port*. He was one year shy of making the move to TV for the first of 217 episodes of *The Life of Riley*.

Louis King, who had helmed the popular *Bulldog Drummond* film series, was tapped to direct, with production set to begin the following week in Montana.

Victor Mature had just finished acting in *The Robe* and *The Gladiator* and was planning a much-needed vacation. But after reading the script for "Rangers of the North," he decided to have a working vacation at Glacier National Park instead, and took his family along for the scenery and fun.

What did Mature like best about "Rangers of the North"? He jokingly told columnist Jimmy Fidler, "I wear long pants and short hair. In my last two pictures, *The Robe* and *The Gladiator*, I wore long hair and short skirts."

Fidler described another perk for Mature:

> Irwin Allen of RKO had gone to Montana's Glacier Park hotel with his company for location scenes in "Rangers of the North." Allen noticed a boy in the lobby whom he thought would be fine for a role in the picture. He approached the lad and asked his name.
>
> "Mike," was the answer. "Would you like to do a part in a picture?" "Sure," was the reply, "if it's all right with my dad." "Where's your dad?" "He'll be down soon – oh, there he is – coming down the stairs."
>
> Allen stared. Dad was Victor Mature, star of "Rangers of the North." Vic had arrived late the night before with his wife, Dorothy, and son Mike, and they had retired without meeting Allen. Vic smiled when his son was proposed for a part in the story. "Sure," he said – and Mike is now portraying a bratty kid who is nuts about bows and arrows, and who is always losing his arrows on the hotel grounds. (VM-ES53)

Location filming lasted two weeks, and then the cast returned to RKO studios for sound-stage work.

Irwin Allen, like Cecil B. DeMille and Alfred Hitchcock, was grabbing headlines because of an oversized set he had built on a Hollywood soundstage. For *Daily Varity*'s August 13th issue:

The Ice Age is coming to RKO and it's costing a small fortune to bring it there. The climactic scenes of "Rangers of the North" take place on a glacier, which is being reproduced on Stage 10 at the studio. When completed, it will be the most mammoth ice set ever built, covering the entire stage and towering 55 feet into the air and descending 15 feet below floor level. Over 100 tons of snow will be needed to cover it. A complicated engineering structure is being built beneath part of the glacier so that it will give way at the right time, causing a tremendous cave-in in which the "heavies" of the film will be trapped.

(A historic note concerning RKO Stage 10: By the 1960s, the studio had been sold to Desi Arnaz and Lucille Ball, who renamed the facility Desilu Productions. *Star Trek* was filmed there, and assigned two soundstages – Stage 9, for the Starship Enterprise, and RKO Stage 10, for alien planet sets. For one episode, 1968's "Spock's Brain," Stage 10 would again be transformed into a glacier environment.)

On December 7th, *Daily Variety* reported that the title of the movie would be changed again – to *Dangerous Mission*. While Allen liked provocative titles derived from the story, Howard Hughes preferred more generic titles signifying action or suspense – especially for a film that might not live up to its dramatic title.

The newly christened *Dangerous Mission* had been shot in 3-D. This cumbersome process was the movie industry's latest attempt to woo audiences away from their television sets, back into vacant theater seats. However, by the time *Dangerous Mission* had a trade-show screening and was scheduled for general release, the timing was no longer good for cashing in on the 3-D craze.

Prospective exhibitors balked over being billed twice for movies filmed with the process – two separate prints and two projectors were required to screen a single 3-D title. Theater owners were coming to the conclusion that they could reap more profit by exhibiting a 3-D movie with standard projection equipment, which completely eliminated the 3-D effect. In fact, Allen's movie would have far more play dates in 2-D than 3-D. This often meant that *Dangerous Mission* was forced to stand on its own merits, without the gimmick of 3-D. For many critics, this simply wasn't enough.

Dangerous Mission went home to Glacier Park for its premiere – for a six-day run at the Civic Theater in Great Falls, Montana. Piper Laurie was on hand with Irwin Allen to mark the occasion. One week later, it opened in numerous U.S. cities.

For its February 24, 1954 issue, the critic for the *Hollywood Reporter* said:

> With the bulk of the film taking place in Montana's Glacier National Park, *Dangerous Mission* has plenty of impressive scenery to offer, beautifully photographed in Technicolor and 3-D by William Snyder. It also has a story that strains credulity... among [the writers] they have worked out a string of episodic adventures that carry little conviction but do successfully utilize the beauties of the locale.

On the same day, "Brog," reviewing the movie for *Variety*, wrote:

> Picture gets rolling with high promise of being a strong suspense meller [melodrama], well-plotted, but settles down to a routine unfoldment about the halfway mark. Had the starting flavor been sustained, it would have been a real taut thriller set against colorful Glacier National Park site of much of the footage. ... Irwin Allen's production guidance gets neat values from the outdoor locations and tossed in for thrill action are an avalanche, a forest fire and the glacier bit.

Boxoffice magazine wasn't nearly as enamored by Allen's everything-but-the-kitchen-sink approach to filmmaking. Its February 27th issue reported:

> Into its comparatively brief footage is packed, in king-size quantities, a diversity of story ingredients – mobsters on the lam, outdoor action, forest fires, avalanches, romance, and what else would you like?

Also on March 6th, Jane Corby, writing in New York's *The Brooklyn Daily Eagle*, gave her verdict. She admitted to liking the Technicolor, the 3-D, and the stars. But, as for the script…

> The story itself is dwarfed by the scenery and the amount of action and accidents, which is just as well. It's not a credible tale. …
>
> The Montana Glacier National Park cooperates beyond the call of duty with this film, lending its grandeur to a story that doesn't really deserve it.

Filmindia, from May 1954, was the harshest, reflecting its political-activist editorial stance:

> *Dangerous Mission* is another ill-tasting concoction served in a Technicolored goblet. Portrayed against some interesting natural scenery, the picture is filled with disgusting contents and deals with crooks and criminals, their criminal, violent activities, and their victims. The theme, of course, is murder. Beginning with one murder, the rest of the picture is devoted to showing a long, sinister, planned attempt by a criminal to commit another murder. … What a useful, instructive and educative story!

With these reviews, and its generic-sounding title, Allen's first attempt as a commercial producer of action films tanked. *Variety* and its sister trade paper, *Daily Variety*, tracked the film's performance at the box office. It started on a good note on March 8th, ranked as "fairish" at the 950-seater Holiday Theater in New York (one of the smaller premiere houses on Broadway), then up to "fine" the following week, and then "good" for its third. Elsewhere, it was rated merely as "average" in Providence; "okay" in Cincinnati; "fair" in Chicago; "slow" in Los Angeles; "mild" in Minneapolis; "poor" in both Montreal and Cleveland; "dull" in Seattle; "light" in Toronto; "thin" in San Francisco; and "limp" in St. Louis. These weren't the adjectives that Allen and RKO wanted to hear in connection with *Dangerous*, or any other project.

In its best week during a three-month first-run tour, the movie ranked at Number 20 on the national box-office register.

Irwin Allen's tenure at RKO was coming to an end. Fortunately for him, by the time *Dangerous Mission* was faltering in the movie houses, his next project was in development … at a different studio.

***

Daily Variety reported on January 13, 1954:

> Two producers abruptly resigned from RKO yesterday as the studio appeared to be entering another full-scale economy drive. ... Exiting producers are Irwin Allen and Sam Wiesenthal. Both make their resignations effective within the next few weeks to give themselves time to clean up their desks. Allen reported immediately that he would enter independent production... Allen, who wrote and produced the Academy Award-winning feature length documentary, *The Sea Around Us*, is finishing up *The Dangerous Mission*, his final assignment after five and one-half years as a writer-producer. He owns three properties which he intends to produce independently.

Allen wasn't waiting for the reviews for *Dangerous Mission* to hit before setting up his next picture deal. In early March, 1954, he formed his own company – Windsor Productions – and hired former Cinerama treasurer Ernest Scanlon to arrange New York financing for a movie that his investors were banking might bring about a second Academy Award acknowledgment. *The Animal World* was pitched as a sequel to *The Sea Around Us*; it would trace the movement of life from the ocean to the land.

On June 28th, *Daily Variety* reported that a deal had been finalized over the previous weekend for Allen to distribute through Warner Bros.

Interviewed by United Press for an April 1955 wire-service article, Allen said of *The Sea Around Us*, "It was the biggest financial success RKO had – *twice as big as Jane Russell* – and *it* won an Oscar! So I decided to make another picture without actors – a documentary on animals. ... *I love to make pictures without actors.* No temperament and [animals are] always on time in the morning because they're the only actors you can lock away at night." (IA-UP55)

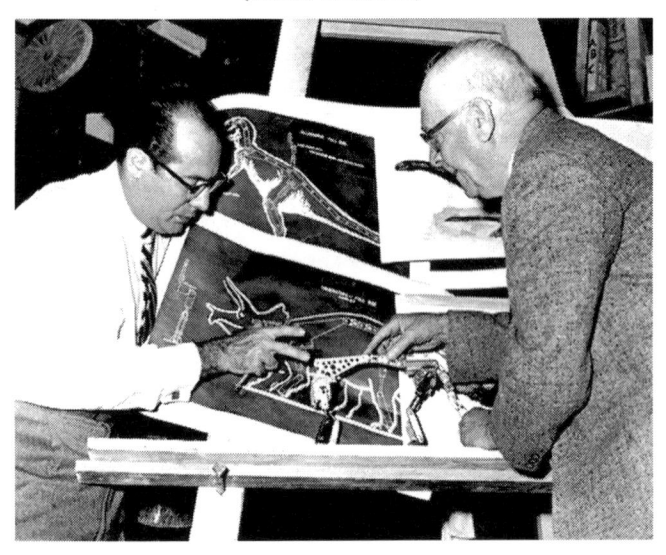

On September 2, 1954, the trades announced that Allen would have to vacate his RKO digs immediately, but that was fine with him. His Windsor Productions moved in to their new complimentary offices at Warner Bros. the next day.

Weeks later, on September 24th, *Daily Variety* reported that Allen had lured post-production coordinator George Swink from RKO to work for Windsor on *The Animal World*. Swink had worked on *The Sea Around Us* as assistant to the producer. In years to come, Swink would stay at Allen's side, as post-production supervisor on *Voyage to the Bottom of the Sea*, *Lost in Space*, *The Time Tunnel*, and *Land of the Giants*, as well as occupying that post on many of Allen's movies from the 1970s and '80s.

Allen playing with his latest toys, with his technical team members, for *The Animal World*.
(Warner Bros., 1956)

From *Daily Variety*, January 20, 1955:

> Jack L. Warner last night approved final production plans and an international schedule of operations for the production of Irwin Allen's *The Animal World*, to be released through WB. Film, to trace the two billion year history of all living things on Earth, will be lensed in

Technicolor and wide-screen, and will be at least twice the 61-minute length of Allen's *The Sea Around Us*.

Already in pre-production for over a year, sked includes more than two months of filming on a pre-historic sequence, one week of shooting the dinosaur fossils at NY's Museum of Natural History, as well as a 10-month production operation in more than 17 foreign countries.

A special unit, headed by Willis O'Brien and Ray Harryhausen, who did animation work on *The Lost World* and *King Kong*, and by cameraman Harold Wellman, stop-motion expert, will shoot the pre-historic scenes showing the Earth when the dinosaur was king of the animal world. Meanwhile, Allen, production associate George Swink and cameraman Wellman leave Friday for film's first location jaunt to NY's Museum of Natural History.

Tracking down his background, Allen has requested and received the active participation of friendly nations in addition to the cooperation of various departments of the U.S. Government. World-wide production includes animal sits in Africa, India, Australia, Brazil, Venezuela, Peru, New Zealand, Mexico, Saudi Arabia, Sweden, Turkey, Norway, and Denmark.

Oscar Godbout, writing in the February 13th edition of the *New York Times*, said:

The eerie nocturnal silence of the Museum of National History was broken unnaturally the other night as a movie troupe under producer-director-writer Irwin Allen moved into the Age of Man Hall to film sequences for the feature-length documentary, *The Animal World*. Mr. Allen, busily supervising the camera crew working on a shot of the skull of Neanderthal Man, took a break in the shooting to explain politely that the picture could not strictly be described as a documentary on the evolution of animal life.

Allen told Godbout, "We don't use the word 'evolution.' We hope to walk a very thin line. On one hand we want the scientists to say this film is right and accurate, and yet we don't want to have the church picketing the film. However, I think we're safe, since both science and the Bible agree on the fundamental point – life began in the sea [Genesis, i, 20]." (IA-NYT55)

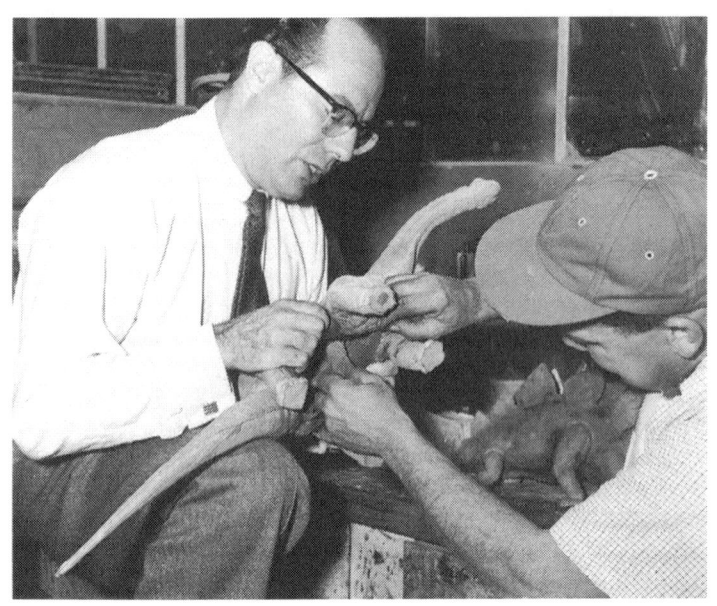

Allen and his technicians, making *The Animal World*.
(Warner Bros., 1956)

This new project, from inception to distribution, occupied two years of Allen's life. Eighteen months alone were spent in active production. For this workaholic, it was an inordinately long period of time to spend on a single motion picture.

As part of that production, seventy-three days alone were needed to create the sequences involving dinosaurs. Using stop-motion animation, Ray Harryhausen, working from designs by Willis O'Brien, carefully and painstakingly moved the models a fraction of an inch for each exposed frame of film, producing the illusion of movement when the footage was projected at normal speed. Those seventy-three days created only twelve minutes of the finished film. In comparison, Harryhausen's shooting time was nearly double the typical forty days of principal photography for an ordinary live-action film from the same period.

On July 29th, *Daily Variety* reported that *The Animal World* had completed filming and was being readied for a Christmas release. The running time, as Allen had predicted, was about two hours. After watching the final edit, however, Jack Warner felt that was at least 30 minutes too long.

More delays resulted when Allen agreed to edit out more than a quarter of the film – cutting it down to a trim 81 minutes. This meant that the proposed Christmas 1955 release was pushed back into early summer of 1956 – a gap of more than two years between the release of Allan's last picture, *Dangerous*

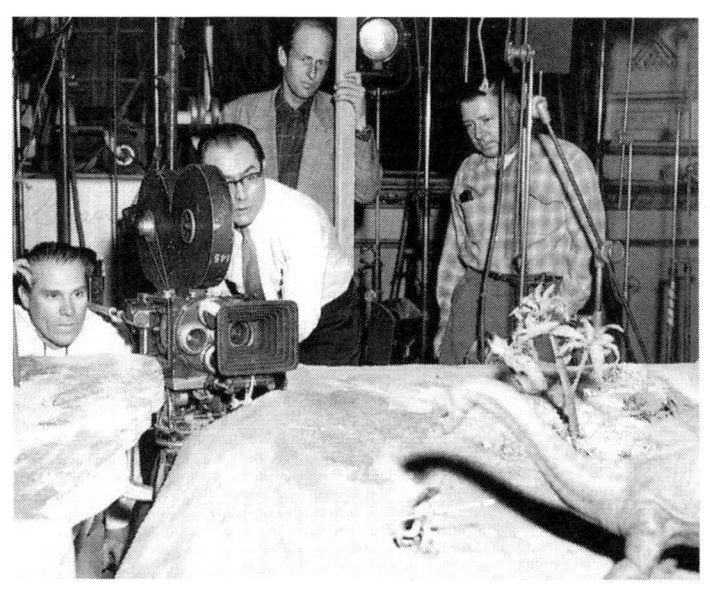

Mission, and *The Animal World*. In the 1950s, a career could cool off considerably in that period of time.

Allen explained his box-office absence to Edwin Schallert of the *Los Angeles Times* this way, "We had to secure film from sources all over the world. A total of more than 3,000,000 feet was exposed in order to obtain the material that we wanted from many different points of origin. … It required all of two and a half years to bring *The Animal World* to fulfillment. About a year and a half was needed for the camera work, preceded by a year of research. However, that is comparatively little to spend on a film which attempts to cover some two and a half billion years in its story – that is, we assume there have been things living on this Earth for that long." (IA-LAT56)

Irwin Allen behind camera ... and directly behind him, a young Ray Harryhausen. (Warner Bros., 1957)

For a March 16, 1956 *Variety* article, writer Fred Hift said:

> Has Hollywood run out of variations on the seven basic plots? Indie Irwin Allen, who releases through Warner Bros., thinks maybe the time is at hand, and he knows just what to do about it. He started solving the problem with *The Sea Around Us* and he's now following up with the as yet unreleased *The Animal World*, which

81

traces animal history and the animal world's relationship to man. In Gotham last week, Allen said it was his aim to entertain *and* educate.

Allen told Hift, "If we can sugarcoat a piece of information, and get them to like it, we've accomplished something.

"We are going to translate the picture into seventeen languages, even though there won't be any subtitles. It'll be understood *everywhere*. In an ordinary Hollywood picture, you have always the problem of getting overseas audiences to adjust to American relationships. Here we have a common language, an international language." (IA-V56)

"Whit," of *Daily Variety*, was one of the first to rate the movie, for the trade's April 18, 1956 issue.

> Irwin Allen's follow-up to his Academy-winning documentary *The Sea Around Us* is marked with the same interesting and often fantastic revelations of nature and her work. ... Feature has both its violent and lighter moments, all shaken together to give spectator a vivid impression of the subject. Some of the most interesting scenes are the fights between various types of dinosaurs, animated with surprising realism by Willis O'Brien and Ray Harryhausen. Real-life scenes show a lioness bringing down an impala and two lions attacking a zebra; giraffes fighting; charge of a rhino upon the camera; a ferret and cobra in combat; a giant eel and octopus locked in death embrace. Actual birth of baby starfish is caught, and there's the film vignette of a bear cub and fawn to delight the eye. Realistic sound effects accompany various sequences.

Writing in the *Hollywood Reporter* on April 18th, James Powers said:

> [T]his is a major work, in conception and in execution, and the achievement is correspondingly great. ... If there is pathos and tragedy, there is also humor. It is no discredit to Allen's originality and creative ability to say that there is the same sort of humor here that Walt Disney achieves so well in his much smaller-scaled animal pictures. This is the kind of anthropomorphic humor that the critics invariably denounce and that audiences invariably take to enthusiastically. It is good pacing, because it gives *The Animal World* needed variety to contrast the fierceness and brutality that is so much a part of any depiction of animals in any age or time.

> The film has no human actors, although two voices are used to very good effect, the narrators Theodor Von Eltz and John Storm. Allen seems to be using one voice for chronological account and the second for comment. It is a good device because it allows him simultaneously to tell his story and to comment upon it.

On May 18th, a United Press wire article made the rounds in newspapers across America, stating in part:

> Irwin Allen is a most unusual type of film producer. He has combined science and entertainment well enough to win an Academy Award. He did this although he usually flunked or just barely passed science courses in high school or college.

Allen told the UP correspondent: "Journalism and advertising were my majors at Columbia University and City College of New York. However, I had a great interest in show business, although it wasn't until after years of working in radio and TV as a writer and producer, and then in films, that I became interested in science as a theme for pictures." (IA-DIJ56)

For his next film, Allen would turn science into science fiction. For now, however, he added, "Our stuff is *not* science-fiction. It's science *non-fiction*." (IA-AR56)

Warner Bros. gave *The Animal World* a wide release. It went into hundreds of theaters across North America simultaneously, as the "A" feature in a double bill. The studio/distributor ran a newspaper ad campaign touting the film as being "Two Billion Years in the Making." And, unlike *The Sea Around Us*, which was booked into smaller movie houses, *The Animal World* went into medium-size theaters, ranging from 1,000 to 3,000 seats.

On May 30th, Allen flew to New Orleans on the first leg of a 28-day cross-country tour promoting his new film. The last documentary he made had won critical praise and an Oscar; this one needed to win something more tangible – money. As it transpired, *The Animal World* brought home the bacon for Warners and Allen.

Then came the reviews.

On May 31st, "A.W." wrote in *The New York Times*:

> ... Mr. Allen's portrait of *The Animal World* is far from definitive. But if it does not continually enthrall the mind it does catch the eye.

On June 2, 1956, Jesse Zunser, of *Cue* magazine, said:

> Writer-producer Irwin Allen has set himself the enormous task of trying to picture in 82 minutes the development of animal life on Earth (exclusive of man) from almost the beginning of time. Considering the difficulties, he's done a fairly creditable job – although to many this film may seem more like a grab-bag of odds and ends of briefly interesting film clips, than a cohesive zoological record. ...

Alice Hughes, writing for King Features Syndicate in the first week of June, raved:

> How exciting! The world of animals must be seen in the breathtaking, noteworthy Technicolor film, *The Animal World*, written, produced and directed by triple-threat Irwin Allen. This new Warner Bros. presentation, just opened at New York's Little Carnegie Theater and soon to be nationally released is a fitting follow-up of *The Sea Around Us*, which won Allen the Academy Award and many other honors. ... Whether showing dinosaurs or microscopic molecules, this picture combines authentic zoology with wonderful color photography. When the prehistoric dinosaur stampede becomes a bit scary, or the eternal battle for survival too grimly realistic, producer Allen is quick with a touch of humor. He thus keeps the film exciting yet palatable for young and old. Educationally, this movie gives biology, zoology, ornithology and paleontology a fast and fascinating approach.

On June 15th, Boyd Martin, in the Louisville, Kentucky's *The Courier-Journal*, commented:

> ... It must be admitted that Allen has covered this world thoroughly. By means of miniatures, underwater photography, animation, and every device known to picture making, he gives you the story of animal life from its prehistoric beginning to the present day. Of course, this is a story that never ends, and that's just about what you will feel in viewing Allen's film.

On June 21st, the film critic for the Los Angeles *Mirror News* wrote:

> Dinosaurs and other great reptiles provide the most excitement in the early scenes. These monsters are more realistically duplicated and better animated than usual in sequences showing us how lucky we were to have been absent billions of years ago. The live animal shots are good, too, but repetitious in view of Walt Disney's True Life Adventures series and the plentitude of film's about Africa. In any case, the subject is almost too overwhelming. ...

Terry Turner, writing in the June 21st edition of the *Akron Beacon Journal*, praised the movie, but also noted:

> Incidentally, the narration is very carefully worded to prevent any involvement in differences of opinion between church and science about history of mankind.

The same comment would be made by more than one critic concerning Allen's next film, *The Story of Mankind*.

The June 27th issue of *Variety* tallied the box office take: Business was "hefty" in Cincinnati; "fine" in Buffalo; "good" in Cleveland; and the movie was also doing good business in Providence, Washington D.C., and St. Louis. In fact, the film did well enough across the nation to claim the No. 2 slot in the *Variety*'s National Box Office Survey for the week ending June 26th.

Allen had conquered the animal world. Now he was ready to take another shot at the biped kingdom.

***

For his next film, Irwin Allen mixed science fiction and fantasy with pseudo-history. Louella O. Parsons had the scoop for her Hearst Syndicate column on March 31, 1955:

> Producers are finally convinced that movie audiences have come of age when such a classic as Hendrik van Loon's *The Story of Mankind* is bought (by Warner Bros.) for a picture. The book, published in 17 languages, including Braille and Esperanto, has won over 40 awards in literature and has passed the 5,000,000 sales mark.
>
> Jack Warner could have made no better selection than Irwin Allen to bring this undertaking to the screen. Allen won an Academy Award for *The Sea Around Us* and is currently completing *The Animal World* for Warners. He

> will script, produce and direct *The Story of Mankind* – a gigantic task of tracing man's history through the one million years of sojourn on the three billion years old Earth. ...

The acclaimed book, written by Dutch-American journalist and author Hendrik Willem van Loon, was first published in 1921. One year later, it was the first book to be awarded the Newbery Medal for outstanding contribution to children's literature – for Van Loon had in fact written the book for his own children, Hansje and Willem. In selecting his subjects, Van Loon's criteria was, "Did the person or event in question perform an act without which the entire history of civilization would have been different?" The book began with primitive man, then proceeded to cover the development of writing, art and architecture, the rise of major religions, and the formation of the modern nation and state.

On March 31st, *Daily Variety* reported that Allen had already spent a year researching the project, and would roll cameras following the completion of *The Animal World*. On the heels of *The Sea Around Us* and *The Animal World*, *The Story of Mankind* would complete Allen's "film trilogy of the history of the sea, the land and now of man."

On March 16, 1956, Fred Hift of *Variety* caught up with Allen while he was in New York promoting *The Animal World*. Allen told Hift that his goal with his trilogy of the history of the Earth remained to educate and entertain. He said, "People sense whether something is accurate or not. It adds to their enjoyment of a picture."

Hift added:

> *The Story of Mankind* [will] again be done in partnership with WB, even though Allen made it plain he considered it nobody's business just what his relationship with the company was. Nor did he think it pertinent to reveal the budget on his picture.

Allen had good reason to keep the specifics of the business deal between his Windsor Productions and Warner Bros. a secret. He had definitely gotten the better of Jack Warner, as later trade magazine reports would reveal.

Allen co-wrote *The Story of Mankind* with Charles Bennett, who grumbled, "Irwin Allen was the living end! After *Danger*, I wrote his every picture until *The Poseidon Adventure* [1972]. I was his favorite writer, but I couldn't *stand* him – an impossible man with the most horrible swollen head." (CB-HPIS14)

Despite these feelings, Bennett was always happy to accept work from Allen, who appreciated and felt friendly toward the writer. But these feelings weren't reciprocated.

After Allen's death, Bennett scoffed, "*Nobody* could ever be a personal friend of his. But he had tremendous respect for *me*, and he never dared cross me in any way. … He would come to my house for drinks occasionally, yes, but then, so did many people." (CB-SL93)

In truth, Allen had many close friends, including Groucho Marx, Red Buttons, Ernest Borgnine, Henry Fonda, Steve Allen, Robert Wagner, Roddy McDowall, Fred Astaire, and Walter Pidgeon. Allen believed that Bennett too was a friend, or at least a friendly collaborator. But the bitter writer saw himself as above those he worked for. While many may agree with his assessment of *The Story of Mankind*, it nonetheless said more about the speaker than the film-maker when Bennett fumed, "That dreadful picture! I came back from England, and Irwin Allen implored me to work on that thing. I didn't realize quite how dreadful it was going to be, or when I was starting off that it was really going to be just a collection of snippets from old pictures and things like that. I *hated* the picture. But I'm a writer; I wrote it; I was being paid quite handsomely, so that was that." (CB-SL93)

Allen – and Warner Bros. – had also paid the estate of Hendrik Willem van Loon handsomely for the rights to the title and book to serve as the basis for the film. However, the film had little or nothing to do with the book besides its world-famous title.

When asked by interviewer Tom Weaver if the script followed the book, Bennett snapped back with a laugh, "Certainly not! In fact, I never read the book – and I don't think Allen did, either!" (CB-SL93)

Irwin Allen and art department assistant pose for studio publicity photo during pre-production for *The Story of Mankind*. (Warner Bros., 1957)

For those familiar with Allen's voracious and wide-ranging reading habits, it is certainly possible that he had read *The Story of Mankind*. And, even though his co-writer dismissed the project as merely a well-paying job, Irwin Allen considered it a labor of love.

On March 21, 1956, Edwin Schallert, writing in *Los Angeles Times*, said:

> No fewer than 42 nations will be represented in *The Story of Mankind,* to be produced by Irwin Allen as a two-and-a-half-hour spectacle for Warners. Full-scale plans for this picture, based on the book by Hendrik van Loon, were announced yesterday by Jack L. Warner. *The Story of Mankind* is the third best seller of all time and will be the maximum-effort project of the studio in all probability. Various departments of the United States government will assist in addition to such educational institutions as Yale, Princeton, SC, Dartmouth, and Harvard. The studio expects to assemble an advisory board of eminent historians, theologians and philosophers for the mammoth picture. Allen, who won an Academy Award for *The Sea Around Us*, which was filmed in various countries, is to be represented next by *The Animal World*. So he has been building up in evolutionary style to this *Story of Mankind*.

Even with such an immense undertaking before him, Allen had to leave the project for months to aggressively promote his current film in release. Edwin Schallert reported in the June 18th edition of the *Los Angeles Times*:

> Irwin Allen, producer of *The Sea Around Us* and *The Animal World*, who has boasted of the fact that he is able to make films without actors, is bound to face the issue of dealing with human performers in a big way in his next undertaking.
>
> Scheduled for this daring creator of unique cinema subjects is *The Story of Mankind* by Hendrik van Loon, which will deal with the whole panorama of humanity.
>
> At the moment Allen can rest briefly on his honors, and concern himself with the exploitation of *The Animal World*, now in release. He has been out on a second tour to promote interest in this remarkable follow-up to *The Sea Around Us*, which won him an Academy Award as a documentary.

A couple of months later, Allen was back to work on his next "big event" film. On October 17th, for her Hearst Syndicate column, Louella O. Parsons reported that Vincent Price had agreed to play Lucifer, with Sir Cedric Hardwicke appearing as the High Judge (in the heavens), and Peter Lorre set to fiddle while Rome burned, as Nero. Diana Lynn was also penciled in to play Joan of Arc, but a scheduling conflict – or a bigger star becoming available – would remove her from the cast.

On October 26th, Parsons reported that more stars had been added, including Ronald Colman (as "The Spirit of Man"), Hedy Lamarr (as the new Joan of Arc), Charles Coburn (as Hippocrates), and Marie Wilson (who was the lead female in Allen's *A Girl in Every Port*) set to play Marie Antoinette.

On November 1st, *Daily Variety* announced that Agnes Moorehead had joined the cast, set to play Queen Elizabeth, a part that Greer Garson had turned down. Also up for a role – Bette Davis. But Miss Davis, like Garson, would give the venture a thumbs down.

The all-star cast of *The Story of Mankind* grows, with the addition of Vincent Price and Ronald Colman (above) and Virginia Mayo (below), as Cleopatra. (Warner Bros., 1957)

Five days later, *Daily Variety* added more names to the roster: John Carradine (as Khufu, the Pharaoh who ordered the building of the Great Pyramid), Melville Cooper (Major Domo), and Franklin Pangborn (as Marquis de Varennes). It was also announced that Allen had formed a new company for this venture – Cambridge Productions.

The following day, *Daily Variety* added two more names to the roster – Helmut Dantine, to play Marc Anthony, and Ziva Rodann, as an Egyptian Concubine.

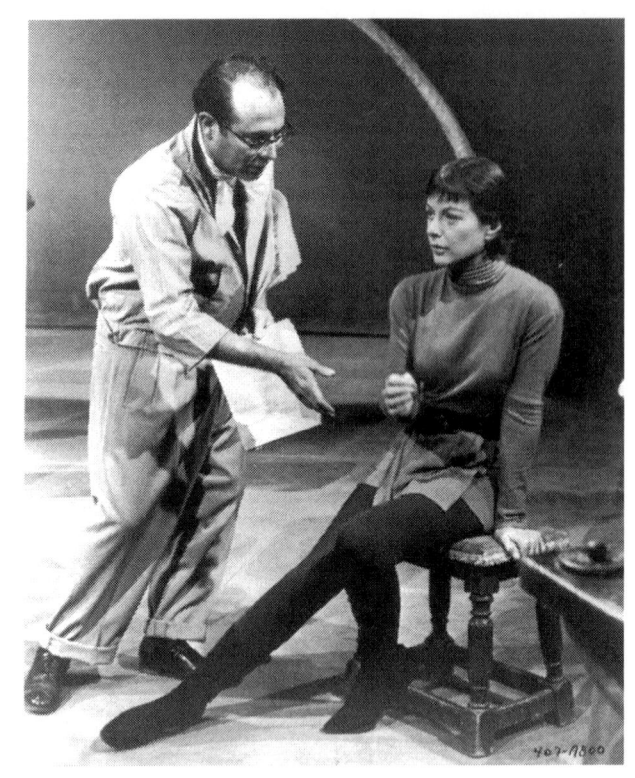

Allen giving direction to Hedy Lamarr for *The Story of Mankind* (Warner Bros., 1957)

The Hollywood trades and syndicated entertainment columnists were having a field day as the cast of "big names" grew almost daily. Allen was putting together his first all-star (human) spectacle.

Two days later, on November 9th, Philip K. Scheuer reported for the *Los Angeles Times*:

> Somehow *The Story of Mankind* wouldn't be complete unless Groucho Marx stuck his inquisitive mug into it somewhere. That's how Irwin Allen figures, too, so he has penciled the comedian in for the part of Peter Minuit, the shrewd real-estate operator who conned the Indians into selling Manhattan Island for the equivalent of 24 bucks. The *You Bet Your Life* star worked for Allen before in a couple of pictures at RKO, *Double Dynamite* and *A Girl in Every Port*, but this will be his first appearance in eye-filling Technicolor.
>
> And that isn't all. *Mankind* is rapidly turning into another *Around the World in 80 Days* as far as big names are concerned. Allen has also signed Cesar Romero for a vignette (Mike Todd calls them "cameos") as Spanish Ambassador to the court of Queen Elizabeth. Romero is in *80 Days* and has his own TV series, *Passport to Danger*.

Veteran George E. Stone will play an Elizabethan court attendant in *Mankind* and Robert Dupont and Tony Randall aides to Napoleon. That brings us right up to deadline.

Not entirely. Within a week's time, more cast additions: Dennis Hopper (yes, *that* Dennis Hopper) would play Napoleon Bonaparte; Virginia Mayo was set to play Cleopatra; Reginald Gardiner was tapped for William Shakespeare; Reginald Sheffield for Julius Caesar; Anthony Dexter to set sail as Christopher Columbus; and Marvin Miller cast as Armana, a figure in Egyptian history.

On November 18th, Philip K. Scheuer wrote in the *Los Angeles Times*:

> Irwin Allen, who conceived *The Sea Around Us* and *The Animal World*, says he has finally graduated to people with *The Story of Mankind*. He is filming the picture from the Hendrik van Loon book – world's best seller, according to him, after the Bible and *Gone With the Wind*. ...
>
> Securing the rights from Van Loon estate was "very complicated," but Allen swung it two years ago. He will not attempt to encompass the book's 600 pages: "Where we can't do justice to a time and place, we won't brush them off summarily. We just won't use them. There have been 400 or more giants of history in all fields. Our big problem has been to bring them down to some 50, asking about each: 'Was what he or she did lasting – and how long did it last?'"

Dennis Hopper as Napoleon Bonaparte, in *The Story of Mankind*.
(Warner Bros,. 1957)

Scheuer reported that the cast now also included Don Megowan and Nancy Miller as Adam and Eve, and Dani Crayne as Helen of Troy.

By the time the movie was released, the names Adam and Eve were stricken from the credits and replaced with "Early Man" and "Early Woman,"

Groucho Marx as Peter Minuit, in *The Story of Mankind*. (Warner Bros., 1957)

perhaps to avoid accusations from Bible schools that he had strayed from the written Word.

One day later, on November 19th, *Daily Variety* reported that *The Story of Mankind* would reunite the Marx Brothers. Groucho, already in the cast, would be joined by Chico and Harpo. Being responsible for a Marx Brothers reunion was a joyous accomplishment for Irwin Allen, even though the three brothers would appear in separate vignettes.

Interviewed while on set, Harpo, the "mute" Marx Brother, said, "I'm a lazy-type guy. The only reason I took this job was that it required only one day's work. The Marx Brothers as a team are through because I found moviemaking took too much energy. One day's work is about my limit." (HM-AR56)

A syndicated Associated Press article, carried in Michigan's *Kalamazoo Gazette* on December 9, 1956, caught the real Irwin Allen at work (or play, depending on one's perspective).

> Nothing seems to faze the films these days. Now they're attempting to tell the entire story of man. The man behind this ambitious project is Irwin Allen, an energetic young radiocaster turned film producer. He is directing *The Story of Mankind* for Warner Brothers. As a film-maker, Allen is strictly out of the TV dramas about Hollywood. He dashes from a countryside set of a pirate ship followed by a crew of technicians. He climbs to high points for inspiring camera angles. He alternately yells at his underlings and pats them on the cheek fondly. As he leaves the stage, he spies an elaborate window grill in a pile of props. "I like that," he exclaims. "Find me a scene I can shoot through it." Then he rumbles off in his high-priced car to his office. He shouts orders to more underlings and gazes at the gallery of his historical figures on his office wall. "All of them will be portrayed in the picture," he explains. "By the time we finish, we

expect to have a bigger cast than Mike Todd had in *Around the World."*

"More stars than there are in Heaven," MGM boasted. *The Story of Mankind* **sought to use most of them.** (Warner Bros., 1957)

Explaining his approach in filming the book, Allen told the AP correspondent, "Van Loon had a rare ability to put history into popular terms, to make it understandable to children. But with all due respect to van Loon, history is still something like hearing a joke for the second time. The punch is gone out of it. So, we have added a gimmick. We start out with two stars in the sky. They pulsate as they talk to each other and tell how the people on Earth have developed the gamma bomb, which with one blow could destroy the world. Should it be exploded? Now, we go to someplace in outer space. It's not heaven, because we wouldn't want to offend any religious groups. Here, a trial is held to determine whether Earth should be destroyed. Many of the heroes and the villains of history appear to testify, and we flash back to see their deeds." (IA-AP56)

The "gimmick" could have been used in any episode of Allen's *Lost in Space*. In fact, it was – in a 1966 episode entitled "Prisoners of Space." A similar cosmic trial of humankind provided the plot for the 1987 pilot episode of *Star Trek: The Next Generation*, sans input from Allen.

Days later, on December 3rd, United Press Hollywood correspondent Aline Mosby wrote:

> Ronald Colman seldom is lured into movies these days because, he says, Hollywood doesn't make "romantic classics" any more. Only two super colossal guest star epics have brought Colman from his hillside home in Santa Barbara, Calif., to the film factory since 1949.

That last starring role Colman had taken was in 1949, for *Champagne for Caesar*. Since that time, Colman only made a cameo appearance in Mike Todd's *Around the World in 80 Days*. Now he was set to play a much larger role in *The Story of Mankind*.

Colman told Mosby, "On the big screen they use a different kind of material than what I used to do. They do circus epics and Bible stories. What I used to do is gone – romantic films, the classics. You don't see pictures anymore such as *A Tale of Two Cities*, *Beau Geste* and *Lost Horizon*."

It was ironic, then, that Colman chose *The Story of Mankind* as a sort of comeback. And Irwin almost had him talked into starring in his next film – one of those circus epics that Colman said he had been avoiding. In fact, if things had turned out differently with *The Story of Mankind*, from a critical and box-office perspective, Colman likely would have taken the lead in *The Big Circus* instead of Victor Mature.

Regarding the temperament of the cast, *Mankind*'s co-writer Charles Bennett said, "I don't know that [Vincent Price] enjoyed playing the Devil in *The Story of Mankind*; I don't think anybody enjoyed any part of it. I know Ronald Colman hated it, and I don't think Vincent Price liked it either. Nobody liked it. It was just a revolting picture, and it should never have been made." (CB-SL93)

But Irwin Allen liked it and labored over it endlessly. Al Gail said, "I'll quote Groucho Marx. One day, Little Irwin was very upset about something that had gone wrong, or doing something with the picture, and Groucho said, 'Why are you getting excited? It's only a movie!' In other words, 'That's not real life; there's no tragedy here. It's a movie; have perspective.' And I guess perspective was what Irwin didn't have." (AG-KB95)

More casting news: *Daily Variety* confirmed on December 5th that Bobby Watson, who previously had impersonated Adolph Hitler in both dramatic and comedy films, would do so again for Allen. And Tudor Owen was announced as the seventy-second of ninety speaking roles to be cast, playing a High Tribunal Clerk. On December 14th, the trade reported that silent film star Francis X. Bushman, after a long absence from the screen, would return to work, playing Moses. And he would wear the same sandals he had worn in 1926, in *Ben Hur*.

Two days later, on December 16th, for a syndicated newspaper story, Harold Heffernan wrote:

> History's vilest villains – each an Oscar winner in his own era and particular brand of viciousness – are getting together for the first time. They'll march across the screen in a big movie, *The Story of Mankind*, which traces the development of man from the earliest days right up to the present. As a result of the widespread search for film counterparts, the casting office at Warners the past few weeks has taken on the appearance of a mug show-up at police headquarters. Even though the roles are brief and episodical, the cream of Hollywood's "nastiest," and of both sexes, have been bidding for the jobs – each an important showcase in itself. Right from the king of them all, the Devil, down the line to such historic meanies as Nero, Napoleon, Attila the Hun, Hitler, Cleopatra, and Marie Antoinette, they are being portrayed by some of Hollywood's most convincing heavies.

Allen told Heffernan, "It's a wonder that civilization has survived. When one realizes some of the weird characters that have played important parts in the progress of man, it's almost incredible that we have been able to reach this point in our development. However, as shown in our story, the good in the world has outweighed the evil, and whenever someone has come along to heap death and destruction upon the world, two others are there to help repair the damage and to give us courage and faith in that wonderful day when peace will truly reign supreme everywhere." (IA-PP56)

The filming finally came to an end on January 24, 1957. The final sequence shot was, as *Daily Variety* called it, a Roman "orgy," with Peter Lorre as Nero.

Despite all the free advance publicity newspapers, trade magazines, and radio commentators had been providing, *Daily Variety*'s Army Archerd revealed on March 3, 1957:

> Irwin Allen and Warners probably won't renew their deal after *Story of Mankind*, which could be a blockbuster. And, Allen owns 25%.

Rumors spread that Jack Warner had now seen the completed film, and was concerned about the hefty profit participation points he had allowed Allen.

If nothing else, Allen was trying to earn his 25%, promoting his new venture at every opportunity.

On May 6, 1957, *Newsweek* said:

> If there is anything to the Hollywood theory that one way to get people into the theaters is to stun them with sheer

size, the beaches this August are going to be deserted. For last week, Irwin Allen, producer and director of Warner Brothers' *The Story of Mankind*, had finished shooting on the most pretentious-sounding movie in recent history. He figures to have the whole thing wrapped up and ready for the public in time for the summer slump. The grandiose movie is based on historian Hendrik Willem van Loon's best seller, which producer Allen has, of course, consulted ("I enjoyed the whole million years in history," he says. "Each one became a challenge.")

Allen, quoted further in the *Newsweek* piece, remarked, "I said to our research department, 'Find me the giants of history – those people who affected mankind more than anyone else.' We found four hundred so-called giants. Obviously, if we were to devote only a minute to each of these giants it would be impossible to tell the story. We boiled it down to fifty-eight people." (IA-NW57)

Allen's on-again, off-again relationship with Jack Warner now seemed back on. *Daily Variety* speculated:

> Looks like Irwin Allen and Warners will get a new pact, result of the sneak preview of his *Story of Mankind*. Only 18 feet are to be snipped. [Audience opinion] cards favored the "cameo" appearances of Groucho Marx, as Peter Minuit, Peter Lorre, as Nero, and Vincent Price, as the Devil. Pic goes out in August as a roadshow.

Charles Bennett said, "[I]t was way too long. I remember the sneak preview at a theater in the Valley, and the wretched Jack Warner – who owned Warner Bros. – was there. At the end, we all went and talked about it around a table in a pub, and I said, 'It has to be cut; this is no good in its present form.' Jack Warner said, 'Oh, let's just put it out.' And all his yes-men said, 'Yes, Jack's right, let's put it out.' So, they did." (CB-SL93)

Regardless, cuts would be made – far more than the 18 minutes of trims *Daily Variety* was told about. By the time it was released, Allen's promised three-hour epic timed in at a mere 100 minutes.

Despite the cuts, Allen the ballyhoo man was still beating the drum.

On October 8, 1957, *Daily Variety* ran the headline, "WB *Story* Winds A-Bomb Pix Race, Declares Allen." Allen told the trade that *The Story of Mankind* was coming at "psychologically the right time" with all the worry in America about a nuclear war with Russia. He was also proud to divulge that his new movie was made with 100% Warner Bros. financing. Of course, this made his 25% profit participation deal all the sweeter, yet all the more sour for Jack Warner.

THE BIGGEST STAR CAST EVER ON ONE SCREEN!

RONALD COLMAN • HEDY LAMARR • GROUCHO MARX • HARPO MARX • CHICO MARX • VIRGINIA MAYO • AGNES MOOREHEAD • VINCENT PRICE

PETER LORRE • CHARLES COBURN • CEDRIC HARDWICKE • CESAR ROMERO • DENNIS HOPPER • MARIE WILSON • HELMUT DANTINE • EDWARD EVERETT HORTON

REGINALD GARDINER • MARIE WINDSOR • CATHY O'DONNELL

THE STORY OF MANKIND

TECHNICOLOR from Warner Bros. · A CAMBRIDGE PRODUCTION

One day later, in sister trade *Variety*, Allen projected that *The Animal World* should clear between $500,000 and $1,000,000 in profits worldwide. He was confident *The Story of Mankind* would do even better, with its sixty-two speaking parts, many of them Hollywood stars. "A star," said Allen, "is a name personality whose name is quickly recognized by the public. In recent years, the term 'star' also has come to mean someone who can 'sell' a picture. It's almost like a brand name." (IA-DV57)

One of the newest brand-name stars: Irwin Allen.

On October 23, 1957, James Powers, writing for *The Hollywood Reporter*, said:

> It is difficult to tell sometimes if Allen is playing it straight or tongue-in-cheek, and the dialogue does not always help. ... The most serious criticism of *Story of Mankind* is that it does not live up to its title. How could it be a presentation of mankind, which means the human race, and omit Christ, Mohammed, Buddha, Plato, Galileo, Luther, Marx and Lenin? This *Story of Mankind* is a Sunday supplement of a story in which the characters have been chosen for their superficial glamour rather than any other value.

On November 9th, Jesse Zunser, of *Cue* magazine, criticized:

> To compress the whole history of man into a brief 100 minutes is no mean trick, but producer-director-writer Irwin Allen is not one to be abashed by the challenge. He has taken Hendrik Van Loon's popular, simplified, narrative history, culled from it the title and a smattering of slices, and has hashed the whole into a celluloid compôte. With unending chatter sandwiched between a hundred clips from old "historical" movies, he now presents this picture as the story of mankind. It is, in fact, merely an immensity of superficial, slapdash film clips, with a hundred characters flashing briefly upon the screen. The "big names" parading through this schoolboyish charade are all made to look and sound foolish by the inane dialogue and the sophomoric level of the picture's pretense to intellectual stature. Ronald Colman and Vincent Price are seen most often as advocate and denouncer of Man's right to live. Mr. Allen doesn't help our side much.

Philip K. Scheuer, writing in the *Los Angeles Times* on November 14th, bemoaned:

> In *The Story of Mankind*, a High Tribunal is called in heaven to decide whether or not we folks down here have done anything to make us worth saving. It is my personal observation that if the High Tribunal ever catches this picture, we're goners.

On the same day, S.A. Desick, writing in the *Los Angeles Examiner*, sighed:

> Poor Van Loon is probably standing in his grave and banging on his coffin in protest as the caricature to which his serious work has been reduced here. ... History was never duller.

On November 15th, Hubert C. Luft, who had spoken so highly of Allen earlier in the year for his "On the Screen" column, now wrote in *The Wisconsin Jewish Chronicle*:

> Irwin Allen's star-studded production of *The Story of Mankind* proved to be quite a disappointment when previewed at Warner Bros. studios. The picture did not live up to our own expectations. ... [T]he bulk of the movie illustrating world history and the dubious

progress of civilization in an all-too-sketchy picture postcard format with a great deal of stock footage from earlier historical spectacles, is embarrassingly bad in every respect.

On November 18th, under the heading, "Bomb and a Bumble," *Newsweek* said:

What starts out as a rather interesting, if extrawordly, polemic turns into a Technicolor riffle through the pages of history and a poor excuse to use a bunch of available actors in some of the weirdest casting ever committed.

Irwin Allen was perplexed by the hostile reaction from the critics. His cousin Al Gail said: "He liked [*The Story of Mankind*]. We felt, naturally, that some of the reviews were unfair. But the film did fairly well. No blockbuster, but, for the type of thing it was, it did fairly well." (AG-KB95)

To put it kindly, Gail misremembered. Irwin Allen's "all-star epic" wouldn't even make the national Top Ten list. According to *Variety*, the best *The Story of Mankind* could do on the trade's National Boxoffice Survey was No. 17, during the first week of November. It stayed there, at No. 17, for the second week. Then it seemed to drop off the radar. The adjectives describing its performance in various big-house theaters across the country were: "poor" and "a new low" in Philadelphia; "drab" in Boston; "mild" in Chicago and San Francisco; merely "okay" in Washington D.C.; "terrible" in Seattle; "so-so" in Buffalo; "sad" in Denver; and "wobbly" in Los Angeles.

Allen could not accept that he had made a bad film. Trying to explain the failure, he told a newspaper reporter, "I think the title scared the customers away." (IA-IAPC62)

Allen's nephew, Michael, said, "It was a lousy movie. It bothered Irwin a lot because he wasn't used to losing. He was a winner in a whole lot of different ways. And he was a competitor. And when you lose due to your own failings, it is no fun at all." (MA-AI15)

In fact, Allen had lost big. In Hollywood, there is a saying that you are only as good as your last picture. And, to be honest, Allen hadn't ever "made" a really good picture. He wasn't the maker of *Double Dynamite*, merely the packager. His freshman film, *Where Danger Lives*, was a minor box-office success but a critical dud. *A Girl in Every Port*, his first movie as lead producer, barely snuck by with mixed reviews; the box-office returns were good, but the trades felt it didn't truly deserve them. *The Sea Around Us* was arguably his best effort to date, and it won a grand prize with an Oscar as Best Feature Length Documentary to prove it. Allen was helped along by an industry that wanted to like the film because they had loved the book and its author. That trophy, along with the reputation of the book, helped it become a "fine arts theater" hit. However, when it had its general release in 1954, the reviews were far more critical and, at best, mixed. But people remembered the Oscar win. And that made Allen a winner, and enabled him to survive the convoluted *Dangerous Mission*. *The Animal World* was an obvious move, and the right move to get a new studio deal after his last picture at RKO had misfired. *The Animal World* didn't win any awards, but it did win decent reviews and a respectable box office return. This gave Allen had his big chance, with his first all-star spectacle. He reached for the sky, but came back with a handful of stardust.

As a result, Allen's relationship with Jack Warner was over. And none of the major studios in Hollywood – known as "The Big Five": MGM, 20th Century-Fox, Paramount, Warner Bros. and RKO – were interested in a relationship.

A studio just on the outside of the Top 5, both in the 1950s and 1960s, was Harry Cohn's Columbia, the lone survivor of the struggling "Gower Gulch" studios, long demeaned by the majors and the trade magazines as being the tenants of "poverty row." That would be Irwin Allen's next stop.

***

The Big Circus was Irwin Allen's first movie spectacle, and second all-star cast. From left to right: Vincent Price, Gilbert Roland, Rhonda Fleming, Victor Mature, Red Buttons, Kathryn Grant, David Nelson, and Peter Lorre.
(Allied Artists, 1959)

Irwin Allen's next film seemed the one he ran off to Hollywood to make. Nephew Michael Allen said, "Irwin had a love and a passion for the circus, because it was great show business. *And he loved show business.* He understood the nature of the circus, and entertainment, in general." (MA-AI15)

The public's perception of circuses centered around animal acts and exotic feats. The artifice, pretense, and pageantry were ready-made for drama or comedy. Several notable films had been set under the big top. They included:

- 1928's *The Circus*, written, directed by, and starring Charlie Chaplin, in which his beloved Tramp character found work, humor, and the girl of his dreams under the big top.
- 1932's *Freaks*, directed by Todd Browning, presenting a curious oddity of real-life human oddities, individuals Browning and the general public considered "freaks of nature." The plot was a maudlin story of untrue love, but Browning presented the title characters with typical human emotions and motivations. To some, this was almost as disturbing as the climax, in which the handicapped characters wrought a terrible revenge on the woman who had cheated one of them.
- 1939's *At the Circus*, in which the Marx Brothers tried to save a failing circus from bankruptcy.
- 1941's *Dumbo*, Walt Disney's animated classic about a flying baby elephant.
- 1952's *The Greatest Show on Earth*, directed by Cecil B. DeMille. The actors trained to perform the acts of their characters; actual circus performers were also used throughout the film. Many Hollywood insiders felt that DeMille's film lived up to its name. It earned two Oscars, for Best Picture and Best Screenplay. Nominations also went to DeMille, as Best Director, as well as a nod toward costume designers and film editors.
- 1956's *Trapeze*, from director Carol Reed, and starring Burt Lancaster, Tony Curtis and Gina Lollobrigida, and featuring a love-triangle on the high wires.

What Allen needed to proceed with his circus movie was financing … and a distributor. In other words – a studio. That didn't seem too big a problem, as *The Story of Mankind* was being readied for release by Warner Bros. If it did well, Warners might be interested in *Circus*. If not, Allen was a high-profile producer/director who was a darling of the press, a seemingly unstoppable force.

On July 3rd, *Variety* told the motion-picture industry more about the next Irwin Allen project:

> Fourth production in the Todd-A-O process will be *The Big Circus*, which Irwin Allen will produce as a multi-million-dollar Technicolor extravaganza in which a total of 62 stars will appear. Each speaking part, the producer said, will be handled by a star name.
>
> Allen, who recently completed *The Story of Mankind* for Warners, said no release arrangement has been set, but *Circus* will be offered to Warners first. ...

On July 29th, Army Archerd reported in *Daily Variety* that the quirky, flamboyant producer had hired a clown to deliver copies of the script for *The Big Circus* to potential cast members and other interested parties. Since he had yet to hire a screenwriter, one must assume the "script" was a typical Irwin Allen movie proposal – a screen treatment written by Allen and Al Gail, complemented by artists' sketches of the spectacular visuals to be expected in the film. Whatever the presentation was, at least one mogul liked it.

On August 27th, *Daily Variety* announced that Allen would be making his *Big Circus* for Harry Cohn's Columbia Pictures.

But in late October, *The Story of Mankind* was released and savaged by the critics. Negative word of mouth spread quickly, resulting in a disappointing box-office return. As the movie traveled across America in true roadshow fashion during November and December, and into the first several months of 1958, the reception remained lukewarm to downright hostile.

Harry Cohn may have lacked social graces and been unpopular among his peers, but he was no fool when it came to the business of motion pictures. He'd now seen the directing job Allen had done with *The Story of Mankind*. Prior to this, the only two movies directed by Irwin Allen had been *The Sea Around Us* and *The Animal World*, documentaries both. It seemed apparent to Cohn that Allen had a lot yet to learn when it came to directing two-legged actors, telling a human story. Cohn felt Allen should practice his craft on a smaller canvas, with smaller pictures. Perhaps even B-pictures. *The Big Circus*, then, became "The Small Circus," as the budget was slashed. And this meant there would be no "all-star" cast.

Allen balked and chose to take his dream project elsewhere. The five Hollywood "majors" – RKO, Warner Bros., MGM, Paramount, and 20th Century-Fox – had all passed, as had Cohn's Columbia, the leader of Hollywood's Poverty Row. Undaunted, Allen set his sight on the "minors," including another Poverty Row studio – Monogram Pictures Corporation, recently rechristened as Allied Artists Pictures Corporation.

On September 9, 1958, the front page of *Daily Variety* reported:

> Irwin Allen's upcoming production, *The Big Circus*, originally planned as a Columbia release, may wind up at Allied Artists. Allen is currently in negotiation with AA regarding moving the property to that company. Producer is also negotiating for Rhonda Fleming and Victor Mature for the leads.

What went unreported – because Allen didn't want it made public – was that Allied didn't want to give Allen the director's chair. But it *was* willing to consider a large budget, provided the right director and stars were attached. At least Allen wasn't starting at the bottom again. But he was nowhere near the top. He would have to prove himself as a producer of a spectacular drama, something he'd failed to do with RKO's *Dangerous Mission*. At least he was being given a second chance, in a town not known for its generosity.

Helping Allen lock in the deal with Allied Artists was Charles Bennett, assigned to rewrite Irving Wallace's script, from Allen's screen story. Another plus was the addition of director Joseph M. Newman, who had received two Oscar nominations in his early career as assistant director, and then gained praise for his work as a director for 1950's film noir *711 Ocean Drive*, 1952's *Red Skies of Montana*, and 1955's cult sci-fi parable *This Island Earth*.

Then came the stars. For its day, *The Big Circus* featured an impressive cast – especially considering its studio.

Victor Mature, who had starred in Allen's *Dangerous Mission*, was given the lead.

Red Buttons had second billing. At 40, he had been a star on Broadway, as well as having his own TV series, 1952's *The Red Buttons Show*. Now he was a hot item in the movies. For his role in the 1957 Marlon Brando film

Rhonda Fleming and friend pose to promote *The Big Circus*. (Allied Artists, 1959)

Sayonara, Buttons won an Oscar as Best Supporting Actor. Several months later, he went to work for Irwin Allen.

Rhonda Fleming was 35. She had starred in many popular films, such as 1949's *A Connecticut Yankee in King Arthur's Court*, opposite Bing Crosby;

1957's *Gunfight at the O.K. Corral*, co-starring with Burt Lancaster and Kirk Douglas; and 1953's *Pony Express*, sharing the bill with Charlton Heston.

Paul Zastupnevich, Irwin Allen's personal assistant and wardrobe designer for three decades, said of his boss, "At one time he was a disc jockey. He had a program from the old Hawaiian Theatre in Hollywood, on the boulevard there. It was at that time that he met Marilyn Louis, who was Rhonda Fleming. While he was doing his program with her, he said, 'One of these days I'm going to put you in a picture.' And that's how Rhonda agreed to be in *The Big Circus*." (PZ-KB95)

The Big Circus, with Gilbert Roland and Kathryn Grant (above), and Vincent Price (below). (Allied Artists, 1959)

Of course, Allen remembered this incident more dramatically. He recalled the moment, and his exact line to Marilyn Louis. During the radio broadcast, he told her, "I want to go out on the limb with three predictions. Some day I'm going to be a motion picture producer. You're going to be a star. And I'm going to star you in one of my pictures." (IA-DP59)

Kathryn Grant was another actress Allen predicted would be a big star. She was already on her way, and was married to a big star as well – Bing Crosby. Grant was 26, and had top billing in the 1957 sci-fi film *The Night the World Exploded*, and then starred opposite Jack Lemmon that same year in *Operation Mad Ball*. She also had the female lead in 1958's *The 7th Voyage of Sinbad*.

Irwin Allen said, "Bing actually acted as Kathy's agent for this part. He read the script and told her, 'Take it. It will make you a star.'" (IA-RMN59)

Vincent Price was 48, and had worked for Irwin Allen before, in *Dangerous Mission*, and then played the Devil in *The Story of Mankind*. *The Big Circus* would be the third of four acting jobs Price took from Allen.

Gilbert Roland, cast as flying trapeze performer Zach Colino, was 54, and had been a leading man in Hollywood since the late 1930s. His most famous screen character was the Cisco Kid, which Roland played in six films, beginning in 1946 with *The Gay Cavalier*.

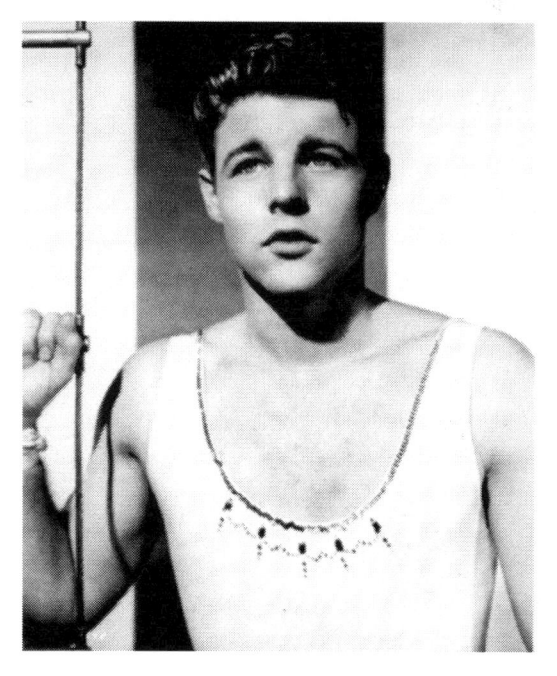

Peter Lorre gained fame in 1931 with the lead in the German-produced thriller, *M*. Alfred Hitchcock cast him in his first English-speaking part – another good villainous role – for 1934's *The Man Who Knew Too Much*. That standout performance brought Hollywood calling. Lorre was soon starring in his own film series, as the crime-solving Mr. Moto, beginning with 1937's *Think Fast, Mr. Moto*. Irwin Allen was impressed with Lorre's turn in the 1954 sci-fi film *20,000 Leagues Under the Sea* and cast him for a cameo in *The Story of Mankind*. However, Lorre was not Allen's first idea in casting the role. He had approached someone else – Ed Wynn. Then Wynn fell ill.

Peter Lorre (above) and David Nelson (below) in *The Big Circus*. (Allied Artists, 1959)

Allen said of Lorre, "I never would have thought of casting him in the part. It happens that Lorre and I have our barber appointments in the same shop at the same time, in adjoining chairs. One day we were talking about the picture, and he jokingly said, 'Why not make *me* the clown?' I thought it was a great idea." (IA-RMN59)

Also in the cast was David Nelson, son of Ozzie and Harriet Nelson. David had been overshadowed on *The Adventures of*

Above: Irwin Allen with Vincent Price on the set of *The Big Circus*. Below: Director Joseph M. Newman, Victor Mature, Irwin Allen, Rhonda Fleming, and Peter Lorre.
(Allied Artists, 1959)

Ozzie and Harriet by his younger brother Ricky, who became an immensely successful pop singer, second only to Elvis Presley in the late 1950s and early 1960s. Before the movie's release, Irwin Allen said, "Maybe David can't sing, but he has a million dollar personality. When I signed him, his father asked me for 50 percent of the billing [in respect to the size of Nelson's name compared to the film's lead actors]. We said we would have to wait until he made the picture. Now that the picture is finished, he gets 100 percent and is billed equally with Vic Mature, Red Buttons and the other top stars." (IA-ADB59)

As a result of making *The Big Circus*, David Nelson became an active aerialist.

Another familiar face in the cast was late-night TV talk-show host Steve Allen. Irwin Allen got him at a great rate – $90. Since the two men were friends, Steve Allen was not willing to accept anything more than the minimum price set by SAG for a mere cameo appearance.

On December 10th, after the full cast had been announced in the Hollywood trade magazines, *Variety* revealed that the production would be a joint venture between

Irwin Allen and Allied Artists. This meant that each was putting up an equal share of the financing. Since Allied Artists was a production and distribution company, and not a studio, the production would be renting space at Metro-Goldwyn-Mayer. The budget had been set at $2,000,000.

On December 23rd, *Daily Variety* reported that Victor Mature, Red Buttons, Rhonda Fleming, Kathryn Grant, Vincent Price, Peter Lorre, and Gilbert Roland would all check onto the Metro lot on December 29th to begin rehearsing for their circus roles. It was also finally revealed that Irwin Allen would not be directing, but that Joseph Newman had been hired to helm the movie.

Regardless of who sat in the director's chair, this was to be an Irwin Allen film.

Al Gail said that the only other filmmaker doing Irwin Allen-type movies during this period was Cecil B. DeMille. Or, more correctly, Allen was doing Cecil B. DeMille-type movies. Gail said of Allen, "DeMille and he were also, in a sense, compared to Samuel Goldwyn, because Goldwyn, as you know, took great pride in his sets and his costumes, and everything [to do with] the look. And so did Irwin. And we were always under a lot of pressure, because we always ran over budget, because he wanted it to look right. Sure, you could save money by cutting this and cutting that, or taking 20 people out of a crowd scene, but that was not his way. He said, 'If you're going to do it, you do it right.' And that led to front office problems." (AG-KB95)

Translation: More money than the studio wanted to spend. Allen finally internalized this lesson after making the move to television. With *Voyage to the Bottom of the Sea*, Allen had no choice but to change his approach to production, learning to compromise and slash costs. Many critics, of course, felt that once Allen learned to cost-cut, he couldn't stop. After reading this book, you can decide for yourself.

The Friday, January 2, 1959 edition of *Daily Variety* indicated just how big *The Big Circus* would be:

> An 18-acre set is being built at Metro for Allied Artists' *The Big Circus*, which producer Irwin Allen will start Monday at the Culver City lot. Tent interiors will be facilitated on Stages 27 and 30, and outside there will be six large circus tents and six small ones in addition to 40 circus wagons, eight animal cages, and two railroad cars.

For a January 11, 1959 article in *The New York Times*, Thomas M. Pryor wrote:

> Never let it be said that Hollywood actors aren't versatile. Take Kathryn Grant, Gilbert Roland, Adele Mara, and

> David Nelson as types of performers who are doing things that just don't come natural and are doing them with an impressive degree of competence. They are playing circus people – aerial specialists – in *The Big Circus*, which Irwin Allen promises will be a "colorful, big, blary, noisy show – the biggest circus ever seen anywhere." ... The producer, who also wrote the screenplay with Charles Bennett, was not the least inclined to backtrack when reminded that Cecil B. DeMille didn't spare the tanbark in filming *The Greatest Show on Earth*. Mr. Allen just smiled and pointed to a slogan nearby that proclaimed "The *Biggest* Show on Earth."

For a syndicated newspaper article, Allen stressed, "The DeMille movie, remember, was made before VistaVision and CinemaScope. [My] picture was filmed in the biggest tent in the world – 400 feet long, and specially constructed on MGM's biggest sound stage. In it we have tried to recreate the circus as it is seen through the eyes of a child – one of the most beautiful things in the world, seen in a kind of fantasy-scope." (IA-RMN59)

Interviewed by the *Denver Post*'s Larry Tajiri for a July 1, 1959 article, Allen boasted, "I believe we have the biggest, most colorful circus film ever made. Ours is no ordinary three-ring tent show. It is the circus of our childhood dreams, when everything was greater and grander than they could be in real life. This is the most commercial film I have ever produced, but one which I believe has elements which will appeal to every age group." (IA-DP59)

Of course, Allen had also wanted to direct. And, while taking no credit, he nevertheless made his presence known on the set of *The Big Circus* in a big way. *Daily Variety*'s Army Archerd, after visiting the set, wrote in the trade's February 12th issue:

> Joe Newman, directing *Circus*, is getting plenty of "assistance" from producer Irwin Allen, always on the set.

This was the movie for which Paul Zastupnevich joined Irwin Allen's team as a wardrobe designer. He was a native of Pittsburgh, Pennsylvania, and was active in local theater and opera, designing costumes and acting in supporting roles for the Civic Opera. After helping to produce musical comedies that entertained World War II troops stationed at Fort Benning, Georgia, Zastupnevich borrowed from the G.I. Bill program to further his studies at the Pasadena Playhouse in California. For five years he worked on 75 productions creating costumes, but he also acted (under the name of Paul Kremin). He grew a moustache and goatee for a role as an Amish, and liked the look so much that he kept it the rest of his career. And, with a last name that was a challenge for most people to remember and pronounce, he became known as "Paul Z." During his early years in wardrobe design, Zastupnevich learned to create costuming out of makeshift materials, ideal training for the challenges ahead for him in television.

Performing and designing costumes for the theater was creatively satisfying work, but was hardly paying his way. For this reason, Zastupnevich was close to giving up on a career in show business. And that's when Irwin Allen entered his life.

Paul Zastupnevich, circa 1950s.

Zastupnevich admitted, "I had been in Los Angeles just over nine years at the time, and had given myself until Christmas. If I didn't make it, I was going home to Pittsburgh. I had a boutique in Beverly Hills, doing gowns and dresses for actresses, and was introduced to Rhonda Fleming, who needed a gown for a TV awards ceremony within four days! I created a gown with a special feature that showed off her legs when she walked, and it was a hit. Rhonda then told me that she and the costume designer on her new picture, *The Big Circus*, weren't getting along. She suggested that I give it a try and said she would get me in to see the producer, Irwin Allen." (PZ-SL93)

Zastupnevich created a "presentation" folder with watercolor illustrations of his designs, including drawings of Fleming in several different outfits. Each drawing had the actress's name, the name of the character, and the presentation had a hand-lettered *Big Circus* title on its cover.

Zastupnevich declared, "Irwin loved it! He looked at me and said I had 'showmanship.' I was on cloud nine, because it was unheard of at the time for an unknown to walk in and get a picture." (PZ-SL93)

Zastupnevich said of Allen, "My first dealing with him was through my agent, who at that time was Harry Bernsen. And Harry said to me, 'Whatever *he* says, he's right, and he's *never* wrong. Don't ever argue; just agree with him.' So I got to the point where I learned all of his little idiosyncrasies. I knew his color preferences; I knew what kind of shirts he liked to wear; I went shopping with him at times. That was a very funny thing about him – every time he went away on a trip, he never took a laundered shirt; he had to have brand new shirts. We would go to Carol's and Monty Factor's and get him a half a dozen shirts to pack in the suitcases. Everything had to be brand new – new shirts, new socks, new everything. I don't know what that was all about. I think that harks back to the days when he was a little boy and didn't have much. He came up the hard way."

Zastupnevich added, "The job was supposed to be for only three weeks. I ended up staying approximately thirty-two years. I'm like the proverbial man who came to dinner – *I never left!* A lot of people say to me, 'Why did you put up with him? Why did you stay if you were so unhappy at times?' And I said, 'Well, you know, after all, I had been in Hollywood for nine years knocking on the doors; I'd been at the Pasadena Playhouse doing things; I'd been an actor and whatnot, and this was the first time that I got a chance to do a picture. He gave me a three [sic] million dollar picture! I hadn't done any movie work up till this time. But, on the basis of that presentation of mine, he gave me the chance." (PZ-KB95)

The Big Circus was also Allen's first time working with director of photography Winton Hoch, who had won three Academy Awards as Best Cinematographer – for 1948's *Joan of Arc*, 1949's *She Wore a Yellow Ribbon*, and 1952's *The Quiet Man*. He had also been the "D.P." on other classics, such as 1955's *Mister Roberts*, 1956's *The Searchers*, and 1959's *Darby O'Gill and the Little People*. Allen was so impressed with Hoch's work that he arranged his production schedule to be sure the talented

Unknown studio executive with Irwin Allen.
(Allied Artists, 1959)

cinematographer could shoot the rest of his 1960s films – *The Lost World*, *Voyage to the Bottom of the Sea*, and *Five Weeks in a Balloon*. He would also convince Hoch to make the move to television, as cinematographer for fifty-one episodes of the television version of *Voyage*, as well as several episodes of *Lost in Space*, and all the episodes of *The Time Tunnel*.

As filming progressed, stories began to emanate from the set.

For Hedda Hopper's February 27, 1959 column:

Gilbert Roland and Kathryn Grant play aerialists. Harry Lillis Crosby, Jr., now six months, should see ma in spangled white leotard and flesh-colored tights. She coached for the trapeze work with Del Graham of the Flying Viennas, who vouches for her proficiency: "She studied ballet all her life," he said, "and it's a great help. Then, too, she's not afraid of anything. You know what? She'd make a great flyer."

Bing [Crosby] hasn't been over to watch her work. Kathryn explained: "He thinks that would be too unprofessional."

Roland still has his 28-inch waist, not only swings on the trapeze but also walks the tight wire. "Fifteen feet on five-eighths of an inch of cable," he boasts. "Of course I can do it, but only a foot and a half above ground. Think I'm crazy?"

For Associated Press, on March 4th, Bob Thomas shared:

Well, sir, it was just like the good old days. The mammoth stage was filled like the interior of a circus tent; brightened by yellow sawdust and three multicolored rings. Hundreds of extras cheered from the stands as the floats and elephants and clowns paraded by. Scores of dancing girls twirled and whirled. You'd think there never had been a depression in Hollywood!

There has, of course. Evidence: There wasn't another movie being made at MGM that day. And even the makers of *The Big Circus*, who were bucking the trend, were renters of space at the once-thriving studio.

The sly producer was finding ways to promote his upcoming movie even before the promotional campaign kicked in. *Variety* reported on June 17th:

[Irwin] Allen refrained from dropping titles, but notes off the record a few recent examples of blue-chip productions, in terms of cost, which have been unsatisfactory at the b.o. He cites a few reasons, foremost among them being the impact of audience identification with the screen characters, or the lack of it. Speaking in generalities, Allen said a sadness theme and ultimate tragedy is the type of material with which the average

> customer can't liken herself to. No names, please, he asked, but the allusion apparently was to *Diary of Anne Frank*, which is the 20th [Century]-Fox release now doing disappointedly. Allen persisted in not naming titles but another case apparently could be Warners' *Old Man and the Sea*, which proved a commercial disaster.
>
> Now comes the commercial. The filmmaker, uninhibited about discussing his latest enterprise, *The Big Circus*, for Allied Artists, stated in New York this week that the audience wants escape and, at the same time, a certain amount of identification with the on-screen characters. This, he figures, he's got, along with some extra angles. Latter include casting of Peter Lorre as a circus clown. Seemed startling at the outset, said Allen, but Lorre comes out a natural tanbark performer.

Allied Artists held a sneak preview of *The Big Circus* on June 21st at the Academy Theatre in Hollywood, decked out in Big Top dressing. Many of the stars, as well as Irwin Allen, were present. *Daily Variety* reported that Vincent Price was there to hear the audience hiss every time he came on screen … even though he wasn't the film's villain, merely its red herring.

The following day, "Ron" reviewed the film for the trade. He wrote in part:

> Irwin Allen's *The Big Circus* is a rousingly lavish film, stocked with tinted elephants, snarling lions and three rings of handsome production. While at times it looks too much like Hollywood's view of the big top, rather than reality, it is shrewdly calculated to satisfy the peanut-and-sawdust yen of the millions to whom circus-going is a less frequently available diversion than in past generations.

Of the cast, "Ron" felt that "Victor Mature does best. He's strong, exhibiting an underlying softness, and he's sincere in achieving what he alone can achieve, in this case setting the wheels in motion to save the circus."

The Daily Variety critic said that Red Buttons "is excellent, mild as the cold banker, strikingly human as a substitute clown and minute-man aerialist."

"Ron" found that "Rhonda Fleming's beauty is an asset to *Circus*; her portrayal of a femme flack an honest, highly skilled one."

The praise continued:

"[Gilbert] Roland adeptly combines confidence and fear as the star attraction, creating a sharp characterization. Kathryn Grant is thoroughly appealing as Mature's sister, coming across as sweet, yet strong and indicating her abilities in the future star category. Vincent Price is perfect as the ringmaster, his voice bellowing through the big tent with precision and authority. Peter Lorre is tops as a clown, and in more than one scene he is more the circus performer than any of his cohorts. David Nelson, in an off-beat role, is very good, keeping his early character a mystery so his later actions won't be tipped off."

Consider yourself tipped off.

The critic continued:

> If most of the creative forces of *The Big Circus* are bent toward the mass audience, the technical credits should excite the most artistic film devotee. Photographically, the picture is, or comes close to being, the finest CinemaScope film yet made. Its Technicolor hues are vivid, the color being a strong part of the production's feeling. And the technical quality of the shots themselves, photographed with warmth and excitement by William [*sic*: Winton] Hoch, are excellent, the Panavision lenses producing a clarity which should be noticeable even to the average viewer.

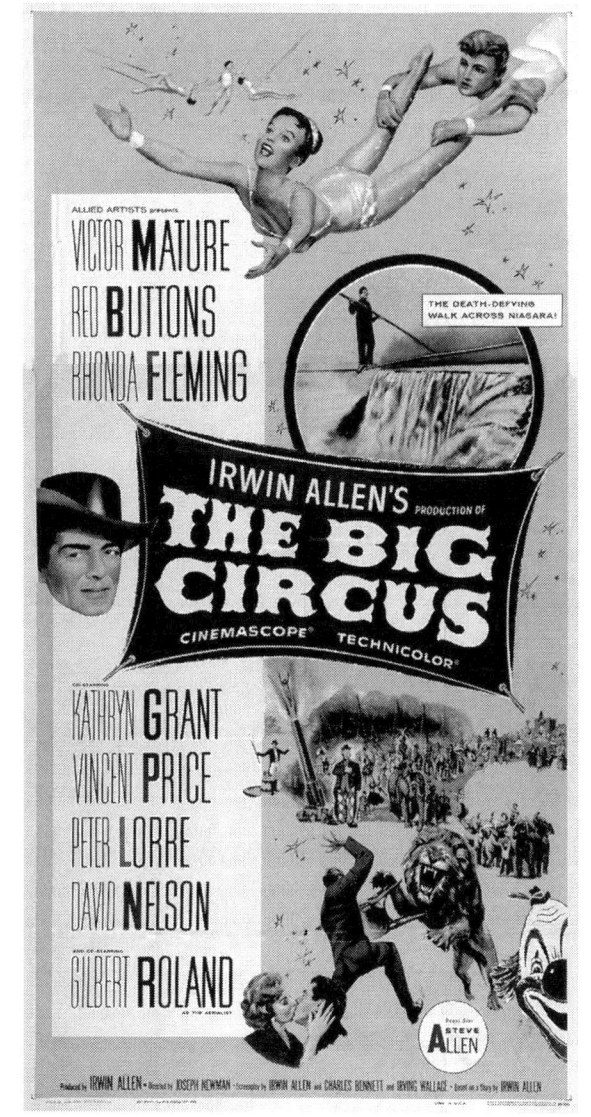

Praise was also given to Paul Sawtell, who with Bert Shefter provided music which was "a potent asset" to the film. Sawtell had composed the score to Allen's *The Sea Around Us* and *The Story of Mankind*, and would become best known among Irwin Allen aficionados as the composer of the theme music for TV's *Voyage to the Bottom of the Sea*.

Days later, *Daily Variety* reported that *The Big Circus* would get the grand treatment in its distribution from Allied Artists, with saturation bookings in many cities, including 45 theaters in the Los Angeles area alone, opening in all on August 5th. But first, the world premiere would take place on July 1st in Baraboo, Wisconsin, the home of the Ringling Brothers Circus. Rhonda Fleming would be on hand. Later that same day, Irwin Allen would be in Denver, with the film having its official opening immediately following the Baraboo premiere. He'd then hop a flight to Peru, Indiana for the premiere in that city the following day.

The Denver Post picked up the story on Wednesday, July 1st. Larry Tajiri wrote:

> Irwin Allen is not the button-pushing type of Hollywood producer, and his work on *The Big Circus*, opening Wednesday at the RKO Orpheum, is proof of his complete involvement in a movie project. Allen, once a writer – he had a Hollywood column syndicated in 73 papers – wrote the original story of the perils of the sawdust trail which became *The Big Circus*. He collaborated on the screenplay with Charles Bennett and Irving Wallace, and followed the picture through every phase of production, including cutting and scoring. Now that the film is ready to show, Allen showed up at *The Denver Post* the other morning, drum-beating for his $2 million picture.

Concerning *The Big Circus*, Allen told Tajiri, "If you look closely, you might find the [kitchen] sink as well." (IA-DP59)

New York Times writer Bosley Crowther looked closely enough to decide he didn't like the movie. Clearly it was too low-brow for him. In the newspaper's July 18th edition, Crowther sniffed:

> There is nothing very subtle about a circus. If you will keep this fact in mind – and also the fact that the world's record in spectacular circus films is held by a most unsubtle champion, *The Greatest Show on Earth*, of the late Cecil B. DeMille – then you can better be prepared for the beating you are going to have to endure when you take the kids to see Irwin Allen's *The Big Circus*, which opened at the Roxy yesterday. One hour and forty-nine minutes of riotous clichés – that's what you're in for, ladies and gentlemen and children of all ages, as they say, with the tiresome assurance of old showmen who persist in thinking you can't insult the intelligence of a kid. One hour and forty-nine minutes of acts, among which, we must say, the [animal] ones are a little more convincing than the ones performed by the human beings!

On July 30th, Brian Sullivan wrote in Rochester, New York's *Democrat and Chronicle*:

> While it isn't exactly *The Greatest Show on Earth*, this one should please a lot of moviegoers and circus fans.... The plot may creak a bit under its own weight, but it serves mainly as a vehicle for some fascinating views of circus performers at work – including some genuine acts.

Meanwhile, Irwin Allen was in Chicago on the 30th, appearing as grand marshal of a parade featuring clowns, stilt walkers, floats, and dancing girls.

On August 3rd, *Time* said:

> *The Big Circus* is an attempt by producer Irwin (*The Sea Around Us*) Allen to shoot the rapids of the old DeMille stream. ... But *The Big Circus* often looks like a gaudily colored CinemaScope production of *The Ed Sullivan Show*. The plot is as hard to swallow as a 3-ft. sword dipped in cotton candy.

Philip K. Scheuer said for the *Los Angeles Times* on August 6th:

> It's hokum, but DeMille's *Greatest Show on Earth* was hokum, too. The difference was that DeMille had a showman's instincts. Nor has Allen the cinematic gift of a Carol Reed, whose *Trapeze* camera floated through the air with the greatest of ease. ... There is nothing exceptional about *The Big Circus* – except, maybe, its use of the word "big." A greater artist [Charlie Chaplin] was once content to call his concept simply *The Circus*.

Although the reviews were mixed, *The Big Circus* gave Allen the box-office hit he'd been striving for. According to *Variety*, it was "wow" at Denver's 2,043-seat Orpheum; "excellent" in Washington, D.C., at the Uptown, with 1,100 seats; "loud" in Baltimore at the 2,300-seat Hippodrome; "swell" in Detroit, at the Palms, with 2,296 seats; "fine" in Portland, at the Orpheum, with its 1,600 seats; "big" in Indianapolis, at the Circle, with 2,800 seats; "fancy" in Buffalo, at the Lafayette, with 3,000 seats; "socko" at the Omaha Theater and its 2,066 seats; "great" in Kansas City, at the Uptown, with 2,093 seats; and, on Broadway, rocking the Roxy, with the theater's biggest first day, biggest second day, biggest third day, and biggest fourth day. For its July 22, 1959 issue, *Variety* ranked *The Big Circus* as the seventh highest-grossing movie in America. One week later, it was the fourth biggest. A week after that, down to fifth place.

Irwin Allen had recovered from *The Story of Mankind* and could now reach for a bigger brass ring – a production deal with one of Hollywood's true "majors" … and a second chance to direct a non-documentary feature film.

***

Pre-production art for *The Lost World*. (20th Century-Fox, 1960)

For Allen's next film, an August, 1960 press release from 20th Century-Fox promised:

> Stranger than the wildest science fiction dreams is the land of the "lost world" where Jurassic monsters from 150,000,000 B.C. roam at will, where dinosaurs rule the land and man-eating plants reach out at every bend in the trail.
>
> This is the untamed and untouched place that zoology professor Challenger (Claude Rains) takes his unforgettable expedition to. Accompanying him on this journey into the past are Lord Roxton (Michael Rennie), a playboy and big game hunter; Jennifer Holmes (Jill St. John), daughter of an executive who finances the venture; David Holmes (Ray Stricklyn), Jennifer's brother; Ed Malone (David Hedison), American newsman, and Professor Summerlee (Richard Haydn), a scientist.

> Joining the expedition at a remote trading post on the Amazon are Gomez (Fernando Lamas), who pilots the helicopter to the plateau of *The Lost World*, and Costa (Jay Novello), a jungle agent and guide.
>
> Unknown animals menace the party at every turn. A large animal blocks their path upon arrival and knocks the helicopter over a cliff. It is identified by Prof. Challenger as a brontosaurus, but still the party plunges deeper into the unknown. ...
>
> *The Lost World*, Irwin Allen's remarkable production of Sir Arthur Conan Doyle's gripping story of a trip to a prehistoric land, filmed in CinemaScope and DeLuxe Color. ...

Screenwriter Charles Bennett said, "It was as simple as the fact that somebody suggested to Irwin that he should make *The Lost World*. He liked the idea of prehistoric monsters and things like that, so he asked me to write the script. ... I knew the novel by heart; I know *all* Conan Doyle's stuff by heart. I loved him." (CB-SL93)

On November 6, 1959, in *Daily Variety*, staffer Ron Silverman wrote:

> The price of thrills has gone up, according to producer-director Irwin Allen, who yesterday termed his forthcoming *The Lost World* the most expensive "exploitation" picture ever made. He said the 20th-Fox release will cost a minimum of $2,000,000. The film will abound in prehistoric monsters, Allen pointed out, and kids want to be fooled by them, but he explains it takes more to fool them these days. "The special effects, the story and the entire production must be done with such expertness that audiences accept them even though they know it couldn't happen." That, opined Allen, can't be done satisfactorily on a small budget. The filmmaker admitted a $100,000 exploitation pic can get back its cost by appealing to only a small segment of the motion picture public. "But to return a significant profit, the film must appeal to the entire family," he added. "We start off by saying, 'I want to get the kids into the theaters,' and we know that every third kid is going to bring an adult. By giving adults something that will entertain them, we'll get other adults."

This time out, Allen was allowed to direct, as well as produce, and co-write the screenplay. *Variety* reported on July 6, 1960:

> Whenever possible, a producer should serve as his own director. "It's part of the modern way of filmmaking," according to producer Irwin Allen who directed his current 20th-Fox release, *The Lost World,* as well as his 1957 production, *The Story of Mankind*, released by Warners. By functioning in this dual capacity, a producer simplifies the chain of command, Allen said in New York last week, "eliminating all those little frictions which are bound to arrive in the course of a production between a producer and a director." There should always be great harmony between a producer and a director and "what better way to achieve this than by having the harmony in one beast?"... As to the future of theatrical films, he is optimistic. The population is exploding all over the place, and more customers are being born than are being lost through death or other unnatural causes.

Regarding the cast, Allen had to compromise on many roles. For Lord John Roxton, the playboy game hunter with an ulterior motive for the adventure, Allen had first considered Richard Ney and Richard Greene, but finally decided on Michael Rennie. Rennie was fifty, and had starred as Klaatu in the 1951 sci-fi classic, *The Day the Earth Stood Still*. Immediately following *The Lost World*, he would have his own television series, *The Third Man*, which co-starred Jonathan Harris (later Dr. Smith in *Lost in Space*). Allen would hire Rennie for *Lost in Space*'s only two-part episode, 1966's "The Keeper."

Jill St. John was Allen's first choice for Jennifer Holmes, the girl along for the ride. She had made her big-screen debut in 1958's *Summer Love*. St. John moved up from fourth billing to third, and then second, with her next few films. She was 28 at this time, and Allen's only concern was her fluctuating weight.

On January 6, 1959, Allen wrote to 20th Century-Fox Casting Director Lew Schreiber:

> I am hoping to see additional film of Margo Moore today or tomorrow. I also looked at additional footage yesterday on Jill St. John (*The Remarkable Mr. Pennypacker*). <u>She must have been fifteen pounds lighter</u> than she was in *Holiday for Lovers* and looked far better to me. She's coming in to see me sometime this afternoon. I certainly think she could handle the role. My concern after seeing *Holiday for Lovers* was that she had put on a great deal of weight and hardly looked the "sophisticated,

devil-may-care, worldly-wise Jennifer." I will report to you right after I see her.

Allen liked what he saw and St. John was offered the role.

David Hedison met Irwin Allen with this acting job, playing Ed Malone, the newspaperman assigned to accompany the adventurers. He was thirty-one, and, as Al Hedison, had been featured prominently in the 1957 hit *The Enemy Below*, and played the lead in the 1958 sci-fi classic, *The Fly*. Allan wanted only Hedison for the role of Ed Malone from the very start. He told Lew Schreiber:

> As you know, I am in complete accord with you regarding David Hedison. He's certainly young enough, clean cut, and has had just enough exposure for good marketing and exploitation.

Hedison said, "I read the script and it was funny at the beginning, with Claude Rains and what he had to do, and I was a photographer, a journalist, all of that. It was nice; it took on something good. But then, once we get on the helicopter, it became a kids' show." (DH-PE17)

Under contract to 20th Century-Fox, Hedison had little choice in the roles assigned to him. And, part of the script, at least, had struck him as funny. He went into the project hoping for the best.

In the same year as *The Lost World*, Hedison starred in his own hour-long TV series, *Five Fingers*, as a U.S. Intelligence agent working in Europe. And, you probably already knew, he achieved international fame as Captain Crane in TV's *Voyage to the Bottom of the Sea*.

David Hedison, in *The Lost World*
(20th Century-Fox, 1960)

Fernando Lamas played Manuel Gomez, the helicopter pilot. Allen had lobbied hard for Gilbert Roland but was unable to made a deal. Lamas was 43 and had been a film star in his home country of Argentina before being brought to America with an MGM contract. The studio featured him as a romantic lead in 1952's *The Merry Widow*; opposite Lana Turner in 1953's *The Girl Who Had Everything*; opposite Elizabeth Taylor; and in *Dangerous When Wet*, opposite

Esther Williams. Like others in the movie, his character, Manuel Gomez, had ulterior reasons for joining the expedition.

Popular character actor Richard Haydn was added for comedy relief, as Professor Summerlee. Haydn had been Allen's first choice above Felix Aylmer, Wilfred Hyde-White, and Sam Jaffe. Haydn was fifty-four, and known for playing pompous types. He is perhaps best remembered as the freeloading theatrical agent Uncle Max, from 1965's *The Sound of Music*.

The beautiful native girl was played by twenty-two-year-old Vitina Marcus, who would become associated to Irwin Allen and work often in his productions. She said, "I was a dancer, and I'd studied with Lee Strasberg, learning Method Acting for four years. I had one small part [on stage], and then starred in a live television show in New York." (VM-AI15)

She was Dolores Vitina then, appearing on Christmas night, 1957, in the *Kraft Theatre* presentation of "The Other Wise Man." She followed that with an episode of *Schlitz Playhouse*, then played John Drew Barrymore's sister in the 1958 Barrymore/ Steve McQueen starrer, *Never Love a Stranger*. A handful of TV westerns followed, including *Have Gun – Will Travel*, *Death Valley Days*, and *Wagon Train*, in which she was usually cast as an American Indian. In 1960, Dolores Vitina became Vitina Marcus.

Marcus recalled, "After that, Jackie Gleason's manager signed me up. He wanted to put me under contract with one of the studios, even though I never wanted that. But he sent me to Hollywood and my agent there took me to 20th Century-Fox for an audition. A short while later he took me back, this time to meet Irwin Allen. Irwin asked me if I knew why I was there. I said, 'No,' just that my agent brought me. He had me sit down in his office and he told me this little story about how he had seen me at 20th once before, but only from the back when I stepped into an elevator."

After getting that glimpse of Marcus, Allen learned her name from a security guard. Then he contacted her agent. Marcus said, "He wanted me to test for *The Lost World*. That was fine with me, until I saw the costume he wanted me to wear! I had actually just had a baby six months prior to that. Fortunately, I had been able to get my figure back." (VM-AI15)

Marcus passed the test with Allen, but he still needed to convince "New York." He told Lew Schreiber:

> In the role of the "NATIVE GIRL" – I believe I have found the perfect choice and Billy agrees with me. The girl's name is Vettina [sic] Marcus. I made a color still test of her yesterday and it turned out great. I will bring the pictures to you at our meeting today. As a matter of fact, I suggest that Fox might want to take an option on her services or put her under contract.

This was only the first time that Marcus played a "wild girl" for Irwin Allen. She commented, "As it turned out, Irwin used that costume I wore in *The Lost World* in three different shows. The first three times I worked for him, I wore the same outfit!" (VM-AI15)

The next two turns in the skimpy outfit were for episodes of *Voyage to the Bottom of the Sea*. After that, Allen would have Marcus painted green and costumed in glistening tights for a pair of *Lost in Space* episodes. He would also cast her in two episodes of *The Time Tunnel*.

For the top-billed role in the movie, Prof. George Edward Challenger, Allan had wanted James Mason. The problem was, Mason had just starred in *Journey to the Center of the Earth*, another big-budget sci-fi film dealing with prehistoric creatures.

Allen told Schreiber:

> I remind you that there will be at least seven months between the release date of Journey and The Lost World, and while I was originally concerned about having Mason in both pictures, I do not feel that that is now a serious consideration in view of the lapse of time between the two pictures, plus the fact that Mason would play the "CHALLENGER" role <u>with a beard</u>.

20th Century-Fox, who also had made *Journey to the Center of the Earth*, disagreed. Screenwriter Charles Bennett then recommended his friend Claude Rains, whom Allen also knew from having worked together in *Where Danger Lives*. Rains was 59 and had already been nominated four times for an Oscar: as Best Supporting Actor, with 1940's *Mr. Smith Goes to Washington*, 1944's *Casablanca*, 1945's *Mr. Skeffington*, and 1947's *Notorious*. He was also the first to play *The Invisible Man* (in 1933). While Mason did not get the part of Challenger, the beard stayed … transplanted onto Claude Rains.

**Above: David Hedison, Michael Renie, and Claude Rains.
Below: Irwin Allen (far left) holding court with cast on the set of *The Lost World*. To Allen's right: David Hedison, Michael Rennie, Fernando Lamas, Claude Rains, Jay Novello, Ray Stricklyn, Jill St. John, and Richard Haydn. (20th Century-Fox, 1960)**

Regarding Rains, Paul Zastupnevich groaned, "[Irwin Allen] chastised me once for calling Claude Rains 'Claude,' and proverbially bawled me out. Claude

Is David Hedison pointing his rifle at the camera ... or at Irwin Allen, immediately behind camera?

overheard and said 'I made the request. I want Paul to call me Claude. I don't want to be called Mr. Rains; it makes me feel like an old man, and I want to feel young.'"

Allen didn't think it was respectful for underlings to address stars, or, for that matter, celebrity producers, by their first names. Rains may have been fine

Filming in the cavern set built on the Fox backlot near the Moat.

with it, but Allen was not. However, in Hollywood of this era, it was acceptable, and even traditional, to address major film producers and studio moguls by their initials – such as Cecil B. DeMille – aka "C.B." – whom Allen relished comparison. Zastupnevich revealed, "So, I never called him 'Irwin.' I never referred to him as 'Mr. Allen.' I always used his initials whenever I had any dealing with him. I always called him 'I.A.'" (PZ-KB95)

Someone else who went by their initials was L.B. Abbott, 20th Century-Fox's special effects/photographic effects wizard. His friends called him "Bud," but Allen did not. This was L.B.'s first dealing with I.A.

Abbott was 50, and worked exclusively for Fox at this time. He would soon receive an Academy Award for his special effects in the studio's 1959 feature film, *Journey to the Center of the Earth*. Before retiring, Abbott would win the award on three more occasions, including Allen's 1972 film, *The Poseidon Adventure*. He would also win three Emmys, all as a result of his involvement with Allen. Two were for the TV version of *Voyage to the Bottom of the Sea*, and the third was for *The Time Tunnel* series. He also worked on *Lost in Space*.

Abbott later said, "I personally feel that a great many of us in the industry owe Mr. Allen a sincere 'thank you' for all the employment his tireless organizational efforts provided for us."

For his book, *Special Effects: Wire, Tape and Rubber Band Style*, Abbott wrote of his first encounter with Allen, saying, "One evening at about six in the late summer of 1959, my boss, Sid Rogell, called and asked me to come posthaste to the production meeting room. When I entered the room, I was confronted by ten strangers. Everyone, including Sid, nodded, and I sat down. After some thirty minutes of listening, I realized that the leader of the group was a

Jim Dannaldson (above) with the lizards before filming, and one of those lizards (below) after getting out of makeup.

gentleman named Irwin Allen. He held an option on a property called *The Lost World*, based on the novel by Sir Arthur Conan Doyle. The issue was that the option would expire in New York about two-and-a-half hours hence. The studio's involvement, as I recall, meant an immediate investment of $10,000. Mr. Rogell turned to me and asked, 'Bill, can we make this picture?' I said, 'Yes.' That ended my dialogue and I was excused. ... Little did I imagine that my one-word commitment was the start of the Irwin Allen syndrome for me."

Now that the job was his, Abbott needed to find a way to realize the commitment that he had made. He revealed, "Having experienced problems with the rhinoceros iguanas in *Journey to the Center of the Earth*, I had a talk with Jim Dannaldson, an animal man in the industry who is well-versed in the reptile field. Inasmuch as we needed a variety of monsters, I concurred with his suggestion and we used monitor lizards from the Singapore area for the large dinosaurs. They are six to seven feet long and weigh 70 to 150 pounds. Unlike the iguanas, they are voracious flesh eaters descended from the ancient line of varanian reptiles which, in prehistoric times, attained gigantic size. They naturally move the way monsters should." (LBA-SE84)

For scenes featuring the lizards moving through the tropical terrain and joining in combat, a large miniature tabletop jungle set was built, twenty feet deep and forty feet wide. It was raised three feet above the stage floor, with a sloping "apron" in the front. The raised set helped to contain the lizards, but also gave the camera operator a better chance to track the subjects.

Abbott admitted, "On the second day of shooting, I stupidly put myself in a precarious position. I was standing close to a camera that was set up near the foreground apron. The lizard was being very cooperative as it trudged left to right through the jungle, knocking down the upside-down grape vines. When it got directly in front of the camera it stopped to look either at the camera or me. It apparently decided that one or the other should be destroyed, and suddenly it charged us. As it lunged down the slope of the apron, I impulsively grabbed the lizard by the scruff of the neck. Luckily, my grasp was close enough to the back of the monitor's head that he couldn't turn and get his teeth into my arm. The monitor's teeth are formidable, being sharp both at the front and back, like those of a shark. I'm certain that I would have lost the struggle but for the increased flow of adrenaline. As it was, before the lizard could have its way with me, my friend Jim grabbed its tail and jerked it back into the set. Believe me, I was very grateful." (LBA-SE84)

Immediately following this close call, a glass sheet was placed between the camera crew and the "monsters."

As graphic as the lizard fights were, Abbott recalled that none of the animals featured in the movie were injured.

Others reported differently. A famous scene in the film features a monitor lizard and a Cayman alligator "fighting to the death." The reptiles are clearly exchanging real bites, leaving actual wounds. As a result, the American Society for the Prevention of Cruelty to Animals lodged a formal complaint against 20th Century-Fox.

One of the human cast who took away no fond memories of the production was David Hedison. He said, "It was terrible. The alligators with horns and the rhinoceros iguanas were the stars of that picture. Irwin totally wasted the top-notch cast: Michael Rennie, Claude Rains, Fernando Lamas, Jill St. John. We spent the whole film running around from one contrived disaster to another. None of the relationships were thought out or even that conflicted." (DH-DM13)

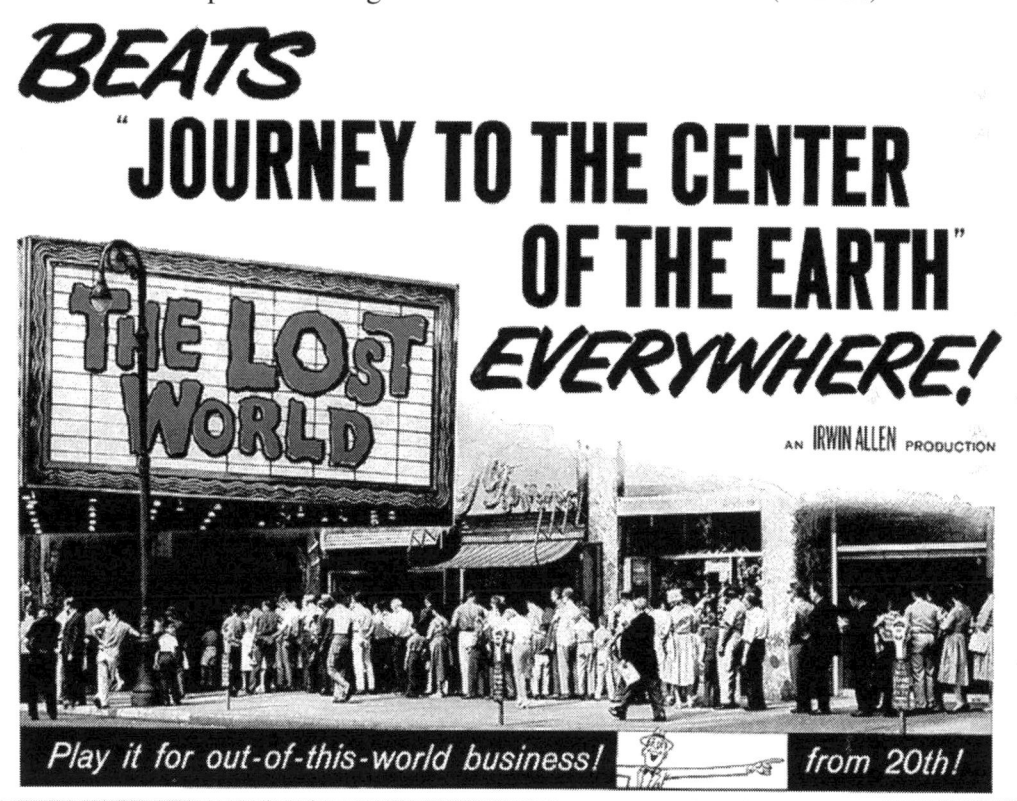

The Lost World had a trade screening in Los Angeles in the first week of July 1960.

On July 6th, Variety opined:

> Watching The Lost World is tantamount to taking a trip through a Coney Island fun house. Like the latter, the Irwin Allen production should appeal primarily to teenagers which, what with the World War II and post-

war birth rate, is a good group to be appealing to these days, from a fiscal standpoint. Although basically as plodding and cumbersome as its dinosaurs, the 20th-Fox release contains enough exploitable spectacle and innocent fun to generate a respectable box office return.

The Motion Picture Herald said in its July 9th issue:

> While the picture is a bit slow in getting started – it's about one-third of its running time before the adventurers meet their first dinosaur – it more than makes up for this in the closing reels. The prehistoric animals are presented with fierce realism and should draw gasps from all audiences.

The "world premiere" took place at the Warner Theatre in New York City on July 13, 1960 (although the film also opened on that day in Los Angeles, at the Iris, Olympic, Century, and the Los Angeles, as well as other theaters across the city). Irwin Allen was in New York at the Warner, along with his friend Groucho Marx, and,

The world premiere took place at the Warner Theatre in New York City. Groucho Marx was on hand with his pal Irwin Allen, giving out *Lost World* comic books.

despite his misgivings about the film, David Hedison, who had been dispatched by 20th Century-Fox. Columnist Walter Winchell was also there, and reported that the 35-foot-high sign over the theater's marquee was one of the largest – if not the largest – "animated electricksters in Broadway lights history."

Above: Groucho buys a ticket from Irwin Allen at the New York City premiere. Below: David Hedison, also on hand, entertains children with a toy dinosaur.

Hedison greeted hundreds of children outside the theater and handed out *Lost World* comic books. Groucho and Irwin Allen hammed it up for publicity stills at the ticket booth. Then all went into the theater as the lights dimmed. Regarding his reaction to watching the film, Hedison said, "It gave me the willies. I didn't really like it, you know. I sat through it and I was ashamed. At that time I had so many aspirations of doing so many wonderful things on film, and I'm looking at this, and I say, 'Here you are, David, at 30, and look at this nonsense you're doing." (DH-PE17)

In time, Hedison would learn that Irwin Allen was more interested in entertainment by broad strokes than in his actors' aspirations. If "nonsense" sold tickets, Allen would produce it. Surely the young at heart would appreciate his efforts.

The morning after the premiere, A.H. Weiler of *The New York Times* sounded more like a grumpy grown-up than Allen would have liked.

> Hollywood's rediscovery of *The Lost World*, as illustrated in flamboyant colors on the Warner Theater's wide screen yesterday, should be far from historic for moviegoers past voting age. The Jurassic Age monsters, to put it neatly into a dinosaur eggshell, have it all over the principals, the director, and the script of this obvious, plodding and often heavy-handed remake of Sir Arthur Conan Doyle's noted contribution to science-fiction. ...
>
> ... A viewer can nod through the first half of this labored adventure. Irwin Allen, who produced, directed and collaborated on the screenplay appears to have been more enamored of palaver than action. His strangely assorted actors engage in a wearying amount of cliché-ridden badinage before their helicopter drops them into something resembling the business at hand. ...
>
> Claude Rains, transformed by a somewhat pinkish hairdo and beard, is a caricature of the dedicated, belligerent zoologist. Michael Rennie is phlegmatic and wooden as the playboy, who is resented by Fernando Lamas, the guitar-playing helicopter pilot. ... Jill St. John, as the daughter of the backer of this junket, is dressed in tight-fitting fuchsia pants and is as out of place here as a manikin in a mudhole. David Hedison, as the handsome reporter she comes to love; Ray Stricklyn, as her brother; Richard Haydn, as Claude Rains' fellow-scientist, and Vitina Marcus, as the native girl, also act as if they thought the trip wasn't necessary.
>
> They can't be blamed. They and the artificial plot are no competition for the prehistoric monsters and lush tropical and volcanic backgrounds of *The Lost World*.

Also on July 14th, after the West Coast premiere, John L. Scott wrote for *The Los Angeles Times*:

> Deep thinkers who might like to slip away from their TV sets and the Democratic convention for a couple of hours of no mental strain can find same in a film program that includes a fantasy, The Lost World, and an even lighter piece titled Bobbikins.

In counterpoint to *The New York Times* review, Scott liked the film, saying that Sir Arthur Conan Doyle's novel had been "turned into a rather surprising adventure film by Irwin Allen," and that the special-effects department "deserves a special accolade," citing "a fight between two prehistoric monsters that should raise blood pressure a bit, mammoth caves whose floors bubble with steaming lava, fierce natives," among other visual delights. Scott wasn't bothered by Claude Rains's playing a caricature of the expedition leader. His take: "Rains plays vigorously and also provides humor in his conflict with a fellow scientist, amusingly performed by a dour Richard Haydn." Nor did he see Michael Rennie as wooden, but said that the actor "does well as a playboy English lord," and, concerning Jill St. John, Scott noted that she was "appropriately decorative."

David Hedison chats with a happy theater exhibitors and studio executive at the New York City world premiere.

Back to the East Coast now. On July 15th, *The Lost World* opened at the Paramount Theater in Rochester, New York, The following morning, Stephen Hammer wrote in that city's popular newspaper, the *Democrat and Chronicle*:

> "Every kid in town is in there," said the ticket taker as I went into the Paramount yesterday for the first showing of *The Lost World*. He was right, too. By the time the show was over, I came to the conclusion that, at 40, a man's too old to figure out what elements in a movie provide it with the drawing power on the young that this one obviously has.

Irwin Allen would certainly have disagreed. At 43, he trusted those instincts constantly. He didn't feel too old or out-of-touch to figure out what might sell to a broad audience.

Determined to feel the weight of his 40 years, Hammer continued:

> As adventure movies go, this one – based on Sir Arthur Conan Doyle's classic – is decidedly long on the

grotesque, but more than slightly short on realism and genuine suspense. True, the chief characters undergo some unusual trials; but this is more than offset by the fact that there are few surprises in the outcome of each. When they emerge from what seems like 72 horrible hours in a prehistoric jungle, they are practically as clean, cheerful and peppy as they were going in.

In the interim, they have encountered dinosaurs of majestic proportion and fierceness, man-eating vegetables, cannibal Indians, a cave filled with bubbling lava, and any number of other weirdies. ...

Lacking the necessary scientific background for honest appraisal, I have to accept most of the special effects as authentic, although generally not unduly exciting. An exception to the latter is a battle to death by two giant dinosaurs, a breathtaking spectacle. On the other hand, a flood of red-hot lava breaking out of its confines looked more like red paint than molten stone. ...

On July 16th Helen Bower's review appeared in *The Detroit Free Press*. After spending two hours at the Fox Theater in Detroit, the girl in Ms. Bowers was alive and well, and happy. She raved:

Everyone who got fun and thrills from *Journey to the Center of the Earth* should go for *The Lost World* .... No finer or more lifelike prehistoric monsters have ever been seen on the screen than those in the Irwin Allen picture ....

Like John L. Scott of *The Los Angeles Times*, Helen Bower connected with Allen's playful side – something many thought he didn't possess:

Claude Rains in red hair and beard, looking like Van Heflin with horn-rimmed glasses, is the first surprise. As a temperamental professor he is a short-tempered, amusing figure. ...

Giant spiders, strangling vegetation, capture by natives, hazardous escape around a lake of fire, and a final bout with a fire monster are some of the horror goodies in store.

Never mind how the group, minus Lamos and Novello, expect to find their way back into civilization after they reach the base of the plateau. What matters is the escape possibilities for movie fans who can lose their own troubles and problems in *The Lost World*.

Bingo.

On July 18th, the film critic for *Time* quipped:

The Lost World exhibits Claude Rains in a red fright-wig, and Jill St. John in – just barely – a pair of pink slacks. These wonders notwithstanding, the most intriguing performers, as is only proper in a Good-Lord-Professor-Can-It-Be? film, are several dinosaurs. Their eyes blaze, their mattress-sized tongues flick menacingly, and their lank green hides glisten in squamous grandeur. They thrash about like lovers in a French art film, roar like convention orators and, when they are hungry, give new depth and meaning to scenery chewing. When two of them duel, Fairbanks-fashion, on the edge of a cliff, they very nearly succeed in bringing to life this tired old Sir Arthur Conan Doyle story of scary Jurassic doings way off in the Amazon rain forest. The human supporting cast, which includes Michael Rennie and Fernando Lamas, adds very little. But then, the reptiles get all the good lines.

Frights and laughs often make good companions. But, as we have seen, not all were amused. David Hedison himself has remained one of the film's harshest critics. He said, "When I finished *The Lost World*, I said I will never work with Irwin again – he's impossible! All he knows is photo effects and banging up against the furniture and fights and everything else [of that type]. He doesn't know anything about character, or simple little moments; nothing. He didn't know anything about that. It was just horrific and very hard. And he was a bit of a crazy man." (DH-PE17)

Regardless, the movie-going public ate it up.

When *The Lost World* opened in New York at the Warner Theatre on Broadway, it was proclaimed a "smash" by *Variety*. When the film was held past its original engagement at the Warner, its reception was called "bang up." A week after the New York premiere, in Washington D.C., in two key movie houses, *Variety* called the picture "socko." In Detroit, at the immense 5,000-seat Fox, business was "swell." In Buffalo, the take was ranked as "great." In Los Angeles, business was "sharp." At the Denver Theatre, the take was "lofty"; a "smash" in Philadelphia; "fast" in Portland; and "good" in Boston. In other cities, and always booked into large theaters, *Variety* deemed *The Lost World* to be "big," "fat," "bright," "loud," "happy," "socko," "boffo," and "solid." During the film's peak week, *Variety*'s National Boxoffice Survey ranked it as the fifth biggest in the nation.

    This was Irwin Allen's greatest triumph to date, solidifying his deal with new partner 20th Century-Fox. Allen would have no resistance from the studio when he announced plans to direct his next feature … the first incarnation of *Voyage to the Bottom of the Sea*.

3

Voyage to the Box Office

VOYAGE TO AMAZING ATOMIC ADVENTURE...ON LAND...IN OUTER SPACE...AND UNDER THE SEA!

[Movie poster: Irwin Allen's Voyage to the Bottom of the Sea, starring Walter Pidgeon, Joan Fontaine, Barbara Eden, Peter Lorre, Robert Sterling, Michael Ansara and Frankie Avalon. Produced and directed by Irwin Allen. Screenplay by Irwin Allen and Charles Bennett. Ride A Fabulous Nuclear Super-Sub! See The Van Allen Radiation Belt Explode! Battle Prehistoric Octopods! Flee A Crashing Rain Of Icebergs! Depth-Dive With The Fearless Aquanauts Of The Deep! Hear Frankie Avalon sing: "Voyage To The Bottom Of The Sea". CinemaScope and breathtaking Color by De Luxe.]

On November 1, 1960, Louella O. Parsons's column, carried by the *Lubbock Avalanche-Journal*, reported:

> Any movie these days that earns $10,000,000 profit for a company, as *Lost World* has for 20th Century-Fox, deserves a repeat call on the services of its producer – in this case, Irwin Allen. [Fox executive] Bob Goldstein, who is closing so many deals he's a one man boom in himself, has signed Allen to produce and direct *Voyage to the Bottom of the Sea*, which Allen also co-authored with Charles Bennett.

As with Allen's other projects, this one began as a simple high-concept topic. Screenwriter Charles Bennett claimed, "Irwin's girlfriend had said, 'Why not a movie about a big submarine?' and he told me that this was a good idea for a movie." (CB-SL93)

Bennett was again happy to take Allen's money without granting much respect. Al Gail felt differently. He said of Irwin Allen and *Voyage to the Bottom of the Sea*, "It was an original idea. It was probably an off-shoot of Jules Verne,

135

but it was an original idea of *his*, and we just developed it as you would normally develop a script." (AG-KB95)

Quoted by Kevin Kelly in *The Boston Globe* of June 14, 1961, Allen said that the concept for his new movie began with a dream. "I had a nightmare," he told Kelly. "Not last night; several months ago. I got up, wrote it down, and turned it into the story that's the basis of the film. You see, there are two belts of radiation surrounding the Earth which were discovered by a scientist named Dr. Van Allen, and I dreamed that one of the belts caught fire. I got to thinking what would happen to a space ship trapped in the blaze at the 300-mile level. I wrote the story and set it in 1967, and if you want to know the solution, you'll have to see the film." (IA-BG61)

Some reviews of *The Lost World* had criticized the movie as sluggish in its first third. As Allen rewrote his script for *Voyage to the Bottom of the Sea*, he deleted material that might postpone the audience's first glimpse of the spectacular effects awaiting them.

Al Gail said, "He liked excitement. He liked explosions. He liked train wrecks. He liked things that would give you a jolt if you were a moviegoer. And he didn't have too much patience for 'talk scenes,' so our scripts were never overloaded with conversation. He was primarily an action producer, and our audience *wanted* action. And we gave 'em action." (AG-KB95)

Allen avoided the "talk," and mixed four of his favorite things: sci-fi spectacle, underwater photography, special effects, and an all-star cast. He co-wrote with Bennett. Then, as producer, he hired himself to direct.

The cast assembled by producer/director Allen was impressive.

On the short list of actors Allen considered to play Admiral Harriman Nelson were Claude Rains, Franchot Tone, Joseph Cotton, Robert Young, Dana Andrews, and the man who won the role, Walter Pidgeon. Looking older than his 53 years, Pidgeon had been a star in Hollywood since 1941 when, after nearly 20 years of working his way up on stage and in films, he had the lead in the popular and critically-acclaimed film *How Green Was My Valley*. The following year, he was nominated for an Academy Award as Best Actor in a Leading role for *Mrs. Miniver*. He received a second nomination as Best Actor for 1943's *Madam*

Curie. Allen fancied casting Pidgeon because of the actor's lead role in the 1956 sci-fi classic, *Forbidden Planet*.

For the role of Dr. Susan Hiller, Allen had considered Patricia Neal, Joan Crawford, Joanne Dru, Ruth Roman, Maureen O'Hara, Arlene Dahl, and Ida Lupino. But always at the top of his wish list was Joan Fontaine, who got the role, second billing in the picture, and a paycheck even bigger than Walter Pidgeon's. Fontaine had catapulted to stardom in 1940 thanks to her role in Alfred Hitchcock's horror-romance epic, *Rebecca*. It brought her the first of three Academy Award nominations as Best Actress in a Leading Role. The second, also under the direction of Hitchcock (1941's suspense thriller *Suspicion*), won her the Oscar. Fontaine's third Academy Award nomination was for her lead performance in 1943's *The Constant Nymph*. By 1960, when *Voyage* began production, Fontaine was 43.

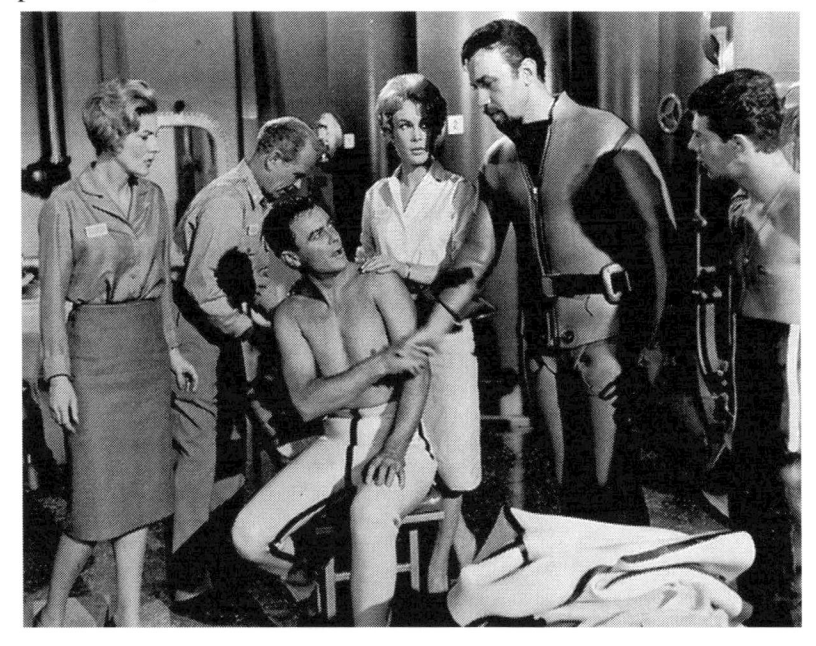

For the role of Lt. Cathy Connors, Allen had considered Mona Freeman and Anne Francis, but first on the list of candidates was always Barbara Eden. She was 30 when given third billing in *Voyage*. Eden had second billing (under Merry Anders) in the 1957-1959 sitcom *How to Marry a Millionaire*. She also had second billing and played opposite Elvis Presley in the

1960 film, *Flaming Star*. Her most famous role was four years away, when she began a five-year run with *I Dream of Jeannie*.

Interviewed for this book, Eden said of *Voyage*, "That was my first movie with Allen, and it was a good experience. The only thing I was a little bit uncomfortable with was the camera zooming in on my bottom. I thought, 'Why are we doing this?' I was under contract to Fox, so I didn't say 'yea or nay' about anything. But I think that was something the audience liked. And the reviews said the best part of the film was Joan Fontaine and myself in high heels on this submarine! They just zeroed in on our legs. And so Irwin was going to show those legs, and those high heels." (BE-AI15)

Eden worked for Allen again in his next film, *Five Weeks in a Balloon*.

For the role of Admiral Nelson's loyal friend and fellow scientist, Lucius Emery, Allen wanted Peter Lorre. The two had worked together for 1957's *The Story of Mankind* and 1959's *The Big Circus*. Lorre, 56, was given fourth billing.

Charles Bennett said, "[W]hen an actor was as good as Lorre, you would naturally employ him whenever you possibly could! It was as simple as that. But, Irwin couldn't always get the actors he wanted. For example … we had wonderful actors in [*Voyage*], but none of them played again for Irwin Allen, except Lorre, because they didn't like Irwin. Joan Fontaine was in it, and she couldn't stand him!" (CB-SL93)

This catty Bennett

remark is disproven by the facts. Three of *Voyage*'s seven stars did in fact work for Allen again. Of the four who didn't, Walter Pidgeon had no problem considering more work. He negotiated with Allen to play Admiral Nelson again in the

Above: Allen, surrounded by Joan Fontaine and Barbara Eden. Below: Eden with Robert Sterling.

television version of *Voyage*. And many other stars became "repeaters" for Irwin Allen projects: Groucho Marx; Paul Newman; William Holden; Victor Mature; Richard Chamberlain; Robert Wagner; Shelley Winters; Barbara Eden, Leslie Nielsen; James Darren; Robert Duvall; Mel Ferrer; Patty Duke; Bradford Dillman; Michael Rennie; Burgess Meredith; Warren Stevens; Martin Milner; and Ralph Bellamy, among others. Some worked for Allen in three, four, or more projects, such as Vincent Price; Ernest Borgnine; Red Buttons; Francine York; Vitina Marcus; Michael Ansara; Whit Bissell; John Crawford; Cameron Mitchell; Albert Salmi; and Richard Basehart. It's a shame that Bennett's slanderous statements haven't been rebutted before now.

Fifth billing was reserved for the actor who would play Captain Lee Crane. Allen wanted David Hedison, who admitted, "[1960] was the most depressing time of my life. I was very low; went home every night depressed, because I was working with Irwin Allen in a film called *The Lost World*. It was one of those pictures that the studio wanted me to do and I felt I had to do, [because] I didn't want to go on suspension. … I was on that film for about eight weeks or so, and I was truly, really, really depressed. So, about a year later, I wasn't depressed anymore, but Irwin called, and he wanted me to do a film called *Voyage to the Bottom of the Sea*. And, after my experience on the *Lost World*, I just couldn't face it, because it was basically the same thing." (DH-TCF07)

Allen had several other candidates. He considered Lloyd Bridges, Steve Forrest, and Cliff Robertson, before offering the role to Robert Sterling, who was 43. In the 1940s, Sterling had been married to Ann Southern, with whom he co-starred in 1941's *Ringside Maisie*. After divorcing in 1949, Sterling married again, to actress Ann Jeffreys. Later, the two were cast to star as mischievous ghosts in the TV series *Topper* (1953-1955), where they tormented Leo G. Carroll.

Allen with Joan Fontaine and Michael Ansara.

Michael Ansara was 38 when given sixth billing in the film, to play Miguel Alvarez. Allen had also considered Ricardo Montalban, Fernando Lamas, John Ireland, and Richard Conte. Ansara had starred in his own television series, as noble Indian Chief Cochise, in the 1956-58 western *Broken Arrow*. He had the lead in a second series, the half-hour western *Law of the Plainsman*, for the 1959-60 TV season. He was married to Barbara Eden during the time that *Voyage* was made.

Frankie Avalon had just turned 21 when he played Lt. Danny Romano, sang the title song, and was given seventh billing. He'd begun acting the year before, with fourth billing in *Guns of the Timberland*, under Alan Ladd, Jeanne

Crain, and Gilbert Roland, and also fourth billed in *The Alamo*, under John Wayne, Richard Widmark, and Laurence Harvey. Avalon's entrée into acting came via his popularity as a pop singer. He scored Top 10 hits in 1958 with "DeDe Dinah" and "Ginger Bread." In 1959, "Venus" hit No. 1 in the pop charts, followed by a second No. 1 hit, "Why," and three more Top 10 entries: "Bobby Sox to Stockings," "A Boy Without a Girl," and "Just Ask Your Heart."

Above: Irwin Allen with 21-year-old Frankie Avalon. Below, giving direction to Mark Slade and Del Monroe. (20th Century-Fox, 1961)

Also in the *Voyage* cast:

Howard McNear, who had previously worked for Irwin Allen in *The Big Circus*, played Congressman Parker. McNear, 55 at this time, was seen often in television and films, and is best known as Floyd the barber on *The Andy Griffith Show*.

Del Monroe played Seaman Kowski (as the name was spelled in the film). He was 24 here. He was brought back as Kowalski, for the TV version of *Voyage*, appearing in 98 episodes.

Mark Slade played Seaman Jimmy "Red" Smith. He was 21 at this time, and would also return for the TV's *Voyage to the Bottom of the Sea*, appearing in five episodes. Slade is best remembered for playing Billy Blue Cannon in the 1960s Western series *The High Chaparral*.

Allen wanted Don Rickles for the role of "Cookie," but the stand-up comedian was unavailable. Allen saved some money, casting a relatively unknown actor named Anthony Monaco.

Mark Slade's memories of Allen as a director: "Irwin's focus was on the spectacle, not the performances. He was a no-nonsense director and expected actors to be prepared. He and his technicians took months to prepare every detail. He became quite volatile if things didn't go his way. He was also a problem-solver. When Frankie Avalon had trouble with a very technical speech, Irwin shouted for cue cards to be made up. They were rushed in and Frankie did the scene perfectly." (MS-TVC99)

Barbara Eden recalled, "He had a lot of energy; he *loved* what he was doing; and got a hundred percent enjoyment out of it. I didn't really know him socially; it was all about work. They were long days; even for *that* time they were long. But I think the thing that stands out in my memory the most is that Irwin didn't say 'Action'; he shot his pistol. And hopefully they were blanks! He'd come on to the set with the boots, and the ballooned pants that directors used to wear, and his pistol, and then 'Boom!' Peter Lorre would jump ten feet and curse, 'What's the matter with that man?! Can't he just say Action?!'" (BE-AI15)

Voyage began production on December 28, 1960, filming miniatures of the Seaview and various other underwater shots and effects. This work, conducted by a second-unit team, continued as principal photography began on January 25, 1961. According to *Daily Variety* on April 10, 1961, Allen and L.B. Abbott collaborated on the longest and most expensive special-effects shooting schedule in 20th-Fox history, spending $860,000 over 36 days.

Designing the Sub of Tomorrow

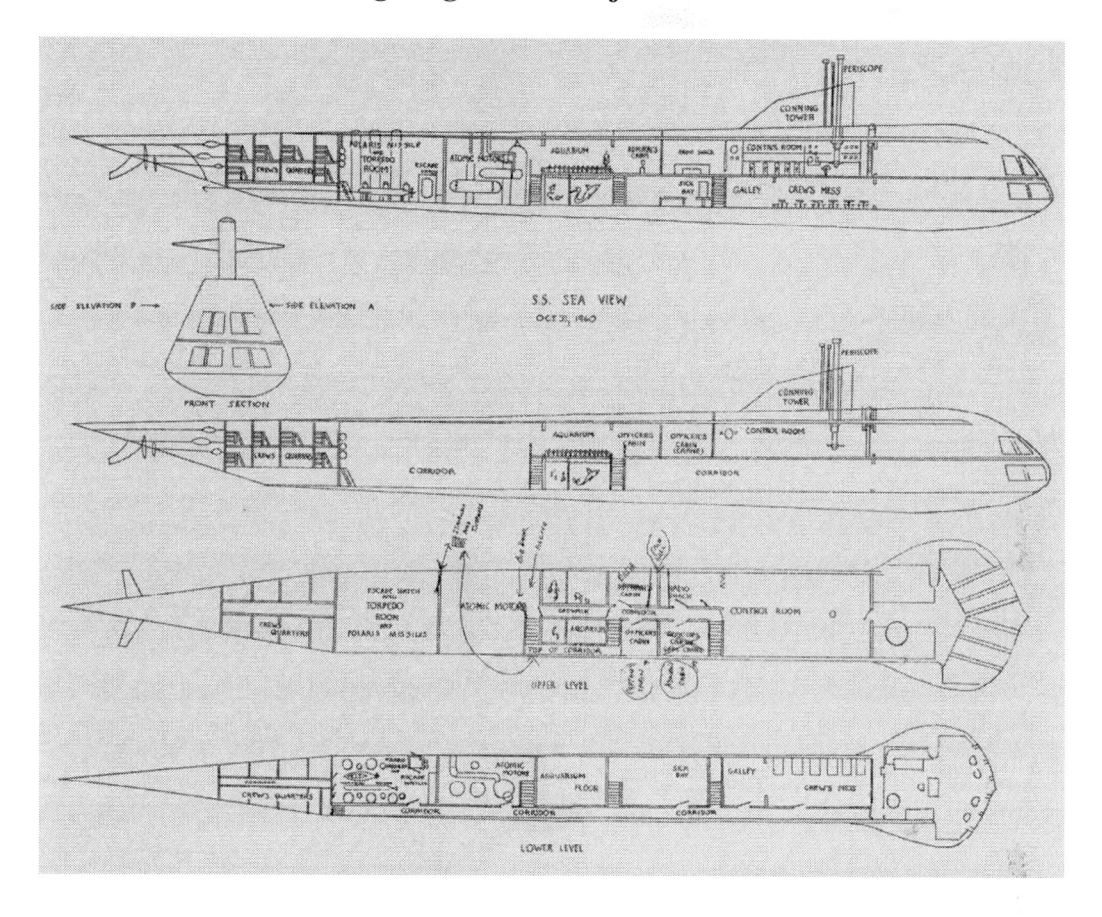

L.B. Abbott said, "*Voyage to the Bottom of the Sea* provided a challenge somewhat greater than that of *The Lost World*. ... The story required a submarine presumably 350 feet long, utterly unique in design and visually exciting. It also had to be theoretically feasible. The onus for the design fell on Jack Martin Smith and Herman Blumenthal, the art directors." (LBA-SE84)

Allen's ideal sub would not only seem "believable" but have a touch of the futuristic. He wanted it instantly distinctive to viewers. You only have to recall the "futuristic" auto designs of the time – featuring streamlining and rocketlike fins – to understand Allen's desire for sleek-looking lines and sweeping contours.

Jack Martin Smith, newly promoted supervising art director at Fox, assigned staff artist Herman Blumenthal to *Voyage to the Bottom of the Sea*. The team of L.B. Abbott, Blumenthal, and Herbert Cheek began graphic design for the project. Cheek's participation was invaluable – as head of Fox's miniatures department, he could advise on how well any designs could be recreated in reduced-scale form.

Under Allen's direction, several Seaview designs were developed. One of the earliest schematics resembled the then-contemporary Skipjack class – the submarine model which introduced the "teardrop hull." Blumenthal's biggest change from current versions of this body would be the addition of a glass-domed observation/control room ... located just behind the conning tower. That concept fell from favor due to cost estimates for set-building.

Another early Seaview design featured more than a dozen bay windows in the front, with a projecting bow. The ship was driven by two propellers in the rear. This layout also depicted a conning tower with diving planes, an access hatch in the belly for launching smaller craft, and a sonar dome just aft of the glassed-in nose.

After Allen gave tentative approval for this version, blueprints and graphic workups were created. Miniatures were made, and Blumenthal and Smith began set design. Their initial request to the U.S. Navy for blueprints and other designs was rebuffed. Now, in the Cold War's chilliest hours, the military wasn't going to be providing accurate information about active nuclear submarines to *anybody*. After Allen's *bona fides* were established and the television *Voyage* was on the air, the Navy consented to provide some reference material.

Despite the military's proscription against documentation, an in-person look wasn't out of the question. The Nautilus was stationed in San Diego, and a few Allen staffers were able to come on board. Jack Martin Smith, interviewed for the book, *Seaview: The Making of Voyage to the Bottom of the Sea*, remembered, "What interested me from a show-business point of view was their 'grand staircase' where two crewmen could walk abreast as they went to different levels of the boat." (JMS-MOVTTBOTS92)

Military-surplus items were used throughout the Seaview's sets, especially the Control Rom and other "tech" areas. The reference book *Jane's Fighting Ships* was also consulted.

Besides scrapped military hardware, some equipment was appropriated from other studio projects. The "missile tracking computer" was a retooled prop from several earlier films – it was seen in *Desk Set* and *The Invisible Boy*, both from 1957, and 1958's *The Fly*. The Control Room's equipment was put together with enough verisimilitude that several Navy visitors to the set were impressed. The devices didn't really make sense, but they certainly *looked* as if they meant business.

Even so, showman Allen wasn't satisfied with a "realistic" setting, and he demanded the addition of more flickering lights to signify power and modernity. The final Control Room set also featured a video display, explained as being linked to exterior cameras, to replace the traditional periscope. No officer draped over the handles of a periscope port for *this* sub of tomorrow! Needless to say, this idea was soon scrapped. Thankfully, there would be a periscope. But the video monitor would also remain.

Seaview's arched, steel-framed observation nose resembled the apse of a medieval cathedral, projecting forward to provide a 180-degree visual range through its reinforced windows. For practical reasons, though, the on-set "windows" contained no glass. Outside their empty frames were rear-projection screens. Two separate projectors simultaneously provided the planned visual sequences – diving, surfacing, sea-level views, and the like.

Other interior sets were Seaview's aquarium, home to Peter Lorre's shark; the ship's mess; and cabins to be redressed as necessary. Another important set, the Missile and Escape Room, housed weaponry and provided egress for scuba men, as well as access to the mini-sub.

A real handicap for the designers was laying out sets that *looked* like the cramped quarters of a submarine, yet allowed access for the operation of cameras and other equipment. Fox's Smith put it this way: "When you're trying to build sets that look like the inside of a submarine it's like you're inside a telephone booth. You have to peel away one wall [the "wild wall"] to make more room for the camera and lights and the seventy-five or so people who are standing around. … [S]o we devised a way where we could take apart the submarine in twelve- to fifteen-foot sections from the floor to the ceiling." (JMS-MOVTTBOTS92)

These sections were also on wheels, so cabins and corridors could be easily swapped about.

The design and construction of real-seeming sets for filming was much more difficult and involved than any miniatures needed. Now you understand why it was necessary for Smith and Blumenthal to work closely with Abbott and Allen in all phases of designing the "look" of *Voyage*.

While hammers echoed on the stages, those miniatures were crafted by Herb Cheek's miniatures department. The Mini-Sub and the Seaview were first sculpted in clay for Allen's approval. After all modifications, the final versions were cast in fiberglass.

Changes had become necessary in the initial "final" design. Over a period of time, Seaview's bow was further rounded, and the number of fore windows reduced to eight. A large searchlight assembly, the "forward lamp," was mounted below the observation ports, replacing several smaller ones that had been originally proposed.

Side fins – like truncated bat wings – swept from the sub's bulbous nose to the body. Abaft, two manta-ray fins below and a smaller pair above completed the ship's missile-like, futuristic appearance. If you compare the Seaview's tail to a 1960 Caddy, you might think that the car's designers were emulating Allen's sub!

This similarity wasn't lost on the *Voyage* graphics team. Smith recalled, "We had these long fins coming out of the back of the sub, and then we added lights on the tips of those fins so it started to look like the back of a Cadillac." (JMS-MOVTTBOTS92)

Smith and Blumenthal built three models of the submarine, dubbed the Seaview – one was seventeen feet, two inches long (not the nineteen feet claimed by some Fox press releases), used for surface shots; another was eight feet long and used for underwater shots; and a third, measuring four feet, was used during the battle with a giant octopus.

Filming and Effects

The miniature work on the *Voyage* feature (as opposed to the TV series) was filmed on "Lake Sersen," named after the studio's prior special-effects head, Fred Sersen. Disney had used this location in 1954 for its *20,000 Leagues Under the Sea*. Lake Sersen was not a natural lake – it was a small body of water on the Fox backlot, with a large sky backdrop and an area for pumps to create waves.

Abbott said, "The scene near the opening [of the movie] when the submarine thunders to the surface at a 30 degree up angle, rising half its length out of the water like a jumping swordfish before the bow crashes back into the sea, is very exciting. We had miniature icebergs in the old tank and a blazing red backing. We had dug a pit in the tank floor some years before in order to sink the Titanic in the picture of that name. The Seaview was sunk in the pit, riding on rails that came to within three feet of the surface. These rails gave it the 30 degree up angle. Attached to the sub's stern were two steel cables that ran underwater over pulleys to the rim of the tank where they were fastened to a truck. On cue, the truck would make a fast start, run the proper distance, and make a quick stop. This made it possible to make the sub leap to the surface. Added to this for effect there were several high pressure fire hoses placed in the hull and directed at the ports of the ballast tanks. These made it appear that the tanks were blown as the ship came out of the sea. The concept of the shot was Irwin Allen's, stemming from his having viewed some U.S. Navy film on Polaris submarines in which a Polaris did a maneuver similar to the Seaview's action."

Another memorable effects shot involved a giant octopus battling the Seaview. Abbott said, "The reason for using a four-foot model of the Seaview for shooting the octopus attack was that the only octopus available at the time were just slightly larger than one's hand, and the four foot model made the octopus appear huge. We shot the sequence in a tank eight feet by four feet by four feet on a stage. This amount of water was easily filtered and also easily cooled and salinated to make the octopus feel at home. Before each take, the handler would place the octopus we were going to use in a large tub and tease it until it expended its supply of ink. The handler would then, very slowly and carefully, place the octopus on the nose of the sub, which was being held by its tail by an effects man standing in the tank just off screen. Obviously, the octopus would not get on the submarine's nose of its own volition. When it seemed attached to the sub, the handler would make an exit very slowly, and the effects man would carefully position the sub for the camera. Often the octopus would fall off the sub before we had any usable footage and the handler would retrieve it in a net and the procedure would be repeated." (LBA-SE84)

This mollusk manhandling continued for an entire day. For the scene of the octopus latching onto the sub, one of the fall-off shots was reversed.

While promoting his new film, Allen crowed, "The filmmakers never had so great an opportunity to profit from television's shortcomings as they do today. The reason is that TV can't produce anything better than stuff for mass communications and it frankly isn't good. What's more, it isn't likely to get better." (IA-EB61)

At least, not until Irwin Allen returned to TV.

Principal Photography

Above (left to right): Irwin Allen, unknown executive, Joan Fontaine, Robert Sterling, Barbara Eden, and Frankie Avalon.

Production with the main unit and the human cast spanned January 25 through March 14, 1961. The interior of the Seaview was built on 20th Century-Fox's Stage 5. The first sequences filmed were in the Observation Nose and Control Room, followed by Int. Missile Room and "Escape Room," Sick Bay and outside corridor. Next came the Aquarium (where Peter Lorre "exercised" his pet shark); the Admiral's Quarters and outside corridor, Interior Crew's Quarters and outside corridor; Crane's Cabin; and "Int. Cathy's Door" and Stairway. Also filmed on Stage 5, beginning in February, was the Ext. Bridge set and surrounding arctic area, the Exterior Derelict Yacht, and "Underwater Close Ups," utilizing the 8-by-4-by-4-foot tank.

Stage 3 was used for the U.N. Conference Room, and TV Booth.

Above (left to right): Regis Toomey, Paul Zastupnevich, and Robert Sterling. Below (l-r): Allen with Sterling and Peter Lorre.

At Sersen Lake, they filmed the U.N. Dock and "Runner – Seaview," and more sequences with the Ext. Bridge of the Seaview, plus "Ext. Raft and Ocean."

The "Lower Moat" on the Fox backlot was utilized for "Ext. Conning Tower and Deck."

The last shots taken by the main unit involved the shark attack in the Sea Aquarium on Stage 5.

The budget that 20th Century-Fox approved on September 28, 1960 was for $1,488,200. By the time the last of the post-production had been completed, the cost had increased to close to $2,000,000. In 2018, after adjusting for inflation, this equals about $17,000,000. Of course, today it would be impossible to make a movie like this for a mere $17 million. How did they manage to do it in 1961? First, Walter Pidgeon, the top-billed star, was only paid $40,000. Joan Fontaine actually did better, receiving $45,000. Peter Lorre was the next highest paid in the cast, receiving $16,000. Robert Sterling was paid $14,000. Barbara Eden was in the budget for $6,700. Michael Ansara was next, making $6,000.

Allen with Peter Lorre (above) and showing Barbara Eden (below) how *not* to put out a fire.

Interviewed by Brooks Yarborough for North Carolina's *Charlotte News*, Allen talked about his all-star casting technique. "The pressure is on in Hollywood. When we put two million dollars into a movie as we did in this one, we've got to make over four million to even break even. We do everything possible to ensure that four million, too. That's why, perhaps, the unknown might not get as good a chance as someone even a little known. We've got to do everything we can to sell a picture. It's a product. We're businessmen, first of all."

Allen admitted to loving the pressure of the entertainment business, saying, "I'd probably fall apart without it. I really don't know what I'd do if I *weren't* under pressure." (IA-CN61)

To a different journalist, Allen explained how he selected titles for his movies: "You read the title and you immediately know what the film is about." As to why he had no interest in making "message films," he said, "My business is to entertain and that's just what I try to do. I have no deep message for the public. I promise them no psychological probe, no social study. Just fun." (IA-AJC61)

Talking to Nora E. Taylor, of *The Christian Science Monitor*, Allen said, "Messages are for Western Union. Films are to make money." (IA-CSM61)

Allen was borrowing. The origin of this saying has been attributed to both Samuel Goldwyn and Moss Hart.

Asked by interviewer Mike Clark what kind of movies he personally liked, Allen coyly responded, "I like successful pictures." (MC-AI15)

Early indications were that *Voyage* would make that list.

Allan takes to the road, wining and dining exhibitioners ... and exhibiting a little something extra to ensure a full roster of engagements.

Irwin Allen delivering the film for the world premiere.

Philip K. Scheuer of the *Los Angeles Times* caught the trade-show preview, and wrote for his newspaper's June 18, 1961 edition:

Voyage to the Bottom of the Sea – for such, indeed, it is – seems to me very probably the most effective big-scale science-fiction film since *Journey to the Center of the Earth* and *The Time Machine*. ... For *Voyage* is crammed with climax after climax; the initial rain of ice rocks in the Arctic; encounters with not one but two octopuses, the second wider across than the sub itself; the slow-speed penetration of a floating mine field, and the destruction of the Seaview's mini-sub itself when it collides with one such mine; and even an attack by another sub which pursues a zig-zagging, fleeing Seaview with irrevocable orders from the United Nations to shoot (torpedoes) to kill. More, Adm. [Walter] Pidgeon is harassed not only by a saboteur or saboteurs on board but also by a growingly rebellious crew who finally persuade even the handsome young captain (Robert Sterling) that the admiral ought to be relieved of his command; and by a religious fanatic of a passenger (Michael Ansara) who keeps shouting that "what will be, will be" and that Pidgeon is flouting the will of God by his high-handed actions. ... [O]f all the artists assisting Mr. Allen the loudest salute should probably go to Jack Martin Smith and Herman A. Blumenthal, who have designed such a practical, workable sub that even *we* get a pretty good inkling as to what those knobs and levers and flashing dials are all about.

Jack Muffitt, writing for *Motion Picture Limelight* on June 29th, compared Allen's film to the Disney 1954 megahit *20,000 Leagues Under the Sea*. He raved:

> This fine adventure story, which 20th is releasing for saturation booking, is so good that it may reasonably be expected to do *20 Thousand Leagues* business. Produced, directed and written by Irwin Allen (who adapted it in collaboration with Charles Bennett), it is a new, convincing type of science-fiction, in which blobs, monsters, and ladies who turn into crocodiles are fortunately absent. Laid in the near future, it deals with conditions whose possibilities already are causing many people a shivery concern – the predicted melting of the Polar ice caps and the ignition of the recently discovered Van Allen radiation belt which, 3000 miles out in space, encircles our Earth.

Jonah M. Ruddy, writing in *The Hollywood Diary* on July 1st, declared:

> Irwin Allen will probably be acclaimed as this generation's Jules Verne of the Mighty Screen. Highly imaginative, marvelously composed with all the magic of special effects and miniatures, his *Voyage to the Bottom of the Sea* is universal entertainment. It's a blend of the sublime and the ridiculous. ... In brief, [the film] is swell, submarine science-fiction and by far the most fascinating nuclear-powered submarine – since the Polaris – that we have seen on the wide, wide screen.

Voyage kicked off to good box office. Given the ballyhoo of its promotional campaign, how could it have been otherwise?

In Washington D.C., at the massive 3,420-seat Capitol, *Variety* rated the movie as "tall." In Toronto, at the 3,348-seat Imperial, and in Detroit, at the huge 5,041-seat Fox, it was "good." In Denver, at the Centre with its 1,270-seats, *Voyage* was "big." And the film was playing in New York City on Broadway, at the 3,665-seat Paramount, where it was rated as "nice." Irwin Allen's movie was the eleventh biggest in the nation.

The following week, it moved up to the seventh spot in the box-office derby. The new city to get *Voyage* was St. Louis, where the colossus Fox Theater, with 5,000 hungry seats, reported business was "fine."

In *Voyage*'s fourth week of release, *Variety* ranked it as the seventh top-grossing movie in the nation. In Chicago and Los Angeles the film was "boffo." In Portland, it was "fast."

On August 11th, according to *Variety*, Fox crowed that the movie had made in excess of $1,000,000 in its first four weeks of release. That left $3,000,000 additional revenue to hit "break-even" (between film costs, advertising costs, and exhibitor shares). Once the film turned a profit, Fox was required to split that revenue down the middle with Irwin Allen.

In week five, *Voyage* slipped down to tenth place on the national scene. It was new in Kansas City, at the 2,043-seat Uptown and the 1,217-seat Granada, where the word was "fancy." In St. Louis, at the big 5,000-seat Fox, business remained "fast." In Chicago, patronage was "solid."

Hear the record! See the picture! Irwin Allen's "VOYAGE TO THE BOTTOM OF THE SEA"

Boxoffice magazine presented Irwin Allen with its Blue Ribbon award, acknowledging that the magazine's editors and critics felt *Voyage to the Bottom of the Sea* had the most potential of both creating family entertainment and, at the same time, earning exhibitors money.

Nephew Michael Allen remembered, "Irwin was very pleased with *Voyage to the Bottom of the Sea*. It was the first of his disaster style movies, with an all-star cast. He felt very strongly about that – that it was the closest to the course his future was going to take." (MA-AI15)

With *Voyage*, Allen had successfully combined facets of his earlier success: high concept, big-name stars, and underwater spectacle. By his sights, he had nowhere to go but up.

4

From the Big Screen to the Small Tube

After completing *Voyage to the Bottom of the Sea*, the second of back-to-back "one-off" picture deals with 20th Century-Fox, Allen began negotiations with legendary producer Joseph Levine, founder and head of Embassy Pictures. The buzz around Hollywood indicated a deal was close at hand. On June 7, 1961, *Variety* reported:

> Whether producer-director Irwin Allen will accept what he terms to be a "fabulous" offer from Joe Levine to join Embassy Pictures, or will continue on with 20th-Fox, will be decided within the next week or so, Allen said in New York Monday. ... Allen said he expected his agent to meet on the coast [Los Angeles] either yesterday (Tues.) or today (Wed.) with 20th-Fox prexy Spyros P. Skouras to receive 20th's counteroffer for his future services. ... A new deal, he said, would certainly be a multiple pic

arrangement. No matter with whom he signs, Allen intends next to make Jules Verne's *Five Weeks in a Balloon*.

Allen's real intent for these talks with Embassy was to leverage more money from Fox. On June 27th, *Variety* reported:

> Turning down Joe Levine and two others, producer-director-writer Irwin Allen wrapped up new five-pix deal at 20th-Fox. Returning yesterday from cross country tour before exhib groups plugging *Voyage to the Bottom of the Sea*, Allen said [Fox] prexy Spyros P. Skouras' offer was best of all; too good to be ignored. Two pix are set under new pact, each to cost $2,000,000: *Five Weeks in a Balloon* and "Passage to the End of Space." Allen will direct and do screenplay with Charles Bennett, who has done eight others with him.

At this time, the studio was thrilled with *Voyage to the Bottom of the Sea*, expecting it to become the hit of the summer season. Allen, always a shrewd negotiator, inked his new deal while expectations were high, before the excitement of *Voyage*'s opening faded. But *Voyage*, despite respectable business, never rose higher than No. 7 in the *Variety*'s National Box Office Survey, and by the end of 1961 had not passed its joint production and distribution-promotion cost of $4 million.

The studio's mood began to shift against Allen. About the same time, Allen's thoughts began to shift, as well. Always a strong believer in research and surveys, his own polls told him that the box-office falloff was due to the science-fiction genre itself. After the incursion of cheap sci-fi B-films throughout the 1950s, an oversaturated public was leaning toward other genres.

Interviewed for a newspaper article at this time, Allen said, "My back goes up when I'm identified with science fiction. I'm a commercial movie-maker, and I enjoy making money at my job. I enjoyed making *Voyage to the Bottom of the Sea*; but something happened that I don't want ever to happen again – mature women and teen-aged girls stayed away in droves. They stay away from all science fiction films. So, remember, *Voyage* was my one venture into that field."
(IA-IAPC62)

Allen chose not to consider *The Lost World* science fiction, or, for that matter, *The Story of Mankind*, with its tribunal in "The Great Court of Outer Space." He maintained that these films were "fantasies," splitting a very fine hair.

Allen's term-switching was driven home in a studio press release from August 1962:

> *Five Weeks in a Balloon* is straightforward adventure-comedy, without the science fiction elements that so preoccupied Verne later in his career. It details the hilarious adventures of seven would-be explorers (five men, two women) who stage a madcap, 4,000-mile balloon race across Africa. ...

Meanwhile, the executives at 20th Century-Fox were preoccupied. Paul Zastupnevich said, "They didn't pay that much attention to Irwin. They were too wrapped up in *Cleopatra* and the problems that they were having. I always felt they tolerated him, because his product did make some money for them and it was keeping them afloat. And it gave a semblance of activity at the studio." (PZ-KB15)

Five Weeks in a Balloon was the last film Charles Bennett co-wrote with Irwin Allen, although Bennett did return to contribute scripts to the TV incarnation of *Voyage to the Bottom of the Sea*. The writer said, "Eventually, I became irritated at continually seeing Irwin's name co-credited with mine, and I finally rebelled after I wrote my final film for him – *Five Weeks in a Balloon*. I insisted that my name only be mentioned as screenwriter, but he *still* placed his name after mine as screenwriter. ... You can hire someone to write something, but that doesn't give

you the right to say that *you* wrote it. No, hiring a writer does not give the producer or anyone hiring the writer to a credit as screenwriter. But Irwin did it."
(CB-LISTTS96)

Nevertheless, Bennett was happy to take several script assignments on the TV version of *Voyage to the Bottom of the Sea*. By 1966, Allen seemed the only producer in Hollywood still willing to give work to the embittered writer. And Allen was the last – assigning Bennett a script job in 1968 on *Land of the Giants*.

With the film's story set, Allen next sought its players.

Red Buttons was given the lead. He had previously appeared in Allen's 1959 film, *The Big Circus*. Now he starred as Donald O'Shay.

Barbara Eden had appeared in Allen's previous movie, *Voyage to the Bottom of the Sea*. Here, she was cast as Susan Gale.

Sir Cedric Hardwicke was sixty-nine when hired to play Fergusson. He was a successful character actor who had third billing in classics such as 1935's *Les Misérables*, 1939's *Stanley and Livingstone*, and 1941's *Suspicion*. He also played the High Judge in Allen's *The Story of Mankind*.

Fabian was only nineteen when hired to play Jacques. He had

**Above: Barbara Eden and Red Buttons.
Below: BarBra Luna and Fabian.
(20th Century Fox, 1962).**

started his film career as the lead of 1959's *Hound-Dog Man*, then received second billing under Bing Crosby in the 1960 musical comedy *High Time*, and was cast in the same year in the John Wayne comedy/western *North to Alaska*. For 1961, he shared top billing with another teen idol, Tommy Sands, in the musical comedy *Love in a Goldfish Bowl*. Fabian was also a pop star, with three Top Ten singles in 1959: "Turn Me Loose," "Tiger," and "Hound Dog Man" (from the movie).

Interviewed at the time of filming, Irwin Allen said, "This kid wants to be an actor, and he's a *good* actor. We even had to persuade him to sing the title song." (IA-IAPC62)

Peter Lorre was now fifty-eight, and had appeared in *The Story of Mankind* and *Voyage to the Bottom of the Sea*. He was given the role of Ahmed.

Richard Haydn was fifty-seven, and had worked for Allen in *The Lost World*. In this film, he played Sir Henry Vining.

BarBara Luna (billed as Barbara) was only twenty-two when cast to play Makia. She had already made a couple of dozen appearances on TV, including four episodes in Guy William's series *Zorro*.

Interviewed for this book, Luna joked, "My audition was really tough. 'Irwin Allen wants to meet you.' 'Okay.' So I go to the office and he says to me, 'Say Me Makia.' So I said, 'Me Makia.' He said, 'Okay, I want you to do my film.' He liked my look. But I had to do something that, to this day, if I ever see *Five Weeks in a Balloon* on the TV, I shudder, because he had a thing about hair. He didn't want hair flying all over the place, because we

159

were going to be outside. In fact, I think we were outside *all the time*. And up in the balloon *all the time*. And he didn't want hair blowing in my face. So he made me wear an invisible hair net. You know, like those things that waitresses had to wear back at that time. So, if you look at my hair, you'll see that it never moves, because it was plastered down with this horrible net. And that was a deal breaker. 'Either you wear the hair net or you're not in the movie.' That was his attitude. Actually, come to think of it, that was his attitude about everything." (BL-AI15)

In an uncredited role as a harem girl was actress Sheila Mathews. She would later date Irwin Allen and, in the mid-1970s, become his wife. She was 33 in 1962.

Paul Zastupnevich said, "That [movie] was the first thing that Sheila did. Irwin met her and became enamored of her, and, at that time, Sheila was slim enough that I was able to put her in a costume that had been made for Susan Hayward, and re-adapted it for her. So, she was very trim in those days and quite beautiful. She has a gorgeous singing voice, which later was utilized in *Lost in Space*." (PZ-KB95)

Mathews recalled, "We were introduced at a restaurant by a mutual friend, and he [Allen] invited me out to the studio. He was shooting *Lost World* at the time. So, he sat me in his director's chair, and let me watch the shooting. After about an hour, he said, 'You can leave your picture and résumé with my secretary.' So I did. About a year later, I was out there being interviewed for something, and I was looking for the office I was to go to, and I was standing downstairs in what later became the 'Irwin Allen building.' I was reading the board, and three or four men walked in, and Irwin said, 'Can I help you?' I turned around and I said, 'Yes, I'm looking for so-and-so's office.' And he said, 'Oh, that's upstairs and down the hall.' As he turned to go up those stairs, he looked familiar, and I said, "Pardon me, but aren't you Irwin Allen?' He said, 'Yes. Have we met?' I told him we'd met a year ago, and he said, 'Well, when you're finished with your interview, why don't you stop up and see me. I'm right upstairs, and let me know how you've been doing.' So, I actually did; I stopped in and we had a chat, and two weeks later he invited me out to dinner, and my dinner date was at Groucho Marx's house, which was quite interesting, to say the least. So then we started dating." (SM-KB95)

According to nephew Michael Allen, "Groucho reminded Irwin a lot of my father [Irwin's brother Rubin]. They looked a lot alike, and had the same kind of attitudes. And Irwin and my father liked one another. Groucho liked that Irwin was young, brash, bright, and heading for success. And I also think he was always respectful of Groucho." (MA-AI15)

Sheila Mathews: "I feel Groucho was almost like a second father to Irwin. And they had a really good time together. Groucho was, of course, quite funny. And Irwin had his moments, too. But they really enjoyed each other for many, many years. I guess we had dinner at Groucho's about three times a week. Evidently Groucho figured I was okay, because I don't think we would have been seeing each other if it [the first dinner with Groucho] hadn't worked out." (SM-KB95)

That first date with Allen, and a nod from fatherly Groucho Marx, led to Mathews being cast in *Five Weeks in a Balloon*.

As for working with Allen, BarBara Luna recalled, "Thankfully, everything I did was okay – it was not problematic. I don't remember him ever yelling at anybody, other than he just yelled, in general, before a take. He would just scream. And this was a comedy, or, at least, it was supposed to be a comedy. I don't know if it ended up being funny. But he was definitely a screamer. If I remember, he was a Gemini. Not that I have anything against Geminis, because I have great fun with all of my Gemini friends, but they are especially hyper. And, he was from New York. He knew exactly what he wanted and it was his way or the highway." (BL-AI15)

Barbara Eden concurred. "He was always high energy, so you didn't know if he was nervous or if he was happy. But he got everything done. And he was never mean spirited. Never. But it is also a matter of how flexible you can be. The older actors, like Peter Lorre, even though he worked with Irwin a lot, were just aghast over his style. The gun that he would fire instead of calling 'Action' was one reason. I don't remember him using the gun in the scenes with the lion, but, otherwise, that gun was always on set. And Peter would jump every time and curse and mumble about it. Irwin also had one of those things you'd talk through – a megaphone. But he was enjoying every minute of it. I've never seen anyone enjoy their job so much. And he got it done." (BE-AI15)

BarBara Luna: "I don't ever remember getting direction. I'd already done a fair amount of TV, not that you get a lot of direction in TV, but I don't remember Irwin ever really directing me, other than technical. And it was a very technical film, obviously. He was about, 'Let's just blow up everything!' But who's really going to direct Peter Lorre or Cedric Hardwicke? It was such an interesting cast. So I think that Irwin Allen maybe, *maybe*, might have been at his very best behavior because of the actors in that.

"Despite Irwin's craziness, it was fun, because the people were so much fun. I think once you get that massive dose of Irwin Allen, you just kind of know what you're in for. But it is tough being a director. In a sense, the director is in *every* shot. But, yes, he would fire a gun instead of saying 'Action!' My gosh, what a character." (BL-AI15)

Left to right: Fabian, BarBra Luna, Richard Haydn, Sir Cedric Hardwicke, Peter Lorre, Barbara Eden, and Red Buttons. (20th Century-Fox, 1962)

Five Weeks in a Balloon was released on August 22, 1962.

Margaret Harford, writing for the August 24, 1962 issue of the *Los Angeles Times*, yawned:

> Although *Five Weeks in a Balloon* seems more like five years (to adults), it isn't because producer Irwin Allen hasn't loaded this color aerial fantasy with a full gondola of Hollywood actors (Fabian, Red Buttons, Herbert

> Marshall, etc.) and enough African wildlife footage to stock three or four "Tarzan" pictures. ... *Five Weeks in a Balloon*, now at local theaters and drive-ins, is mostly hot air, an adventure film inflated from an early Jules Verne novel and sent aloft as a summertime family film. It fills that bill nicely. Children will enjoy it, but adults may find the whimsy heavy and repetitious before the balloon bursts.

On August 15th, after catching a pre-release trade screening in Los Angeles, *Variety* said:

> Allen has taken a conventional balloon-adventure and dealt with it tongue-in-cheek style – in effect approaching Verne in a kind of wild "Road" picture vein. Goal of the kidding approach seems to be to make it more palatable for adults. ... At any rate, *Five Weeks in a Balloon* has been designed with a something-for-everybody, "whole family" commercial concept: spoofery for the adults, romance and high adventure for the older youngsters, African wildlife and aerial fantasy for the tykes. There is, however, an inherent danger in the film that aims a bit too ambitiously to span and please all age groups. Each separate facet tends to subtract from the impact of the others.

On August 18th, the movie critic for *Cue* magazine groaned:

> Jules Verne's science fiction fantasies have for 60 years provided drama and amusement for movie audiences. However, there is nothing in the Verne public domain to suggest that his work need be brought down to kindergarten level; and that is what, with no apologies, producer Irwin Allen has done here.

In early October, *Boxoffice* once again singled out an Irwin Allen movie – this time *Five Weeks in a Balloon* – as a movie the editors and critics felt had the most potential of both creating family entertainment and, at the same time, earning exhibitors money. It was awarded the magazine's Blue Ribbon Award for September.

Five Weeks in a Balloon peaked in the *Variety* National Box Office Survey in seventh position.

During its fourth week of release, *Five Weeks* slipped down to the ninth spot in *Variety*'s National Box Office Survey. One week later, it was missing from most first-run downtown theaters. The neighborhood houses would get it next, and business in those venues was spotty. When all was said and done, it would take overseas sales and, later, television, to turn this one into a moneymaker.

***

Because of the marginal returns of *Five Weeks in a Balloon*, Allen's next two feature-film projects at Fox – the sci-fi "Passage to the End of Space" and the costume adventure "The Big Pirate" – stalled out.

A big reason for Fox's skittishness: It was overextended, due to its commitment to a hoped-for blockbuster that nearly bankrupted the studio instead.

Cleopatra – the Elizabeth Taylor-Richard Burton epic movie – had become a runaway train, and a runaway drain of resources. Its production spanned 1960 and '63, with massive cost overruns and production troubles, including changes in directors, cinematographers, actors, and locales. Health problems with Taylor delayed the production more than once. Sets were built, discarded, then built anew. *Cleopatra* was the most expensive movie ever made up to that time. Though it was the highest-grossing film of 1963, even these returns couldn't

Cleopatra, starring Elizabeth Taylor and Richard Burton, cost 20th Century-Fox its backlot ... and Irwin Allen his movie deal. (20th Century Fox, 1963)

offset its combined production and marketing cost of $44,000,000. In 2018, this cost equates to over $350 million. By comparison, the 2011 release *Pirates of the Caribbean: On Stranger Tides* clocked in at $378 million in production costs.

Another 1961 Fox production hemorrhaging money was *Something's Gotta Give*, which paired Marilyn Monroe and Dean Martin. Monroe caused delays on a daily basis, and the production descended into a costly debacle. After weeks of script rewrites and very little progress, Monroe was fired, then rehired and promised a hefty bonus upon the completion of filming. This never came about, for she was found dead in her home on August 5, 1962. Doris Day replaced Monroe, prompting Martin to exit the project. The film was finally completed the following year and released as *Move Over, Darling*, starring Day and James Garner.

Marilyn Monroe in 1962, filming what would have been her last film, 20th Century-Fox's *Something's Got To Give*.

In the meantime, Fox sold its backlot (now the site of Century City) to Alcoa in an effort to raise the cash needed to complete both films. Despite this, in 1962, the studio released nearly all of its contract stars, including Jayne Mansfield.

The situation at 20th Century-Fox was bleak. Al Gail said, "Up front, the executives kept turning over. You never knew when you came back into work the next day who was running the studio. They were in bad shape. *Cleopatra* almost knocked them out completely. It was strange but, when we'd go out to lunch, we'd never go out the front gate; we'd always go out the back. We didn't want to remind them [that we were still on the lot], because they had no money. … We'd all climb into [Irwin's] Rolls Royce, and we'd sneak out the back gate and hope none of the executives saw us." (AG-KB95)

The studio would soon receive a lifeline, ironically, from television – the same industry often treated in the past as the bastard child of motion pictures. In a practice continued through the 1960s, most TV was produced by production companies established solely for that purpose – ZIV (*Highway Patrol*, *The Cisco Kid*, *Sea Hunt*), Desilu (*I Love Lucy*, *The Andy Griffith Show*, *The Dick Van Dyke Show*, *The Untouchables*), Mark VII (*Dragnet*, *The D.A.'s Man*), Filmways (*The Bob Cummings Show*, *The Beverly Hillbillies*, *Petticoat Junction*), Revue (*Wagon Train*, *Leave It to Beaver*, *Alfred Hitchcock Presents*) and Four Star (*The Rifleman*, *Wanted: Dead or Alive*, *Richard Diamond - Private Detective*). These companies would lease studio or stage space from the majors. Until the last half of the 1950s, this was as close as Paramount, Warner Bros., Universal, MGM, United Artists, RKO, Columbia, and 20th Century-Fox consented to come. For the movie industry, television remained the sibling born on the wrong side of the blanket. Even so, TV was growing hungrier for product, even as the major studios were hurting for revenue.

The door to producing for television was cracked open when the studios began selling their older movie libraries to TV distributors. Columbia was the first to take a bold step toward making TV in the late-1940s, but did so by setting up a new studio – Screen Gems. They made *Father Knows Best*, *The Adventures of Rin Tin Tin*, *Jungle Jim*, *Dennis the Menace*, *The Donna Reed Show*, and *Naked City*, among others – all hits in their day, and destined for long lives as syndicated repeats.

Twentieth Century-Fox tested the television waters in the fall of 1955 with *My Friend Flicka*, which spent one year on CBS and one on NBC, and *The 20th Century-Fox Hour*, which had a two-year run on CBS. Neither hit big, but *Flicka* would stick around on Saturday mornings for a few years in syndication. In 1957, the studio sold the half-hour western *Broken Arrow* to ABC, where it stayed for two years. The kids loved it; the series stayed around for another two years on the network as early-evening repeats, earning extra returns.

In the fall of 1959, Fox undertook a major push to break into TV. It had *Five Fingers* on NBC, starring David Hedison, but only for a half season. Doing better were *The Many Loves of Dobie Gillis* for CBS, and *Adventures in Paradise* on ABC. The latter starred Gardner McKay as the captain of a freelance schooner, traveling the South Seas in search of passengers, cargo, and adventure.

Bob Chandler, for his *Daily Variety* "Sound and Pictures" column on June 26, 1959, said:

> 20th's TV activities have been somewhat shaky since the start, when the company first went into production with *Twentieth Century Fox Hour* and *My Friend Flicka*, neither

of which were exemplary examples of television production.

As for *Paradise*, the critic for sister trade *Variety* called it an "elementary hour which took off … like a lead balloon."

But then Fox stole CBS's head of development – William Edwin Self.

Bill Self started as a film actor in 1945. He used his showbiz contacts to get a job on the 1952 TV series *China Smith* as assistant to the producer, later moving up through such shows as *Schlitz Playhouse*, *The Frank Sinatra Show*, to oversee the making of *The Twilight Zone* pilot.

At the end of 1959, Self made the move to 20th Century-Fox, as "executive producer" for all its current series except *Dobie Gillis*. In this role he oversaw the launch of a dozen or more new titles, some respectable, some folding quickly. In 1961 Self became head of the TV division.

Left to right: Paul Monash, Dorothy Malone, and William Self, celebrating the 400th episode of *Peyton Place*. (20th Century Fox)

By November, 1963, the studio was growing desperate. William Self put three pilots into production. This time out, all would make it to series. One starred Anthony Franciosa – a comedy called *Valentine's Day*. Executive producer Quinn Martin had a green light to make *12 O'Clock High*, starring Robert Lansing. And a certain studio feature film producer who hadn't gotten a project off the ground in more than a year was going to make the move to television – writing, directing, and producing a pilot that would take TV viewers to new depths.

Irwin Allen had been considering television as far back as 1960, prior to Hurricane *Cleopatra*. It was part of the new-and-improved deal he had obtained from the studio after his flirtation with Embassy Films. *Variety* had the scoop on October 12, 1960:

> Producer-director Irwin Allen has completed initial plans on a $9,000,000 motion picture and television production

slate to encompass the next two years. First project will be [the feature film] *Voyage to the Bottom of the Sea.* ... On Allen's TV slate are "Safari," an African adventure series, and "The House of Ghosts," a spook [show]. ...

The studio could not find interest at the networks for Allen's "Safari" or "The House of Ghosts." "The Big Pirate," a film project, was likewise set adrift. The same fate came to his expensive sci-fi property – "Passage to the End of Space."

Finally, in late summer, 1963, Allen had a green light for one of his proposals. His television voyage to excitement was about to begin.

5

Voyage to Television: Premise and Pilot

Television agent Herman Rush with Irwin Allen in 1965, with a mockup of the Flying Sub.

Irwin Allen's television agent, Herman Rush, began representing him in 1962. Interviewed for this book, Rush talked about Allen's switch to television storytelling: "The accelerated pace of television appealed to him. In addition, he saw the value and the importance of television as a medium, and felt it could be as lucrative as motion pictures. Another reason he chose to go into television, I think, is that I and others who represented him had the opinion that he *should*, and that he could be a pioneer; he could be an initiator; and he could use his motion picture expertise in this new medium of television. And I think the combination of those reasons is what got him to do it." (HR-AI15)

Al Gail said of Allen, "He was always fond of television, and he had been comfortable in television [with *Hollywood Merry-Go-Round* and *Irwin Allen's Hollywood Party*]. We had a television background. He was happy being in action – that was the important thing. So, when the opportunity came, he took it. He got the idea for *Voyage to the Bottom of the Sea* and 20th Century-Fox thought it was a good idea and said develop it." (AG-KB95)

Paul Zastupnevich put in, "I think he realized that television was the up and coming thing and that films were not going to be that predominant, right at that particular moment. And where the buck was, that's where he went. I think he was approached by his agent, that this would be a good time to go into a TV series. And they had felt that *Voyage to the Bottom of the Sea* would make a proper jump off. They had all the component parts from the main picture. They would be able to do a TV series for peanuts, supposedly – and we did. You know, it's surprising, if you look at *Voyage to the Bottom of the Sea* and you check the budget out, compared to *Star Trek* and other things that came later, you'll find that it was done on a shoestring. And, because he had all those pieces around, and the various component parts – wardrobe, whatnot – he was able to utilize everything, and cut [costs]. He proved that he could do a series for a low figure, and Fox went for it." (PZ-KB95)

In August, the Hollywood trades announced that Allen would write, produce, and direct a pilot film based on *Voyage to the Bottom of the Sea* for 20th Century-Fox Television, and that ABC-TV had "already manifested interest in the project."

Allen worked on his teleplay throughout August, and continued to tinker with it as late as November, 1963. He also played around with alternative titles for the series to distinguish it from the movie, as well as to allow for stories away from the submarine. The ones he considered were "Voyage to the Unknown," "Voyage to Danger," "Dangerous Voyage" and, simply, "Voyage."

In September, *Daily Variety* reported that Walter Pidgeon would be repeating his role as Admiral Nelson from the feature film. Both Irwin Allen and Pidgeon seemed to want it that way at first. It seemed Pidgeon did too. But this announcement, leaked from Allen's office, was premature. The problem was not entirely over money. Pidgeon's asking price to do a TV series was $5,000 per week (with a raise each season that could get him as high as $7,000). This was on the high end of what was normal at the time, but hardly excessive. In the end, it was more a consideration of age and stamina – selecting an actor who could survive long days of production, spread over several months a year.

Al Gail said of Pidgeon, "He couldn't do it. He wasn't ready to do television. It was too tough for him in those days." (AG-KB95)

Another guide for Allen was his use of audience surveys, to learn viewer preferences.

Allen's agent Herman Rush said, "*Voyage to the Bottom of the Sea* was cast in consideration of the time period and the network. It was not a vehicle for a motion picture star. It would have taken the series in a different direction. It was cast for a good performer who could play that part." (HR-AI15)

Allen made a wish list of "good performers" to play Admiral Nelson. Among the names bantered about: Joseph Cotton, Macdonald Carey, James Whitmore, Joel McCrea, John Forsythe, Don Ameche, and Richard Carlson.

Days later, after more consideration, a list of nine possibilities was prepared. In Allen's order of preference:

1. Dana Andrews, a film star from the 1940s and '50s, who shared top honors with Gene Tierney in 1944's *Laura*;
2. Howard Duff, a film star of the late 1940s and '50s (*film noirs* mostly, such as 1949's *Johnny Stool Pigeon* and 1950's *Shakedown*), plus his own television series, *Dante* (from 1960-61);
3. Philip Carey, who starred as Lieutenant Michael Rhodes in the 1956-57 action series, *The Tales of the 77th Bengal Lancers*, and as Phillip Marlow in the 1959-60 series of the same name;
4. Richard Basehart, acclaimed character actor of stage and screen, who had the lead role in numerous prestigious films;
5. Gary Merrill, who had worked with Bette Davis in *All About Eve*, and had starred in the 1954-55 series, *Justice*;
6. John Russell, who starred in the 1955-57 adventure series, *Soldiers of Fortune*, and the 1958-62 Western, *Lawman*;
7. Sterling Hayden, who had starred in *film noirs* such as 1950's *The Asphalt Jungle*, 1954's *Johnny Guitar*, and Stanley Kubrick's 1956 *The Killing*;
8. Victor Mature, big-screen star of the 1940s and '50s, best known for the 1947 *film noir*, *Kiss of Death*, and Cecil B. DeMille's 1949 epic, *Samson and Delilah*; also a veteran of Allen's 1954 *Dangerous Mission* and 1959 *The Big Circus*;
9. James Gregory, who starred in the 1959-61 crime drama, *The Lawless Years*, but was more respected for hundreds of character roles in films and television dating back to 1948.

For Captain Crane, Allen's wish list, in order of preference, included:

1. Don Murray, who had been nominated for an Academy Award for his supporting role in 1956's *Bus Stop*;
2. Philip Carey, who had been on Allen's list for Admiral Nelson, as well;
3. Patrick O'Neal, who starred as Dick in the 1957-58 television series, *Dick and the Duchess*, and had been working steadily as a guest star in TV;

4. David Hedison, who had his own series, *Five Fingers*, in 1959-60, and whom Allen had directed in *The Lost World*, and who had been offered the role of Lee Crane for the 1961 film version of *Voyage*;
5. John Ericson, an in-demand actor in television and films;
6. Dewey Martin, who had second billing under Kirk Douglas in 1952's *The Big Sky*, then played Daniel Boone in four episodes of *Walt Disney Presents* in 1960 (no relation to the Fess Parker series);
7. Bruce Yarnell, who co-starred in the 1961-62 TV western, *The Outlaws*;
8. Van Williams, who had co-starred in the 1959-60 crime drama series, *Bourbon Street Beat*, then had the lead in the 1960-62 detective drama, *Surfside 6*.

By October 1st, the list for Crane had been cut back to five, with Hedison now up to third spot, followed by Williams and Ericson. The No. 1 and No. 2 choices were new: Allen Case and Steve Forrest. Case had co-starred with Henry Fonda in the 1959-62 TV Western, *The Deputy*, for which he played the title role under the marshal played by Fonda. He would soon play Frank James in the 1965-66 ABC series, *The Legend of Jesse James*. Steven Forrest had won the Golden Globe Award as Most Promising Newcomer (Male) in 1954, for his supporting role in the 1953 film, *So Big*. He would soon have the lead (and title character) in a series of his own, *The Baron*, for the 1966-67 TV season. A decade later he would star in *S.W.A.T.*

Come October, even without a cast under contract, it was announced that the pilot film, to be written, directed and produced by Allen, would begin filming on November 18th. The October 15 press release read:

> Shooting starts Monday, November 18 on the season's biggest and most expensive pilot for the new adventure series "VOYAGE" which Irwin Allen will direct and produce in partnership with 20th Century-Fox for airing over the ABC Network.
>
> The announcement was made by William Self, 20th Century-Fox Television Production chief, and Richard Zanuck, Vice President in Charge of the Studio. Self reported that the hour-length shows will be filmed in color at both the main studio and a half-dozen local locations. The big-budget project is scheduled for televising during the 1964-65 season. Allen, who had produced and directed a long list of exploitation-

adventure feature motion pictures, will serve as producer of the series as well as write and direct every fourth segment.

The Academy-Award winning producer-director-writer said "VOYAGE" would be "an explosive combination of science-fiction and action-adventure, with generous sprinklings of the Ian Fleming school of romantic espionage." ...

An all-star cast will be announced within a week.

Allen and Fox were not exaggerating the cost of the pilot. The projected budget, from October 25, 1963, was $284,772. It was only this low because the main sets, those of the Seaview, were already built. Additionally, it was planned to extract several effects shots from the film for use in the series. These sequences included the Seaview in action; a giant squid attack; and crumbling ice falling onto the ship.

Allen was paying himself $12,500 for the script, another $7,500 to direct, and $10,750 to produce. By November 4th, the pilot's budget had climbed to $339,545, despite the producer taking a pay cut to $7,669.

Also by the start of November, Allen and 20th Century-Fox had set their sights on Richard Basehart for the role of Admiral Nelson. Both Allen and William Self were scheduled to take Basehart and wife to dinner at Dominick's restaurant in West Hollywood, a favorite hangout of Frank Sinatra and his Rat Pack, followed by an 8:30 p.m. screening of the *Voyage* movie at Fox.

Richard Basehart

Of his early life, Richard Basehart said, "Well, there isn't much to tell. I was born in Zanesville, Ohio. My father was editor of our local newspaper, *The Times Signal*, and I started out as a reporter."
(RB-CST49)

Those years were far more eventful than Basehart let on. When interviewed in 1949 by Louella O. Parsons for International News Service (syndicating articles to various newspapers), she wrote:

> I've never had so much trouble writing an interview in my life as I had trying to get a story out of Richard Basehart. He doesn't mean to be difficult; he just doesn't like to talk about himself. He's modest that way.

Part of the untold Basehart story was personal loss. He confided to one interviewer, "My mother died when I was six and I was brought up in an orphanage." (RB-FITM64)

The understatement raises questions, considering Basehart's father was alive and, for a brief period, Richard would try to follow in his father's footsteps. It was after an acting fling with a home-town stock company at 13 that Richard Basehart tried his hand at reporting, at the very newspaper for which his father worked as an editor. He said, "As a kid just out of high school, I got a job as a reporter on the *Zanesville Times Signal*. ... There was a murder – and I saw the body. It was an earth-shaking thing. 'This,' I said, 'is not for me.' My dad, who at one time had headed a stock company, suggested that I try the stage." (RB-LAT49)

At 19, Basehart joined the troupe of the Hedgerow Theatre near Philadelphia, where he performed in roughly 40 plays, including Shakespeare, Shaw, Chekhov, and Ibsen. He also married at this time. Basehart said, "I met her when I was with the Hedgerow Players in Philadelphia. She was Stephanie Klein, a costume designer. I stayed with the Hedgerow Players for five years, and we were married while we were both with them." (RB-CST49)

Behind many men who achieve greatness is a greater woman. It was Stephanie who challenged Basehart to reach for an acting career. In 1942, she took a trip to New York City, got herself a war industry job, found an inexpensive apartment, and then wrote to her husband telling him to join her, to take a chance.

Once in New York, Basehart wrote a letter of his own, to Margaret Webster, a well-known stage producer, asking for an audition. He attended open auditions, where each hopeful came onstage alone. Webster sat in the orchestra area and took in Basehart's audition. Then he was excused.

Just as Basehart was about to take a job on the waterfront, Webster sent for him again. He recalled, "This time she called me to her office. And I could see she was disappointed as soon as I stepped into the room. 'Why, I thought you were much taller, Mr. Basehart,' she said. 'I wanted a long, lean actor for this role.'" (RB-BDE47)

According to his own résumé, Basehart's height was five feet, nine inches. Terry Becker, who played Chief Sharkey on *Voyage to the Bottom of the Sea* and shared a great deal of screen time with his admiral, said that this five-foot-nine

figure was greatly exaggerated. When asked about Basehart's true height, he said, 'Maybe 5' 4". He was 5' 6" in elevator shoes. I'm 5' 8" and I was taller than he."
(TB-SE98)

After Webster's comment about his height, Basehart related, "My hopes suddenly vanished. But then [theatrical producer] Lee Sabinson, who was sitting in the corner of the room, leaped to his feet and rushed over to me, all five-foot-five of him. 'Well, he *is* tall,' said Sabinson to Miss Webster after looking up at me. Miss Webster smiled and, eventually, recalling the audition, took me on."
(RB-BDE47)

The Hasty Heart opened on Broadway the first week of January, 1945. In its July 24, 1945 issue, *Daily Variety* said that Basehart gave a "flawless performance … in portrayal of Scotch Highlander, doomed by an incurable ailment, who transforms from self-sufficient misanthrope to one who falteringly finds love in his heart." The critic called Basehart's work "the most thoroughly professional performance to date [as] a dour Scot who disdains his fellow man until his wall of bitterness is melted in a Burma convalescent hospital."

Basehart said, "It received critical awards, but it only played on Broadway for six months." (RB-CST49)

Above: Richard Basehart in *He Walked by Night*. (Eagle-Lion Films, 1948)

The "critical awards" included Basehart receiving the New York Drama Critics' "Most Promising Actor of the Year" Award. And that, in turn, won him a Warner Brothers film contract.

When Basehart stepped in front of the cameras, it was more often than not for dark roles. His first, for 1947's *Cry Wolf*, starring Barbara Stanwyck and Errol Flynn, was as Stanwyck's psychopathic husband, who escapes from an asylum to make an attempt on her life. Next, he was given top billing in the 1948 *film noir* thriller, *He Walked by Night*, as a loner responsible for a wave of burglaries and a cop-killing. In its November 11, 1948 issue, *Daily Variety* called *He Walked by Night* "tense" and "exciting," saying:

... Performance of Richard Basehart, as the cop killer, is worth the price of admission. He plays the part to the hilt, gathering dramatic momentum from stark beginning to the stock inevitable finish.

In 1949, Basehart had the lead as a similarly unsavory character in *Tension*, this time as a meek pharmacist who plots murder against a bully who has become his wife's lover. In its November 23, 1949 issue, *Variety* said *Tension* "lives up to its title" and that Basehart "turns in a thoughtful performance." Sister trade *Daily Variety*, for its November 17 issue, said the movie "has the nervous energy of a high-strung thoroughbred," and that the "cuckold role, as played by Richard Basehart, is a finely limned one."

Regarding his many turns as lead in a film playing offbeat, dark, and troubled characters, Basehart said, "I couldn't be a straight leading man. You've got to be bigger and prettier than I am." (RB-IMDB)

Above: Basehart played yet another dark character in *Tension*. (MGM, 1949)
Below: The latest in a string of neurotics, in *Fourteen Hours*, with Paul Douglas (to his immediate right). (20th Century-Fox, 1951)

For 1951's *Fourteen Hours*, Basehart was nominated as Best Actor by the National Board of Review (NBA) for playing a man on the ledge, *literally*, as his character threatens suicide and spends 14 hours on the ledge of a high-rise.

It was during this success that tragedy struck. Stephanie, Basehart's wife of 10 years, died after surgery to remove a brain tumor.

Interviewed by Jerry Asher for a syndicated newspaper story, the actor admitted that, after the death of his wife, his personal world had grown increasingly dark. He said, "I felt and acted as if I was living on an exclusive diet of lemons. In all fairness to myself I must say there were circumstances and situations that left me a bit groggy. However, it's always the same old story – things are as important as the importance we give them. With a conspicuous lack of humor, which there often is when we get too subjective about ourselves, we really ask for trouble." (RB-JA56)

Basehart, though heartbroken, returned to work as another dark character, this time a murderer, in 1951's *House on Telegraph Hill*. His co-star was Italian actress Valentina Cortese. Although still recovering emotionally from the death of his wife, Basehart felt an attraction to Cortese. She responded, and they were married that year.

In 1951, Basehart starred in *Fixed Bayonets!*, as a former Army officer who issued orders that resulted in the injuries of several men. Busted to corporal, he wants nothing to do with command. But, after the deaths of three superiors, he is left in charge during battle conditions. On November 21, 1951, *Daily Variety* said, "Basehart dips deep into his characterization, injecting it with naturalism and socking it across in good form."

In 1952, Basehart took the lead in *Decision Before Dawn*, a World War II drama which garnered an Academy Award nomination as Best Picture.

Basehart in 1951's *Fixed Bayonets!*
(20th Century-Fox, 1951)

Around this time, Valentina Cortese bore Basehart his first child – a son. In his interview with Jerry Asher, Basehart said that the troubling feelings he had experienced had, for the most part, passed. He told Asher, "Add to this a certain amount of progress – such pictures as *Fourteen Hours*, *Fixed Bayonets!*, and *Decision Before Dawn* to bolster one's ego, and, last but very far from least, a very great personal happiness. I'm referring of course to my marriage to Valentina Cortese, who has given me young John Anthony Carmine Michael Basehart to complete the picture." (RB-JA56)

Second wife, Italian actress Valentina Cortese, and son, Jackie, circa mid-1950s.

Basehart agreed to move with Cortese and their son to Rome, Italy, where she could resume her film career. He hoped that past accomplishments would allow him to continue working in American movies being shot abroad, as well as foreign pictures. The adjustment was not easy. He said, "I learned Italian in self-defense. Whenever my wife entertained any of her friends they began yapping away in Italian and it made me feel left out. Even our son speaks perfect Italian." (RB-HT60)

It was also a period of great personal drama. After losing his first wife to illness, it looked as if Basehart might lose his second. In April, 1953, an AP wire story from Rome announced:

> Italian actress Valentina Cortese, a star of a number of Hollywood films, was reported recovering today from a nearly fatal attack of peritonitis. The 28-year-old wife of American actor Richard Basehart entered Salvatore Mundi International hospital 11 days ago and later underwent surgery. At the time of the operation she was given her last rites of the Catholic church.

Fortunately, Cortese made a full recovery.

From this period, Basehart was featured as a defrocked alcoholic priest in 1953's *Titanic*, and as an acrobatic clown in Fellini's dark 1954 ode, *La Strada*. He won the National Board of Review Award (as Best Supporting Actor) for his role in 1956's *Moby Dick* as Ishmael, the sailor (and narrator), and the sole survivor of the Pequod, who served under Captain Ahab (played by Gregory Peck).

Basehart was enjoying the change in roles spurred by his move to Europe. While working abroad (on the set of *The Extra Day*), he told a writer for England's *Picturegoer* magazine, "I've had my fill of twisted neurotics. I got into a terrifying rut playing psychopathic killers, half-wits, complex kids, and hot-heads. Maybe I was scared I would get as nutty as the characters I played." (RB-PG55)

Upon his return to Hollywood for a film role in 1957's *Time Limit*, Basehart told Hedda Hopper, "I wanted to work with Dick Widmark, but there was also the pull of the home country after being away for so long. Valentina also had a longing to see Hollywood again; and we both wanted to show 'Jackie' to the various members of my family who'd never seen him." (RB-LAT57)

Above: Basehart in *Moby Dick*.
(Warner Bros., 1956)
Below: With Dolores Michaels in *Time Limit*.
(United Artists, 1957)

More accolades came as Basehart won a BAFTA Award (Britain's version of the Oscar) for the lead in *Time Limit*, as a Korean War POW on trial for treason. *Daily Variety* said that Basehart's performance as "the soul-tortured major" was "a fine characterization of a man torn between humaneness and duty as exemplified by the Army code."

David Hedison said of Basehart, "*La Strada… Moby Dick; Fourteen Hours; Time Limit* – Richard had fabulous range and was always worth watching in anything he did." (DH-CR10)

Basehart as "The Fool" in Federico Fellini's *La Strada*.
(Trans Lux, 1954)

While in America, Basehart accepted a role in the new medium of television, on the prestigious *Studio One* anthology series – a two-part episode, running the length of a feature film, called "Mutiny on the Shark." Seeming to foreshadow *Voyage to the Bottom of the Sea*, the story involved the highly trained crew of an atomic submarine and, not too unlike Admiral Nelson in certain episodes, their gruff commander who demands perfection.

Basehart returned to Italy with wife Cortese and settled into a routine of taking third or fourth billing in movies. When he was given the lead, the movie would never see release in the United States. His star status was waning.

One high-profile Basehart film made in Europe was 1958's *The Brothers Karamazov*, for which he played the intellectual atheist Ivan Karamazov. The critics embraced the film, and Basehart's performance. In February, 1958, Bosley Crowther of *The New York Times* said, "Basehart is icy and forbidding as the second cantankerous son." *Variety* said, "Richard Basehart manages to glow with anger and resentment, using only his eyes and voice to suggest his great hatred." But it was Yul Brynner's film. Basehart had fifth billing.

Basehart returned to Hollywood to accept third billing in the 1960 crime thriller, *Portrait in Black*, starring Lana Turner and Anthony Quinn. Interviewed by United Press International from the set, he said, "When I'm in Hollywood I get homesick for Rome, but when I'm in Italy it's the other way around. … From the standpoint of money and work, I'm okay, but the bad thing is that all my European pictures aren't shown in the United States. That means I don't have much exposure to American audiences as a Hollywood actor." (RB-AH59)

It was at this time that Valentina Cortese took their son and returned to Italy. Close friend and fellow actor Warren Stevens, who later appeared in a couple of episodes of *Voyage to the Bottom of the Sea*, was concerned over Basehart's well-being and got him an apartment adjoining his own. According to Stevens, Basehart called Italy often, and this continued for months, but Cortese would not respond. When Basehart finally filed for divorce, Stevens was on hand to serve as a witness.

Basehart would marry again in 1962, to Diana Lotery. The third time seemed the charm; they stayed together the rest of his life.

Richard Basehart on the set of *Hitler*. (Allied Artists, 1962)

Also in 1962, Basehart had the title role in *Hitler*. At first he was excited about the role, telling syndicated entertainment correspondent Erskine Johnson: "Hitler was a genius. Don't ever think he was a clown. He was a man of tremendous drive, force and intelligence, a ruthless but perfectly sincere visionary animated by a dream, and a great leader of men. How else do you imagine he accomplished so much? Naturally, he was a matchless egotist. What would you expect, with all Germany 'heiling' his name as though he were some kind of god? And then, you know, he was psychotic."

Basehart, a method actor, said, "I am just trying to become the person I am playing. I've got to. I'm no good at pretending at all. I've got to 'be' the guy – and, believe me, that can be a pretty rugged experience." (RB-PL61)

In the end, the movie wasn't what Basehart had hoped. He said, "I researched, I read volumes, I evolved a characterization of this man – a genius, if a psychopathic one. The producer exploded. 'Too sympathetic,' he said. We did it *his* way." (RB-TVG65)

The film was a critical and financial failure. Basehart returned to his first love – the stage, especially Shakespeare. On June 18, 1962, *The Bridgeport Post* said:

> Pageantry, drama and poetry of the downfall of a corrupt king are presented excitedly by a skilled cast in *Richard II*. The drama moves quickly with no breaks in the rapidly shifting scenes. ... A great deal of this is due also to Richard Basehart's extremely telling performance in the title role. Basehart keeps his performance sharply to the Shakespeare plot, and his portrait grows in intensity as

well as stature as Richard turns from cynical, dissolute ruler to the badgered, beleaguered king and finally to the deposed, imprisoned and murdered ex-monarch. In physical appearance he certainly looks like a king and his lines frequently spark fire.

The actor also began accepting roles on television. At first, he managed to confine his video activities to high-profile guest starring roles on prestige series, such as *Studio One, Playhouse 90,* and *DuPont Show of the Month.* There was no shame in taking part in television "events." He even made a TV pilot called "The Judge," which was given a test run on *The Dick Powell Theatre.*

After years of jumping from one movie or country to another, and traveling with touring stage productions, Basehart felt like settling down, perhaps even ready to commit to a series. He told syndicated entertainment columnist Harvey Pack, "I can still remember the time when I liked living in hotel rooms. But I'm cured. Actors are always knocking the old days when they were under contract to major studios and had to make a certain amount of pictures every year. Now that I look back on my contract days, it really wasn't so bad. At least you went home every night."

On the other hand, he added, "I just can't see myself playing the same part every week in just another series. Of course, there have been offers, but nothing exciting." (RB-HT60)

Therein lay the key – it would have to be something other than "just another series," and a format which would allow the actor to play variations on his character. Perhaps sci-fi would prove to be the answer, as Basehart considered Irwin Allen's offer of a lead role in a futuristic underwater drama.

The November, 1963 dinner meeting between Richard Basehart, Irwin Allen, and William Self went well, as did their screening of the *Voyage* movie for Basehart later that night on the Fox lot.

No one was pushing Allen in the specific direction of Richard Basehart. Allen's television agent Herman Rush said, "Irwin would never cast somebody who he did not feel comfortable with; did not have respect for, no matter what kind of pressure was put upon him at the time. But Irwin also knew that the submarine was the star, and he could amortize that cost and he could afford to pay Basehart a little more than normal." (HR-AI15)

Paul Zastupnevich said, "The reason he went for Richard Basehart is that, at that time, before Sheila, he was dating a gal by the name of Jodi Desmond. Now, Jodi came from Italy and she knew Basehart, and she mentioned to Irwin, 'Why don't you get Richard Basehart?,' because she was friendly with Basehart and his former wife, Valentina Cortese." (PZ-KB95)

A deal was soon struck. And it was a good deal for Basehart – $7,000 per episode – top dollar for 1964. Two years later, William Shatner would be making $5,000 per episode of *Star Trek*, a sum more in line with industry standards. On the other hand, Shatner was given a small piece of the *Trek* action – a five percent ownership in the series. For cash-poor Desilu Studios, it was the only way to bring in a medium-sized fish like Shatner. Irwin Allen and 20th Century-Fox weren't interested in sharing ownership. Herman Rush said, "I am not familiar with anything that we did with Irwin where a star had a cut; a participation. To give out a partial ownership was absolutely an unusual arrangement back then." (HR-AI15)

A bigger paycheck was offered instead. And it was one of the biggest for its time. Basehart was being treated like a movie star. He was 49.

Assistant Casting Director Larry Stewart said, "Richard got himself screwed up with the amount of money he had to pay for his divorce. *Voyage* was a way to make money." (LS-SFTS2)

A short while later, when asked for a *Los Angeles Times* article why he agreed to do a series, the ex-Shakespearean actor said, "I was surprised myself – still am – but the deal offered was too good to resist. It came at a time when the last half dozen pictures I made weren't satisfying experiences; so I'd done a few guest shots, enough to convince me the medium now had possibilities." (RB-LAT66)

The big question remained, who would play Captain Crane, the series second lead?

On Friday, November 1, as dinner and a movie were still being arranged with Richard Basehart and wife, Allen wrote to William Self:

> Dear Bill: The moratorium "not to panic" over the casting of Captain Crane for the pilot of "VOYAGE" expires at 6 PM tonight. To avoid such panic I am reviewing herewith the situation so that we might mutually move forward to a quick decision.
>
> Together with [studio casting director] Cliff Gould and additionally on my own, I have interviewed, seen on film or still pictures, virtually all the young leading men in town who would be available, believable and within the budget. While there are still three or four pieces of film I hope to see with Cliff before the day is over, I do not have much hope of filling the bill by the deadline hour. You are even more aware than I am that every such young actor is being sought by every television operation in town.
>
> All of the above brings us to the David Hedison situation.

1) Hedison has been approved by ABC which simply means that we can move forward immediately with a deal without showing them film on any new player and going through all the requirements of the presentation problem.
2) Hedison has turned down our first offer (which was $3,500 for the pilot and $1,500 per segment).
3) I propose that we make a new offer to Hedison as follows:
   a) $3,500 for the pilot. (We will also pledge to use our good offices to secure two or three guest appearances on other Fox TV shows over the course of the next year to make up the additional monies he wanted guaranteed from the pilot.)
   b) $2,500 per episode.

I have reason to believe that Hedison may very well accept this offer over the weekend which would wrap up our casting problem and leave us free to move forward on the thousands of other details that need our attention.

Please advise. Regards, Irwin.

Come Monday, Allen wrote to Self:

David Hedison is in London and is supposed to let the producers of "ESPIONAGE" know whether or not he will do a guest spot for them. His doing this show would eliminate him from doing "VOYAGE." He has promised not to give them a commitment until he hears from us by cable tomorrow. May we meet and discuss this sometime today?

Herman Rush said, "I think his [Allen's] biggest supporter was Bill Self, who was the CEO of Fox Television. I think they understood each other; they were friends; but they worked together very closely, and Irwin always accepted whatever was being advised by the studio. He debated it, he argued it; he talked about it; but he never got pissed off and said, 'I'm going to pay no attention to it.' It was a very good relationship." (HR-AI15)

David Hedison

Allen had always wanted David Hedison for Captain Lee Crane. He'd first caught glimpse of Hedison as Lt. Ware, the Executive Officer of the U.S. Navy Destroyer commanded by Robert Mitchum in the 1957 classic *The Enemy Below*. He was Al Hedison back then (his real name), and had third billing. Hedison looked good with short hair and in the Navy uniform, and Allen was sure he was the right man to serve as Captain of the Seaview.

Hedison grew up in Providence, Rhode Island, and kept growing until he stood six-foot-one. His father had a prosperous jewelry-enameling business, and hoped young Al would eventually choose to take over. Hedison was sent to an Ivy League university (Brown College in Providence), where he majored in English and languages. He stayed for three years, later saying, "I just couldn't reach anybody at Brown. It was really my fault. I just wasn't interested. I hated every minute of it." (DH-TR59)

Hedison wanted to succeed on his own. He later told entertainment columnist Hedda Hopper, "My first gesture of independence was a job as Fuller Brush salesman. I sold a woman $30 worth of goods and she told me, 'Boy, you oughta be in pictures.' In one winter, I saved $1,000 and took off for New York and the Neighborhood Playhouse. At the end of my first year I was one of 200 students who auditioned for the Barter Theater Award. I won, which took care of my summer. But when I returned to New York, my finances were so low I became a bellboy at the Waldorf. Later, I was an assistant to Albert in the Empire Room, which financed my second year with the Playhouse. I was so broke when I graduated, I sold a pint of blood at a 96th St. clinic to get cash." (DH-LAT60)

Al Hedison also served in the Navy, stationed for two years in Jacksonville, Florida. When he was discharged as a Seaman Second Class, he heard that John Ford was to make a movie in Mexico. Hedison wrote to the famed director, offering his services in any capacity. In order for Ford to know that he had "the right look," Hedison enclosed a snapshot of himself with his Navy cap cocked on the back of his head. Ford was a former Navy captain who had served in World War II. The letter and picture did catch the director's attention, enough so that he actually wrote a reply. Ford said that the movie was not to be made after all, and then, David Hedison recalled, closed his letter with the admonition, "And next time you send your picture to an ex-Navy four-striper, square your hat, sailor!" (DH-TVG66)

Above: "Al" Hedison (right) with Robert Mitchum (center) in *The Enemy Below*. (20th Century Fox, 1957)
Below: With Patricia Owens in *The Fly*. (20th Century-Fox, 1958)

In 1958, Hedison returned to the stage and was named "Most Promising Newcomer" for his role in an off-Broadway play, *A Month in the Country*. That acknowledgement got him the lead in the film *The Fly*. He told interviewer Harvey Chartrand, "I read [James] Clavell's script and got terribly excited about it. I knew, from the start, I could play it. Once you know that about a character, you can do it. I did a lot of thinking about this role, coming up with things that I thought my character would do, given his circumstances. And [director Kurt] Neumann let me do most of them." (DH-DM13)

186

Hedison talked about the film's dramatic ending: "I remember totally being terrified, because I was in this web, and they had a pointer, and the pointer would move slowly down the web, which is supposed to be the spider, and I had to react to that. Well, I was terrified; I was truly terrified. And I was screaming 'Help!' I mean, it really came from the gut, screaming 'Help me; help me, help me!' Very good. They applauded afterwards; they liked the scene. I was satisfied.

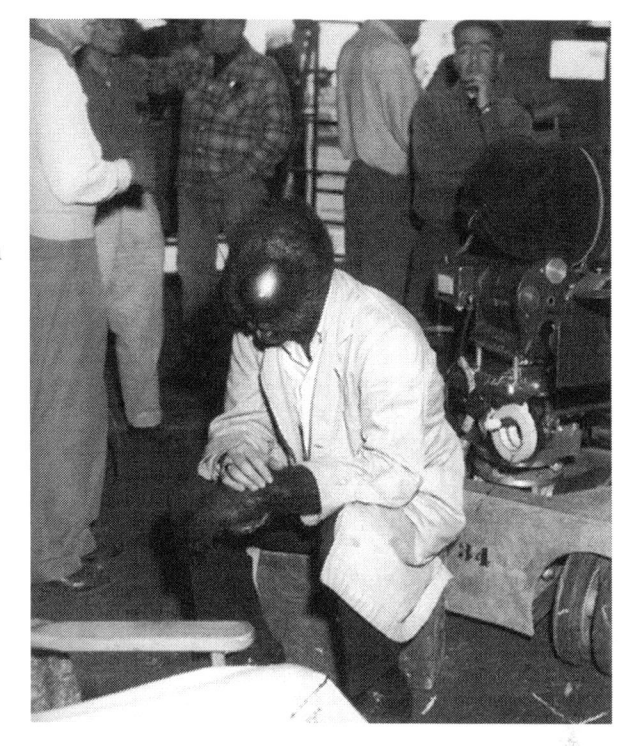

"Then, when I came back from [an acting assignment in] England, and I saw the film, they had taken that terror out of my voice, and they had cranked up the sound. And out came, 'Help me!' way up there high. And I said, 'Jesus, why did they do that; why didn't they just keep that voice; why did they make it smaller, not a person, this silly sound?'

"Except, you know, look, it's easy for an actor to complain, 'They should have done this.' The film worked. Everybody was happy; nobody ever said, 'They should have done this; they should have done that.' They did what they had to do, and what they thought was right for the film. And I bow to them." (DH-PE17)

You may recognize the ring on the right hand. That is Hedison ... perhaps contemplating his future. (20th Century-Fox, 1958)

Hedison told Hedda Hopper, for her *Los Angeles Times* column, "*The Fly* cost $450,000, made $5 million. It's the kind of picture you dream of." (DH-LAT60)

187

Also in 1958, Hedison turned to action-adventure when he took the lead as the title character in *The Son of Robin Hood* – the film he traveled to England to make immediately following *The Fly*. He dreaded it, later saying, "Avoid at all costs." (DH-LAT11)

June Laverick, "Al" Hedison, and Marius Goring in *Son of Robin Hood*.
(20th Century-Fox, 1958)

On June 18, 1958, the film critic for *Daily Variety* differed:

> Although the action isn't as dashing as it was in the Errol Flynn days, it's fast enough to hold the juvenile trade in a flurry of bows and arrows and swords. ... David Hedison (his first name used to be "Al" and, in fact, remains so in the film's main titles), [is] a strong hero, intriguingly youthful yet sufficiently mature. He shows a good deal of promise which 20th [Century-Fox] should continue to develop.

The studio *did* continue to develop Hedison. A short while later he was starring in his own TV series for NBC, as an American counterspy in Europe. His code name was the series title. *Five Fingers* co-starred Paul Burke as Fingers' American contact. For this TV assignment, per the network, Al became David.

Hedison recalled, "They said they wanted me [for the series], with the stipulation that Fox change my name. They hated Al. They said, 'We can't make him a star with the name of Al. It was absolutely ridiculous. So they said, 'How about John Hedison?' I said, 'If we are going to change it, use my middle name, which is David.' So I became David Hedison." (DH-LAT11)

Five Fingers premiered opposite the top-rated CBS line-up of half-hour Westerns *Have Gun – Will Travel* and *Gunsmoke*, and, on ABC, the popular *Lawrence Welk Show*. It was formidable competition: *Gunsmoke* and *Have Gun* had ranked No. 1 and No. 3, respectively, in the previous year's Nielsens (this continued for two more years). Knowing he was under the gun, and likely to be outgunned by fast-drawing Paladin and Marshal Dillon, Hedison told UPI correspondent Vernon Scott, "We have twice as much show to film every week as they do, and I'm anxious to make it twice as good."

The weight on young Hedison's shoulders was immense. He told Scott, "Ours is an hour show, and we're supposed to turn out a complete program every seven days. With a schedule like that we rarely have time for more than two or three takes. Personally, I don't care for that kind of pressure, and if I think I'm not reading my lines as well as I should, I goof. I'm up at 6 a.m., at the studio by 7, and get home at 8 and 9 at night. Then, when I do

Hedison – now David – played double agent Victor Sebastian in *Five Fingers*. Below, he poses with co-star Luciana Paluzzi. (20th Century-Fox, 1959)

get home, I have to study the next day's script for several hours. Even the old 'B' movies didn't move as fast as a modern TV series." (DH-UPI59)

On October 7, 1959, *Variety* rated the premiere, saying:

> The high gloss of *Five Fingers* is ruined by an inept, complicated script and ditto plot to give it a four-flush film based (loosely, it is apparent) on 20th-Fox' James Mason starrer of 1952. But whereas that was one of the sleeper theatrical pix of the year, this one just bears the similarity in the title. ... The series fronts handsome, Wildroot-groomed David Hedison, who has appeared in films, and his *vis-a-vié* is attractive, shapely Italian pic actress Luciana Paluzzi in her U.S. video debut.

On October 9, sister trade *Daily Variety* said:

> Sex and romance and expensive-looking production are fine and all that, but for a public geared to the rapid, get-to-the-point tempo of television, *Five Fingers* had better start knuckling down. It took 22 minutes before the premiere episode even revealed the general posture of the plot. By that time, "Paladin" on CBS-TV's opposing *Have Gun, Will Travel* had probably cut down four or five heavies and a viewer already could hear Marshal Dillon [on *Gunsmoke*] warming up. ... The series is pegged on Hedison's activities as a theatrical agent who doubles in counter-espionage as an employee of the U.S. government. Off the initial sampler, he's going to be in plenty of trouble, both battling the enemy agents and the scripts. ... Hedison does competently.

Hedison took the reviews to heart. He pushed himself even harder to make the series everything it could be, despite scripts that felt as rushed as the direction and performances. He said, "The old 'B' actors were learning their trade, but for a small audience. But on a series such as mine, you're seen by 25 million people or so every week. You can't afford to do less than your very best. ... Another thing, in the second-rate movies, if the actor was bad, they didn't bother putting him in another film. They can't do that in a series. You just have to keep going." (DH-UPI59)

Hedison felt the series was too grim. Talking with interviewer Mike Clark for this book, he said, "There were some great comedic things that could have been done. And I had a producer who was a really nice guy – Herbert Baird Swope – but he didn't really appreciate what I was trying to do. I was trying to keep it light and funny, and all that stuff, and still being this wonderful James Bond kind of character. And I had Luciana Paluzzi, and we got on very well, but a lot could have been developed between the two of us, I thought, and nothing was ever done." (DH-PE17)

Peter Lorre with Hedsion, in "Thin Ice," an episode of *Five Fingers*. (20th Century-Fox, 1959)

Five Fingers struggled in the ratings from the start. For the week ending October 18, 1959, it only managed a 12.7 Nielsen rating, against *Have Gun – Will Travel*'s 33.1, and, from 10:30 to 11 p.m., *Gunsmoke*'s 35.7. Two weeks later, *Variety* published the Nielsen findings for the first two weeks of November. *Five Fingers* had dropped from 12.7 to 8.7. The number improved slightly by December, to 11.0, but, against *Gunsmoke*'s 38.7, there was no hope of survival. In fact, the series had already received its pink slip from NBC. Production stopped after sixteen episodes, and *Five Fingers* left the network in January.

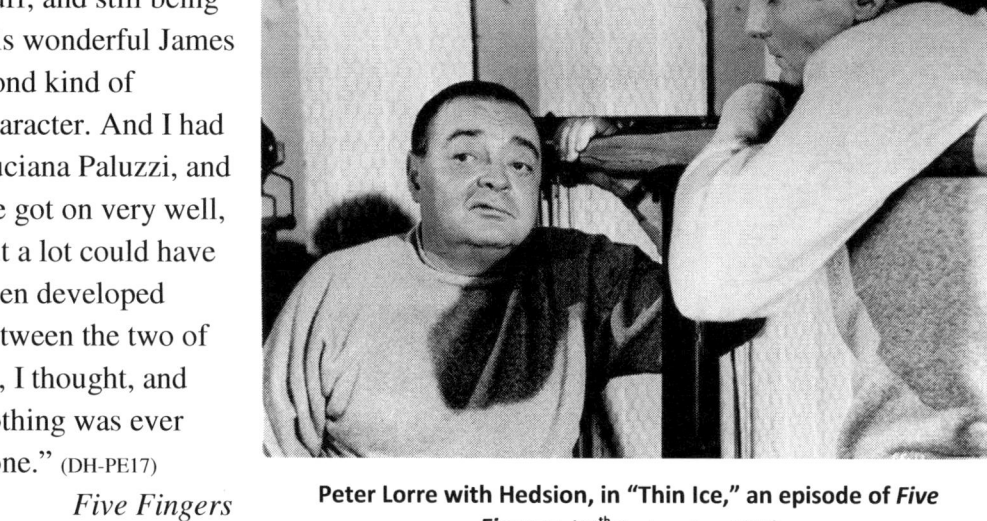

Hedison later said, "But I learned more while making sixteen shows than anything I'd done on Broadway, summer stock or anywhere else." (DH-LAT60)

Shortly after his release, Hedison went to work for Irwin Allen in *The Lost World*. In 1961, during the casting period for the big-screen *Voyage to the Bottom of the Sea*, Allen sent a copy of the script to Hedison. The actor said, "I read it. I didn't like it; I didn't believe any of it. I didn't think it would be good for me to do because it was so much like *Lost World*, so I told Irwin that I couldn't do it, that I had another film I was going to be doing, which was a huge lie. So I got out of it, and then Robert Sterling played the part, and he was very good." (DH-PE17)

A short while later, Hedison took second billing in a war movie for 1961 called *Marines, Let's Go*. It wasn't a good career move. Hedison said, "Working with the Master, Raoul Walsh, was a great experience for me, but even Walsh admitted that the script he and John Twist came up with for that film was not up to par." (DH-DM13)

In an interview for this book, Hedison admitted that not all his career choices had been good ones. "Unfortunately, I had turned down a couple of wonderful opportunities to play comedy. And I would have been very good in them … but I didn't think I would be right. *But I would have been right*. As actors, we make some stupid decisions; we turn down things we should never have turned down. I think, 'God, what the hell did I do that for?' And what did I do instead? I turned that down to do this piece of shit.

Above: Tom Reese, Fumiyo Fujimoto, and David Hedison in *Marines, Let's Go*. Below: Fujimoto comforts Hedison.
(20th Century-Fox, 1961)

"But I had no mentor. I wish I had someone like Cary Grant on the sidelines saying, 'You do it your way, David; do what you wanna do. Oh, change that line; do this.' I knew him personally and I liked him a lot, and I think he would have been a great mentor.'" (DH-PE17)

Irwin Allen made his submarine movie without Hedison's participation. But despite a good performance from Robert Sterling, Allen still believed Hedison was the man meant to play the part. He was determined to get the right Crane aboard the Seaview for the TV incarnation.

Hedison said, "So then, a year or so after the film came *Voyage to the Bottom of the Sea*, the television show, and Irwin wanted me for it. And I turned it down again. I said, 'It's not the kind of thing I want to do, Irwin. I want a doctor show, or some other kind of show, but, really, it's not for me and I'd rather work on something else.'

"So then he called me again. I was in Providence, Rhode Island, visiting my parents, and he called there. 'No.' Then I was invited to an international television festival in Egypt, and I went there for *Five Fingers*, and Roger Moore went there for *The Saint* – and that's where I met Roger, my old, dear friend. And it was just such a great experience." (DH-PE17)

Hedison and Moore hit it off immediately, and Moore offered him a role in an upcoming episode of *The Saint*. Hedison traveled to England to take the part, and was soon offered another role, a play which was to be filmed for the BBC.

He remembered, 'So then who calls on the telephone? Irwin Allen, from America. 'I want you to reconsider the *Voyage to the Bottom of the Sea*.' I said, 'Irwin, please, I've got something going on now, which is *Camino Real* and the BBC; it's an interesting play; it's a wonderful part, and I think I'd be very good in it.' He wouldn't give up." (DH-PE17)

Harry Harris, who worked as a director for Allen on all his 1960s TV series, said, "When he wanted you, if he wanted you for something, and you said, 'No, I can't,' it drove him crazy. He had to have you! If he wanted somebody, he stuck in there until he got you. I don't care whether it was an actor or director, whoever, he would never take no, till the very last. I mean, he'd hang in there." (HH-KB95)

Allen defended his obsessive pursuit. "Hedison looks like the type of modern, thinking, fighting man that we have come to recognize through the brilliance of the image created by the astronauts." (IA-TC09)

But Hedison didn't want to play an astronaut ... especially one underwater. He still wanted to be considered a serious actor, and now had a chance to do a play.

He recalled, "And then, again, he called one day. I said, 'Irwin, not again! All right, what is it?' He said, 'All right, look, I have Richard Basehart as the part of the Admiral.'

"Tick, tick, tick, tick, tick, tick. 'Irwin, look, I'll call ya back in the morning. I promise; I'll call ya in the morning; it'll be your time in the afternoon.'

"I talked to Roger [Moore] about it. He says, 'Look, take it; it's not gonna kill you. See what you can get out of it. This play you want to do on the BBC, my God, you'll do that and it's gone; nobody will ever see it. Do it. Do the series.'

"And I did it because of Roger. I called Irwin, and said, 'Irwin, we're on. I'll be there and we'll do it." (DH-PE17)

So, it wasn't a big paycheck that got David Hedison to catch the next flight back from London – it was the presence of Richard Basehart, and the counsel of Hedison's new friend Roger Moore. Hedison said, "Richard Basehart and I, we got on tremendously well. From the first day we met. I got his telephone number from Irwin, and I called him and I asked if I could come to his house. I met his wife, and we sat down and had some coffee, and I told him how proud I was to be working in a show with him because I always thought he was a fabulous actor. I was always a great fan of his. And he appreciated that, and we began to talk about what we could do to make it a good show. This is *before* the pilot." (DH-TCF07)

In a recent interview, Hedison told of his first meeting with Basehart. "I thought as a good spirit; as a good guy, I would meet with Richard. And I said to him, 'Richard, look, you're a fine actor; you've done wonderful films, brilliant films in Italy, at Fox, wonderful. Now you're going into a new medium, which is television, and you're going to be working with a gentleman called Irwin Allen. Now, you're not used to this, but he'll go in there, and say, '*You*, stand there. *You*, stand there, say your lines.' And off we go. And you won't know what hit you. He hasn't had the chance to really develop the character, and whatnot, so be patient. … I'll always be there [for you], because I'm used to this crap. I've been doing it for years; playing this junk. And, you know, it's going to be new to you." (DH-PE17)

Hedison continued, "[We discussed] what we could do with our characters. And we were sort of in agreement with everything, and we just hit it off – [*with a snap of his fingers*] – like that. And we became very, very close friends. And I'm so glad that I was finally able to do *Voyage*, especially because of Richard, who was a sensitive, generous, beautiful soul. Very, very shy, didn't get on too well with a lot of people, but, oh, so intelligent, and was a wonderful actor. And such a nice guy to have as a friend."

Hedison was given that contract for $2,500 per episode – very good money in 1964 for the secondary lead in a series on ABC. That would be something like $20,000 a week, in twenty-first century terms. Hedison was 36.

Preparing to Sail

On November 10, William Self, head of 20th Century-Fox TV, announced the signings of Richard Basehart and David Hedison. It was a last-minute save – the pilot was set to begin filming in eight days.

Allen got busy selecting his supporting cast.

To play the Seaview's executive officer, Robert Dowdell was signed. He was recommended by his real-life neighbor – David Hedison. Dowdell, 31, had just finished appearing in 32 episodes of *Stoney Burke*, which starred Jack Lord as a contemporary rodeo cowboy.

Henry Kulky was signed to play Chief Curley Jones. Kulky had been a boxer in his teenage years. After six bouts, he stopped when offered a position training wrestlers. By 1939, he was competing and became known as "Bomber Kulkavich," in hundreds of matches – some sources say thousands. Kulky turned to acting in the 1940s. Because of his background and looks, Kulky specialized in playing military men, thugs, bartenders, truck drivers, and, of course, wrestlers. His gift was making the tough guys friendly and even lovable. Among the soldiers he played was one in *Fixed Bayonets!*, which starred Richard Basehart. In 1953, he was cast in the television series *The Life of Riley* as Otto Schmidlap, a coworker of Chester Riley (played by William Bendix), who worked as a wing riveter at an aircraft plant. From 1959 to 1962 Kulky played Chief Max Bronsky in 47 episodes of the military sitcom/drama *Hennesey*, starring Jackie Cooper. Kulky felt comfortable and looked right in a Navy uniform for *Hennesey* and

Robert Dowdell (standing with Jack Lord) in *Stoney Burke*. (United Artists, 1962-63)
Henry Kulky played Chief Max Bronsky in 47 episodes of *Hennesey*. (CBS-TV, 1959-62)

Voyage because he had served as a deck seaman in the Navy during World War II. He had also served on a sub before, as Chief Petty Officer York, in the 1959 film, *Up Periscope*, starring James Garner. His *Voyage* deal was for $750 per episode – the equivalent of a $6,000 paycheck in 2018. Kulky was 52.

Del Monroe transferred over from the movie version. He played "Kowski" there, and was now given the name of Kowalski in the series. Monroe was offered $150 per day, or $500 for up to five days, per episode. He was 27.

Mark Slade also shipped aboard from the film version, although his stay would be short (five episodes). He was Seaman Smith in the movie; Seaman Malone in the series. Slade was 24.

Above: Mark Slade became popular on the late 1960s NBC-TV one-hour Western series, *The High Chaparral*. Below: Paul Trinka got to kiss the buxom babe in director Russ Meyer's 1965 exploitation film, *Faster, Pussycat! Kill! Kill!*

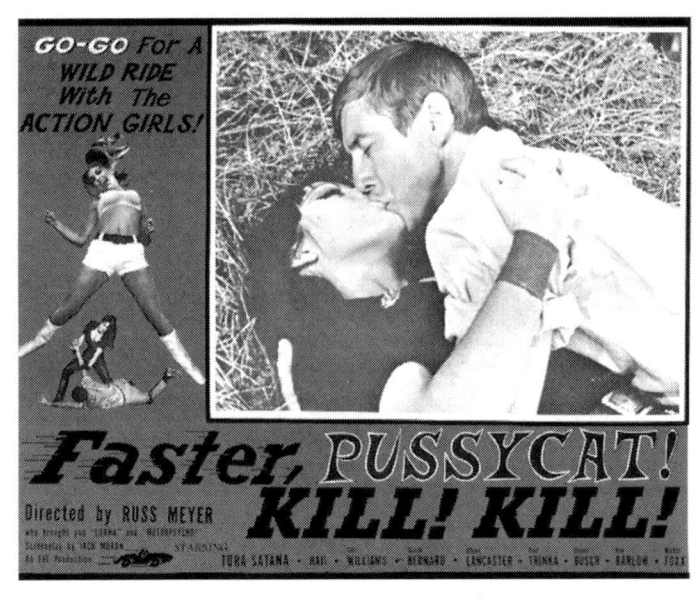

Other regulars:

Paul Trinka was given the role of Patterson. He was 31 and had just finished filming an exploitation film with many dangerous curves – director Russ Meyer's *Faster, Pussycat! Kill! Kill!*

Arch Whiting was cast as "Sparks," the radioman. He was 27.

Richard Bull, the last of the Season One recurring players, would be added several episodes into the first season, to play the ship's doctor, known only as "Doc." He had been active in TV since 1956. He was 39.

Eddie Albert was hired to play Dr. Fred Wilson, the series' first "guest star." He was 52 and best known for 1953's *Roman Holiday*, which earned him an Academy Award nomination as Best Supporting Actor; 1956's *The Teahouse of the August Moon*, which brought him a Golden Globe nomination as Best Supporting Actor; and Robert Altman's 1956 film *Attack*, as a cowardly, psychotic army officer. Shortly after appearing in the *Voyage* pilot, Albert would film "Cry of Silence," an episode of the original *Outer Limits*. He was one year away from having his own series – *Green Acres*, as Oliver Wendell Douglas, a New York lawyer who gives up the high life to become a farmer in rural Hooterville.

On November 12, just two days after William Self announced that Basehart and Hedison had been signed, Irwin Allen sent each a letter, along with freshly written pages for their scripts. He told both:

> The enclosed blue pages are to be inserted in your new bright orange script of "VOYAGE." As you will note, some added speeches have been put into the Briefing Room to add more bite to the sequence. The other changes are of a minor nature.
>
> If there's any question about any of this, please phone me. Warmest regards, Irwin Allen.

Allen's excitement for this new project was contagious. Hedison said, "Irwin had fantastic enthusiasm for his projects and got you excited, too. He took you into his office and showed you his sketches, models and costume designs. You got caught up, and it was just fantastic." (DH-SL86)

Production

While Allen wore three hats as writer, director, and producer, he wasn't in the trenches by himself.

Costume designer Paul Zastupnevich was also the production illustrator, and worked as Irwin Allen's assistant in nearly all ways. Allen depended on Paul Z. for much. The two had worked together since *The Big Circus*.

Al Gail was given the title of assistant to the producer, shouldering a vast variety of duties. In time, he would also be elevated to a writing post – first as assistant story editor, and then occasional scriptwriter.

Gaston Glass was hired to serve as Production Manager. He was a Fox man, having performed this duty for some of the studio's other series: *Hong Kong*, *Adventures in Paradise*, *Bus Stop*, and *Follow the Sun*.

Winton C. Hoch was the Director of Photography. He had worked for Allen often, as cinematographer on *The Big Circus*, *The Lost World*, *Five Weeks in a Balloon*, and the big-screen *Voyage to the Bottom of the Sea*. He had plenty of awards on his mantel, including Oscars for 1948's *Joan of Arc*, 1949's *She Wore a Yellow Ribbon*, and 1952's *The Quiet Man*.

Jack Martin Smith, one of two art directors responsible for the Seaview, inside and out, had worked for 20th Century-Fox for decades, and was among a team of set designers who shared an Oscar for their work on the studio's 1963 *Cleopatra*. A few years later, he would also work on the studio's sci-fi epic, *Fantastic Voyage*.

William J. Creber worked with Smith, and was more directly answerable to Irwin Allen. He stayed with *Voyage* for 37 episodes, and was instrumental in establishing the look of the series. Allen would also use Creber to help launch *Lost in Space* and *The Time Tunnel*. Before this, Creber had served as Art Director on *Rio Conchos* and *The Greatest Story Ever Told*.

Walter M. Scott decorated the sets. He was a 20th Century-Fox man, having worked on many of the studio's films and all of its TV series.

L.B. Abbott provided the photographic effects, including the work done with the various Seaview models (mostly lifted from the movie). He had also served Allen well, for *The Lost World*, the big-screen *Voyage*, and *Five Weeks in a Balloon*. He survived the experience of working on the 20th Century-Fox runaway train, *Cleopatra*. He had already won an Oscar for his work in *Journey to the Center of the Earth*. There were more in his future.

Lionel Newman would supervise the music for the series. As vice president in charge of music for Fox, he selected composers and, at times, conducted. He had composed title themes, including those for *The Many Loves of Dobie Gillis* and, yet to come, *Daniel Boone*.

Paul Sawtell was Irwin Allen's choice for staff composer. He provided the pilot's score, including the memorable theme and title music. Sawtell had been composing movie soundtracks since the late 1930s and had worked on several of Irwin Allen's films – *The Sea Around Us*, *The Story of Mankind*, *The Big Circus*, *Five Weeks in a Balloon*, and the movie version of *Voyage*. He also scored David Hedison's sci-fi hit, *The Fly*. Another sci-fi cult classic featuring Sawtell's music was 1958's *It! The Terror from Beyond Space*. On TV, he wrote the theme song for Michael Ansara's 1950s series, *Broken Arrow*. He would work for Allen again on *The Time Tunnel* and *Land of the Giants*. (See the Appendix A: "The Composers of *Voyage to the Bottom of the Sea*, for information on the series' scores.)

In putting together his story and pilot film, Allen harvested a great deal of footage from the 1961 feature-film version of *Voyage*, including the depth-charge explosions, along with many shots of the crew being tumbled about (such as scenes in the kitchen and corridors). For the scenes involving the reattachment of the sonar antenna, Allen selected film sequences showing shark and squid attacks. Also harvested from the film was footage depicting large chunks of ice raining in front of the observation windows. This thrifty practice seemed a perfect way to add big-picture production values to the TV footage.

***

Above: First day of principal photography, November 18, 1963. Below: On the second day, Allen and Winton Hoch (on camera crane) prepare to shoot the X-marks-the-spot scene at the 20th Century-Fox Santa Monica Blvd. gate.

Production began on Monday, November 18, on 20th Century-Fox Stage 5. It was the six and one-quarter page briefing-room scene featuring Admiral Nelson (Basehart); Dr. Fred Wilson (Albert); an Air Force General (Hal Torey) and an Army General (Barney Biro); a "chairman" (Booth Colman); Dr. Selby (John Zaremba); and a token scientist, played by Walter Reed. They were all seasoned pros.

Day 2: Tuesday, November 19. David Hedison first played Captain Crane on this day, joining Basehart, Albert, and William Hudson (as Seaview's

From Day 2: The Ext. Nelson Institute Wharf and Seaview were filmed on giant Stage 5, with a large open tank filled with water. Allen is on the camera crane (above) with megaphone.

original commander, Captain Phillips), although all were not featured in the same scenes. Hudson was with Basehart, filming at the Santa Monica Blvd. gate for 20th Century-Fox, which served as the exterior entrance gate for the Nelson Institute. The Admiral's Cabin was on Stage 16. Curiously, the production schedule lists the Ext. Nelson Institute Wharf and Seaview for Stage 5 and not at the outdoor Moat – perhaps done this way for better light and sound.

Before his termination with prejudice as the outgoing captain of the Seaview, Hudson had a recurring role as Ranger Clark on 1954's *Rocky Jones, Space Ranger*, and appeared as Special Agent Mike Andrews in several episodes of the Cold War espionage drama *I Led 3 Lives*. He played over 100 other roles in TV and film, coming to a dramatic death in many of them.

Of his first day on the Seaview, David Hedison said, "They were great sets; very well done. I wasn't in awe, but I could appreciate the hard work that went into them." (DH-CB12)

Day 3: Wednesday, November 20. The whole gang was present now, for the first time, on Stage 5 and the Int. Missile Room set. Basehart, Hedison, and Albert were joined by Robert Dowdell, Henry Kulky, Del Monroe, and Mark Slade.

201

Day 4: Thursday, November 21. Stage 16 was the location, for the Int. Control Room of the Seaview. William Hudson worked, as the doomed captain. David Hedison was there, to take over as the new skipper. Also present: Basehart, Dowdell, Kulky, Monroe, Slade, and Eddie Albert.

David Hedison experienced his first round of the Seaview lurching from side to side on this day. He later said, "There was a guy on set with a metal pail and a hammer. When he hit the pail the first time we all lurched to the right. On the second hit we'd fall to the left as the camera tilted to the right. A hammer and an old tin pail. Can you imagine!" (DH-CB12)

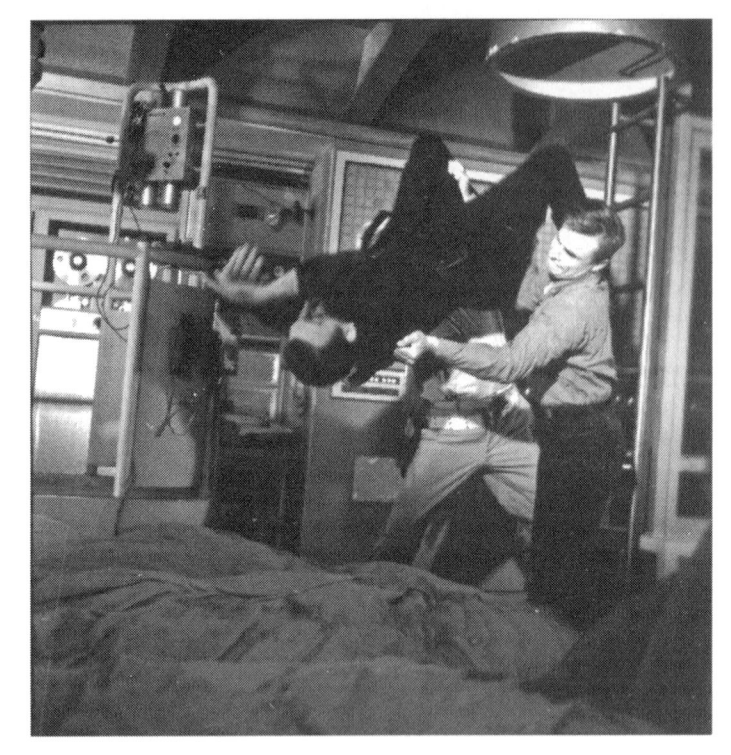

Day 4: Captain Crane takes a tumble on board the Seaview (above). Note the cushions laid on the floor of the set to insuring a safe landing. They also filmed the first instance of the Seaview rock and roll (below).

Day 5: Friday, November 22. More work on Stage 16 in the Control Room, with the presence of William Hudson. Gordon Gilbert, Chris Connelly, and Jim Goodwin were manning the controls. Goodwin, as the helmsman, would play the

same role, with the same title, on the bridge of the Enterprise during several episodes from the first season of *Star Trek* (in 1966). Also filmed this day were scenes in the Admiral's Cabin.

David Hedison: "I did the pilot and I loved the people I was with: Richard Basehart – I had so much to talk to him about; Henry Kulky; Bob Dowdell; a lot of wonderful people. And the terrific crew, like Winnie Hoch – you know, who won the award for *The Quiet Man* – I mean, an illustrious group of people. So, I was very lucky to be on it.

Day 5, November 22, 1963: More work on the Control Room set. Robert Dowdell joins Hedison above. Below, Henry Kulky with Hedison. Production came to a sudden halt at a little after 11 a.m. when news arrived on the set that President Kennedy had been shot.

"Then they were lining up for my close-up, and Henry Kulky came running by and saying something about the President's been shot. Well, we didn't hear what the hell he was talking about, so I continued my conversation with Richard." (DH-PE17)

Within minutes, work was interrupted by breaking news out of Dallas, Texas. At 10:48 a.m. (Pacific Time), Walter Cronkite interrupted the broadcast of *As the World Turns* on CBS-TV to announce, "Here is a bulletin from CBS News. In Dallas, Texas, three shots were fired at President Kennedy's motorcade in downtown Dallas. The first reports say that President Kennedy has been seriously wounded by this shooting. …

203

"More details just arrived. These details about the same as previously: President Kennedy shot today just as his motorcade left downtown Dallas. Mrs. Kennedy jumped up and grabbed Mr. Kennedy; she called 'Oh, no!' The motorcade sped on. United Press says that the wounds for President Kennedy perhaps could be fatal. Repeating, a bulletin from CBS News, President Kennedy has been shot by a would-be assassin in Dallas, Texas."

Actor Mark Slade said, "I was walking outside the soundstage. Someone said President Kennedy had been assassinated. I ran back to the stage and told an older crew member. He got angry and said, 'That's not funny!' A few minutes later, everyone knew it was true. The reaction on the set of the Seaview was the same as it was around the country." (MS-SFTS2)

As word spread through the company, work slowed, and then stopped, as radios and TV sets were switched on.

At 11:38 a.m. PST, a solemn Walter Cronkite broke the news to a national television audience: "We just have a report from our correspondent Dan Rather in Dallas that he has confirmed that President Kennedy is dead. There is still no official confirmation of this. However … it's a report from our correspondent Dan Rather … in Dallas, Texas."

Five minutes later, a somber Walter Cronkite said to the TV camera, "The priests … who were with Kennedy … the two priests who were with Kennedy say that he is dead of his bullet wounds. That seems to be about as close to official as we can get at this time."

Eleven minutes after the first announcement, Cronkite was handed a sheet from the AP News ticker. He put on his glasses, took a few seconds to read the sheet, and then said to the camera: "From Dallas, Texas, the flash apparently official: President Kennedy died at 1 p.m. Central Standard Time, 2:00 Eastern Standard Time, some 38 minutes ago."

David Hedison: "We were numb. It was awful. And I'll never forget that moment. All the work stopped on the pilot; they sent everyone home. We went home and we grieved. We missed Kennedy so much. We grieved. It was so sad. Terrible. Terrible." (DH-PE17)

Lee Harvey Oswald, Kennedy's accused assassin, was himself cut down, on Sunday, the 24th. His murder by Jack Ruby happened live on television, as Oswald was being taken from the Dallas Police Headquarters to the Dallas County Jail. Also on Sunday, 300,000 spectators, and a live television audience, watched the horse-drawn caisson with the flag-covered casket of President Kennedy proceed along Pennsylvania Avenue in Washington, D.C. from the White House to the Capitol Rotunda, where the slain president would lie in state, before burial at Arlington National Cemetery.

Day 6: Monday, November 25. Numb production personnel and performers returned to 20th Century-Fox to pick up where they had left off on Friday, filming in the Seaview Control Room on Stage 16, then moving on for the process shots taken in the Observation Nose of the Seaview. Also filmed were process shots in the "Int. Limousine" (with Basehart and Hudson being shot at, and returning fire, as the assassin's helicopter chases their car).

Day 6: In an eerie coincidence, the first day of filming after the assassination of President Kennedy involved Captain Phillips (John Hudson) being shot in the head by an assassin while sitting in the backseat of a motorcade limo.

Tuesday, November 26. There was no filming on this day. It was apparent to all involved in the previous day's work that cast and crew needed a period of mourning.

Day 7: Wednesday, November 27. Back onto Stage 16 for an entire day in the Observation Nose of the submarine. Basehart, Hedison, Albert, and Kulky were called in to work. Also present was a last-minute additional crewmember.

Derek Lewis played an unnamed Seaview officer for the pilot, and would return as Lt. O'Brien in half a dozen first-season episodes. Regarding his casting,

Day 7 (above): Filming on the Observation Nose set, with Basehard, Hedison, and Albert.
Day 8 (below): A second day on the Observation Nose, with Allen giving direction to Hedison, Kulky, Basehart, and Lewis.

Lewis said, "It just so happened that my 'sub-agent' was married to Cliff Gould, the casting director at 20th Century-Fox. I had met him on something else at one point, and he was really a nice guy. He called me in. They were well into shooting the pilot, and they needed someone that day! The part was for one of the crewmen – a helmsmen, I think. Cliff walked me onto the set to meet Irwin Allen, who was directing. It was literally, 'Excuse me, Irwin, you want to have a look.' Irwin looked me up and down. I felt like he was buying a used car. And then he said, "Oh, all right." Just like that.

"They rushed me off to wardrobe. Trouble was, I didn't fit into the crewman outfit, and they couldn't find one that did fit me. But they had this officer's uniform there, and it was a perfect fit. So, they said, 'Well, we'll just use that.' And I got an instant promotion in the wardrobe room.

"I was surprised Irwin let that go. He was a stickler to his vision, so it was odd that he didn't pass on that. But what I found out later was the guy that evidently had the role dropped out for one reason or another. I was there, and I fit the uniform, so I was established as an officer on the Seaview. Right place; right time; right fit." (DL-AI18)

Lewis's instant promotion was interrupted for a day. Production was

206

again suspended as bugs were worked out for the process shots needed in the observation nose.

Day 8 with the Main Unit: Friday, November 29. More work on Stage 16, in the Observation Nose. Again, only Basehart, Hedison, Kulky, Albert, and Lewis were needed.

Lewis said, "For television of that time, the shooting sets were certainly impressive. I'd been acting since I was 13, and you're used to creating this reality, and believing what you're doing, but, on this show, everything was *there* – the props, the controls, the various electronic screens – and it wasn't so flimsy that it was laughable. I mean, you can go back to see shows from the '50s, like *Captain Video*, and the sets *are* laughable, but not on *this* show. I don't think I realized at the moment when we were shooting that this was the set from the movie. I don't even think I had seen the movie at that point. I've seen it since, but not before working on the show. So, it was all kind of amazing to me.

"Of course, they looked better on film than they did when you were there. And everything broke apart – all the sections could be moved in and out. But with all the wiring that powered the flashing lights on the screens and boards, it was quite an undertaking." (DL-AU18)

The Fantasy Worlds of Irwin Allen features home movie footage shot on the set this day by Sheila Mathews (who married Irwin Allen in 1974). Allen can be seen having a ball, showing his stars how to fall about the ship as it rocks and rolls. Derek Lewis is one of those taking lessons from "The General." Lewis related, "Irwin was very hands on. And very animated! In television, with a lot of the directors, you hardly even see them! They're behind the camera, or they're over on the far side of the set, having

Days 9 and 10 were spent on Stage 8 for the very hot "Ice Caps" set.

private conversations with their technical crew. But Irwin was right there in the middle of *everything*. He was quite amazing. But he was also intimidating. That's a word that probably comes up a lot; at least for me. I have made the point in my life to try not to be intimidated by anybody, and to stand my ground, but Irwin was definitely intimidating. He had a brusque manner about him; a very sharp and fast way of speaking and doing things, and he was always telling you what to do, *every moment*, and you didn't dare interrupt him; you just had to listen. Irwin was 'The General.'"

Others would refer to him as the Emperor.

Also shot on this day, pickup shots needed in the Admiral's Cabin.

Additional camera work took Basehart outside, for the Ext. Shoulder of a Highway, where he lands after tumbling from the car, and returns fire on the helicopter. This shot was taken on the studio backlot.

From Production Days 9 & 10: Kulky and Hedison bundled up, despite the hot environment of a brightly lit sound-stage set.

Day 9: Monday, December 2. An ice set had been created on Stage 8, for "Ext. Seaview & Ice Fields." Present: Basehart, Hedison, Albert, Dowdell, Kulky, Monroe, and Slade.

Day 10: Tuesday, December 3. They were still on the Ice Fields of Stage 8, with Hedison, Albert, Kulky, Slade, and, later in the afternoon, Basehart, Dowdell, and Monroe. By day's end, the

regular cast, as well as Eddie Albert, were finished.

David Hedison left the set excited by the accelerated working conditions with some true legendary Hollywood pioneers. He was also conflicted over his impressions of the job they had done, and emotionally numb from the assassination of President John F. Kennedy. One other lasting impression pertained to the nucleus of the whole project – Irwin Allen. Despite Allen's limitations as a director, Hedison was nonetheless in awe of the man. He said, "Irwin was very specific – he knew what he wanted to do. If there wasn't enough grass on the set, he'd be screaming, 'Get me some crab grass! I need some more crab grass!,' and all of that. I mean, the guys would be running around getting him crab grass. And he was a nutcase. But, the thing is, he's a hell of a salesman. He got you so enthusiastic about this thing you were doing; this voyage to the bottom of the sea. 'It's gonna make you a star!' He'd, like, mesmerize you; hypnotize you. He was amazing. He's very good that way. He was a showman." (DH-PE17)

Day 11: Wednesday, December 4. Back on Stage 16 now for pickup shots in the Control Room, not requiring any of the regulars (close-ups on panels, etc.), then onto a new set built there – "Int. Gamma's Headquarters" – where Theodore Marcuse was needed, along with several bit players.

Marcuse, 43 when cast as Dr. Gamma for the pilot film, was a familiar villain on the small screen in the 1960s.

Day 11: Theodore Marcus stands on a "half-apple box" for height as he steps into the role of Dr. Gamma.

Shortly after his brief appearance in the *Voyage* pilot, Marcuse had stand-out villainous roles on *Get Smart*; *I Spy*; *The Man from U.N.C.L.E.*; *Star Trek*; *Hogan's Heroes*; *The Wild, Wild West*; *Batman* (as Van Bloheim, a nod toward Blofeld from the James Bond films), and, for a little movie on the big screen,

1966's *The Last of the Secret Agents?* He appeared again for Irwin Allen on *The Time Tunnel* in 1966.

On Thursday, Allen and his team reviewed the last of the dailies, making sure nothing more was needed. It wasn't; all previously filmed scenes had sufficient coverage. But a last bit of business remained.

Day 12: Friday, December 6. The second-unit team took over for the attack of the helicopter on the highway (near the 20th Century-Fox Ranch in the hills above Malibu). Motorcycle stunt performer Bud Ekins, who often doubled for Steve McQueen (it was Ekins, not McQueen, who made the jump over the barbed wire fence the year before in *The Great Escape*) was one of the military-guard cyclists who took a spill. The other, George Dockstader, pulled double duty, also playing the driver of the staff car. Ronnie Rondell, Jr. doubled for Basehart. Hubie Kerns was the assassin in the helicopter.

Regarding taking direction from Irwin Allen, David Hedison said, "He was wonderful to his 'stars.' You know, 'Where are my starrrrs?' All of that stuff. He was terribly generous. But he couldn't direct actors. He loved photo effects; he loved all that kind of thing, but he didn't know what to say to an actor. But he was wonderful; he was great to me; I liked him, but we were always arguing. I'd say, 'Irwin, what a great idea it would be if we tried it *this* way.' He thought I was mad. I think Irwin was a great salesman; a great producer, but not a director." (DH-TCF07)

Most of the scenes with the miniatures and other underwater shots were harvested from the 1961 *Voyage* motion picture. New sequences for the pilot were filmed by a second-unit team.

In post-production, Allen brought in Dick Tufeld to provide the narration for the opening of the first episode. Tufeld would also serve as the narrator (and the voice of the Robot) on *Lost in Space*.

During his editing of the pilot, Allen felt he needed some additional shots of Dr. Gamma, but Theodore Marcuse was not available. Therefore, Werner Klemperer (soon to become famous as Colonel Klink on *Hogan's Heroes*) was brought in, put into a skull cap, then shot in the shadows. Allen didn't think anyone would notice that he had two different actors, with two different body types, and two different voices, playing the same character in the same episode. Did Allen really think so little of his audience?

Launching the Series

According to *Variety*'s September 1, 1965 issue, the pilot for *Voyage to the Bottom of the Sea* was the most expensive filmed so far, costing $550,000. It was in color, though aired in black-and-white.

It was an easy sell to ABC. Interviewed for this book, network executive Lew Hunter said, "The presentation was made on film. Afterwards, I

complimented Bill Self on selling the show. I asked him, 'Was that particularly hard?' He said, 'No, I have the tendency to show the pilot to the suits,' whom I was one of them, 'and then stand up and ask if there are any questions.' And I said, 'Yes, but you didn't go on about the show.' He said, 'One: I thought the show spoke for itself. And, two: I have seen a lot of people talk themselves *out* of a sale. And I was not going to do that.' That's the kind of man he was. And Irwin would sit there with a smile on his face, wearing those coke-bottle glasses. And he'd say, 'Wasn't it great?!' And then someone would usher him out of there."
(LH-AI15)

***

The first order of business was to hire a rewrite man or two for the series. But before these new wordsmiths could commence reworking scripts, they worked with Allen writing the Series Bible, also known as the Writers Guide.

William Welch was a meat-and-potatoes writer, and had cut his teeth on TV series which attempted to spook the viewer, such as *Lights Out* (from 1950 and '51), and those that appealed to youth, such as *Sky King* (in 1957 and '58). He wrote the screenplay for a 1963 low-budget (and somewhat trashy) Jane Mansfield movie called *Promises, Promises*. He also tried his hand at being a playwright, with the 1960 way-off Broadway sci-fi *How to Make a Man*, starring Peter Marshall (later of *Hollywood Squares* fame), as a robot. *Daily Variety*'s December 30, 1960 review for *How to Make a Man* sounds a lot like one for an Irwin Allen production:

> *How to Make a Man*, a new comedy by William Welch which premed [premiered] tonight at the Cass Theatre [Detroit], provides an ironic lesson in how not to make a play. In attempting to show the difference between man and robots, the comedy carries with it all the faults of man which tend to make him robot-like. Thus, it is obvious that most of the creative effort went into material things – ingenious moving stages, a wondrous home electronic console with a widescreen rear projection color TV set that was an important part of the action, stunning, futuristic sets and gorgeous costumes. Unfortunately, very little substance was given to the words and actions of the human actors.

Because of the play's failure, Welch needed a job. He said, "Through a combination of incredible circumstances which merit a book of their own, the venture was a cataclysmic bomb which all but destroyed anyone who had

anything to do with it. As the author, I was the particular target of vengeance."
(WW-TWTD75)

By virtue of his varied writing background, Welch was a perfect fit for the Allen TV production company, and was signed up to serve as Script Editor.

Al Gail had been working closely with his cousin Irwin since the two had moved to Los Angeles in the late 1930s. Without credit, he collaborated with Allen on his various movies, and now he would again be at Allen's side with this new venture, as Welch's assistant.

Welch and Gail worked with Allen, fleshing out the series and committing ideas to paper to serve as a road map for the freelance writers who would be given script assignments.

Artwork included with Irwin Allen's version of a "Series Bible," the *Voyage to the Bottom of the Sea* "Series Proposal."

Allen, ever the showman, was making a big show of trying to intrigue and educate the writers he would use for the series. Every television series has a Series Bible, but, with Allen's first TV spectacular, it was more of an entertainment package. The work of Allen, Welch, and Gail grabbed the prospective writers with the bold title, "NOW THAT YOU'VE SEEN THE PILOT …" The first page was THEME. Considering what followed, a more accurate title would have been LACK OF THEME. It said:

> *Voyage to the Bottom of the Sea* is an exercise in action-adventure. It has dash ... verve ... an honest, high-hearted approach to exciting entertainment. In spirit, each episode contains the rapidly sputtering fuse, the breathless, desperate race against the clock, the gripping suspense of overwhelming danger.
>
> Obviously, then, this is not a show of social crusades, satirical comments or probing searches into the human psyche. Such themes, fascinating and worthy as they may be, are outside the province of a series dedicated to the heady business of high adventure.
>
> But the very fact that the themes required are straightforward and fundamental means that great skill is called for in their development. Motivations must be clear. Events must proceed logically. Plausibility is a key note.
>
> In a practical sense, themes may be divided into three broad areas: struggle against the forces of nature; struggle against the enemies of mankind; any combination of the two. Such themes lead naturally to stories of pure adventure, stories of mystery-adventure and stories with overtones of science fiction-adventure.

Sadly, stories of Man Against Nature, or Man Against Man, without the addition of Man Against *Himself* – the element of introspection – often lack depth. They don't ask the audience to think; merely cheer. They are a video rollercoaster ride, which is fine for a while. But can a rollercoaster ride last five years? Eventually, the thrill wears off and the rider begins to crave a different means of amusement – something with substance. With all his talent and accomplishments, Allen never seemed to understand this fundamental rule of entertainment.

Sheila Mathews Allen said of her long-time companion and husband of 17 years, "He loved to put people in jeopardy, and have them rise to the occasion and succeed. He used to call it the 'Walter Mitty Syndrome.' And if you look at most of his work, that's the theme that I think ran through it, where people would overcome great hardships and some would [make it] and some wouldn't." (SMA-KB95)

Allen had read James Thurber's story "The Secret Life of Walter Mitty," and empathized with its theme of unfulfilled daydreams. Within a few years of the tale's 1939 publication in *The New Yorker*, the name Walter Mitty had become cultural shorthand for anybody who was prone to dream big and prefer those dreams to reality. The story was filmed, with many additions and changes, in 1947 as a vehicle for Danny Kaye's hijinks. A different approach to the theme was filmed, starring Ben Stiller, in 2013. While Allen entertained big goals like the story's namesake, he at least had attained success in the real world – unlike Thurber's nebbish character.

Mathews said, "He was a very moral, ethical man, and he was making pictures in the days that he did, when it was a little different than it is today. We didn't have to deal with as much, you know, sex. Can we say that? And that would not have been his cup of tea, really. So he was a very moral movie-maker. I don't think you can find anything in anything he ever did that was not acceptable to all, the whole range of audience." (SMA-KB95)

The next subject in the *Voyage* Series Bible was "Style." Allen and his helpers wrote:

> The style of writing desired for the series is deceptively simple. Its main ingredients are action, pace, economy, and tense excitement. Talk for talk's sake – even talk for the development of depth of character – [is] considered expendable.

Most writers will tell you that "character" is a prerequisite for a successful story. A story is about a character with a problem to solve, and an urgent need to make something happen … or not happen. The key words are "character," "problem," and "urgent." Allen understood the urgency factor. What he didn't realize was that the best story problems have to do with characters, not things … things like enemy spies, enemy aliens, and enemy monsters.

The page on "Style" continued:

> The language used must have the ring of authenticity and dialogue exchanges will be used in all cases to advance the story, heighten the tension, increase the excitement, grip the audience. Taut drama is the prevailing mood. When there is romance, it must impel, not hinder, the relentless progress of the story. Humor is welcome but it must proceed from the action and be part of the headlong dash that carries the viewer from the intriguing teaser to the crashing climax of each show.

The next page was headed "LOCALE," followed by: "Where do we play our stories? <u>Everywhere!</u>"

Allen and his team wrote:

> This is not a submarine series, *per se*. Its plots are not confined to a group of sweating men surrounded by the intricate plumbing of a sub interior as they listen breathlessly to the shattering explosions of depth charges. Not that such scenes won't have a place in the series. They will. But they will be the exception rather than the rule. In the vast majority of stories, the sub is merely a conveyance to get our principals to the scene of the action. The greatest part of any one specific story will take place off the submarine. Unlike the pilot, the typical submarine-type scenes – when they occur – will be incidental for the big climax of the story.
>
> And where is the big climax likely to occur? Literally anywhere in the world. The men from the Seaview may find themselves on some remote mountain peak, in a deep, unexplored cavern, on a desert or in the glittering jungle of some great capitol city.

One might wonder, then, why the series was called *Voyage to the Bottom of the Sea*. It transpired that, as with many adventure shows whose individual budgets might vary widely, the need to reduce costs would necessitate "bottle shows," shot entirely on the sub. But for now, for this first season, the canvas was wider.

The next page had the heading of "Characters." Why, then, was the first name in the list "Seaview"?

Allen wrote:

> Although, strictly speaking, not a character, Seaview is definitely a strong motivating force in the series. It is a huge, radically designed nuclear submarine which carries a complement of twelve officers and one hundred twenty-five men. Its most distinctive feature is a fantastic glass nose which makes the forward lounge an ideal place from which to view the awesome wonders of the undersea world. It is the great glass nose which gives the ship its distinctive look of a "Submarine of Tomorrow." But even more important, although less immediately apparent, are its other features ... its missile room with

> its arsenal of nuclear warhead rockets ... its mini-sub which permits two-man scouting trips below the operating range of the deepest diver ... its escape hatch which permits individual frogmen to explore ocean bottoms ... its rows of efficient computers which can perform all the magic of the new machine brains ... and its amazing ability to dive deeper and move faster than any ship ever designed. These are a few of the features making Seaview the world's most efficient device for scientific research, exploring and defense.
>
> Seaview is <u>not</u> a regular Navy ship. It is privately owned by the Nelson Institute of Marine Research – an organization of scientists with headquarters at Santa Barbara, California. Its crew members are civilian employees, although nearly all of them are former naval submariners.

This was a good move on the part of Allen. It gave him freedom from having to seek approval from the Department of the Navy for his series. Allen wouldn't have to submit his scripts to military red-liners, and military policies could be observed or ignored in the best interests of a story. The Seaview would cooperate with the Navy of 1973, perhaps even be drafted into service for specific missions, but otherwise travel to the beat of its own drum ... or sonar.

Here's how the Series Bible delineated Admiral Nelson:

> Even to those who knew him best, it came as a distinct surprise when this dedicated and gifted officer gave up his naval career to devote the rest of his life to science. But only a handful of people know that Nelson's retirement was in name only. Actually, he and his Institute of Marine Research serve as a powerful and secret intelligence force, ranging the world under the cover of scientific research on missions of vital importance to the security of their country.

The next characters were Commander Lee Crane, who "has a rule, amounting almost to a fetish, of never ordering a man to tackle a dangerous assignment that he would not risk doing himself"; Lieutenant Chip Morton, "the efficient Executive Officer of the submarine"; and Chief Petty Officer Curley Jones, "a jolly yet rugged old time Navy man who occasionally forgets that he is no longer a part of the Fleet."

The next two recurring characters fell on the villainous side of the ledger. One, seen in the pilot, was Dr. Gamma.

> This shadowy figure is the adversary who opposes the men of the Seaview in many of the stories which unfold as the series progresses. "A riddle wrapped in a mystery inside an enigma," Gamma is an individual of awesome power and unlimited ambition. Even his name is unknown -- "Dr. Gamma" of course being merely a nickname. But his power is all too well known in the secret councils of every government in the world. He seems to have at his command a veritable corps of skilled scientific brains ... an elaborate network of secret agents ... a seemingly endless arsenal of weapons ... and a body of fanatically devoted followers – men and women who have pledged their lives to the furtherance of his cause.
>
> Gamma's ultimate goal is world domination. He seeks it through the spread of disorder and dissension ... through the promotion of disaster and death and the undermining of civil authority.

The other recurring character was Professor "X," the most feared of Gamma's lieutenants.

On a separate page, in a box devoted to "Taboos," Allen told his future writers:

> The taboos are few but implacable.
>
> A. All the ordinary taboos set up in the interest of taste and morality;
> B. No spy stories in which the adversary is a representative of any recognizable governments, even by implication (Gamma is the adversary we use in stories with an international spy flavor);
> C. No supernatural stories;
> D. No story in which the element of romance, psychological study or personal drama are permitted to bring the action to a halt.

Why no supernatural stories? The 1960s continued the West's tradition of rigid rules of propriety and strict public morality. ABC was reluctant to tell ghost stories during the family hour, for fear of offending sponsors. The sponsors, of course, were afraid of offending mainstream sensibilities. Somehow monster stories, however, were okay. And so were subplots involving curvy, provocative women.

In his summary, the key points Allen highlighted were:

- "The action takes place a few years in the future, giving wide latitude in technical matters";
- "There is a James Bondian flavor to the series, which, of course, means that seductive attractive women often play a part and may involve Crane, Nelson, Chip Morton or – in fact – any one of the twelve officers and 125 crewmen of the sub";
- "The teaser of each episode is vitally important. It must shock the audience – grip them – literally force them to watch the show":
- "And the keynote is … ACTION!"

On March 10, using stationery from the Herzlia-On-Sea Hotel, Israel, Theodore Marcuse wrote a four-page letter to Irwin Allen, saying, in part:

> Dear Irwin: Carl Forest writes me that "Voyage" is setting to sail, and I am <u>very</u> pleased, for you – and for me. I wanted to work on that role with you. Congratulations.
>
> Would you, or have you, thought of Dr. Gamma, in his fight for Evil, appearing in disguise to the others? I have played so many varied characters on TV, mainly because my ear is so good and my [physical appearance] so easily changed – with makeup & wigs. Dutch (*The Islanders*), Amish (*Have Gun*), German (*DuPont Show of the Week*), Chinese (*Peter Gunn*), British (any number), even Malayan Pirate (that first Rick Jason for Ziv – forgot the name [*Case of the Dangerous Robin*] but there's good film in it – Jim Goldstone directed), and so on. Plus any number of Hungarians (*77 Sunset*), and even some Texans (again, *Have Gun*). All this by way of my playing an Arab in this present film [*Harum Scarum*]. The first day of shooting, after watching some scenes, the Arab advisor came up and started talking to me in Arabic! Of course it may have been because I was riding a <u>wild</u> Arabian stallion! On the other hand – ? Do consider it. Fond best, Ted. P.S. Let me know starting date when you can. I want to stay in London until.

Allen wrote back on March 25, saying:

> Dear Ted: Thank you so much for your letter and forgive me for this belated response. As of this moment, there is every indication that the show will go, but we do not, as yet, have the final green light. However, we have assigned writers and are well into preparation for the first group of shows.
>
> Your idea about doing a variety of villains is intriguing and well worth consideration. We will certainly talk about it when you return.
>
> As soon as I have definite news about the start of the show and the further appearances of Dr. Gamma I will immediately make you aware.
>
> Kindest regards, Irwin Allen.

The struggle at this point was to make sure "Voyage" (or, as it was once again called, *Voyage to the Bottom of the Sea*) could be produced on a TV budget, and delivered on a weekly basis to the network without missing any air dates. The same battle against time took place for *Lost in Space* one year later, and for *Star Trek* a year after that. Television had never produced a one-hour dramatic science-fiction series with recurring cast members and regular sets on a weekly basis. Anthology series had been attempted in this genre before, with shows such as *The Twilight Zone* and *The Outer Limits*. If one episode fell behind, producers could shoot different episodes simultaneously, since the same sets and cast members would not be needed in each. But in many ways Allen was exploring uncharted lands in television production. Each *Voyage* episode would be the equivalent of half a science-fiction movie. These requirements for futuristic sets, costumes and props – not to mention special effects – loomed as nigh-impossible tasks.

Irwin Allen was the pioneer of this new territory of television production. It is fair to say that without *Voyage to the Bottom of the Sea*, there might not have been a *Lost in Space* or *Star Trek*.

Allen's agent, Herman Rush, was involved in much of the wrangling with the network and studio in setting a budget for the series – a magic number that was just high enough, but that wouldn't waste a single thin dime. He said, "The budgets were different for different shows, depending on the time period they would be put in to. ABC needed programming for, in those days, 7:30 time periods, where they were getting a young audience, but they had limited budgets. I think ABC had lower budgets than CBS and NBC would have had, but one of Irwin's great assets was the ability to make things on a budget that other producers had difficulty with. Irwin had a system; he had a way of addressing these things. ... Those budgets were a little higher than the licensing fee that the network was paying, with 20th Century-Fox doing a little deficit financing, recouping that loss in the foreign sales which took place with this kind of content. What helped him with those small budgets was 20th Century-Fox had the back lot, which is now Century City, and that included the water area [known as 'The Moat'], where he had filmed portions of the movie version of *Voyage to the Bottom of the Sea*. So he was able to use that same setting to do the television series, saving money and thereby making it a feasible venture to the thinking of the studio and network executives." (HR-AI15)

On April 2, 1964, after a production meeting between Allen and his staff, notes were typed up and circulated to the department heads.

Regarding the "Basic Set":

> CONTROL ROOM – as is. Need the wild pieces for shooting up the alley. It was ascertained that they still exist. Some pieces have been altered for *Fate Is the Hunter* [feature film] so they will have to be revamped back (Approximate cost $475 - $500).
>
> STAGE B is to be the home base for sets only if the sound problem is checked out.
>
> Set cost to include cost of reassembling and putting everything back in working order – also transportation.
>
> MISSILE ROOM: Could be conceivably smaller, but, since third side is open, [Fox set supervisor] Jack Smith feels not necessary.
>
> ADMIRAL'S CABIN: Use it as is, and redress for Crane and other quarters.
>
> WHARF OF NELSON RESEARCH INSTITUTE: Set it permanently at the "moat" and create a set since it will be in practically every episode. Analyze the feasibility of building the underwater tank at the moat. After the tour of the moat, it was temporarily decided to use the Moat for basic sets, shoot underwater scenes with people at

Catalina, Sea World or Marineland. Bill Abbott to utilize the use of the Green Tank for the miniatures with additional shots at Sersen when needed. Green Tank will take about $2,000 to refurbish. $1,000 – Ivan [Martin], $1,000 – Dave [Anderson].

GREEN TANK: Needs a transformer and some plumbing. As noted, Ivan Martin roughly estimates $1,000 to put his end into shape and Dave Anderson needs roughly $1,000 to do the necessary electrical work.

PORTABLE TANK: To be used on the stage for actor's close-ups.

ONE DAY FOR PROCESS – possibility of even sharing crew for this.

Plan to use stock footage for various foreign cities – then jump into the foreign street section for punching up the completion of the shots. Don't figure in the budget, for this would fall in the episodic cost of the budget.

IN ADDITION TO THIS: I.A., Ivan Martin, Jack Smith & Gaston Glass will sit down and figure average cost per episode.

OBSERVATION NOSE: Not really possible on STAGE B. Requires more angle room for Process shots. Should possibly share another stage with someone else rather than attempting a tight squeeze on Stage B.

We will have to wait for [Financial Director] Sol's budget since final determination has not yet been reached as to color or black and white.

The battle over the budget continued. It was decided that the Observation Nose, with the Process Shot screen, would remain on Stage B, along with the Control Room, the Radio Hut, the Missile Room, the Admiral's Cabin (which could be redressed as other cabins), Sickbay (which could be redressed as crew quarters), and corridors.

With these compromises, there would be a series ... but, sadly for Allen and Theodore Marcuse, no Dr. Gamma. ABC felt the evildoer was too imitative of Dr. No and Blofeld from the James Bond movies.

Now that the potential series had been deemed feasible as a TV production, and with the network already impressed with the pilot film, a deal was struck between Irwin Allen Productions, 20th Century-Fox Studios, and the ABC television network. Fox and ABC made a commitment for 16 one-hour episodes, with options in place for ABC to extend that order to 26 or more, as well as additional seasons of the series.

Thomas Moore, former president of ABC, said, "Allen was one of the most creative people in the science fiction arena. He grasped the Jules Verne material with an immediate recognition as to its convertibility to television. He surrounded himself with talented young writers, directors and special effects people." (TM-SFTS2)

Allen had one more thing going for him – as David Hedison had noted, he was remarkably impassioned.

Dave Kaufman of *Daily Variety* was also struck by Allen's enthusiasm. Interviewed for Kaufman's May 5, 1964 column, Allen said, "Like every motion picture producer, you're dying to bring to TV a motion picture technique. They say you don't have the time or money in TV. I think it can be done. In my movies, I've always had about 2,000 sketches made on each project – sketches of all the action in pictures. This is literally cutting a picture before it goes on stage. This way, every department – wardrobe, special effects and so on – knows exactly what I need, and they know long in advance of production. It keeps hysteria to a minimum. I am doing the same thing on the series." Regarding the scope of his first television project since his 1950s panel show, Allen told Kaufman, "I have 21 permanent sets. We will have a second unit on location all over the world. We plan extensive use of miniatures. Our 102-foot submarine will go into the block-long moat – now occupied by Tiki, the *Adventures in Paradise* ship, which will be removed. We have seven smaller subs, in different sizes for proportionate shooting. We can run them by remote radio. They are the most expensive toys ever made. We will reproduce the sub in sections for indoor shots. We even have a Polaris missile room in the sub, largest in the world!

"In the pilot, we had an advanced seismograph, which foretold earthquakes. Since we made it, the government has revealed they are just a step away from such an instrument." (IA-DV64)

(The 102-foot submarine Allen was referring to was actually the full-upper deck/conning tower mockup. The overall length of the largest Seaview miniature was 350 feet.)

Allen was having a ball with his expensive toys, even if the seven remote-controlled models only existed in his imagination. But to his disappointment, it was dictated that the show, including his much-hyped sets and props, would be filmed in so many shades of gray.

In April, 1964, *Variety* reported "No Tint for 20th's *Bottom of the Sea*." It had been calculated that color processing would have added another $20,000 per segment, about $600,000 over the season. The conclusion, from the studio and network, was that there simply were not enough color TV sets in America to warrant this added expense. So far for the series, the network was already committed to deficit financing, with only Coca-Cola committed as a partial sponsor. The studio was also into deficit financing: The network was paying about two-thirds of the cost of each episode, with additional money to be paid later, if and when episodes were repeated.

Black-and-white could, if nothing else, give *Voyage to the Bottom of the Sea* a *film noir* look. And with the themes Allen had in mind, this might not be an entirely bad thing. Allen told *Daily Variety* that his *Voyage* would be "a damp cloak-and-dagger series, centered about the glass-nosed sub."

He added, "In the series, the sub is owned and operated by a Santa Barbara institute as an oceanography lab, but actually that's the cover for 'the top CIA of that day.'"

The sub would be manned by "the super-commandos of the world, the most brilliant scientist-soldiers ever created."

Allen said he planned to write and direct three episodes out of every 13, and that the series would appeal to adults as much as children. He said, "While we hope we will have the teenage kids, we are also reaching for an adult audience. Youngsters alone can't support a show." (IA-DV64)

***

Twentieth Century-Fox was suddenly back in the TV game, with four series scheduled for the 1964-65 season. NBC was taking the one-hour *Daniel Boone*. And ABC had ordered three hours per week: *Peyton Place* (one hour broken into two segments), *12 O'Clock High,* and *Voyage to the Bottom of the Sea.*

William Self was interviewed by Cecil Smith for a June 28, 1964 *Los Angeles Times* article. Smith wrote:

> The biggest resurgence of television production in Hollywood is at 20th Century-Fox, the studio that went suddenly from nowhere to be the second largest producer of programs on the networks next season. Though still far behind the production of the Universal-

Revue colossus, which will supply 8½ hours weekly to the networks, the 4 hours from Fox is a major coup. It's also very gratifying to young [studio head] Richard Zanuck, who says, flatly, no major film studio today can survive without a strong television arm, and to William Self, who guides its TV fortunes.

Self is the first to admit that Fox has never done really superior television, though the studio had great success with *Dobie Gillis* and produced one series far better than its single-series deserved, the robust *Hong Kong*. But *Follow the Sun, Bus Stop, Adventures in Paradise*, etc., are not particularly missed.

Self told Smith, "I love to make comedy, but you can get lost when nearly everything around is comedy. There are only nine new dramatic shows, and we're doing four of them." (WS-LAT64)

Jack Hellman interviewed Irwin Allen and then filed a report for his July 9, 1964 *Daily Variety* "Light and Airy" column. Irwin told him that, with TV's *Voyage to the Bottom of the Sea*, his goal was "every week, *Perils of Pauline*!" Hellman reported:

> No show next season can boast such far-flung production as *Bottom*. Four units will be at work on every segment and seven cameras will be used ("more than in feature pictures"). One unit will work in the Bahamas, where the water is crystal clear, and another around Catalina. Says Allen, "If this sounds like a kid show, well and good, but once the elders take a look they'll be confirmed repeaters. Similar pictures of mine have always drawn a family trade and the nights were just as strong as the Saturday matinees. It's targeted, however, for adults and our 11 sponsors are confident they'll be selling their wares in the right places."

Bob Suhosky, TV Publicity Director for 20th Century-Fox Television, got busy next, telling the TV press corps:

> No producer in history ever approached a television series with more knowledge of his subject and the materials for making the subject into an exciting series than has Academy Award winner Irwin Allen, producer, director and writer for his 20th Century-Fox Television

series, *Voyage to the Bottom of the Sea*, for ABC-TV. *Voyage* has been a preoccupation with Allen for five years, from the time he first began researching an original story about a submarine of the future ("Let's say the late 1960s or early 1970s," said Allen) and this grew to the fantastically successful motion picture, *Voyage to the Bottom of the Sea*, which was a blockbuster for 20th Century-Fox. It is important to the series that *Voyage* initially was a motion picture, for Allen will be the first to admit that it would be impossible to obtain the production values for the TV series had it not been for the motion picture version absorbing the initial costs of sets, props, costumes, and underwater film, to say nothing of such intangibles as research, drawings, conception, and a myriad of etcs. "For example," Allen pointed out, "the three main underwater sections of our Seaview submarine cost more than $400,000 to build – more than most television pilot films in their entirety. Yet when we were ready to make the television pilot we had at our disposal, and in perfect working shape, the intact sections of the control room, the viewing room (the only submarine with a glass nose) and the missile and torpedo rooms fully equipped with more than two dozen of the latest atomic warhead-carrying missiles."

Of the costumes designed by Paul Zastupnevich, Allen said, "We had to have a military appearance, yet we could not duplicate any existing uniform or any army or navy in the world. In addition we had to take into account the ever-changing modes and modernization of military uniforms. I think Paul dreamed up Department of Marine Science uniforms one night when rotating his nocturnal thoughts between World War II and a space trip of the future."

For the pilot film, "Eleven Days to Zero," Allen had 1,100 sketches prepared to guide the production. He approached the making of a TV series with the kind of strategic planning only seen in motion pictures – until now.

Thanks to the plentiful publicity, industry anticipation was high. For a syndicated newspaper article, printed in the *Abilene Reporter-News* on July 7, 1964, entertainment correspondent Erskine Johnson wrote:

> A block-long maze of colored lights in the submarine's master control room blink like the eyes of a thousand owls on a roost. No electric sign on Times Square is as busy or as colorful. Men in uniforms operate a long panel of dials, gauges, levers, scanning viewers, electronic

meters and hundreds of control buttons. This is the "Seaview," a glass-nosed submarine conceived in the mind of a Hollywood art director and so bizarre he owes Jules (*20 Thousand Leagues Under the Sea*) Verne no apology at any level.

A 20th Century-Fox press release touted the series this way:

> *Voyage*'s unparalleled production (which includes probably the most elaborate studio sets ever created for a TV series, such as the futuristic interior of a submarine and an amazing *Lost World* where prehistoric animals still roam) will come over impressively on the home screen.

Irwin Allen said, "Call us lucky. No other series has ever been handed a million dollars' worth of sets and props to work with right from the start." (IA-TR64)

Richard Basehart said, "All this is an enormous help to the actor. When Hedison, as the skipper, tells me that we're at a depth of 2,400 feet, proceeding at 65 knots on a 70 degree course, I can flick my eyes around the instruments, and those *are* the readings. If the script calls for us to change depth, speed, or course, the instruments immediately adjust – even when the camera isn't looking. It's not at all difficult to get caught up in the excitement and tensions with which the scriptwriters have so kindly furnished us. Maybe the critic who said actors are just tall children was right. If so, 'us kids' in this series should be happy. We've been given the most expensive toys ever made." (RB-TR64)

On the other hand, don't forget that in the Series Bible, the first "character" was the Seaview. Basehart told interviewer Erskine Johnson, "Fighting the submarine – that's the challenge to all the actors in this show. With all those lights and dials the submarine is bigger acting competition than a child or a dog. … With our crazy glass-nosed sub, no one will notice the actors in the first show. After that, my only problem will be to make the character believable. SOMETHING has to be believable in this show." (RB-ARN64)

Basehart continued to worry about being upstaged by his ship. In an interview from September 1964, after several episodes had been filmed, he commented, "I'm talking about the challenge to me or any other actor to play against the leading lady of our series, the Seaview, our submarine of the future. In many ways, she can be a metal monster. If you're not careful, she'll steal a scene right from under you." (RB-PPI64)

Over the next couple of years, things would only get more challenging.

6

Season One: ABC's Initial Order of 16

> Mission for viewers: sit on the edge of your seat, hold your breath, and enjoy the most unique, most spellbinding television series your senses have ever experienced.... on the **ABC TELEVISION NETWORK**

An ABC press release, carried by Maine's *Biddeford-Saco Journal* on September 12, 1964, summed up the fledgling series this way:

> *Voyage to the Bottom of the Sea*, starring Richard Basehart and David Hedison, and dealing with the action-filled, dangerous missions of the submarine Seaview in the year 1973, debuts Monday. ... Basehart plays Admiral Harriman Nelson, USN (Ret.), director of a marine research institute and designer-builder of the atomic-powered, glass-nosed submarine. Ostensively a research vessel, the Seaview is actually the most effective weapon afloat, and is often assigned top secret missions by the U.S. Government.
>
> Hedison co-stars as Commander Lee Crane, skipper of the Seaview. Henry Kulky appears as Chief Curley Jones, and Robert Dowdell as Lt. Commander Chip Morton.

And then it was time for America to join TV's *Voyage to the Bottom of the Sea.*

Episode 1: "Eleven Days to Zero"

(Prod. #6008; first aired Monday, September 14, 1964)
Written, directed, and produced by Irwin Allen.
Guest Star Eddie Albert
(with Theodore Marcuse as Dr. Gamma)

From the same ABC press release quoted above:

In "Eleven Days to Zero," the premiere episode, Eddie Albert guest stars as Dr. Fred Wilson, a seismologist who accompanies the Seaview crew as they speed to the North Pole. The mission is to detonate a nuclear device at the precise instant of an accurately predicted earthquake. The explosion is planned to set up opposing lines of force and break the back of tidal waves before they form. Otherwise, the waves will inundate half the coastal areas of the world. Enroute, the Seaview is attacked by a submarine and aircraft dispatched by the brilliant Dr. Gamma (Theodore Marcuse), head of an international ring bent on world domination.

Assessment:

The reviews were mixed but ... if nothing else, Irwin Allen had a knack for making big, flashy pilots which were tense and filled with high drama. They were all inspired by the Saturday-morning matinee serials Allen had watched as a kid in his local movie houses, with one cliffhanger after another, stories driven by Man Against Nature and Man Against Man situations. Rarely did Allen bother with the most demanding and introspective, but also most rewarding of the three story categories, Man Against Himself. Perhaps this was one reason for the mixed reviews he received for his films and television series. His characters were, for the most part, standard hero types, responding to the latest crisis. An Irwin Allen production was rarely – and never intentionally – a "message" story. It was always action-adventure. In this regard, "Eleven Hours to Zero" is a resounding success. It is a big production for the standards of 1960s television. The story moves like gangbusters, never slowing down long enough for audience attention to drift. The characters are quick to display conflict, and just as quick to shrug it off and shake hands. What drives them are sudden impulses, as they react, and overreact, to one another and the events around them.

Production:
(Filmed November 18 through December 4, 1963; 12 days)

Even though the pilot was filmed in color, the broadcast version, with some cuts and a handful of new sequences, including those featuring Werner Klemperer as Dr. Gamma, was from a monochrome print (allowing the new scenes to be filmed in black-and-white, saving money).

"Eleven Days to Zero" was the most expensive TV pilot made up to this time (a record that would soon be broken by *Lost in Space*, and later by *Star Trek*). The networks and studios had good reason to think that a science-fiction series, with futuristic sets and special effects

Irwin Allen discussing a scene about to be filmed with Richard Basehart and Robert Dowdell.

requirements, was unaffordable. Allen tried to prove this belief wrong, through the reuse of common sequences. This sometimes-effective tactic became a routine practice in later series, from *Star Trek* to *Battlestar Galactica*. Among these cost-saving tricks:

- When the Seaview first dives and Captain Crane looks through the periscope, the exterior effects shot seems to depict a WWII-era vessel, which doesn't match the Seaview's sleek, futuristic body style;
- When the sub dramatically emerges from an arctic sea, as if about to launch itself out of the water;
- When Captain Crane suits up for a swim, he dons a yellow wetsuit. This was done to match shots from the *Voyage* feature which showed Robert Sterling in yellow scuba attire, allowing for the recycling of the giant squid attack;
- When the Polaris-type submarine chases the Seaview, firing torpedoes, then imploding from the pressure of the depth;
- When chunks of ice plummet deeper into the sea, clobbering the Seaview;
- Also, according to *Seaview: A 50th Anniversary Tribute to Voyage to the Bottom of the Sea* (Alpha Control Press, 2012), the Seaview dock was originally built for the 1954 Richard Widmark submarine film *Hell and High Water*.

When it came to creator credits for the pilot, Irwin Allen was listed as creator ... and producer ... and writer ... and director. Paul Zastupnevich was given one credit ... and not even for wardrobe. He is "Production Assistant" here.

Zastupnevich said, "There was always a phrase around the office – 'I'll get Paul to do it.' Whenever someone would turn him [Allen] down, if he felt that they weren't going to follow through for him, he said, 'That's all right; forget about it; I'll get Paul to do it.' But when I wanted a double credit, I didn't get it. That's why, all of a sudden, I ended up with an 'assistant to the producer' credit, and no costume designer credit. He said,

'You can't have two credits, and, besides, your name is too long. You should shorten your name.' I said, 'What do you want me to change it to?' He said, 'You can call yourself Paul Zaza.' I said. 'I'm not going to be Zsa Zsa Gabor, by any means.' ... And, all of a sudden you see Irwin Allen Production, directed by Irwin Allen, produced by Irwin Allen, conceived by Irwin Allen. ... If Irwin did three things, Irwin got three salaries, and he got three credits." (PZ-KB95)

Release / Reaction:
(Only ABC broadcast: 9/14/64)

"The House of the Rising Sun" by the Animals was in its first of three weeks as the most-played song on American Top 40 radio, having knocked the Supremes' "Where Did Our Love Go" from the top spot. Disney's *Mary Poppins*, starring Julie Andrews and Dick Van Dyke, was the big hit in the movie houses, having displaced *A Hard Day's Night,* starring the Beatles. Walt Disney had a second victory, as he was awarded a Medal of Freedom at the White House by President Lyndon Johnson. The Beatles, meanwhile, were touring the U.S. and, on this particular night, playing a public auditorium in Cleveland, Ohio. Tickets ranged between $2 and $8.50. Prior to their concert, they may have been watching *Voyage*. David Hedison told interviewer William Anchors his surprise on discovering a special group of fans: "The Beatles. They wouldn't come out for their interview until our episode had ended." (DH-S50)

Also making their premieres on TV this week were *The Addams Family, Peyton Place, Shindig, Bewitched, 12 O'Clock High,* and *Jonny Quest*. All were on ABC, which was launching its fall season one week ahead of the other two networks, hoping to get a foothold in the ratings. In the following week, NBC would premiere *Flipper, Daniel Boone* and *The Man from U.N.C.L.E.*, while CBS gave us our first look at *Gomer Pyle, U.S.M.C., The Munsters,* and *Gilligan's Island*.

ABC had high hopes for *Voyage to the Bottom of the Sea* and gave it a great send-off with many on-air promotions, as well as print ads in newspapers and TV magazines.

The day of the premiere, the NEA (Newspaper Enterprise Association) syndicated column "TV Scout," edited and often written by Joan Crosby, and carried in numerous newspapers throughout the United States and Canada, reported:

> *Voyage to the Bottom of the Sea*, an action-filled series set in 1973 about an atomic-powered, glass-nosed submarine, should delight the youngsters, who aren't overly spoiled on comic books, and adventure-loving adults who haven't read Jules Verne too closely.

Also on September 14, Steven H. Scheuer, for his syndicated preview column, 'TV Key," circulated by King Features Syndicate to as many as 300 newspapers, said:

> Though adults may end up scratching their heads in bewilderment after seeing this, it shapes up as ideal non-provocative entertainment for the kids. Produced in the technique of the early Saturday morning movie serials, this far-fetched, science fiction adventure pits the American supersub "Seaview" against a certain unnamed power headed by the mysterious villain Dr. Gamma (Theodore Marcuse).

On September 15, Cynthia Lowry reviewed "Eleven Days to Zero" for the Associated Press:

> This 60-minute drama was so full of various elements on so many fronts it was pretty hard to follow the plot, if any. There was a super-powerful nuclear submarine and its brave crew on a secret mission to the Arctic to balance with atomic explosions a couple of earthquakes that were going to destroy the Western world. There was also the evil "powerful worldwide force" that wanted the disasters to occur, represented by shadowy bald-headed men with Oriental features. The hostile force – unidentified – kept bombing the submarine and shaking up the crew but didn't seem to hurt things much. There was also an undersea battle between divers and the biggest, phoniest octopus ever seen on the small screen. Small boys of all ages may find it fun.

Lowry also famously panned *A Charlie Brown Christmas* when it premiered on CBS in 1965.

Vince Leonard, the TV critic for *The Pittsburgh Post*, was another Tuesday-morning quarterback. He started:

> Why are the teasers so good and the rest of the hour so mediocre? Again it happened last night, this time on *Voyage to the Bottom of the Sea*, the first of four premieres sent our way by ABC-TV via Channel 4.

Leonard, on the edge of his seat, loved the idea of an innocuous painter spraying a nice, big "X" on the roof of the military car. "Suddenly, like a bolt from the blue, as they say in the funny papers, this helicopter assaults the car like a giant insect attacking its prey The cyclist go over the hillside; so does the car."

But then, for Leonard, the rest of the plot went down too, with "a bored Richard Basehart" … "an apple-green David Hedison" … and a wasted Eddie Albert along for the ride."

> Between nautical clichés like "well done," "mission accomplished," and calling the radio man "sparks" …. [and] a certain fascination it may hold for youngsters, Voyage will be a long, tedious trip for early (7:30) viewers. …

Los Angeles Times critic Don Page was the most vicious *Voyage* gainsayer. The headline for his review in the newspaper's September 15 edition read, "ABC Sinks to New Depths with *Voyage to the Bottom of the Sea*."

> *Voyage* was released Monday night as part of the network's Wide World of Entertainment (slogan for ABC's new season). Well, stop the world, we want to get off. Richard Basehart, an outstanding actor, and David Hedison are co-stars of this disaster and must be secretly cringing at every cliché in the script. … In the premiere episode, "Eleven Days to Zero," guest star Eddie Albert (a seismologist) is assigned to detonate a nuclear device at the North Pole. The explosion will stop a predicted earthquake and tidal wave. (oh brother). Meanwhile, under the seaweed, the crew battles an octopus (giant size) and "opposing powerful world forces" with their torpedoes and bat-winged bomber planes. After a number of "we can't risk the lives of an entire crew for the lives of two men" and "we're under secret orders but

the crew has to know" and other monumental clichés, they set off the bomb and escape Davey Jones. Stay tuned next week folks, because they've got another big squid to fight. The kids will like it. Maybe.

David Hedison's disheartened comment regarding the review: "What can I say? I thought that was obviously the end of the series." (DH-DM13)

They weren't all bad. Bill Summers, writing for the *Orlando Evening Star* on September 15, wrote:

> ABC's new season started last night with *Voyage to the Bottom of the Sea*, an adventure tale that combines the imagination of Jules Verne, the late Ian Fleming (author of James Bond spy stories) and science fiction. It also reminded this writer of the 13-episode serials we watched in the movies 25 years or so ago.
>
> Richard Basehart as Adm. (yes) Nelson and David Hedison (as Cmdr. Lee Crane) are featured in series dealing with missions of atomic-powered submarine Seaview in year 1973.
>
> A group bent on ruling the world provides the conflict. Last night this nefarious crew attempted to stop a Seaview mission to North Pole intended to prevent a world-wrecking tidal wave ....
>
> The enemies used an attack from helicopter on an automobile, undersea sub attack, an aerial depth charge try, and a drone raid from sky, but were naturally unsuccessful.
>
> In addition, Capt. Crane was attacked by a shark and giant squid, something you might expect, but not necessarily in the opening hour. I can scarcely wait to see what sea creature is dished up as an encore.

In the months to come, Summers would be treated to a giant octopus, a giant jellyfish, a giant whale, and a giant stingray, among other giant problems for the crew of the Seaview.

TV syndicated columnist Bob Foster called *Voyage* "a better than average adventure series." For his review, printed in the September 15 edition of the *San Mateo Times*, he added:

It isn't exactly a science-fiction story in the true sense, but it has a bit of the future in it. In fact, what we saw was supposed to have happened about 10 years hence. *Voyage to the Bottom of the Sea* will have its followers, and plenty, too. This is a natural for the older teenagers and the younger "elder citizens" as well, as all those who so enjoyed *Outer Limits* which formally occupied the time slot.

The critic known as "Pit" commented for the September 16 edition of *Variety*:

No question but that triple-credit [writer, director, producer] Irwin Allen has the credentials for all that sci-fi jazz herein abundantly displayed. Expectedly from this cinema craftsman of the Jules Verne genre, all the imposing folderol was in place and slickly mounted – but then virtually squandered by a script that was Saturday serial stuff. For all that, *Voyage* stands a Nielsen chance precisely because of its obvious play-to-the-kids strategy as ABC's Monday night tee-upper. Yet even the kids might get wise to the conning in double-time, and if that happens, the super A-sub Seaview of this 20th-Fox bromide goes down for keeps. The Allen formula calls for paper-mache characterizations, blinking gizmo lights, a sinister unspecified "enemy power" (who's either back-to-camera or faceless in the shadowy light), and frequent cuts of the sub nosing down to ocean bottom.

The same day, "Daku," writing for *Daily Variety*, presented a contrasting view, saying that *Voyage* was:

... a series with a setting fresh to TV, and an actionful, slam-bang show which races along at a sizzling pace. Richard Basehart plays the Admiral with restraint and skill, and is given a good assist by his co-star, David Hedison, as Captain of the sub. ... Technical credits, particularly the camera work and special effects, are top-drawer. There is an exciting fight wherein a helicopter attacks a car; an enemy drone plane attacks the sub; there is an underwater fight with an octopus; and, finally, a walloping finale at the North Pole, where the mission is carried out successfully. With its combined elements of futuristic inventiveness, science, intrigue, suspense, *Sea* is off to an excellent start.

Lawrence Laurent, of *The Arizona Republic*, shared his opinion on September 17:

> *Voyage to the Bottom of the Sea* didn't do much harm to its characters, but the premiere this week left one to wonder, "What next?" The opening episode included just about every hazard a man can encounter on land or sea.
>
> Let's see: there were two earthquakes, one atomic explosion, and a submarine that exploded. There was a giant squid, a bombing by a remote control drone airplane (shot down on its second run), depth charges, and a perilous swim to recover a lost sonar antenna. Then there was a battle between heroes in automobiles and villains in a helicopter. The heroes had to use automatic pistols and the villain had a machine gun. But with one well-aimed shot, the bad guy fell from the skies.
>
> The good guys operate a super atomic submarine for the United Nations. The bad ones are identified as "agents of a certain evil power, the name of whom we all know too well" ... because they have shaved heads, beards and dark clothing. The good ones wear khakis or dungarees and are clean shaven. ...
>
> Still, *Bottom of the Sea* is not a new low for television. It is simply the greatest collection of sure-fire tricks and gimmicks to reach the TV set in this young season. ...
>
> Nearly every 60-minute television series these days needs a father-and-son relationship. Dr. Kildare has Dr. Gillespie. Ben Casey has Dr. Zorba. And the new Lassie has a forest ranger played by Robert Bray.
>
> So it is with *Voyage to the Bottom of the Sea*. The older one is played by Richard Basehart and his character (honestly) is named Adm. Nelson. The younger one is Cdr. Crane, played by David Hedison.
>
> These are chin up, stiff upper lip types who accept hazards and catastrophe as part of any journey. Personal safety is never a concern. "Just look after the enlisted men" and "We dare not fail." ...

Voyage, etc. is out of the television film factory of 20th Century-Fox and it is an expensive show. The price is high for all those visual effects, and the underwater scenes are expensive. Too bad that a little of the budget wasn't saved for a script. The plot and dialogue is exactly what one would expect from wooden men and iron ships.

Terry Vernon said in his "Tele-Vues" column in the September 21 edition of the California *Long Beach Press-Telegram*:

[T]he series has going for it good acting, photography and action. However, the storyline in the opener attempted to encompass too much. As a result, the continuity was ragged. The whole thing just didn't hang together – or maybe it did hang itself. My final impression is that the series should succeed. If it ever finds that missing continuity, it has one big factor to its advantage – it offers lots of action and adventure in a relatively adventureless season.

The reviewer for *Time*, in the magazine's September 25, 1964 issue, was also onboard:

For one hour, on land and at sea, machine guns chattered, torpedoes schlurped through the deep, and missiles sang in the air. *Voyage* is all it tries to be: fast-moving calisthenics for young eyeballs.

As these reviews clearly demonstrate, the fan folklore that *Voyage to the Bottom of the Sea* premiered to mostly negative reviews is clearly not true. But then, folklore – especially when spread across the no-facts-checked internet – can be wildly inaccurate. The contemporary reviews were, in fact, mixed. For every bad one, there was one that was primarily positive. This doesn't mean that Irwin Allen ignored the negative notices.

Allen's television agent, Herman Rush, said, "It was a frustration for him when the critics were negative. The critics were always looking at things like they should be classics; they should be *Playhouse 90*; they should be that type of product. They always were critical of adventure, children's shows, that type of thing. Irwin understood that; he accepted it. It was frustrating, but that was the world he lived in. He paid attention to those reviews. He may have been unhappy with them, but he'd say, 'Maybe they have something here; let's analyze it.' He faced it. A lot of those weekends we spent at his house were reading reviews. He had a clip service that gave him the reviews from all over the country. So he had a lot of local newspaper reviews, as well, not just the national ones from the various TV guides. But what Irwin really respected was Nielsen." (HR-AI15)

This is also what the networks most respected – the TV ratings from A.C. Nielsen.

ABC's premiere of *Voyage to the Bottom of the Sea* was pitted against the CBS one-two punch of *To Tell the Truth* from 7:30 to 8 p.m., followed by *I've Got a Secret*, from 8 to 8:30. This was the fifth year for *To Tell the Truth* in the lead-off Monday-evening position, and it had always been a winner for the network.

Ironically, NBC's Monday Night at the Movies was a repeat showing of Irwin Allen's *The Lost World*, co-starring David Hedison.

Voyage won hands down with a 39.6% audience share, compared to 23.4% for the movie. As for the competition from CBS, the panel shows did not fare well. The previous season, *To Tell the Truth* finished No. 24 out of more than 80 prime-time series. *I've Got a Secret* had placed at No 12. Now, with *Voyage* as their opposition, neither show would make it into the Top 30.

Nielsen ratings report from Sept. 14, 1964: 7:30 – 8 p.m.:	Rating:	Share:
ABC: *Voyage to the Bottom of the Sea*	**22.0**	**39.6%**
CBS: *To Tell the Truth*	14.2	25.6%
NBC: Monday Night Movie: *The Lost World*	13.0	23.4%
8 – 8:30 p.m.		
ABC: *Voyage to the Bottom of the Sea*	**23.2**	**39.0%**
CBS: *I've Got a Secret*	14.1	23.7%
NBC: Monday Night Movie: *The Lost World*	14.8	24.9%

Episode 2: "The Village of Guilt"

(Prod. #7202; first aired Monday, November 2, 1964)
Written by Berne Giler
Directed and produced by Irwin Allen
Story Editor: William Welch; Associate Producer Joseph Gantman
Assistant Story Editor: Al Gail
Guest Star Richard Carlson
Also Starring Anna-Lisa

The ABC-TV press release read:

> Richard Carlson guest stars in this tale of a sea monster that overturns a fishing boat in a Norwegian fjord. When Admiral Nelson and Commander Crane start to investigate, they are blocked by the mysterious death of the sole survivor and by the hostile silence of the villagers.

Here's Allen's one-sentence synopsis of the plot, from his files:

> A scientist's discovery to increase the size of fish for the benefit of mankind is used by his unscrupulous assistant to create a monster which Nelson has to destroy before it destroys the Seaview.

Sound Bites:

Crane: "Sea monsters? Even if I saw one, I wouldn't believe it."

Oskar Dalgren: "But three men dead. They died!" *Lars Mattson*: "Three drunken fishermen going someplace they had no business to go. Is it our fault they ignored our warnings?" *Sigrid*: "The authorities will not look at it that way." *Mattson*: "The authorities will never know." *Sigrid*: "Every fisherman in the village knows." *Mattson*: "They won't talk. We pay them well for their help. They share in the guilt of these deaths." *Sigrid*: "Lars, please…" *Mattson*: "I have done nothing I'm ashamed of!" … *(after their reactions, and a moment of solemn contemplation)* … "We are making a great contribution to science. Are we to throw it away just because of some idiotic accident?"

Assessment:

"The Village of Guilt" makes a fine "guilt"-y pleasure. It has all the ingredients of a splendid 1950s "B" sci-fi movie. Take one mad scientist, a whole bushel of hostile villagers, a giant sea monster, and add a straightforward presentation. As genre writer Mark Phillips noted, you have a concoction which is "dramatic and supersedes the clichés." Icing on the cake: a startling scene in which a school of giant catfish press up against the Seaview nose and gives us a looking-over.

The rousing battle between the sub and the monster – a giant octopus – was too good for television at this time … and wasn't originally intended for TV. It is recycled from the motion-picture version of *Voyage*. But for those who had not seen the movie, it was an unexpected thrill to see in a TV episodic series.

There are moments of surprising humor in this episode, mostly between Nelson, Crane, and, in one scene, between Crane and Morton. These lighter moments spring naturally from the characters, never feeling forced or artificial.

Also effective: the wonderfully calm and understated performances by Richard Carlson and Anna-Lisa, and also from Basehart, Hedison, and Dowdell. They save the dramatics for the big climactic moments, but, until then, are surprisingly subdued for this genre. Some of these effectively understated scenes occur between Basehart and Anna-Lisa in the tavern; between Basehart and Hedison on the shoreline (while under fire); between Carlson and Anna-Lisa during two moments of confrontation, one in which Mattson tries to explain his motives and his lack of guilt; and when Sigrid reveals to him that she knows he has committed murder. The characters are not one-dimensional, like many in horror tales. The villain in this story began his experimentations to increase the size of sea life with the most noble of causes – to feed a hungry world. He is not even aware that somewhere along the way he has changed and become a monster himself – a stereotypical Dr. Frankenstein. Consider how Sigrid grieves over the darkness that has overtaken her husband, withdrawing from him as he attempts to comfort her, and saying that she feels "cold" and is "shriveling inside." It confuses and hurts Mattson to hear this. It's easy to feel empathy for this villain, even when his psychodrama becomes overt. Consider when, with blood on his hands, he tells his wife and her uncle, "This hasn't been easy for me."

Given these less flamboyant touches, you might be surprised that this episode was directed by Irwin Allen. With all we have heard about him – his inability to direct actors and his resistance to dialogue scenes – he seemed to have handled the direction with an assured hand. Some of the later tales from the set – with Basehart storming off the set in frustration at one point – indicate a clumsy and insensitive director. But the end results are what matters, and "Village of Guilt" makes for a worthwhile voyage.

Script:
Berne Giler's writers contract: March 4, 1964.
Giler's story treatment and 1st and 2nd draft teleplays: Dates unknown.
Mimeo Department's reformatted Shooting Final: May 11, 1964.
Revised Shooting Final teleplay (by William Welch or Al Gail): Date unknown.
2nd Rev. Shooting Final by writing staff: June 9.
Page revisions by the staff (pink): June 10.
Page revisions (yellow): June 12.
Added scene (by William Welch or Al Gail): September 21.

Irwin Allen, with the help of William Welch and Al Gail, concocted the springboard for this tale, including it in the Writers Guide. They wrote:

> A thick blanket of fog covers the still waters of a Norwegian fjord when a small excursion boat is suddenly attacked by a mysterious force. Screaming tourists leap into the icy waters as the little steamboat is crushed and sent to the bottom.

It would have made an exciting teaser, but this sort of action was hardly within the budget of a TV series on ABC, which expected each episode to be brought in for under $120,000. A rowboat with three drunken fisherman would be substituted when the script was written – a typical example of the network's expense-versus-drama compromises.

The story springboard continued:

> The sea tragedy makes world headlines when the captain of the lost boat tells a weird tale of having been attacked by a gigantic sea monster. Maritime authorities scoff at

> the story and accuse the captain of inventing it to exonerate himself in the loss of the ship and many of its passengers. He is arrested and charged with the full blame of the catastrophe.
>
> Seaview, on a world cruise, puts into the port of Bergen for supplies and shore leave. A Norwegian girl comes to see Captain Crane and identifies herself as the daughter of the accused captain. She begs to be allowed to tell her story to Admiral Nelson in the hope that, somehow, a way can be found to prove her father's weird story. Although skeptical, Crane brings the girl to Nelson and the Admiral agrees to investigate. If her story of a sea monster should prove true, the scientific data would be invaluable.

This part of the story was not utilized in "The Village of Guilt," but, instead, used to kick off the story for another episode, "City Beneath the Sea."

For "Guilt," freelance writer Berne Giler was put on assignment to spin the initial concept provided by Allen, Welch, and Gail into a story of his own.

Giler was 55. He had worked throughout the 1940s and '50s as a writer of short subjects, and a few screenplays, such as 1949's *C-Man*, a *film noir* starring Dean Jagger and John Carradine, as well as some low-budget Westerns, including 1959's *Westbound*, starring an aging Randolph Scott. In other words, B-flicks. Giler did better in TV, writing for popular anthology series of the 1950s, such as *Playhouse 90* and *Ford Television Theatre*. He then moved into writing for the episodics, especially Westerns, with multiple assignments on *Cheyenne*, *Bronco*, *Lawmen*, and an adventure show starring Preston Foster called *Waterfront*. "Village of Guilt" was the first of two assignments for Giler on *Voyage* (the other was "Hot Line").

Giler, in conference with Allen and Welch, worked out the roadmap for the rest of the teleplay. On May 11, after Dorothy Brown of ABC Continuity Acceptance Department (the network censor) got a look at that script, she wrote to Irwin Allen. Among her "requests" for changes:

> Page 1, Sc 4: Keep scream of terror to living room tolerance. Also, remember time period – so this huge tentacle is not so scary in appearance, the family can't look. ...
>
> Page 2, Sc 8: Here and thru-out the story, be sure the towns and fjord's allll [sic] are fictitious.

Page 3, Sc 8: In deference to cigarette sponsors, caution that Nelson doesn't smoke too many cigars – maybe *none* would be best.

Page 18, Sc 50: Delete the last line of action and dissolve out on the pillow over his face. We do not want to see him struggle as he dies.

Page 20, Sc 57: Close Rolvaag's eyes. No open-eyed dead men on TV please.

Page 20, Sc 59: Caution make-up that this circular welt is not too livid and ugly for family viewing.

Page 35, Sc 107: Clarify it is the "arm of the monster" that was hacked off. If they find an arm, we do not want to think it is a human arm. ...

Page 50, Sc 148: In deference to the mentally ill, try to avoid such words as "nut" and "crazy." Suggest "out of his mind" and "ridiculous" in this instance.

Page 59 and 61, Scenes 174, 176, 183, 185: These scenes can only be approved on film. Don't make them too scary – and be prepared to delete the "BALEFUL EYE" if it's too much of a shock.

The script was toned down in a series of rewrites from William Welch on June 9, 10, 12, and 21. And director Irwin Allen made sure that men always died with their eyes closed.

Production:
(Filmed June 15-24, 1964; 8 days)
(Budget: $132,552)

Joseph Gantman began his work on the series here, as one of two alternating associate producers. This role was known in the TV industry of the day as the "nuts & bolts producer," now more commonly referred to as the "line producer" – the one responsible for taking the finished script and overseeing the physical production. In 1958, Gantman had served a stint as associate producer on the hour-long anthology series *Studio One in Hollywood*. He did likewise for one season (1961-62) on another anthology series, *General Electric Theater*. For the 1963-64 TV season, he worked in the same capacity for the hour-long drama, *Channing*.

As associate producer, Gantman often gave notes on the scripts as they were developed, primarily from a perspective of production. But Welch was in charge of the writing of the scripts, assisted by Irwin Allen's cousin, Al Gail. Gantman, on every other episode (alternating with Associate Producer Allan Balter) had to then find the means of realizing what had been written, which also meant being involved in the casting process.

As of May 14, actors considered for the role of Mattson included James Whitmore, Dan O'Herlihy, Arthur Kennedy, Macdonald Carey, Joseph Cotton, and Richard Carlson.

On May 20, 20th Century-Fox Production Manager Gaston Glass, assigned to oversee *Voyage*, wrote to William Self:

> Dear Bill: After many meetings with Irwin Allen, the attached [budget] is the final outcome and the best we can do with this particular show. Irwin will try his best to save additional money in the casting. Please advise. GG.

This finalized budget meant no Joseph Cotton … or James Whitmore. But they could afford one name from the wish list.

Richard Carlson was 52 when cast as Lars Mattson. He broke through in 1950 as third-billed in the very successful *King Solomon's Mines*, under Deborah Kerr and Stewart Granger. By 1953, he had top billing in sci-fi "classics" such as *It Came from Outer Space*, *The Magnetic Monster*, and 1954's *Creature from the Black Lagoon*. Also beginning in 1953, he was seen regularly on the small screen, as the star of *I Led 3 Lives*, playing Herbert Philbrick (a real-life FBI undercover agent fighting communism in America). After a three-year run, Carlson traded in his contemporary wardrobe for

Richard Carlson in publicity photo for *Creature from the Black Lagoon*.
(Universal International Pictures, 1954)

vintage Western garb for a second series, the 1958-59 *Mackenzie's Raiders*. With two series under his belt, and several feature-film leads, Carlson had earned the billing of TV "guest star."

Among the actresses considered for the part of Sigrid were Antoinette Bower and Mariette Hartley, but, according to memos and "wish lists" from the producers, the favorite throughout the casting process was Anna-Lisa.

Anna-Lisa was 29 when she played Sigrid. She had co-starred (under Peter Breck, later of *The Big Valley*, and Russell Johnson, later of *Gilligan's Island*) in the 1959-60 TV Western *Black Saddle*. And she had worked with the Three Stooges in their 1959 sci-fi comedy *Have Rocket – Will Travel*. But Anna-Lisa was mostly known for her work on stage, and, with that, she could carry the title of "guest star" in television from this era.

The three stars of TV's *Black Saddle* series – Russell Johnson, Peter Breck, and Anna-Lisa.
(Four Star Production, 1959-60)

Anna-Lisa told interviewer Mark Phillips, "I remember this episode was afloat with dark, dramatic events, and that Richard Carlson's character had created some sort of dreadful sea monster. I must admit I found the whole yarn a bit fabricated and I worked extra hard on my character's interpretation to make her believable. But I rather enjoy challenges of those kind.

"Richard Carlson was a charming person, a dream to work with and very supportive. Director Irwin Allen was a soft-spoken, gentle man, and he left us alone to work out our scenes without interference. In the 1960s, there was no time for directors to give actors instructions. It was, 'These are your marks, hit 'em, roll 'em, and action!'" (AL-VTTBOTS)

Many would tell Anna-Lisa that this was how Allen directed his feature films too. But few would have agreed with her observation that he was a "soft-spoken, gentle man." For some reason, this episode contains many surprisingly un-Allenesque moments of calm and sensitivity. Allen didn't seem his typical self.

Ray Didsbury was hired to serve as Richard Basehart's "lighting double." This job also guaranteed him a place among the "background" crew of the Seaview. The two had met on Basehart's last film, 1965's *The Satan Bug* (shot in

1964). Didsbury told Mark Phillips, "I realized if an extra wanted to work five days per week, he would have to become a stand-in. These jobs were difficult to come by. When I had landed a three-day job on *The Satan Bug* as an extra, we were in Palm Springs doing exteriors, and the assistant director, Jack Reddish, asked if I would stand in for Richard. ... The door really swung open for me. During the filming, I had become friendly with Richard Basehart. One day, I spotted a small blurb in *Daily Variety* about a pilot film Dick had shot, which had sold to ABC. I pointed it out to him and he said, 'Oh, that piece of shit.' Being somewhat naïve, I asked him why he was doing it if he felt that way. He just smiled and said, 'Contract.' ...

"Since he didn't have a regular stand-in, I asked him if I could be his on *Voyage*. He said, 'Yes, but how do I go about getting you on?' Knowing how studio politics work, I told him to inform Irwin Allen, in no uncertain terms, that I was to be his stand-in." (RD-FF01)

Basehart exerted the requisite influence on Allen, and Didsbury was hired to serve as Nelson's lighting double. This resulted in Didsbury's appearance in over 100 episodes as one of the seamen. In a short amount of time, he also became the series' dialogue coach. Didsbury explained, "A dialogue coach reads the off-camera lines for actors who might not have a set call that day. It's their job to help actors run lines between takes. *Voyage* didn't have a dialogue coach, and since I knew the show, and was fortunate to be in the right place at the right time, it fell to me." (RD-FF01)

Production began on Monday, June 15, 1964, in and around the 20th Century-Fox backlot "Moat," with the Ext. Seaview deck, and the "Int. Underground Room" set, followed by a mid-day company move to Stage 3, for the "Int. Mattson Lab" set.

Mark Slade recalled, "Richard Basehart was a genuine actor's actor and a pleasure to be around. For some reason we hit it off. He didn't think the

Day 1 of production: Filming the Seaview deck on the Fox backlot Moat.

pilot for *Voyage* would sell and on the first day of filming the series, he said to me, 'My God, it sold!' I think he was secretly pleased that it had." (MS-TVC99)

Allen had the cast on set from 8:30 a.m. to 7 p.m.

Day 2: Tuesday, June 16. Work continued on Stage 3, for "Int. Mattson Lab" from 8:30 a.m. to 7:05 p.m. David Hedison told interviewer William E. Anchors, Jr., "Richard and Irwin had a major fight on the set during the filming of the first season episode 'Village of Guilt.' It wasn't a very good script and Richard didn't like what he was being asked to do. He got so mad he stormed off the set." (DH-S50)

Hedison understood Basehart's disappointment. In a different interview he said, "It was a very difficult thing for Richard, because I think Richard had always done fine films; worked with good directors, for the most part, and suddenly to go into work like this … doing a TV series, and doing it in six days, and working very hard. … So, he walked off the set, which I knew was a dangerous thing to do in Hollywood. He went out the emergency door, and I remember chasing him, calling him, and I opened one door, and then I opened the other inside door where there was a glass thing. But I couldn't open that door, so I pushed it, and broke the glass, and I got this big cut here [on my arm]. And, suddenly, everyone's coming over to me,

Day 1: "Mattson's Underground Room" was filmed on a corner of the Moat. Below: Irwin Allen prepares Richard Carlson for a scene.

because I've got this blood all over the place. And then Richard comes on the set, and he sees what happened, and saw that I was chasing him and trying to get him. And, I don't know, I think that maybe that's what sealed our friendship. I could see the pain that he was going through, and it was terrible." (DH-TCF07)

With their bond struck, Hedison recalled, Basehart "forgot all about leaving and stayed with me until the set

Above: Allen chats with Richard Carlson and Anna-Lisa on the side of the Moat. Below: Another sequence shot on Day 1 – Anna-Lisa at the top of the trap door looking into the "Mattson's Underground Room."

doctor came and stitched me up. It was not fun, but I healed and Richard didn't get fired that day, so I guess it was worth it." (DH-S50)

Day 3: Wednesday, June 17. Irwin Allen filmed from 8:30 a.m. to 5:45 p.m. at Paradise Cove, including "Ext. Beach," "Ext. Shore," exterior shots on Tana Road, the cliff stairs, and, as a set-up for a matte shot, the "Ext. Shore" (village to be matted in later). Any time a TV show went on location, filming with the Main Unit off the studio lot or backlot, the production costs increased significantly. In the initial order of 16 episodes, *Voyage* often went on location. In time, as both money and time became in short supply, it happened less often.

Above: Filming at Paradise Cove on Day 3.
Below: From Day 5, filming on the Observation nose, using the rear projection screen to show cast members exactly what they are reacting to – GIANT CATFISH!

Day 4: Thursday, June 18. They were back on Stage 3, for "Int. Revolving Bedroom," "Ext. Tavern," "Int. Tavern," "Ext. Cottage," and "Int. Cottage." All this, from 8:30 in the morning until 7 p.m.

Day 5: Friday, June 19. A very long day on Stage B, where the Seaview sets had been built. The company filmed in the Observation Nose (including process shots) from 8:30 a.m. to 9:35 p.m. They covered eight and three-eighths pages.

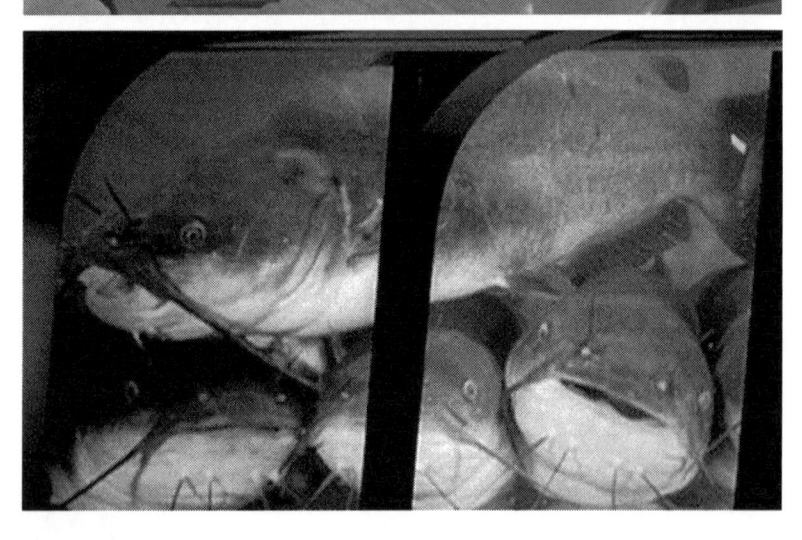

Day 6: Monday, June 22. A worse day, as Allen fell further behind in shooting. They filmed from 8:30 a.m. to 10:15 p.m., covering nine and a half pages on Stage B with scenes in the ship's Control Room, Radio Shack, Missile Room, and the "Fish Tank" where they could do close-ups on the faces of the regular cast members for underwater diving scenes.

The underwater sequences utilized stunt divers, and were handled by a Second Unit team. They filmed in the murky waters off the shore of Santa Catalina, Channel Islands, California, which is a one-hour powerboat ride from Los Angeles's San Pedro Harbor.

Even with a Second Unit team's help, the Main Unit was not able to finish their part of the production within the prerequisite six-day shooting period for one-hour TV episodes.

Day 7: Tuesday, June 23. The company filmed from 8:30 a.m. to 9:15 p.m. on Stage B, and still didn't finish.

Day 8: Because the previous day's filming had extended into a partial night's filming, Allen allowed the exhausted cast and crew to sleep in. The call times were pushed back from 6:30 to 8 a.m.

Day 6: Filming Arch Whiting as "Sparks" in the Radio Hut (above) and Del Monroe and Mark Slade (below) in the Control Room.

They didn't start filming until 9:45 a.m. and worked until 3 p.m. when the next episode, "The Mist of Silence," was finally allowed to start production.

Irwin Allen had planned to direct one out of every three episodes. But, after failing to complete a one-hour episode of his own series in the allotted six days, he limited his directing to pilot episodes and feature films. Richard Basehart and David Hedison no doubt breathed a sigh of relief.

After filming was complete, Paul Sawtell was paid $1,500 to compose the score; recording commenced on July 22, 1964.

The production cost ended up being on the high end of what ABC and 20th Century-Fox wanted to spend, adding up to $132,552. That equates to $1 million and change in 2018. By industry standards, even this would be considered cheap. The average one-hour TV episode of the present day costs $3 million or more.

Cynthia Lowry, in an Associated Press wire story, published in the *Warren Times-Mirror* on September 15, 1964, wrote:

> Irwin Allen, the series' producer, originally dreamed up, produced and directed the adventure story as a movie. Even then he realized its potential as a TV series and squirreled away the elaborate submarine sets which he said cost over $500,000. It would have been economically impossible to make the current series without them. With all the special photography, each episode still costs around $150,000 to turn out, says Allen.

ABC was shown a rough cut on October 13. The final Air Print was screened for the network on October 20th, and on the air less than two weeks later.

Release / Reaction:
(ABC premiere broadcast: 11/2/64; network repeat airing: 5/17/65)

"Baby Love" by the Supremes was getting more spins on DJ's turntables than any other song on U.S. Top 40 radio. It would stay that way for four weeks, with former champ "Do Wah Diddy Diddy," by English band Manfred Mann, now in second position. While the kids stayed home to watch *Voyage*, some of their folks and older siblings were off to the movies, making *The Naked Kiss* the top grosser in the nation. It didn't have any big Hollywood stars (Constance Towers had the lead), but it did have a sordid poster and the come-on line, "SHOCK and SHAME STORY of a NIGHT GIRL!" You could get a ticket to see it for a buck. And the adults could smoke in the movie houses, which 60% of the population in 1964 did, with a pack of cigarettes costing $1.60. The day after this episode aired, President Lyndon B. Johnson defeated Republican Senator Barry Goldwater and won his first full term in office.

Although "Village of Guilt" was the second episode filmed (the first to follow the pilot), and the only other episode of the series besides the pilot directed by Irwin Allen, it was pushed back to be the eighth to air.

In the syndicated "TV Scout," Joan Crosby said:

> *Voyage to the Bottom of the Sea*, with its nuclear submarine Seaview, is involved in another make-believe episode in "The Village of Guilt." The crew tonight (headed by Richard Basehart and David Hedison) visit a tavern, have a glass of good Norwegian beer and talk of monsters of the deep. It appears Norway's fjords are

plagued by watery creatures so big they can turn over fishing boats with a flip of a fin. Richard Carlson and Anna-Lisa are involved in the make-believe outing.

New on NBC was *90 Bristol Court*, a 90-minute block of three sitcoms linked together because the principal characters of each series lived in the same apartment complex. The first of the two to go head-to-head against *Voyage* were *Karen*, starring Karen Valentine and Denver Pyle. From 8 to 8:30 was *Harris Against the World*, starring Jack Klugman (still several years away from becoming a household name as Oscar Madison through the success of *The Odd Couple* series, and later, as *Quincy, M.E.*) as the plant superintendent of a large movie studio.

The A.C. Nielsen ratings report for November 2, 1964 named *Voyage* the champ by a mile, with the following numbers:

Nielsen ratings report from Nov. 2, 1964:	Rating:	Share:
7:30 – 8 p.m.:		
ABC: *Voyage to the Bottom of the Sea*	**22.0**	**35.4%**
CBS: *To Tell the Truth*	14.4	27.9%
NBC: *90 Bristol Court: Karen*	14.3	22.7%
8 – 8:30 p.m.		
ABC: *Voyage to the Bottom of the Sea*	**25.4**	**42.7%**
CBS: News special on President Johnson	11.0	17.7%
NBC: *90 Bristol Court: Harris Against the World*	15.3	23.3%

A more detailed report conducted by Nielsen (a result of a broader survey), covering the first week of November, was published in the November 30 issue of *Broadcasting*. It put *Voyage* inside the National Top 20 prime-time TV programs. The shows were ranked as follows:

Program/Network:	Rating:
Bonanza (NBC)	35.2
Bewitched (ABC)	31.2
The Ed Sullivan Show (CBS)	28.7
The Red Skelton Show (CBS)	27.0
The Dick Van Dyke Show (CBS)	26.1
Peyton Place (Thursday) (ABC)	26.0
The Virginian (NBC)	25.6
The Andy Griffith Show (CBS)	25.4
The Addams Family (ABC)	25.1
The Munsters (CBS)	25.1
The Beverly Hillbillies (CBS)	25.0
Petticoat Junction (CBS)	25.0

My Favorite Martian (CBS)	24.9
Gomer Pyle, U.S.M.C. (CBS)	24.9
Peyton Place (Tuesday) (ABC)	24.7
Combat! (ABC)	24.6
***Voyage to the Bottom of the Sea* (ABC)**	**24.5**
The Fugitive (ABC)	24.5
McHale's Navy (ABC)	24.1

Despite being pushed back from the second episode filmed to the eighth to air, "Village of Guilt" was nonetheless given a repeat broadcast by ABC. Irwin Allen felt little guilt in making sure that "Guilt" was one of the 19 that repeated. As director of this episode, he was entitled to a residual check when it aired again on the network.

Episode 3: "The Mist of Silence"

(Prod. #7203; first aired Monday, October 5, 1964)
Written by John McGreevey
Directed by Leonard Horn
Produced by Irwin Allen
Story Editor: William Welch; Associate Producer Allan Balter
Assistant Story Editor Al Gail
Guest Star Rita Gam
Guest Star Alejandro Rey
(with Edward Colmans, Henry Delgado, and Mike Kellin as "Steban")

From the October 4, 1964 edition of *The Cullman Times* in Cullman, Alabama, by TV Editor Bill Shelton:

> Drama and action both are intermingled on the *Voyage to the Bottom of the Sea*... as the Seaview atomic submarine goes in search of a ship with a Latin-American President aboard. Upon its destination, the Seaview finds the ship empty.

The authorized synopsis in Irwin Allen's Papers Collection put it this way:

255

The President of a recently liberated South American country, held prisoner by dissident generals, appeals to the U.S. for aid. The Seaview has secret orders to bring him to this country. Crane and several seamen are captured while trying to rescue the President. All are to be shot. ...

Sound Bites:

General Steban: "Now, how about Señor Presidente?" *Captain Serra:* "Resting quietly." *Oriental Colonel:* "And will be for several hours." *Steban:* "Apparently the lithium gas is as effective as you predicted, Colonel. Thanks to your country's generosity, we have the weapon of tomorrow ... today."

Crane (waking up after being gassed): "Oh ... what a headache." *Kowalski (suffering):* "I have the world's worst hangover ... and I haven't even had a drink." *Farrell:* "What was that fog, sir?" *Crane:* "Some kind of new nerve gas, I guess."

Steban (to Seaview captives): "To celebrate the first anniversary of our liberation, I promised that every hour one traitor will die, from now until midnight tomorrow. Names are being drawn by lot from the condemned men here. Your four names are already included and will remain so until you advise me that you are ready to make the public confession of your guilt."

Assessment:

William E. Anchors and Frederick Barr, writers of *SEAVIEW: A 50th Anniversary Tribute to Voyage to the Bottom of the Sea*, said in their book, "This was the first and one of the best of the *Voyage* political thrillers: intense, grim, raw, shocking in its portrayal of evil; a stark choice for the Captain – a marvelous episode."

"The Mist of Silence" would have made a good *Mission: Impossible*, with emphasis on action, adventure, and espionage. In other words, "Mist" contained much of what the Series Bible called for at this early period of the show's history. But there certainly is little of that other element mentioned in the Bible – a dash of science-fiction flavoring in the mix. The only thing remotely close to a sci-fi element, besides the Seaview, is the titular mist which works like a knockout gas.

Alejandro Rey is featured well as Ricardo, the patriot determined to eliminate his former leader. Mike Kellin is wonderfully sleazy as the corrupt General Steban, with his oily hair and pencil-thin mustache. Kellin's acting choices, such as Steban's slothy posture, swagger, sadistic glee, and hedonistic mannerisms (as he munches food with smacking lips and sucks at his greasy fingertips) combine to deliver a mega creep-out factor. And Joe E. Tata, as Farrell, one of the Seaview crewmembers held captive, is electrifying in the scene in which his character is dragged off to be executed.

There are many excellent moments for Del Monroe (Kowalski), Paul Trinka (Patterson), and, especially, David Hedison, as they are imprisoned and awaiting execution. Richard Basehart gets to go into a covert operation, and charges in like the cavalry. But it is Rey's character, and that of Kellin, who drive the story.

Script:
John McGreevey's writers contract: March 25, 1964.
McGreevey's treatment and 1st and 2nd draft scripts: Dates unknown.
Mimeo Department's reformatted Shooting Final teleplay: May 20.
Revised Shooting Final teleplay (by William Welch or Al Gail): Date Unknown.
2nd Rev. Shooting Final teleplay by the writing staff (blue pages): June 11.
Page revisions by the staff (pink paper): June 22.

John McGreevey provided the script. He was 41, and a former writer of pulp science fiction, including short subjects for *Amazing Stories*, *Fantastic Stories*, *Weird Stories*, and *SF Quarterly*. McGreevey was also a prolific writer in television, having cut his teeth on such 1950s prestige anthology series as *Studio 57*, *Schlitz Playhouse*, *General Electric Theater*, and *Climax!* He wrote for many TV Westerns, such as *Zane Grey Theater*, *Bat Masterson* and, with 12 episodes, *Wagon Train*, and was co-creator of a Western, *Black Saddle*, starring Peter Breck and Russell Johnson. In the field of TV comedy, he had just been nominated for an Emmy Award for co-writing an episode of *The Farmer's Daughter*, and was in the middle of writing a hefty load of 35 episodes for *My Three Sons*. Later in his career, McGreevey would win an Emmy for one of the 20 scripts he wrote for *The Waltons*. But he only worked once for Irwin Allen … and this was it.

McGreevey pitched the story to William Welch, and later told *Starlog* writer Mark Phillips, "One of the most famous stories in sea-going life was the Marie Celeste [1872]. They found food cooking and everything in order, but nobody was aboard. They never figured out what happened to those people. Could they have been carried off to another planet? It's possible. So I said, 'What if Seaview found, in contemporary terms, a ship like the Marie Celeste? That was the springboard for 'The Mist of Silence.' I was thinking purely in terms of a SF approach. The Latin American plot wasn't a part of it." (JM-SL92)

One reason for the ship's fame is the 1884 story, "J. Habakuk Jephson's Statement," by Arthur Conan Doyle. In his fictional attempt to explain the mystery, Doyle changed the brig's actual name from Mary Celeste to Marie Celeste.

McGreevey clearly knew the tale of the Mary Celeste well, but he did not bring this mysterious element of the story to *Voyage*. The idea had already been included in the Series Writers Guide. That version read:

> In the eerie half light of dawn, Seaview lookouts sound an alarm. A freighter in the mist, speeding toward the surfaced sub on collision course. Quick action by Crane avoids disaster. When the freighter fails to answer, the Captain orders a boarding party to investigate. They are astonished to discover the freighter is completely deserted: There is no evidence of a struggle. Food is cooking in the galley and everything is normal ... except that there is no sign whatever of life! In the ship's log, a last entry reads: "Entered small patch of fog, Expect..."
>
> Chip Morton, Seaview's Exec, is put in command of a prize crew to take the freighter to port on the larger of a nearby Fuji islands while the submarine searches for survivors. Hours later, the freighter's radio abruptly goes dead and all contact is lost. Crane, aboard the Seaview, orders full speed pursuit of the mystery vessel. Overtaking the ship, they are amazed to find it again deserted. Chip Morton and his crew have vanished!

The person behind the disappearances, and the mist, is the intended series villain Dr. Gamma. But this part of the story was dropped. The mist of the episode's title and the drifting ship were inserted into McGreevey's tale. McGreevey's story is a good one, but it is a shame that this tale of people vanishing from boats into a mysterious mist didn't reach its original potential as the core of its own episode. That would have been a "mist-erious" voyage worth taking!

Of the episode that transpired, McGreevey said, "The story was based loosely on the events in El Salvador. It was a look at a military-dominated, oppressive, fascist government. Obviously, the story is saying that democracy will overcome, even though it will demand heavy sacrifices. The people, in the long run, won't be held down by tyrants like Esteban, Adolph Hitler or Joseph Stalin." (JM-SL93)

The episode is effective in many ways, with some gripping scenes in which Captain Crane decides to allow the execution of one or more crewmembers, rather than divulge classified information. But it is very atypical for *Voyage*. McGreevey said, "They hadn't decided on what direction the show was going in and, as a result, I wasn't locked into any specific formula. Irwin was quite concerned about the Seaview's lack of involvement in 'The Mist of Silence.' This was, after all, a voyage to the bottom of the sea and we were spending our time in the middle of some South American country! [But] the Seaview wasn't that important to the story, and I felt it was very claustrophobic to spend most of your time on a sub." (JM-SL92)

McGreevey was not bending the format. The Series Bible had told him that *Voyage* was "not a submarine series," and that, "In the vast majority of stories, the sub is merely a conveyance to get our principals to the scene of the action."

McGreevey appreciated the support of Story Editor William Welch, saying, "Bill was a very literate, well-read man and a good story editor. He was very specific in his criticisms, and that's a blessing for a writer. He really wanted to help you improve your script. He wasn't out to impose his ideas [just] because he had some authority." (JM-SL92)

After McGreevey delivered his second-draft teleplay, William Welch took over. There were notes from ABC to address.

Dorothy Brown, Director of the network's Continuity Acceptance Department, wrote to Irwin Allen on May 21, saying:

> To assure the viewing audience that this [is] completely fictional, there must be no alluding to the Cuban affair. This would include likenesses of character, names and accents, uniforms, flags and bunting, insignia, etc. With that thought in mind the remaining minor modifications are necessary:
>
> Page 5, Sc 26: There must be no visual or audio reference identifying any member of the CONFERENCE TABLE as a "State Department" man or "CIA" man.
>
> Page 26, Sc 91: Line STEBAN "...paralyze a city as large as Miami". Please substitute any other city of equal size – but not in the state of Florida.
>
> Page 27, Sc 91: I think you know of our policy, re: hyp [sic] needles – no insertions on camera. Either keep it below camera frame level or block with body shots.
>
> Page 42, Sc 133: RICARDO knifes DRIVER. Again out of camera frame or block with body shot. Same for Page 58, Sc 209 – and do not play the "spins slowly around" for shock or horror.

The episode would have shocks enough, courtesy of the Seaview men's captivity and possible execution by firing squad.

Production:
(Filmed June 24 through July 3, 1964; 7½ days)
(Budget: $133,316)

This was the first episode made under the supervision of alternating associate producer Allan Balter. While Joseph Gantman was serving as line producer on his first episode, "The Village of Guilt," Balter had between six and seven days to prepare "The Mist of Silence" for the camera. Then, during the six- to seven-day period in which Balter was involved in the filming of "Mist," Gantman was prepping the next to come down the chute (in this case, "The City Beneath the Sea"). It made for an efficient operation – much needed in this process of turning out what was, in a sense, half a science fiction movie a week.

Balter didn't have the experience that Gantman did, having only worked as an associate producer in 1963 on *Stoney Burke* (the series which featured Robert Dowdell in the cast). But he had been involved with a few other series – as a writer – including one science fiction – *The Outer Limits*, for which he wrote two episodes. This last job had given him an appreciation for the demands in production for a science-fiction show. Balter also had a training period, observing and assisting Gantman during the prep for "The Village of Guilt." Now he would be tested in action. He soon learned that being the on-set producer for a science-fiction series is akin to going into combat.

Leonard Horn, who also directed the upcoming episode, "The Fear-Makers," began his work on *Voyage* here. Despite his good work, it was somewhat surprising that Irwin Allen asked Horn back. This episode was far more edgy than most Allen fare.

Alejandro Rey was 34 when he appeared as Ricardo Galdez. He made over 100 appearances in TV and films between 1953 and 1986, appearing more than once on series such as *Thriller*, *The FBI*, *That Girl*, and *Gunsmoke*. He is best known for his featured role in *The Flying Nun*, as Carlos Ramirez.

Rita Gam was 32 when cast as Detta Casone. She had won the Golden Globe award as Most Promising Newcomer for the 1952 film *The Thief*. One year after that she was the title character in *Saadia*. In 1956, she had the top female role in

Alejandro Rey, from one of his 75 episodes of *The Flying Nun*, with Sally Field. (Screen Gems Television, 1967-70)

Mohawk, a movie that did respectable business upon its release. In 1962, she won as Best Actress in the Berlin International Film Festival, for performances in *No Exit* and *Sinners Go to Hell*.

Writer John McGreevey was impressed by Gam's performance: "Usually, women of that TV era were there to look pretty and ensure a few female viewers. They were often the romantic interest, but they were rarely the motivators or activators. But from the very first draft, Detta was a strong woman." (JM-SL92)

Mike Kellin played General Esteban d'Alvarez. He was 42 and had been busy in front of the camera since 1950, including playing Chief Petty Officer Willie Miller in the 1960 film *The Wackiest Ship in the Army* (starring Jack Lemmon and Ricky Nelson). He returned to that role for the 1965-66 TV series of the same title, under skipper Jack Warden. Kellin did submarine duty on *The Twilight Zone* for the gripping episode, "The Thirty-Fathom Grave," and had a horrific death scene in the 1962 Steve McQueen movie, *Hell Is for Heroes*. Irwin Allen liked Kellin enough in *Voyage* to bring him back for the lead guest-star role in "The Deadly Games of Gamma 6," a 1966 episode of *Lost in Space*.

Edward Colmans played President Alejandro Fuentes. He

Above: Rita Gam, pinup girl, circa mid-1950s. Below: Mike Kellin in a 1966 episode of *Lost in Space*.

was 55, and appeared in more than 150 movies and TV episodes during the 1950s, '60s and '70s.

Joe E. Tata played Farrell, the Seaview crew member who is executed by firing squad. Director Leonard Horn recommended Tata after giving him direction in two episodes of *The Outer Limits* ("The Zanti Misfits" and "The Children of Spider County"). Tata was 27, and early in a career that included 238 episodes of *Beverly Hills, 90210*, as Nat Bussichio. Tata said, "Irwin was a tough S.O.B. but I got along with him fine. During *Voyage* I was also in a TV series called *No Time for Sergeants*. Irwin joked, 'So, you've got your own TV series now, Tata? You're a big shot, huh?' I never had an intimidation from him, but 99 percent of other people did because Irwin was loud and he ruled. Nothing escaped his attention. [But] I loved working with him." (JT-TVC99)

Above: Joe E. Tata in "The Zanti Misfits," an episode of *The Outer Limits*. (United Artists Television, 1963)
Below: Henry Darrow as Monolito Montoya in 97 episodes of *High Chaparral*. (NBC Productions, 1967-71)

Allen brought Tata back for two more episodes of *Voyage* (as different characters, obviously), as well as five episodes of *Lost in Space* (usually in voiceover only), and trips into *The Time Tunnel*, playing Napoleon Bonaparte in one ("Reign of Terror"). Concerning "Mist of Silence," Tata said, "From a writing standpoint, that was my favorite episode. There wasn't an ounce of camp in that show. It was a great script; very serious, very adult and exciting. That entire first year of *Voyage* was very serious." (JT-TVC99)

Henry Darrow, billed here as Henry Delgado, played Captain Serra. He was 30 and a prolific actor with hundreds of credits in television and films. Darrow was a regular on the late 1960s TV Western, *The High Chaparral*, as Manolito Montoya.

Darrow told Mark Phillips, "It was a fun show to work on and a real treat to work with Richard Basehart. I had seen a lot of his work and he was a fine actor. Rita Gam was rather different, a very exotic lady, and Alejandro Rey was fun and energetic. … Mike Kellin was a solid actor. We joked that here he was, a New York-accented actor, playing a Latino dictator. Joey Tata is a great guy."
(HD-VTTBOTS)

Paul Zastupnevich, the costume designer on *Voyage* and all-trades assistant to Irwin Allen, appeared briefly as one of the villagers.

Production began on Wednesday, June 24 on the home base of Fox Stage B, for filming in the Control Room, the Admiral's Cabin, and then the Ext. Flying Bridge of the Seaview, against a screen allowing for a process shot.

Day 2: Thursday. They were on location at Paradise Cove, Malibu, filming the Ext. Pier and Shore Road, the Cliffs and Shore, the Shore Top, and the Jungle Road. The company arrived at 6:30 a.m. The camera began rolling a little after 8:30 in the morning and they finished at 7:40 p.m.

Days 3 and 4: Friday and Monday. The company took over Fox Soundstage 5 for two days, beginning with the sets for Int. D'Alvarez Office, Int. Large Cell, and Int. Jail Corridors.

Joe Tata recalled, "The magnificent jail cells in 'Mist of Silence' were

Day 3: "Int. D'Alvarez's Office," with Henry Darrow watching in guarded disgust as Mike Kellin sucks his fingertips while eating, and contemplating torture and murder.

263

Days 3 and 4: The gripping jailhouse scene, with a delightfully slimy Mike Kellin (above), and an intensely dramatic performance by Joe E. Tata (below).

from a film called *The Reward*, with Efrem Zimbalist, Jr. There was no way we could have built those sets on a TV budget." (JT-TVC99)

The prison scene, featuring excellent acting by Tata in particular, was filmed on this day. *Voyage* was often dismissed as a kids show, but this scene is as gripping and adult as anything on television during this period. Tata recalled, "Lenny Horn directed that episode. Lenny was a terrific guy, but very driven and competitive. It was that sense of angst that killed him at such a young age [in 1975]. He was a great dramatic director. He whispered to me, 'Joey, we're really going to go to town with your death scene.' He explained to me how this bad-ass general, played by Mike Kellin, has me dragged from a jail cell and shot. Lenny said, 'When the guards grab you, fight them for real.' And so I screamed and yelled and kicked. After it was over, there was dead silence from everyone. They were in shock. A couple of the crew got upset. One of them took Lenny aside and said, 'Leonard, are you crazy? Irwin will never allow this to go in.' He did, but the scene was so disturbing that it was almost cut out during editing." (JT-TVC99)

Tata added, "After it was all over, Del Monroe [Kowalski] said, 'Holy shit, Joey ... I got a terrible feeling watching that." (JT-SCTS2)

Also, on Monday, they filmed on the sets identified as Int. Presidential Bedroom and the Hall Outside Bedroom.

Day 5: Tuesday. The company filmed outdoors all day, beginning on the lot for the Ext. Presidential Courtyard, then moving to the Moat on the backlot for Ext. Banyon Cove and Ext. Jungle Edge. The last shot was taken at 7:20 p.m. while the summer sun was still high enough in the sky to provide daylight. The extending shadows were fought back with carbon arc lights – high-intensity bulbs designed for TV and film, so powerful that they had been known to cause temporary blindness.

Day 6: Wednesday. More production in and around the Moat, and then onto the Olympic Boulevard Bridge. Again, the company filmed right up to the loss of daylight at 7:25 p.m. They knew going into this day's filming that Leonard Horn would not finish within his six-day schedule. Waiting director John Brahm was told to stand down until Friday before beginning his episode, "The City Beneath the Sea."

Day 7, Basehart with Alejandro Rey and Rita Gam on the "Int. Cabin La Libertad" set.

Day 7: Thursday. Back on the controlled environment of Stage B, for a sequence identified as "Int. Cabin La Libertad." Camera rolled until 7:30 p.m.

Leonard Horn almost finished, the next episode on the production schedule was pushed back again, this time until a late-morning start on Friday.

Day 8: Friday, July 3. Horn got his last shots between 8:30 and 10:45 a.m., finishing one day and four hours behind schedule, and finally making way for director John Brahm to take over the company and break ground on "The City Beneath the Sea."

Del Monroe said, "I thought we got some of our best scripts in the first year. The story I heard was that when Richard Basehart was first contacted about the series, Irwin Allen described it originally as an action/adventure-type show and we were going to be involved in different political uprisings wherever around the world – The Bay of Pigs – wherever. And then we'd use the Seaview as the means to get from one destination to another. But, there again, cost was one of the issues and when we were off-set, it cost more money. So, as time went on, we spent more time on-set." (DM-SE98)

From the déjà-vu department: To save money, some recycled footage was cut into this episode, most notably the bomber dropping depth-charges on the Seaview. It was lifted from "Eleven Days to Zero."

Release / Reaction:
(Only ABC broadcast: 10/5/64)

"Oh, Pretty Woman," by Roy Orbison, was the song getting the most plays on the radio. Richard Widmark's Western *Cheyenne Autumn* was tops in the movie houses. And many potential TV viewers in Louisiana, Mississippi, and Georgia were preoccupied, as Hurricane Hilda slammed the coast, resulting in power outages and 38 deaths.

Writer John McGreevey, safely watching TV in Los Angeles, was happy with his one *Voyage to the Bottom of the Sea*. He said, "I was pleasantly surprised. I thought it was unusual for series television, for Detta, Ricardo and Esteban to have the dimension they did. Part of that was because Gam, Rey and Kellin were excellent. Since the story was so concentrated on those characters, it was effective. Alejandro Rey, poor man, later ended up as a regular on *The Flying Nun*. I wrote several of those and he said that 'The Mist of Silence' gave him a rare opportunity to play a character that had some substance. Mike Kellin did a very good job as Esteban. ... Mike had a great time doing that role. He was totally despicable, yet quite creditable. Mike conveyed what made the character tick. You understand his motivation."

McGreevey was less impressed with the series star. "Basehart was the least convincing. He looked like he wished he were somewhere else, and probably did. As I recall, he wasn't terribly happy about doing *Voyage*. I had the feeling he was slumming. I didn't feel that way about Hedison. The irony is that Basehart was a much finer actor, but Hedison brought lots of credibility to those scenes in the cell." (JM-SL92)

"TV Scout" said, in the October 5th edition of Texas's *San Antonio Express*:

> *Voyage to the Bottom of the Sea* has Admiral Nelson (Richard Basehart) and commander Crane (David Hedison) taking the Seaview south on a rescue mission. The man they want to bring back alive is Edward Colmans, a Latin-American president, who is under fire by dictator Mike Kellin, who wants to blot him out. The S.O.S. is brightened somewhat by the presence of Rita Gam.

The syndicated "TV Key," in the October 5, 1964 edition of Arizona's *Tucson Daily Citizen*, among other newspapers, said:

> Remembering that this series is strictly for adventure-minded kids, tonight's episode should keep them on the edge of their seats. Once again gas is used against the valiant crew of the Seaview [as in the previous week's "The Fear-Makers"], but, this time, not aboard the sub. Most of the action takes place in another of those Red revolution-dominated Latin-American dictatorships and involves the attempted rescue of the leader of the revolt, now a prisoner.

A.C. Nielsen, the leading nose-counter of TV viewers, gave *Voyage* a "thumbs up." For the week ending October 11, 1964, *Voyage* was floating high at No. 22 (of more than 80 prime-time series) in the national ratings. It was the eighth best-rated new series, under *Bewitched*; *Gomer Pyle, U.S.M.C.*; *The Addams Family*; *The Munsters*; *No Time for Sergeants*; *Peyton Place*; and *Flipper*, but placing above other newcomers such as *Daniel Boone* and *Gilligan's Island*.

Nielsen ratings report from Oct. 5, 1964: 7:30 – 8 p.m.:	Rating:	Share:
ABC: *Voyage to the Bottom of the Sea*	**20.7**	**32.6%**
CBS: *To Tell the Truth*	12.7	20.0%
NBC: *90 Bristol Court: Karen*	19.5	30.7%
8 – 8:30 p.m.		
ABC: *Voyage to the Bottom of the Sea*	**22.2**	**32.6%**
CBS: *I've Got a Secret*	15.5	22.8%
NBC: *90 Bristol Court: Harris Against the World*	19.9	29.2%

Despite getting a nod from the writer, and the indisputably tense scenes involving Captain Crane and his men sitting on death row, "The Mist of Silence" was pushed back (just slightly) from the third episode made to the fourth to air; it was not given a network repeat. Even though McGreevey went by the Series Bible in choosing to stage all the action off the Seaview, and involving non-regular characters as leads, by the time all the first-run episodes had aired, the direction for the series had shifted. Stories of this type were more likely to be passed over.

Episode 4: "The City Beneath the Sea"
(Prod. #7204; first aired Monday, September 21, 1964)
Written by Richard Landau
Directed by John Brahm
Produced by Irwin Allen
Story Editor: William Welch; Associate Producer: Joseph Gantman
Assistant Story Editor: Al Gail
Guest Star Hurd Hatfield
Co-Starring Linda Cristal

From the *Voyage to the Bottom of the Sea* show files (Irwin Allen Papers Collection):

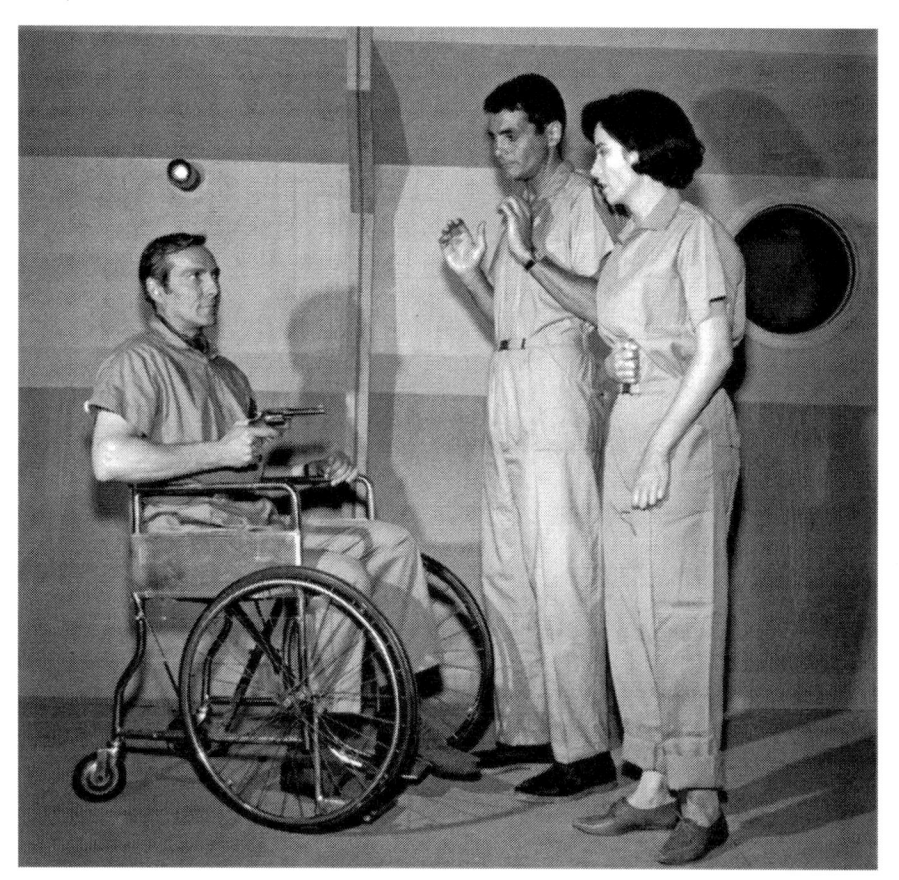

A power-hungry despot has built himself a kingdom under the sea and plans to make himself master of the riches of the oceans. Boats and divers, accidentally stumbling on his secret, are ruthlessly eliminated. Crane, attempting to solve the mystery, finds himself imprisoned in a fantastic underwater city while Nelson, looking for him in the Seaview, unknowingly approaches the undersea citadel and narrowly escapes destruction.

Sound Bites:

Nelson (undercover; to Melina): "Name: Harriman Jones. Occupation: Lee Glenn's friend, enemy, partner, rival, big brother, blood brother, and sometimes I'd like to bash his head in."

Leopold Zeraff (after greeting Crane in the underwater city): "I was beginning to enjoy our little game; I was beginning to like you. You have a strong character." *Crane (enraged):* "And you have a nice bit of antiquity down here. Relics everywhere you look – storage tanks of explosives; ski sleds; underwater missile pad; wall-to-wall push-buttons. What are you trying to do anyway, take over the world!" *Zeraff:* "*This* is my world. I explored it and I built it at the bottom of the sea. Man has decided to conquer outer space, Captain. Here, in this inner space, I am building a new world."

Zeraff (after Crane's escape attempt): "Don't try your luck again, Captain." *Crane:* "And suppose I do?" *Zeraff:* "Alright. There's a deep trench at the edge of the city. It goes into frigid cold, utter blackness. I have often gone diving into that trench to observe the various species of marine life. Some of the tragedies that take place there are unbelievable. Do you know what happens to a fish that makes an effort to rise to a level that is higher than its evolutional depth? It's like tearing lose from gravity. There's nothing to stop it. It literally dies falling upwards; it explodes. The lower depths; the pressures of the sea respect neither fish nor human beings. ... *(noting alarmed reacts from Crane and Melina)* ... I must persuade you to see my point of view. I hope I don't have to demonstrate with the young lady. It would be a pity."

Assessment:

The series hadn't yet settled on its formula. It was clear *Voyage* would be action-adventure with an underwater setting. But would the main emphasis be on James Bond-inspired espionage ... or mystery ... or science fiction? And how, if at all, would romance fit in?

The first few episodes produced were all over the map. Despite the dramatic intensity of "The Village of Guilt" and "The Mist of Silence," both Irwin Allen and ABC felt that "The City Beneath the Sea," with its mix of action-adventure, mystery, science fiction, and even a brief flirtation with a member of the opposite sex, seemed to fit the bill for what the pilot episode had established – what the network promotions were promising.

Overall, "The City Beneath the Sea" is a fair hour of entertainment, although uneven and at times awkwardly paced. The covert excursion by Captain

Crane to the Greek islands, passing himself off as a deep-sea diver seeking employment and adventure, is hardly realized. Many parts of this sequence, and its characters, are underutilized and therefore ineffective. These are the moments within the story that drag the most … along with one too many underwater fight sequences in the murky waters, where it is not always clear who is fighting whom.

Hurd Hatfield is wasted as the villain of the story, Leopold Zeraff. It's a shallow and undefined role, not only poorly drawn but lacking any real menace. Does his being in a wheelchair advance the character or the story? It certainly detracts from the believability in the underwater fight scene that does the character in. Further, what exactly is Zeraff looking to accomplish with his city beneath the sea, which he says is to serve as the prototype for an underwater kingdom? There's no explanation of how this will help him conquer the land.

Another missed moment is that the antagonist dies in an underwater struggle with Captain Crane. Underneath the obstructive scuba mask, Zeraff's face is a cipher. A better ending might have featured Zeraff waiting, impotent, in his control room, as Seaview's torpedoes approach. How would the villain face the inescapable destruction of his city and himself?

The assets and liabilities of this episode very nearly cancel one another out. The technicians did their job, with the underwater city under attack, and one domed structure after another imploding. The actors, struggling with some remarkably bad dialogue and rushed direction, fluctuate from good to poor. The scenes in the Seaview work, as do those filmed in the Greek village hotel and in Zeraff's home. But nearly everything filmed in the underwater facility is horrid. Also poorly executed are the underwater scenes filmed off the coast of Catalina Island. The stunt director/camera operator and the diver playing Zeraff must have been out of the loop regarding the rewriting of the script. The stunt diver makes the mistake of using his legs to swim, and the director lets him. But how could this be? Zeraff, for whatever reason in the minds of Irwin Allen and script editor William Welch, is paralyzed from the waist down. Here is the greatest fumble in an episode which drowns in mediocrity.

Script:
Richard Landau's contract: March 3, 1964.
Landau's treatment and 1st and 2nd draft scripts: Dates unknown.
Mimeo Department's reformatted Shooting Final teleplay: Date unknown.
Revised Shooting Final teleplay (by William Welch or Al Gail): Date unknown.
2nd Rev. Shooting Final by writing staff (yellow pages): June 17.
Page revisions by the staff (blue): June 23.
Page revisions (pink): July 2.
Page revisions (gold): July 7.
Page revisions (beige): July 8.

Irwin Allen and William Welch came up with the title and springboard for this episode. It is unclear how much of the story was originally by Allen, and how much came from Welch's pen. Here's how it was summarized in the Series Bible:

> The warped genius of Dr. Gamma has conceived the most outlandish extortion plot in history. He flatly warns all nations that henceforth any ship using the Strait of Gibraltar between the Atlantic and the Mediterranean must pay a tribute – or be sunk! At first, shipping interests laugh at the audacious demand but then a merchant vessel approaching the Strait is torpedoed and sunk. A great hue and cry is raised around the globe. Gamma's warning and demand are repeated. When the tribute is again refused, a second ship is torpedoed.

The combined naval forces of the free world cannot find the attackers, and so the Seaview is called in. This leads to the discovery of Dr. Gamma's underwater city, and a torpedo battle between it and the Seaview.

The title and springboard were then handed off to a freelance writer.

Richard Landau was 50 when he wrote his first of two episodes of *Voyage to the Bottom of the Sea* (the second: "The Indestructible Man," later this season). His first film (as a co-writer) was the 1945 World War II story *Back to Bataan*, starring John Wayne and Anthony Quinn. He wrote the screenplay for a movie Irwin Allen no doubt liked – the 1951 sci-fi *Lost Continent*, about a South Pacific island inhabited by prehistoric beasts. In 1953, he wrote an outer-space adventure starring Howard Duff, called *Spaceways*. Another sci-fi movie was 1955's *The Quatermass Xperiment* (aka *The Creeping Unknown*). And then there was 1957's *Voodoo Island*, starring Boris Karloff. Another qualification for *Voyage* was a 1959 action-adventure film called *Up Periscope*. And one more: In 1964, he wrote the "Wolf 359" episode of *The Outer Limits*. Giving a script assignment to Landau for *Voyage* was a no-brainer.

Landau said, "They were desperate to get a script and they showed me a couple of story ideas. One was 'City,' which I selected."

As for Dr. Gamma, the Dr. No/Blofeld-type villain from "Eleven Days to Zero." Landau said, "Irwin loved the idea of this guy, but the network didn't, and they got rid of him fast. They felt that kind of villain was old hat – and he was!" (RL-SL92)

Within a year, Landau was writing and serving as associate producer on the first season of *The Wild, Wild West*, another series that mixed mystery, espionage, and science fiction … in a Western format. He would also write and briefly produce for *The Six Million Dollar Man*, and receive a Hugo nomination for Best Screen Adaptation (shared with a co-writer and director) for Disney's 1979 juvenile, campy sci-fi film *The Black Hole*.

William Welch, under the direction of Irwin Allen, took over the rewriting. The first changes required by an ABC directive was to lose Dr. Gamma, not only in name but in characterization. He was not to resemble James Bond's adversary, Dr. No. To accomplish this, the underwater city was no longer built for the purpose of terrorizing the world and controlling the seas, but for harvesting the wealth of the organic and mineral wealth from the bottom of the oceans. Because of this, the idea of Leopold Zeraff ordering the destruction of two freighters because they may have uncovered what he was building had to be implemented. It may have worked if better explained ... but, then, there would have been much to explain, such as how one could build such an enormous facility, dozens of structures, underwater, off the coast of a major western power, without detection. And how could such a thing ever be cost effective?

Placing Zeraff in a wheelchair comes across as a tawdry attempt at making the villain distinctive.

After rendering the characterization of Zeraff and the story ineffective, Welch turned his attention to more unhelpful meddling from ABC. The network's Dorothy Brown wrote to Irwin Allen on May 19:

> Page 11, Scene 30: DIMITRI GOUNARIS -- Please do not make him the stereotype hunchback or "Lenny" type character. A victim of the "raptures of the deep," yes – but please not something horrible to look at. And his guttural sounds should not pain the viewing audience.

In an effort not to "pain the audience," the character, who had suffered minor brain damage after a deep-sea dive and could no longer speak, was merely bland.

Brown continued:

> Page 13, Sc 32: ("meaningful tap at the head") – We try to discourage this kind of visual reference – it is a malicious thing when copied by children and young viewers of TV – and your audience will be loaded with impressionable youngsters.
>
> Page 53, Scene 130 and Page 60, Scene 184: Please keep the blood flow from the spear gun tips at the absolute minimum necessary for story. Blood, underwater, in color, magnifies beyond acceptability.

Dorothy Brown clearly did not know that *Voyage to the Bottom of the Sea* was being filmed in black-and-white.

On June 18, Brown was writing to Allen again, saying:

Confirming fone [sic] conversation this date with Mr. Gantman; the use of the plastic bag as an instrument of death is both too imitative to a possible fringe member of any audience and a mis-use [sic] of a sponsor product, Dupont, whom I believe hold the basic patent.

Associate Producer Joe Gantman was playing it safe when, on June 26, he bypassed Dorothy Brown and wrote to a member of the ABC Continuity Acceptance team, Tom Kersey:

Dear Tom: This is to confirm our phone conversation of today in which I informed you that, in the VOYAGE segment titled "City Beneath the Sea," the girl, Melina, in Scene 37 thru 51, will wear a bikini bathing suit. Of course we will handle this with appropriate good taste. Thanks for your approval and cooperation.

ABC wasn't buying it. The bikini – with the idea of making Linda Cristal as pleasing to the male eye as Ursula Andress was in *Dr. No* – was a no-show. Cristal ended up wearing a far less becoming one-piece scuba outfit.

Production:
(July 6-14, 1964; 7 days)
(Budget: $134,033)

This was Joseph Gantman's second episode as line producer.

John Brahm was hired to direct. He was 71 and had been directing Hollywood movies since the late 1930s, including the 1944 remake of *The Lodger* (following Alfred Hitchcock's silent-movie version), and the 3-D 1954 Vincent Price movie *The Mad Magician*. After moving to television, Brahm directed 15 episodes for Alfred Hitchcock's two series; 12 for *The Twilight Zone* (including "Time Enough at Last," for which he received a Directors Guild Award nomination); 12 for *Thriller*; and 15 for the gritty New York-based cop show *Naked City*, as well as a couple for *The Outer Limits* ("ZZZZZ" and "The Bellero Shield"). But he would only do two episodes of *Voyage* (this and "Hot Line," later in the season). He switched to *The Man from U.N.C.L.E.* (with eight episodes) and *The Girl from U.N.C.L.E.* (with six) before retiring after his swan song, the 1967 exploitation film *Hot Rods to Hell*, starring Dana Andrews.

Hurd Hatfield was cast to play Leopold Zeraff. He was 47 and had gained fame as the title character in the 1945 Oscar-winning horror film, *The Picture of Dorian Gray*. He received an Emmy nomination one year before appearing in this *Voyage* for the 1963 TV Movie, *Invincible Mr. Disraeli*. Like Dorian Gray,

Above: Hurd Hartfield in *The Picture of Dorian Gray*. (MGM, 1945)
Below: Linda Cristal appeared in 96 episodes of *The High Chaparral*. (NBC Productions, 1967-71)

Hartfield would go from young to old in the span of another sci-fi story, "The Night of the Man-Eating House," a 1966 episode of *The Wild, Wild West*. *The Picture of Dorian Gray* had made Hatfield a star, but it brought the curse of being typecast. He later said, "I never understood why I got the part, and have spent my career regretting it." (HH-IMDB)

He added elsewhere, "The film didn't make me popular in Hollywood. It was too odd, too avant-garde, too ahead of its time. The decadence, the hints of bisexuality and so on, made me a leper! Nobody knew I had a sense of humor, and people wouldn't even have lunch with me. ... But not many actors are fortunate enough to have made a classic. (HH-TI15)

Linda Cristal played Melina Gounaris. She was 30, and was one of the few women in the cast of 1960's *The Alamo*, starring John Wayne and Richard Widmark. She had the lead in another 1960 film, *The Pharaoh's Women*, as well as 1959's *Legions of the Nile*, as Cleopatra. She was prominently featured in the 1961 James Stewart-Richard Widmark Western, *Two Rode Together*, and she shared a Golden Globe award that year as "Most Promising Newcomer,

Female" with Susan Kohner and Tina Louise. She would soon be playing Victoria Cannon, the female lead in the NBC western *The High Chaparral*, a series that also featured Mark Slade, who appears briefly in this episode as Crewman Malone.

Al Ruscio, 40 at this time, played "dumb" Dimitri Gounaris. The noted character actor's so-so work here hardly betrays that he would have roughly 200 screen appearances over his career.

John Alderson was 47 when he put on the shades and played Zeraff's henchman, "Round Face." He had played Sgt. Bullock in 37 episodes of the 1957-58 cavalry series, *Boots and Saddles*, and was in the middle of a career in TV and film which would bring him roughly 150 screen appearances.

Paul Zastupnevich, the series costume designer, makes a cameo appearance as Giorgio.

Production began on Monday, July 6, 1964, filming on Stage B and the Seaview sets (Control Room and Radio Shack, followed by the Observation Nose). Also filmed on Stage B were the various close-ups of Hurd Hatfield, David Hedison, and Linda Cristal in the Green Tank, wearing scuba suits and masks, to be inserted into the footage filmed off Catalina Island by the Second Unit team. The cast had a 6:30 a.m. call time. Filming began at 8:30 in the morning and continued until 7:30 p.m., covering eight pages from the script. Another 30 minutes were needed for changing out of wardrobe and removing makeup from the cast, as the crew wrapped the set. Most of those working had been at it for 14 hours by the time they left the studio.

On Day 2, the company began on Stage B for scenes in the Missile Room at 8:30 a.m., then moved to Fox Stage 14 and the sets for Int. Zeraff's Home, where Crane, undercover, first meets Leopold Zeraff. John Alderson worked on this set, this day and the next, playing "Round Face." Also filmed were the scenes between David Hedison and Linda Cristal, in the "Int. Hotel Room & Corridor" set, as well as those between Hedison and Alderman.

Day 2 of filming included the scenes with David Hedison in the hotel room, built on Stage 14.

Hedison is delightful in these scenes, bringing a uniquely playful character to life as the fortune-seeking deep sea diver in search of adventure. Nine pages from the script had been filmed by the time "that's a wrap" was called at 7:30 p.m.

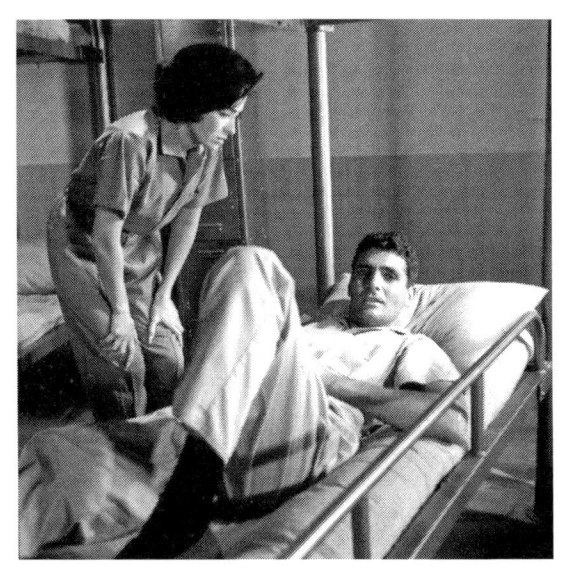

Day 3, Wednesday, July 8th, was another split day, with work beginning at 8:30 a.m. on Stage B for the "sleeping quarters" set required for the underwater city, from which Crane and Melina escape. Also filmed on this set, Zeraff's speech about the perils for fish and humans alike in the deep depths of the trench surrounding the underwater city.

Day 3: Physical action with David Hedison and Linda Cristal ... and a battle of wills between Hurd Hatfield and Hedison.

Little time was left for the scene in the control area of the underwater facility, in which Zeraff first reveals himself to Crane as the ruler of this underwater "kingdom," and boasts of his evil plans. The scene was not terribly well written, and the rushed direction did no favors to the actors. They were given too few takes in order to get comfortable with the awkward dialogue.

After a lunch break, the company moved back to Stage 14 and the "Int. Hotel Room & Corridor" set, this time for the scenes between Richard Basehart and Linda Cristal.

Basehart seems very at ease here, appearing to enjoy Nelson's undercover assignment, as well as working with Cristal, even if he looks ill at ease holding a lit cigarette. The actor preferred cigars but was mandated to switch to cigarettes to pacify one of the series' sponsors. A real smoker can instantly spot Basehart's unfamiliarity at holding the cigarette, as well as his reluctance to inhale the smoke when taking a puff.

They called for a wrap at 7:30 p.m., after 11 hours of production, having covered eight pages from the script with mixed results.

On Day 4, the company made the journey north to Paradise Cove, in Malibu, an area featured in Sally Field's 1965-66 Screen Gems series, *Gidget*. Once on location, the company filmed in the Cove, as well as the small pier and the cliffs, rolling camera from 8:30 a.m. to 7:15 p.m. It was still light out, so the last scene shot, of Hedison and Cristal, talking under the pier, was staged to shield the actors from what sunlight was left. Added darkness was created by a special camera lens and filter. This, however, resulted in the murkiness of the shot.

Day 4: Cristal and Hedison (above), on location at Paradise Cove.
Day 6: Filming the booby-trapped raft scene on at the backlot Moat.

Day 5: On Friday, they were back on Stage 14, filming on the Hotel Lobby set, then made a company move to Stage 8 where the access chamber for the underwater facility had been built. Under the hot stage lights, David Hedison, Linda Cristal, and Hurd Hatfield donned uncomfortable wet suits for hours. Filming wrapped at 7:30 p.m.

Day 6 Monday, July 13, the company spent most of the day outdoors on the 20th backlot, filming in and about the "Moat" for the "Ext. Deck Seaview." Work began at the standard time: 8:30 a.m.

A terrible accident was narrowly

278

avoided while filming this episode's Teaser on the deck of the Seaview. Actor Mark Slade told writers Mark Phillips and Frank Garcia, "We were ready to shoot a scene where the submarine is hit by a torpedo [sic]. We rehearsed the scene on the deck of the plywood sub on the backlot tank, and the explosives were set. For some reason, Richard [Basehart] asked to see the explosion go off before the scene was shot. His request caused some tension because it would delay filming, but Richard held out." (MS-SFTS2)

The reason for the request was because Basehart, a seasoned pro, had done his share of action movies, war movies in particular. He had been on enough sets and been exposed to enough dangerous explosive effects to know that sometimes things do go wrong, causing severe injury to actors and stunt crew. Mark Slade, relatively wet behind the ears, was trusting. Basehart was not.

Slade recalled, "The special effects crew set off the explosives, and it blew out a large chunk of the sub's deck, right where the actors would have been standing. Richard just stood there and began singing, 'There's No Business Like Show Business,' and he went to lunch." (MS-SFTS2)

Day 6: Stunts that involve regulars are routinely saved for the last day of production ... just in case anything goes wrong. Above image: a split-second before the explosion. Below: The big bang.

With this delay, Director John Brahm did not finish filming his episode by the end of the day as planned. Regardless, the company continued to work until 7:30 p.m. on Stage 14 and the "Int. Water Front Saloon" set.

On Tuesday, July 14, after director Alan Crosland, Jr. filmed for a day on his assignment, "Turn Back the Clock," John Brahm returned to finish his episode, filming from 8:30 until 10:15 p.m.

Lyle B. Abbott and Howard Lydecker, and their special-effects department, had their work cut out for them with this episode.

The undersea city was built and filmed in the studio's "Green Tank" by Abbott and Lydecker, working with a Second Unit team. Associated Press entertainment correspondent Cynthia Lowry visited during filming. For an AP wire service story, she wrote:

> The series will specialize in dramatic undersea action which requires delicate, special camera work. There will be collisions between subs, underwater explorations, even attacks on cities built on the ocean floor. All this violent action takes place in a cement tank on the studio back lot the size of a small swimming pool but considerably deeper and equipped with portholes for the cameras' eyes. All the props, from subs to rocks and buildings are carefully constructed scale miniatures.

The larger scale model of the Seaview, too big for the Green Tank, would be used in the studio's larger body of water on the backlot – "The Moat." Or at the Studio's Ranch in the mountains above Malibu, which included a lake.

The cost for "The City Beneath the Sea" was $134,037. Included in that budget was the $1,500 Paul Sawtell was paid to score the episode.

Release / Reaction:
(ABC premiere broadcast: 9/21/64; network repeat airing: 9/6/65)

The Animals, with "House of the Rising Sun," and Roy Orbison, with "Oh, Pretty Woman," had been vying for the top spot with radio airplay and sales of 45 RPM singles in America for weeks. The Newbeats, with their catchy "Bread and Butter," had to settle for second position. This was the week *Fiddler on the Roof* opened at the Imperial Theater in New York City for the first of 3,242 performances. *Mary Poppins* continued to be the top attraction at the movie houses. *The Man from U.N.C.L.E.* premiered on NBC, and CBS launched *The Munsters*, *Gomer Pyle*, and *Gilligan's Island*. ABC, which had jumped the gun and kicked off a week early, was already giving America a second look at its new series.

Joan Crosby, for her syndicated "TV Scout" on September 21, 1964, said:

> The new adventure series *Voyage to the Bottom of the Sea* continues on its less-than-merry scavenger hunt with "The City Beneath the Sea." Opening scenes are suspenseful enough as the Seaview investigates the whereabouts of a missing research ship. But all too soon, we discover that a gloomy scientist (Hurd Hatfield) is building his own town (and empire) in the murky depths off the Greek Isles, and is taking prisoners, as if catching flies. It's all a bit farfetched for even the 1970s.

Steven Scheuer, in the rival entertainment column "TV Key," opined in other newspapers:

> The kiddies for whom this show has been created aren't going to appreciate the inclusion of beautiful Linda Cristal in the cast, but she'll help pass the time for any adult males who tune in. The story involves another nut bent on world domination who is intent on accomplishing this from his home-made underwater fortress. Hurd Hatfield is the chief villain, Jay Novello is a victim, and series stars Richard Basehart and David Hedison continue to appear as a couple of naval Rover Boys.

"The City Beneath the Sea" aired early in the season. NBC televised a movie; its portmanteau series *90 Bristol Court* had not yet premiered. On hand was a repeat of the 1957 John Ford film *Wings of an Eagle*, starring John Wayne and Maureen O'Hara.

The movie went down for the count against the CBS powerhouse panel-show combo of *To Tell the Truth* and *I've Got a Secret*, and the new Monday-night champ, *Voyage to the Bottom of the Sea*.

Nielsen ratings report from Sept. 21, 1964: 7:30 – 8 p.m.:	Rating:	Share:
ABC: *Voyage to the Bottom of the Sea*	**24.8**	**41.1%**
CBS: *To Tell the Truth*	14.2	23.5%
NBC: Monday Night Movie: *Wings of an Eagle*	13.3	22.1%

8 – 8:30 p.m.
ABC: *Voyage to the Bottom of the Sea* **26.5** **42.0%**
CBS: *I've Got a Secret* 15.2 24.1%
NBC: Monday Night Movie: *Wings of an Eagle* 13.8 21.9%

"The City Beneath the Sea" was one of the 19 episodes from the first season to be repeated on the network.

Episode 5: "Turn Back the Clock"

(Prod. #7205; first aired Monday, October 26, 1964)
Written by Sheldon Stark
Directed by Alan Crosland, Jr.
Produced by Irwin Allen
Story Editor: William Welch; Associate Producer: Allan Balter
Assistant Story Editor: Al Gail
Guest Star Nick Adams
Also starring Yvonne Craig
(with Vitina Marcus)

From the *Voyage to the Bottom of the Sea* show files (Irwin Allen Papers Collection):

> Nelson, Crane, Jason and Carol are in a diving bell in the Arctic when a strange thermal surge breaks them loose from the Seaview and they surface at a tropical island amid waters heated by volcanic action. This island has remained cut off and hidden there since the Mesozoic Period and the travelers find themselves threatened by dinosaurs and primitive savages.

Sound Bites:

Naval Doctor: "Impossible! As a man of science, you must know that there's no such thing as a tropical region in the Antarctic." *Nelson:* "As a man of science, Doctor, you should be as careful as I am about using the word 'impossible.'" *Doctor:* "Facts are facts." *Nelson:* "I'll give you a fact: At the center point on the coast of Antarctica, there's no ice; the ground temperature is 50 degrees Fahrenheit. I could cite other facts – the hot springs in Iceland for example. No, no, Doctor, the existence of a pocket of tropical terrain in Antarctica is far from impossible."

Assessment:

This episode's springboard – warmth and strange creatures in a lost land at Earth's poles – has a long heritage, usually as part of the Hollow Earth theory. According to this fringe belief, verdant patches of Arctic and Antarctic land are warmed by air flow through (supposed) holes in the poles. Such gaps are also passages for life forms to enter and leave the surface world – even flying saucers, according to some.

"Turn Back the Clock" deserves its reputation as being cut from the same cloth as *The Lost World* – a shameful example of recycling. Even so, writer Sheldon Stark, supported by Allen, Welch, and Gail, did an excellent job of weaving various film sequences from that movie into a new story. The end results contained high adventure, excitement, and at least one interesting character turn, although Nick Adams's performance is criminally over-the-top.

Some bumps in the road are hard to ignore, most notably Captain Crane's choice to wear a tropical safari outfit with scarf tied around his neck when he enters the diving bell. He even has a notebook in his breast pocket (you will recall Hedison played a reporter in *The Lost World*, on an expedition to tropical South America). The outfit and notebook seemed appropriate in the movie, but hardly so in this situation, as they board the diving bell for a trip into the turbulent deep waters under the icy edges of Antarctica. Of course, the reason for the outlandish get-up, and the snug (and, we must assume, pink) pedal pushers worn by Yvonne Craig, is to match footage from the film.

If nothing else, the episode provides a fascinating lesson in how to effectively recycle earlier material.

Script:
Sheldon Stark's teleplay, "Once Upon a Dinosaur": April 30, 1964.
Mimeo Department's reformatted Shooting Final teleplay (green pages): May 7.
Page revision by William Welch or Al Gail (pink paper): June 30.
Page revisions (dark green paper): July 10.

Writer Sheldon Stark was 54 and had been scripting for television since the early 1950s, including two episodes for producer Gene Roddenberry's first series, *The Lieutenant*. Stark wrote multiple episodes for *The Man from U.N.C.L.E.*, *The Rat Patrol*, *Batman*, and *The Fugitive*. He received an Emmy nomination in 1974 for an episode of *The Waltons*. This was his only script for *Voyage*, but Irwin Allen would bring him back in 1969 to write an episode of *Land of the Giants*.

Stark, interviewed by writer Mark Phillips, said, "Initially, I pitched four story ideas to Irwin Allen, but the only thing that excited him was this old volcano footage he had. He asked me to write a story around it, and that helped me come up with a basic story, because they needed a script fast. It was a very simple story, and, besides, my agent always told me not to write anything too serious!" (SS-SL92)

The springboard for the story was already in the Series Bible, as written by Irwin Allen, William Welch, and Al Gail. Their one-page story summary said in part:

> With Captain Crane commanding, Seaview probes the deep, uncharted waters when suddenly the ship is gripped in an amazingly powerful underwater current. Its great nuclear engines are unable to resist the pull of the unbelievable strong undertow. The mighty submarine is swept along like a toy into a mammoth underground cavern and, finally, to the surface of a calm lagoon. The men of the Seaview are astonished to find themselves in tropical waters. Palms and lush vegetation surround them in startling contrast to the mountains of ice everywhere on the horizon. They finally discover that they are in a saucer-like plateau on the frigid Antarctic continent where volcanic action has produced a weird prehistoric "land that time forgot."

After taking on the assignment, Sheldon Stark called his script "Once Upon a Dinosaur." The title was changed to "Turn Back the Clock" during a series of rewrites.

Al Gail wrote to Irwin Allen on May 11, 1964:

> Billy Abbott brings to our attention that in the script "Turn Back the Clock," shots 67, 71, 74 are marked "stock," but it is his opinion that these shots do not exist. The shots are <u>the sub at dead stop</u> and <u>the sub gliding forward after a dead stop</u>. The closest thing to these shots in stock I can recall is when the sub stops, hovers, then

settles to bottom to let frogmen go out to search in the scene when the squid attacks Crane.

In any case, these are the type of shots we will need probably in several shows, so, when Billy gets into the green tank with the sub, he'll shoot the sub at dead stop, start, nosing up, diving down, etc.

Two days later, on May 13, Dorothy Brown wrote on behalf of the ABC Continuity Acceptance Department. Remarkably, the network censor was actually concerned that young audience members would think the prehistoric monsters and giant spiders in the episode were actually coming through the TV sets to eat them up.

In the use of stock footage for your gigantic prehistoric monster, huge spider, and the fire monster – please try to select footage that will give the younger members of your viewing audience a frame of reference. In particular Scene 14, Page 2 – "As it roars and heads directly for CAMERA". If the footage were to include the monster coming into full frame and completely filling the TV tube, this would be too frightening to both the very young and the very old. In the Central Time Zone (Chicago), you will be telecasting at 6:30 PM – to an audience very susceptible to shock. A frame of reference (trees, buildings, people, door frames, etc.) permits the viewer to separate himself from the action – he is an observer rather than a participant. ...

Page 43, Sc 153: GIRL wearing patchwork of skins. But all points covered in propriety please.

Page 49, Sc 176: Please substitute for "... what hell it was..."

William Welch had taken over the typewriter keys for rewrites by this point, making the changes ABC wanted, and addressing any other concerns from the production people.

Production:
(Filmed July 15-22, 1964; 6 days)
(Budget: $130,966)

This was Allan Balter's second turn at producing for the young series.

Alan Crosland, Jr. was hired to direct – and was paid more than the average *Voyage* director, commanding $2,750 ($250 above standard). Why did the 45-year-old director rate a higher salary? Perhaps because of his wide-ranging areas of expertise. Before directing, Crosland had been a film editor during the 1940s and early '50s; he had directed 19 episodes for Alfred Hitchcock's TV series; his outré directorial accomplishments also included four *Twilight Zone*s and two *Outer Limits*; he had also directed 19 episodes of the stylishly dark *Peter Gunn* and was well represented at other popular series such as *Bat Masterson* (22 episodes) and *Sergeant Preston of the Yukon* (11 episodes). Crosland had the directorial chops to ask for, and get, a pay bump.

Nick Adams was 33 when paid top guest-star rate, $2,500, to play Jason. He had already starred in two TV series – as Johnny Yuma, *The Rebel*, from 1959-61, and then as Nick Alexander in *Saints and Sinners*, for 1962-63. He had a prominent role in the 1962 Steve McQueen war film, *Hell Is for Heroes*, and received an Oscar nomination as Best Supporting Actor for the 1963 film *Twilight of Honor*. One season before appearing here, he was top guest star in the excellent "Fun and Games" episode of *The Outer Limits*.

Above: Nick Adams got the cover of *TV Guide* during the run of his western series, *The Rebel*. Below: Yvonne Craig would soon gain fame as TV's Batgirl.

Yvonne Craig was 27 when she played Carol Denning and had been working feverishly as a guest player in TV since 1957. She'd soon be back working on the Fox lot, from 1967 to '68, in the campy *Batman*, as "Batgirl." Also in 1968, she played a green-skinned Orion woman and have a love scene with Captain Kirk, in the *Star Trek* episode "Whom Gods Destroy." Irwin Allen would bring Craig back for "Wild Journey," an episode of *Land of the Giants*. She was paid $1,500 for her six days' work here.

Les Tremayne played Yvonne Craig's missing father/scientist, Denning. He was 51, and had come from radio, where he worked as an announcer, actor, and even star, of the weekly drama, *The First Nighters*. On TV, along with countless guest appearances, he'd been a regular on two series – *The Further Adventures of Ellery Queen* (1958-59), as dad Richard Queen, and, doing double duty during the same TV season, *The Adventures of Rin Tin Tin*, as Major Stone. Tremayne would work regularly in a third series in the future, *Shazam!*, from 1974-76, as Mentor.

Vitina Marcus was 26 at this time and had appeared in *The Lost World* as "Native Girl." Some of her footage from that film was added to this episode, along with the new sequences, so Marcus was costumed and coiffed to match.

Marcus said, "Irwin knew I was a single mom, and he thought I had a darling little daughter. He always wondered how I was managing, and he respected me for being a good mother. I had somebody bring her to the set sometimes. And when Irwin had gatherings at his home, I brought her with me. He had a barn with the merry-go-round type of horses serving as seats around it, and she liked to sit on those. She fell off once and he was beside himself until he knew that she was okay. He was very generous with her. He sent her Christmas gifts, like a motion picture projector and a screen, and different things. And he talked about his cat with her. I think he was very kind to animals, and I liked that because I'm into animals, too. He had a very kind side; a sensitive side; and he told me he was my best friend. I felt that he had a very strong affection for me, and he might have had other thoughts also." (VM-AI-15)

Vitina Marcus would soon play a second iconic role for Irwin Allen, as the Girl from the Green Dimension on a pair of 1966 *Lost in Space* episodes.

Perhaps because of Allen's regard and their previous acquaintance, the lovely 27-year-old was paid a healthy $1,000 for her one day's work on this episode.

This was the last of four episodes to feature Mark Slade (the pilot, "The Village of Guilt," "The City Beneath the Sea," and here, although he would be seen briefly in "The Fear-Makers" thanks to a stock shot). Slade said, "My agent felt the series would help my career. However, I was never signed on as a regular. Unknown to Irwin, my agent had a balancing act going with my recurring role on *Gomer Pyle*. My *Gomer* role was being expanded and I wanted to do more comedy. When the inevitable scheduling conflicts arrived, I discussed the situation with Irwin. I decided to leave. It was a good choice. *Gomer* led to being cast in *The Wackiest Ship in the Army* the next season." (MS-TVC99)

Day 1: Filming alongside the Moat in the "Ext. Jungle Locations 1, 2, and 3."

Slade spent one season on *Wackiest Ship*, before attaining a co-starring role on the long-running Western, *The High Chaparral*.

Production began on Wednesday, July 15 in and around the Moat on the backlot. They filmed the "Ext. Jungle Clearing & Pool," "Ext. Jungle Locations 1, 2, and 3," "Ext. Rocky Clearing" and "Ext. Diving Bell," finishing at 7:05 p.m., before sunset.

Day 2: Thursday. A second full day at the Moat, this time shooting scenes identified as "Ledge and Lava Cave," "Int. Fire Monster Cave," "Int. Cavern Tunnels" and "Ext. Seaview."

The production crew did an excellent job of dressing their sets so that the four-year-old footage from *The Lost World* could be matched to the new sequences filmed both this day and the next. The caves – actually, caverns may be a better word – had been made from concrete and wood sprayed with a stucco-like covering many years earlier, and these sets, used in the movie, were now revisited. Watching this episode gives you perhaps the best sense of how immense these covered artificial caves and caverns were. There were sections on top which could be opened, allowing lights to shine in, and other sections which remained closed off from above.

Vitina Marcus recalled a frightening situation which occurred on this day because of the lack of air movement in the caverns, and due to a miscalculation by the part of the special-effects crew as to how much flame and smoke were safe for the cast members

She said, "The colored smoke kept getting thicker as we were making our way past the various fire pits and lava pits. And suddenly we saw a look on Richard Basehart's face which told us we were in trouble. I mean, we were engulfed in smoke, which was really more of a gas. It smelt awful, and everyone was coughing, and Richard's look told us we needed to get out of there."

Above: David Hedison, Jill St. John, Vitina Marcus, and Michael Rennie from *The Lost World*. Below: Flash forward two years, with the same costumes on Hedison, Yvonne Craig (dressed as St. John was), and Marcus; the same ledge, on the same set. And, presto, a near-perfect match.

With his experience making war movies, Basehart had been exposed to countless dangers through special-effects explosions and gasses. He motioned for the others to exit the caverns. Marcus said, "It was most serious. The looks on

everyone's faces conveyed that. And once people start rushing out, everyone else follows. When someone like Richard Basehart tells you to get out, you listen." (VM-AI-15)

The set had to be "scrubbed" – thoroughly aired out. For the next attempt to get the required shots, less fire and smoke were used.

The company took their last shot at 6:35 p.m.

Day 3: Friday. It was a third full day at the Moat, with "Ext. Exit from Cave," "Int. Prison Cave" and "Int. Denning Cave." These were manmade caves adjoining the Moat. They could be opened at the top for placement of lights or closed when it rained. Helping to keep costs down, these were the same caves used during the filming of *The Lost World,* allowing for easy matching shots. Filming continued until 7:05 p.m.

Day 4: Monday. Finally, the company was able to work in the controlled environment of a sound stage, with their first day's work at home base, on Stage B. Filmed this day: Ext. Bridge of Seaview (against process screen), Int. Missile Room, and Int. Diving Bell. They filmed until 7:45 p.m.

Day 5: Basehart and Craig on the "Observation Nose" set. Day 6: Basehart, Craig, and Nick Adams on the "Int. Hospital Room" set.

Day 5: Tuesday. Work resumed on Stage B, with the claustrophobic Control Room set, then onto the Observation Nose.

Day 6: Wednesday, July 22. The company worked on Fox Stage 2 this day, for sequences in "Carol's Darkroom & Living Room," "Int. Hospital Room," "Int. Doctor's Office," and "Int. Laboratory." Director Alan Crosland, Jr. proved he was worth the extra $250, finishing this ambitious episode in six days. He was

helped, of course, by the stock footage that padded his production. But to make the stock footage work required a great deal of craft to be sure the newly shot footage could be matched to the footage from *The Lost World*. And, with three full days of outdoor production (always more time-demanding than soundstage work), Crosland earned his pay.

The budget was set at $130, 966, of which Hugo Friedhofer was paid $1,500 to provide the musical score. He started recording on September 1.

ABC got its first look with the rough edit on August 20. The network required substantial changes, and the Final Air Print wasn't ready for screening until October 14 – twelve days before its scheduled broadcast.

"Turn Back the Clock" was the fifth episode to film; the seventh to air.

Release / Reaction:
(Only ABC broadcast: 10/26/64)

Would the sleight-of-hand trick of sneaking in whole chunks of *The Lost World* fool the audience? Hardly.

Manfred Mann's "Do Wah Diddy Diddy" had a second turn as the most-played song on America's radio stations. Shut out from the top position: "Dancing in the Streets" by Martha & the Vandellas. And *Mary Poppins* continued to out-earn all the other movies showing across the country.

A press release from 20th Century-Fox announced:

> Irwin Allen, the producer of *Voyage to the Bottom of the Sea*, 20th Century-Fox Television's new hour action-

> adventure series, is a past member of fantasy and science fiction and you can be sure that a few of Allen's famous prehistoric monsters will turn up now and then in this new and exciting series. ... In fact, just such a battle between a Stegosaurus dinosaur and a Edaphosaurus dinosaur will take place in the "Turn of the Clock" segment of *Voyage*, which stars regular topliners Richard Basehart and David Hedison, and guest stars Nick Adams and Yvonne Craig.
>
> Producer Allen, when asked recently about his favorite prehistoric monster, produced this quotable quote: "I never met a monster I didn't like."

Syndicated newspaper entertainment column "TV Scout," running in hundreds of newspapers on October 26, said:

> This one's off on another science fiction fantasy with "Turn Back the Clock." The Seaview, on one of its hunting junkets (this time to find a missing scientist), runs into a lost world strictly out of Walt Disney's *Fantasia* that is swarming with Stegosauruses and other dinosaurs of unbelievable proportions.

Rival syndicated column "TV Key," also on the 26th, said:

> This could make a good science fiction "B" picture. Somewhere in the bowels of the Antarctic, the Seaview, in its search for the missing members of a scientific expedition, comes across a prehistoric world, complete with savages, monsters and active volcanoes. The cast effectively goes through the motions of pretending to believe all of this and if parts of the show look familiar, they should. They've been used in earlier films. Credit goes more to the editing than to the special effects. ...

The A.C. Nielsen ratings service declared *Voyage* the winner in its ratings survey report from October 26, 1964:

Nielsen ratings report from Oct. 26, 1964: 7:30 – 8 p.m.:	Rating:	Share:
ABC: *Voyage to the Bottom of the Sea*	**23.8**	**36.2%**
CBS: *To Tell the Truth*	15.8	24.0%
NBC: *90 Bristol Court: Karen*	14.9	22.7%

8 – 8:30 p.m.
ABC: ***Voyage to the Bottom of the Sea***   **26.0**   **39.2%**
CBS: *I've Got a Secret*   14.9   22.5%
NBC: *90 Bristol Court: Harris Against the World*   15.6   23.5%

The day after the network broadcast of "Turn Back the Clock," Frank Wilson, of Indiana's *The Indianapolis News*, called out Irwin Allen and ABC for their blatant pilfering from *The Lost World*.

> ... If the viewers at 7:30 p.m. on ABC-TV (WLW-I) got the feeling they had been there before, they were right. The thing was lifted almost bodily from the movie, chase scenes and all. It's the first time in memory that such a gigantic theft has been foisted on the public without some mention being made of original credits. [A. Conan] Doyle wasn't even mentioned.
>
> With it all, however, the series is just improbable enough to become an old reliable. It has all the flavor and nonsense of the old-fashioned movie house serial. The dialogue at times is ridiculous to adults, and yet the program has its own kind of fascination. ...
>
> It is aimed at the younger audience, doesn't push the imagination and has a good level of excitement. Somehow, though, one believes they'd better watch what they are about. If they pull much more of what happened last night, they'll be hearing from the audience they want to pull.
>
> The 13-year-old in the house spotted the whole thing immediately. He then pulled out the book and said, 'This thing is *The Lost World*, just like the movie."

Later that same day, Bill Summers, the TV critic for Florida's *Orlando Evening Star*, also took a shot at *Voyage* for its thievery:

> *Voyage to the Bottom of the Sea* apparently ran into script problems. What else can you say about an hour practically lifted from a movie, *The Lost World*, seen recently on TV!
>
> In ABC's series, our stalwart submariners discovered Mesozoic flora and fauna in Antarctica. Michael Rennie, the film hero, found the same beasts in south America. ...

And, wonder of wonder, the same native girl (with lipstick and eye makeup) was chased by Rennie and David Hedison, although continents apart.

Nick Adams looked a little pained – probably wished he was back on *The Rebel*.

In the weeks to come, numerous letters from viewers noticing the similarities between *The Lost World* and "Turn Back the Clock" turned up in various newspapers and TV magazines.

Steven B. Scheuer, in his syndicated "TV Key" column, carried in the *Winona Daily News*, of Winona, Minnesota, shared one such letter:

> My sister and I disagree on something and we would like you to settle it for us. I say that some of the scenes on a recent episode of *Voyage to the Bottom of the Sea* titled "Turn Back the Clock" were cut from the movie *The Lost World*, which starred Michael Rennie and David Hedison. My sister thinks they were filmed expressly for the series. Which of us is right? A.D.C., Meriden, Connecticut.

Scheuer responded:

> You win the argument. Many of the scenes used on the science-fiction series are from various films made by Twentieth Century-Fox, which also produces *Voyage* TV series. Most of the footage comes from the feature film *Voyage to the Bottom of the Sea*, but scenes from *The Lost World* have also been used.

On November 7, *The Kansas City Times*, in Kansas City, Missouri, printed a letter which said:

> My wife and I were watching *Voyage to the Bottom of the Sea* October 26 in which the story evolved around the finding of a lost island in the Antarctic. We believe some of the scenes from this episode were film clips from the movie *The Lost World*, starring Michael Rennie and Jill St. John. Could it be? – J. and S.G.

Answer:

> Since 20th Century-Fox made the movie and is making the TV series, it is likely that the company dipped into its film library.

Two days later, in *The Cincinnati Enquirer*, "V.R.H." wrote:

> The setting and savages in the *Voyage to the Bottom of the Sea* film about monsters and cavemen in Antarctica looked just like those in a Saturday Night at the Movies I once saw. Can you tell me the name of the movie?

James Devane, the *Enquirer*'s TV-Radio Editor, answered:

> The film was called *Lost World*. Incidentally, it also starred David Hedison, which made it easy to incorporate its footage into the *Voyage* adventure.

And these were just the ones we happened across. There was no doubt that plenty more viewers, young and old, had noticed. Allen's rejoinder might have been, "Is it stealing when I use my own material?" But, judging by many of the clippings filed away in the Irwin Allen Private Papers Collection, we know that he was aware of these observations and complaints. The flurry of grumbles may have been part of the reason that "Turn Back the Clock" was passed over for a network repeat.

Episode 6: "Hail to the Chief"

(Prod. #7206; first aired Monday, December 28, 1964)
Written by Don Brinkley
Directed by Gerd Oswald
Produced by Irwin Allen
Story Editor: William Welch; Associate Producer: Joseph Gantman
Assistant Story Editor: Al Gail
Guest Star Viveca Lindfors
Also starring John Hoyt, Malcolm Atterbury, Edward Platt.
(with James Doohan and Nancy Kovack)

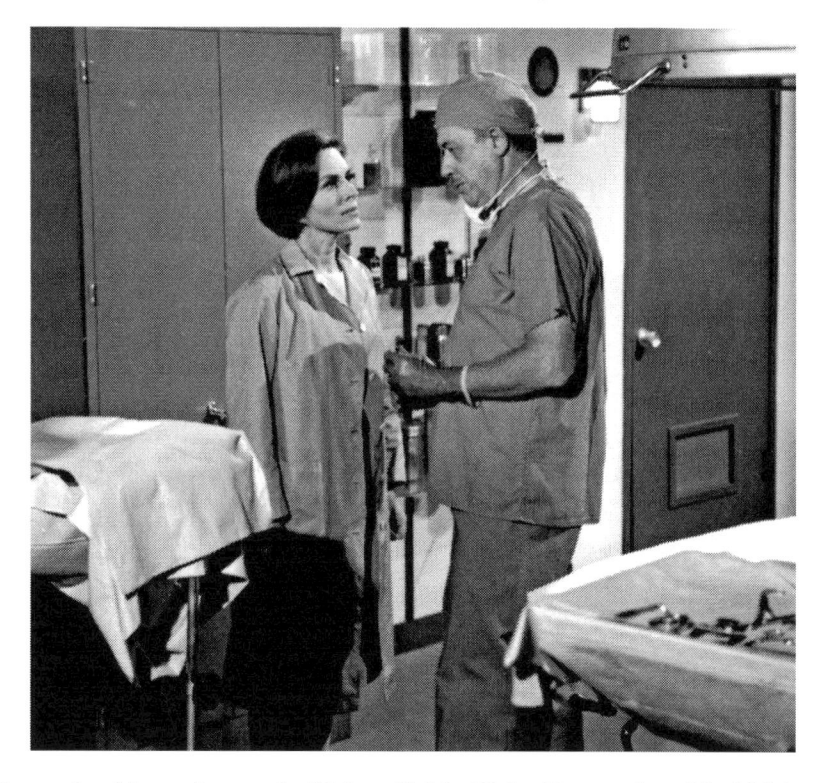

From the *News Journal* of Mansfield, Ohio, December 28, 1964:

"Hail to the Chief." Viveca Lindfors guest-stars as an enemy agent in tonight's episode, in which the President of the United States is accidentally injured during a South American visit and placed aboard the submarine Seaview for special treatment to enable him to attend an important peace conference.

Dr. Laura Rettig (Lindfors), having replaced the true team specialist, intends to use the experimental treatment machine to kill the president. On board, Rettig alters the machine's settings so that it will cook the President's gray cells like a microwave hard-boiling an egg.

Sound Bites:

Laura: "See, the magnetic ray brings the radioactivity of the isotope into play on the malignant tissue, or the hematoma, or whatever it is we wish to dissolve." *Senior Foreign Agent:* "At normal intensity. But if the ray intensifies to this extent, surely they will know that something's wrong." *Laura:* "No. See, they won't know. They'll have no idea that I've increased the power of this machine to a destructive level. Because the gauges and the dials, they show normal readings. When I turn on this designated switch, the power shows normal intensity. Now, when I turn on this hidden switch, the curing ray becomes, in effect, a death ray."

Crane (into intercom mike): "What's the course on your gyro repeater?" *Crewman's Voice (over intercom):* "Two-three-four-two, Captain." *Crane:* "Mr. Morton, what course are we steering?" *Morton (surprised by the reading):* "One-seven-oh, sir." *Crane (to Nelson):* "This is a better ship than we thought – we're going in two directions at once."

Assessment:

Former *Starlog* writer Mark Phillips called it "The most boring episode of Year One."

Voyage historian Mike Bailey said, "The idea of frying the President's brain is horrendous." (vttbots.com)

While clearly not a favorite of many *Voyage* fans, primarily because of the deliberately slow pacing, "Hail to the Chief" still has many fine moments.

Viveca Lindfors, as Dr. Laura Rettig, makes for an out-of-the-ordinary villainess, delightful to watch. She is elegant and sophisticated, yet sinister. It's especially bemusing to watch her operate intricate, deadly electronics with a cigarette dangling from her lips. And she is ruthlessly cold-blooded. Even the actress's choice to hiss the line "Don't touch me!" at the conclusion is refreshing. As befits her rich background in TV and film, Lindfors exudes star appeal.

One eerie scene involves Dr. Rettig demonstrating the electron surgical device on an egg, turning the egg's interior to dust. Then, with as much emotion as most people display when zapping a cup of coffee in a microwave, she suggests using this machine on a human brain. This "healing ray" has echoes of the mysterious beams of the Shaver Mystery's "Teros" and "Deros," as well as the Purple Ray invented by Wonder Woman in the comics, to resuscitate Steve Trevor.

Another dramatic scene occurs when Seaman Clark (Paul Carr) volunteers to go into the water-filled ducts to conduct repairs on a jammed mechanism, knowing that he has only minutes to accomplish his task and exit before the compartments will flood. Tension and claustrophobia mount with the spewing steam and flares of electrical sparks as Clark crawls deeper into the winding ducts, then gets his arm jammed in the mechanism he has been sent to repair. Crane, a ticking clock sounding louder with each moment, goes in next to help Clark. It's an impressive scene, and both actors, soaked to the skin, certainly earned their paychecks. As time runs out, Nelson is forced to order Chief Curley Jones to seal the two men inside the duct and flood the compartment. The drama is nearly unbearable. When the moment of resolution finally comes, and we realize the men inside will not perish, Richard Basehart delivers a most authentic-sounding laugh of relief.

More eerie and effective moments occur when the gauges in the control room malfunction, each giving different readings, prompting Crane's line about Seaview's course bifurcation.

Along with all of this, we get a trio of femme fatales, as beautiful as they are evil, a rarity for this show.

With all due respect to the naysayers, and despite the slow start, this episode delivers the goods.

Script:
Don Brinkley's treatment and 1st and 2nd draft teleplays: Dates unknown.
Mimeo Department's reformatted Shooting Final teleplay: Date unknown.
Rev. Final Shooting, by William Welch or Al Gail (green pages): September 25, 1964.
Page revision by Welch or Gail (pink paper): July 22.
Page revisions (gold paper): July 23.
Page revisions (blue paper): July 28.

This was Don Brinkley's first *Voyage* writing assignment (to be followed by the excellent "The Sky Is Falling"). He said, "I tried to be a little outrageous and spooky. We went through many story possibilities with Irwin Allen and finally I said, 'Look, why not go the whole route? Let's make the victim the President of the United States!' Irwin said, 'No! You can't do that.' I said, 'Let's try it.' He thought it over and said, 'Okay, go ahead,' and it worked. I thought it turned out well." (DB-SL92)

Brinkley was 42 and had written 15 episodes for *Highway Patrol*, 14 for *Bat Masterson*, and several each for other hit series, such as *Wanted: Dead or Alive* and *The Fugitive*. He was also supermodel-actress Christine Brinkley's dad.

Brinkley *pater* said of *Voyage*, "That whole production company was chaotic. Irwin set the mood for everything and there wasn't much sanity going on there. It was fun for a while, but then it got crazy and it was hard to get any work done."

According to Brinkley, Allen was "a strange man." He elaborated: "Actually, I think Irwin was a decent guy. He wasn't a bad fellow, but he didn't know how to deal with people. He came on very strong with everything and he had no consideration for anybody else's feelings. But he had a certain talent and he used it well. I admire him for that. They say the squeaky wheel gets the most attention in this business, *and Irwin squeaked*." (DB-SL92)

ABC made sure that script editor William Welch included the story's futuristic date in the teaser, before we see that the President of the United States is gravely ill. The President's aide, played by James Doohan, mentions difficulties at the Geneva Conference having occurred in the recent past, in 1971 and "again last year," establishing a timeline that puts this story in 1973 or later. Elsewhere, the date pops up again – more specifically – as June 24, 1973. The reason: The network didn't want anyone watching to be confused that perhaps they were watching a news show and the real President of the United States was in danger of dying. It was also imperative to the network that the actor chosen for the part had no resemblance to Lyndon B. Johnson.

Production:
(Filmed July 23-31, 1964; 6¼ days)
(Budget: $138,594)

Gerd Oswald was hired to direct. He was 44 and had helmed 14 episodes of *The Outer Limits*, including "Soldier," written by Harlan Ellison and starring Michael Ansara. He would go on to do a pair of *Star Trek*s ("The Conscience of the King" and "The Alternative Factor").

For the role of Laura Rettig, Irwin Allen's first three choices were Vera Miles, Barbara Rush, and Anne Francis, in that order. Joseph Gantman suggested Anne Baxter, Carolyn Jones, Piper Laurie, Hope Lange, and Susan Oliver. They were all A-listers. But so was the actress that was eventually hired.

Viveca Lindfors was 43 when she played Laura. She had starred in many films in Sweden before being brought to Hollywood to top-line features. Among many others, she shared star billing with Errol Flynn in 1948's *Adventures of Don Juan*; Ronald Reagan in 1949's *Night Unto Night*; Glenn Ford in 1950's *The Flying*

Viveca Lindfors, circa early 1950s.

Missiles; Sterling Hayden in 1951's *Journey into Light*; and with James Cagney in 1953's *Run for Cover*. She played the wife of Richard Basehart's character for the 1962 movie *The Paradine Case*, a TV version of the 1947 Alfred Hitchcock film of that name. She won the Best Actress award at the Berlin International Film Festival for her starring role in the 1962 film *No Exit*. Lindfors also appeared in an episode of David Hedison's first series, *Five Fingers*.

John Hoyt was 58 when cast as General Beeker. He was a well-respected character actor in television and films with over 250 different roles. He stayed clear of doing a series until late in his career (as Grandpa Kanisky in the 1980s series *Gimme a Break!*). He was however the first doctor on the Starship Enterprise, for the 1964 *Star Trek* pilot film, "The Cage." He and producer Gene Roddenberry were in agreement that someone else should play the role if the pilot went to series.

Above: John Hoyt, the first of four *Star Trek* alumni to appear in this episode, from the pilot film "The Cage," also shot in 1964. Below: Ed Platt with Don Adams in *Get Smart*.

Malcolm Atterbury was given third guest-star billing to play Commander Jamison. He was 57, back in the day when that age often looked like 67. His face should look familiar; he made close to 200 film and TV appearances, including multiple appearances on many of the shows you may have grown up watching: *Wagon Train*, *Dragnet*, *Twilight Zone*, *Perry Mason*, *The Fugitive*, *Bonanza*, and *Gunsmoke*, to name a few.

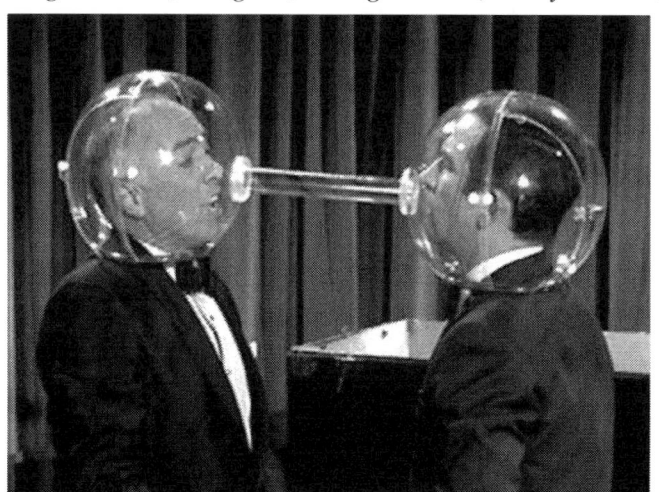

Edward Platt was 47 when he played Morgan, for fourth guest-star billing. He was another busy character actor who could play almost any type of role, and was busy in both film and TV, including a trip into *The Twilight Zone* and three encounters with *The Outer Limits*. He had so far managed to stay free from being locked in to one specific part, but that would change one year after this, when he became the Chief of CONTROL on *Get Smart*.

The large and impressive cast had several other performers yet to reach their greatest fame.

David Lewis was Dr. Kranz. He was 48 and several years away from winning a slew of Emmys for his regular role on *General Hospital*. At this time he was a well-employed guest performer, and occasionally repeated work on *The Farmer's Daughter*, as Senator Ames, and on *Batman*, as Warden Crichton.

Nancy Kovack played Monique, the third of the femme fatales, who pretends to come to Kowalski's rescue on the back road. The stunning actress was 29 and had just won the Golden Laurel Award as Best New Face – Female. That face was only part of the anatomy she displayed in the 1968 *Star Trek* episode "A Private Little War," as the bewitching Nona. She would receive an Emmy nomination for a 1967 episode of *Mannix*.

Susan Flannery, the second of the three gorgeous female villains (in order of appearance) to figure into the tale, was 25, and had only recently begun working in television. This was the first of three appearances on *Voyage* for Flannery, who returned for "The Traitor" and "Time Bomb." There was even talk of her becoming a recurring character. More on her illustrious career when she returns later in the season in a bigger role.

Above: Nancy Kovack goes brunette for a 1968 episode of *Star Trek*. Below: James Doohan in his most famous role.

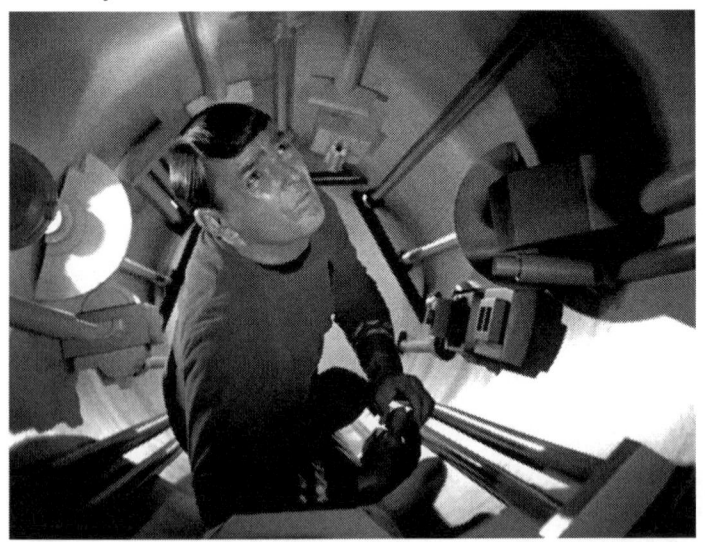

James Doohan makes his first of two appearances in the series as Lawrence Tobin, a top aide to the President of the United States.

302

He'll return for "Hot Line." Doohan was a frequently employed guest actor on television at this time, showing up in *The Twilight Zone*, *The Outer Limits*, *Gunsmoke*, *The Fugitive*, *Ben Casey*, *Bewitched*, *The Man from U.N.C.L.E.*, you name it. He even had a 27-episode stint on *Peyton Place* before winning fame and becoming permanently typecast as Scotty on *Star Trek*. And he wasn't even Scots, but born in Canada to Irish immigrants.

Paul Carr, 30, took his first of six turns as Seaman Clark. He too would soon have a *Star Trek* experience, appearing in the series' second pilot, "Where No Man Has Gone Before." Carr had the dubious honor of being the first Enterprise crewman to die in the line of duty – strangled telekinetically by an electrical cable. Irwin Allen liked Carr and, besides having him reprise the role of Clark five more times, cast him in a seventh episode of

Above: Paul Carr was the fourth cast member of this episode to jump ship and take a ride on the Enterprise, in 1965, for "Where No Man Has Gone Before" ... while he was still working as a semi-regular on *Voyage*.
Below: Del Monroe and Nancy Kovack at the Rancho Golf Course Club for the "Isolated Highway," where Kowalski takes a spill from his motorcycle.

Voyage as another character (Benson in "Terror of Dinosaur Island"), as well as a pair of *Time Tunnel* episodes, plus one *Land of the Giants*. You had over 160 other opportunities to catch Paul Carr on television in the 1960s, '70s and beyond, with prominent guest roles on many popular shows.

This tale featured a big cast ... and it was a busy period on the 20th Century-Fox lot. Besides *Voyage*, and the studio's other TV series (*12 O'Clock High*, *Daniel Boone*, *Valentine's Day* and *Peyton Place*), three feature films were in production: *The Sound of Music*, *Von Ryan's*

303

Express, and *Hush, Hush, Sweet Charlotte*.

Filming for "Hail to the Chief" began Thursday, July 23, 1964 at the Rancho Golf Course Club for the "Isolated Highway" sequence. This was where Kowalski took his fall from the motorcycle.

Next they filmed on the lot, outside the Administration Building on Studio Street, then on to the backlot Moat, with camera rolling between 7:30 a.m. and 7:45 p.m. All of Friday was spent at the Moat location – a long day at that, with the camera rolling from 8 in the morning to 11:20 at night. Cast and crew would have the weekend to recover.

Day 3: Monday –

From Day 3: Femme fatale Viveca Lindfors (above), dangling cigarette and plenty of wicked sex appeal. Below: Del Monroe and John Hoyt stand before the camera; and the camera's perspective.

an ambitious day as the crew worked on two separate stages. Filming began on Fox Stage 8, for "Int. President's Anteroom," "President's Bedroom" and "Int. Radiology Clinic," with a cigarette-smoking Viveca Lindfors demonstrating how she planned to cook the President's brain ... like an egg. The company then moved to Stage 5 for "Int. Foreign Legation" and "Int. Conference Room." Remarkable, Gerd Oswald got it all done, with the last shots taken at 7 p.m.

Day 4: Tuesday. Now on home ground – Fox Stage B, and the scenes in Sickbay. There were a lot of them – taking up seven and a half pages in the script, including the near assassination of the President of the United States. Covering it all took from 8 a.m. to 7:12 p.m.

Day 5: Wednesday. Filmed were scenes in the Observation Nose, as well as in the Admiral's Quarters, Exam Room, Missile Room, and the ship's corridor – all in a little more than 11 hours, spanning 8 a.m. to 7:12 p.m.

Also from Day 3: The grim "Int. Conference Room" scene.

Day 6: Thursday was spent on the Control Room set, and an area used for the ship's inner ducts, partially filled with water. Paul Carr, followed by David Hedison, spent hours on their hands and knees under hot lights and in room-temperature water. It was a grueling process. The

305

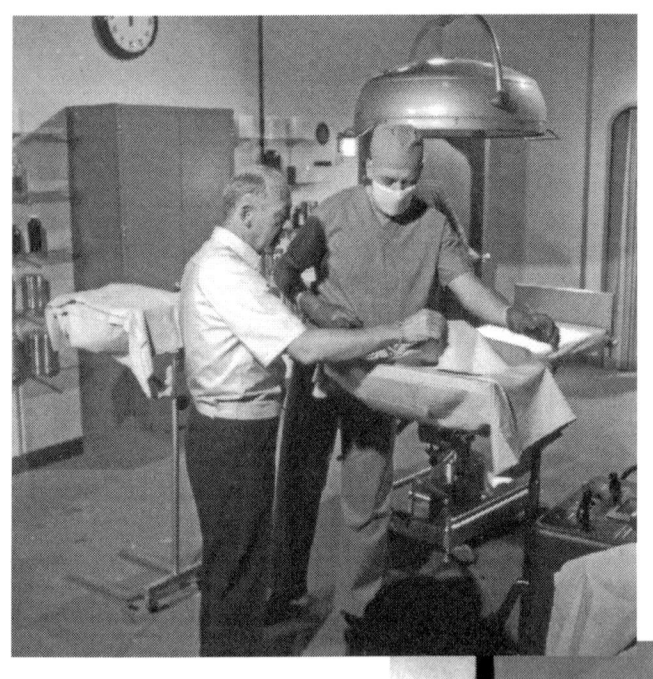

lighting crew had the difficult task of finding ways to illuminate the tight passageways, while the special-effects team kept pumping water and simulating the flashes of electrical wiring shorts. David Hedison and Paul Carr deserved an award for their torturous half-day spent in the ducts.

Director Oswald had fallen behind. The next episode scheduled, "The Fear-Makers," had to be delayed, now set to begin filming on Monday of the following week. The company filmed from 8 a.m. to 8:05 p.m. Del Monroe said, "The people who would be the most irritated about working late were the crew. Many times we'd break up laughing – the longer you work, the punchier you get. Whenever an actor would break up, the crew would say, 'You're laughing us

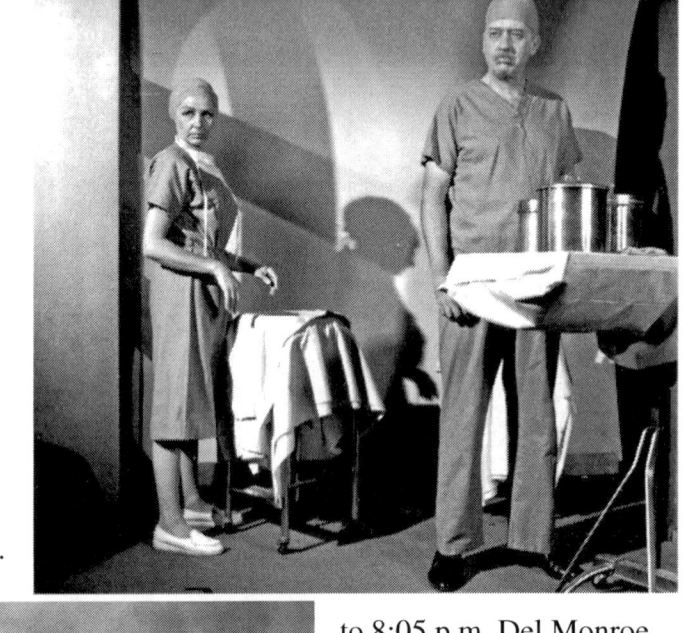

Above: Former *Outer Limits* director Gerd Oswald prepares a scene on the fourth day of filming, and then shoots it (right) in true *film noir* fashion. Below: David Hedison earns his pay in the Seaview's flooded lower ducts.

306

into overtime!' They weren't interested in overtime. We were, but they wanted to go home." (DM-SE98)

Day 7: Friday, July 31. The push was on to get this one finished. Oswald had gotten so far behind in filming that it appeared he might not even wrap the production with a full extra day. Still on Stage B, they rolled camera between 8 a.m. and 9:35 p.m., completing the sequences needed for the Control Room. A special dinner had to be arranged for cast and crew, then back into the Admiral's Quarters for pickup shots. It was finally a wrap ... except for a few additional "inserts," which would be filmed on September 29 by another director.

Release / Reaction:
(Only ABC broadcast: 12/28/64)

"Hail to the Chief" was the sixth episode filmed, but pushed back in the broadcast order to No. 16. And it was not given a network repeat airing.

When it aired on ABC, syndicated "TV Scout" told us:

> This show surfaces with a reasonable exciting adventure, "Hail to the Chief," with a vivid performance by Viveca Lindfors as an enemy agent. She is out to assassinate the president of the U.S., who has been injured on a South American visit. The plan is to do away with the only doctor capable of mending him. It is not all highly improbable but it is taut science fiction stuff.

"TV Time," syndicated to newspapers, including the *Troy Record*, in Troy, New York, on December 28, said:

This one concerns a diabolical plot against the life of the President of the United States, using an electronic substitute for brain surgery as a death ray. When the President hurts his head in a fall, it is essential to international diplomacy that the news be suppressed. The scheme is so far out that this series and *Jonny Quest* are the only two on which it might seem passable.

Nielsen ratings report from Dec. 28, 1964:	Rating:	Share:
7:30 – 8 p.m.:		
ABC: *Voyage to the Bottom of the Sea*	**19.7**	**32.0%**
CBS: *To Tell the Truth*	19.5	31.7%
NBC: *90 Bristol Court: Karen*	11.7	19.0%
8 – 8:30 p.m.		
ABC: *Voyage to the Bottom of the Sea*	**20.7**	**33.1%**
CBS: *I've Got a Secret*	18.0	28.8%
NBC: *90 Bristol Court: Harris Against the World*	13.4	21.4%

On January 4, 1965, days after "Hail to the Chief" aired, the *Portsmouth Times*, among other newspapers, carried syndicated columnist Hal Humphrey's seventh annual "10 Worst" list. In the category of "Worst Adventure Series," Humphrey picked *The Man from U.N.C.L.E.*, saying that it "suffocates under threadbare stories and a hero with no style." He added:

> Almost in a dead heat for the same honor is *Voyage to the Bottom of the Sea* (ABC) with dialogue exhausted decades ago by the Rover Boys.

Along with *U.N.C.L.E.* and *Voyage*, Humphrey singled out *Bonanza* ("Worst Western") and *Gilligan's Island* ("Worst Comedy"). Of course, the preteen viewers devoted to these shows up might have retaliated by naming Humphrey "Worst Critic."

Episode 7: "The Fear-Makers"

(Prod. #7207; first aired September 28, 1964)
Written by Anthony Wilson
Directed by Leonard Horn
Produced by Irwin Allen
Story Editor: William Welch; Associate Producer: Allan Balter
Assistant Story Editor: Al Gail
Guest Star Lloyd Bochner
Special Guest Star Edgar Bergen

Official synopsis from Irwin Allen Private Papers Collection:

The men of the "Polidor," a sub designed by Nelson to explore the ocean depths, inexplicably panicked at a certain point and the sub and its crew went to the bottom. Against all advice, Nelson is determined to take the Seaview to the same place to find out what went wrong. He doesn't know that an insidious fear-gas was planted on the "Polidor" by the enemy, who want to exploit the ocean riches for themselves. An enemy agent with fear gas is now aboard the Seaview....

Dr. Arthur Kenner (Edgar Bergen) is on board observing the crew under stressful conditions. Also, along for the ride, his assistant, Dr. Martin Davis (Lloyd Bochner). One of them is up to no good.

Sound Bites:

Nelson (unwilling to cancel further test dives): "It will mean surrendering untold wealth in minerals, food and scientific information to other countries with greater courage and more vision."

Davis: "Does it frighten you to be going down forty-five hundred feet in an eggshell?" *Patterson:* "Well, sir, I've never thought about it that way." *Davis:* "Well, you think about it, Patterson."

Curley: "They think they found something. It might be the Polidor on the ledge, right out there." *Patterson:* "So close you can almost … *(reacts to sounds created from water pressure outside the hull; a banging)* … it's like … like somebody's out there."

Davis (to Crane): "It's difficult to accept, Captain, but fear takes many forms and it's always destructive … even in a man like Nelson. You have to take over, Captain … for the sake of the crew and the Seaview itself. He'll push us down to destruction if you don't."

Crane (to Nelson): "There's no evidence that Polidor was deliberately sunk." *Nelson*: "There's got to be … there's no other answer." *Crane*: "Why? Because any other answer would lay the deaths of 85 men at your feet? You may be willing to die rather than admit you made a mistake, but I'm not going to die with you. And neither are the men on this ship!"

Assessment:

"The Fear-Makers" was advanced from the seventh filmed to the third aired, and you can see why. Writing, direction, and acting are all top notch – not just by the standards of *Voyage to the Bottom of the Sea*, but for any hour-long drama from this period. And the episode is still tense and compelling more than 50 years after its first broadcast.

There isn't a bad performance in sight, but Lloyd Bochner, all over the TV dial in this era, has never been better. Edgar Bergen, adept at comedy, seems less assured as a dramatic actor … until the scene in the Control Room when he has his nervous breakdown. It is performed so well that it is uncomfortable to watch, a result of both Bergen's conviction and the reactions from the Seaview command and crew, with their mix of surprise, awe, concern, discomfort, and even embarrassment. Richard Basehart and David Hedison are particularly excellent in this episode, supported by the expert direction of Leonard Horn.

Note the many but superb choices made by Horn, such as the framing of numerous shots near air vents. While the actors converse in the foreground, the vents behind them flutter with ribbons blowing. It makes an effective silent ticking clock, as we anticipate the fear gas making its way through the vents into every compartment of the Seaview. One of these shots is particularly effective – as the two doctors, Kenner and Davis, are shown into Nelson's cabin. As Nelson greets the men, we see the ever-present and foreboding air vent in the background, while, in the foreground is a model of the Polidor on Nelson's desk. Davis carries his briefcase, which we know contains the fear gas hidden in a tape recorder. Watch as he sets his briefcase down on Nelson's desk, blocking the camera's view of the model of the Polidor. The case containing the gas now dominates the shot, obscuring all else. The shot is worthy of Hitchcock.

"The Fear-Makers" became a good template for episodes to come, in which Nelson, Crane, or other members of the Seaview crew are acting out of character, causing the story's conflict. Here, however, it is handled with skill and believability, from the writing to the acting to the direction and the technical aspects.

Script:
Anthony Wilson's writers contract (as C. Anthony Wilson): April 31, 1964.
Wilson's treatment and 1st and 2nd draft teleplays: Dates unknown.
Mimeo Department's reformatted Shooting Final teleplay: Date unknown.

Revised Shooting Final teleplay (by William Welch or Al Gail):
Date unknown.
2nd Rev. Shooting Final teleplay by writing staff: July 21.
3rd Rev. Shooting Final (on yellow paper): July 30.
Page revisions (blue paper): July 30.
Page revisions (pink paper): August 3.

Writer Anthony Wilson had been in television since 1959. He'd served as producer on *Alcoa Theatre*, *Goodyear Theatre* and the short-lived *Follow the Sun*, about two freelance magazine writers in Hawaii. He had visited other series, writing scripts for *Have Gun – Will Travel*, *The Naked City*, *Bonanza*, *Mr. Novak*, *Combat!*, and *The Twilight Zone* – the less-than-classic "Come Wander with Me," in which "The Rockabilly Kid," played by Gary Crosby, goes into the backwoods looking for new music. Wilson had also served as "story executive" on a short-lived Western, *The Travels of Jaimie McPheeters*. It was a good résumé for five years in TV.

This one and only *Voyage* assignment would make an impression on Irwin Allen. The following year he invited Wilson to serve as story editor on *Lost in Space*. Allen would also hire Wilson to write nine episodes of *Land of the Giants*. Also in the near future, Wilson served as producer for the sci-fi series *The Immortal* (1970-71) and *Future Cop* (1976-78). He created and wrote for the TV version of *Planet of the Apes* (1974).

Associate producer Allan Balter sent his script notes to Irwin Allen on July 17, only some of which Allen and William Welch addressed.

1. Suggest teaser develop so that right up to his last speech Nelson is talking to Polidor and <u>hearing</u> frantic, shouted, aimless commands and then teaser <u>ends</u> with the implosion.

2. <u>Urgently</u> suggest that scene which starts at the bottom of Page 9 (Scene 28) and runs <u>through</u> ¾ of Page 15 (just under six full pages) be drastically cut.

3. In above scene, if speech "certain other countries" on Page 11 is not cut, suggest it be changed.

4. Suggest that Davis be made one of several key men working for Fear Gas project under Kenner. <u>None</u> of the men know the nature of the <u>sum</u> of their work – only Kenner. And it is only <u>he</u> who knows they are developing not <u>just</u> a new gas but a deadly gas as well. In Scene 39 through 41 let Kenner be showing film of latest experiments to this group of men.

5. Suggest that all references to "riches of the sea" be changed to nodules of manganese, uranium, ore, etc., which collect on the ocean floor at extreme depths and could be scooped up by the first power to develop highly mobile submarine-type vessels capable of operating at these depths.

6. Why does the Polidor implode at a depth subsequently reached by Seaview which doesn't implode (at the same depth?) ...

7. Page 61 – Why can't the Seaview surface despite a jammed diving plane? The planes have no relation to the ballast tanks. Surely, they could go straight up!

The caliber of Balter's notes in this one memo reveal the asset he was to the series ... and one reason why the first season of *Voyage to the Bottom of the Sea* is considered by many to be its best. It wasn't really his job to suggest script changes of this type; he was, after all, the nuts-and-bolts producer, in charge of overseeing the physical production. But, as a writer with several screen credits of his own, Balter had trouble resisting the urge to make *Voyage* scripts better.

Incidentally, the scene Balter urgently wanted trimmed was the one in which Laura demonstrates the "death ray" on an egg for her superior. It was reduced by 50%.

On July 30, Dorothy Brown, Director of ABC Continuity Acceptance Department, was giving notes, too. Allen couldn't ignore Brown:

Page 5, Sc A-14: The addition of the FULL SHOT of the men in the submarine and their cries of terror as they are about to all die is UNACCEPTABLE.

Page 13, Sc 39: Do not hold this frightened family pet too long – also it MUST be approved by the Humane Association. ...

Page 42 and 43: This material about "somebody out there" is pretty frightening. Caution you do not go overboard. ...

Kindly remember the early hour for this program – and minimize horror.

They did minimize the horror.

- The full shot of the men of the Polidor panicking and about to die was never shown. Instead, we got a medium shot, limiting our view ... to the point that many in the audience didn't understand that the man whose legs are seen was trying to tighten a valve in order to stop a leak.
- The footage of the "frightened family pet" – a cat – which reacted in terror to a tiny mouse, was kept short.
- "This material about 'somebody out there'" – the excellent scene between Curley and Patterson – was minimized.

Despite this, all involved turned out a script that would provide for a gripping drama that may have been atypical for the "family hour," but was guaranteed to entertain the adults as well as the kids.

Production:
(Filmed August 3-10, 1964; 6 days)
(Budget: $119,484)

Leonard Horn was hired to direct, having impressed everyone with his handling of "The Mist of Silence." Irwin Allen recognized Horn's talent, and brought him back to direct seven more episodes, as well as a first-season entry for *Lost in Space* (1965's "Invaders from the Fifth Dimension").

Lloyd Bochner was 40 when he played Dr. Martin Davis, and received nearly the top pay of the day for a guest star on an hour-long program: $2,500 for six days work. A combination of good writing and excellent acting elevated this

Lloyd Bochner co-starred with Rod Taylor in the TV series *Hong Kong*. (20ᵗʰ Century-Fox, 1960-61)

character above the standard traitorous spy type. It is especially effective when Bochner's character gives in to fear with some fancy panicking of his own. Bochner was a regular on the 1960-61 20th Century-Fox series, *Hong Kong* (second-billed to star Rod Taylor), and turned in a memorable turn on *The Twilight Zone*, in the classic "To Serve Man," as the title character who realizes he is being taken home by aliens who are man-eaters. Bochner would return to *Voyage* for the second-season episode, "The Deadliest Game."

Edgar Bergen, playing Dr. Arthur Kenner, was 61, and the proud papa of future actress Candice Bergen … and of Charlie McCarthy. Ventriloquist Bergen and Charlie, his dummy sidekick, became famous with their own weekly series … on radio, of all things. He had appeared in an episode of David Hedison's previous series, *Five Fingers*. All of this allowed his agent to negotiate $1,500 for his services on five production days, and a "Special Guest Star" title card.

Edgar Bergen with *his* co-star, Charlie McCarthy.

William Sargent, 34, was the skipper of the sub that is lost in the Teaser. It was a small but extremely dramatic role. He would have a memorable turn as eventual murder victim Dr. Tom Leighton in the first season *Star Trek* episode "The Conscience of the King." And he had appeared in *Hitler*, starring Richard Basehart.

Derek Lewis, 23 at the time, returned to the series as Lt. O'Brien. He was seen briefly in "Eleven Days to Zero," as an unnamed officer. Now the character had a name. This would be the second of eight appearances during Season One. A chance second encounter with Irwin Allen won Lewis this recurring role. He recalled, "I watched the trades and found out that the show had sold to the network, and they were about to start the series. But no one called me. Then, one day, I had lunch with a friend at the studio. Irwin Allen was filming one of the first episodes on the back lot at the Moat, and I was standing on the small hillside, watching. Suddenly, Irwin looked in my direction, and then he stopped everything. He charged up the hill toward me. I didn't move; I just froze, and Irwin comes right up to me, his face right up to mine. The first thing out of his mouth was, 'Where the hell have you been? We've been looking all over for you!' I didn't know what to say. It's hard to believe he couldn't reach me; his casting people had all my contacts; but, evidently, these things move in strange ways, and fast. At least, that's how things seemed to move with Irwin.

"If it hadn't been for that lunch on the Fox lot with a friend, I wouldn't have ever been put into the series." (DL-AI18)

Filming started on Monday, August 3, 1964, lasting six days.

Lewis later recalled, "What I liked about the shooting was that all these wonderful actors – Richard, David, Robert, and Henry – were so serious; everyone was totally into what they were creating. Richard obviously had lots to memorize – a lot of the script – and so did David. I was just happy that they were personable. And the other thing was that they accepted me immediately into that group. They looked at me as a fellow actor, and a good actor.

"Irwin made a point of noticing the good actors that were on the scene at the time. I say this because, a lot of the actors who were on *Voyage* – small roles or big – were pretty damn good. Even the supporting players could have carried part of the action, and they would do that at different times, with each of the supporting players stepping forward to be featured in portions of the episodes. And I had a chance a couple of times."

Lewis had worked for director Leonard Horn once before, in an unsold television pilot. He said, "Leonard was really good. As a TV director, I remember him really working with the actors, and having a little bit of a sense of humor … even though there wasn't a lot of humor on the *Voyage* set!"

Regarding his fellow actors in this episode, Lewis said, "Lloyd Bochner was a very intense actor. He had his character right in place. And maybe it was because we

High tension in the Control Room. Below: Robert Dowdell with Edgar Bergen. Bottom image: Lloyd Bochner with Basehart and Hedison.

didn't have a lot of time, but, when you hit the set, everybody was *in* character. I cannot remember very many times when we just sat around and laughed and scratched; it just wasn't happening there, except for Edgar Bergman. He joked around. On a submarine, you have what's called the 'Poop Deck.' Well, Edgar

317

would say, 'Let's go up to the Poop Deck and take a poop!' I can remember things like that because he was one of those people who I worked with from time to time who I knew so well from television or films. I'd be talking to him, and I would stop mid-sentence and look at him and think, 'My God, I'm talking to Edgar Bergen!' I got so I didn't get intimidated by most actors, but every now and then I would meet someone, and I would be just stunned, because of my admiration for them.

"I will say this – there was something wonderful about working with Richard Basehart. His focus, his intensity, and his basic acting chops just made you a better actor, because you could look at each other and actually get into the moment – *act the scene*. There were a number of times on that show where, just for the moment, it felt real. You had the confines of the submarine, and could feel that, and react to that. I mean, obviously, the sets were open to the camera, but they were built so that they encompassed you. And when you're acting opposite someone like Richard Basehart, or Lloyd Bochner, in a tense story like this, it could feel very real." (DL-AI18)

The entire episode was filmed on Stage B, even though three scenes were not written for the Seaview sets.

The first of those, filmed on Day 5, Thursday, August 7, was the control room of the Polidor. It was merely the Seaview Control Room with minor changes. Also filmed that day, Dr. Kenner's Laboratory. Now you know why Kenner's door resembled those leading into Sickbay and the Admiral's Cabin on the Seaview. On the final day of production, when the Observation Nose scenes were filmed using the process screen, they also shot the interior of the limousine where the villainous agent talks on the car phone. The interior limo prop was wheeled in and filmed against the same process screen.

As a result of this economical approach, the final expenditure was only $119,484, about $15,000 to $20,000 less than most of the other episodes filmed to date. It was hoped that the technique, later called a "bottle show," might save *Voyage to the Bottom of the Sea* from ending the season with too great a production deficit ... and, worse, missed airdates. All the previous episodes filmed were meant to take six days each but had run over to seven or eight days. If this trend continued, *Voyage* would not be able to keep up with its broadcast schedule on ABC. That could result in cancellation.

In the post-production phase, the score was provided by selections written by both Hugo Friedhofer and Alexander Courage, both soon to be scoring for *Star Trek*.

Several months after the production, Richard Basehart told *TV Guide* writer Marian Dern, "Oh, there's a lot of challenge in this role. I mean it. Really wild things happen to the admiral. Once I remember the script called for the heavies to do away with the Seaview by giving the commander, me, a fear-producing drug. I spent half the show in a state of euphoria, the other half in a horrible depression. That's acting, television-style." (RB-TVG65)

The Polidor miniature used in this episode was seen in the 1961 *Voyage* feature film, although new sequences are presented here. The design is very similar to "Skipjack class" of U.S. nuclear submarines, which began with the U.S.S. Skipjack, commissioned in 1959. Five more of this class submarine – the Scamp, Scorpion, Sculpin, Shark, and Snook – were launched in 1959 and 1960, and they most certainly were prowling the oceans in the fictional time of the *Voyage* series (1973-78). The Scorpion was lost with all hands – 99 crewmembers – in 1968, cause unknown. But the others stayed in service through the late 1980s. The last to be decommissioned was the Shark, in 1990.

We would see the sub design again in later episodes of *Voyage*.

Release / Reaction:
(ABC premiere broadcast: 9/28/64; network repeat airing: 8/30/65)

"Oh, Pretty Woman" by Roy Orbison led the hit parade on U.S. radio stations. *Mary Poppins* continued to be the big cash winner at movie-house box offices. The night before, the Beach Boys, Leslie Uggams, and Robert Goulet all took turns singing on the *Ed Sullivan Show*. Alan King and Topo Gigio, the Italian puppet mouse, provided the laughs.

On September 28, 1964, syndicated "TV Scout," overseen by NEA's Joan Crosby, said:

> This show again submerges to the lower depths of high dramatics with "The Fear-Makers," which has the Seaview diving to the bottom in search of sister sub Polidor. On the way down, the crew gets a heavy dose of nerve gas released by some sinister foreign agent aboard. The ride is hysterical all the way. Calmest man aboard, for good reason, is guest star Edgar Bergen.

"TV Key," also syndicated to newspapers across America, took the material far more seriously. Steven Scheuer's take:

> This is possibly the most exciting episode of the young series, despite a certain amount of confusion at the beginning and hysteria toward the end. Mysterious evil forces are out to sabotage our undersea work so that they can get to the riches of the deep first. The sabotage takes the form of a newly created, unstable gas which gets into the hands of an enemy agent. Scenes aboard the Seaview showing the entire crew in the grip of the gas are nail-chewers and the hour builds up a lot of tension. Edgar Bergen guests as a good scientist, with Lloyd Bochner as an assistant who's really in the employ of the enemy. The series regulars are on hand giving capable performances.

Nielsen ratings report from Sept. 28, 1964:	Rating:	Share:
7:30 – 8 p.m.:		
ABC: *Voyage to the Bottom of the Sea*	**23.0**	**34.1%**
CBS: *To Tell the Truth*	17.2	25.5%
NBC: Monday Night Movie: *Ask Any Girl*	18.0	26.7%
8 – 8:30 p.m.		
ABC: *Voyage to the Bottom of the Sea*	**25.7**	**36.4%**
CBS: *I've Got a Secret*	19.0	26.9%
NBC: Monday Night Movie: *Ask Any Girl*	18.2	25.7%

NBC had David Niven, Shirley MacLaine, and Gig Young in a repeat of the 1959 comedy *Ask Any Girl*, which trailed the CBS panel shows during the first hour, giving *Voyage* the victory.

The Nielsen Top 20 report for the week covering September 28 through October 4, 1964, as printed in the October 12 issue of *Broadcasting* magazine, ranked the series this way:

1. *Bewitched* (ABC)
2. *The Fugitive* (ABC)
3. *The Addams Family* (ABC)
4. *My Three Sons* (ABC)
5. *Peyton Place II* (ABC)
6. *Valentine's Day* (ABC)
7. *The Patty Duke Show* (ABC)
8. *The Bing Crosby Show* (ABC)
9. *Ben Casey* (ABC)
10. *McHale's Navy* (ABC)
11. *Bonanza* (NBC)

12. *No Times for Sergeants* (ABC)
13. *The Munsters* (CBS)
14. *Wendy and Me* (ABC)
15. *Peyton Place I* (ABC)
16. ***Voyage to the Bottom of the Sea*** **(ABC)**
17. *Combat!* (ABC)
18. *The Beverly Hillbillies* (CBS)
19. *The Dick Van Dyke Show* (CBS)
20. Saturday Night Movie (NBC)

We liked "The Fear-Makers" then, and we like it now. But not all agreed. Two days after the first broadcast of "The Fear-Makers," James Devane, the TV-Radio Editor of *The Cincinnati Enquirer*, said "goodbye" to *Voyage to the Bottom of the Sea*:

> … I've sampled the program twice. I found its premiere childishly melodramatic, full of clichés and so tiresome I kept drifting toward dreamland. This week's adventure came up a fraction, but only a fraction. Melodrama and clichés had lessoned as foreign agent Lloyd Bochner and some deadly gas raised underwater pandemonium, but the episode was pedestrian and predictable. I still kept drifting toward dreamland.
>
> It's too bad. I'm all for science fiction when it's cleverly and imaginatively done. I've sat through many *Outer Limits* and *Twilight Zone* happily gnawing my nails. But *Voyage to the Bottom of the Sea* doesn't seem destined to have what it takes. The program has adventures with mysterious monsters and strangling plankton coming up but I can't imagine they'll be handled any better than past hours.
>
> So far as I'm concerned, *Voyage* and I have had it. … I've had my two sittings with David Hedison and his crew, and things didn't improve enough. The Seaview can go on without me. …

Episode 8: "Hot Line"

(Prod. #7208; first aired Monday, November 9, 1964)
Written by Berne Giler
Directed by John Brahm
Produced by Irwin Allen
Story Editor: William Welch; Associate Producer: Joseph Gantman
Assistant Story Editor: Al Gail
Guest Star Everett Sloane
Special Guest Star Michael Ansara
(with Ford Rainey and James Doohan)

From the *Voyage to the Bottom of the Sea* show files (Irwin Allen Papers Collection):

> The Russians discover that due to sabotage, their nuclear test rocket just launched will fall close to the California coast, with enough power to blow up San Francisco. With no time to evacuate the city, the President, when he gets the news over the Russian "Hot Line," tells Nelson that everything depends on the Seaview reaching it fast enough to render it harmless. But one of the Soviet technicians supposedly helping to dismantle the mechanism is a secret saboteur.

As word of their mission spreads through the sub, the volatile seaman Clark is desperate to warn his wife and child who live in San Francisco. After tussling with Kowalski, he attacks Sparks in an attempt to get out a message.

Sound Bites:

Nelson: "They just heard from the Kremlin. Russian intelligence has just captured one of the ringleaders of the sabotage plot. They now have reason to believe that one of our Russian technicians is an imposter." *Crane:* "Which one?" *Nelson:* "They don't know. The prisoner died before they could get a full statement." *Crane (realizing):* "The satellite hasn't been disarmed. It's still going to blow up." *Nelson:* "That would be the only purpose in sending an imposter."
(Note Nelson's implication that "the prisoner" probably died under Russian torture.)

Assessment:

It's all a bit stagey, marred by sections of stilted dialogue and the usual melodramatics. But don't let that stand in the way of your enjoyment of this fine tale of espionage, betrayal, and double-dealing. Several mainstream novels of the era, such as *Fail Safe* and *Alas, Babylon* concerned the dreadful consequences of accidental nuclear war. This episode was highly representative of society's Cold War anxiety. Fifty years later, it's sad to note that its theme is still relevant.

Script:
Berne Giler's writers contract: May 12, 1964.
Giler's treatment and 1st and 2nd draft teleplays: Dates unknown.
Mimeo Department's reformatted Shooting Final teleplay: Date unknown.
Revised Shooting Final teleplay (by William Welch or Al Gail): Date unknown.
2nd Revised Shooting final teleplay by writing staff: August 7.
3rd Revised Shooting Final teleplay (yellow pages): August 11.
Page revisions (blue): August 14.

This was Berne Giler's second and last *Voyage* writing assignment, following "Village of Guilt." The inspiration for the episode's title, also known as "the red telephone," was established between Washington and Moscow on June 20, 1963, in the wake of the Cuban Missile Crisis. It really wasn't a phone, but used teletype technology (later replaced by "telecopier," later known as a fax machine, and then electronic mail).

Associate Producer Joseph Gantman, like Allan Balter, felt compelled to give notes during the creative development of the scripts. On July 17, he wrote to Irwin Allen, with copies sent to script editors Bill Welch and Al Gail:

1. Suggest that scenes 1-12 in the Russian Block House control center be dropped, and that the Teaser start close on a TV Monitor showing the launch and pull back to reveal the scene in the Kremlin Conference Room. This scene can be built with the tension of the viewers ... their reaction and shock at the launch going wrong.

   They and we will hear the control room dialogue on their closed circuit system.

   They must demand that every effort be made to destroy the missile and that another effort be made.

   It must be made clear that the instant computations have determined that the missile will land in the area of the U.S. and that this could be the accidental beginning of a terrible war.

   The dialogue should be in English.

2. The start of Act I ideally should be continuous. Start on the phone in the White House (a unique sound signal). Pull back to see the reaction of the man on duty. The first reaction would be real shock. The President is awakened and called in immediately. He is in pajamas and a robe.

   The scene between the President and the Kremlin will have tremendous impact. The catastrophic possibilities overshadowing them could make this a great scene.

   This scene must be in English.

3. Page 8, Sc. 28 reference to Security Council is confusing.

4. Suggest dissolving from Sc. 23 to scene on P. 14 in which Seaview is on way to meet Russian Trawler. Play the scene here only to point on P. 15 where Crane says "we'll know soon enough."

   This construction will give is the feeling that something is afoot, but we're not sure yet what it is.

> 5. From scene above go to Sc. 24 with the President presiding (as now written the President seems ineffectual).
>
> Pages 13, 14, 15: The entire airport scene is too big, too confusing. The use of the "men's room" is unsavory. It is never made clear whether the men in the "waiting Soviet limousine" are in on the abduction or completely fooled by it. ...
>
> Page 15: This is too late, too mild, too confusing an introduction of Nelson. Reconsider putting him back in the Washington meeting. ...
>
> Page 16: Crane's speech – "<u>Not much doubt which one's the boss, is there</u>?" – Since they just talked in Russian and no one crawled out on their knees, how the hell does Crane know which one's the boss?
>
> Nelson's speech – "Ours is to get them to the splash area in time?" – This is the first time we have the vaguest notion what the [mission of the] Seaview is about – it's still so vague as to be downright confusing.
>
> Crane's speech – "<u>not a special sea detail</u>." What's a "special sea detail" and to do what?

Gantman's notes went on for five pages. He was appalled by the condition of the script – and wasn't even a writer!

Meanwhile, Irwin Allen was writing script notes of his own (undated), and seemed equally bothered. Note that Allen and Gantman point out some of the same flaws:

> Scene 1, 2, etc.: Voices should be in English, not Russian.
>
> Scene 16 thru 26: This is a confusing sequence – the audience will be confused. There is no audience preparation to the bringing aboard the Seaview of Malinoff.
>
> Scene 28: Spell out what C.N.O. means.
>
> Page 3, Scene 8: In order to build and maintain the later suspense, the final speech on Page 3 of the Russian aide

must contain more specific and alarming information – "critical mass" – "could kill millions" – "start an atomic war."

Page 11, Scene 28: In the aide's first speech – change "level" to "destroy" and add "and kill millions of people in that city."

Page 15: Nelson doesn't enter story until Page 15 – too late! As now re-written, Nelson is not in the Washington meeting with the President and is not on board the sub when Malinoff arrives. Yet Chip refers to "the Admiral's phone call from Washington." This is a carryover [from previous draft].

Page 12: President's speech all wrong – it sums up things never seen, referred to or even hinted at up to this point. It's just too much of a cheat.

On August 7, the representative from ABC Continuity Acceptance Department gave his notes, saying, in part:

Again (as with the "Hail to the Chief" episode) obvious reference to your 1973 date are most important to avoid any duplication of the Orson Welles "War of the Worlds" scare. May I suggest that on page 2 the RUSSIAN AIDE toast the date as "... mark the day, the 27th day of blank, 1973, etc...." and that wherever and as often as possible (whenever a time reference is given with video information) that the 1973 date be included. Calendars could be displayed on the fictional President's desk (sc 139); a time, day, month and year electronic gimmick should be displayed for instance in scene 143; picture calendars in the radio shack; etc. And, without entering into a programming area, any futuristic device employed in this episode which would indicate to the audience that the time is not NOW (such as the HOT LINE telephone should not be a 1964 AT&T model) would greatly improve its acceptability. The alternate to this is to fictionalize the area of location.

And again, for the record, the President may not resemble any past, present or aspirant candidate, nor may any of his Cabinet in any way resemble those currently in office.

It may appear that ABC believed viewers were so ill-informed and easily swayed that this episode's fiction would be taken as fact. While it's indeed hard to underestimate the intelligence of some consumers, these network and censor warnings were typical for the era. The admonitions were a combination of liability avoidance and a legitimate (if overanxious) desire to not "inflame the public." Cautions regarding the casting of government roles were not only due to corporate cowardice, but also an American scene delineated by student protests and political assassinations. (To take a lighter tone – how in the world could Allen make sure that his actor "President" didn't resemble *any future aspirant* to the office?)

The date used for this episode was May 27, 1973.

Production:
(Filmed August 11-18, 1964; 6 days)
(Budget: $119,995)

John Brahm returned to direct his second and final episode of *Voyage*, following "City Beneath the Sea."

Everett Sloan played Gronski. He was 54, and had been nominated for an Emmy for "Patterns," a 1955 episode of *Kraft Theatre* written by Rod Serling. Before that, he had been a member of Orson Welles' Mercury Theatre, and made his screen debut in Welles' classic

**Above: Everett Sloan, circa 1950s.
Below: Michael Ansara as Cochise, in the TV series *Broken Arrow*.**
(20th Century-Fox, 1956-58)

Citizen Kane as Kane's confidant, Mr. Bernstein. He had two more prominent roles working for Welles, in *Journey into Fear* and *The Lady from Shanghai*, as well as an additional standout role acting with his mentor, Welles, and Tyrone Power, in 1949's *Prince of Foxes*. Sloan took a memorable trip into *The Twilight Zone* as a man hooked on gambling and haunted by a Vegas slot machine, in the 1960 episode "The Fever."

Michael Ansara was ranked as "special guest star," playing Malinoff. He was 42 and married to Barbara Eden. He'd starred in two series of his own, *Broken Arrow*, from 1956 to '58, and *Law of the Plainsman*, for the 1959-60 TV season. He appeared in the feature-film version of *Voyage to the Bottom of the Sea*, and would return again to the series (for "Killers of the Deep"), as well as a pair of *The Time Tunnel* episodes, one *Lost in Space*, and one *Land of the Giants*, all for producer Irwin Allen. You may also remember him as Kang, the Klingon commander, in the 1968 *Star Trek* episode, "Day of the Dove."

Paul Carr returned as Seaman Clark. We last saw him in "Hail to the Chief," when he risked his life in water-filled ducts to save the Seaview. Here, he is more concerned with wife and child in San Francisco. Clark, an emotionally charged individual whether working with or against his fellow shipmates, would be back.

Ford Rainey was 55 when hired to play the President of the United States. He was still in office for another first-season episode, "Doomsday," and again played the U.S. President for the *Lost in Space* pilot filmed later in the year. Irwin Allen brought Rainey back to play a different U.S. President – Abraham Lincoln – for an episode of *The Time Tunnel*.

James Doohan reprised his role as a White House aide. He had played this character once before, for "Hail to the Chief," although "Hot Line" aired first. Allen liked Doohan enough to offer him the role of the Seaview Chief for the second season, but

Above: Would you believe John Banner, the future Sgt. Shultz, as a high-ranking Soviet official with a hotline to the Kremlin? No, we didn't either.
Below: The airplane below was one of the bigger props on the Fox backlot, wheeled in whenever the "Craft Center" was needed to pass for an airport.

Doohan had to decline. He'd already been tapped to play Chief Engineer Scott on the Enterprise, in *Star Trek*.

John Banner played the Russian Chairman. He was 54, and had been acting in Hollywood films since 1940, with well over a hundred appearances at this time. One year from now he would win the hearts of TV viewers as Sgt. Schultz in *Hogan's Heroes*.

Filming began Tuesday, August 11 for the outdoor locations, all on the Fox lot. The "Ext. Arline Office Building" and "Int. and Ext. Baggage Shed"

329

were really the area known as the "Craft Center." Note the passenger jet featured here. This was a standing set at Fox, and hap appeared in Irwin Allen's *The Lost World*.

The helicopter pad was a real one on the studio lot. The high-rise buildings under construction in the background were the beginning of Century City, on the land that until recently was the 20th Century-Fox backlot.

Next, the company moved onto Stage B to shoot in the Missile Room. They filmed until 7 p.m.

On Wednesday, the company filmed in the Control Room and Radio Shack, and the crew's quarters, all on Stage B.

On Thursday, the company covered the scenes written for the Observation Nose and corridors.

Come Friday, they were still filming in the Observation Nose, taking up the entire day (until 7:40 p.m.) and most of Monday.

The underwater footage seen outside the windows of the nose, which includes divers swimming away from the sub, was filmed by the Second Unit team off the coast of Catalina. You never see the faces of the divers, because Everett Sloan and Michael Ansara were not asked to jump into the "Green Tank" for close-up shots in scuba gear and masks.

Director Brahm took his last shot with the main unit at 7:55. And that wrapped work on Stage B.

Day 6: Int. White House Oval Office, with, at its center, James Doohan and Ford Rainey.

The sixth and final day of filming took place on Fox Stage 3 (the Kremlin Conference Room set), followed by a move to Stage 14 for the White House Oval Office set. It was a long day. Call times were 6:30 a.m. Filming began shortly after 8 a.m. and lasted until 9:50 p.m., at which point another half hour was needed to wrap the set and for the actors to change and have their make-up stripped off.

John Brahm had brought his second *Voyage* assignment in on budget and schedule, no small feat considering this was far from being a bottle show.

The rough edit was screened for ABC on October 7. Adrian Samish, of the network, sent specific notes to Irwin Allen asking for 13 edits to remove camera shots or lines of dialogue that he felt would either offend or distress members of the viewing audience.

Half of these desired cuts were not made, including Samish's orders that they "Drop struggle between Clark and Kowalski in the mess room, Cut after line, 'Maybe you just haven't the guts to take it.'"

Now why in the world would anyone think to cut after that line? Them were fighting words, after all. Of course a scuffle would follow. We can only chalk it up to Samish's unfathomable irascibility. (Hear writer Harlan Ellison's colorful take on Samish later in this chapter, for the episode "The Price of Doom.")

Irwin Allen and/or Joseph Gantman fought for the scene ... and won.

Release / Reaction:
(ABC premiere broadcast: 11/9/64; network repeat airing: 7/19/65)

"The House of the Rising Sun," by the Animals, was getting the most airplay on U.S. Top 40 radio stations. The film doing the best business in movie houses was an odd one – *Kitten with a Whip*, about juvenile delinquents, and starring Ann-Margret (fresh from *Viva Las Vegas* and *Bye, Bye Birdie*).

"Hot Line" was the eighth episode to film; the ninth to air.

Syndicated "TV Scout," carried in hundreds of newspapers across America, said:

> "Hot Line" on *Voyage to the Bottom of the Sea* is a murky but often exciting adventure. Mission of the Seaview is to disarm a nuclear satellite which has crashed into the ocean. Object here is to save a million lives. Good acting in this one, with a cast headed by Everett Sloan and Michael Ansara.

Nielsen ratings report from Nov. 9, 1964:	Rating:	Share:
7:30 – 8 p.m.:		
ABC: *Voyage to the Bottom of the Sea*	**19.1**	**30.9%**
CBS: *To Tell the Truth*	15.8	25.5%
NBC: *90 Bristol Court: Karen*	15.3	24.7%
8 – 8:30 p.m.		
ABC: *Voyage to the Bottom of the Sea*	**22.4**	**37.3%**
CBS: *I've Got a Secret*	16.6	25.0%
NBC: *90 Bristol Court: Harris Against the World*	16.6	25.0%

Within days of the airing of "Hot Line," ABC picked up additional episodes of *Voyage*, making for a full season.

Episode 9: "The Sky Is Falling"

(Prod. #7209; first aired Monday, October 19, 1964)
Written by Don Brinkley
Directed by Leonard Horn
Produced by Irwin Allen
Story Editor: William Welch; Associate Producer: Allan Balter
Assistant Script Editor: Al Gail
Guest Star Charles McGraw

From the *Voyage to the Bottom of the Sea* show files (Irwin Allen Papers Collection):

> A U.F.O., seen over various parts of the U.S., causes alarm and terror. When it dives into the Pacific, the Seaview is commandeered by Admiral Robin [Tobin] to find and destroy it. But Nelson discovers that it is a spaceship from another planet with no ill-intentions. He prevents "Trigger-Happy Tobin" from starting an interplanetary war by an attack on the helpless space craft, an attack which would bring about immediate retaliation from the other planet.

However, Nelson's action leaves the Seaview at the mercy of the alien. This soon comes under question as the submarine loses power, is unable to surface, and the crew is in jeopardy of suffocating.

Sound Bites:

Kowalski (to Patterson): "Well, that's the neatest trick of the week – chasing a flying saucer with a submarine!"

Nelson: "Maybe they're trying to communicate with us." *Crane:* "Maybe they are. How do we communicate with *them*?" *Nelson:* "Something tells me they'll find a way."

Alien (to Nelson): "You are obviously a man of courage, otherwise you would not have accepted the invitation that brought you here. Are you also a man of curiosity?" *Nelson:* "I'm a scientist, if that term has any meaning for you." *Alien:* "A vast meaning – I am delighted to hear it."

Kowalski (standing in front of air ventilator when power is restored): "I finally found something I like better than girls."

Crane: "We can expect to see them again someday. I hope they'll remember they were treated as friends." *Nelson:* "They'll remember all right. I wonder if we will?"

Assessment:

Shades of *The Day the Earth Stood Still* … visually … and thematically. Two years before *Star Trek* gave us "The Devil in the Dark," and more than a decade before Steven Spielberg gave us *E.T.*, *Voyage* introduced a benevolent alien of its own – a chance for mankind to react in a manner other than violence triggered by fear. As another alien from *Star Trek* would say (in 1966's "Arena"), "Perhaps, in several thousand years, your people and mine shall meet to reach an agreement. You are still half savage … but there is hope."

Writer Mark Phillips said it best: "This is *Voyage* at its most rational and at its best. Ultimately, this story is a vote of confidence for humans AND extra-terrestrials. Nelson's last line of dialog really makes the show." (vttbots.com)

Another point in this story's favor is that the alien takes the form of Admiral Nelson – a vivid depiction of man's possibility for wisdom or violence.

A *Star Trek* with more than a passing resemblance to this episode was "The Corbomite Maneuver," written by Jerry Sohl. In that, the U.S.S. Enterprise encounters a giant alien spaceship in uncharted space. The Enterprise is remotely paralyzed, Kirk and crew stymied. After a tension-filled series of useless ploys by Kirk, it transpires that the alien is benevolent, merely testing the humans to see if they can respond without rushing to violence. "Corbomite" was nominated for a

Hugo Award, the Oscar of the science fiction community. And it came two years after this particular voyage.

This episode represented a pair of "firsts" for *Voyage to the Bottom of the Sea*. It was the Seaview's first encounter with aliens from outer space, and also the first instance of a doppelganger "Admiral Nelson" and/or a doppelganger "Captain Crane" – something we would see a *lot* of in future seasons.

Everyone involved could be proud of "The Sky Is Falling," in all ways – from the writing, the direction, the acting, and the visual effects, especially impressive for this time. The sky may have been falling, but *Voyage to the Bottom of the Sea* was soaring to new heights.

Script:
Berne Giler's writers contract, for "The Lost Treasure": July 2, 1964.
1st draft teleplay by Giler, addressed in July 6 report.
Don Brinkley's new 1st draft teleplay, and 2nd draft teleplay: Dates unknown.
Mimeo Department's reformatted Shooting Final teleplay: Date unknown.
Rev. Shooting Final teleplay (by William Welch or Al Gail): August 7.
3rd Rev. Shooting Final by writing staff (on green paper): August 18.
Page revisions (pink paper): August 20.
Page revisions (yellow paper): August 27.

Script assignment 7256 was originally given to Berne Giler, who had written "The Village of Guilt" and "Hot Line"; it had the working title "The Lost Treasure." This assignment was cancelled after the first draft, and handed off to Don Brinkley, who had written "Hail to the Chief."

Brinkley said, "They wanted to do a show with an alien, and I said, 'Well, rather than have a bad alien, what about a good one?' And that was a fresh idea for television. ... The story fell into place easily. I remember trying to avoid clichés because there were enough built into *Voyage* as it was. Let's face it, the series' concept was a little hokey. It was designed like the old Saturday afternoon movie serials." (DB-SL92)

The title was changed to "The Sky Is Falling," with a theme of fear – both warranted and unjustified. The new title was based on the familiar children's tale about Chicken Little, who is struck by a falling acorn and hysterically cries, "The sky is falling!" The phrase has become an instant signifier of unfounded fear of imminent catastrophe.

In the script, there were description of reactions from people looking up into the sky and seeing the flying saucer. Some were children. ABC wasn't going to sit still for that. Dorothy Brown, the network censor, wrote to Irwin Allen on August 10, saying:

> To avoid overtones of "child jeopardy" – Page 2, Sc 6 – the children must not recognize the potential danger – must

not register fear. Otherwise you will have to use teenagers – or woman and poodle – or some other effect.

The substitute of teenagers and "woman and poodle" were made. Some younger kids are seen in stock footage from *The Day the World Stood Still*, but efforts were made to not include shots in which the young were unduly fearful.

Despite the quality of both of Brinkley's scripts for *Voyage*, he chose not to seek additional work. The reason was Brinkley's attitude regarding Irwin Allen. "He wasn't the easiest guy in the world to deal with," said the writer. "He was very temperamental, impulsive and certainly not the most rational human being I've ever met. He had a huge ego and he always had to be right. If you had an idea, it had to be *his* idea; that sort of thing. He would throw temper tantrums, and either you accepted his behavior and walked away from him, or you got upset. Some people got upset. I didn't! I just walked away. That's why I only did two episodes. He wanted to put me under contract, but the thought of being tied to his coattails was too much for me." (DB-SL92)

Charles McGraw and Marie Windsor in *The Narrow Margin*. (RKO Radio Pictures, 1952)

Production:
(Filmed August 20-28, 1964; 7 days)
(Budget: $118,125)

This was Director Leonard Horn's second of nine *Voyage* assignments. His work, as usual, is top-notch.

Charles McGraw was 50 when he played Rear Admiral Tobin. He had his own series from 1954 to '56, in *Adventures of the Falcon*. At this time he was pulling double duty, also appearing in a series for the 1955-56 series, *Casablanca*, as Rick Blaine, the role played by Humphrey Bogart in the 1942 film. Shortly before appearing on *Voyage*, McGraw played the sadistic gladiatorial trainer Marcellus, who repeatedly taunted slave Kirk Douglas in *Spartacus*, just one of many memorable film roles.

Adam Williams was the Chief on watch, under the scrutiny of his Captain (watching from behind). The first three days of production covered the remarkably tense – and darkly lit – scenes in the Control Room.

Adam Williams stood in for Henry Kulky as the Chief of the Seaview. Williams was 41, and was a respected character actor, often playing military types and heavies. He had an occasional lead, such as the 1952 *film noir*, *Without Warning*. Williams worked often in television, appearing in dozens of popular series, including six appearances on *The Rifleman*; four turns each on *Bonanza* and *77 Sunset Strip*; three each on *The Detectives*, *Surfside 6*, *Rawhide*, and *Have Gun – Will Travel*; and two trips into *The Twilight Zone*. But this was his only voyage on Irwin Allen's Seaview.

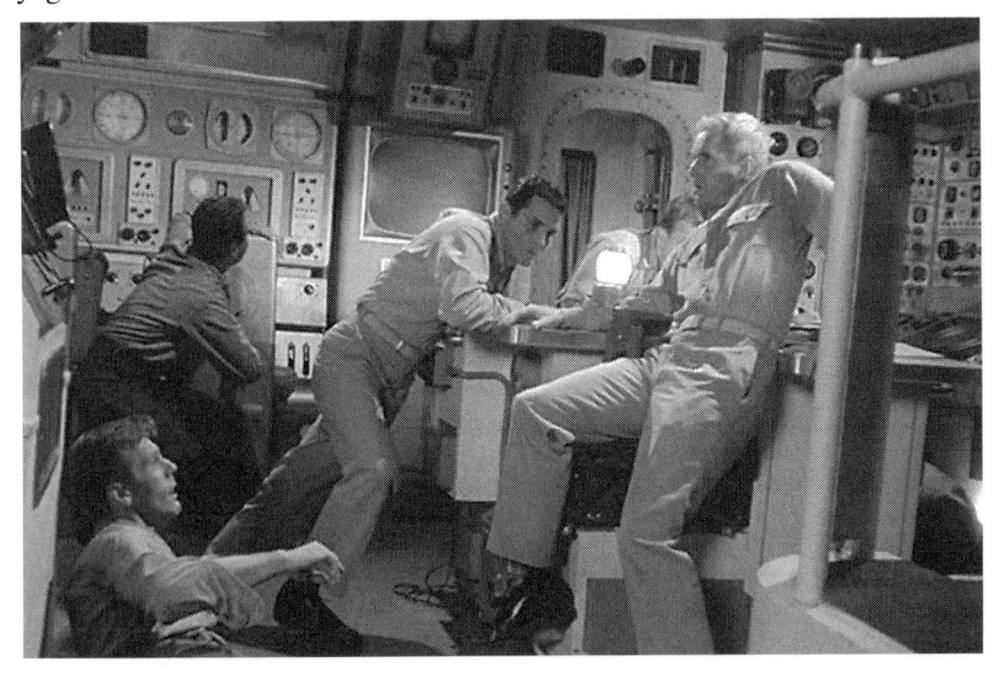

The scenes in the episode's teaser which depict frightened citizens dashing around in a flying-saucer frenzy came from 1951's *The Day the Earth Stood Still*, also from 20th Century-Fox and therefore subject to harvesting by Irwin Allen. The frugal producer also "borrowed" bits of the film's classic Bernard Herrmann score. Effects shots and music from the movie were later "liberated" for a few episodes of *Lost in Space*.

Under Leonard Horn's excellent direction, and with the Seaview's power system on emergency battery, the sub never looked darker ... or more dramatic.

Filming began on Thursday, August 20, 1964, for three days on Stage B, shooting all the scenes required for the Seaview's Control Room and Admiral Nelson's Cabin.

Filming went like clockwork the first few days, with the set wrapping at 6:40 p.m. on the first day, and 7:20 on both Days 2 and 3.

Day 4, Tuesday, August 25th, also went smoothly, as the company took over Fox Stage 16 for filming in the "Int. Tracking Room," with a 5:40 p.m. wrap. Following this, test shots were taken of the plankton monster for the next episode to film, "The Price of Doom."

Day 5, Wednesday: Remaining on the borrowed Stage 16, the company was to film all of the "Int. Saucer" scenes. Even though it was a simple set – just one room -- they ran out of time. The necessities of costume and makeup changes for the two stars, plus intricate blocking, and double-shooting for split-screen shots, all conspired to make production fall behind.

For 1960s television, the split-screen process was hardly cheap – requiring hand-drawn "masks" and an optical printer, especially primitive.

Above: Richard Basehart acting opposite his lighting double, Ray Didsbury. After shooting this angle, the two actors would exchange places and do the scene again, putting the real Basehart on both sides.
Below: The alien in its true form.

Above: From Day 6, the Observation Nose scenes, utilizing the rear view projector, took an entire day to film.
Below: The reaction from those in the Control Room, through the magic of film editing, was actually filmed days earlier.

When it comes to this episode, imagine yourself in Richard Basehart's shoes. You have been a film star; a stage star; you've also done high-profile television and radio. You've played the classics and earned renown as a Shakespearean actor. Presently you star in a weekly TV series. Now comes this story, with its depiction of an encounter with a being from space. One of the elevating aspects of science fiction for an actor is the unique roles one can play. And what more unique role than opposite yourself – as the "Other"? Although appearing twice-at-once via split screen was a novelty for Basehart, this technique would soon become a virtual cottage industry for TV, enhancing plots on shows such as *The Man from U.N.C.L.E.*, *Lost in Space*, *Star Trek*, *Land of the Giants*, and forming the entire basis for *The Patty Duke Show* (1963-1966).

Then came Hedison's turn to "double up." He had acted opposite prehistoric monsters before ... or reacted to something that wasn't yet there (in *The Lost World* and "Turn Back the Clock"). Now he was acting against another version of himself, which would be realized through the magic of post-production. Episodes like this, while exacting technically, nevertheless gave a performer a chance to stretch his acting muscles by presenting a different lookalike character.

With the extra time needed for staging the split-screen technique, the company did not wrap until 7:25 in the evening ... and with a few pages from this day's shooting schedule not yet covered.

Director Horn would have to return to finish this work, but Stage 16 was needed by another company the following day. Therefore, the *Voyage* team headed back to Stage B, with a return to Stage 16 on Friday. "The Price of Doom," the next episode to film, was pushed back until the following week.

Day 6: Thursday. The company was back on Stage B, rolling camera between 8 a.m. and 6:20 p.m., first on the Observation Nose (including process shots), then on the "Flying Bridge," also filmed against a process screen. They took their last shot by 6:20 p.m.

Day 7: Friday, August 28. They were back on Stage 16, for the last of the shots needed inside the Saucer. Also, the scene in which Nelson, Crane and Rear Admiral Tobin climb into a compartment above the control room which gives access to a hatch that, in turn, would take Nelson up into the alien shuttle. Horn wrapped at 5:20 p.m.

A second unit was used to film the miniature of the saucer splash-landing into Lake Sersen, as well as the saucer miniature appearing in the same shot as the four-foot Seaview miniature, and the sequence in which the transport leaves and returns to the saucer.

ABC screened the rough edit on September 18, 1964. The Final Air Print was approved on October 9 and televised 10 days later.

Release / Reaction:
(ABC premiere broadcast: 10/19/64; network repeat airing: 5/3/65)

"The Sky Is Falling" was the ninth episode to film but was advanced in the broadcast schedule to be sixth to air. And it was repeated on the network during the summer months.

Writer Don Brinkley said, "The little I did see of that first year was rather special. Instead of being a straight action-adventure show, they tried to expand TV's horizons a little. The SF/fantasy approach opened up the perimeters and gave it added dimension. 'Sky' was fun to do and it got some good reviews. ... I remember enjoying what they did with my script. The director, Leonard Horn, did a fine job." (DB-SL92)

On October 18, 1964, the day before "The Sky Is Falling" first aired, entertainment columnist Bill Sheriton wrote in Alabama's *The Cullman Times*:

> Did you ever think about the scientific phenomena involved with the *Voyage to the Bottom of the Sea*? Well, in Monday night's episode at 6:30 over Ch. 6, you will see what happens when the Seaview uses its atomic power to destroy an enemy spaceship that sank to the bottom of the ocean. Regulars Richard Basehart and David Hedison also portray spacemen in this story.

The syndicated column "TV Key," carried on October 19 in the *Tucson Daily Citizen*, among other newspapers, said:

> Pretty exciting science fiction hokum. A disabled spaceship falls into the sea and our first thought is that it's an invading enemy. When contact is established and help solicited, a trigger-happy admiral (Charles McGraw) wants to proceed with the attack anyway. Richard Basehart and David Hedison are at their noble best and

the show benefits tremendously from some well executed special effects.

Also on October 19, rival syndicated column, "TV Scout," carried in the *Monessen Valley Independent*, among other newspapers, said:

> The heroic atomic sub, Seaview, is faced with an old problem: flying saucers. In "The Sky Is Falling," the Seaview goes as berserk as Chicken Little when the spacecraft's powerful rays disable its power and light system.

Days after the episode aired, syndicated newspaper columnist Charles Witbeck gave his overview of the series. For his column, printing in the *Waterloo Daily Courier* on October 25, 1964, Witbeck said in part:

> It's clear to all that *Voyage* is a kid's show, filled with stern men concentrating on dials, conversing in thin-lipped tones, using dialogue sprinkled with pseudo-scientific jargon. The high adventure comic book material has come to the TV screen, produced with care and effort. Actor Basehart, a man who didn't have to jump for the first offer to come along, read a script and said "yes," he'd do it. Basehart's presence will help a good deal.
>
> The real stars are the prop men, the special effects crew working in miniature, and the writers who are dreaming about plot possibilities underwater ten years from now. If the visual effects look phony, the actors won't have a chance, but producer Allen says he has this angle beaten. Where did Allen, a New Yorker, begin his big love affair with the sea? Allen laughed and said, "When I was a kid, an epidemic of whooping cough swept through the city. Many of us were taken over to Brooklyn Navy Yard and put in a sub. It seems there was a theory that the change in pressure from going up and down would relieve the cough, so hundreds of us went through it. I don't remember if the change in pressure had any effect, but it's my first memory of the ocean."

Between this and the Saturday-morning movie serials watched by the young Allen, part of his future was set. And now he was passing along his love for high jinks adventure in weekly doses.

Witbeck continued:

In last month's opener, the sub went to the North Pole to explode a nuclear device to offset a forthcoming earthquake. The explosion was expected to break the back of tidal waves about to be formed by the earthquakes. Eight-year-old minds will certainly buy this heady stuff and homework may be junked. Just calling out signals from all those sub dials, a dependable segment in every show, will have the kids hopping.

A.C. Nielsen reported more than kids were jumping to tune in *Voyage*.

Nielsen ratings report from Oct. 19, 1964: 7:30 – 8 p.m.:	Rating:	Share:
ABC: *Voyage to the Bottom of the Sea*	**25.8**	**38.1%**
CBS: *To Tell the Truth*	16.4	24.2%
NBC: *90 Bristol Court: Karen*	15.0	22.1%
8 – 8:30 p.m.		
ABC: *Voyage to the Bottom of the Sea*	**28.0**	**40.3%**
CBS: *I've Got a Secret*	17.7	25.5%
NBC: *90 Bristol Court: Harris Against the World*	13.1	18.8%

Episode 10: "The Price of Doom"

(Prod. #7210; first aired Monday, October 12, 1964)
Written by Harlan Ellison (as Cord Wainer Bird)
Directed by James Goldstone
Produced by Irwin Allen
Story Editor: William Welch; Associate Producer: Joseph Gantman
Assistant Story Editor: Al Gail
Guest Stars David Opatoshu and John Milford
and Jill Ireland as "Julie"
(with Steve Ihnat and Pat Priest)

From the *Voyage to the Bottom of the Sea* show files (Irwin Allen Papers Collection):

> Nelson, visiting one of his scientists working on methods of synthesizing plankton for food, finds the Arctic ice-station a shambles and the scientist and his wife vanished. Then, to his horror, samples of the plankton brought aboard the Seaview mysteriously expand to gigantic size and threaten to swallow the whole ship. Nelson, working desperately against time, has to discover the secret of the grotesque transformation before it is too late.

Sound Bites:

Nelson: "Doctor Reisner, Mr. Wesley is here because money is necessary for this project. That is a fact of life."

Dr. Reisner (to Nelson): "If I have forgotten my manners, it is because this is so important to me." *Dr. Julie Lyle (asserting herself):* "Important to all of us, doctor." *Reisner (with annoyance):* "I have given 15 years of my life to this project." *Julie:* "I have spent only five. But we're all after the same thing." *Reisner (angry):* "What do you know about it?! Have you ever seen people starving? Have *you* ever starved? If we can break through, plankton can be a source of food that can save the lives of unborn millions!"

Assessment:

This episode, along with "Turn Back the Clock," "Village of Guilt," and "The Sky Is Falling," put *Voyage*'s monster episodes at forty percent of the first ten. Not surprisingly for a series that hadn't quite settled into its format, this episode is uneven. The formula mixing espionage with monsters isn't entirely successful. But "The Price of Doom" is always entertaining, and has several effective – even frightening – moments. They aren't hair-raising so much because of the monster – it rarely rises above silly – but because of the impassioned acting. Several fine performances – with just the right mixture of awe and horror – turn this possibly goofy retread of *The Blob* into an enjoyable thrill ride. Steve Ihnat's desperate attempts to rescue his wife, and effectively dramatic (not melodramatic) turns from David Hedison and Del Monroe, among others, combine to elevate the hokey premise to a blast from our more innocent past.

Harlan Ellison's original tongue-in-cheek title was "Meal Time." You can be sure that "Cord Wainer Bird" took devilish glee in thinking about his viewers' conundrum. For this "Meal Time," with its man-eating plankton, who is the diner, and who will become dinner?

Script:
Harlan Ellison's writers contract: April 17, 1964.
Ellison's "Meal Time" treatment and 1st and 2nd draft teleplays: Dates unknown.
Mimeo Department's reformatted Shooting Final teleplay, now "The Price of Doom": Date unknown.
Revised Shooting Final, and 2nd and 3rd Rev. Shooting Final teleplays (by William Welch and/or Al Gail): Dates unknown.
4th Rev. Shooting Final teleplay by writing staff: August 25.
5th Rev. Shooting Final: August 27.
6th Rev. Shooting Final (green paper): August 31.
Page revisions (pink paper): September 1.

Harlan Ellison with Leonard Nimoy and William Shatner on the set of *Star Trek* in 1966.
(Photo credit: Harlan Ellison collection)

This was Harlan Ellison's only script for *Voyage to the Bottom of the Sea*. He was a highly sought-after science-fiction writer of short stories and novels. His TV credits included *Burke's Law*, *The Alfred Hitchcock Hour*, and *The Outer Limits*. In the future, his work would grace the TV series *The Man from U.N.C.L.E.*, *Star Trek*, *The Starlost*, *Logan's Run*, *The Twilight Zone* (1980s version), and *Babylon 5*.

For decades, rumors have circulated around Hollywood that Ellison became frustrated by Irwin Allen's notes on his script to the point that he picked up a large model of the Seaview and hurled it down the long boardroom table in Allen's direction.

When interviewed for this book, Ellison said, "As with all of these stories, they get distorted in time. I didn't throw it at Irwin Allen. I was at one end of a long conference table at a meeting with Adrian Samish, who was the head of ABC network continuity, at the other. He was the censor at the time. And both sides of the table were filled with about 20 people – 'yes men' of all sorts, including an unforgettably named Paul Zastupnevich. And [Samish's] suggestions were so goddamn stupid. Censors of the type of Adrian Samish had no idea what they're asking. They'll say, 'Well, just change that,' meaning it's no longer an airplane, it's an *egg-beater*. And, finally, I couldn't take it anymore and I got furious and I jumped up on my chair and ran down the length of the table. It was a long table, about 30 feet long, and I slipped on the memorandum pages that were laid out, and fell flat on my ass, but with my fists outstretched. And I hit Adrian Samish right in the throat. He went backwards in a swivel chair, and it went out from under him and he hit the wall with a giant thump. And a model of the Seaview, which was very long – I think it was the 10-foot model – came unshackled from its moorings and fell on him and broke his pelvis. And I'm hanging over the edge of the table to try to get at him to kill him, with four people literally on me to get me onto the floor and into the next room and into a chair to keep me down, otherwise I'd gone back in to finish the job.

"Irwin Allen avoided a lawsuit by getting his producer friend Quinn Martin to offer Adrian Samish a job at Warners, and Samish went to work for him there.

"Adrian Samish made sure I didn't work at ABC for a while – I think it was at least seven years before I had another script assignment at ABC. The last day of his work, before he went to work for Quinn Martin, he killed a *Batman* script that I had written, which broke my heart. I was sitting in Bill Dozier's office when he took the call from Samish, and Samish said 'yes' on 15 treatments, but said 'no' on the Ellison one." (HE-AI13)

As a result of the "boardroom incident," Ellison was not asked to make the rewrites on his script. William Welch – the anti-Harlan Ellison – did them instead, and what likely would have been an intelligent handling of science fiction – as Ellison's other scripts from this period, such as "Demon with a Glass Hand" and "Soldier" for *The Outer Limits*, and "The City on the Edge of Forever" for *Star Trek* – became something a bit less cerebral.

Production:
(Filmed August 31 through September 8; 6 days)
(Budget: $128,888)

James Goldstone was 33 when hired to direct his first of four episodes of *Voyage*, and paid the standard fee of $2,500 for pre-production and production, spanning a combined total of two weeks. He had proven his abilities in the half-hour Western genre, with multiple assignments on series such as *Tombstone Territory* and *Death Valley Days*, and in the genre of intrigue, with 10 directing chores on the 1960-1961 *The Case of the Dangerous Robin*. He graduated to hour-long drama with repeat assignments on *Route 66*, *The Fugitive*, and *The Outer Limits* (the classic "The Sixth Finger" and the two-part "The Inheritors"). Goldstone went on to direct a pair of *Star Trek*s (including the second pilot, "Where No Man Has Gone Before"), and was nominated for an Emmy for an episode of *The Bold Ones*. He won one for the 1981 TV movie *Kent State*.

Interviewed by Mark Phillips, Goldstone said of his work on *Voyage*: "The episodes I directed were done on assignment during an early period of my career, at which time I was taking just about whatever job I could get. I had a commitment to direct a show for 20th Century-Fox, but, when it was cancelled, that commitment was transferred to *Voyage*, which I had no prejudice for or against. I was trying to get out of episodic TV and into theatrical films, and this was hardly a step in the direction I wanted to go." (JG-SLP94)

David Opatoshu had top guest billing as Dr. Karl Reisner. He was 46 and a highly respected character actor in TV and films. Among hundreds of roles, he had standout scenes with Paul Newman and Julie Andrews in Alfred Hitchcock's *Torn Curtain*. If you needed a scientist type, especially one with an accent, Opatoshu was your man. He also appeared in *The Brothers Karamazov*, which co-starred Richard Basehart, and he appeared in an episode of David Hedison's series, *Five Fingers*.

Above and below: David Opatoshu and Jill Ireland, in separate *Star Treks*.
(Desilu Productions, 1967)
Right: John Milford, guesting on one of three episodes of *The Fugitive*. (QM Productions, 1963)

John Milford shared top honors as Philip Wesley. He was 34, and had played Ike Clanton in 14 episodes of the 1959-60 series, *The Life and Legend of Wyatt Earp*. He also had a recurring role, as Sgt. Kagey, in producer Gene Roddenberry's first series, *The Lieutenant*, for the 1963-64 TV season. But with close to 200 screen appearances, Milford was all over the TV dial, with three turns each on *Tales of Wells Fargo*, *The Fugitive*, *The Invaders*, and *Bonanza*; four each on *The Big Valley* and *Mannix*; five on *The F.B.I.*; six on *The Virginian*; seven on *Gunsmoke*; and eleven on *The Rifleman*. Irwin Allen brought Milford back too, but only once, for an episode of *Land of the Giants*.

Jill Ireland was 27 when she played Dr. Julie Lyle. At this time, she was married to David McCallum, who was filming segments for another new fall series – *The Man from U.N.C.L.E.* Ireland had already appeared in a couple of its episodes. She had starred in a handful of movies made in Great Britain, such as *Jungle Street Girls* (with McCallum) from 1960; *So Evil, Young*, from 1961; and *The Battleaxe*, from 1962. She would soon play a love interest for Mr. Spock in the 1967 *Star Trek* episode "This Side of Paradise." After divorcing McCallum and marrying Charles Bronson, Ireland had second billing under her new husband in some of his films from the 1970s and '80s, such as *Riders on the Rain, Violent City, Chino, From Noon Till Three, Love and Bullets, Death Wish II*, and *Assassination*.

Steve Ihnat was only seen in the Teaser, as Robert Pennell. He was 30, and would soon be a top guest star in his own right, appearing in "The Inheritors," the two-part episode of *The Outer Limits* directed by Goldstone. He would also be top villain in "Whom Gods Destroy," a 1968 episode of *Star Trek*, and bad guy Gen. Carter in the 1967 James Coburn spy spoof, *In Like Flint*.

Steve Ihnat (above, with Yvonne Craig), would take a *Trek* of his own, in "Whom Gods Destroy."
(Paramount Pictures, 1968)
Clockwise: Yvonne De Carlo, Al Lewis, Pat Priest, Fred Gwynne, and Butch Patrick in *The Munsters*.
(CBS-TV, 1964-66)

Pat Priest is also confined to the Teaser. She was 27 and made this appearance on a day off from playing Marilyn Munster in *The Munsters*, which was scheduled to premiere on CBS in the fall.

Paul Zastupnevich, wardrobe designer and assistant to Irwin Allen, appeared briefly as a technician. He's the one with a mustache and goatee.

Filming began on Monday, August 31, for the first of six days on Stage B. Besides the Seaview sets, they made room for Ext. Ice Station and Ext. Ice Area on the same stage.

Above: Steve Ihnat and Pat Priest, home sweet home at the North Pole. Below: What is left of that home.

After five days of production, Labor Day brought a three-day weekend, then a final day of filming on Tuesday, September 8. The longest day of the shoot was Friday, September 4, from 8 in the morning until 11:15 at night.

The budget had been set for $121,459, but it was raised to $128,888.

James Goldstone said, "To put it in the most objective and charitable fashion, Irwin and I didn't get along. It was like talking different languages or coming from different planets. There were certain ways he wanted the show done, and he told me, 'When the submarine lurches, you must have the camera as well as the actors tilt to the right. And then Irwin showed me this beat-up water bucket and a ball peen hammer and said, 'And when you want them to tilt, hit the bucket with the hammer!'" (JG-SLP94)

Ray Didsbury said, "They actually

352

began by blowing a whistle for our cue, and Richard rebelled. No whistles! He wasn't enamored with the can either, but he found it far less offensive than the whistle." (RD-FF01)

Above: The hungry thing. Below: Its intended meal ... and another example of David Hedison's excellence as an actor.

Regarding the can and hammer, Goldstone said, "Well, I did that. Why not? It was just as good as shooting off a gun or snapping my fingers, but then it became absurd. I felt like some kid on a playground holding this beat-up tin pail and hammer. I finally decided to say, 'Go!' and 'Now!' Well, the word got back to Irwin that I was defying his edict, and we had an argument about that." (JG-SLP94)

Allen was notorious for being a backseat director. Al Gail said, "He wanted it done his way. And he liked to direct. I think, given his choice, where he had one choice of being a writer, a director, or producer, he probably would have chosen directing. He enjoyed it. He loved it, and it was a challenge to him." (AG-KB95)

Goldstone said, "Irwin Allen was much more interested in special effects and monsters than he was in the characters. I was working with the actors, trying to establish their character relationships, and Irwin kept looking over my shoulder and saying things like, 'Jim, where's the plankton? Remember, this story is about killer plankton.'" (JG-VTTBOTS)

Al Gail concurred. "I think there is probably some truth to that. ... But he took an interest in every aspect of the production. There was nothing that he didn't have his eyes on, or his fingers into, and sometimes to the annoyance of the particular 'experts' he would be working with. But that was his way. And he was decisive. If somebody wanted an answer, he didn't say, 'Come back in a couple of days and I'll tell you.' He told 'em. Right or wrong, the guys got an answer. So, he was very decisive in that respect." (AG-KB95)

This trait definitely rubbed some people wrong.

Lighting double Ray Didsbury said, "My only exposure to Irwin was on the set, either when he was directing or during one of his visits to the stage. He was very good to me, but he was almost a caricature. He ranted and raved so much that I couldn't take him seriously. He always wanted an answer right away, right or wrong. You didn't take time to think, you just said what you figured he wanted to hear. One of his favorite expressions was, 'You're out of the will.' Or, if he was pleased, he'd say, 'You're back in the will.' He was very loyal to those who worked for him." (RD-FF01)

Despite his troubled dealings with Allen on this episode, Goldstone was pleasantly surprised by the results. He told Mark Philips, "I was really amazed at how good the plankton looked. On the set [it] looked terribly fake ... made out of big balloons, and the air pumps that made them move were so noisy we had to loop all of the actor's lines. The secret was not to stay on it too long, and instead to play the people's reaction to the danger ... not that the plankton is terrifying, but that the people are terrified." (JG-SLP94)

Pat Priest said, "I had never been eaten by plankton before. When they told me what the story was about, I thought, 'Come on! How can I be eaten by plankton? It's practically microscopic. It would take great special effects to pull it off.' But I liked how they did it. The problem was to act fearful when you see a guy crouched under the plankton, supporting it as it comes after you. We had a lot of rehearsals because it had to be timed perfectly. Jim Goldstone was a wonderful director. I had never done science fiction before. *Voyage* was really one of the forerunners of the genre." (PP-SFTS2)

Above: Jill Ireland ... about to become a tasty morsel.
Below: Richard Basehart and Robert Dowdell can't believe it ate the whole girl.

Goldstone recalled, "That scene really worked. I played it absolutely against what you know is going to happen, which is kind of Hitchcockian. I let the audience see that something's growing out of these test tubes, and they want to say to this young couple on their honeymoon, 'Hey, look around! Look over your shoulder!' … Like I said to Steve Ihnat, 'You're in love, you're on your honeymoon, and you've chosen a lousy place!' That scene worked on one criterion, and that's whether you cared about the human beings. That's how the plankton either worked or didn't work. You did feel something for the couple, and that was a great testimony to Steve, as well. He was a discovery of mine and he was enormously talented, a marvelous natural actor." (JG-STP94)

Ray Didsbury said, "James Goldstone had to prove himself to the crew before he was taken seriously, because of his youth. He *did* prove himself, and had a good imagination."

However, this attribute did not endear Goldstone to his producer/boss. Didsbury added, "Irwin wouldn't let directors experiment or use imagination, because it cost time, and time was money." (RD-FF01)

What saved time and money was stock footage, including the "emergency blow" into an area of open sea surrounded by an ice field, from the 1961 *Voyage* feature film, which had already been recycled for "Eleven Days to Zero."

Alexander Courage, later famous for the *Star Trek* theme and the scoring of several *Trek* episodes, including both pilots, composed music for half of this episode. Hugo Friedhofer scored the other half. The two composers split the $1,500 fee down the middle.

Release / Reaction:
(ABC premiere broadcast: 10/12/64; network repeat airing: 4/26/65)

"The Price of Doom" was the tenth episode to film, but advanced in the broadcast schedule to be the fifth to air.

James Goldstone: "I considered myself a friend of Harlan's at the time and I thought the episode turned out very well, with strong performances." (JG-VTTBOTS)

Harlan Ellison didn't agree about the merits of the episode, and opted to use the pseudonym Cordwainer Bird as a screen credit (although spelled "Cord Wainer Bird" in the titles). He said, "When I was just starting in science fiction, they had just rediscovered a guy who had only one story published from many years before. His real name was Paul Linebarger. He worked for the CIA, as did his wife, and he couldn't write fiction because of that embargo – not under his name – so he invented the name 'Cordwainer Smith.' And Cordwainer Smith was a writer above the range of most writers, and he became very much an icon.

"When it came my turn to come up with a pseudonym, I wanted to pay homage to Cordwainer Smith, but I also wanted to give the bird to the person who had rewritten me – Here's the finger in your face!' So it's sort of a love/hate pseudonym. I've used it with some regularity. I used it on *Voyage to the Bottom of the Sea*. And I used it on *The Flying Nun*." (HE-MC)

Goldstone said, "Nobody – and I don't mean Irwin – took *Voyage* terribly seriously. We took it seriously as a craft, but nobody said, 'This is a work of art.' *Voyage* was a little cartoonish, but my attitude at the time was, 'Hey, get performances and relationships from the actors to make up for the plot and FX,' especially in the plankton episode. By and large, they're fun and interesting." (JG-SLP94)

Syndicated "TV Scout," carried in *The Daily Intelligencer*, in Doylestown, Pennsylvania, on October 12, 1964, said:

> *Voyage to the Bottom of the Sea* again takes a rocky ride that any experienced salt would avoid. In "The Price of Doom," the Seaview, a sub that has more perils than Pearl White had in a lifetime, faces a murky finale when samples of marine life mysteriously expand. The big search is to find the foreign agent that brought the plankton aboard.

Those who had watched *The Outer Limits* in the Monday night ABC slot several weeks earlier might have eaten this *Voyage* up ... if they had known about it. There was no push by the network to promote this as an out-and-out horror story. In fact, the print ad campaign leaned more toward the espionage elements of the story, with mere lip service given to "mysterious expanding plankton." All in all, as described in network press releases and newspaper TV listings, it sounded like a less-than-thrilling voyage. The CBS panel shows gained ground as a result, but *Voyage* still nudged ahead of its competition.

Nielsen ratings report from Oct. 12, 1964:	Rating:	Share:
7:30 – 8 p.m.:		
ABC: *Voyage to the Bottom of the Sea*	**18.6**	**29.2%**
CBS: *To Tell the Truth*	17.7	27.8%
NBC: *90 Bristol Court: Karen*	16.7	26.2%
8 – 8:30 p.m.		
ABC: *Voyage to the Bottom of the Sea*	**22.3**	**31.7%**
CBS: *I've Got a Secret*	19.9	28.3%
NBC: *90 Bristol Court: Harris Against the World*	18.5	26.3%

It was becoming a closer race for the top spot from 7:30 to 8:30 p.m., but *Voyage* won by the skin of its teeth, beating *I've Got a Secret* with a 31.7% audience share to the panel show's 28.3%.

Like most of *Voyage*'s sci-fi-oriented episodes, "The Price of Doom" was given a network repeat broadcast in the summer.

Episode 11: "Long Live the King"

(Prod. #7211; first aired Monday, December 21, 1964)
Written by Raphael Hayes
Directed by Laslo Benedek
Produced by Irwin Allen
Story Editor: William Welch; Associate Producer: Allan Balter
Assistant Story Editor: Al Gail
Guest Star: Carroll O'Connor
Co-Starring Sarah Shane and Michael Pate

From the *Voyage to the Bottom of the Sea* show files (Irwin Allen Papers Collection):

> All set for Christmas leave, the crew of the Seaview is suddenly given a top secret mission. The king of a middle-eastern kingdom has just been assassinated; the job is to bring his 12 year-old son, presently on a visit to California, back safely to take over the throne. The child behaves like a spoiled brat, but a mysterious castaway, picked up near the Christmas Islands, effects a surprising change of heart in him.

Sound Bites:

Countess (encountering Nelson leaving his quarters): "Oh, Admiral, I'm looking for the King's quarters." *Nelson (frustrated):* "*This* is now the King's quarters." *Countess:* "But it was yours, wasn't it?" *Nelson:* "Mmm." *Countess:* "He's an interesting little boy, isn't he?" *Nelson:* "Tell me, Countess, exactly what are your duties to the King?" *Countess:* "Well, I'm his teacher – in French, in English, manners, deportment; I teach him to be a royal gentleman." *Nelson:* "Really? And who's teaching him how to be a royal human being?"

Crane (regarding the boy Prince): "Well, in my opinion, there is only one person aboard who'd be likely to attack him." *Nelson:* "Who?" *Crane:* "Me!"

Prince Ang (re: Crane): "Admiral, I want this man arrested." *Crane:* "Your Highness, why don't you shut up."

Assessment:

Sci-fi authority Mark Phillips said: "An episode where individual scenes are better than the whole – such as the crew cheerfully anticipating shore leave, Cookie defending his kitchen with a knife while Christmas music plays in the background, and Chief Jones losing a card game to Prince Ang. There's also a great scene where Nelson and Crane are trying to uncover the spoiled Prince's would-be killer, and Crane says, 'I know one person aboard this ship who wants to kill him!' And Nelson, thinking Crane has solved the mystery, says, 'Who?' and Crane says, 'Me!' Nelson's reaction, a guffaw of relieved laughter, is spontaneous and genuine and it plays well. Otherwise, slow going, although Carroll O'Connor's singing certainly takes this show into a different realm."
(vttbots.com)

Script:
Raphael Hayes's writers contract (for "If I Were King"): July 8, 1964.
Hayes's treatment and 1st and 2nd draft teleplays: Dates unknown.
Mimeo Department's reformatted Shooting Final teleplay, now "Long Live the King":
September 1.
Rev. Shooting Final, by William Welch or Al Gail (pink pages): September 8.
Revised pages (blue): September 10.
Revised pages (yellow): September 4.

While being developed, and while filming, this episode was called "If I Were King."

Writer Raphael Hayes was 49 and had just written the screenplay for a movie that would be nominated for an Academy Award the following year (*One*

Potato, Two Potato). He was a former radio writer who made the move to television in the 1950s with multiple assignments on prestigious anthology series such as *Studio One, Suspense*, and *U.S. Steel Hour*. By the early 1960s, he was a regular contributor to Western series like *Riverboat, Laramie*, and *Sugarfoot*. This was his only time working for Irwin Allen.

Hayes said he was specifically asked to write a Christmas story, which prompted him to come up with the idea for "Long Live the King." He told Mark Phillips, "I was never a shoot 'em up or hardware writer. I prefer tales with human relationships. The countess was my favorite character. I find a woman's villainy much more interesting than a man's. She's a much more complex character and she carried in herself villain, lover, seductress, and mother. Conspirators are always more dramatic and colorful than heroes. To wit, Satan." (RH-SL92)

As for the character played by Carroll O'Connor, Hayes said, "Old John was me and my view of life. Christ, love, affection, the joy of laughter, kindness. It all has to be somewhere. Why not me?" (RH-SL62)

The development of this script was more problematic than most others, prompting Irwin Allen to not only rely on staff meetings to convey his wishes, but to become more involved in the note-giving process. One undated memo in particular well demonstrates Allen's story savvy, and his abilities as a writer and a dramatist. His memo reads, in part:

> TEASER MUST BE COMPLETELY RE-WRITTEN – more excitement and less expensive. ...

Rewriting to make use of stock footage of the kingdom and the cheering crowds, and limiting production otherwise to one set – the Throne Room – would solve this problem.

Allen continued:

> Page 11: Rewrite to build up shock value when Nelson and Crane find out Prince is only twelve years old. ...
>
> Page 12: The Prince should show his anger with the Col. and Countess who have not told him why he's there and his mistrust of everyone. ...
>
> Page 13: ... COL. MEGER: "Admiral Nelson, I think it is time to explain to Prince Ang the reason for his being here." ... The Countess knows King Vayan is dead, therefore she wouldn't reassure Prince Ang that he's all right. It must be decided whether or not the Countess and Colonel Meger know of the King's death -- if they do not

know, then they too would be upset and demand to know why they have been spirited away. It seems illogical that they would not have been informed by their government.

It was decided – the Countess, a spy, knows of the King's death, but keeps her lips sealed. The Colonel, loyal to the prince, is as surprised and upset by the news as the Prince is.

> Page 13-14: Carter should find a more sympathetic way of breaking the news to Ang, and his following speeches simplified and shortened. He is talking to a twelve-year-old boy.
>
> Prince Ang should <u>not</u> be referred to as "your highness" until he is informed that he is now the king. <u>Check this point</u>. ...
>
> Page 18: Why on a sub the size of Seaview is it necessary for Nelson to share Crane's cabin?

An easy solution was not to mention where Nelson would be sleeping. The audience would naturally assume that the Admiral could commandeer, say, Morton's cabin and have the exec officer bunk with the Captain.

More notes from Allen:

> Page 18: Some snub should have been given by Prince to Crane in previous scenes to build up justification for Crane's dislike personally of Prince.
>
> Don't have Crane say he <u>hates</u> the Prince.
>
> Page 19: Countess and Col. Meger should be coming out of separate cabins as Crane and Nelson arrive. So that either one could have been guilty of the attack. ...
>
> Prince shouldn't call Countess "you fool." ...
>
> Page 33: Man on raft scene should follow Ang's shouts of "A man! – etc." and Crane would naturally look first to see what Ang is talking about before giving orders to complete surfacing.
>
> Page 34, 35, 38: Examine consistency of John's attitude – he appears to be a mad man who has never seen a sub before. How does this fit in with his intelligent handling

of the boy later and the mysterious way he disappears at the end. Also, he tries to use force to keep from being taken aboard, but later cautions boy about not being brutal.

In the next draft, any lines showing John to be unfamiliar with submarines were removed, as was the depiction of John's use of force to restrain the Prince.

> Page 38, 39: This scene can be cut in half and the static stop and start dialogue is not good for Nelson or Crane. Crane especially seems like an idiot in this scene. Perhaps this scene should be played more between Nelson and John – some chance for interesting type of dialogue here establishing mutual respect between them. ...
>
> Page 48: In view of the attempt on Ang's life, it is unlikely he would be running loose on sub without a guard. I think the guard should come in looking for Ang. Certainly Nelson would not send the boy up on deck by himself. And the sub would not be on the surface in dangerous waters without a look-out stationed above. How about the look-out getting stabbed by assassin?
>
> Page 50: Take into consideration that John is supposed to be a very old man. Don't make him look too good in the battle. ...
>
> Page 54: <u>Ang's Cabin</u> – This scene is much too long. Needs only one page instead of three. Better to show some of divers under water and what happened to the artillery fire? More peril to sub and divers needed. Crane should contact representatives on land and return with new plan for getting boy to safety. Possibly another rendezvous is arranged. It must be assumed that the enemy has control of the Harbor.

Instead, and much cheaper, the U.S. 7th Fleet (courtesy of stock footage) came to the rescue.

Allen's comments continued:

> More action and danger needed. The fact that the rebels can't be stopped until the new King is known to be on the throne safely. ...
>
> Page 59: Under the dangerous circumstances, I hardly think Ang would be in pajamas.

> Col Meger has very little to do – something should be done to bring him more into the story – meetings with Nelson about the landing – perhaps he has a secret code to contact friends on land or perhaps he should go along with Crane on underwater dive to make contact.
>
> Page 59: Since teaser will be re-written, so probably will be the ending. It's much too long and too expensive.
>
> Col Meger must play a bigger part at the end, as he is the one entrusted from now on with the safety of the king. ...
>
> An emotional parting between John and boy would be good so that boy doesn't once more feel rejected.

This memo reveals Allen as a man who understood that a story's biggest bang can come from internal combustion ... and firsthand experience at what it felt like to be abandoned.

ABC didn't want the conflict *too* intense, especially in a story featuring a child. Dorothy Brown, in various memos to Irwin Allen, cautioned against violence too fierce or too continuous, and that the child should never fear for his safety.

Raphael Hayes commented, "I'm not a SF writer. I have a feeling for black and white humor. When I wrote it, I never expected it to become history! At the time, I had bigger fish to fry." (RH-SL62)

Production:
(Filmed September 9-16; 6 days)
(Budget: $121,389)

Laslo Benedek was hired to direct his first of two episodes of *Voyage*. He had won a Golden Globe award for his 1951 movie, *Death of a Salesman*. He also directed Marlon Brando, in 1953's *The Wild One*. But while these movies received positive attention and made money, Benedek wasn't able to follow up his earlier successes. He made the move to television, where he had multiple directing assignments with series such as *Perry Mason* and *Stoney Burke*. He tinkered with the sci-fi genre, directing three episodes of *The Outer Limits* ("Wolf 359," "Tourist Attraction" and "The Man with the Power").

Carroll O'Connor led the guest cast, as Old John. He wasn't really that old – only 39. But he had been around on TV, and in films, since 1951, and was well respected as a character actor with great versatility. A standout performance from this period was for "The Night of the Ready-Made Corpse," for *The Wild, Wild*

West (filmed two years after his appearance here). Allen would bring O'Connor back twice for *The Time Tunnel*, and even offer him the role of Dr. Zachary Smith in *Lost in Space*. O'Connor wasn't ready to be tied down to one series, and waited until 1971 when the role of a lifetime – the bigot Archie Bunker – was offered. He would win several Emmys and one Golden Globe for his portrayal of the iconic character.

A solid supporting cast: Carrol O'Connor gained fame as Archie Bunker; Sara Shane was a 1950s glamour girl; and Michel Pate (carrying Kathleen Crowley) in 1959's *Curse of the Undead*.

Sara Shane played the countess. She was 36 and poised to become a star, first with a contract with MGM, then Universal. But the career-defining roles never materialized; her onscreen work in a couple of dozen films was both minor and forgettable. Director Benedek worked with Shane on a few occasions, including for the *Outer Limits* episode "Wolf 359," and recommended her for this role, her last before an early retirement from acting. She became an author of nonfiction and went into business.

Michael Pate was 44 when he played Colonel Meger. He had over

Above: Sara Shane, Michael Petit, and Michael Pate, in the-old-car-half-of-a-car-interior-sitting-in-front-of-a-process-screen trick. Below: Two of the scenes with Michael Petit filmed on the first day of production, with Michael Pate and, then, Carrol O'Connor.

200 roles in TV and film, starting in 1940. He was featured in 192 episodes of the 1971-75 Australian series, *Matlock Police*. Allen would bring him back for two more *Voyage*s ("The Traitor" and "Flaming Ice") and two trips into the *The Time Tunnel*.

Michel Petit played the Prince. He had been busy in TV since 1959 as a juvenile performer.

Filming began on Wednesday, September 9, 1964 and lasted for six days. Director Laslo Benedek did well at staying on schedule. Allen's suggested changes had eliminated many extras, dialogue, and onshore sequences. Now we saw a car (filmed in front of a process-shot screen), and a throne room (on Stage 8 at 20th Century-Fox), both requiring less than a day's work. The balance of the six-day production took place on Stage B, with the Seaview sets. Benedek began filming at 8 a.m. each day, rolling camera until 6:40 (the earliest) and 7:30 (the latest) on the first five days of filming. On the final day, there was a big push to

365

complete the production, and Benedek filmed until 11:30 at night.

Actor Michael Pate said, "Laslo was a wonderful, sensitive director. He was terribly patient with the young boy. When Michael Petit began to behave as a nasty little boy on the set, most everyone was lining up to kick him!" (MP-SFTS2)

While this episode was being filmed, *Voyage to the Bottom of the Sea* premiered on ABC-TV with its pilot, "Eleven Days to Zero." It was a strange evening for David Hedison, since his new series was scheduled opposite one of his old movies – *The Lost World*.

Filming on Stage B and the Seaview sets. Above: Hedison ad-libs a line about wanting to get rid of a certain problem, causing Basehart to burst out laughing. Below: Captain Crane dealing with that "certain problem."

The next morning, morale was shaken throughout the company as the reviews came in. A few were good, most mixed, but some, including the *Los Angeles Times*, were extremely negative.

Hedison said, "*Voyage* premiered on a Monday night. The review from the *Los Angeles Times* appeared in the Tuesday morning edition with the headline, 'ABC Sinks to New Depths with *Voyage to the Bottom of the Sea*.' ... Richard Basehart and myself were depressed and not at all optimistic about the chances of lasting past Christmas." (DH-DM13)

Hedison later told the *L.A. Times*, "I stopped reading after that." (DH-LAT65)

Days later the ratings arrived, and spirits lifted. *Voyage* had won its time slot.

Release / Reaction:
(Only ABC broadcast: 12/21/64)

"Come See About Me" by the Supremes was the song getting saturation airplay from U.S. Top 40 radio stations. Twentieth Century-Fox's own *Hush ... Hush, Sweet Charlotte* was No. 1 at the movie houses. It starred Bette Davis, Olivia de Havilland, and Joseph Cotton. This was the week that comedian Lenny Bruce was convicted of obscenity charges due to material he performed on stage. Production began on "The Cage," the first of two eventual pilots for *Star Trek*. This one starred Jeffrey Hunter as Captain of the Starship Enterprise ... and a woman as his first officer (Majel Barrett, as Number One).

"Long Live the King" was the eleventh episode made, but the Christmas-themed episode was the fifteenth to air.

Syndicated "TV Scout," in the *Post-Crescent* of Appleton, Wisconsin on December 21, 1964, said:

> "Long Live the King" is a lively adventure on *Voyage to the Bottom of the Sea*. An updated "Arabian Nights" yarn, it concerns a boy prince of some far Eastern country whose father, the king, has been assassinated. It is up to the Seaview to take the young heir back home before his country is overrun by anti-Americans. Michael Petit is fine as the sturdy, 12-year-old prince and Carroll O'Connor offers some surprises as the enigmatic stranger the Seaview picks up in the mid-Pacific.

Nielsen ratings report from Dec. 21, 1964:	Rating:	Share:
7:30 – 8 p.m.:		
ABC: *Voyage to the Bottom of the Sea*	**18.8**	**31.4%**
CBS: *To Tell the Truth*	13.1	21.9%
NBC: "The Story of Christmas"	16.6	27.7%
8 – 8:30 p.m.		
ABC: *Voyage to the Bottom of the Sea*	**20.1**	**32.7%**
CBS: *I've Got a Secret*	13.5	22.0%
NBC: "The Story of Christmas"	17.5	28.5%

The episode was filled with references to Christmas and peace on Earth, and therefore not appropriate for a summer repeat. We wouldn't have an opportunity to see it again until *Voyage* went into syndication in late 1968. Even then, because of the double whammy of a Christmas theme, and being in black-and-white, the episode was rarely aired.

Episode 12: "Submarine Sunk Here"

(Prod. #7212; first aired Monday, November 16, 1964)
Written by William Tunberg
Directed by Leonard Horn
Produced by Irwin Allen
Story Editor: William Welch; Associate Producer: Joseph Gantman
Assistant Story Editor: Al Gail
Co-starring Carl Reindel, Eddie Ryder, Robert Doyle, Wright King

Synopsis:

From the *Voyage to the Bottom of the Sea* show files (Irwin Allen Papers Collection):

> The Seaview, damaged by a mine explosion as it enters an uncharted minefield, has sunk to the bottom. There is only enough air to last 8 hours and the only hope of escape is the diving bell which is presently undergoing repairs. The problem is: Can the men survive until help arrives?

Sound Bites:

Harker: "I couldn't hold him, sir. I just couldn't hold him. He's still down there." *Nelson*: "Dog the hatch." *Harker*: "He's still alive down there." *Nelson*: "Dog the hatch! That's an order."

Nelson: "Engine room, Nelson, report. Engine room, this is Nelson, report your condition!" *Harker:* "They're all dead. They're dead. Just floating out there. Dead."

Collins: "Give it to us straight, sir, can we get out?" *Nelson:* "Well, we've got one chance. It's a pretty good one. Our position is known; we're not far from New London. When the radio quit, the Coast Guard must've started a search for us. They can't fail to see our marker buoy." *Collins:* "Suppose the Coast Guard don't find us?" *Nelson:* "Suppose you're crossing the street in Los Angeles a month from now and a car hits you?"

Assessment:

Voyage historian Mike Bailey said, "This is one of those *Voyage* episodes where you can lift virtually any frame from the film, and you've got a terrific still shot, so finely executed is the camera work. It was perhaps *Voyage*'s reputation as a kid's show based on critical reaction to the pilot that kept this episode and/or Richard Basehart from being nominated for an Emmy. I don't believe it's too far off the beam to suggest that it and he are that good. The entire cast shines."
(vttbots.com)

Indeed! "Submarine Sunk Here" is just about as taunt as a drama gets. The episode's intensity is only increased by the fact that *Voyage*'s first season was black-and-white. The cinematography is crisp, and suitably dark. The tension is so thick you can cut it with a knife. Superb in nearly all ways.

Script:

William Tunberg's writers contract: July 17, 1964.
Tunberg's treatment, and 1st and 2nd draft teleplays: Date unknown.
Mimeo Department's reformatted Shooting Final teleplay: September 15.
Revised Shooting Final teleplay, by William Welch or Al Gail (dark green pages): September 16.
Page revisions by writing staff (on pink paper): September 17.
Page revisions (on gold paper): September 17.
Page revisions (on blue paper): September 21.
Page revisions (on light green paper): September 22.

William Tunberg was 50 and had written the screenplay for the 1957 film *Old Yeller,* as well as the 1963 Disney Western *Savage Sam,* which co-starred

Marta Kristen (soon to be cast in *Lost in Space*). This was his only script for *Voyage* and Irwin Allen.

After reading one of the early drafts of the script, Irwin Allen sent his notes to associate producer Joseph Gantman, script editor William Welch, and associate script editor Al Gail:

> Page 1, Sc. 1: Change Ward Room to Observation Nose – (What do we see out the front window?). ...
>
> Page 8, Sc. 10: Change "door" to "hatch." ...
>
> Page 18, Sc. 33: Phone going dead so fast is phony.
>
> Page 19, Sc. 35: <u>Bishop</u>'s first speech is peevish – should be hard and tough. Collins would never say what he does.
>
> Page 21, Sc. 35: <u>Baine's third speech</u> – Change "If we save" to "If we hope to save".
>
> Page 22, Sc. 36: <u>Crane's third speech</u> – Re-write! ...
>
> Page 27, Sc. 40: <u>Crane's second speech</u> – Change "lately" to "within the hour!"
>
> Page 32: Act Two <u>does not</u> have an exciting ending.
>
> Page 33: Why does Morton speak "(absently)". He should be vital, alive, anxious!
>
> Page 34 & 35: All the dialogue sounds like Mrs. Minerva's finishing school instead of a race against death to save a friend. ...
>
> Page 42: <u>Bishop's first speech</u> – Typo – <u>Bishop's second speech</u> – What does "only those six" mean?
>
> Page 51 thru 53: Wouldn't Nelson bring a couple of tanks of oxygen?
>
> Why doesn't someone in the submarine pound back on the hull?
>
> SUMMATION:
>
> 1. Weak ending.
> 2. The show doesn't build.

3. No personal stories.
4. Too much talk and all too polite.
5. Not enough action.
6. Everything predictable.

In time, the script became a taut, suspenseful episode. It just took a bit of rewriting to get there, matched with effective direction, production and, especially, dynamic acting.

Production:
(Filmed September 17-25; 7 days)
(Budget: $122,323)

There were no stars hired for "Submarine Sunk Here," but the episode did feature some very familiar faces from television at this time.

In the order of their "co-starring" billing:

Carl Reindel played Evans. He was 29, and had been working regularly in television, with multiple appearances on *Gunsmoke* and *Perry Mason*, among other series. His contract was also for $1,000 for up to six days.

Eddie Ryder played Harker. He was 41, and had been a regular on two series: *The Dennis O'Keefe Show* (1959-60) and *Dr. Kildare* (1961-65). He also received $1,000 for a six-day contract.

Robert Doyle was 26 when he played Blake. He had appeared on *12 O'Clock High*, *The Fugitive*, and in two episodes of *The Outer Limits*, as well as series such as *Stoney Burke* and *The Untouchables*. He was paid $1,000 for up to six days work. He would return to the Seaview, in the second-season episode "… And Five of Us Are Left."

Wright King played Dr. Baines. He was 41, and, from 1959-1960, had been Steve McQueen's sidekick during the final season of *Wanted: Dead or Alive*. He had also been a regular in the 1953-54 sci-fi series, *Johnny Jupiter*. His contract was for $375 for a single day's work. He ended up staying four days.

Also in the cast:

George Lindsey, the future Goober on *The Andy Griffith Show*, played Collins. In his pre-Mayberry days, he was paid $750 for five days work.

Paul Comi was assigned the role of Bishop, and budgeted at $300 for one day before the cameras. He was 32, and had been a regular on the 1960-61 Western series, *Two Faces West*, as well as the skydiver series *Ripcord*, airing from 1961 through '63. Comi had also appeared in three episodes of *The Twilight Zone*, and shortly after this *Voyage* would go into space as Styles, the bigoted navigator in the *Star Trek* episode "Balance of Terror."

Production began on Thursday, September 17, 1964, at the studio's "Mill Area" and the backlot "Moat." The Mill, where the props and sets were made,

Henry Kulky and Robert Dowdell on the first day of production, at the Moat location.

served as the location for the "Ext. Repair Shed" and "Ext. Hospital." This location served for New London, Connecticut, home of the U.S. Coast Guard Academy. After rehearsals, blocking, and lighting set-ups, filming began at the outdoor locations at 10:10 a.m. A trip to the Moat provided the location needed for "Ext. Buoy" and "Ext. Salvation Vessel." And then the company moved to Stage B to film the scenes involving the "Int. Escape Bell." The last shot was taken at 7:45 p.m.

Day 2, Friday. They filmed on Stage B and the Int. Observation Nose, as well as starting work in the Int. Control Room. Outside the bay windows, the underwater minefield footage from the *Voyage* feature film gets a good dusting off. It's augmented with many additional shots of exploding mines, which were not from the film. The company filmed from 8:30 a.m. to 7:05 p.m.

Del Monroe told interviewer Mark Phillips, "One of the main criticisms of the pilot, 'Eleven Days to Zero,' was that these were plastic characters. And that was true. Many of the scripts were like that because Irwin wanted an action-adventure show. The relationships between the characters came out through the dedication of the actors. We were always trying to find ways to make the show believable, which is the job of an actor anyway." (DM-SLY98)

With this episode, all the components clicked to form a top-notch *Voyage*.

Day 3, Monday, September 21. The company spent the entire day in the ship's Control Room, with the usual 6:30 a.m. call time, and on set by 8. Since the lighting set-up was in place from the day before, the camera rolled at 8:05 a.m.

Derrik Lewis, present here in his recurring role as Lt. O'Brien, said, "'Submarine Sunk Here' was probably the standout of my work on that show. You wait to get something to do on these things, and the hardest thing in Hollywood is to only have a few lines. At least in a play you can have a lot of dialogue. But a lot of the time in TV episodics you just have a few single lines, and it's harder. But when you're given something to do, then you have a chance to reach for something. The scene where O'Brien is choking, for instance, now that was wonderful. I can remember Leonard walking us through – a little bit of rehearsal on what was going to happen – and then, when the cameras were rolling, we were on our own. And I liked that; I've always liked not knowing exactly what was going to happen. And everybody went right with it. I mean, David was wonderful, in how he jumped in at that point when O'Brien starting choking. He was an 'actor' in every sense of the word. That was the thing – these people were

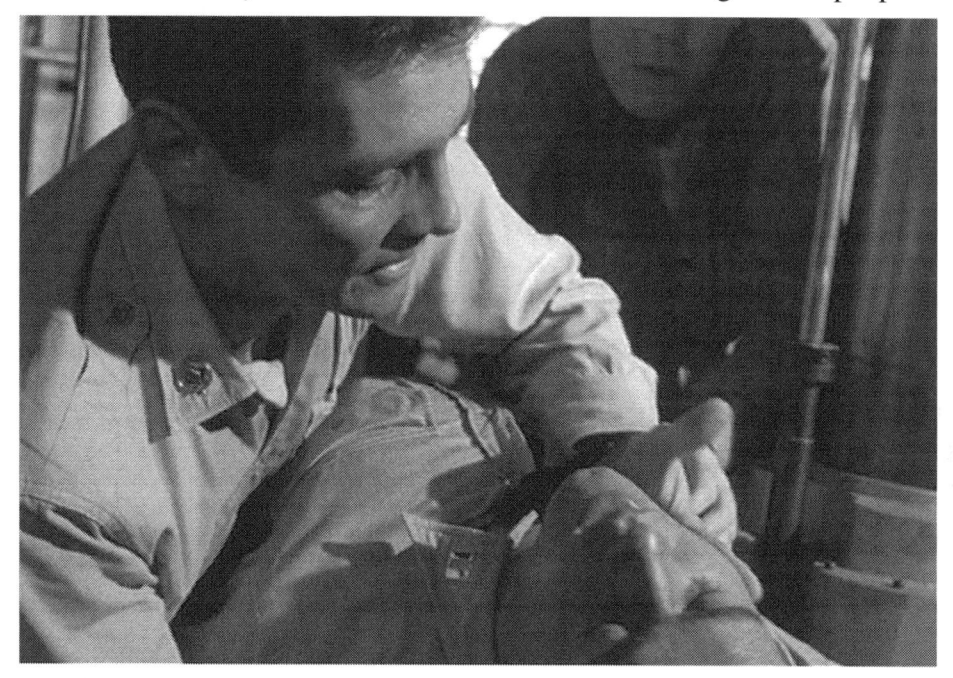

David Hedison and Derrik Lewis – the dramatic choking scene.

all trained actors, not just a character, or a celebrity, or a pretty face – and that's what was exciting about working on that show." (DL-AI18)

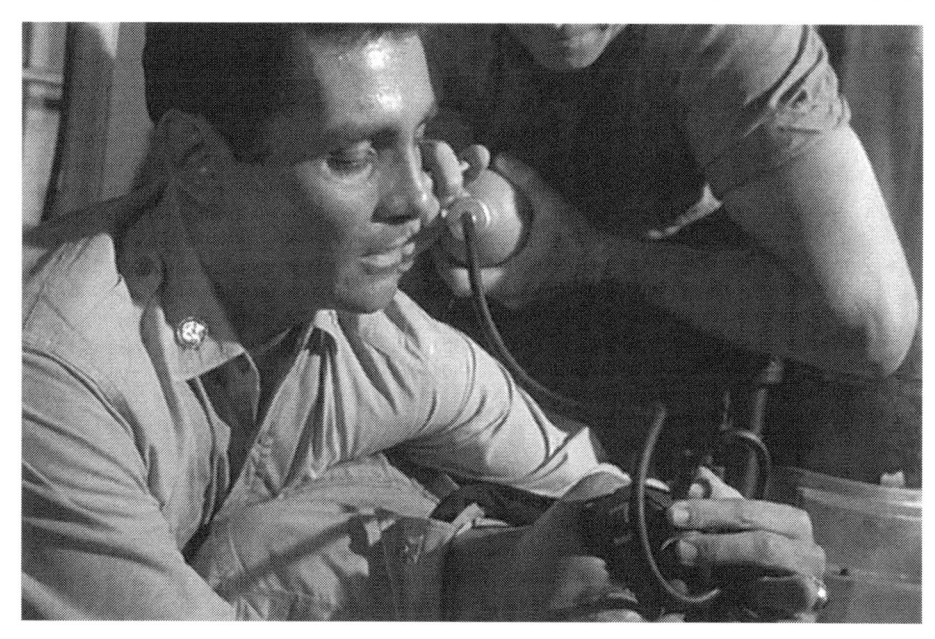

The company stopped filming at 7 p.m. The second episode of *Voyage* to air, "City Beneath the Sea," had its premiere broadcast on ABC this night, at 7:30 p.m.

Days 4 and 5. Tuesday was another day spent in the Control Room, with production then moving to the Sickbay set, the ship's corridors, and a set area called "Hatch to Turbine Tunnel." They filmed until 7:15 p.m., then returned on Wednesday, filming all the "water sets," including Int. Small Compartment, Int. Turbine Tunnel, Int. Storage Locker, and Int. Brig ... all flooded, with the production

Robert Doyle has a very wet day of filming. Note the camera crew to his right ... and, below, the camera's perspective.

crew as waterlogged as the actors. The men had been in the water from 8 a.m. to 6:45 p.m.

Actor George Lindsey said, "It was one of the best shows they ever did. I was cold and wet all of the time, but it was a fun show. Richard Basehart was a real pro." (GL-SFTS2)

Days 6 and 7. Thursday and Friday, were drier days, working in the Int. Crew Quarters, Int. Missile Room (at Mini Sub), and numerous sections of ship's corridors. By 7:30 p.m. on Friday, after a seventh full day of production, this difficult, effects-driven story had wrapped.

Money was saved by some serious "recycling" of footage – the mine field scene, prompting the destruction of the Mini Sub. However, some shots of the chain reaction of underwater mines exploding did not appear in the 1961 *Voyage* feature film.

After the excellent work involved in making "Submarine Sunk Here," cast and production crew deserved a rest, and they would get one – two weeks off for the industry-wide hiatus known as the Labor Day Break. During this interruption in production, TV series often sent their stars on the road, promoting the premieres of the Fall TV season. Richard Basehart, in particular, made the rounds, granting interviews to local newspaper writers in several U.S. cities. Meanwhile, the production people could rest after several months of working 12-hour-plus days, five days a week. The editors would have time to catch up on making their deliveries to the network. And, finally, with the premiere of the series, and the early ratings reports, producers would have an idea as to whether they might expect to see a midseason renewal and, therefore, need more scripts.

David Hedison jumps in. For the flooding scenes, multiple cameras – including hand-held models – were rolling to catch different angles in as few takes as possible.

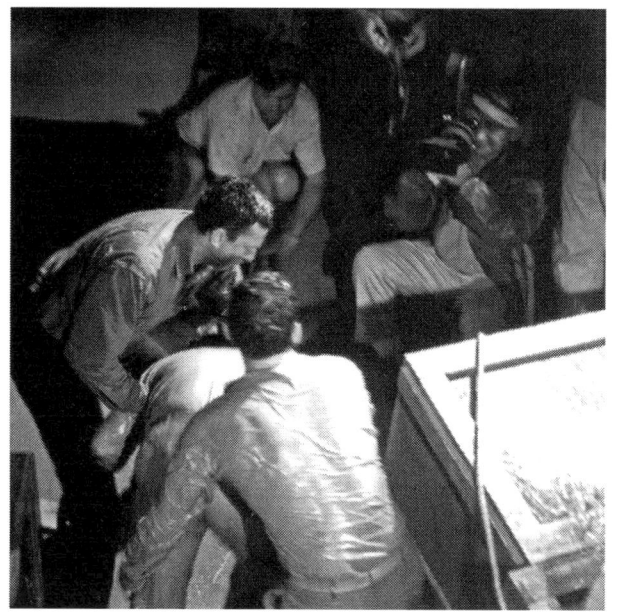

Release / Reaction:
(ABC premiere broadcast: 11/16/64; network repeat airing: 5/24/65)

"Submarine Sunk Here" was the twelfth episode to film, the tenth to air on ABC. It was well liked and given a repeat broadcast by the network. When it premiered, "Baby Love" by the Supremes was the song playing the most on the radio, and *Roustabout*, starring Elvis Presley, was No. 1 in the movie houses. And you could buy a can of Coke for 12 cents.

Steven Scheuer of syndicated "TV Key," from November 15, 1964, and printed in Indiana's *Kokomo Tribune*, liked what he saw:

> Best in weeks. Less stress on visual gimmicks and more on plot as the Seaview sinks to a level of 600 feet and is unable to surface. The rescue scenes are very well handled.

Over at "TV Scout," syndicated to other newspapers on November 16, such as Arizona's *Tucson Daily Courier*, Joan Crosby said:

> *Voyage to the Bottom of the Sea* is REALLY a voyage to the bottom of the sea in "Submarine Sunk Here." Though circumstances under which the Seaview gets itself damaged and sunk in the middle of an uncharted mine field are completely incredible, once you accept the situation it's nail-chewing time. Can the ship and its men escape, and how, particularly since everything seems to be fouling up, the air is running out and the men are at each other's throats?

A TV series involving a submarine might have been expected to do at least one episode like this, which exploited the limitations of the craft's artificial environment. Audience support seemed clear. According to A.C. Nielsen, the ratings from November 16, 1964 gave *Voyage* the win for its time period:

Nielsen ratings report from Nov. 16, 1964: 7:30 – 8 p.m.:	Rating:	Share:
ABC: *Voyage to the Bottom of the Sea*	**23.6**	**35.1%**
CBS: *To Tell the Truth*	17.0	25.3%
NBC: *90 Bristol Court: Karen*	14.2	21.1%

8 – 8:30 p.m.
ABC: ***Voyage to the Bottom of the Sea***   **24.7**   **36.0%**
CBS: *I've Got a Secret*   16.4   23.9%
NBC: *90 Bristol Court: Harris Against the World*   14.8   21.5%

The day after "Submarine Sunk Here" first aired, it was announced that *Voyage* had been picked up for broadcast in Canada. It was also announced that the series, along with *To Tell the Truth* and *I've Got a Secret* on CBS, had knocked off the NBC competition. According to a UPI story:

> The failure of *Harris Against the World* is especially hard for its star Jack Klugman who moved from New York complete with family to appear in the series. He'll probably move back East.

Klugman would return west in time. He'd have better luck in 1970 with his second series, *The Odd Couple*, followed in 1976 by a third, *Quincy, M.E.*

Episode 13: "The Magnus Beam"

(Prod. #7213; first aired Monday, November 23, 1964)
Written by Alan Caillou
Directed by Leonard Horn
Produced by Irwin Allen
Story Editor: William Welch; Associate Producer: Allan Balter
Assistant Story Editor: Al Gail
Co-starring:
Mario Alcalde, Monique LeMaire, Malachi Throne, Jacques Aubuchon,
and Joseph Ruskin

From the *Voyage to the Bottom of the Sea* show files (Irwin Allen Papers Collection):

> A belligerent Middle-Eastern country is preparing for war that will involve the whole Arab world; confident that its secret weapon will bring it victory. The only force capable of combating this amazing new weapon, which can immobilize any object containing metal that comes within its radius, is the Seaview. An army officer, posing as a defector, is sent to lure the sub to its doom in the subterranean cavern under the Red Sea where the "Magnus Beam" is housed. Captain Crane goes ashore in disguise in an attempt to ferret out the secret of the magnetic ray.

Sound Bites:

Kowalski: "All the hatches are jammed tight!" *Nelson:* "Amadi, what are they using on us? ... *(off Major Amadi's silence)* ... Patterson! ... *(as Patterson puts a gun to Amadi's head)* ... You have five seconds to make up your mind, Major. Just five seconds." *Amadi:* "Have him pull the trigger, Admiral. ... *(off their surprise)* ... Your gun will not fire. Nothing made of steel will move. While our weapon is in operation, your motors, your pumps, every piece of machinery on board is immobilized." *Nelson:* "Magnetism?" *Amadi:* "The Magnus Beam, Admiral." *Nelson:* "Now I understand why you were so anxious to get away on the mini-sub." *Patterson (frustrated that his gun won't fire):* "I never wanted so much to pull the trigger." *Amadi (with sad irony):* "Why bother, Patterson. I'm already a dead man, gentleman – just as you are."

Assessment:

A giant magnet that pulls planes out of the sky? Why not? If it helps to validate the tale, the weapon isn't really a giant magnet, but a large magnetic-field generator.

The actions and assorted conflicts in this story are relentless. *Voyage to the Bottom of the Sea* historian Mike Bailey said, there is "enough automatic weapons fire in this episode to satisfy any NRA member in good standing." Bailey added, "Oddly uninvolved direction from the brilliant Leonard Horn, whose work on *Voyage* seemed to shine most brightly when telling stories of a more personal nature. 'The Magnus Beam' is anything but a personal story. Jacques Aubuchon is great as comic support, his character similar in function to Jonathan Rhys-Davis' character (Sallah) in the Indiana Jones movies." (vttbots.com)

We'll take the counterpoint. The cast is top-notch. Malachi Throne is commanding, as always, bringing great power, and a nice swagger, to his role. As Major Amadi, Mario Alcalde creates a nicely fleshed-out characterization which is far from being a one-dimensional villain. The lovely Monique LeMaire also delivers a character who is both smart and motivated. And, while Joseph Ruskin seems to walk through his role, few did the menacing walk-and-talk better than the vulpine Ruskin.

On the technical side, the underwater footage, and L.B. Abbott's work with the Seaview miniature as it as it makes its way through underwater caves, is highly accomplished and well executed. No stock footage in this one!

Lastly, due to being filmed mostly at night, "The Magnus Beam" stands apart from most episodes of the series – more intense, fresher, and distinctive.

Bailey was right – from a story perspective, it's little more than enjoyable escapism. But the bells and whistles dress this one up quite nicely for the party.

Script:
Alan Caillou's treatment and 1st and 2nd draft teleplays: Dates unknown.
Mimeo Department's reformatted Shooting Final teleplay: Late September 1964.
Revised Shooting Final teleplay (by William Welch or Al Gail):
Date unknown.
2nd Revised Shooting Final teleplay, by writing staff (on pink paper): October 7.
Page revisions (on blue paper): October 7.

Writer Alan Caillou said of his teleplay: "I recall that it was written in the golden years of TV and, while there was nothing particularly golden about *Voyage*, those days were a great time for writers. They left us alone to write. In later years, we had to write for committee." (AC-SL92)

Caillou was 49, and an actor as well as a writer. He wrote scripts for *Behind Closed Doors* and *Thriller*, as well as seven for *The Man from U.N.C.L.E.* After this one *Voyage*, he moved on to films, writing the screenplays for 1965's *Village of the Giants* and *Clarence, the Cross-Eyed Lion*.

Regarding the episode's title, *Magnus* is a Latin word meaning "great." Its most familiar use as a name is for Charlemagne, the Frankish emperor whose Latin name became "Carolus Magnus."

After reading Caillou's teleplay, Irwin Allen sent eight pages of notes to associate producer Allan Balter and script editor William Welch, including:

> Page 2 ... "High flying spy plane" – sounds childish – "unauthorized foreign plane" would be better. ...

Allen called the term childish, but it was more specific, and therefore better writing, than his suggested substitute.

The notes continued:

> Page 4 ... Can you not bring Amadi into story importance sooner – as it is now, we think everything is being explained to him as to other officers. We are not aware of him until he takes gun from officer saying "leave this to me"....

Allen was bothered that Amadi, one of the two primary villains, was not revealed until well after boarding the Seaview. Writer Alan Caillou made it appear that Amadi (Mario Alcalde) was truly defecting, and that the only true adversary for our heroes was General Gamal (Malachi Throne). In this case, the writer's instincts may have been better than the producer's. The story might have worked better, and delivered a nice surprise toward the end, if Amadi's villainy *wasn't* unmasked so blatantly early on. This would have also made Nelson's suspicions of him all the more interesting.

Allen wrote:

> The Teaser has 6 almost solid pages of dialogue with the exception of film at beginning – young officer with gun – and planes blowing up – I feel that the explanation of Magnus Beam should not be in the teaser. ...
>
> They have reason to believe that Seaview can produce a magnetic field – Seaview never does so, this looks bad for Seaview. Maybe should say, "We know very little about the Seaview – It is just possible that ... etc..." ...
>
> In all the talk no one has mentioned the spying country, and all of a sudden they start talking about Seaview – never even mentioning the fact that it's American! Or why America would even be interested in sending Sub into area.

Clarifications were inserted into the script by William Welch. America was spying on the unnamed Latin country because of rumors that it had been developing new and dangerous weaponry. U-2 spy planes were looking to verify this, and one was pulled down by the Magnus Beam. This prompted the Seaview's mission to being sent in to investigate.

Allen asked:

> Page 9... General: "No sub can enter our caverns." Why not???

Explanation was added into the script that the depth of the underwater caverns was too deep for a normal submarine.

Allen had another question:

> Page 9... Amadi: "And this, gentlemen, is our one weakness." Seems like trite way of setting up Seaview entrance into story. How can he be so definite about sub's ability? ...

The line was changed.

> Page 12 – Nelson: "Maybe it's time to bring it out again, etc." This sounds a little dirty?

Well, now that you mention it ...

> Page 12 – The important point of the whole story is to get Seaview into a trap. Therefore, it must be Major Amadi who requests that Washington send the Seaview and he must give a good reason for such action. The agent (girl) should be a side issue at first. Otherwise, it is highly unlikely that anyone seeking asylum would be afforded the use of the Seaview – and also highly unlikely that an agent of the U.S. would not be able to trust anyone other than Crane and therefore be allowed to send for Seaview. ????? ...

All of this was streamlined ... and seemed to work fine.

> Page 28 – Rewrite Nelson's long speech to make clear Major Amadi's reason for needing Seaview. Reason – He has not been able to get close to machine by land and the only other way is to go in through the 3,200 foot deep cavern.

Something was lost in the rewriting. In the first drafts, as stated earlier, it was unknown whether Amadi was sincere in his wish to defect. If taken at his word, he wanted to guide the Seaview through the underwater cavern in order to orchestrate a surprise attack on General Gamal and make off with the Magnus Beam weapon. With William Welch's rewriting, Amadi's motivation, and the story itself, became muddled. We can understand why Nelson wants to take the Seaview into the caverns – to stop General Gamal from using his Magnus Beam on more American aircraft. But Amadi's true motivation is never made clear. He says the Seaview would be destroyed – crushed like a tin can. Wouldn't capturing the ship make more sense than destroying it? You'd think that an enemy power would rather take possession of the super sub, and its technology ... and its nuclear warheads. Now why didn't someone think of that? (Actually, read on ... it seems that someone did, even if the suggestion was ignored.)

> Page 28-29: Let Nelson give Chip Morton the order to take Seaview to 3 thousand feet – then Morton will go to squawk box and repeat order. Have more complete diving instructions given such as "Dive All Dive" etc. This is exciting for audience and should be used whenever possible. ...

And now we know why, in so many episodes of *Voyage to the Bottom of the Sea*, we were treated to this repetitive sequence. Nelson would tell Crane, "Dive!" And Crane would then turn to Morton and tell him "Dive! All dive!" And then Morton would say into the squawk box, "Dive! All dive!" Allen thought it was exciting. What do you think?

> Page 31 – Sc. 55 – Nelson's question to Chip, re: "Divers ready?" should be made clearer. As a matter of fact, Chip couldn't possibly know if they were ready or not. So why not have Curley in Missile Room report that they are ready over squawk box. ...
>
> Page 38 – Sc. 72 – Stage direction "Nelson grins." I don't think he would. He is in doubt about Amadi and the fate that awaits the Seaview. He should be very tense.
>
> Page 38 – Nelson (last speech) needs work. Again the use of the word "hatches" – any diver at 3,000 or 1,000, would need to enter a compression chamber before leaving sub, wouldn't they??? ...

The "escape tank" was used instead.

> Page 39 & 40 – ??? When the General ordered the Magnus Beam used in the Teaser – no objects in the room flew to any steel objects. Is this logical that they would behave this way on the sub? ...

Allen had a good point. Regardless, his staff ignored the note. It was a fun-sounding concept, in the abstract. But to have the guns fly across the room would not only disarm the men, it would probably be very hard to convincingly rig for special effects. So it was science that flew across the room ... and right out the window.

> Page 40 – Do you want Amadi smoking? And would he be calm? I think he would be extremely unhappy and disturbed that he didn't get off sub before they used Magnus Beam. ...

They got rid of the cigarette, but allowed Amadi to remain calm ... with an expression indicating him accepting the inevitable ... with a certain sense of irony.

> Page 46 – Sc. 78 – In this scene Amadi should explain the reason it was necessary to trap Seaview. (They had to know if Seaview was a match for their weapon before they undertook to overthrow all the surrounding nations

as they knew America would come to the aid of the besieged countries). He should show contempt for the Seaview's inability to cope with the situation. Nelson can look like he'd like to kill him and taunt him with the fact that his country doesn't seem to think Amadi's very important as it appears they are willing to let him die with the rest of the Seaview crew. Also it is unlikely that they intend to destroy a sub like Seaview which they could use themselves.

And there you have it. Allen *had* seen the obvious. Co-producer Allan Balter and script editor William Welch ignored his observation, and left in the line about crushing the Seaview like a tin can.

ABC's Tom Kersey wrote to Allen on September 30. Kersey wasn't concerned with what might make the story better ... only worse.

> Please research GENERAL GAMAL to determine there is no "middle-east" head-of-state of that name, appearance, uniform, etc.
>
> Page 27, Sc A-45 – "He points gun at Amadi's face" – please move gun down to chest or neck area.
>
> Page 36, Sc 53 – Caution on blood exposure CRANE's face.
>
> Page 54, Sc 93 – This entire scene must be MASKED FOR PERISCOPE; the soldier firing into camera must be in a long shot (perspective) and of course at no time can the rifle barrel zoom in full and fill the TV screen.
>
> Page 56, Sc 98 – At best, the use of the spear-gun as a land weapon is a violent thing, so that the two soldiers "hit" by the spears must be nothing more than wounded in the arm, leg, shoulder area. They must not be fatally shot thru the body with accompanying fall, screams.

Credit director Leonard Horn for maintaining a good amount of grittiness in this tale, despite ABC's efforts to help ... or censor.

Production:
(Filmed October 8-16, 1964; 7 days)
(Budget: $123,951)

In mid-November, 1964, Irwin Allen was showing off his office to Hollywood syndicated newspaper correspondent Aldine Bird. He called Bird's attention to a wall full of different colored filing books. Allen said, "Pick a number – any number. Pick a color, any color. Go ahead, pick any one of them."

Bird picked No. 13, in blue. Allen pulled the file and presented it to Aldine, saying, "Here is a complete record of episode No. 13 in *Voyage to the Bottom of the Sea*. It contains every piece of information pertaining to its production, including the days it was filmed, the number of hours and film footage [needed] every day, costs, script used by the director and script girl, and everyone appearing in or producing it."

Allen then motioned about the room, saying, "Here in this office and around these walls is a complete record of everything I have done for movies as well as television. … I have always tried to make a creative business into a business, without losing any creativity." (IA-IAPC)

For "The Magnus Beam," Leonard Horn was paid $2,500 to direct, from a budget of $123,951. However, money was saved by hiring respected TV actors just short of "star" status, and then offering them "co-starring" billing during the episode's opening title sequence.

Mario Alcalde was 38 when cast as Major Amadi, the first of five names sharing a title card at the opening of Act 1. He was a well-regarded guest performer in an era when there was not a great deal (or variety) of work for actors of Hispanic background on American TV,

Mario Alcalde (in uniform), with Joseph Ruskin.

outside of stereotypical roles. Alcalde played his share of Mexican banditos in TV westerns, and he also played many American Indians, such as Yellow Hawk in several episodes of the Western series *The Texan*, Chief Bloody Hand for one segment of *Overland Trail*, and Lazyfoot in an episode of *Laredo*. He also played South Seas Islanders, like Too-Chee-La in an episode of *The Great Adventure*. In exchange for $900, top guest star billing, and a role a bit more intriguing than many of the others he'd been offered, Alcalde accepting the five-day job for *Voyage*.

Monique LeMaire was 29 when cast as Luana. Her career in front of the camera was relatively brief, spanning 1963 to 1970. In exchange for her five days on the set, LeMaire received second "co-star" billing, $800, and, as a bonus two years later: a part in *The Time Tunnel* ("Reign of Terror"), as Marie Antoinette. It was good casting. LeMaire had been born in France, and English was her second language.

Malachi Throne was 35 when he played General Gamal. Throne deserved his "co-star" billing, for he was a highly sought-after guest performer. During this TV season, he also had a recurring role in several episodes of *Ben Casey* (as Dr. Martin Phelps), and would soon co-star in *It Takes a Thief* with Robert Wagner. He would have top billing as a guest star, and a wide variety of roles in many popular series, from *The Wild, Wild West*, to *Star Trek* (with the two-part "The Menagerie"); *The Man from U.N.C.L.E.*; *Batman* (as the villainous "False Face"); *The Fugitive*; *I Spy*; *The Outer Limits*; and *Mission: Impossible*, among others. Irwin Allen and his people liked Throne so much that he would be brought back for two more

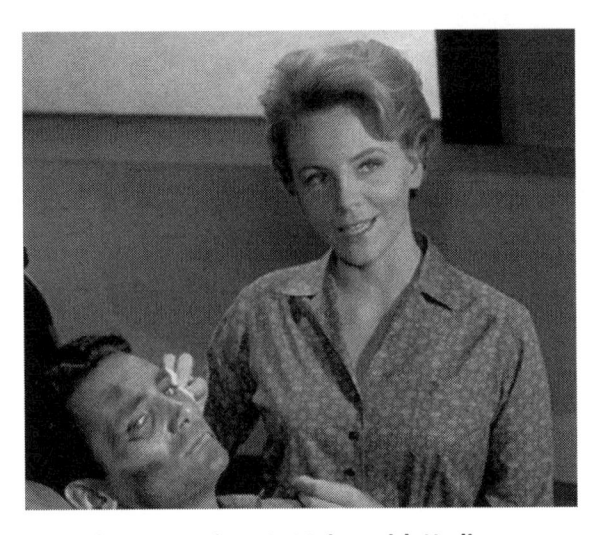

Above: Monique LeMaire, with Hedison.
Center: Malachi Thorne co-starred with Robert Wagner in the late 1960s espionage series, *It Takes a Thief*.
(Universal Studios, 1968)
Below: The versatile Jacques Aubuchon.

episodes of *Voyage* ("The Enemies" later in the first year, and a scenery-chewing role as Blackbeard the Pirate in "The Return of Blackbeard"), as well as two episodes of *Time Tunnel*, and one each for *Land of the Giants* and *Lost in Space* (the latter as "The Thief from Outer Space"). He was paid $750 for two days … and a death scene.

Jacques Aubuchon played the helpful, and comical Abdul Azziz. He was 39. Where have you seen him? A better question would be, "Where *haven't* you seen him?!" Aubuchon had well over 100 appearances in just about every show that was popular in the 1950s, '60s and '70s, from *Hogan's Heroes* to *F Troop*, from *The Man from U.N.C.L.E.* to *Bewitched*, from *The Monkees* to *The Green Hornet* and *Land of the Giants*. The year before, he had a recurring role in *McHale's Navy*, as Chief Urulu. For *Voyage*, he was paid $750 and given fourth billing for three days work.

Joseph Ruskin, as Inspector Falazir, was 40. The sinister-looking Ruskin was in high demand for villainous types. Among a couple of hundred roles, he played a not-very-nice Genie in "The Man in the Bottle" segment of *The Twilight Zone*, the drill instructor Galt in *Star Trek*'s "The Gamesters of Triskelion," and an unsavory character named "Viper Black" on *The Wild, Wild West*. He made $700 and was given fifth billing in exchange for four days work. Ruskin worked for Irwin Allen again, in an episode of *The Time Tunnel* ("Revenge of the Gods) and two episodes of *Land of the Giants* (Secret City of Limbo" and "Terror-Go-Round").

Below: Joseph Ruskin, with an interesting look of his own, for an episode of *Star Trek*.
(Desilu Productions, 1967)

This was the first episode to go before the cameras in three weeks, since "Submarine Sunk Here" had wrapped on September 25. Some of the cast had been out promoting the series.

Right before the break had come the premiere of the series, "Eleven Days to Zero." In the three weeks since, "The City Beneath the Sea," "The Fear-Makers," and "The Mist of Silence" had aired. While "City" was an uneven affair, the next two episodes were above-average productions based on solid scripts. And *Voyage* had continued to win its time slot. Now, the order had come from ABC for additional episodes to extend the series beyond the initial order of 16. Cast and crew were returning to work knowing that they had a hit show.

Production began Thursday, October 8, 1964, on the backlot at the studio Moat. It was a night shoot, with call time at 6:30 p.m. They started filming right after the sun went down at 8 p.m. and didn't stop until 5 the following morning.

Day 1: Late-night filming on the backlot Moat area ... and the battle over the Magnus Beam machine (above); and, below, one of the many fatalities.

Cast and crew slept in on Friday, arriving on the set by 3 p.m. – again in the outdoor Moat area, this time for the "Ext. Beach" scenes, the schedule's only daylight sequence. The camera rolled at 4:10 p.m. as a raft from the Seaview brings Captain Crane to the shore – which was really the edge of the Moat. When Crane looks up at the flat-faced towering cliffs, this was not a trick shot. Those cliffs, made of concrete and painted to look like rock, were also part of the backlot.

Once the sun had set, the company began

filming on the "Studio Street" for "Ext. Arab Street," "Ext. Golden Parrot," and "Ext. Curio Shop." The last shot was in the can by 11:50 p.m.

For the third day of production, on Monday, October 12, cast and crew were due at the studio at 9 a.m. for make-up and set preparation. Call time on the outdoor Moat set was 10:30 a.m., with camera rolling by 11. They filmed "Int. Cave and Corridor" first – the same cavernous area seen in "Turn Back the Clock" – and then, after dark, they shot the "Ext. Magnus Room" set, a cavernous area with a window-like opening which looked out toward the moat, as well as a corner of the moat itself – the potion which was bordered by a ramp, concert steps, and a landing. (This same area was also often used as the dock area to the Nelson Institute). The last shot was completed at 11:30 p.m. No one was going to get home to see the fifth episode aired – "The Price of Doom." That was probably a good

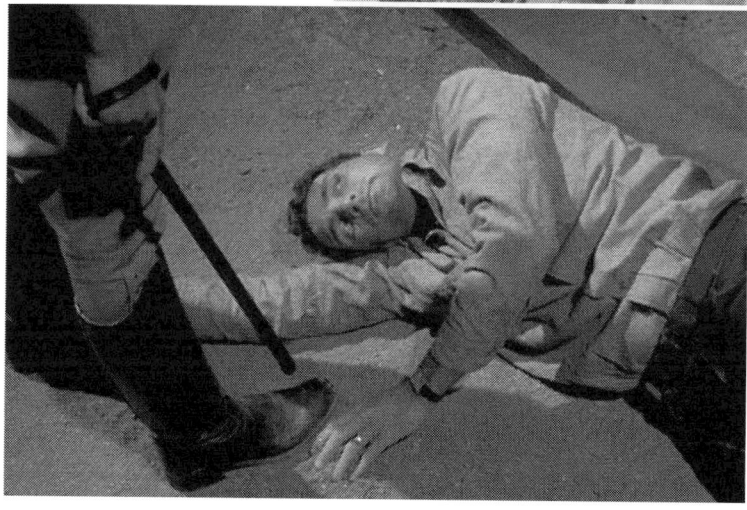

Day 3: Filming in the man-made caves and caverns adjacent to the Moat, with Jacques Aubuchon (above) and Monique LeMaire (below), with Aubuchon and Hedison.

Day 3: The Magnus Beam Control Room (above), filmed at night in the Cavern area adjacent to the Moat, with Mario Alcalde and Joseph Ruskin. Center: Alcalde with Malachi Throne. Bottom: Monique LeMaire with Hedison on Day 5.

thing.

Tuesday was another atypical day of production for this atypical episode. Call time on the Moat set was 10:30 a.m. (after 90 minutes of make-up for the cast, and time for the crew to prepare the filming location). Camera rolled at 11 for yet another scene in one of the caves. At midday, the company moved to Stage 3 to film the sequence in the Int. Golden Parrot. For this we see a large section of the stage itself, passing for the performance stage and backstage area of a theater. Give David Hedison and Monique LeMaire credit for demonstrating no fear of heights, as they climb the three sections of stairs up toward the stage rigging, with nothing on either side or below, except a drop to the concrete floor three stories down. They had the last shot by

390

7:40 p.m.

Day 5 of the production, on Wednesday, began on Fox Stage 3, for the "Int. Curio Shop" sequence, then "Int. Dressing Room" at The Golden Parrot, and the "Int. Living Room" set. Then a quick move to Stage B – home of the Seaview – to take some pick-up shots needed for the "Submarine Sunk Here" episode.

Day 6: Unknown extra, with Richard Basehart, Del Monroe, Paul Trinka, and Mario Alcalde.

Thursday finally brought a more typical production day, with the usual 6:30 a.m. call times. Everyone was expected on set by 8 a.m., cameras rolling by 8:30, and the last shot of the day came at 6:18 p.m. But this sixth day wasn't the last. The ambitious production was running late.

Day 7, Friday, October 16. It took a full day of filming, on Stage B in the Missile Room, to finish. With an 8 a.m. set call, and camera rolling at 8:35, "The Magnus Beam" finally wrapped just after 6 p.m.

Release / Reaction:
(Only ABC broadcast: 11/23/64)

"The Magnus Beam" was the thirteenth episode to film, and the eleventh to air on ABC. With only 19 episodes making the cut for summer repeats, it was passed over.

"Baby Love" by the Supremes was still the song getting the most spins on radio stations' turntables, now in its fourth week at No. 1. And *Roustabout*, with Elvis Presley was still king in the movie houses, for its second week. You could see it as a matinee for a buck.

Syndicated "TV Scout," carried on November 23, 1964, in the *Monessen Valley Independent*, in Monessen, Pennsylvania, said:

> The setting this time is the Middle East where one of those twirly-whirly dancers (Luana Rossi) has more than gyrations on her mind. In her spare time, she has been

391

watching the skies and informs Seaview's commander (David Hedison) all about a high flying secret weapon that could upset the peace in the world. But before they can do anything about it, both are captured by a power-hungry general. It's hokum, but fun.

According to A.C. Nielsen, 1964 was a fine year for fun hokum.

Nielsen ratings report from Nov. 23, 1964:	Rating:	Share:
7:30 – 8 p.m.:		
ABC: *Voyage to the Bottom of the Sea*	**22.5**	**35.0%**
CBS: *To Tell the Truth*	18.7	29.1%
NBC: *90 Bristol Court: Karen*	13.0	20.2%
8 – 8:30 p.m.		
ABC: *Voyage to the Bottom of the Sea*	**23.7**	**35.9%**
CBS: *I've Got a Secret*	21.4	32.4%
NBC: *90 Bristol Court: Harris Against the World*	11.1	16.8%

Although it walloped its competition on this night, *Voyage* had slipped out of the Nielsen Top 20. It was now in the low end of the Top 30. Basehart said, "Television rating systems are a fallacy. None of the rating systems are consistent. The Top 20 shows in three different ratings systems sometimes are as unalike as night and day." (RB-HN64)

The day after "The Magnus Beam" aired, it was announced that *Voyage* had been sold to Australia, Mexico, Venezuela, Uruguay, the Philippines, and Egypt. Indications were that Richard Basehart was not regretting his decision to take the plunge into TV. He told one newspaper interviewer, "It's amazing. Everyone realizes what a powerful medium television is, but until you feel the result of a series, you are still unaware of what a monster it is – and a wonderful monster I might add." (RB-BC64)

Episode 14: "No Way Out"

(Prod. #7214; first aired Monday, November 30, 1964)
Teleplay by Robert Hamner
Story by Robert Hamner and Robert Leslie Bellem
Directed by Felix Feist
Produced by Irwin Allen
Story Editor: William Welch; Associate Producer: Joseph Gantman
Assistant Story Editor: Al Gail
Co-starring Jan Merlin and Danielle De Metz

From the *Voyage* show files, part of the Irwin Allen Papers Collection:

Anton Koslow, an important secret agent working in Indonesia, defects to the west. Nelson has to get him, and his girlfriend, Anna Ravec, safely to the U.S.

Koslow is badly wounded during the escape and Washington flies out a man from the Intelligence Department to board the Seaview and learn Koslow's secrets in case he dies en route. But the enemy, discovering the scheme, substitute one of their top agents for the American. Although Nelson discovers this ruse in time to save Koslow from the enemy agent, he doesn't know that Anna, whom Koslow trusts implicitly, is also out to murder the defector.

Sound Bites:

Col. Lascoe (checking body of fallen agent after training exercise): "Very impressive, Victor – Vasula is dead. You snapped his back." *Victor Vail (with sadistic pride):* "Isn't it better to weed out the incompetent here rather than in the field?" *Lascoe (with a hint of a smile):* "Are you the perfect pupil? Or is it that I'm the perfect teacher?" *Vail:* "Well, I suppose …" *Lascoe (interrupts):* "It doesn't matter. What is important is that now we have need for your … very special talents."

Assessment:

"No Way Out" is a taut espionage drama highlighted by Jan Merlin's sinister portrayal of the sadistic enemy agent.

TV historian Mark Phillips said, "A high energy saga, easily the best of *Voyage*'s spy capers. Richard Webb's character falls prey to one of the most gruesome deaths ever seen on TV. I'm amazed it got past the censors." (vttbots.com)

Webb's character – Parker – was killed by the old-knife-plunging-through-the-back-seat-of-a-limo trick. We'd soon see this type of thing playing out on shows such as *Get Smart!* and *The Wild, Wild West* many times over in the next few years to come. But there is indeed something frightening about it here – due in part to Webb's spot-on look of horror after he gets that "stabbing pain," but also because, after he slumps forward, the blade of the knife is shown to be stained with blood. Mark Phillips is right – this absolutely went against ABC Broadcast Standards policy in 1964 … even when in black and white. The censor must have nodded, or looked away for a split second during the screening of the episode, or this jab would never have made it onto the air.

Phillips added, "Jan Merlin is excellent as a deadly karate expert who is loose aboard Seaview." (vttbots.com)

Indeed, Merlin's "Victor Vail" is no one-dimensional killing machine. He is a true sadist who has taken to heart the old adage from Confucius: "Choose a job you love and you will never have to work a day in your life." On the other hand, another sage warned, "He who lives by the sword may die by the sword."

"No Way Out" is one of the best from *Voyage*'s first season.

Script:
Robert Leslie Bellem's writers contract: August 7, 1964.
Bellem's "Writers draft": Early October, 1964.
Robert Hamner's 2nd draft: Date unknown.
Mimeo Department's reformatted Shooting Final teleplay: Date unknown.
Rev. Shooting Final teleplay by William Welch or Al Gail (on pink paper): October 14.
Page revisions by writing staff (blue paper): October 16.

Page revisions (gold paper): October 19.
Page revisions (green paper): October 20.
Page revisions (beige paper): October 21.
Page revisions (yellow paper): October 21.

Robert Leslie Bellem was hired to write the script and given the standard contract, compensating him with $630 upon delivery of the story treatment, an additional $1,870 upon delivery of the first draft, and a final payment of $1,000 upon acceptance of his final rewrite, if the story and script proceeded that far. They did not.

Bellem was 61. He was a former journalist turned pulp-detective writer. He created "Dan Turner, Hollywood Detective," which ran in mystery magazines in the 1930s and '40s. One movie was made with the character – 1947's *Blackmail* – based on one of Bellem's stories. Bellem cut his teeth in TV during the early 1950s writing for *Dick Tracy* (with 23 assignments), and the similar themed *Boston Blackie* and *Front Page Detective*. By the middle of the decade, he had moved into other genres and was writing scripts for *The Lone Ranger*, and for anthology series such as *Schlitz Playhouse*. He wrote eight episodes of *The Adventures of Superman*, then took multiple assignments on Michael Ansara's first series, *Broken Arrow*. Next, Bellem returned to the sleuth genre, with 11 scripts for *Man with a Gun*, starring Rex Reason as a newspaper publisher and amateur detective. By the early 1960s, Bellem had found success at *Perry Mason* (five shows) and *77 Sunset Strip* (four shows). That's when he got the chance to write for *Voyage*. However, his product was unacceptable to Allen; it was handed off to another writer.

Robert Hamner, who had just completed work on his first script assignment for *Voyage* ("The Ghost of Moby Dick"), was asked to give Bellem's script a rewrite. Hamner not only got the "teleplay by" credit but half of the "story by" credit, as well.

Hamner got his start in screenwriting by penning the "B" film *13 Fighting Men* in 1960, then another cheapie – 1961's *The Long Rope*. Those two films served as his calling card, and Hamner immediately found employment in television, where producers appreciated writers capable of turning out scripts that could be filmed fast and cheap. Among Hamner's early 1960s TV stops: *Klondike*, *Cheyenne*, and *Hawaiian Eye*. *Voyage* came next, where he saved the day with this script, and was rewarded with five more assignments, as well as six on *Lost in Space* and one for *The Time Tunnel*. He'd also do one for *Star Trek* – 1967's "A Taste of Armageddon." In the 1970s, Hamner created and produced the commando/cop series *S.W.A.T.*

Tom Kersey, from ABC Continuity Acceptance Department, wrote to Irwin Allen on October 8, 1964:

Page 4, Sc. AHMED'S HAND. The strangling must be off camera as indicated. Please keep accompanying death rattles to minimum. And keep resulting blood on Walden's face from razor sharp kris to minimum.

Page 8, substitute for use of "scotch" in any dialogue reference. And of course "Highland Fling" must be fictitious.

Page 10, whenever possible please substitute for the use of the word "assassin". The Kennedy thing is still of too recent date for a vast majority of viewers.

On October 16, Kersey sent more notes:

Page 5, Sc 14 -- TWO HARD LOOKING MEN with MACHINE GUNS – will be cut to one man and one machine-sub-gun.

Page 5, Sc 20 – they both fall limply aside – will be cut to he falls limply aside.

Page 9, Sc 33 – CIA will be deleted. ...

Page 35, Sc 122 – "Blue Cross" will be deleted.

As we discussed, the total violent action is of great concern in this episode. The karate blows will not be new or teaching a new imitative form – rather they should be a stunning instead of fatal type – and covered with concealing block shots. In all uses of the sub-machine-gun, the pistols, the knives, and the karate please hold to the absolute minimum to tell the story without furthering the criticism of "violence for its own sake".

Allen disliked using obviously made-up names for foreign nations or government agencies, but it was a requirement at the time. CBS was inflexible in this respect, as well, as evident in so many episodes of *Mission: Impossible* that took place in some nondescript Eastern European Communist bloc nation. When *I Spy* came to NBC the following year, Executive Producer Sheldon Leonard had the clout to name names, ally or enemy. But his case was an exception.

Production:
(Filmed October 19-27, 1964; 7 days)
(Budget: $125,950)

Felix Feist was hired to direct, at the standard rate of $2,500 for two weeks work (pre-production and filming). He was 54, and had been a "short subject" director throughout the 1930s and early '40s. He got to direct full-length feature films after that, and hit big with 1952's *The Big Trees*, starring Kirk Douglas. He also directed 1953's *Donovan's Brain*, about a scientist who keeps the brain of a ruthless dead millionaire alive in a tank. For television, he directed *The Outer Limits* episode, "The Probe." Feist was well liked by William Self, and had directed numerous episodes of 20th Century-Fox series, such as *Adventures in Paradise*, *Follow the Sun*, and *Bus Stop*. It was Self's idea that Feist be put to work on *Voyage*. This was his first of six assignments for the series.

Lighting double and background cast member Ray Didsbury said, "Felix Feist was tough, demanding, and there was no bullshit. He had very little humor, but he did bring some imagination to the show." (RD-FF01)

Jan Merlin (left) with Frankie Thomas and Al Markim in *Tom Corbett, Space Cadet*.

Jan Merlin was 38 when hired to play Victor Vail, the foreign assassin impersonating Parker. He was no stranger to Navy ships, including submarines, having served in the Navy during World War II as a torpedoman, and having accumulated ten "battle stars." He had been a regular in two TV series (as Cadet Roger Manning in *Tom Corbett, Space Cadet*, from 1950 to '53, and as Lt. Colin Kirby in 1959's *The Rough Riders*). But Merlin could also be a threatening heavy. He was paid $1,250 for his six days work.

Merlin told interviewer Mark Phillips, "Once Hollywood discovered I could do foreign accents, I was always cast as a bad guy, and [the character of] Victor Vail was a good example. The karate bits came off pretty well. I was instructed how to make the moves between breaks. It was important that I do the stunts myself so that the camera could get in close during the fight sequences.

"It was also a pleasure to work with actors I admired. Richard Webb was a good friend, and Richard Basehart was a delight. I told [Basehart] how much I loved his work in the film *La Strada*.

"Science fiction was my passion as a youngster, so working on a show like *Voyage* was interesting. Irwin Allen had a wonderful enthusiasm. I really believed he loved his shows as much as the public did." (JM-VTTBOTS)

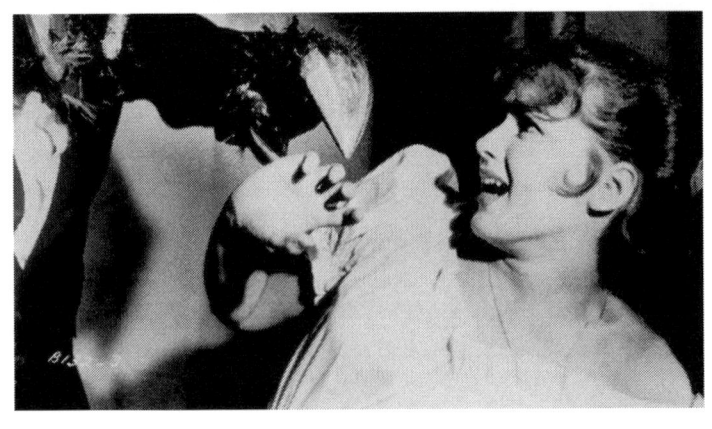

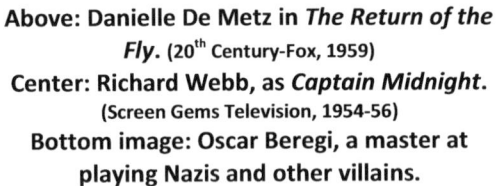

Above: Danielle De Metz in *The Return of the Fly*. (20th Century-Fox, 1959)
Center: Richard Webb, as *Captain Midnight*. (Screen Gems Television, 1954-56)
Bottom image: Oscar Beregi, a master at playing Nazis and other villains.

Danielle De Metz was 26 when given $1,000 (on a one-week deal) to play Anna, the sweet and innocent-looking girl with a vial of deadly serum in her pocket. She and David Hedison had something in common. He had starred in *The Fly*; she appeared in its 1959 sequel, *Return of the Fly*.

49-year-old Richard Webb was cast as Parker, the poor fellow knifed in the back of a chauffeur-driven car. He had played Captain Midnight on television from 1954 through '56. He had a second series in 1959, *Border Patrol*.

Than Wyenn was paid $750 for three days work, playing Koslow, the defector who becomes a target for assassination aboard the Seaview. His face should be familiar to anyone who grew up with the TV set in the 1950s and '60s. He made some 200 appearances on the tube.

Oscar Beregi was cast as Col. Lascoe, the high ranking (Soviet?) official behind the assassination plot. Beregi had a sinister look to him which kept him well-employed in TV and movies throughout the 1960s and '70s, playing Nazis and other heavies, and various European dignitary-types, on shows like *The Man from U.N.C.L.E.*, *The Wild, Wild West*, and *The Twilight Zone*.

Richard Bull began playing the Seaview's doctor here. He was 40, and had been a frequent character actor in television since 1956. Joseph Gantman had recommended him for the role. Bull would return 26 more times over the course of the series, whenever a trip to Sickbay was warranted and Bull was available. He would later play Nels Oleson in 147 episodes of *Little House on the Prairie*.

Filming began on Monday, October 19, 1964. It was mostly a day of exterior shooting on the Fox lot, with the North Gate area serving as "Ext. Jakarta Airport," with a view of the big commuter passenger plane they kept on the lot; the Moat area (providing for "Ext. Country Road"), and the Old Writers Building (providing the look desired for "Ext. Mansion"). The company then moved onto Fox Stage 3 to film the sequences needed in the "Int. CIA Office" and "Int. Bedroom Mansion." And they did all this by 6:30 p.m. An hour after that, ABC aired *Voyage* for the sixth time, with the excellent "The Sky Is Falling." Again, the series won its time period.

Day 2 of filming took place on Tuesday, picking up from the day before, on Stage 3, now on the "Int. Apartment & Hallway" set. The company

Above: Richard Bull played Nels Oleson in 147 episodes of *Little House on the Prairie*. (NBC-TV, 1974-83)
Day 1: Ext Moat/Jungle Area for the "Ext. County Road" ... in which Richard Webb takes a double knife stab to the back ... and his imposter, Jan Merlin, fools Crane.

then moved to their home base, Stage B, for the "Int. Simulated Seaview Corridor" scene in which the homicidal enemy agent practices his invasion inside a mockup of the sub, and kills one from his own side while doing so. Next came "Int. Sect. Mansion Study," and finally the familiar sets with the Control Room and Radio Hut. They

Above: Jan Merlin and Oscar Beregi plot their fiendish scheme on the second day of production.
Below: From Day 4, Danielle De Metz with Merlin on the Sickbay set, then caught in the arms of David Hedison.

wrapped at 6:45 p.m.

Day 3, Wednesday, was spent in the Control Room set on Stage B, then into sickbay, wrapping at 6:50 p.m.

All of Day 4, Thursday, was spent in Sickbay, with the last shot taken at 7:45 p.m.

Day 5: Friday. Exteriors were needed this day on the Fox lot, including many "night-for-night" sequences. On schedule: "Int. Mortuary Garage," "Ext. Mortuary Garage & Jakarta Street," and "Ext. Anna's Apt. House & Street." The latter allowed Richard Basehard to slip into skivvies, and, ironically, rescue the very person assigned to serve as a backup

400

Day 5 sequences included "Int. Mortuary," with Danielle De Metz and Than Wyenn; and (bottom image) "Int. Anna's Apt. House," with Richard Basehart going undercover.

assassin for the injured defector on the Seaview. Cast and crew arrived at noon, for make-up and set preparation. The set call was 1:30 p.m., with camera rolling until 11:45 at night.

Day 6: Monday, October 26. Cast and crew were back on familiar ground – Stage B, on the Int. Observation Nose set and that of the Int. Missile Room. Felix Feist filmed between 8 a.m. and 6 p.m., allowing anyone in the company who was interested in seeing "Turn Back the Clock" home in time to warm up the TV set. David Hedison, in particular, would have been curious to see how old footage (from *The Lost World*) was interwoven with new footage from the series. It was a seamless, if not shameless, job.

Also scheduled (but unattained): Int. Corridor and Int. Ventilation Duct. Both set-ups would carry over to a seventh day of filming. The former involved Jan Merlin's efforts to gain entrance into Sickbay, ending with a

401

shooting rampage. The latter sequences were happily saved until last – and quite hard on the knees for Jan Merlin and David Hedison. The action required them to crawl around in the vitalization ducts for several hours. It took this extra full day to finish "No Way Out."

Day 6: Jan Merlin and David Hedison spent a good portion of the day crawling on their knees in the Seaview's vitalization ducts.

ABC watched a rough cut on November 10, then approved the Final Air Print on November 19, 1964. "No Way Out" would make it onto the air eleven days later.

Release / Reaction:
(ABC premiere broadcast: 11/30/64; repeat airing: 5/31/65)

"Leader of the Pack," by the Shangri-Las, was the most popular song on American radio. Another girl group, the Supremes, was in second position, with "Come See About Me." The Elvis Presley vehicle *Roustabout* was still leading the pack in the movie houses. It would be the eighth top-grossing movie of the year, and its soundtrack album was at the summit on the

Publicity photos taken of Richard Basehart and Robert Dowdell during production of "No Way Out."

Billboard album chart.

"No Way Out" was both the twelfth episode to film and the twelfth to air on ABC. It was liked enough by the producers and the network to be given a repeat broadcast.

Syndicated "TV Scout" previewed the episode in the November 30, 1964 edition of Appleton, Wisconsin's *Post-Crescent*:

> The *Voyage to the Bottom of the Sea* has a script that seems better geared for *The Man from U.N.C.L.E.* It's a cloak and dagger epic with the heroic sub Seaview playing host to a defective Red agent from one of those Communist infiltrated Oriental lands.

On the night "No Way Out" first aired, CBS pre-empted its popular panel shows for a music special presentation of the "Young People's Concert." However, it appeared that the young people across America weren't interested.

403

They were watching *Voyage to the Bottom of the Sea*, giving the series its highest rating to date.

Nielsen ratings report from Nov. 30, 1964:	Rating:	Share:
7:30 – 8 p.m.:		
ABC: *Voyage to the Bottom of the Sea*	**24.1**	**38.7%**
CBS: Music Special: "Young People's Concert"	9.6	15.4%
NBC: *90 Bristol Court: Karen*	15.9	25.5%
8 – 8:30 p.m.		
ABC: *Voyage to the Bottom of the Sea*	**27.5**	**41.2%**
CBS: Music Special: "Young People's Concert"	9.3	13.9%
NBC: *90 Bristol Court: Harris Against the World*	17.1	25.6%

Shortly after "No Way Out" aired, Basehart told Hollywood correspondent Edgar Penton, "A Shakespeare play or an action-adventure story are alike in this respect – either can be dull or exciting, good or bad, depending on the approach. The action movie or television series has been terribly abused at times. Wildly illogical stories, cheap production, bored or incompetent actors, a general feeling, all along the line of 'Don't care.' In this series, we *do* care. As an actor, I do my best in every scene. Otherwise, I would be just wasting my time, and the viewers' time. Hedison, Bob Dowdell, Henry Kulky – they feel the same way. We're playing it the hard way – *for real*. It's not the only way. Action-adventure can be done with the light touch, spoofing as you go. That style seems popular at the moment. But we believe that we can catch the viewer up on a feeling of authentic danger. We're not aiming for the amused smile. We aim for hearts that beat a little faster, for the big sigh of relief when the hole in the side of the Seaview is repaired just in time, when the villains are foiled again." (RB-LCT64)

Basehart knew that a key to success for *Voyage* was treating the unbelievable in a believable way. A year in the future, Guy Williams, June Lockhart, Mark Goddard, and Marta Kristen would approach their *Lost in Space* roles in much the same way. Jonathan Harris would not.

Basehart elaborated: "To the conscientious actor, it's very demanding. I think it's difficult for an actor to give a really bad performance of *Hamlet*. He has so much going for him – time to reveal a complex character, to build up strong relationships with the other characters, along with the most spellbinding language ever written. But what about the hero of an action piece? No time for soliloquies or comment; he has a tough and dangerous job to do, perils and villains to overcome. And yet he knows that unless he creates, between the lines, a fully rounded and believable character, the audience won't care whether he gets thrown off the cliff. That's where the job of the actor comes in. To project a human being, not a robot." (RB-LCT64)

Episode 15: "The Blizzard Makers"

(Prod. #7215; first aired Monday, December 7, 1964)
Story by William Welch and Joe Madison
Teleplay by William Welch
Directed by Joseph Leytes
Produced by Irwin Allen
Story Editor: William Welch; Associate Producer: Allan Balter
Assistant Story Editor: Al Gail
Co-starring Werner Klemperer, Milton Selzer

From the *Voyage* show files, in the Irwin Allen Papers Collection:

A mysterious change in the Gulf Stream results in freakish snowy weather along the Florida coast. Nelson persuades Dr. Melton, a world famous authority on the subject, to join his expedition to check into the causes. On reaching the Gulf Stream they find that an enemy country is secretly testing nuclear bombs, hidden in the caves of a small island. The next bomb, due to be exploded within the hour, will blow the Seaview to bits. Nelson's attempts to stop the enemy are frustrated by Dr. Melton who, unknown to all, has been secretly brain-washed by the enemy.

Sound Bites:

Dr. Melton: 'Admiral Nelson ... where am I? What ... happened?"
Nelson: "You'll be all right." *Melton:* "All right? ... (remembering) ... No, not all right. Never all right. I'm beginning to remember. That plane; that pilot; I killed him. And I tried to kill you." *Nelson:* "No. No, you didn't. You're no more guilty of murder than a gun is. The guilt belongs to the man that pulled the trigger."
Morton (playing translation of signal sent to Melton): "Admiral, listen to this."
Fredric Cregar (transmitted voice): "You failed me, Doctor. Radar indicates that submarine hasn't been disabled. The job is even more difficult now – deliver Nelson to my Central Center. This is imperative. Deliver Nelson to me at once."
Nelson: The man who pulled the trigger."

Assessment:

The story doesn't sit still for a moment. It exemplifies Irwin Allen's recipe for audience thrills: action, action, action ... and then a little more action. Guest performers Werner Klemperer (as the curiously charismatic but ruthless evildoer), and Milton Selzer (as the scientist programmed to kill) bring unexpected dimension to their characters. The story is just odd enough to keep the viewer reasonably spellbound. And credit Richard Basehart for making all the mumbo jumbo about the Gulf Current sound plausible. Credit Joe Madison and William Welch for the tall tale, and the entire supporting cast for their top-flight job in selling us this plot of frozen swampland.

Script:
Joe Madison's writers contract for "The Blizzard Makers": July 1, 1964.
Madison's story treatment and 1st draft teleplay: Date unknown.
Don Brinkley's writers contract: August 3.
Brinkley's new 1st draft ("writers draft") teleplay turned in on October 20.
2nd draft teleplay (first by William Welch): Date unknown.
Mimeo Department's reformatted Shooting Final teleplay: Date unknown.
Rev. Shooting Final teleplay, by William Welch or Al Gail (on pink paper) October 23.
Page revisions by writing staff (on blue paper): October 26.
Page revisions (on green paper): October 27.
Page revisions (on yellow paper): October 27.
Page revisions (on gold paper): October 27.
Page revisions (on beige paper): October 28.

Louis Pollock (aka Joe Madison) was 59 when assigned the story and script for "The Blizzard Makers." He had been Director of Advertising and Publicity at United Artists until 1945, when he decided that what he really wanted to do was write. He sold a few stories to films that would be written by others, including *Stork Bites Man*, about a talking stork and the arrival of a baby, and *The Gamma People*, about the dictator of an Iron Curtain country who uses gamma rays to mutate children into zombie henchmen. Pollock moved into television, selling scripts to the anthology series *Suspense*. Then, as a result of Joseph McCarthy's witch hunt for communist sympathizers in Hollywood, Pollock was blacklisted. His name was removed from screenplays he had contributed to, including *The Jackie Robinson Story* and *Lady and the Tramp*. To sidestep these restrictions, Pollock began writing under pseudonyms, including Joe Madison. During this period he sold a script to *Alfred Hitchcock Presents*, the classic "Breakdown," which starred Joseph Cotton as a paralyzed accident survivor who cannot prevent his impending autopsy. Pollock also wrote several scripts for *The Richard Boone Show*.

Pollock's *Voyage* script was problematic. Don Brinkley was hired to rewrite the script. His draft was also deemed unacceptable, so William Welch took over, and ended up doing enough rewriting that the Writers Guild of America determined he should receive a co-writing credit.

Tom Kersey, of ABC, talked to William Welch on the phone (or "fone," as Kersey liked to spell it), then wrote to Irwin Allen on October 20, saying:

> The script indicates both "... the keys ..." and "... Pensacola in two hours ..." putting you near the Cuban thing – we must avoid all references of innuendo Cuban-wise – and neither Cregar or the telephone lineman can appear Cuban in descent.
>
> Page 4, Sc 8 & 9 – Please check with Vic Bickerstaff of the fone [sic] company, 463-0073, on the telephone gag gimmick [sic]. It being a utility you should extend the courtesy or again, disguise it 1973 style.

All of this meant that the number acquired from the "fone" company had to be an otherwise unused number – a "utility" number designated by the AT&T (aka "Ma Bell") as a test number, which could also be assigned to a TV show or movie; a dummy number which went nowhere. (Any kid growing up in the 1960s quickly deduced that a phone number with the "555" exchange was a fake. They showed up in TV and movies all the time.)

Kersey continued:

> Page 9, Sc 22 – You will have to employ some other device rather than "... raises pistol against his own temple ..." and the following directions in Sc 24, "... pulls the trigger & click of hammer" are unacceptable.

> Page 26, Sc 63 – In difference [sic] to a network sponsor, please use another device than the cigarette (it does not seem to be a particular story point that it be a cigarette).
>
> Page 38, Sc. 94 – Since the Kennedy assassination, the use of cross-hairs and telescopic sights on rifles has been unacceptable.

The assassination of President John F. Kennedy was but one of many reasons why violence on television had become cartoonish in nature. People watching television had no idea why TV "violence," when it appeared at all, had become so fake-looking. Often we young viewers felt that the makers of television dramas, even those in the action-adventure genre, didn't have a clue as to what a real fist fight, knife fight, or gun battle, looked or felt like. The truth was, they did know – they were grown-ups after all, and many had served in the military – but part of their job nowadays was to shelter us from such knowledge.

Production:
(Filmed October 28 through November 4; 6 days)
(Budget: $121,706)

Joseph Leytes was hired to direct. The 63-year-old director was from Poland, where he had made movies prior to World War II. He won the Fascist Industry Confederation Cup at the 1935 Venice Film Festival for his *The Day of the Great Adventure* (U.S. title), and was nominated for the Mussolini Cup at the 1937 Venice Film Festival for another Polish film, *Love or a Kingdom*. After the war, Leytes migrated to Israel where he stayed active as a film director, and received three more Venice Film Festival nominations (in 1949, '50 and '52), this time with no mention of "fascist" or "Mussolini" in the award category. By 1959, Leytes had migrated to America, and Jack Warner put him to work directing ten episodes of the TV Western *Sugarfoot*. Zanuck at 20th Century-Fox was also supportive of Leytes, and brought him to that studio for eight episodes of *Adventures in Paradise*. He would only do one *Voyage* before moving on to the studio's *12 O'Clock High* for several assignments.

Werner Klemperer was 44 when he played Fredric Cregar. He had worked for Irwin Allen once before, standing in for Theodore Marcuse for some pickup shots needed in the *Voyage* pilot, "Eleven Days to Zero." He was 44, had garnered critical acclaim for his role in 1961's *Judgment at Nuremberg*, and was just one year away from TV fame and two Emmy awards, as Colonel Klink in *Hogan's Heroes*. He plays Cregar here.

Milton Selzer was 45 when cast as Dr. Melton. Between 1951 and 1995 he made over 200 appearances in TV and films, including playing Parker,

Werner Klemperer was only one year away from fame ... and Emmy Awards ... for playing Col. Klink on *Hogan's Heroes*.
(Bing Crosby Productions, 1965-71)

Milton Selzer – seen here in "The Masks," an episode of *The Twilight Zone* – was equally adept at drama and comedy.
(Cayuga Productions, 1964)

CONTROL's gadget maker, in seven episodes of *Get Smart*. He's an amiable assassin here, but you can see him play a more sinister one in the *Wild, Wild West* episode "The Night of the Death Masks."

Sheila Mathews plays Dr. Melton's wife. She was 35 and the new girlfriend of the producer, later becoming Mrs. Irwin Allen. She would also appear in three episodes of *Lost in Space* (most notably as the singing Brynhilda in "The Space Vikings"), and two episodes of *Land of the Giants*. She had small roles in Allen's 1971 TV movie and pilot film *City Beneath the Sea*, plus many more of her husband's projects: 1972's *The Poseidon Adventure*; 1974's *The Towering Inferno*; the 1975 TV movie and pilot *Adventures of the Queen* (which co-starred David Hedison); 1977's *Viva Knievel!*; 1980's *When Time Ran Out...*; 1985's two-part TV event, *Alice in Wonderland*; and the 1986 TV movie *Outrage!* She also had a recurring role in a series *not* produced by Allen – *The Waltons*, as Fanny Tatum.

This episode's set-up required a great deal of exposition. Much of this burden fell on Richard Basehart. Admiral Nelson explains to his crew (and the TV audience) what is happening with the Gulf Stream, climate change, etc. Basehart said, "It's a fun show. But we have a format and we must stick to it and that limits you. I get into so much trouble fighting the lines. But I want it to be the best we can make it."

Of David Hedison, Basehart added, "He's one of the most promising young actors in television. When David has something to say, he'll show what he's got. But it's hard to be great with 'Up periscope; down periscope.'" (RB-FITM64)

Filming started on Wednesday, October 28 on Stage B for Int. Cregar's Cab (a limo, actually, filmed against a process screen), followed by the fire scene in Nelson's cabin, including Crane in the corridor outside.

On Thursday, they filmed on Stage 3 (Int. Melton Bedroom and Int. Melton Study) and Peyton Square (from the *Peyton Place* TV series) for Florida Street.

Day 2: Milton Selzer and Werner Klemperer (above) on the "Int. Melton's Study" set.
Day 4: Hedison, Monroe and Kulky in the "Cave Cell."

Friday was spent on Stage 3, filming Int. Bunker and Cave Cell, both on the island.

On Monday, November 2, they worked outdoors at the Craft Building (M.A.T.S. Terminal and Ext. Road), the Moat (Ext. Beach, Jungle Clearing and Mouth of Cave), and then, finally, onto Stage B for additional work on the Seaview sets. They finished at 7:38 p.m., after "The Village of Guilt" began airing on ABC. Though the makers of the episode couldn't get home in time to watch, *Voyage* won its time period for the eighth consecutive week.

410

Day 5: Filming on the beach area of the Moat and the surrounding jungle (above), as well as the large cave opening (below), with Hedison, Monroe, and Kulky. Day 6: Utilizing the Seaview Lab to serve as the operating room for the foreign spies, with Klemperer and Selzer.

Tuesday, November 3, was Election Day, and cast and crew were not expected on set until 9 a.m., theoretically allowing time to vote before starting work. Filming started at 9:23 on the Observation Nose set (shooting toward the process screen), then onto the Seaview Lab set, the Missile Room and, lastly, into the Control Room. Production stopped at 7:10 p.m. The early election returns were coming in.

Lyndon B. Johnson, having served two years in office since the assassination of President John F. Kennedy, won re-election with 61.1% of the popular vote, defeating Republican candidate Barry Goldwater by a landslide.

The sixth and final day of production was Wednesday, November 4, back on Stage B for more work in the Seaview's Control Room and Radio Hut, and a trip to Sickbay. Production wrapped at 7 p.m.

The Second Unit played a big part

in the impressive look of this episode. With an early renewal received from ABC for further episodes, Irwin Allen dispatched L.B. Abbott to film new transitions scenes with the various models of the Seaview. Some of the new "sail by" sequences seen in this episode are spectacular. They demonstrate that the filming of miniatures – especially when some of those miniatures are several feet long – could look far superior to what is commonplace today. No matter how detailed the CGI, there's something about model work which provides weight and scale, when it's done well. In these effects shots, the Seaview feels real ... because it was.

Day 6: One of the last scenes filmed for the episode was Selzer's attempt to take over the Control Room, holding Robert Dowdell at gunpoint.

Release / Reaction:
(Only ABC broadcast: 12/7/64)

"Ringo," by Lorne Greene, was the song getting more radio airplay than any other in the United States. It had been released on an album several months earlier which hadn't even dented the charts. Perhaps its surprise-hit status was because its title was also the name of the drummer in the No. 1 pop band in America, and the world – Ringo Starr. Also this week, the seasonal special *Rudolph the Red-Nosed Reindeer* first aired on television. And Dr. Martin Luther King was presented with the Nobel Peace Prize.

"The Blizzard Makers" was both the fifteenth episode filmed and aired. But it wasn't quite fantastic enough to get a network repeat broadcast.

Steven Scheuer, in his nationally syndicated column, "TV Key," wrote:

> Comic strip science-fiction. Someone's been tampering with the Gulf Stream and there are severe blizzards in Florida. Lurking behind the trouble is a nasty little foreign power which not only destroys Florida's tourist trade, but manages to entrap the mind of a scientist working to clear up the program. So, naturally, the Seaview is enlisted to get to the source of the trouble.

Joan Crosby, in her syndicated "TV Scout" column, said:

> "The Blizzard Makers" is enough to make any Florida tourist agent shake in his sandals. It appears the sun baked peninsula has suddenly turned colder than an iceberg. So, the tireless crew of the Seaview investigates. But the scientist they've taken along turns out to be a yes man robot for a foreign agent. This episode is strictly for science fiction buffs who don't take their plots too seriously.

We're not sure, but we think we've just been insulted. Regardless, it turned out that we plot-insensitive sci-fi buffs were in the majority. On this night, as with most others, *Voyage to the Bottom of the Sea* won its time slot.

Nielsen ratings report from Dec. 7, 1964:	Rating:	Share:
7:30 – 8 p.m.:		
ABC: ***Voyage to the Bottom of the Sea***	**19.5**	**32.0%**
CBS: *To Tell the Truth*	18.2	29.8%
NBC: *90 Bristol Court: Karen*	11.5	18.9%
8 – 8:30 p.m.		
ABC: ***Voyage to the Bottom of the Sea***	**21.1**	**32.7%**
CBS: *I've Got a Secret*	20.2	31.3%
NBC: *90 Bristol Court: Harris Against the World*	12.5	19.3%

Richard Basehart was the subject of a feature newspaper article, "Basehart Plays *Voyage* for Real," carried in the *Courier Times* of Levittown, Pennsylvania, on December 5, 1964, among other newspapers. Syndicated entertainment correspondent Edgar Penton wrote in part:

> At first thought, Richard Basehart would seem a surprising choice to star in an action-packed underwater series. ... Basehart is not the iron-jawed-hero type. Since his first Broadway appearance in the heart-wrenching role of a doomed Scottish soldier in *The Hasty Heart*, he has been the actor producers sent for when they needed a sensitive, thoughtful, highly-skilled acting job. He has been called "the thinking man's actor." One critic, in a flight of lyricism, described Basehart's voice as one that "seems to seek unceasingly for the lost and wondrous tones of the English language." David Hedison, the lean, dark-eyed actor who plays the Seaview's skipper, Commander Lee Crane, declares, "Dick is one of the five best actors in America." So what is Basehart doing in an action series, as designer-builder of the Seaview, atom-powered, glass-nosed submarine? An interviewer gets a basic answer from Basehart: "Working at my trade."

Challenged with the question, "What does *Voyage* say?," Basehart answered: "[W]e must not be fooled by the trap of words: The test of a morality or philosophy is not how eloquent a man may be on the subject, but what action he takes. Morality is action; the rest platitudes. Analyze most *Voyage* stories. Someone is in deep trouble. The men of the Seaview do not look the other way. Despite the danger, they go to help him out. They demonstrate that people can rise above concern for their own skins, that they care, that they take the trouble. In these times, or in any times, I think that's an important statement to make."
(RB-LCT64)

Episode 16: "The Ghost of Moby Dick"

(Prod. #7216; first aired Monday, December 14, 1964)
Written by Robert Hamner
Directed by Sobey Martin
Produced by Irwin Allen
Story Editor: William Welch; Associate Producer: Joseph Gantman
Assistant Story Editor: Al Gail
Guest stars Ed Binns and June Lockhart

The official synopsis from the *Voyage* show files:

> A brilliant ichthyologist was badly mutilated and his own son killed when their boat was attacked by a gigantic whale they were pursuing. Now, obsessed by the idea of tracking down the creature and revenging himself, the scientist, who was prepared to sacrifice the Seaview, its crew and his wife, deliberately engages in a duel to the death with his monstrous foe.

Sound Bites:

Walter Bryce: "Somewhere here in the South Atlantic, I happened on one of the great scientific finds of all time – a huge … a gigantic whale, many times larger than any other sighted before." *Crane (cynically):* "Moby Dick?" *Walter Bryce:* "Moby Dick was fictional, Captain." … *(putting a hand over his crippled arm)* … "This whale was very real." *Crane:* "Well, the largest I've ever heard of was a sperm whale, caught off Bering Straits, about 800 feet long." *Ellen Bryce:* "This whale is more than twice that size." *Crane:* "Well, that's incredible. That would make it bigger than the largest dinosaur that ever lived." *Walter Bryce:* "It's probably the largest of its species ever to draw a breath on this planet – a vast storehouse of knowledge that must be unlocked." *Crane (skeptical):* "Dr. Bryce, do you have any pictures of this whale, or ship's logs documenting all of this? How about an eyewitness, present company excluded?" *Bryce (taking offense):* "I think Admiral Nelson will verify that we are scientists of some standing, and not weekend fishermen bragging about the big one that got away."

Chip Morton: "We do any faster maneuvering and this old sub is going to be the 'Sea' and the 'View' with both ends going in opposite directions." … *Crane*: "How does it feel getting pushed around by a fish?" *Morton*: "Fish? That's like saying Babe Ruth was just another baseball player."

Assessment:

Who would have expected that yet another variation on *Moby Dick* could succeed?

June Lockhart demonstrates a stunning range of emotions. Her character expresses in turn poise; distress; confrontation; despair; and calm resolve. The scene in which she confronts her husband and is knocked to the deck is especially effective, showcasing Lockhart's talents beyond anything we would ever see on *Lassie* or *Lost in Space*. The whale is a wonderful effect, remarkably realistic in appearance for a 1964 TV production. And it is not merely a monster; it is motivated. It responds when attacked and attempts to flee when hurt. You may find yourself feeling an odd mixture of fear and compassion for the beast, and similarly conflicting feelings toward Dr. Bryce, effectively portrayed by Ed Binns. The terror felt by the crew as the whale attacks, and as Seaview takes a beating, is so well depicted from all involved that we spectators easily find ourselves lost in the drama. Not an easy trick when it comes to this tale of a whale and a sub, shot in six days for TV.

While all of these aspects are assets, it's a shame that the production crew used a distracting number of close-up insert shots that were supposedly visible through Seaview's stern camera.

One stagnant, murky nose-camera shot would have been sufficient, not multiple close-up angles of the action. At least the blunder is short-lived, then we're back to all that works in this engrossing tale.

Another wonderful moment worth mentioning: Richard Basehart reading aloud from *Moby-Dick*. Basehart had starred in the 1956 film version as Ishmael, the narrator of that story. He tells the story again, as Nelson is forced to realize that Dr. Bryce, whom he both likes and respects, may be mad. With this scene, we get a nice inside joke. Crane asks, "Have you read this?" Nelson answers, "*Moby Dick*? Every word of it."

Script:
Robert Hamner's treatment and 1st draft teleplay: Dates unknown.
Hamner's Final Draft teleplay approved on October 21, 1964.
Mimeo Department's reformatted Shooting Final teleplay: Date unknown.
Revised Shooting final teleplay (by William Welch or Al Gail):
Date unknown.
2nd Rev. Shooting Final by writing staff (on pink paper): November 2.
Page revision (on blue paper): November 3.
Page revisions (on yellow paper): November 9.
Page revisions (on gold paper): November 3.

Robert Hamner said, "The first script I wrote was ripped off from *Moby Dick*, and that turned out well…. It was fun." (RH-SL92)

Hamner began his work for *Voyage* here (although his rewrite of "No Way Out" was filmed first).

Hamner said, "The first thing you had to understand about Irwin was that even though he was doing, by today's standards, very cheesy special FX, to him, *Voyage* was *Gone with the Wind*. That was his saving grace. He felt he was doing the most wonderful, fabulous thing ever. Irwin's TV shows, and everyone who worked on them, were Irwin's family. He had no other family except for actress Sheila Mathews, whom he later married, and Al Gail, his cousin. Irwin had no other life. Monday mornings were the happiest times of his life because he could have his family around him all week. When the weekend came, he invented crises so that he could call you up. If I had a problem with Irwin, he would say, 'You're out of the will.' And, if you did something good, he would say, 'Hey, you're back in the will.' He was very special, and anything I say is with great affection." (RH-SL92)

Production:
(Filmed November 5-12, 1964; 6 days)
(Budget numbers unavailable)

Sobey Martin was hired to direct with the standard pay rate of $2,500 for five to six days of preparation, and six to seven days of production. He was 55, and this was his first of 14 episodes of *Voyage*. Irwin Allen was very loyal to Martin, who also directed 14 episodes of *Lost in Space*, 14 of *The Time Tunnel*, and 21 of *Land of the Giants*. Ray Didsbury said, "Sobey Martin struck me as being somewhat incompetent. He had very little imagination, and he must have worked cheap, since he did so many shows. He spoke with a thick accent. One of our running jokes was a 'Sobeyism.' For instance, if an actor was to be karate-chopped, Sobey's direction was that the villain was to 'Karachi' him. He was a nice man, but he was not an actor's favorite." (RD-FF01)

June Lockhart was 39, and just off of six years of *Lassie*, when she appeared as Ellen Bryce. Lockhart had also appeared as Richard Basehart's wife in the 1957 film *Time Limit*. She received top guest-star billing here, and $1,500 for six days of service.

This appearance led to another important step in her career. Lockhart recalled a voice asking her, "You want to do another series?" She said, "It was Irwin Allen asking me the question after having seen the first day's rushes of my guest appearance on *Voyage to the Bottom of the Sea*, entitled 'Ghost of Moby Dick.' The script he gave me to read was for 'Space Family Robinson,' as it was then called. It was high adventure, very provocative science fiction. NASA was launching astronauts into space – space was hot – and this series would be completely different to the *Lassie* show I'd finished doing the previous six years. I was delighted to say 'yes' – and was the first actor cast in the show." (JL-LISM)

She would begin filming the *Lost in Space* pilot six weeks later, in late December, 1964.

June Lockhart, circa early 1950s.

Edward Binns was 48 when he played Walter Bryce. He got second guest-star billing, and a $1,750 paycheck for six days work. One of those days included pretending to be drowning in the 20th Century-Fox Moat. Binns made close to 200 appearances in TV and films over his career, which included his own series – *Brenner* (1959-64) – for which he played the title character, a veteran NYPD cop, assigned to work with his son, an idealistic rookie.

This was Del Monroe's fourteenth appearance since coming aboard for the pilot. Speaking before a sci-fi convention crowd in England, Monroe said, "The first year, before Allan [Hunt] joined the show, Irwin had about eight or nine of us actors – myself, Paul Trinka, Paul Carr, Nigel [McKeand]. Irwin didn't know whose role to embellish; there were all these characters. The stunt people and the special-effects people would always get the script first because they had to prepare, so we used to run to the stunt people and the special-effects people to see if we were in the next week's script, because we didn't know from week to week. As a matter of fact, I was working the graveyard shift – which was 12-midnight to seven-thirty in the morning – at the Lockheed aircraft plant the first year of *Voyage*. I didn't know if I was going to work from week-to-week, and I had two kids, who were toddlers. Sometimes I would have a call at 7 o'clock in the morning. I worked about thirty miles from the studio. I would give them some kind of fictitious excuse to get off early from the plant to get to the studio on time. I ran out of excuses and my agent at the time said, 'Hey, give the kid a contract, he's killing himself trying to get from work to here.' Irwin did. He gave me a contract for 13 shows. We did 32 shows that first year and I did more than 13. At last I was sure of an income. I quit my job, which is every actor's dream – to quit your job and know that you're going to work every day at the studio. That was marvelous." (DM-SE98)

Production for "Ghost" began on Thursday, November 5, 1964. One of the hard scenes was up first – hard for guest stars June Lockhart and Ed Binns. Set in

Edward Binns and Virginia Gregg in *Portland Expose*. (Allied Artists, 1957)

the Bryces' Seaview cabin, it involved an argument between the couple that ends with Bryce knocking his wife against a bulkhead; she slides weeping to the floor. The acting in this scene is still affecting, 50 years later.

Also filmed: scenes in the corridors, the Missile Room, and the Forward Torpedo Room.

The Control Room scenes were filmed on Friday and Monday, the second and third days of production. They wrapped at 6:55 p.m. on Monday evening, with "Hot Line" premiering 35 minutes later on ABC-TV's local affiliate, Channel 7.

Day 4 included Int. Pilot's House, Ext. Bow" and "Flying Bridge," shot against a process screen.

Again, for the ninth week, *Voyage* won its time period in the all-important Nielsen ratings.

Tuesday was busy, with work beginning on Stage 15 for the various shots on the Bryces' motor cruiser, including "Int. Pilot's House, Ext. Bow" (with the harpoon cannon). These were all process shots, filmed against a screen that would show the ocean when broadcast. The other process shot of this type, the "Flying Bridge" of the Seaview, was taken on this day as well. After this, the company moved back to Stage B, to begin

420

filming scenes needed on the Observation Nose of the Seaview, also requiring a process shot. Wednesday was also spent on the Observation Nose.

Thursday, November 12, was the sixth and final day of production, as they filmed Observation Nose scenes and camera angles not

Captain Crane prompts Admiral Nelson to read out loud from Moby Dick ... the very lines Richard Basehart narrated in the 1950s feature-film version.

requiring process shots, then moved to the "Fish Tank" to get close-ups of Ed Binns underwater, in his scuba mask. Now that everything else had been filmed, they dared the sequences which features Binns in close-up, being pulled by the whale and with water splashing over him. This was also shot in the "Fish Tank."

Interviewed for an article in Massachusetts' *North Adams Transcript*, Edward Binns told how one scene for the episode "called for him to be dragged through the water to his death." Binns said, "I'm in a wet suit and flippers and they turn the hoses in my face, and I'm being pulled through the water, and I scream and die. When the scene is over, I get out of the tank where it was filmed and the producer says to me, 'You're a wonderful swimmer.' That's fine, but I wonder what kind of an actor I am. I wanted to say, 'Good, call me the next time you need a swimmer.'" (EB-NAT65)

Before the episode went into post-production, a phone call was made to United Artists to see if shots of the whale from *Moby Dick* could be licensed as stock footage. UA politely said no. This meant more work for L.B. Abbott, Allen's special-effects wizard.

Robert Mintz told interviewer Mark Phillips, "My job at Fox was to make sure that the post-production process was on schedule so that the studio would make all of its airdates. *Voyage* was a major challenge because of the sizable amount of special effects. Whether we were working with giant lizards or giant whales, these kinds of effects took time and they took longer to deliver them to the network. If we did have airdate problems, I would go to Bill "L.B." Abbott, who was in charge of special effects at Fox, and I would whine, beg and negotiate to get whatever effects shots we needed. He and his department were tremendously cooperative and we never missed an airdate. Irwin Allen had a wonderfully keen mind and he was a showman through and through." (RM-VTTBOTS)

Another part of post-production is "looping" voices onto previously filmed scenes. Irwin Allen had been providing some of these dubbed-in voices, and Allen is heard in this episode over the ship's intercom exclaiming, in a Brooklyn accent, "If that whale hits us again, we've had it!" Costume designer Paul Zastupnevich and post-production supervisor George Swink had also been contributing their voices when needed. Ray Didsbury, who filled roles as Richard Basehart's lighting double, as one of the Seaview's nondescript crewmen, and also as the series dialogue coach, was about to be handed a fourth duty. He told interviewer Mark Phillips, "One day, in the dailies, I must have been closer to the mike than usual, because Irwin and the post-production people heard my voice loud and clear, and they liked it. Joe D'Agosta, the casting director, said they wanted me to do the voices over the Seaview's intercom. Irwin did some of the voices until someone had the courage to tell him that he didn't sound right. Paul Zastupnevich had an unfortunate high voice, and Irwin realized Paul was wrong for the voiceovers." (RD-FF01)

Release / Reaction:
(ABC premiere broadcast: 12/14/64; network repeat airing: 6/7/65)

"Mr. Lonely," by Bobby Vinton, was the song getting the most spins on radio station turntables across America. "She's Not There," by the Zombies, came in second. Both would be moving down in the days to come, because the Beatles had a new release flying up the charts, "I Feel Fine" b/w "She's a Woman." *Roustabout* was still king of movie box offices. And Julie Newmar, who starred as a robot in *My Living Doll*, had the cover of *TV Guide*. A bigger bomb than *My Living Doll* went off in the Pacific and in Nevada, as the United States conducted separate nuclear-bomb tests. Perhaps less damaging to the world's environment,

"The Pink Panther" cartoons began showing in movie theaters as opening attractions, starting with "The Pink Phink." It would go on to win an Academy Award as Best Animated Short Film.

"The Ghost of Moby Dick" was the sixteenth episode filmed; the fourteenth to air.

Syndicated "TV Scout," in the December 14, 1964 edition of Appleton, Wisconsin's *Post-Crescent*, said:

> What may have been a whale of an adventure in "The Ghost of Moby Dick" on *Voyage to the Bottom of the Sea* turns into a lot of scientific blubber before the outing is over. Nevertheless, there are some exciting moments as the Seaview prowls the South Atlantic to trap "the greatest ichthyological find in history" – a 160-foot whale. Edward Binns is the scientist aboard who wants to take an electro-cardiograph of the monster's huge heart and June Lockhart is his aide who thinks he is more interested in revenge.

Also from the 14th, in "TV Previews," Steven Scheuer gave the series a backhanded compliment:

> Give the show credit for integrity. The story is a blatant parallel to Melville's classic and admits it. In this one a scientist (Edward Binns) is after the biggest whale in history, ostensibly for scientific purposes, but actually to revenge himself against the brute for killing his son and maiming him. There are some good special effects in this one, including the shock of a whale ramming a submarine and undersea battle pitting man against whale. June Lockhart, who can't seem to get away from wild life, guests as the scientist's wife.

On December 16, Duku, of *Daily Variety*, surveyed the series again. With "The Ghost of Moby Dick," the trade critic still liked what he was seeing, calling it "exciting and suspenseful," with an episode that was "loaded with action and the bizarre qualities which have maintained a healthy rating for the Irwin Allen-20th-Fox TV series."

Nielsen ratings report from Dec. 14, 1964: 7:30 – 8 p.m.:	Rating:	Share:
ABC: *Voyage to the Bottom of the Sea*	**23.9**	**38.0%**
CBS: *To Tell the Truth*	17.3	27.5%
NBC: *90 Bristol Court: Karen*	11.9	18.9%

8 – 8:30 p.m.
ABC: ***Voyage to the Bottom of the Sea***   **25.4**   **40.0%**
CBS: *I've Got a Secret*   17.4   27.4%
NBC: *90 Bristol Court: Harris Against the World*   11.6   18.3%

During the same week, *TV Guide* ran this letter in its December 12, 1964 issue:

> As members of the US submarine force, we have been appalled by the reflection on us by the actions of the crew aboard the submarine in *Voyage to the Bottom of the Sea*. We are referring to the panic that takes place every time something goes wrong on the Seaview. If this happened on submarines every time something went wrong, there would be very few submarines afloat today. The prestige of our crew and the whole submarine force is high and we believe that the actions of the crew of the Seaview are degrading to us. – Crew Members, USS Jack, New York, N.Y.

7

Fathoming Irwin Allen

As Season One of *Voyage to the Bottom of the Sea* reached its midway point, some behind-the-scenes changes were taking place at Irwin Allen Productions. The company was growing by leaps and bounds, with *Voyage* picked up for another 16 episodes; the *Lost in Space* pilot on order; and a third potential series on the drawing boards – *The Time Tunnel* – with interest from ABC. 20th Century-Fox had other series in production for ABC with *12 O'Clock High*, *Valentine's Day*, and *Peyton Place*. The studio was also producing *Daniel Boone* for NBC. Pilots in production included three that would become series the following year – *The Legend of Jesse James* and *The Long, Hot Summer*, for ABC, and, along with *Lost in Space*, Rod Serling's *The Loner*, for CBS. More help was needed from casting, and more "help" was needed from the network.

The first order of business: Joe D'Agosta was assigned to work under Cliff Gould in the casting department of 20th Century-Fox. D'Agosta had held a similar position at MGM, where he handled the casting for producer Gene Roddenberry's pre-*Star Trek* series, *The Lieutenant*. At Fox, his responsibilities were much greater. Among his series assignments were *Voyage to the Bottom of the Sea* and *Lost in Space*, followed later by the pilot film for *The Time Tunnel*. Interviewed for this book, Joe D'Agosta said of Irwin Allen, "He was not as much a producer as he was an emperor.

"He worked me from 7 in the morning till 11:30 at night. I didn't mind; I loved my work. I was the same as Irwin in that regard. I loved Monday mornings and hated Friday afternoons. I didn't like *not* going to the studio. And I understood that about Irwin. That's what I respected. The fact that he was a little rigid, I didn't care about. And I didn't care that he was a bit of an emperor, for lack of a better term, with his Napoleonic way. I didn't mind that. I like tough guys. You know what you're dealing with. It's the nice guys that criticize you behind your back that you have to worry about. So I always liked working with him."

There was a stumbling block, however, for D'Agosta. "One thing Irwin wanted from his employees, other than that they agree with him, was absolute exclusive loyalty. When I went to Fox, my deal was that I would cast features as well as television. So, I was assigned *Stagecoach* by my boss, Cliff Gould, the head of casting. And Irwin saw me on the grounds of Fox with the script. He said, 'What's that?' I said, 'I'm casting a movie; it's a remake of the John Wayne movie.' I was very proud when I said it. But he walked away off that comment, and the next thing I get is a call from my boss. I was asked into his office, and he said, 'Irwin wants to meet with us.'"

D'Agosta was about to see how this emperor acted when his subjects displeased him. D'Agosta said, "We went into this meeting, and there was this long table – probably 10 to 15 feet long – and on one end sat Irwin, and on the other end sat my boss. And on one side of the length of the long table sat Frank La Tourette, an associate producer who I always had casting sessions with, and Harry Harris, a director who worked on many of the episodes. I sat on the other long side. Irwin proceeded to talk about how he wasn't getting enough of my time, and then turned to the associate producer and said, 'You tell Cliff Gould what it is like to work with Joe.' And this guy went on with a bunch of complaints about my unavailability, how it took me a little longer to get the interviews set up. I don't remember the arguments, but he had a whole list of things that he was programmed to complain about. Then Irwin turned to director Harry Harris and said, 'Tell Cliff about how it is to work with Joe,' and a similar list was presented." (JDA-AI15)

Harris was hoping to pacify Allen, who might send further directing assignments his way. But he certainly understood D'Agosta's difficultly. He told interviewer Kevin Burns, "The experience of working with Irwin did a lot for me, because you have to have a tremendous amount of patience to keep from blowing your stack. Getting through that kind of experience over all those years working with him, that's what I think about. I don't think about *Lost in Space* or *Voyage to the Bottom* – the product doesn't mean anything to me; the fact that I worked with him stays with me. I think about him all the time. I hated him, and I liked him. Sometimes it was a love-hate relationship. But I learned a lot from him, and I learned to keep my mouth shut, and I learned to have patience and how to go about my business and do my work and not do anything to hinder my relationship with him." (HH-KB95)

Joe D'Agosta had not yet learned that lesson. Continuing his story of the meeting, he said, "I was a young man at the time, around 26. I sat there and I just started shaking, and my lip was tightening, and my anger was building. And Irwin just sat there, very superior like. Finally, I got up and I stared out the window. I tried to hold my temper, but, when Irwin started to speak again, I verbally attacked him. I put my finger right up to his nose, and said, 'Let me tell you something, you! I come here; I work with you till 11:30 at night. I've got a family at home, but I'm *here* at 7 o'clock in the morning, pulling your casting together.' He just sat there; he froze, and he wouldn't meet my stare. He knew that I was ready to explode. I was scary. I scared *myself!* And it was all because I was hurt. I was *hurt* that I'd been set up – with that table and the way he placed us and then presided over that kangaroo court. I just attacked him verbally, then I walked right out the door. As I passed Cliff, I said, 'I'm sorry, Cliff, I couldn't keep it in,' because Cliff was a gentleman; a truly nice guy and I felt bad for whatever trouble this would create for him."

Anyone who knew Joe D'Agosta – everyone interviewed for this book and books on *Lost in Space* and *Star Trek* (where D'Agosta also worked) – always remember him as friendly and even-tempered. D'Agosta's response to the meeting shocked even him. He said, "I went back to my office, and I was shaking. I thought, 'That's it; I'm done here,' because Irwin Allen had more shows on the air than any company in town. I was doing three shows with him. So, the phone rings, and Cliff says, 'Can you come in to my office?' I went into his office and said, 'Just fire me. Don't worry about it, Cliff. I'm sorry; I just couldn't hold it in.' He said, 'Boy, you sure can get mad.' I told him, 'Cliff, I worked my ass off for that guy, blah, blah, blah, blah.'" D'Agosta apologized to Gould for losing his temper, then braced himself for the worst. Was his career at Fox over? To his surprise, Gould asked, "Well, can you work with him again?"

D'Agosta said, "What are you talking about?" Then, he recalled, "Cliff says, 'He wants nobody but you.' I said, 'What about the feature?' He says, 'You can keep the feature.' 'Really?!'

"Now, if Irwin was the emperor I thought he was, he could have had my head chopped off. I would have been finished in the business, not just at Fox. So, I went back to Irwin and, from that point on, he never made a casting decision based on the director's or the associate producer's opinions, but only on my opinion. He'd say, 'What do you think, Joe?' And we had this father/son relationship that was just amazing. It always remained a professional relationship;

we didn't hang out; it was within the walls of the office, but when I say father/son, I'm saying he treated me kindly, with respect, and he wouldn't make a move in casting without getting my approval." (JDA-AI15)

Now that *Voyage to the Bottom of the Sea* had a full season of 32 episodes on order, another change involved the control ABC exercised. During the first half of Season One, which included the early script development of some later season episodes, Adrian Samish had been the primary liaison between the series and the network. And Samish was a hands-on production manager. Since the show was not yet a hit (with nearly half the first-season episodes filmed before the series premiered), the network had the power to mandate many elements of the series. But when the ratings reports started to come in, proving that *Voyage* was winning its time slot and bringing in well above a 30-percent audience share, the emboldened Allen started paying more attention to his own narrative instincts. At first, this change was not a dramatic one, and Samish tried to keep a firm hand on the show. By the latter part of Season One, however, Samish had moved up at the network. Harve Bennett was in charge of overseeing the numerous details for many of ABC's series, including *Voyage*. Bennett soon learned that he wasn't going to make much of a dent on Allen's decisions. He took a step back and assigned one of his junior executives the headache of trying to rein Allen in. Handed this touchy job was Lew Hunter.

Interviewed for this book, Hunter related, "Harve Bennett was the one that hired me and got me into programming. And I jumped up in pay from an $8,000 annual gig – being the Director of Broadcast Promotions – to $35,000. And, my God, I thought I'd died and gone to heaven. He says over the phone, 'I'm going to give you $35,000 a year.' I gulped and said, 'That will be fine, Harve.'" (LH-AI15)

Irwin Allen admired Hunter. The two men had come from different parts of the United States but otherwise had much in common. Both were tireless workers. And their achievements had been earned the hard way.

Hunter remembered, "I started in television back in 1952 when I was a floor manager at KOLN, Lincoln, Nebraska. I was a self-confessed farm boy way back then, and I went to Chicago to attend Northwestern. I also did some work in advertising there. So, I think Irwin had an identification with my own background, because when I was going to Hollywood from Chicago, I knew *nobody* in Hollywood. I had an aunt and uncle that lived in Long Beach and that was it.

"I'd been in town for three weeks, and I was a failure. Particularly when I was at the gas company, trying to sign up for gas service, and the form said, 'Occupation?' I put down 'Producer.' The woman who was dealing with me put a line through 'producer' and she wrote, 'unemployed.' I laughed then, and was shook up at the same time. So I wrote 95 letters – and that was back in the time when you typed up each letter, because you didn't have the ability to copy them or to readjust the heading. So I wrote 95 letters to 95 different people at the studios and networks, and at advertising agencies, and I got 15 responses. Of those, five people agreed to meet with me. One was this wonderful man named Ed Cashman, and Ed said, 'You need to get in the door. Whether it's the 'Page Cap' or the mail room, you just get in the door, and from then on you can fly.' He was absolutely right. I worked as a page at ABC, starting in 1956, and did that for two weeks, then five months in the mail room, then I went into music clearance, and up the ladder, and up, up, up, and I got into broadcast promotions, where I did the trailers. I won an award for one of those trailers, and that led to me being transferred to work under Harve Bennett. Somehow, Irwin got hold of that information, and that gave him a little more respect for me. That energy that Irwin saw in me, from how I came out with no contacts and then worked my way up, from the bottom, was something that he admired." (LW-AI15)

Allen had similarly clawed his way up a different showbiz ladder upon his own arrival in Hollywood. Like Hunter, Allen had been one of the few to succeed, but he always remembered that his career could have gone the other way. Vitina Marcus, closely associated with Allen at this time, said, "Irwin told me he had a recurring dream that he was in a strange city without any money. There was no one he could go to; nowhere for him to turn. And no money to get home. This was a recurring nightmare; he was always telling me about that dream. He had it often. So this had been a big fear for him." (VM-AI15)

Even with his own hard-working ethic, Lew Hunter was in awe of the even longer days that Irwin Allen put in. He said of Allen, "He worked 18 hours a day. I can't imagine how he had time for anything else. I never got the impression that he had personal friends; only business friends. He wasn't married at that time, and he never did have children. His movies and television shows *were* his children. He was so consumed with what he did that it almost cut out everything else in his life. It was a seven-day-a-week gig. He just loved to work. And I did the same thing."

Despite liking Hunter, Allen wasn't willing to enter another situation in which an ABC man would have control – especially a network man with far less experience in the business than he did. Hunter recalled, "I was going over the notes on this particular script with Irwin one day, and I said, 'We have to have this scene in the middle of the script moved toward the beginning of it, rather than so far back.' Irwin said, 'I'm not going to do it.' I said, 'Now, Irwin, you don't understand, I am the authority here; I am representing ABC, who funds your series.' 'No,' he says, 'I'm not going to do it.' He said, 'Let me tell you, Lew, I was dealing once with Columbia Pictures, and I was preparing a movie called *The Big Circus*, and I sat in a chair in [Columbia Head] Harry Cohn's office, and Cohn taught me a very important lesson.'

"Now, to Irwin's thinking, part of that lesson was how Cohn had set the stage for the meeting. He told me that Harry Cohn's desk was on a riser about a foot or a foot-and-a-half tall, so that people who sat in a chair across from the desk would be on the lower level. Not only on a lower level, but there was a spotlight aimed at their chair! So Irwin was sitting there, and Harry Cohn lifted up the script and said, 'Allen, this is a piece of shit!' He threw the script at Irwin, then looked at him and said, 'You know how that asshole [Gilbert Roland's character] walks across fucking Niagara Falls on a tightrope on Page 6?' And Irwin said, 'Yes, Mr. Cohn.' And Harry Cohn said, 'Put him on Page 45 and you got a deal.' Well, I broke out and laughed, because I knew exactly what he meant. Because, on Page 6, you don't give a shit if this character falls into Niagara Falls. You don't know this guy. But on Page 45, the audience is terrified, because they've invested themselves in the character. That was the kind of thinking that Irwin had. He was outrageous and wonderful."

What Allen *did* want to put into a story early on was something that would grab his youthful audience. Hunter said, "Irwin did not want to do Hitchcock. He wanted to show the monster – 'Pow!' – right up front. Hitchcock liked to play with the audience, and then put the reveal of whoever it is that's the biggest threat as deep into the movie as possible. But Irwin wasn't that way. He was very frontal in his work. There was nothing subtle about him. He got a little calmed down with Stirling Silliphant, who wrote *The Poseidon Adventure* and *The Towering Inferno*, because he had a good way of communicating and, basically, dealing with Irwin. So Irwin got a little subtler in both of those. But when it came to the TV shows, Irwin would say, 'I'm not serving caviar, I'm serving popcorn!' And it was hard to challenge that when you consider the content of *Voyage*. It was all action and stayed clear of philosophical statements. He'd say, 'You want to send a message, call Western Union. Now get out of the office.'" (LW-AI15)

Regarding those who entered Allen's office domain, Joe D'Agosta said, "I realized he was a tough man. Everybody in his company, meaning his associate producers and his directors, were, in my observation, 'yes men.' You didn't have to salute when you entered Irwin's office, but, yes, you basically *had to salute*. There was a certain protocol, because, after all, he *was* the emperor. I'd never met a man like him. I'd heard that expression about other people in this business, Louis B. Mayer, especially, but Irwin was the only emperor I had dealings with." (JDA-AI15)

Lew Hunter said, "There was definitely an imperial air about him. And every time he'd go someplace, he'd have about six people moving around the lot with him. He'd have Arthur Weiss, who was the Story Editor on one of his shows, and he had Jerry Briskin, who was one of his associate producers, and Frank La Tourette, who used to be at UCLA as one of the professors there. But they were all afraid of him. And they all knew exactly the breaking point with him, and they would back off the minute that was coming up. They all had love/hate for him. The love was the fact that they all knew that they were working for a very different sort of human being, and if they wanted to stick around, they had to love him. Before I came along, in his producing period, he probably fired a number of people in a much more flamboyant way, so they all knew the risk in displeasing him. The best way to put it is they were 'yes men.' But they did it in such a way that he respected them. He would say to me, 'Well, my associate producer here is one of the best men for the job.' He would praise them when he wanted to give them strength with the network. But they all wanted their jobs, so they did what he wanted."

As we've seen, Allen had learned from one of the masters of intimidation – Harry Cohn. Hunter said, "Irwin's desk was on a riser, too. I don't think it was as high up as Harry Cohn's desk, but it was enough so it certainly made him seem bigger. He was probably about five-foot-eight. And I was six-foot at the time. So he would find ways of rising above you." (LW-AI15)

D'Agosta said, "I think he knew everybody's job. And he knew how to suck the last piece of energy out of you, and to get the best idea out of you. I think that was his talent, really. You knew Irwin Allen had a great mind. He was a determined, creative man. I might compare him to Orson Welles. He exuded that sense of command, and brilliance; you definitely got a sense of his creativity. And maybe he was always testing us as to what we would take and what we wouldn't take. The thing about men like that is they attract two kinds of people – strong people and weak people. The weak can be manipulated. And the strong people will make you look better. Anyone in between is just going to go away." (JDA-AI15)

Lew Hunter recalled, "The only time I ever heard Irwin use profanity was during a screening. Clay Daniels, an editor friend of mine, and I were watching a rough cut with Irwin, and Irwin was screaming about the different things he thought were wrong. Clay was sitting there, just as an assistant editor; he didn't have anything to do with the cutting of this particular episode, but he saw how Irwin kept yelling at the screen, 'You're fucking me; you're fucking me!', in terms of whoever the editor was that made the cut. Finally, the lights came up, and the producer of the show – Jerry Briskin was his name – said, 'Hey, I want you to meet our new editorial assistant, Clay Daniels.' Irwin looked at Clay and said, 'Clay Daniels, huh? When are *you* going to fuck me?!'"

When asked how the ABC executives felt about Allen, Hunter said, "We got a kick out of him. I loved him because of his flamboyance, and I think all the people around him were entertained by it. We of course would *never* give him that impression." (LW-AI15)

***

Above: Irwin Allen continues to pioneer science fiction on TV, with his second series, *Lost in Space*. Below: Allen on the sound stage, holding court with the cast of *LiS*, during filming of the pilot (January, 1965).

Irwin Allen felt compelled to entertain, to continually generate stories and ideas to flare the imaginations of his audience. Only a self-driven man could do what Allen did:

In the middle of producing Season One of *Voyage to the Bottom of the Sea*, Allen somehow found the time and energy to launch a *second* prime-time science-fiction series – the now-classic *Lost in Space*. In October, 1964, only weeks after *Voyage* had its premiere on ABC, a presentation was made to CBS executives. Allen was accompanied by his TV agent, Herman Rush, and Guy della-Cioppa, whose production company would partner with him on the

433

venture. Armed with a series proposal, numerous concept sketches, and survey reports showing *Voyage* beating the pants off CBS in the TV ratings, Allen convinced the network to put up money for script development and the filming of a pilot.

Production spanned 20 days (December 28-31, 1964, for 2nd Unit filming around Red Rock Canyon and the Trona Pinnacles in California, and January 6-27 at 20th Century-Fox studios). Allen was again both producer and director, working from a script written by himself and Shimon Wincelberg.

The *Voyage* pilot had cost over $500,000 one year earlier. *Lost in Space* surpassed that, amounting to $689,545 (production cost combined with building the spaceship).

Costing $350,000 to design and construct (interior, exterior, plus miniatures), the Gemini 12, as it was called in the *Lost in Space* pilot, cost more than all other aspects of the production combined.

Also beginning production at the end of 1964 was the first pilot film for *Star Trek*, at Desilu, Culver City. Its cost surpassed topped both of Allen's ventures, with expenses of nearly $700,000. Science fiction did not come cheap.

Despite the heavy price tag, Allen's epic production of the *Lost in Space* pilot dazzled the network executives, and CBS ordered the series for the Fall of 1965.

Of course, ABC was not happy that Allen was casting his net into another network's sea.

Herman Rush said, "There was a major battle with ABC when *Lost in Space* went to CBS. Now, that was a *big* battle. It had high points and low points. ABC wanted to have an exclusive on Irwin Allen. Irwin had all his other shows on ABC in the 1960s, and yet something called *Lost in Space* ended up on CBS. ABC wasn't happy about that." (HR-AI15)

ABC executive Lew Hunter said, "I

Lost in Space meets *Voyage to the Bottom of the Sea* – photo op with the Cyclops and David Hedison.

remember very clearly that we were pissing and moaning about, 'How can he sell this show to CBS when we have the relationship with him and Fox?' I don't think he even gave us a chance to buy it, which was probably a smart move on his part. But we were upset, no questions about that. Irwin had a relationship with Mike Dann over at CBS. Of course, Irwin had a relationship with everybody that he wanted a relationship with. It wasn't what ABC wanted, but we didn't allow it to cause a strain between us; we just shrugged our shoulders and went on trying to win whatever battles we could in persuading Irwin on what he was doing." (LH-AI15)

Partly to appease ABC, and partly because his personality compelled forward movement, Allen began putting together a proposal for a third series – *The Time Tunnel* – which he could offer to the alphabet network. And he did this even as he oversaw the filming of the remaining 16 Season One episodes of *Voyage*.

Irwin Allen was self-driven, a fountain of salable ideas unmatched by no TV producer before, or since.

8

Season One: ABC's Back Order of 16

Episode 17: "Doomsday"

(Prod. #7217; first aired January 18, 1965)
Written by William Read Woodfield
Directed by James Goldstone
Produced by Irwin Allen
Story Editor: William Welch; Associate Producer: Allan Balter
Assistant Story Editor: Al Gail
Co-Starring Donald Harron and Paul Carr

Here's the synopsis from the Irwin Allen Papers Collection:

The DEW LINE system flashes a warning of an impending missile attack. The U.S. activates its retaliatory nuclear missiles from bases all over the world and aboard the Seaview. It's a false alarm and the alert is cancelled. However, the missile aboard the Seaview shorts out and remains activated. The story revolves around the efforts of the Seaview personnel to prevent its firing. (A Fail Safe-type story.)

Sound Bites:

Corbett (staring at Fail Safe key in his hand): "This isn't an exercise, Admiral. It's real. I cannot destroy the world. I can't!" *Nelson:* "It's not you." *Corbett:* "It isn't?" *Nelson (putting his hand out for key):* "It's me."

Crane: "What happened to Corbett?" *Nelson*: "He couldn't activate his Failsafe; he just couldn't do it!" *Crane*: "Every soldier who ever went to war knows that moment. It's one thing to be a crack shot on the rifle range; it's another thing to pull the trigger when there's a man – a real man; a human being – in your sights." *Nelson*: "Corbett's not a coward. He just started to wrestle with his conscience at the wrong time. He should have done that *before* he'd taken his oath of duty." *Crane*: "Admiral, no one – none of us – knows how we'll act when we have to pull *that* trigger."

Corbett: "This is Doomsday, Admiral. Doomsday!" *Nelson:* "If it is, we didn't start it." *Corbett:* "What difference is it who started it? It's one thing to carry a big stick; it's another to bash someone's head with it. I just couldn't do it. But you could; couldn't you, Admiral?!" *Nelson:* "You think because I could do what I had to do, I don't feel; I don't feel for the millions?! Our job is to provide the bone and muscle of our country's deterrent power. Failing that, if we freeze in the clutch, then our country's defenseless. You failed your country once before; don't ever fail her again."

Patterson: "It's like when I was a kid – my mom always used to say, 'Don't go out when you're dirty. Always look right; you might get into an accident and what will the ambulance guy think if you're dirty?" *Clark (concerned about his appearance):* "Yeah, that's it." *Patterson:* "Yeah, well don't worry how you look, Clark. Nobody's gonna see us again. Not ever."

Assessment:

The story was a tense one, a sinister representation of its time. It was also a pretty adult topic for a "kids show," and ABC was nervous about putting it on the air.

Voyage historian and lifelong fan, the late Mike Bailey, said, "William Read Woodfield's powerful cautionary script for 'Doomsday' poses a horrible dilemma for both Nelson and Crane. They are duty-bound to carry out their orders in spite of the fact that to do so is madness. The writer is clearly on the side of missile officer, Lt. Cmdr. Corbett, who pleads the case for humanity, arguing that there is a line past which individuals are not bound by orders. And at the conclusion of the drama, the viewer sides with Corbett in spite of the fact that his military career is ruined, and Nelson is obviously the show's daddy/hero. Fairly bold stuff to air in 1964 during the cold war and a brewing Vietnam. Donald Harron did a remarkable job of facing off against Richard Basehart, a task that many actors were not up to. He was. 'Doomsday' is arguably *Voyage*'s finest attempt to deal with social and moral issues and crackles with tension." (vttbots.com)

The series had touched on social and military issues before, highlighting the pros and cons of putting trust in the rapidly advancing fields of science and medicine. Irwin Allen was not into sending messages, but his writers sometimes succeeded in sneaking hot-topic questions or statements into their scripts. Some of these episodes were:

- "The Village of Guilt" (with man playing God, experimenting to increase the size of marine life to feed a hungry world);
- "The Mist of Silence" and "The Magnus Beam" (the dangers of unstable, third-world nations' acquisition of advanced weapons);
- "The City Beneath the Sea" (the inner-space race);
- "Hail to the Chief" (overzealous medical experimentation);
- "Hot Line" (the dangers of nuclear-weapons testing);
- "The Sky Is Falling" (man's instinctive violence against what he does not understand); and
- "The Ghost of Moby Dick" (with its subtle pro-animal statement).

But "Doomsday" does more than touch on an issue – it is full hands-on. And quite frightening.

Script:
William Read Woodfield's writers contract: November 11, 1964.
Woodfield's treatment and 1st and 2nd draft teleplays: Dates unknown.
Mimeo Department's reformatted Shooting Final teleplay (blue pages): November 10.
Page revisions by William Welch or Al Gail (pink paper): November 11.
Page revisions by writing staff (yellow paper): November 12.
Page revisions (dark green paper): November 13.

This was the first script written for *Voyage* by William Read Woodfield, and the second of his episodes to air. Woodfield was 36 and making a good living as a photographer, who occasionally moonlighted as a TV writer. He had written two scripts for *Sea Hunt*, and two more for *Everglades*, a syndicated series about a lawman patrolling the wilderness area in his airboat. He had also written *The Hypnotic Eye*, a 1960 low-budget film about a serial killer. Then Woodfield's friend, Allan Balter, associate producer on *Voyage*, made him an offer.

Woodfield told interviewer Mark Phillips, "When Balter explained he was doing a TV series called *Voyage*, I asked him, 'How is it?' He said, 'Terrible.

They've got no scripts. Why don't you write one?' He told me when it was on. I started to watch it and couldn't. I found it absolutely unwatchable. I thought it was a terrible show. I asked Balter, 'You'll pay me $3,500 to write one of *these*?' And he said, 'Yeah. We need a script by next Monday.' I said, 'I'll give it to you in two days,' and I handed him 'Doomsday.' Irwin Allen paid me the money and put me under contract."

Woodfield was not expecting to stay in television. He said, "I didn't consider TV writing as a real career. I was doing too well as a photographer. I didn't know anything about the sea and, for *Voyage*, I had to learn what a starboard port was. I never did get it right."

Regarding this particular script, his first, Woodfield said, "I wanted to do *Dr. Strangelove*. Since Seaview was a nuclear submarine, I thought someone ought to show what Fail Safe was and the problem of turning the key. It made for an interesting episode, because showing people what they haven't seen is more interesting than showing what they have."

As for the character of Lt. Corbett, Woodfield explained, "He was a necessity. You had to have somebody aboard Seaview who didn't want to set off the nuclear weapons. Otherwise, you had no conflict. Irwin Allen never quite understood that. It was a principle I taught him. He thought conflict was, 'Admiral, don't run into the [underwater] mountain! There's a mountain ahead!' 'No, there isn't. Full speed ahead!' Irwin had lots of those scenes in *Voyage*."

Balancing these criticisms of Allen, Woodfield added, "He appreciated a good script more than a bad one. He was not a stupid man. He knew the difference between a good script and a bad script. If you had an argument of some substance to it, he found that better than whether there's a mountain ahead." (WRW-SL92)

ABC's Tom Kersey chatted with William Welch on the phone, then wrote to Irwin Allen on November 10th to make his comments official:

> Again, as in the episodes "Hail to the Chief" and "Hot Line," it is very important that your story date of 1973 be exposed both audio and video – at the earliest moment in the episode and as frequently as possible. And again, every futuristic device (hot line telephone) that you can employ to tell the audience that this is not happening now, will favorably enhance its acceptability [for broadcast]. Too, the President must not resemble any past, present, or recent aspirant President.

ABC was also insistent that *Voyage*'s future setting should be plainly stated in the episode. Reference was made to the Orson Welles *War of the Worlds* radio broadcast and the panic it caused on Halloween's eve in 1938. That program had aired on CBS, and the network caught a great deal of flack over it. ABC's executives were adamant about making sure that a dramatic TV episode couldn't be taken for something really happening. (As if the commercial breaks wouldn't be a helpful suggestion of business as usual.)

The year for this story was worked into the Teaser, as Nelson announces that the ship's complement will be conducting the "1973 initiation ceremonies." The actor who played the president in "Hot Line," Ford Rainey, returned to the role for this story. Evidently the suits were satisfied that Rainey didn't look *too* presidential.

Betraying a common mistrust of the intelligence of the American consumer, Kersey continued to fret that a very gullible and ill-informed American TV audience might confuse *Voyage to the Bottom of the Sea* with a news broadcast.

> On the subject of the President – I strongly recommend that you discontinue his use – especially in subject matter of this nature – topical and controversial. And in this particular instance I trust you have researched the "fail-safe" procedures and that the President is involved to this extent. If he is not involved to this extent – it is a SAC or some other GROUP decision, I think we should stay on this level rather than Presidential.
>
> Page 36, Sc 162 – CORBETT's lines at bottom of page: "Then maybe we'll put these monstrous toys away before they destroy us" – DELETE.
>
> Page 20, Sc 95 – Please substitute for the word "geez".
>
> Page 1, Sc 6 – "Popular Mechanics" must be fictionalized title.

Of these concerns:

ABC did not want to risk offending anyone in the U.S. military, or any "hawks" who might have believed that nuclear bombs were a good deterrent to war, by calling them "monstrous toys."

"Geez" could easily be taken as a contraction for "Jesus!", and such sacrilege could not be tolerated.

Popular Mechanics, of course, has been a real magazine for the last century or more. And since real businesses are very defensive about their reputations, fictional substitutes are common in fiction. (Remember that all of Wile E. Coyote's mail-order gizmos came from "Acme"?)

When you consider all of these diversions and sidesteps, the real surprise is that "Doomsday" got made and aired.

Production:
(Filmed November 13-20, 1964; 6 days)
(Budget: $115,479)

James Goldstone returned to direct his second of four episodes. He'd previously helmed "The Price of Doom."

Don Harron was 30 when cast to play Lt. Cmdr. William Corbett, the reluctant crew member with his finger on the launch button. Goldstone recommended him, having recently directed Harron in the two-part *Outer Limits* episode, "The Inheritors." Irwin Allen was impressed by Harron's work here, and brought him back to play Robin Hood in an episode of *The Time Tunnel*. Harron would became widely recognized for his comedy, playing the character of Charlie Farquharson in 83 episodes of *Hee-Haw* from 1969 to 1982.

Don Harron in an episode of *The Fugitive*.
(QM Productions, 1965)

Paul Carr was 30 when given "co-starring" billing with Harron in the opening titles, acknowledging his excellent work as Clark in three previous episodes of *Voyage* ("Hot Line," "Long Live the King" and "Hail to the Chief"). He'd be brought back for three more, starting with "Cradle of the Deep," the second season's "Terror on Dinosaur Island," and for the third season's "No Escape from Death." Carr would also be cast in two episodes of *The Time Tunnel* and one *Land of the Giants*. As mentioned earlier, *Star Trek* fans know him from 1965's "Where No Man Has Gone Before," also directed by Goldstone.

Ford Rainey played the U.S. President a second time on *Voyage*, after "Hot Line." Later, Rainey switched networks and played the President for Irwin Allen in the first episode of *Lost in Space*. He was 56.

Production began Friday, November 13, 1964, and continued through the following Friday, November 20. All six days were spent on Stage B (including the final day when they filmed the President in "The War Room").

While making this episode, the excellent "Submarine Sunk Here" aired on ABC. According to A.C. Nielsen, *Voyage* again won its time period. Cast and crew wouldn't make it home in time to watch the entire episode; Goldstone didn't get his last shot on this day until 7:23 in the evening.

The grim episode opened on a surprisingly humorous note. James Goldstone told interviewer Mark Phillips, "That whole idea of hitting the crisis moment while wearing those silly costumes was a very good stroke, and it worked. There's a marvelous actor in the show, Paul Carr, and Paul was just wonderful, sitting there, slowly taking this makeup off his face and talking in a very real way about his family. The contrast was absolutely marvelous. … Usually, on *Voyage*, there was a crisis within seconds and, by God, you played the crisis with heavy breathing right to the end. This scene was a change of pace and it worked very well dramatically." (JG-SLP94)

The calm before the storm (above), and the storm hits (below), with painted-faced Henry Kulky giving comfort to a blinded Del Monroe.

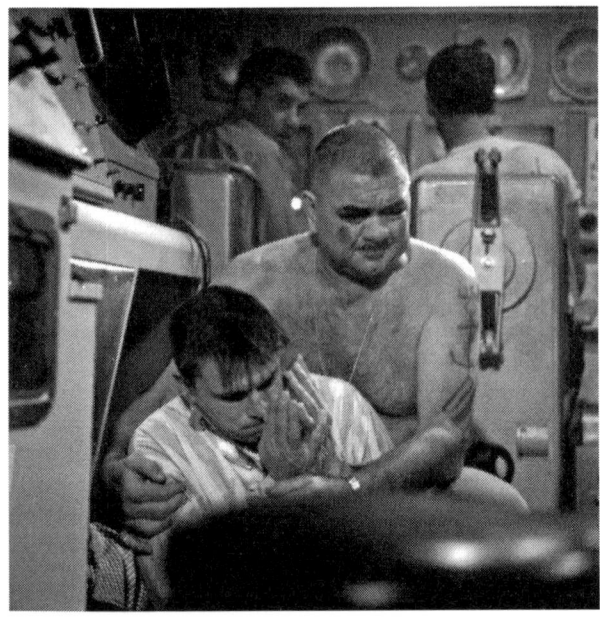

Don Harron, who played the young Navy officer, told Mark Phillips, "To have your finger on the doomsday button is like playing a classical tragedy. It is the reaction human beings have to the possibility that everyone and everything they know may cease to exist. That was interesting to play. But I really tried not to think about the preposterous plot and instead enjoyed the camaraderie with my fellow actors. We got along great and had lots of laughs as we pretended to stumble and fall as the shock waves and depth charges went off. Jimmy Goldstone was a terrific director. His spirit was very enthusiastic and infectious. Richard Basehart was more anxious to talk Shakespeare than *Voyage*. I had always enjoyed his film work. He was a fine actor with a great noble face. He was much too genuine for the shallow politics of Hollywood." (DH-VTTBOTS)

James Goldstone said, "Of the five episodes I directed, 'Doomsday' was the most interesting, thematically. Donald [Harron], Richard Basehart, and I had these long discussions about the possible effects of nuclear war. We were all into the subject, and I even had friends who had moved from the U.S. to live in New Zealand. It was a subject that dominated our lives at the time. With Don's character, you had to have him strong while being weak, weak while being strong, and right while being wrong. Just as important was the stuff with Richard, who has to toe the party line. That is, if the chips are down and you don't do what your country's policy is, then you negate the diplomacy that has taken so long for supposedly sane and sober men to develop. … I found myself thinking, 'Where is that fine line between playing personal abject fear and playing the thematic of 'I cannot do this because I will be the person responsible for mankind's destruction'? … Donald was a consummate, classically-trained Shakespearean actor, and, given the limitations of the time on screen and the production, he did a marvelous job in creating sympathy for the character."

James Goldstone giving direction, as Richard "Doc" Bull listens in.

Goldstone recalled that Irwin Allen kept coming down to the set "because I wasn't going 'by the book.'" The director continued, "At a certain point, I said to [associate producer] Allan Balter, 'Look I can't direct actors with Irwin Allen standing behind me. If Irwin walks on the set, I walk off!' I've never done that before or since, and I have worked with people I didn't get along with. Once or twice, Irwin did walk on the set, and the production stopped. I walked out the other door. Pretty soon, he didn't come down anymore, because he knew filming would stop."

Vitina Marcus, who worked often for Irwin Allen, gave insight into the producer. "He was always lurking around the set. You'd turn around and, bam, there he was, right behind you, watching. He would have liked to direct every episode if he'd had the time. It was a control thing, but it was also how he had fun. He wanted to come out and play. I don't think a lot of people understood that part. He was like a kid who wanted to be in the game too. He had all that power, but the bigger kids still didn't want to play with him." (VM-AI15)

Goldstone added, "Allan Balter was really the producer as far as I was concerned. That is, he dealt with me because I wouldn't deal with Irwin. Allan [Balter] was a sweet, lovely man, and, apparently, Irwin said to him, 'How can Jim do this show if he dislikes me so much?', to which I said to Allan, 'Because I have a contractual commitment, and that commitment doesn't include being in the presence of Irwin Allen.' I mainly dealt with Allan and Billy Woodfield, who was a very good writer. We had as much fun as we could while trying to please this strange egomaniac [Irwin Allen] in his lavish suite down the hall." (JG-SLP94)

Release / Reaction:
(ABC premiere broadcast: 1/18/65; network repeat airing: 6/28/65)

The night "Doomsday" first aired, the songs getting the most airplay in America were "Downtown," by Petula Clark, and "You've Lost That Loving Feeling," by the Righteous Brothers. The top-selling record album was *Beatles '65. My Fair Lady* was leading the way at the movie houses, for the entire month of January. And nuclear weapons were on everyone's minds. Only three days before "Doomsday" first aired, the Soviet Union carried out its first nuclear explosion in its "Program 7" project. The result was a crater that would become "Lake Chagan" in the Kazakh SSR." The body of water is colloquially referred to as the "Atomic Lake" because it remains radioactive. And on the very day "Doomsday" aired, the Soviets accused the United States and West Germany of conspiring to build "an 800-mile curtain belt of atomic land mines" across the borders between West Germany and that of East Germany and Czechoslovakia. It was an absurd notion – perhaps the type of thing that might only happen in an Irwin Allen production.

As the crew and cast committed this tale to film, many were aware of the significance of the storyline. Was it possible for a scenario like "Doomsday" to come true, due to a hardware glitch?

Goldstone said, "Episodic plot television certainly didn't deal with that kind of serious subject. I don't mean to imply that we were pretentious in thinking we were doing something important, but the fact was we weren't *avoiding* the subject." (JG-SLP94)

William Read Woodfield said, "'Doomsday' was a fine show. Richard Basehart and David Hedison both wanted to meet me after they read the script. They said, 'This is the best script we've ever had. Please stay and write more.'" (WRW-SL92)

Syndicated "TV Key," in the January 18, 1965 edition of the *Tucson Daily Citizen*, said:

> Call this one "Reverse Fail Safe." This time an enemy accident involving communications satellites places us on war alert. But, when the mistake is discovered and the alert is called off, one of the Seaview's nuclear computers has passed its point of no return. Can it be recalled or detonated harmlessly in time to prevent disaster? This has the quality and excitement of a Saturday a.m. movie serial. Donald Harron guests as an officer with a conscience.

On the same day, rival "TV Scout," in the *Philadelphia Daily News*, saw it this way:

> The adventure on *Voyage to the Bottom of the Sea* is tense and nerve-shattering as the Seaview goes on war alert when the U.S. mistakes 25 communications satellites for nuclear missiles. The tale is called "Doomsday" and is enough to give viewers the creeps. Richard Basehart and David Hedison, the dour leaders of the Seaview, play their roles with considerably dry-eyed seriousness.

Voyage had new competition on NBC. *The Man from U.N.C.L.E.* had made the move from Tuesday nights to Mondays, now starting at 8 p.m. The lead-in, from 7:30 to 8 was *Karen*, the sole survivor from *90 Bristol Court*. CBS was sticking with its long-established winning combination of *To Tell the Truth* (7:30-8 p.m.) and *I've Got a Secret* (8-8:30).

Nielsen ratings report from Jan. 18, 1965:	Rating:	Share:
7:30 – 8 p.m.:		
ABC: *Voyage to the Bottom of the Sea*	**22.9**	**32.9%**
CBS: *To Tell the Truth*	19.0	27.3%
NBC: *Karen*	15.3	22.0%
8 – 8:30 p.m.		
ABC: *Voyage to the Bottom of the Sea*	**23.2**	**32.5%**
CBS: *I've Got a Secret*	21.1	29.6%
NBC: *The Man from U.N.C.L.E.*	15.6	21.8%

The day after "Doomsday" first aired, Dick Kleiner wrote for his syndicated newspaper column, "Hollywood Today!":

> Richard Basehart and David Hedison, of *Voyage to the Bottom of the Sea*, always wear naval uniforms. And they get a bit bored with the costume monotony of it all. So they've devised tricks to give themselves a bit of variety. You'll note that one week they will wear no tie, the next week a tie with the collar opened, then the tie and the collar buttoned. That way they kid themselves into feeling they're wearing something different.

Twentieth Century-Fox Television was promoting the series by standard Hollywood means: issuing press releases that could pass as "light news." On January 23, a few days after "Doomsday" aired, *The Bakersfield Californian* ran one of these studio-supplied pieces:

> The new fan mail champion of 20th Century-Fox Studios is none other than the "Seaview," the futuristic atomic submarine that stars with Richard Basehart and David Hedison in 20th Century-Fox Television's *Voyage to the Bottom of the Sea*, seen Monday nights over ABC-TV. The fabulous glass-nosed submarine of tomorrow is receiving fan mail at a record pace, which the competent girls of the 20th Century-Fox fan mail department have been able to efficiently handle until the other day when they received an interesting request from a six-year-old boy in Chicago which posed a bit of a problem. The youngster wanted "an autographed picture of the Seaview."

Apparently those "competent girls" couldn't keep up with *all* the letters. Another wire story – code word for studio P.R. piece – which had been showing up in various newspapers, "reported":

> Bob Dowdell, who stars with Richard Basehart, David Hedison and Henry Kulky in 20th Century-Fox Television's *Voyage to the Bottom of the Sea* for ABC-TV, has had to hire a secretary to take care of the flood of fan mail since the first airing of the Voyage series. Bob also still is receiving fan mail from his starring role in the *Stoney Burke* series, now defunct but in reruns throughout the country.

Dowdell was actually a co-star. Jack Lord was Stoney Burke.

Episode 18: "Mutiny"

(Prod. #7219; first aired Monday, January 11, 1965)
Written by William Read Woodfield
Directed by James Goldstone (uncredited) and Sobey Martin
Produced by Irwin Allen
Story Editor: William Welch; Associate Producer: Joseph Gantman
Assistant Story Editor: Al Gail
Guest Star Harold J. Stone

From the *Voyage* show files (Irwin Allen Papers Collection):

The Seaview, searching for a nuclear sub that has disappeared, stops to pick up Nelson, who miraculously escaped death when the sub went down. He says he saw it destroyed by a giant coelenterate as he and Fowler [who later perished] were outside in scuba gear to examine an underwater mountain for magnetite. Nelson's manner becomes strangely erratic and when Crane countermands a dangerous order the Admiral charges him with mutiny.

Sound Bites:

Jiggs: "Tell me more about this creature, Harriman." *Nelson:* "It's not just one creature, Jiggs; it's millions of creatures all combined into one central organism." *Crane:* "Like the Portuguese Man o' War." *Nelson:* "Exactly, Lee. Sit down; sit down. ... *(to Jiggs)* ... Like a Portuguese Man o' War, but much bigger;

more than a thousand feet across." *Jiggs:* "A thousand feet across?!" *Nelson:* "I would speculate that the radioactive energy of the force field has stimulated this organism's ability to combine. It could go to two, three, four times its present size in time." *Jiggs:* "Oh, come on. You've been adrift too long, Harriman. Is it possible you're exaggerating?" *Crane:* "Admiral Nelson doesn't exaggerate. You see, it's like the Seaview, Admiral. Not all of us – the crew, you and I – inside we're like individuals, but outside we're like one big creature." *Nelson:* "Exactly, Lee. But there's one big difference between Seaview and the cnidarian – other than size." *Jiggs:* "What's that?" *Nelson:* "It has only a central nervous system; it can only respond. But we have a brain – many brains combined. We can do more than respond; we can think. We can function together as a team. And that's our strength."

Nelson (to Crane, in front of the crew): "I . . . I treated you like a brother. You drew a gun on me. Get out of here. Get out of my sight! Mr. Morton, you're in command of the Seaview. Set course for home. ... Jiggs, however temporarily, this was a Navy ship. Captain Crane mutinied. I demand a general court martial." *Admiral Jiggs Starke*: "But Lee was right. He saved this ship and all hands." *Nelson (tortured)*: "Mutiny ... mutiny ... he drew a gun on me. He drew a gun on me!" *Starke*: "Harriman, I think we should go to your cabin." *Nelson (ignoring the suggestion, still obsessing over the incident)*: "You ... you were right, Jiggs. You were right. The Seaview is a loose ship, a mutinous ship. ... *(shouting at the crew)* ... Mutineers – ALL of you!"

Assessment:

Mike Bailey, founder of the vttbots.com website, said, "This is an episode loaded with impressive miniature effects, and is an explosive showcase for the talented Richard Basehart. David Hedison, guest Harold J. Stone and the entire cast turn in intense performances in what is one of the series' top entries. Writer William Read Woodfield delivers the goods. ... The episode's 'bear,' a giant jellyfish, is simply out-and-out fabulous miniature photography and holds up as well as anything produced today, be it CGI or whatever. When it gets to emotional crunch time, Basehart's performance is amazing. Even the often-flat direction of Sobey Martin steps up several notches for this episode, although much of the final effect in that department may have been punched in by the editor." (vttbots.com)

The reason for this improvement in "the often flat" direction of Sobey Martin? It's because James Goldstone, filling in for Martin on a couple of the days, directed many of the scenes.

The only problem with the miniature photography of the giant Man-o'-War-type anomaly, which caught Mike Bailey's eye (and will no doubt hold your gaze) is that the smaller (2-foot), less detailed Seaview model was used for the shots that featured both. The creature indeed looks fantastic, but the sub suffers in comparison.

As noted by Bailey, Richard Basehart's performance is captivating. As the Admiral pops the pills responsible for his personality change, Basehart continually dials up the level of manic energy, at first seeming like someone jittery from too much coffee, then resembling an unstable speed freak. After his final bursts of emotion, Basehart's character simply sits staring at the floor, like a burnt-out junkie. (Are we reading anti-drug message into Basehart's performance? Perhaps.)

And here you thought the monster of the story was only a colony of jellyfish!

Script:
William Read Woodfield's writers contract: November 11, 1964.
Woodfield's story treatment and 1st and 2nd draft teleplays: Dates unknown.
Mimeo Department's reformatted Shooting Final teleplay: Date unknown.
Revised Shooting Final teleplay (by William Welch or Al Gail):
Date unknown.
2nd Rev. Shooting Final, by writing staff (on yellow paper): November 20, 1964.
Page revisions (blue paper): November 24.
Page revisions (pink paper): November 27.

"Mutiny" was William Read Woodfield's second script for *Voyage*, albeit the first broadcast. Regarding the inspiration for this second assignment, Woodfield said, "I read some books and found out about a Coelentera, which is essentially what a jellyfish is. It's not a single animal, but a colony of animals that becomes enormous in size and functions like a beehive. It stings and eats other things. I also read a book called *The Abyss*, about all these things at the bottom of the sea, where the sea pressures are tremendous and nobody knows what's down there. Irwin said, 'You mean this thing is hundreds of thousands of animals?' and I said, 'Yeah, sort of like cells, except these are more complacent.' And he was fascinated." (WRW-SL92)

Tom Kersey, of ABC, wrote to Irwin Allen on November 18:

> Please determine that all names (Jiggs Starke, Willie Snyder, etc.) of ComSubPac are fictious; that the court martial procedures and Navy Articles quoted are correct.
>
> Page 46, Sc 144 – and throughout script, substitute for the use of "crazy", "nuts", "crazy-mad as a hatter".

Telecasting in the public interest – it is not in the interest of those who work so hard with the Mental Health Associations to confuse these uses with "mental illness".

Or perhaps the ABC censors just didn't want to offend any viewers who were residents in an insane asylum? More seriously, we might question Kersey's directions about obeying Navy rules. Remember, Irwin Allen had specifically written in the Series Bible, "Seaview is not a regular Navy ship. It is privately owned by the Nelson Institute of Marine Research."

Production:
(Filmed November 23 through December 1, 1964; 6 days)
(Budget: $116,160)

Sobey Martin took directing credit, although the episode also involved the participation of James Goldstone, returning after directing "The Price of Doom" and "Doomsday."

Harold J. Stone was 51 when he played Admiral Jiggs Starke. He was an eminent "guest star," and was paid $1,750. Stone had just been nominated for an Emmy for his guest appearance in the series *The Nurses*. One year earlier, he had been nominated for a Golden Globe Award as Best Supporting Actor for the film *The Chapman Report*. Prior to that, he had been a regular in 40 episodes of the 1959-60 series, *Grand Jury*.

Richard Bull received $600 for up to three days as the Seaview's unnamed "Doctor" – his third appearance in the role.

Filming began on Monday, November 23, for the first of three days on the Control Room set on Stage B.

Goldstone told interviewer Mark Phillips, "I loved the main set. The control room was marvelous. The art director, Bill Creber, was brilliant. They had no budget, but somehow he came up with these wonderful things. *Voyage* also had a famous cameraman, Winton Hoch. He was a genius at black-and-white photography." (JG-SLP94)

Thursday, November 26 was Thanksgiving. Cast and crew had the day off.

Day 4. Work resumed on Friday, on Stage 14 for the scenes in which Admiral Nelson is on the open sea. Yes, these were filmed on a soundstage, in a large tank of water – for better control of light and sound … and the star's safety and comfort.

Day 1: Admiral Nelson has a breakdown in the Control Room, finely handled by Richard Basehart. Day 2 (bottom page): 4, in the Missile Room.

At midday, the company moved to Stage B for "Int. Captain Crane's Cabin" and "Int. Missile Room."

Goldstone said, "The tempo was marvelous and the sense of tension made 'em go. Part of their success was due to Dick Basehart, a wonderful actor. He and David Hedison had a very good

451

working relationship, but Richard really hated doing *Voyage*. He was embarrassed by it, but he was making a lot of money. He considered himself a serious stage actor, and he was, but he was making a hundred times the money he would have made had he been doing *The Hasty Heart* on Broadway, where I first saw him."
(JG-SLP94)

Day 5: Monday. The Admiral was still on the makeshift raft, but this time on the home base of Stage B, in front of a process screen. These were for all the sequences in which Nelson is sitting up, therefore not actually in any water. There was none to be in.

Also filmed, against the process screen, the Observation Nose, then reverse angles of the same set, without the use of the process screen. At the end of the day, they moved back into the Missile Room for pickup shots.

Day 6: Holding on schedule, Director Sobey Martin worked on Fox Stage 2 for "Int. Starke's Office" and the "Int. Hawaii Naval Hospital Room" sets. The company then returned to Stage B for pickup shots in the Observation Nose of the Seaview. Martin took his last shot at 6:55 p.m.

Release / Reaction:
(ABC premiere broadcast: 1/11/65; network repeat airing: 6/21/65)

"Mutiny" was the nineteenth episode to film; the eighteenth to air, during the second week of January, 1965. At this time, *Beatles '65* was outselling all other music albums in the department stores across America. The single from the album, "I Feel Fine," was No. 2 on radio stations, just under "Come See About Me," by the Supremes. You could buy either for 59 cents.

The nightly news reflected more of the Cold War tension that infused many first-season episodes of *Voyage to the Bottom of the Sea*. Air Force Major Wang Shi-chuen, serving Free China, a U.S. ally, was captured when his America built U-2 spy plane was shot down during an attempt to photograph the Paotow uranium enrichment plant in the People's Republic of China. He would remain a prisoner for nearly 18 years, before being released in Hong Kong in November 1982.

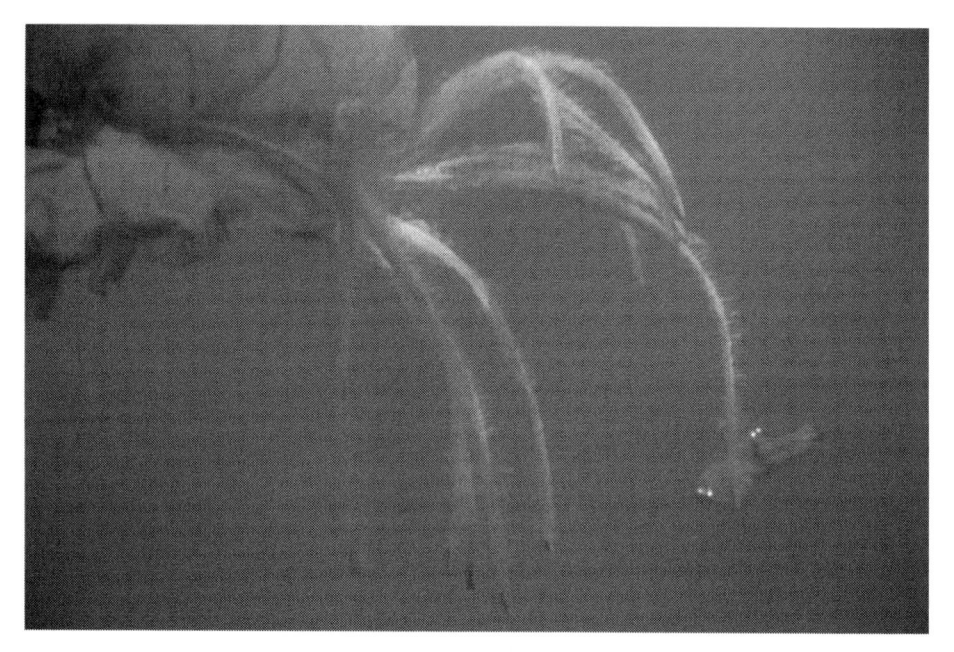

The night "Mutiny" first hit the air, syndicated "TV Scout," carried on January 11, 1965 in Appleton, Wisconsin's *Post-Crescent*, said:

> Admiral Nelson (Richard Basehart) on *Voyage to the Bottom of the Sea* goes scuba diving in an uncharted area of the ocean that is as "deep as the Mariana Trench, with mountains higher than Mount Everest." But while he is swimming about, his experimental submarine is scooped up by a luminescent Coelenterata – a jellyfish 10 times as big as the whale that swallowed Jonah!

Also on January 11, syndicated "TV Key," in the *Arizona Republic*, from Phoenix, weighed in:

> We've heard of TV being populated by jellyfish, but this is ridiculous. The show opens with millions of them, plus one monster, submarine-swallowing jellyfish. The Seaview's search for the monster puts Crane into direct conflict with a half-crazed Nelson, who charges him with mutiny. Not much substance here, but the melodramatic effects are well handled.

On January 12, one day after the episode aired, Associated Press TV-radio writer Cynthia Lowry wrote for the *Idaho State Journal*:

> Now that NBC has moved *The Man from U.N.C.L.E.* into the shank of Monday evening television, relaxation-seekers must make some painful decisions. The difficult question Monday night was whether to watch intrepid Napoleon

Solo suavely confound the evil, clever THRUSH agents or to chill at the sight of a giant jelly fish smothering the nuclear submarine in ABC's *Voyage to the Bottom of the Sea*.

There was a third and less bizarre choice – CBS' *I've Got a Secret*, a pleasant little game, but Monday night even that was clamoring for attention with a double panel of guessers. ...

Was Cynthia Lowry right? Would *U.N.C.L.E.* out-pull *Voyage*?

Nielsen ratings report from Jan. 11, 1965:	Rating:	Share:
7:30 – 8 p.m.:		
ABC: *Voyage to the Bottom of the Sea*	**23.1**	**33.7%**
CBS: *To Tell the Truth*	17.3	25.3%
NBC: *Karen*	14.7	21.5%
8 – 8:30 p.m.		
ABC: *Voyage to the Bottom of the Sea*	**23.5**	**32.9%**
CBS: *I've Got a Secret*	19.1	26.8%
NBC: *The Man from U.N.C.L.E.*	15.3	21.4%

On this night, the Seaview reigned. In the mid-1960s, with many fewer avenues for media hype than today, it often took audiences weeks to find their favorite TV shows, if they had been moved to a different day or time. *U.N.C.L.E.*'s lackluster performance had more to do with the new time, new day, and weak lead-in series, as the ratings for future seasons and the fan mail to its stars would prove. And, in an age when most TV sets did not come with remote controls, having a strong lead-in show on a network was essential to attracting and maintaining a large audience.

At the end of the *Voyage*'s second season, while being interviewed by Tom McIntyre, Weekend Editor for *The Gastonia Gazette*, in North Carolina, Richard Basehart identified "Mutiny" as one of his two favorite episodes from *Voyage*, so far. He said, "Anytime I can do something other than say, 'Up scope,' I'm happy with my role of Nelson." (RB-GG66)

This episode was spoofed in the 1965 *Mad* magazine parody, "Voyage to See What's on the Bottom."

Episode 19: "The Last Battle"

(Prod. #7220; first aired Monday, January 4, 1965)
Written by Robert Hamner
Directed by Felix Feist
Produced by Irwin Allen
Story Editor: William Welch; Associate Producer: Allan Balter
Assistant Story Editor: Al Gail
Co-starring John van Dreelen, Joe De Santis, Rudy Solari

From the *Voyage* show files (the Irwin Allen Papers Collection):

Admiral Nelson, kidnapped from a plane, finds himself on a Pacific Island where a concentration camp has been set up by Schroder, a former ranking Nazi with wild plans to create a Fourth Reich. Here Nelson finds four other kidnapped men, each famous in a different field, whom the Nazis plan to use as the nucleus for their new super-world. They pool their talents to build a short-wave radio to summon the Seaview to their rescue. Schroeder has anticipated this move, planning to capture the Sub and use its missiles to start a war between America and Russia.

Sound Bites:

Colonel Schroder (surveying prison camp): "We are people of habit, aren't we? Give us a few pieces of good timber, a few yards of barbed wire, and what do we do? We do what we know how to do best."

Schroder: "I've been hunted like an animal. I've been in the sewers of the world like a criminal. And through it all, I survived." *Nelson:* "Yes, you people always seem to survive." *Schroder:* "You won the war and you think you are heroes. You call yourselves free, just men, while you label us war criminals." *Nelson:* 'The whole world labeled you war criminals." *Schroder:* "All that is ancient history now. All our concerns are here and now!"

Nelson (to the other captive scientists): "Divide and conquer, divide and conquer some more. How do the Schroders of the world get so good at it?"

Nelson (referring to the Nazis): "It's the idea that has to be destroyed, not just the men."

Assessment:

Voyage archivist Mike Bailey said, "Actually, there are a number of things to like about this show. It at least attempts to introduce some moral concepts into the conflict. The Stalag set is fabulous; the first images of Schroder viewing his Nazis war clips of Hitler are chilling. The guest cast looks authentic and turns in thoroughly believable performances." (vttbots.com)

Consider this the anti-*Voyage* episode; one of the most atypical of the series. With so little time spent on the nuclear sub, so little Captain Crane and other members of the crew, and no science fiction anywhere in sight, it may not make many "Most Popular Episodes" lists. Still, "The Last Battle" is a perfect embodiment of the Series Bible, which stated "In the vast majority of stories, the sub is merely a conveyance to get our principals to the scene of the action." But enjoy the change of pace while you can.

Script:
Robert Hamner's 1st draft teleplay approved on November 12, 1964.
Hamner's 2nd draft teleplay: Date unknown.
Mimeo Department's reformatted Shooting Final teleplay: November 27.
Rev. Shooting Final teleplay, by William Welch or Al Gail (blue pages): December 1.
Page revisions by writing staff (pink paper): December 1.
Page revisions (yellow paper): December 4.

"The Last Detail" was conceived to utilize the prison camp from the recently completed *Von Ryan's Express* ... with very minor alterations, as evident in these two images. Above: Frank Sinatra is told the rules of the camp from a German Captain, played by Sergio Fantoni. (20th Century-Fox, 1965)
Below: John van Dreelen warns Richard Basehart there will be no escape from his camp, either.

"The Last Battle" was the third of six script assignments on *Voyage* for writer Robert Hamner. After finishing "No Way Out" and "The Ghost of Moby Dick," Irwin Allen had a special job for the writer. Hamner recalled, "Irwin called me up: 'Bob, I gotta show you something!' So, we drove up to this little hill on the 20th Century-Fox lot and Irwin pointed to this concentration camp sitting there. Sinatra had just finished *Von Ryan's Express*, and a good deal of that film took place in this prisoner of war camp. Irwin said, 'They paid half a million dollars for this set, Bob. Why don't you write a story around it?' I said, 'Irwin, there's no room for a submarine on this set. It's a war camp!' He said, 'Think it over.'" (RH-SL92)

Hamner came up with a story in which Nelson is kidnapped by renegade Nazis and taken to this camp.

Wardrobe head Paul Zastupnevich said, "The thing was, Irwin used a lot of stock footage. That was one of his trademarks throughout. I mean, *Story of Mankind* actually was a picture that was built on outtakes and stock footage, and *The Time Tunnel* was based a lot on stock footage. And I had to match up costumes and tie in things so that they would carry on through. Wherever he could beg, borrow or steal, he always did. That was one way of his cutting down the budget. … But they were always breathing down his neck. In fact, we were shooting one episode and we got into the set of *Von Ryan's Express* and we stole a background out of it, and there was the devil to pay at the studio. He had cleared using that particular thing, but Frank Sinatra was quite upset at the time that we had been working on that set." (PZ-KB95)

Hamner said, "I wrote the script, we filmed the show, and it's about to go on the air, when Irwin calls, 'Come quick! Come quick! Big problem! Big problem!' I rush over to his office and Irwin's waving a telegram. 'Bob, we're in trouble!'

"It's Frank Sinatra's lawyer putting Irwin on legal notice. The prisoner of war camp is an integral part of *Von Ryan's Express* and Irwin's infringing on the value of their set by airing his episode *before* the film's release. They're going to sue Irwin unless he pulls the show off that night. So, Irwin says, 'Bob, what are we going to do?' Since *Voyage* was a partnership with Fox and the movie was a Fox movie, I said, 'Irwin, stop! Look, you didn't sneak in here in the middle of the night with a camera under your coat. You did it in conjunction with 20th Century-Fox. Go over and see [studio head] Dick Zanuck.' Irwin said, 'You're right!'

"He went over to Zanuck's office. Zanuck read the telegram, laughed and made one call to Sinatra. It was straightened out." (RH-SL92)

Dorothy Brown, ABC's watchdog in the Continuity Acceptance Department, wanted some things lined out too. She wrote to Irwin Allen on December 1:

> Page 1, Sc 1 & 2: There can be no commercial identification on the airliner, interior or exterior, with the exception of footage in-flight, which must be held to the absolute minimum and can be accepted only upon viewing the film. In the cabin interior, there can be no insignia display such as on stewardess' uniform, doily-like napkins on head-rests or arm rests, pieces or baggage, etc.

Page 14, Sc 29: Line "You're as <u>crazy</u> as your Fuhrer was!" Please substitute.

Page 15, Sc 30: ALEJANDRO TOMAS – Since it does not seem to be a story point, please substitute for this Mexican-Latin-American name.

Page 29, Sc 58: TOMAS' hands torn and bloody. Please block this from the viewers' sight, using reaction instead.

Page 30, Sc 62: NELSON cannot send an SOS or MAYDAY signal.

By this point in this book, you may be savvy to the thinking process at ABC. Let's see how you did.

Page 1: No airline identifications were allowed because ABC sold commercial time to various air passenger services. American Airlines ("The choice of the experienced traveler!"), Continental Airlines ("For the man on the way up!"), Eastern ("We make it easier to fly!"), Pan Am ("Don't leave the country without us!"), PSA ("Pure, Sober, Available!"), TWA ("Best bill of fare in the air!"), United ("Fly the friendly skies of United), and Western Airlines ("The only way to fly") were just some of the top companies buying air time on ABC in 1965. There was no way to plug them all, or risk upsetting any, so none would be acknowledged.

Page 14: The network was once again worried about offending any "crazy" people in the viewing audience. More charitably, perhaps they didn't want to demean the efforts of mental-health professionals.

Page 15: Your guess is as good as ours; nearly any name has *some* cultural relationship.

Page 29: No blood allowed on ABC during the Family Hour.

Page 30: If actual Morse Code appeared in the episode ("SOS"), the signal might be picked up and mistaken for a real emergency.

As for the Nazis, however, anything went. World War II was only 20 years in the past, and its horrors had yet to heal. Nazis have been go-to bad guys on TV ever since ... and rightfully so.

It was decided during the making of this episode to promote Nelson – to a full four-star Admiral.

Production:
(Filmed December 2-9, 1964; 6 days)
(Budget: $118,585)

Felix Feist was hired to direct. He was 54, and this was his first of five episodes. Feist had directed 48 feature films before moving to television. One was the 1952 ecologically themed *The Big Trees*, starring Kirk Douglas. Another was the 1953 sci-fi/horror "classic," *Donovan's Brain*. Feist had worked well with small budgets, which made him ideal for the needs of television. He produced, as well as directed many of the episodes for the 1957-59 Western series, *The Californian*. Twentieth Century-Fox brought Feist to its lot to direct numerous episodes of its series, *Adventures in Paradise* (1960-61) and *Follow the Sun* (1961-62), before sending him to work for Irwin Allen. Feist also directed the final episode of *The Outer Limits* – "The Probe" – which aired just days after this episode of *Voyage*. The next stop for Feist, after five more assignments on *Voyage*, was to produce *Peyton Place* in 1965 for 20th Century-Fox.

Above: Seen here in one of six episodes of *12 O'Clock High* in which he played a German officer, John van Dreelen seemed to make a career of playing Nazis. (20th Century-Fox, 1965)
Below: Joe De Santis slaps Sal Mineo's puss in *Dino*. (Allied Artists, 1957)

John van Dreelen made a good Nazi. He was 42 when cast to play Col. Alfred Schroder, and, ironically, had fled Europe to get away from the Nazis, after escaping from a German concentration camp in Holland. Perhaps this experience allowed a deeper level of authenticity. Van Dreelen even appeared as a German officer in *Von Ryan's Express*, the movie that paid for the building of the concentration camp used in this episode. *Voyage* would bring him back to play another Nazi commander, in "Death from the Past."

Joe De Santis was 55 when tapped to play Miklos, and had played over 150 different roles in films and TV. He began in radio and starred in his own series in the 1940s, *Under Arrest*.

Rudy Solari was 30 when cast as Alejandro Tomas, the athlete. He'd already been a regular on the Western *Redigo* and was about to enlist for the WWII comedy/drama *The Wackiest Ship in the Army* – with a third series coming – the WWII/spy series, *Garrison's Gorillas* (1967-68). *Star Trek* fans know him from the 1968 episode, "The Paradise Syndrome."

Ben Wright, 49, played

Above: Rudy Solari in an episode of *Star Trek*. (Paramount Pictures, 1968)
Center: Ben Wright as a Nazi in *The Sound of Music*. (1965, 20th Century-Fox)
Bottom: Dayton Lummis in *Alfred Hitchock Presents*. (Revue Studios, 1956)

Benjamin Brewster, "the world's top authority on electronics." You know you know him. With over 200 screen appearances, Wright appeared on every series imaginable in the 1950s, '60s and '70s, including three trips into *The Twilight Zone*; four turns on *The Outer Limits*; eleven on *Gunsmoke*; and two each on *The Man from U.N.C.L.E.*, *The Wild, Wild West*, and *The Six Million Dollar Man* – and that's only a handful of his appearances! Irwin Allen would bring Wright back for "Night of the Long Knives," a 1966 episode of *The Time Tunnel*.

Dayton Lummis, 61, played Dr. Gustav Reinhardt, the "world's most famous psychologist." Lummis was another of those actors who popped up in nearly everything during the 1960s, and was also featured in the same episode of *The Time Tunnel* as Ben Wright.

461

Rounding out the inmates was Eric Feldary, as Deiner, the nuclear scientist. He was yet another of the reliable guest actors in television who could adapt himself to nearly any series. He was at the end of his run, however, with only an episode of *Mission: Impossible* and *The Man from U.N.C.L.E.* to go before his accidental death at 55 from a gas explosion in his Hollywood home.

With no need to build new sets, this episode could sail by with a miserly budget of $118,585.

Filming began on Wednesday, December 2, 1964 on Stage B for the scenes in the Observation Nose of the Seaview, as well as Control Room and Radio Hut. There wasn't a lot to cover, and Director Feist wrapped at 5:30 p.m.

Day 2: Thursday, December 3. A second day was spent on Stage B, although not on the Seaview. Some of those sets were collapsed to make room for "Int. Schroder's Quarters," part of the concentration camp. They wrapped at 6:15 p.m.

Day 3: Friday, December 4. The company took over the set from *Von Ryan's Express* – the German POW camp that was supposed to be in Italy, filming until 7:30 p.m.

Day 4: Monday. More concentration camp exteriors were filmed in the morning, then the company moved to Stage 3 for sets of the interior barracks. After dark, the company filmed scenes outside the fence of the camp. The last shot was taken at 7:15 p.m. *Voyage* episode "The Blizzard Makers" began airing 15 minutes later on ABC-TV.

Day 5: Tuesday. More filming was needed in the exterior of the compound, then onto Stage 3 for the "Int. Concentration Camp Prison Hut," as well as the "Int. Airliner Cabin."

Day 6: Wednesday, December 9. More filming in the "Int. Concentration Camp Prison Hut" on Stage 3, then pickup shots in the "Ext. Compound," and, finally, pickup shots on Stage B. Felix Feist covered twelve and three-quarters pages from the script in addition to the two company moves, wrapping at 6:40 p.m.

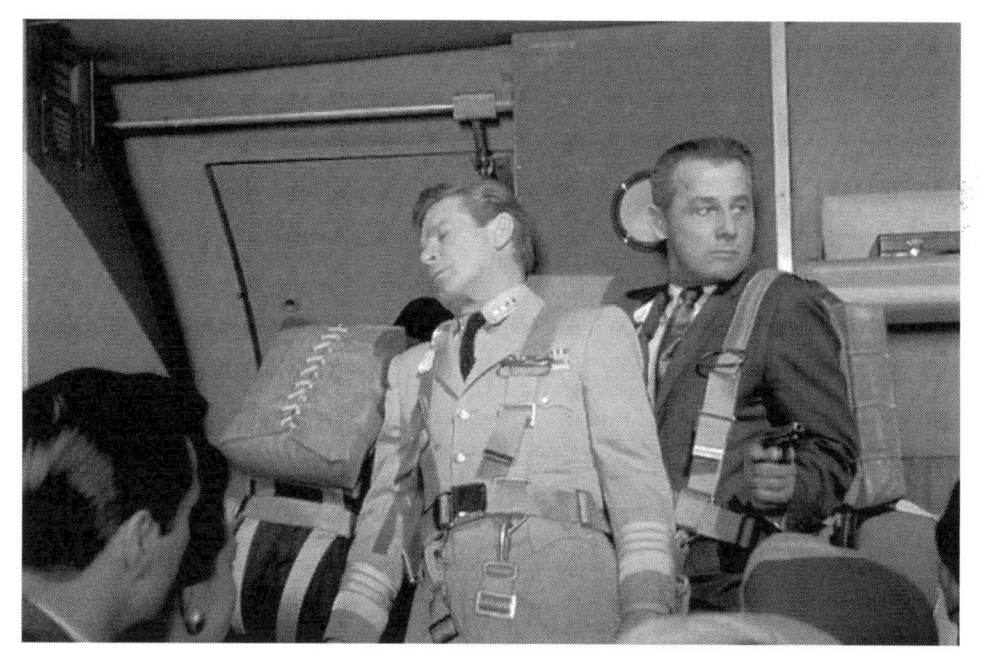

Release / Reaction:
(Only ABC broadcast: 1/4/65)

"The Last Battle" was both the seventeenth episode to film and air. During the week it had its only ABC broadcast, "I Feel Fine," by the Beatles, was the

463

most-played song on American radio stations. Its parent album, *Beatles '65*, headed the *Billboard* album chart. *My Fair Lady*, starring Audrey Hepburn and Rex Harrison, was packing them in at the movie houses.

On January 4, 1965, "TV Scout," in Pennsylvania's *The Pittsburgh Press*, said:

> *Voyage to the Bottom of the Sea* sinks to a new low in its effort to dig up an adventure tale. In "The Last Battle," viewers are led to believe that a group of die-hard Nazis, on orders from their long-dead Fuehrer, are busy taking over the world. With headquarters in South America, they have been fleecing the U.S. and Russia of its great minds – scientists, military geniuses, financial wizards, theoreticians – to build a Fourth Reich on the ashes of the Third. Story opens with their capture of Admiral Nelson (Richard Basehart), who is subjected to the horrors of a concentration camp reminiscent of World War II.

Also on January 4, rival "TV Key," showing up in the *Tucson Daily Courier*, in Arizona, said:

> Since a comparable theme has already been used on *Man from U.N.C.L.E.*, it figures that this comparable series would also be using it. This is about a cult of fanatics attempting a grandiose rebirth of Nazism and the establishment of the Fourth Reich. Only two steps are required to complete the master plan – kidnap Nelson and then capture the Seaview.

Nielsen ratings report from Jan. 4, 1965:	Rating:	Share:
7:30 – 8 p.m.:		
ABC: *Voyage to the Bottom of the Sea*	**23.5**	**35.5%**
CBS: *To Tell the Truth*	18.0	27.2%
NBC: *90 Bristol Court: Karen*	16.6	20.5%
8 – 8:30 p.m.		
ABC: *Voyage to the Bottom of the Sea*	**25.6**	**38.0%**
CBS: *I've Got a Secret*	18.3	27.2%
NBC: *90 Bristol Court: Harris Against the World*	13.0	19.3%

From the Mailbag:

On January 7, 1965, days after "The Last Battle" aired on ABC, Steven H. Scheuer, of "TV Key," printed a pair of dueling letters from viewers.

> Our entire family finds *Voyage to the Bottom of the Sea* a delightful program and we sincerely hope it won't be taken off the air. Richard Basehart is very fine in the role of Admiral Nelson and the stories are always interesting. – Mrs. E.L. Hammond, Ind.

And:

> I can't understand why Richard Basehart is wasting his time and talent on such an empty role in *Voyage to the Bottom of the Sea*. I realize actors have to work and any job is better than no job, but I hate to see an actor of his talent in such a bomb. – V.T., Memphis.

Scheuer responded:

> I'm inclined to agree that Richard Basehart is really too fine a talent to be stuck with the seemingly unchallenging role of "Admiral Nelson" on the *Voyage* series, but most fans must be satisfied because the show is doing very well in the ratings. It has been renewed for the rest of the season and chances are good it will be around for a second.

On January 10th, a syndicated newspaper blurb, with the title "*Voyage Series Is British Hit*," generated by the 20th Century-Fox promotional department, was picked up by *The Fresno Bee The Republican*, from Fresno, California. It reported:

> *Voyage to the Bottom of the Sea*, 20th Century-Fox Television's high adventure series, seen Monday nights over ABC-TV, has become one of England's top shows. The British ratings system, similar to this country's Nielsen and Arbitron ratings, lists Irwin Allen's *Voyage to the Bottom of the Sea*, starring Richard Basehart, David Hedison, Bob Dowdell and Henry Kulky, near the top of their "most popular" parade.

And, as we will later learn, four of *Voyage to the Bottom of the Sea*'s British fans were also that country's biggest current export – the Beatles.

Episode 20: "The Invaders"

(Prod. #7221; first aired on Monday, January 25, 1965)
Written by William Read Woodfield
Directed by Sobey Martin
Produced by Irwin Allen
Story Editor: William Welch; Associate Producer: Joseph Gantman
Assistant Story Editor: Al Gail
Guest Star Robert Duvall

From the *Voyage* show files (Irwin Allen Papers Collection):

Tremors in the ocean reveal a city previously hidden under centuries of mud. Lying in the debris are many metal cylinders. One, brought aboard the Seaview, contains a being from an earlier evolutionary cycle whose powers far surpass those of the present. This survivor, Zar, tells Nelson his job is to judge whether humans of today can live together with his people who are now in suspended animation in the capsules. He discovers that -- biologically -- they cannot co-exist, so he plans to destroy the [human population of the] world. In his blood is a deadly virus that could wipe out all living things.

Sound Bites:

Zar: "What is it?" *Crane:* "It's a bunk." *Zar:* "Bunk? What is it for?" *Crane:* "For sleeping." *Zar:* "Sleeping?" *Crane*: "You do sleep, don't you?" *Zar (understanding):* "Ah, sleeping. What the animals do. I understand. Do *you* sleep?" *Crane*: "Well, of course I do. ... *(beat)* ... Your people never sleep?" *Zar*: "Never." *Crane*: "Well, when they get tired, how do they rest?" *Zar*: "Ah, yes, I see. You – your civilization – has not yet discovered that animals sleep because, when the sun goes down, it is difficult for them to see. Not because the animal needs to sleep." *Crane*: "We sleep because we get tired." *Zar*: "No. You sleep out of habit because the animals you evolved from slept. Aren't there creatures who don't need to sleep?" *Crane*: "Some fish – dolphins, sharks; they don't sleep." *Zar*: "You see. One saves much time by not sleeping."

Nelson: "Nothing's working properly. Sonar, radar, everything electrical has malfunctioned." *Crane:* "I'm having a hard time holding course. We can only dead-reckon." *Nelson:* "Our friend must be responsible. How or why I don't know, but I intend to find out." *Crane:* "Why don't we take that weapon away from him and slam him in the brig?" *Nelson:* "No, let's play along with him. I want to see just what he's up to." *Crane (to himself):* "Well, I hope he doesn't kill us all while we play along."

Assessment:

Captain Crane feels uneasy after conversing with Zar about man's need to sleep ... coupled with Zar's inquisitiveness about the operation of the Seaview. It is hard to trust a humanoid who never gets tired yet seems relaxed and nonaggressive. The 1967 *Star Trek* story "Space Seed" similarly starts with the discovery of members of a lost race in suspended animation. And Mr. Spock's line about Ricardo Montalban's Khan applies equally well to Zar in this episode: "Superior ability breeds superior ambition."

The episode hooks you from the outset. The Seaview discovers the remains of an underwater city ... and hundreds, perhaps thousands, of mysterious canisters. They bring one aboard and discover, through a small window in the otherwise seamless metal canister, that it contains a humanoid creature that appears to be asleep. What a shock when its eyes open!

After the opening credits we watch as the Seaview crew tries to rescue the man within the canister, failing time and again to open it. Drilling doesn't work, nor do blowtorches. Meanwhile, the man on the inside seems to be suffocating – perhaps he was parboiled by the blowtorch! Nelson finally figures out a way to cut through the strange material and free the individual from within – and it's a creature they have never encountered before.

As he had done in "The Chameleon," a recent episode of *The Outer Limits*, Robert Duvall gives us an alien that is truly un-human – in voice, in expression, in movement. And writer William Read Woodfield gives Duvall intriguing ideas and dialogue to work with. The backstory concerning his civilization, as well as his medical exam; the watery blood that kills one member of the Seaview crew and threatens mankind; and the only means of destroying him without contaminating the ship, a death by fire, all make for an interesting hour. Zar's poisonous blood and near indestructability seem to foreshadow the title character in the Alien franchise, as well.

Some fans have stated that Zar should have been given a deeper characterization instead of being "another arrogant villain." We must disagree. For Zar's single-mindedness reflects his mission. His race would prove lethal to humans; therefore, his race and humankind cannot live in harmony. For his people to live, mankind must go.

Script:
William Read Woodfield's story treatment and 1st and 2nd draft teleplays:
Date unknown.
Mimeo Department's reformatted Shooting Final teleplay: December 8, 1964.
Page revisions by William Welch or Al Gail (blue paper): December 9.
Page revisions by writing staff (pink paper): December 14.
Page revisions (yellow paper): December 15.
Added scene (gold paper): January 4, 1965.

This was William Read Woodfield's third script for *Voyage to the Bottom of the Sea*, following "Doomsday" and "Mutiny." They were all written in rapid succession, with eleven more to come. This amount of work is an indication of how appreciated the writer was by Irwin Allen, his co-producers, his story editors, the cast, and ABC. So far, Woodfield's scripts had all been above standard. And to the relief of the overworked William Welch, they had required very little rewriting. Note in the script timeline above that "The Invaders" didn't even require a rewrite by Welch or Al Gail, only page revisions for small changes which addressed production needs and notes from the network. Speaking of the latter:

Mary Garbutt, of ABC Continuity Acceptance Department, wrote to Irwin Allen on December 8, warning him to be sure that "Standard caution on the fight sequence – caution that the gasping for air, the choke hold is not to the point of grotesque facial contortion, etc.," and to "Please keep hypo injection shot off camera or covered." She also cautioned: "Note that Zar's laser gun causes electrical charge and not burning effect."

This was one of the easy ones. Or perhaps Ms. Garbutt was one of the less strenuous censors.

Production:
(Filmed December 12-18, 1964, plus January 5, 1965; 8 days)
(Budget: $114,941)

Sobey Martin returned to the director's chair, where he spent some of the time snoozing, according to some reports. Marta Kristen, who would soon be taking direction from Martin on *Lost in Space*, told this author, "Sobey was a very good friend of Irwin's. Sobey would be sitting in his director's chair and he'd start falling asleep. And the camera person would come up and say, 'Alright, Sobey, we're ready to do the scene.' And his head would snap up, and, in that Eastern European accent, 'Oh, shoooot it; shoooot it!' He was not talented. Everybody else did their job, and did them well, and Sobey would just say, 'Okay, stand der, and der; okay, shoooot it.' He stayed on schedule. And he was under Irwin's thumb. And he just did what Irwin wanted him to do." (MK-AI15)

Robert Duvall as Boo Radley in *To Kill a Mockingbird*. (Universal Pictures, 1962)

Robert Duvall was 33 when cast as Zar. He was paid $2,500 – the top pay for guest stars at this time – for up to six days. He earned every nickel. Duvall needs no introduction now, nor did he in 1965. He'd already been a guest star on a vast variety of popular series, including *The Outer Limits*, *The Fugitive*, *Route 66*, *The Twilight Zone*, *Alfred Hitchcock Presents*, and *Naked City*. And he had played Boo Radley in the 1962 film *To Kill a Mockingbird*. In the future – as of this writing – Duvall would receive seven nominations for an Academy Award. Four were as Best Supporting Actor: *The Godfather* (1972), *Apocalypse Now* (1979), *A Civil Action* (1998), and *The Judge* (2014). Three were for Best Lead Actor, which included *The Great Santini* (1979) and *The Apostle* (1997). He won the Oscar for *Tender Mercies* (1983). But Duvall would be paying his dues for a few more years before the big film roles started to come his way, including another job for Irwin Allen, in "Chase through Time," an episode of *The Time Tunnel*.

"The Invaders" was a "bottle show," taking place entirely on the Seaview. Having only one guest actor saved additional money. The budget was therefore kept down to only $114,941. That equates to over $900,000 in 2018.

Production began on Thursday, December 12, 1964. The entire episode was filmed on Stage B. New to the series, Captain Crane's iconic onyx and gold ring replaced what had appeared to be a large Naval Academy ring. Hedison told interviewer William Anchors, "I didn't like the prop ring. I made the onyx ring. It was mine and was far more comfortable. I'd been wearing my onyx ring for almost 20 years at that point and didn't feel the need to replace it with an ill-fitting prop." (DH-S50)

Above: Director Sobey Martin confers with Richard Basehart. Below: A messy job on the Missile Room set.

William Read Woodfield said, "Duvall played a guy who had been in storage. That was *The Man Who Fell to Earth*, *Stranger in a Strange Land*, Rip Van Winkle. I don't recall if I liked it or not. I only remember that Duvall kept pronouncing 'aluminum' wrong. He would call it 'amminiummmm,'" and we kept breaking up. 'What is this insane person doing?'" (WRW-SL02)

On the third day of filming, Monday, December 14, Martin wrapped at 6:30 p.m., allowing most of the cast and crew members to make it home in time for the 7:30 start of "The Ghost of Moby Dick" on ABC, where *Voyage* easily won its time period.

With all the special effects needed (freezing units, blowtorches, and specialty make-up), Director Martin fell behind, taking a full extra day to finish, turning this into a seven-day production even though it never left the controllable environment of Stage B. "The Indestructible Man," the next episode to film, had to be pushed back a day, now set to begin on Monday. Martin's longest day was Thursday, the originally planned final day of shooting, when he shot from 7:36 a.m. to 7:40 p.m., and stopped with a full day's work still ahead. Even when he had finished, work on "The Invaders" had not. On January 5, director Laslo Benedek had to stop filming his episode, "The Buccaneer," to oversee an eighth day of filming for "The Invaders," with an added scene that had just been written by the writing/producing staff. The reason for the new scene: The episode had timed out short.

Release / Reaction:
(ABC premiere broadcast: 1/25/65; network repeat airing: 6/14/65)

On January 25, 1965, the espionage thriller *36 Hours*, starring James Garner, Eva Marie Saint and Rod Taylor was No. 1 at the movie houses. You may have been reading *You Only Live Twice*, by Ian Fleming, or *The Spy Who Came in from the Cold*, by John le Carré, or *Julian*, by Gore Vidal. They were all on *The New York Times* Best Seller List for this week. Or maybe you were sitting by the "hi-fi," playing *Beatles '65*. Drop the needle on Side 1, Band 1, and you'd hear John Lennon singing "No Reply." Switch on the radio and you'd likely hear Petula Clark singing "Downtown." It was at the top of the hit parade. Or you could watch "The Invaders" on *Voyage to the Bottom of the Sea*.

One day before "The Invaders" first aired, a 20th Century-Fox promotional "filler piece" carried in California's *The Fresno Bee The Republican*, said:

David Hedison, who stars with Richard Basehart in 20th Century-Fox Television's *Voyage to the Bottom of the Sea* action-adventure series, seen Monday nights over ABC-TV, is a Hollywood bachelor who lives like one. The six-foot, one inch, 180 pounder, with jet black hair and hazel eyes, lives in a hideaway canyon home which once belonged to the late Jean Harlow. He has gained recognition in Hollywood as both a thespian and bon vivant, and in the latter role can be seen frequently at filmland's top parties, [with] Hollywood's loveliest starlets. As David explains it when he usually arrives sleepy eyed on the *Voyage to the Bottom of the Sea* set each morning, "Who has time for sleep?"

At this point in the new series' life, the strategy at Fox was to get the title ingrained into the public's consciousness any way possible ... and to increase female interest in one of its stars.

As for the episode itself, syndicated "TV Key," showing up on January 25, 1965 in New York's *Syracuse Post-Standard*, said:

> For the kids and those of you who miss *Outer Limits*, this underwater series comes up with a fairly interesting science fiction yarn and one the kids will probably enjoy. Robert Duvall, who has played many a TV "creature," guest stars as a remnant of a past civilization being revived after his entombment in a capsule at the bottom of the sea.

On the same day, "TV Scout," in newspapers across the nation, said:

> A low budget monster movie, television style. ... In one of their most fantasy-action scripts to date, *Voyage to the Bottom of the Sea*'s nautical heroes, Richard Basehart and David Hedison, discover a creature with reptile like skin in a time capsule after a violent undersea earthquake. He is without a nervous system, heart or blood, but has an "I.Q. of a genius." He is also from another age, and is eager to find out the progress of mankind. Robert Duvall plays the "living time capsule," with seething conviction in this outing that borders on the preposterous.

Nielsen ratings report from Jan. 25, 1965: 7:30 – 8 p.m.:	Rating:	Share:
ABC: *Voyage to the Bottom of the Sea*	**21.5**	**31.2%**
CBS: *To Tell the Truth*	17.6	25.5%
NBC: *Karen*	17.6	25.5%
8 – 8:30 p.m.		
ABC: *Voyage to the Bottom of the Sea*	**21.9**	**31.1%**
CBS: *I've Got a Secret*	19.7	27.9%
NBC: *The Man from U.N.C.L.E.*	18.2	25.8%

The week after "The Invaders" aired, David Hedison told entertainment columnist Dick Kleiner, "*Voyage to the Bottom of the Sea* is a difficult series to play. That's because there is nothing to relate it to in a person's own experience. By contrast, *Peyton Place* should be a snap. Just think of any old love affair you've had and you're in business."

Episode 21: "The Indestructible Man"

(Prod. #7222; first aired Monday, February 1, 1965)
Written by Richard Landau
Directed by Felix Feist
Produced by Irwin Allen
Story Editor: William Welch; Associate Producer: Allan Balter
Assistant Story Editor: Al Gail
Co-Starring Michael Constantine

From the *Voyage* show files (Irwin Allen Papers Collection):

A space capsule containing a robot is sent into outer space where it mysteriously disappears. Sometime later it re-enters the Earth's atmosphere, is recovered and taken aboard the Seaview. But something strange seems to have happened to the robot. It appears to have been programmed to destroy the submarine. A desperate battle of wits is fought out between Nelson and the mechanical man with the fate of the Seaview and its crew depending on the outcome.

Sound Bites:

Dr. Brand: "[The robot] has a brilliant mind. An electronic brain dedicated to killing all of us." *Nelson:* "That's a strange statement coming from you." *Brand:* "No. Listen carefully: I had to program it with emotional reactions closely duplicating a man's behavior. But something happened out there in space; something went wrong. Now its whole intelligence is dedicated to just one thing – our destruction."

Crane: "Have they dogged down all hatches between it and the missile room?" *Kowalski:* "Yes, sir. But that won't help. That thing goes through steel hatches like they were cardboard."

Assessment:

Voyage aficionado Mike Bailey said, "I found the clunkiness of the robot to be the very thing that made this episode scary as all get out. Although slow, the thing seems unstoppable, and on a submarine there are only so many places to hide. I was fifteen when I first viewed this, so maybe I should just profess embarrassment at my own youthful naivety, but I gotta say, I still find the episode spooky. Bernard Herrmann's music (lifted from *Day the Earth Stood Still* and *Journey to the Center of the Earth*) really puts the icing on the cake." (vttbots.com)

Irwin Allen would use Bernard Herrmann's music in several episodes of *Lost in Space* the following year, and if those scenes, partly due to the score, don't make your skin crawl, what could? Without the ominous music, "The Indestructible Man" might have induced snickers. Let's face it, that robot is quite silly-looking. But, as Mike Bailey observed, the inclusion of Herrmann's horror music makes this one of *Voyage to the Bottom of the Sea*'s most fear-provoking episodes.

And who can possibly sit still while watching the big climax, in which the robot clamps a magnetic mine to itself and activates its 60-second detonation "fuse"? This is a kamikaze robot, intent on taking the Seaview out, even at the price of its own destruction. Nelson enters, with less than a minute to find a way to get the mechanical walking bomb off the ship. *Tick ... tick ... tick ...*

Script:
Richard Landau's writers contract: November 6, 1964.
Landau's story treatment and 1st and 2nd draft teleplays: Date unknown.
Mimeo Department's reformatted Shooting Final teleplay (pale green paper): December 15.
Page revisions by William Welch or Al Gail (blue paper): December 16.
Page revisions by writing staff (pink paper): December 18.

Page revisions (yellow paper): December 30.

Richard Landau had written "City Beneath the Sea" earlier in the season, which was based on a "springboard" by Irwin Allen and William Welch. For his second assignment, Landau went with an idea of his own: "I pitched a story to Bill Welch. I knocked out a rough draft, which they instantly approved. That was 'The Indestructible Man.'"

The series was desperately in need of scripts. In fact, more in a hurry than when Landau had written that first script. He told Mark Phillips, "The funny thing was Irwin. He was a charming and talented guy, but he was so nervous about getting the script that he called me at my office two days after I had been given the assignment. I wasn't there. When I got back, the phone was ringing and it was Irwin. 'You weren't in your office! Where were you?!' I said, 'I was out.' 'You shouldn't be out! You should be sitting at your typewriter doing the script!' I said, 'Irwin, go screw yourself. You need a psychiatrist. This is ridiculous! I'm not allowed to even go out of my office?!' I never heard from him or saw him again. It was the end of a beautiful friendship. I just did my two scripts and went on my way." (RL-SL92)

Irwin Allen explained his nervous disposition: "I get jumpy when my backlog of scripts starts getting skimpy. I say to myself, 'Better get a move on.' So I start developing more plot themes for something to be shot six months or even a year away." (IA-HT69)

Contracts between the Producers Guild and the Writers Guild allowed for a freelance writer to take up to two weeks to deliver a first-draft teleplay for a 60-minute series. Series are nearly always behind on scripts. This was especially true in the 1960s, when 30 or more episodes were needed for each season. *Voyage*, still on its shakedown cruise, was farther behind than many shows.

It was not unusual for a producer to try to get a script sooner than the allotted two weeks. But Landau, like many, felt Allen's pressure was more trouble than the job was worth. He said, "Bill Welch was a very nice, laid-back kind of guy, and Joe Gantman was another nice, quiet guy. Irwin only hired people he could manipulate. He beat people down. That was part of his attitude." (RL-SL92)

In its turn, ABC was trying to keep Allen on the straight-and-narrow. It was nothing personal.

Mary Gerbutt, with the ABC censors, wrote to Allen, "There will be the usual care and caution exercised in these scenes of the robot attack and subsequent shots of the bodies," and "There will be no shots of the robot moving to camera and completely filling the screen."

God forbid, the network did not want the kids at home to think the scary robot was coming for them through the TV screen … and bringing that nightmare inducing Bernard Herrmann music with him!

Production:
(Filmed December 21 through 30, 1965; 7 days)
(Budget: $114,449)

Felix Feist returned to direct. This was his third *Voyage*, following "No Way Out" and "The Last Battle." He'd return three more times.

Michael Constantine was 37 when paid $1,750 for up to seven days work and given co-starring billing in the front titles for playing Dr. Ralph Brand. He already had more than 50 appearances on TV and in films during a career that would bring hundreds more (including co-starring in three series, most notably *Room 222*), as well as appearances on stage, both on and off Broadway.

Bernard Herrmann was the real star of this episode, having written scores that could make watching an ant walk across the floor seem frightening. Since the score was taken from the 20th Century-Fox library and not composed for the episode, he didn't get credit for the effective music. The sources were, as noted earlier, *The Day the Earth Stood Still* (1951) and *Journey to the Center of the Earth* (1959). Herrmann had gotten his start in films with Orson Welles, providing effectively moody scores for 1941's *Citizen Kane*, 1942's *The Magnificent Ambersons*, and 1944's *Jane Eyre*. Alfred Hitchcock loved Herrmann's dark scores as well. They were ideal for the Master's *The Trouble with Harry*, the 1956 version of *The Man Who Knew Too Much*, *The Wrong Man*, *Vertigo*, *North by Northwest*, *Psycho*, and *Marnie*. Other movies that benefited greatly from Herrmann's scores were 1958's *The 7th Voyage of Sinbad*, 1961's *Mysterious Island,* the original 1962 version of *Cape Fear*, 1963's *Jason and the Argonauts*, and 1976's *Taxi Driver*. Herrmann also scored seven episodes of *The Twilight Zone* and 17 episodes of *The Alfred Hitchcock Hour*. Herrmann won an Oscar for his score to 1941's *All That Money Can Buy*, and was nominated for *Citizen Kane, Taxi Driver* and 1976's *Obsession*.

Thanks to being a "bottle show," the episode only needed a budget of $114,449.

Filming began on Monday, December 21, 1964 for the first of eight days on Stage B. They shot until 7:25 p.m. Five minutes later, long before anyone could leave the Fox lot, *Voyage* episode "Long Live the King" had its only broadcast on ABC-TV. If the cast and crew hadn't caught this one in a Fox screening room, they were out of luck … until syndicated reruns began in the fall of 1968.

Three more days of production followed (Tuesday, Wednesday and Thursday) before the company was given a three-day weekend to celebrate Christmas.

Work resumed on Monday, December 28. They filmed until 7:03 p.m. Less than half an hour later, "Hail to the Chief" aired on ABC.

Tuesday was supposed to be the final day of production, but at the beginning of that morning's shooting, it was apparent that more time would be needed. "The Buccaneer" was told to stand by for a Thursday start. Come that morning, Felix Feist needed another hour of production time to finish.

ABC screened the rough cut on January 8, 1965. The Final Air Print was approved on January 20. The episode was on the air a little more than a week later. *Voyage to the Bottom of the Sea* was that far behind in its production schedule.

Release / Reaction:
(ABC premiere broadcast: 2/1/65; network repeat airing: 7/5/65)

On the day "The Indestructible Man" first aired, Martin Luther King, Jr. and 700 peaceful demonstrators were arrested in Selma, Alabama. Peter Jennings reported the story, on his first day as the new anchorman for *ABC Evening News*. Inger Stevens, of *The Farmer's Daughter*, had the cover of *TV Guide* for the January 30 issue. Also, in *TV Guide*, *Voyage* had a picture article, showing the three different Seaview models used for the series (4-foot, 8-foot, and 17.2-foot), as well as technician Wesley Lee preparing one for a plunge. There was also a photo of David Hedison, in a red wetsuit, in the 20th Century-Fox Moat, hefting the four-foot model. The unidentified *TV Guide* writer said, in part:

> Riddle: What is sometimes 4 feet long, sometimes 8 feet, sometimes 18 feet; can be found in two indoor tanks, an outdoor moat and a lake; and looks like a 400-foot submarine cruising the seas? Answer: The Seaview, the futuristic sub that is the one indispensable element of ABC's brine opera, *Voyage to the Bottom of the Sea*. On the screen it does indeed look like a 400-foot submarine. This is, of course, an illusion, and a very elaborate one. The Seaview is really three miniature fiberglass models. And the sea they voyage to the bottom of is either of the two indoor tanks at 20th Century-Fox's Hollywood studios. Actually, only two of the model subs – one 4 foot long the

other 8 feet – ever are submerged. The third model – 18 feet long – is used only for surface shots, filmed on a lake at the Fox Ranch in Malibu Canyon, Cal., or on a 5-foot-deep moat on Fox's back lot.... Price of the models: about $200,000.

That would be in excess of 1.5 million dollars in 2018.

Irwin Allen was furious over the *TV Guide* article, fearing the behind-the-scenes effects shots would ruin "the magic." William Creber told interviewer Kevin Burns, "Irwin fought that [article]; Irwin fought the revelation like mad. And he was very upset about showing the miniatures. He just thought that you should never show the audience a miniature in off-camera or documentary style. And I remember he went nuts – they had the cover [sic] of a *TV Guide* that had all of the submarines used in *Voyage* sitting in a tank with an effects guy in a scuba suit standing there, and he just went mad, like, 'How did they get this picture?!' You know, the publicity department thought it was a pretty tricky thing and it would tweak some interest, but he just went nuts." (WC-KB95)

As we know, magicians don't appreciate having their secrets revealed.

Regarding "The Indestructible Man," "TV Scout," in the February 1, 1965 edition of the *Monessen Valley Independent*, said:

> This show is getting to be more and more like a voyage to the bottom of *Outer Limits*, the old science fiction series. In "The Indestructible Man," the Seaview is entangled with a robot which has "emotional reactions closely duplicating a man's behavior." Question here is who is behind the monster, in this monster of a script.

Nielsen ratings report from Feb. 1, 1965: 7:30 – 8 p.m.:	Rating:	Share:
ABC: *Voyage to the Bottom of the Sea*	19.3	26.8%
CBS: *To Tell the Truth*	18.6	25.8%
NBC: *Karen*	**20.4**	**28.3%**
8 – 8:30 p.m.		
ABC: *Voyage to the Bottom of the Sea*	**21.6**	**28.5%**
CBS: *I've Got a Secret*	20.3	26.8%
NBC: *The Man from U.N.C.L.E.*	20.5	27.0%

NBC was conducting saturation on-air promos for its 7:30 p.m. sitcom, *Karen*, and *The Man from U.N.C.L.E.*, now on Monday nights. All the hype was paying off. This was the first time in its short history that *Voyage* had failed to pull in 30% of the viewing audience or better. In the 1960s, with fewer TV channels to watch, anything less than a 30 share didn't guarantee renewal.

Episode 22: "The Buccaneer"

(Prod. #7223; first aired Monday, February 8, 1965)
Written by William Welch and Al Gail
Directed by Laslo Benedek
Produced by Irwin Allen
Story Editor: William Welch; Associate Producer: Joseph Gantman
Assistant Story Editor: Al Gail
Co-starring G.B. Atwater (aka Barry Atwater)

From the *Voyage* show files (Irwin Allen Papers Collection):

A master criminal, calling himself Logan, plans to steal Da Vinci's painting, the Mona Lisa. Faking a fire at the Nelson Institute, he hijacks the Seaview during the confusion, overpowering Nelson, Crane and the crew, and putting his own men in command. A French cruiser is taking the picture to Australia for exhibition at a World Fair. Logan, in the Seaview, overtakes the ship and forces the captain to give up the painting.

Sound Bites:

Morton: "Did you find out anything?" *Crane:* "No, not a lot. We met the chief buccaneer. But, outside of that, we don't know much." *Morton:* "Well, wouldn't he talk?" *Crane:* "Talk? He won't shut up!"

Kowalski: "All this for a picture?" *Morton:* "A picture? Kowalski, if you tried to sell the Seaview on the open market, it wouldn't bring as much money as the Mona Lisa." *Kowalski (disbelieving):* "You're kidding?" *Morton:* "It's the most famous work of art in the world. Wars have been fought over less."

Assessment:

Unlike the Mona Lisa, "The Buccaneer" was no work of art. *Voyage* enthusiast Mike Bailey said, "By the time this episode aired, Season One had produced so many fine shows, so many well written and produced episodes, that this one stood out as being particularly lame in comparison. The fact that the episode had no real point, other than the action itself, foreshadowed what was to so often come in the color years. It's OK to do action for action's sake, but it needs to be more intelligently written and energetically directed than this grade 'C' work piece." (vttbots.com)

There is one saving grace to this pointless yet competently made episode – "Mr. Logan," both as written and played by Barry Atwater, makes an elegant and interesting villain. We don't believe any of it; and we certainly don't believe him as a threat. But he is deliciously ruthless … and quite debonair.

Script:
William Welch's and Al Gail's writers contract: December 9, 1964.
Welch's and Gail's story treatment and 1st draft teleplay: Dates unknown.
Welch's and Gail's 2nd ("Final") draft teleplay approved on December 23.
Mimeo Department's reformatted Shooting Final teleplay: Date unknown.
Rev. Shooting Final teleplay, by William Welch or Al Gail (on blue paper): December 30.
Page revisions by writing staff (yellow paper): December 31.
Page revisions (gold paper): January 11.
Page revisions (beige paper): January 19.
Page revisions (pink paper): January 20.

The script was co-written by Irwin Allen's cousin, Al Gail, in collaboration with Story Editor William Welch. And the boys were running on empty with this one. David Hedison said, "Irwin didn't much care about the quality of the writing, but he always cast good actors. That is why he had so much success." (DH-DM13)

Production:
(Filmed December 31, 1964 through January 13, 1965, and January 20; 9 days)
(Budget: $117,528)

Laslo Benedek was hired to direct, and was paid the standard fee of $2,500 for two weeks of his services (pre-production and production). He had directed "Long Live the King" in six days with Director of Photography Winton Hoch. But the game, and some of the players, had changed.

Carl Guthrie began working on the series here, stepping in as Director of Photography for Winton Hoch for several weeks while Hoch was off filming the *Lost in Space* pilot film with Irwin Allen. Guthrie had an impressive track record. He'd shot scary movies, like 1959's *House on Haunted Hill*, and submarine movies, like 1959's *Up Periscope*, and silly movies, like 1951's *Bedtime for Bonzo*. And he had shot TV, like Mark Goddard's first series, *Johnny Ringo*, and many of the Warner Brothers series from the late 1950s and early '60s, like *77 Sunset Strip*, *Hawaiian Eye* and *Cheyenne*. But *Voyage* would prove a challenge for Guthrie with his first journey on the Seaview. He was 59, but, this week, no doubt felt older.

Barry Atwater was paid $1,000 for a week's work, playing "Mr. Logan." He was 46, and would be remembered for playing Surak in the *Star Trek* episode "The Savage Curtain" and the vampire in the 1972 *Night Stalker* TV movie (which led to the television series of that name). Atwater would return for another *Voyage* – in fact, the very last episode of the series. In "No Way Back," he was cast as Major General Benedict Arnold.

Darren McGavin and Barry Atwater in *The Night Stalker*.
(ABC-TV, 1972)

George Keymas replaced Kurt Kreuger, who had originally been signed for the role of Igor. Keymas was 39 and worked often in television and films. On TV, and on one series alone, *Rin Tin Tin*, Keymas was often cast as Indians, such as Red Wolf, Crooked Leg, and Yellow Wolf, as well as several episodes in which he played Mexican banditos. He was paid $750 for a week's services.

Production started on Thursday, December 31, 1964, on Stage B, for work on the "Officer's Quarters" set. They stopped filming at 5:45, wished cast and crew a "Happy New Year," and sent everyone home.

Work resumed on Monday, January 4, 1965, in the crew's quarters, then on to the Missile Room and "Int. Cabin."

The versatile Ray Didsbury plays a crewman who is gunned down by the hijackers. He told interviewer Mark Phillips, "Irwin realized that, as background crewmen, some of us were getting killed off and then re-appearing the next week. So he nicely informed us we had to make a choice – be a regular crew member and not die, or die, make the big bucks, and leave. We opted to stay." (RD-FF01)

From this time forward, Didsbury was under strict orders not to die.

Day 1, filming in the "Officer's Quarters" (above), with Dowdell, Hedison, and Basehart. They have a plan! Below: Days 2 and 3: "Int. Missile Room."

484

Director Laslo Benedek completed his last shot at 7 p.m., giving anyone who might be interested in seeing the ABC premiere "The Last Battle" a 30-minute head start to get home.

On Tuesday, work on "The Buccaneer" was suspended as director Laslo Benedek was asked to shoot an added scene for "The Invaders," which also took place on Stage B. Benedek wasn't able to get back to his own episode until 5:05 p.m., filming one scene in the Missile Room until 6:55.

Wednesday was Benedek's official third day of production on "The Buccaneer," finishing up the work started the evening before in the Missile Room, then filming sequences written for "Int. Cabin." On Thursday, they filmed in the Control Room and the adjoining Radio Hut.

Above: From Day 3, filming "Int. Cabin," on the French destroyer. Center: Days 3 & 4 on the Control Room set, with Hedison, Atwater, and Basehart. Bottom image: George Keymas getting gassed.

Friday, January 8. More work in the Control Room, then the company moved out onto the studio lot to shoot night-for-night at one of the Administration Buildings, passing

485

for the Nelson Institute. The set call time on this day had been 12 noon (with make-up calls of 10:30 a.m.). The last camera shot was taken at 11:24 p.m. Saturday morning, everyone could sleep in.

The question in the minds of most who watch this episode concerns the teaser, and that stock footage of 1950s-era fire trucks pulling out of a fire station and speeding down a road which doesn't have a car newer than the late 1950s in sight! Certainly 20th Century-Fox had footage of fire trucks from some more recent movie or TV show? Of course they did. The problem was, any "stock" footage had to match the fire truck that was available to the company to film, roaring into the entrance to the Nielsen Institute. And that vehicle was a retired fire truck, about ten years old at the time of filming. So, the upshot was that *Voyage to the Bottom of the Sea*, set 10 years into the future, depicted a twenty-year-old fire truck.

Monday, January 11 was the sixth full day of production. It was supposed to be the last day, but everyone knew going in that it wouldn't be. Director Benedek and D.P. Guthrie had fallen too far behind.

Del Monroe said, "They ran it like a factory, basically. They had storyboards as to which shot they were going to take next. It was pretty well-organized. Irwin did the pilot and the first segment, then he hired directors after that. He was always aware of the time. I remember we had Laslo Benedek, who directed a segment. He had directed *The Men*, Marlon Brando's first film. Irwin came down to the set and told him, 'You've got to shoot faster, we're running too long.' Benedek replied, 'This is as fast as I shoot.' Irwin became upset; he wanted it to move along and get out of there." (DM-SE98)

The company worked on the Observation Nose set, with process shots. Wrap time came at 7 p.m. "Mutiny" aired on ABC-TV this night, starting at 7:30.

Benedek and Guthrie continued to film for two more days, on Tuesday and Wednesday,

Day 6, on the Observation Nose – fine wine, talk of fine art, and some fine overtime.

with the final day of production lasting until 3:30 p.m., when Benedek finally made way for director James Goldstone to begin work on "The Human Computer."

A final day on the Observation Nose ... and then a ninth day of production, with a rewrite sending David Hedison into the "Int. Conduit."

Benedek, learning the ropes on *Voyage* alongside Guthrie, had taken eight days to do the work that had been planned for six. Even worse, the resulting episode was a weak one.

After additional rewriting on the script, Benedek was brought back for a ninth day of production on Wednesday, January 20, with additional filming in the "Int. Conduit" and the crew's quarters. He was again teamed with Guthrie, who was in the middle of running the camera crew on four episodes, including "The Human Computer," "The Saboteur," and "The Exile." Benedek would not return to direct for Irwin Allen again, moving instead to another 20th Century-Fox series, *12 O'Clock High.*

ABC saw the rough edit on January 22, 1965. The Final Air Print was approved by the network on January 28, and put onto the air a week and a half later.

Release / Reaction:
(Only ABC broadcast: 2/8/65)

The week that "The Buccaneers" had its only ABC airing, "You've Lost That Lovin' Feeling," by the Righteous Brothers, was the song playing the most on radio stations across America. The albums that were spinning on the turntables of most American's record players were *Beatles '65*, followed by the soundtrack to *Mary Poppins,* the Supremes' *Where Did Our Love Go*, the soundtrack to *My Fair Lady*, and *Beach Boys Concert*. The hottest ticket in the movie houses was still *My Fair Lady*. On the way home from the movie, you could stop off at Shakey's Pizza Parlor and Ye Public House and get a large pepperoni pizza for $1.95, or a "giant" for only $2.40. And if you had it boxed to go, you could spend the night at home watching *Voyage to the Bottom of the Sea*.

Syndicated "TV Scout," appearing in the January 8, 1965 edition of the *San Antonio Express*, in Texas, said:

> To get into the swing of *Voyage to the Bottom of the Sea*, you must first imagine that it's 1975 and the Mona Lisa is on its way to the Australian World's Fair. So far, so good. But in this highly-charged trifle, the priceless painting has trouble making it to the Aussie shore when a mad art collector decides to pirate her aboard the Seaview. None of the action is as exciting as the lady's smile, although Barry Atwater's performance as the thief is volatile stuff.

Nielsen ratings report from Feb. 8, 1965: 7:30 – 8 p.m.:	Rating:	Share:
ABC: *Voyage to the Bottom of the Sea*	**19.2**	**28.0%**
CBS: *To Tell the Truth*	18.3	26.7%
NBC: *Karen*	19.0	27.7%
8 – 8:30 p.m.		
ABC: *Voyage to the Bottom of the Sea*	20.2	28.5%
CBS: *I've Got a Secret*	**21.1**	**29.8%**
NBC: *The Man from U.N.C.L.E.*	18.7	26.4%

Episode 23: "The Human Computer"

(Prod. #7224; first aired Monday, February 15, 1965)
Written by Robert Hamner
Directed by James Goldstone
Produced by Irwin Allen
Story Editor: William Welch; Associate Producer: Allan Balter
Assistant Story Editor: Al Gail
Co-Starring Simon Scott and Harry Millard

From the *Voyage* show files (Irwin Allen Papers Collection):

Ralph Reston, inventor of a master computer that can guide a sub in peace or war without a crew aboard, is having his invention tested on the Seaview. The sub was to be unmanned but Crane says he will stay on it, as observer only. This upsets the plans of a foreign power who have smuggled an agent aboard to bring the enemy sub to them when the test is over. The agent must now kill Crane before he can accomplish his mission. But Crane becomes aware of a hidden enemy and a battle of wits is fought out between them for stakes of life or death.

Sound Bites:

Crane: "When can we sail, Mr. Reston?" *Reston:* "Not 'we' – it. Or should I say 'she'?" *Crane:* "We. I'm going along." *Reston:* "Captain, the whole point of the test is to prove that an automated submarine can function in battle with absolutely no one on board." *Crane:* "I'm sorry, Mr. Reston, but according to Maritime Law, if a vessel's deserted, anyone can claim it as a derelict ship. Don't worry, I won't press any buttons on your super brain."

Assessment:

Three years from now, "The Ultimate Computer" episode of *Star Trek* would depict Captain Kirk and a skeleton crew standing by as their ship is piloted by an experimental computer. The episodes demonstrate how the same basic scenario can produce wide variations at the hands of two different writers.

Mark Phillips said, "An energetic teaser collapses into an agonizingly slow-moving episode, despite James Goldstone's efforts to liven things up." (vttbots.com)

Mike Bailey said, "When I first viewed this episode in 1965, I was thrilled by the dark, eerie lighting and overall strangeness of the first half of the show, although it did bog down toward the end. Subsequent viewings weren't as enthralling, but man, the cinematography is great." (vttbots.com)

"The Human Computer" is not only slow and dull, it's absurd. While making a nice showcase for David Hedison's acting, this boat is set afloat on a nonsense plot. A computer, which failed in its last test run – due to a 30-cent transistor burnout – now gets full control of the ship. Yes, the biggest, most advanced, most expensive, most secretive nuclear sub in the world is going out to sea with no one on board. And none of the brilliant military minds – including Nelson, who you'd think would be protective of the boat he designed and built – even thinks to send along a skeleton crew … just in case something should go wrong … as it most certainly did the last time. It is good that Captain Crane insists that he'll make the voyage, but he only does so because he knows that if no one is onboard, the ship could be claimed by a foreign power, or a drunken sailor in a rowboat. But even Crain doesn't think to ask, "Hey, who's going to man all these controls if another transistor burns out?"

The absurdities continue. A saboteur – working for one of those unidentified Eastern Block nations – manages to get on board before the Seaview departs its "secure" harbor. How did he get past security? He can't even speak English without that Eastern European accent heard on so many TV shows from this time. And how does he know his way around the Seaview so well – apparently even better than Captain Crain? Perhaps he bought the boat's top-secret plans from Logan, the mad art collector, who picked up a set on the black market for the previous episode.

On the plus side, this episode may have inspired *Star Trek*'s "The Ultimate Computer" – which *was* an hour of TV worth watching. And "The

Human Computer" is not without its supporters. William E. Anchors, Jr. and Frederick Barr, who wrote *Seaview: A 50th Anniversary Tribute to Voyage to the Bottom of the Sea*, gave it a thumbs up: "Director James Goldstone and David Hedison create an extraordinary mixture of action and suspense without dialogue in this remarkable episode."

Others liked it too. David Hedison said, "Another episode I enjoyed was 'The Human Computer.' It was the first episode they let me carry – the episode was me, alone on the Seaview with a Russian saboteur. That was fun to do." (DH-CFTV)

The TV critics of 1965 seemed to go for this change-of-pace episode, too (see "Release / Reaction").

Script:
Robert Hamner's writers contract: November 30, 1964.
Hamner's story treatment and 1st and 2nd draft teleplays: Dates unknown.
Mimeo Department's reformatted Shooting Final teleplay: Date unknown.
Rev. Shooting Final teleplay, by William Welch or Al Gail (blue paper): January 11.
Page revisions by writing staff (pink paper): January 13.
Page revisions (yellow pages): January 15.

The story's villain was originally a female. Writer Robert Hamner told interviewer Mark Phillips, "I found that whenever I wrote a woman into a script, Irwin would say, 'Bob, does it really have to be a woman?' I would say, 'She's a heavy; it'll be a switch.' He would say, 'No, let's make her a man.' 'But why? What have you got against women?'

"So, one night we're having dinner and I said, 'Okay, Irwin, loosen up. What's this thing about women?' And he replied, 'Every woman you have on the set costs you time, and time is money. You need an extra makeup person to do the body makeup and the hair styling. You don't have to do that with a man.' And that's why *Voyage* ended up with no women!" (RH-SL92)

It was a sad fact. Of the first group of 16 episodes, nine prominently featured women. And two of these episodes had more than one female in each. But, for the second batch of 16 episodes, only two would feature women, and their roles were not as developed as in the earlier episodes. Irwin Allen was forgetting that the male segment – teenage boys and the fathers of young viewers – was a valuable demographic too. Granted, boys and men would probably tune in for the action and adventure … and that very cool submarine. But a pretty face and a shapely figure never hurt a series in the ratings.

Regardless, the lack of a distaff guest star (including her wardrobe, make-up, and hairdressing) was one of the reasons "The Human Computer" was the least expensive episode made in the series up to this point. Another reason was that it didn't require any guest stars. Nor hardly any of the series regulars. And it was a "bottle show."

Because there was almost no dialogue in this episode, or any U.S. Presidents, or any Soviet nuclear missiles rocketing toward America – or anything interesting like sex or blood – there were no notes of interest from ABC to be addressed. It was as if the creative staff and the network watchdogs took a nap through this one. You may find yourself taking a nap too.

But *Voyage* needed a script to film in a hurry, when another planned script fell through. So, this one was hastily written over a weekend and put into production.

Production:
(Filmed January 13-25, 1965; 7 days)
(Budget: $110.931)

James Goldstone returned to direct for his third directing assignment, following "The Price of Doom" and "Doomsday." He did his work well with substitute cinematographer Carl Guthrie, giving *Voyage* a *film noir* feel. It's dark. Sadly, it's also a bit empty.

Simon Scott was paid $300 for a single day's work, playing Ralph Reston, designer of the Human Computer. Despite only being needed for a day, he was given top guest-star billing. Why? One answer is the billing helped compensate for the lack of pay. Further, Scott was a character actor with hundreds of credits in films and television, including multiple appearances on popular series such as *The Alfred Hitchcock Hour* and *77 Sunset Strip*. He had been a regular on Ray Milland's 1959 TV series, *Markham*, and also appeared in nine episodes of *McHale's Navy*, as General Bronson. Scott would go on to be featured in 83 episodes of *Trapper John, M.D.*, as Arnold Slocum.

Harry Millard was "The Man" on the Seaview – the episode's villain. He'd been making the rounds on all the usual TV shows – *12 O'Clock High*, *Honey West*, *The F.B.I.*, *The Fugitive* – but what Millard really wanted to do was write and produce movies. He got to do this, in 1968 and '69 with *Kemek*, a thriller costarring David Hedison. Although the movie's release was held up until 1970, it is notable for being one of Hedison's first post-*Voyage* acting jobs. What caused the delay? Millard, while only 41, had contracted cancer. He died in 1969.

Filming began on Wednesday, January 13, 1965, for the first of eight days on Stage B, although only seven of them were spent filming "The Human Computer." The set for the entire day, with more days to come, was the Control Room. Goldstone stopped filming at 7 p.m.

Goldstone spent Thursday and Friday filming additional scenes on the Control Room set, as well as shots in sections of corridor, and spending part of Friday on the Sick Bay set.

It was practically a one-man show for David Hedison, with glimpses of Walter Sande (above, on left) and villain Harry Millard (below).

Monday, January 18, was the fourth day of filming on Stage B, this time in the Observation Nose, including process shots, and then back into the Control Room for pickup shots. Goldstone had his last shot in the can by 6:45, allowing cast and crew time to make it home for the start of the excellent *Voyage* episode "Doomsday" on ABC's Channel 7 in Los Angeles.

Work continued on Stage B on Tuesday, with filming on the sets described in the production schedule as "Corridor of Ballast Pump Room," "Int. Small Arms Locker" and "Int. Other Corridor."

James Goldstone told interviewer Mark Phillips, "I wanted to see what I could do with a zoom lens. The zoom lens wasn't used much back then, and I would dolly in while zooming out. David Hedison and I also decided to play speechless suspense, and we did that by using his body language, the way he moved down a corridor and so on. These things were done to create spookiness, and it worked pretty well." (JG-SLP94)

On Wednesday. January 20, the production crew was commandeered and director Laslo Benedek was put in charge to film a new scene needed for "The Buccaneer." Goldstone spent the morning visiting with the Second Unit, which filmed at the outdoor location known as "the Green Tank." John Lamb was on camera for the underwater footage, but it wasn't being filmed off Catalina as in the past.

A wire story reported from late 1964 reported that Irwin Allen was sending a "27-man permanent second production unit" to Nassau in the Bahamas for underwater filming.

> ... *Voyage*, the only television series with four separate units filming simultaneously, has been doing its underwater shooting near Catalina Island, but according to producer Irwin Allen, the muddy condition of Catalina waters during winter's months necessitates the change.
> ...

On Friday, Goldstone had his crew back and resumed work on "The Human Computer" on Stage 2, for the "Int. Foreign Office" and "Int. Naval War Room" sequences. The company then moved back to Stage B for more filming on the Seaview's Control Room set, with a 6:55 p.m. wrap.

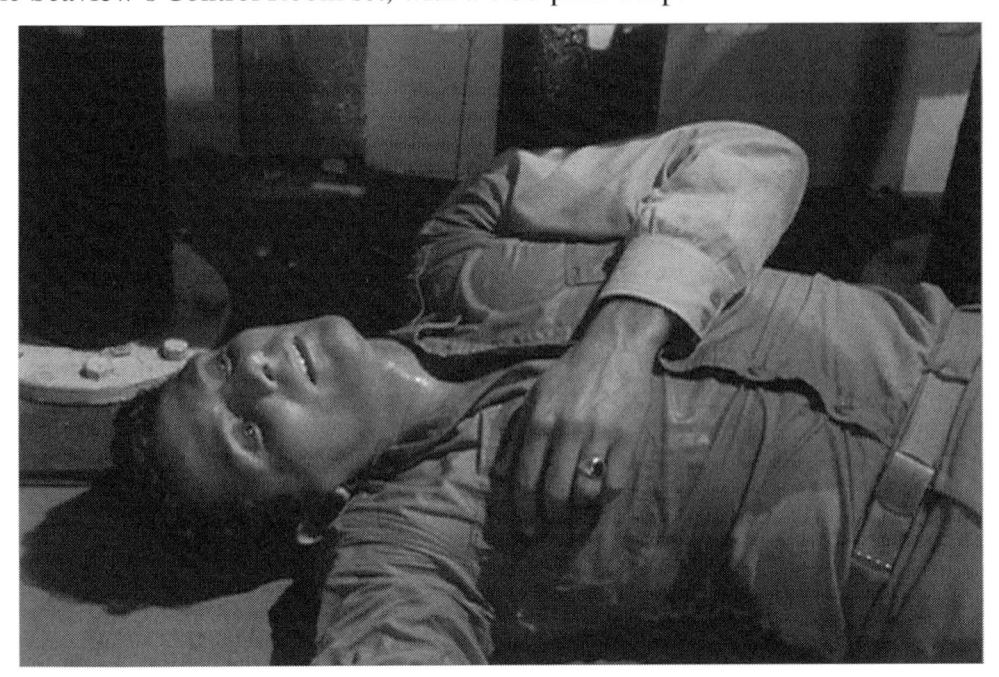

David Hedison with a startling look of near-death for the camera.

Monday, January 25 was the seventh full day of production, and the last, with Goldstone remaining on Stage B for more Control Room shots, then onto the Sick Bay and Missile Room sets. He wrapped at 6:45 p.m., one day behind. At 7:30 p.m., "The Invaders" episode of *Voyage* aired on ABC.

Release / Reaction:
(Only ABC broadcast: 2/15/65)

February 15, 1965 was the day that Canada replaced the Union Jack flag with the Maple Leaf. *The Greatest Story Ever Told*, starring Max von Sydow as Jesus, Dorothy McGuire as the Virgin Mary, Charlton Heston as John the Baptist, and Telly Savalas as Pontius Pilate, was No. 1 in the movie houses. The Beatles still had the top-selling album in America, with *Beatles '65*, being hounded in the charts by the soundtrack albums for *Mary Poppins* and *Goldfinger*. On the radio, Gary Lewis and the Playboys had the song getting the most airplay, with "This Diamond Ring."

Syndicated "TV Scout," carried on February 15, 1965 in Appleton, Wisconsin's *Post-Crescent*, said:

> "The Human Computer" in *Voyage to the Bottom of the Sea* begins with a teaser that will not only shock but mystify fans of the adventure series: The Seaview is sunk. But soon you realize that the Navy is only playing war games, and the invincible submarine is taking part in an experiment in which computers command the ship. No crew is needed, but on the maiden voyage of the test, with only Commander Crane (David Hedison) aboard, we learn that computers have enemies, too. It's a far out tale told well.

Also on February 15, rival entertainment column "TV Key," in West Virginia's *Charleston Gazette*, said:

> A fairly suspenseful entry that should appeal to the kids. It's virtually a one-man show as Capt. Crane (David Hedison) solos on the Seaview, which is being used to test a computer programmed to sail the sub automatically. Of course, there's a stowaway aboard – an enemy agent dispatched to kill Crane and take over.

Nielsen ratings report from Feb. 15, 1965:	Rating:	Share:
7:30 – 8 p.m.:		
ABC: *Voyage to the Bottom of the Sea*	**22.7**	**32.6%**
CBS: *To Tell the Truth*	19.5	28.0%
NBC: *Karen*	14.9	21.4%
8 – 8:30 p.m.		
ABC: *Voyage to the Bottom of the Sea*	**23.50**	**31.9%**
CBS: *I've Got a Secret*	20.6	28.6%
NBC: *The Man from U.N.C.L.E.*	18.2	25.3%

Episode 24: "The Saboteur"

(Prod. #7226; first aired Monday, February 22, 1965)
Written by William Read Woodfield and George Reed (aka Allan Balter)
Directed by Felix Feist
Produced by Irwin Allen
Story Editor: William Welch; Associate Producer: Joseph Gantman
Assistant Story Editor: Al Gail
Co-Starring Warren Stevens and Bert Freed

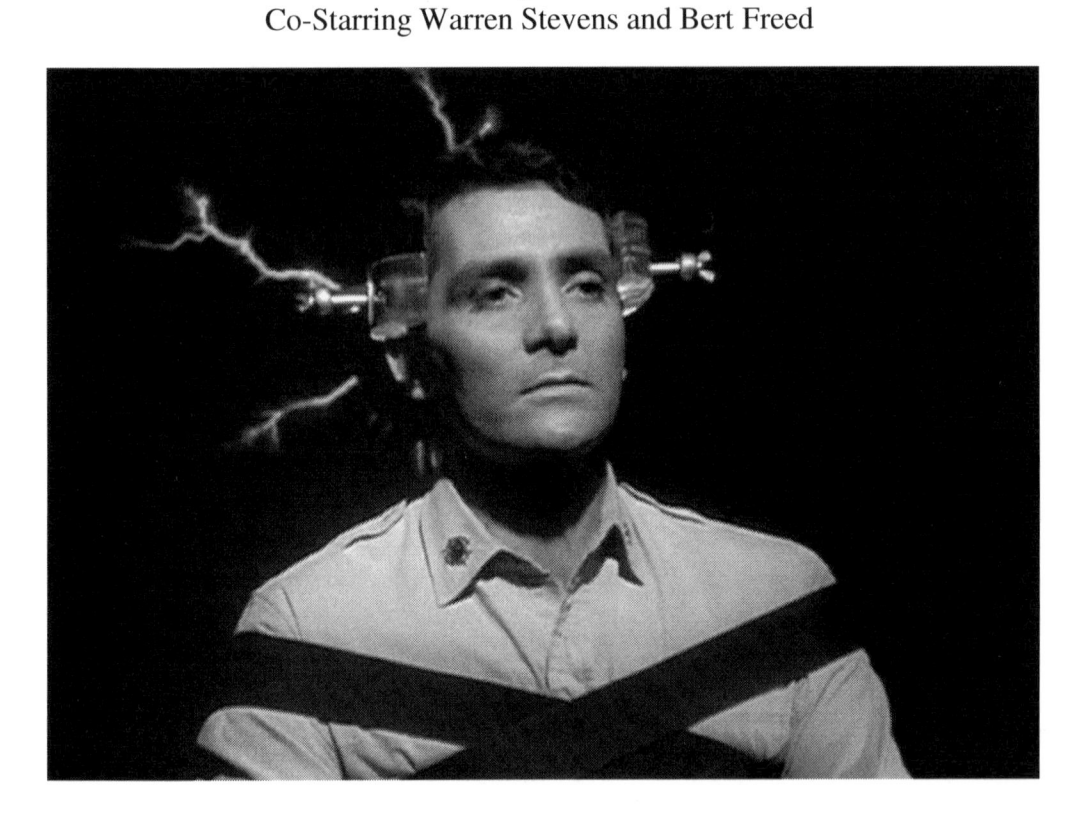

From the *Voyage* show files (Irwin Allen Papers Collection):

Crane is captured by agents of a foreign power who torture and brain-wash him until he is nothing more than an automaton to carry out their orders to sabotage the Seaview's current mission, which is planting a number of ICBM's [Intercontinental Ballistic Missile] in a hidden spot on the ocean floor for future use. Crane tries to abort the mission. When this fails, he deactivates the missiles. By now, Forester, in charge of security, suspects him, and shoots him just as Crane is about to kill Nelson, on orders. Wounded and delirious, Crane reveals the plot. But one of Seaview's radio operators also has been brain-washed and has orders to destroy the ship.

Sound Bites:

Nelson (in Missile Room): "You're drifting right into the mountain, Lee!" *Crane (in Control Room):* "Get off my back, Admiral! I'm in control of this ship! ... (to crew) ... Two more degrees, right rudder!" *Nelson:* "Port your helm, Lee! ... (to Missile Room crew) ... Stand fast for collision!"

Nelson: "How dare you?! How dare you abort this mission without my knowledge? On whose authority?" *Crane:* "On my authority, as Captain!" *Nelson:* "This mission will continue if I have to hang this ship together with spit and glue!" *Crane:* "And risk 125 lives; for what?" *Nelson:* "For the future peace of the world." *Crane:* "Peace of the world? You hypocrite! You don't care about the peace of the world!"

Assessment:

Watching "The Saboteur" now, you will likely feel you've seen this kind of story many times before. But in February 1965, this was pretty novel stuff on American TV. No one can say with certainty, but this episode of *Voyage to the Bottom of the Sea* may have only been the second time in TV history that depicted one lead character programmed to assassinate another ... or, for that matter, programmed to assassinate anyone.

This would become an overworked plot device in later seasons, and on other TV series, but it was pretty fresh, and shocking, stuff for February, 1965.

The intervening years may have lessened the impact of this episode. Mark Phillips said, "There's a group of latter Year-One episodes that, either due to budget crunches or creative fatigue, wearily flex some otherwise interesting ideas. The concept of *two* people on Seaview being brainwashed (one is Crane, the other a crewman) is intriguing, as is the idea of the observation windows being blown apart. Otherwise, routine going. Warren Stevens is always a welcome presence and look quickly for James Brolin – all you see is the back of his head!" (vttbots.com)

We agree concerning Warren Stevens. He is top-notch in this episode. But so are Basehart and Hedison. And, if you take into account the time it was made, "The Saboteur" is quite tense and filled with surprises.

William E. Anchors, Jr. and Frederick Barr raved in *Seaview: A 50th Anniversary Tribute to Voyage to the Bottom of the Sea*, "This great episode written by William Read Woodfield contains suspense and tension with multiple suspects, a sterling performance by David Hedison, and an examination of which is more important – intrinsic character or temporary conditioning."

Who could ask for more?

Script:

William Read Woodfield's and Allan Balter's writers contract: January 21, 1965.
Woodfield's and Balter's story treatment and 1st and 2nd draft teleplays:
Dates unknown.
Mimeo Department's reformatted Shooting Final teleplay (pale green paper):
January 25.
Page revisions by Allan Balter, William Welch, or Al Gail (blue paper): January 26.
Page revisions by writing staff (pink paper): January 27.
Page revisions (gold paper): February 1.

This was the first collaborative effort between William Read Woodfield and Allan Balter … although Balter, because he was also associate producer on the series, used the pseudonym George Reed. Balter had written before, with two scripts for *The Outer Limits* ("The Mutant" and "The Hundred Days of the Dragon"), but Irwin Allen preferred that he stick to his duties in production and leave the writing to Woodfield. But Allen needed Woodfield – especially because Basehart and Hedison were so fond of his writing – and Woodfield wanted Balter.

Woodfield said, "Richard and David were the only two cast members I got to know, and they were delights. They were very grateful to get any kind of a script that was different. It's hard to talk about nothing for an hour, and Richard was a master at talking gibberish and making it sound wonderful. Both Richard and David knew our scripts would at least give them something to discuss and they appreciated it." (WRW-SL92)

With this leverage, Allen reluctantly allowed Balter to work with their star writer.

The subject of brainwashing of a U.S. military officer by a foreign government had only recently become a hot topic in popular novels and movies. The Nazis had toyed with brainwashing during World War II, as had the Japanese, both of which may have influenced the writing of George Orwell's 1949 novel, *Nineteen Eighty-Four*. But it was the North Korean government – and their ally, the Red Chinese – who advanced the technique with captured soldiers during the Korean War (1950-53), conditioning their minds through torture. One year after the war ended, a modestly budgeted exploitation film brought the subject to the big screen. 1954's *The Bamboo Prison*, featured an America POW in North Korea who chooses to stay behind the Bamboo Curtain after the end of the war. One year later, in 1955, Rod Serling wrote an episode of the *U.S. Steel Hour*, called "The Rack," about a decorated U.S. Korean War hero who had been brainwashed. It was strong stuff for TV, better served the following year when it was remade for the 1956 film of the same title, starring Paul Newman. Two years later, Dana Andrews was the Korean War vet who got his brains washed, for 1958's *The Fearmakers*. The following year, Richard Condon's 1959 novel, *The Manchurian Candidate*, was published. It was adapted into a major motion picture in 1962, starring Frank Sinatra, and again focusing on a Korean War vet with scrambled brains ... this time programmed to become an assassin.

It wasn't just in fiction that mind-control research was underway. And it wasn't only being undertaken by "the bad guys." Although it was not revealed until decades later, at this time the CIA sponsored several hush-hush projects, attempting to create the perfect undercover agent. One of the most notorious was MKUltra, which ran from 1950 until 1973, and involved dosing volunteers and unsuspecting subjects with psychedelic drugs.

Amidst this cultural milieu, the stage was set for *Voyage to the Bottom of the Sea*. "The Saboteur" is at the forefront of the depiction of brainwashing on TV. One year later, Kelly Robinson (Robert Culp) on *I Spy* would be brainwashed and sent to assassinate his partner, Alexander Scott (Bill Cosby). And, for the same TV season, James West on *The Wild, Wild West* would be conditioned to become an assassin. But "The Saboteur" has the dubious honor of leading the pack (except for the Serling story from 1955). As far as its 1960s preteen audience was concerned, *Voyage* got there first. It was both novel and daring for a network entertainment program.

Of course, ABC-TV had their concerns. Calvin Ward, from the network, wrote to Irwin Allen and his staff on January 27, 1965:

> Page 1: Please ascertain that "Santa Barbara Van and Storage" is fictitious.
>
> Page 2, 3 & 4: Use extreme care with the "electrodes" business. Keep the flash and spark to a minimum. The effect and Crane's reaction must not be overly gruesome or terrifying. Can be approved only on film.
>
> Page 7: Keep Forester's position more generic, i.e., just "Intelligence Division" rather than a specific agency such as "State Department Intelligence Division."
>
> Page 10: Caution that the contents of the shaving kit are not identifiable as commercial brands.
>
> Page 15: The paperback novel will of course be a mock-up and unidentifiable with any actual publication.
>
> Page 32: Keep sparks, etc., to a minimum when the machine shorts out. Clark must not appear to be suffering in the extreme. Can be approved only on film.
>
> Page 33: As usual, the injection will take place off-camera.

Production:
(Filmed January 26 through February 3, 1965; 7 days)
(Budget: $112,138)

Felix Feist returned to direct this unnerving tale of artificially altered loyalties.

Out of the budget of $112,138, Richard Basehart received his flat fee of $7,000; Hedison his $2,500, Kulky $750, and Dowdell $500.

Warren Stevens was paid $1,250 for up to six days filming, playing Mason Forester. He was 44, and had co-starred in the 1956-57 series, *Tales of the 77th Bengal Lancers*, as Lt. William Storm. He had taken a trip to *The Twilight Zone* ("Dead Man's Shoes"), and to *Outer Limits* ("Keeper of the Purple Twilight"). He would soon do a *Star Trek* ("By Any Other Name"), always as the top guest star. Stevens had played the starship doctor on the movie that helped inspire *Star Trek*, 1956's *Forbidden Planet*. And he was an old friend of Richard Basehart. Stevens would return two more times to *Voyage* ("Deadly Invasion" and "Cave of the Dead"). Irwin Allen would also cast Stevens in *The Time Tunnel* episode "One Way to the Moon," and a pair of episodes for *Land of the Giants*: "Brainwash" and "A Place Called Earth."

Bert Freed was paid $1,000 for a week's work, playing Dr. Ernest

Above: Warren Stevens in *Intent to Kill*. (20th Century-Fox, 1958)
Below: Janice Rule with Bert Freed on *Goodyear Playhouse* (NBC-TV, 1954)

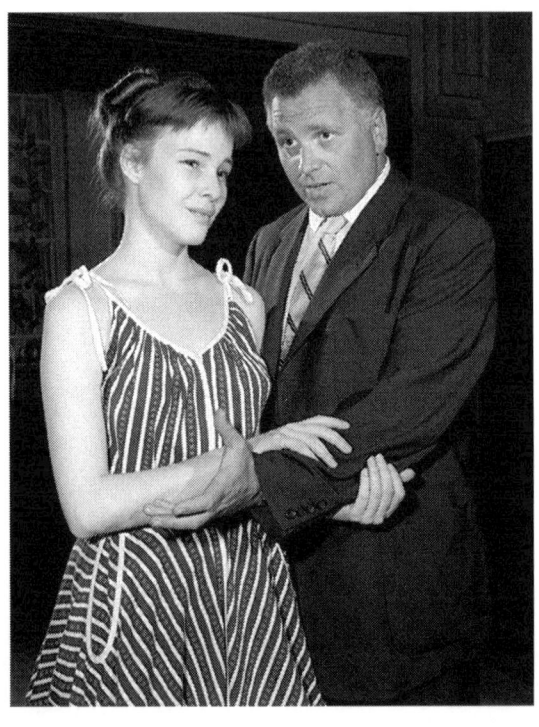

Ullman, and was made to look older than his 44 years. He worked often, playing sheriffs, and crooks, and was the police chief who was taken over by Martians in 1953's *Invaders from Mars*.

James Brolin, who was under contract with 20th Century Fox, was paid $200 to play Spencer.

Werner Klemperer was paid $350 for providing the voice of Crane's tormentor.

Derrik Lewis returned as Lt. O'Brien. This was his sixth of eight appearances during the first season. Lewis considered "The Saboteur" one of the better episodes he appeared in. He added, "They really had the best scripts during that first season. And, also, the fact that it was shot in black-and-white was

Derrik Lewis as Lt. O'Brien in a scene from "The Saboteur."

a plus, because that gives you that film noir feel – with the shadows, and a bit darker slant to it."

While the episodes were rich on drama, Lewis recalls an encounter with Irwin Allen away from the set as one of his most memorable *Voyage* experiences. He shared, "I was a musician by night in those days – a piano player and a singer – and I had a friend who was a wonderful pianist, and we wrote a song together. It was a wonderful love song. The title of the song was, 'On the Journey to the Bottom of the Sea.' And then, a short time later, I'm in a show called *Voyage to the Bottom of the Sea*. Now, I had either forgotten or did not know that the original movie had a song, sung by Frankie Avalon, and that it was called 'Voyage to the Bottom of the Sea.' Not remembering or knowing this, I told my songwriting friend, 'I'm going to take this and show it to Irwin. And, who knows?'

"Well, I went for the first time that day up to Irwin Allen's office. I had been in the casting office, and on the set, and on the lot, but I had never had a reason or was invited into Irwin Allen's inner sanctum. So, I walked up the stairs to the office, and I was talking to the secretary for a moment, and, suddenly, Irwin *bursts* out of his office! He saw me and came straight over, wanting to know what I'm doing there. 'Well, I've come to give you this,' I said, nervously. And I handed it to him. He took it into his hands, and he said, 'What is it?' I said, 'It's a song I wrote …' And, as soon as I got that much out of my mouth, he dropped it on the floor, like it was a hot potato. A very HOT POTATO. He takes a step away from it, and then starts explaining to me something about legalities, and how he couldn't accept something like that; how it could eventually have legal ramifications. And then he said something about they have their own musicians and things at the studio, of course, and to never put anything like that in his hands again. So, I said, 'Well, thank you very much,' and I collected my song from the floor, then I put my tail between my legs and beat it out of there. Of course, since then, I've realized that he was right. You can't do things like that. But this is what I mean when I say that Irwin was a very animated producer – like the Road Runner." (DL-AI18)

Filming began on Tuesday, January 26 for the first of seven days on Stage B. Besides the usual Seaview sets, the torture room was also filmed at this location. It took an entire day – the seventh. The set was described in the script as "Int. Warehouse." What we got instead was a black void set, symbolic of the

Above: Captain Crane prepares to shoot an image of Admiral Nelson after being brainwashed. Below: Real-life friends Warren Stevens and Richard Basehart reunite on camera.

neverland of mental torture.

Friday, January 29, was the longest day, filming on the Observation Nose (with process shots). The camera rolled from 8:55 a.m. (after an 8 a.m. set call) until 9:20 at

502

Above: Top security man Stevens inspects the captain's shaving kit. Center: Hedison with Derrik Lewis. Bottom: The brainwashed saboteur ... gunning for Nelson.

night. The thinking was, if they were going to go late, let it be on a Friday. At least no one had to come in to work the next morning.

During the course of the production – on Monday, February 1 – "The Indestructible Man" aired on ABC. Filming continued until 6:42 that night. The episode aired at 7:30 p.m.

While being interviewed on the set, Richard Basehart asked *TV Guide* writer Marian Dern, "You didn't see the pilot film by any chance? You did? Oh, Lord, forget about that. The scripts have improved. We have some very inventive stories – sometimes. There was one recently about a court-martial – awfully good idea. But I don't know. Somehow, that old monster showed up there at the end. Now, don't get me wrong. I like to work and I like to earn money. Nothing irritates me more than actors who take all the money and then complain about how terribly limited TV is. That kind of talk only reflects on them."

After being interrupted for another take, Basehart returned to Dern. "Sometimes, though, I wonder what it's all about. We knock ourselves out – you know, it's a backbreaking schedule. … But I don't plan to stay in this game forever. A couple more years, a few more dollars, and then I'll go off and do some stage work or something."

Warren Stevens and Richard Basehart lean over David Hedison – three superb actors making life easy for their director.

Dern said Basehart suddenly looked sombre. "I can't help but think about John's death," he said.

John Larkin was an actor like Basehart – serious, from the stage, finally gaining success and recognition, and a decent paycheck, as a regular on *12 O'Clock High*. He was also a friend of Basehart, about the same age. But he suddenly died of a heart attack. Basehart said, "I had an intensely personal reaction to his death. I resented his death. He was just beginning to garner the fruits of his efforts … and boom!"

Basehart shook his head, perhaps recalling the death of his wife, Stephanie Basehart, from a brain tumor, 15 years earlier. He said, "You fight for the moments. You fight for the seconds to live."

Dern's interview was interrupted again, as the director called, "C'mon, Dick, we're ready to shoot. Pick it up at, uh, where you say to Crane, 'This mission won't be aborted, if I have to put this submarine together with spit and glue.' OK?" (RB-TVG65)

ABC screened the rough cut of "The Saboteur" on February 9, 1965. The Final Air Print was approved on February 12, only days before broadcast. They had been cutting it that close.

Release / Reaction:
(ABC premiere broadcast: 2/22/65; network repeat airing: 7/26/65)

The day before "The Saboteur" first aired on ABC, Civil Rights activist Malcolm X was shot and killed by Nation of Islam followers in New York City.

The Bible epic *The Greatest Story Ever Told* was the most popular movie over the weekend in theaters. And on Sunday night's *The Ed Sullivan Show*, Jerry Vale was the musical guest, with Sid Caesar and impressionist Frank Gorshin providing comedy.

"TV Scout," as carried in the Texas *Abilene Reporter-News*, said:

> Pity poor David Hedison on *Voyage to the Bottom of the Sea*. What he has to go through week after week! This time, he is brainwashed in order to deactivate U.S. missiles. There are some suspenseful moments as he tries to wash-those-thoughts-right-out-of-his-head.

That final phrase, of course, is a nod to the Rodgers and Hammerstein song "I'm Going to Wash That Man Right Outa My Hair" from the 1949 Broadway musical *South Pacific*, which became a movie in 1958.

Daily Variety's "Daku" reviewed "The Saboteur" for the Hollywood trade. The critic said, in part:

> Already assured of another voyage next season, *Voyage* demonstrates in "The Saboteur" the qualities that have made this Irwin Allen-20th-Fox TV series a marked success. Teleplay by William Read Woodfield and George Reed is a bizarre one, true to the spirit of series' futuristic vein. *Voyage* is one of the more imaginative, ingenious and provocative series in a medium unfortunately lacking in these qualities. In "Saboteur," captain of the nuclear sub (David Hedison) is brainwashed by the enemy, and as a result, tries to sabotage his own ship, on a highly strategic mission – that of concealing brand-new model ICBMs on the bottom of the sea, as a deterrent to the enemy who might have war on his mind. Action is plentiful and the drama moves at a brisk, suspenseful pace.

A.C. Nielsen ratings report, Feb. 22, 1965:	Rating:	Share:
7:30 – 8 p.m.:		
ABC: *Voyage to the Bottom of the Sea*	**19.7**	**30.4%**
CBS: *To Tell the Truth*	19.3	29.8%
NBC: *Karen*	14.4	22.3%
8 – 8:30 p.m.		
ABC: *Voyage to the Bottom of the Sea*	**20.4**	**28.9%**
CBS: *I've Got a Secret*	20.0	28.4%
NBC: *The Man from U.N.C.L.E.*	18.5	26.2%

Episode 25: "Cradle of the Deep"

(Prod. #7227; first aired Monday, March 1, 1965)
Written by Robert Hamner
Directed by Sobey Martin
Produced by Irwin Allen
Story Editor: William Welch; Associate Producer: Allan Balter
Assistant Story Editor: Al Gail
Co-Starring John Anderson

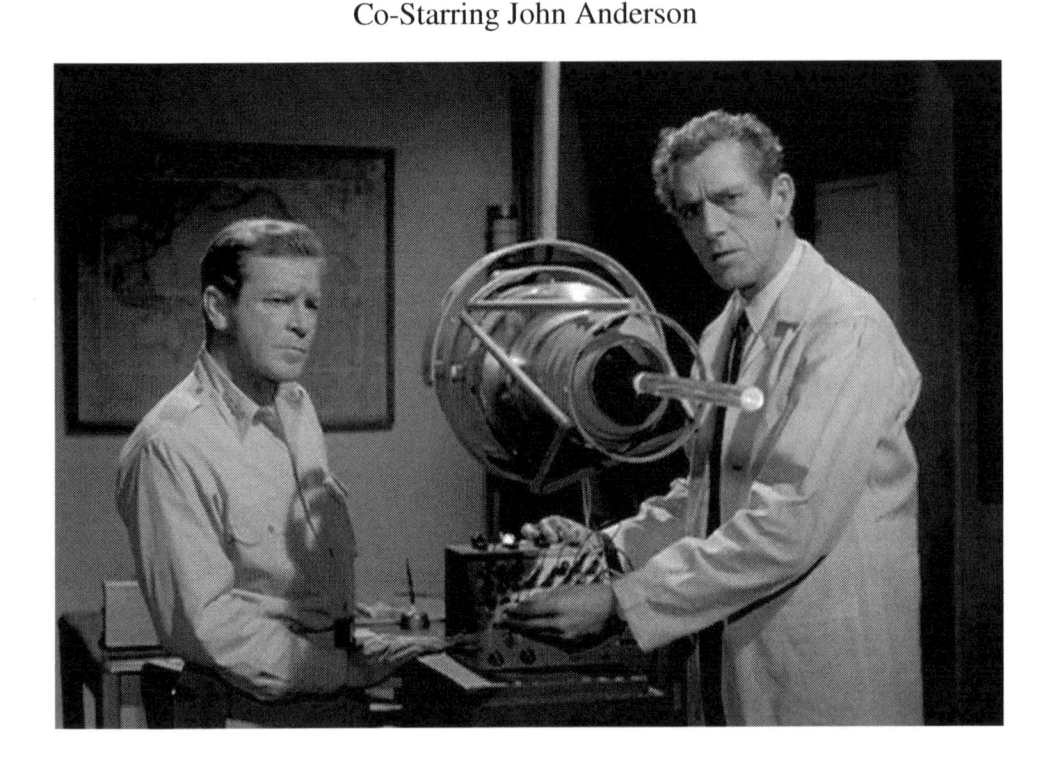

From the *Voyage* show files (Irwin Allen Papers Collection):

Dr. Janus, a brilliant scientist, thinks he has discovered the secret of life. The experiment requires certain elements from the Azanian Sea and the Seaview is commissioned to take him there. He gets the material aboard, despite violent seaquakes that almost destroy the sub, and gets to work. The experiment is successful but the newly created specimen begins to grow at an alarming rate. The sub races for home but now the crew is found to be suffering from nitrogen narcosis. The specimen is feeding on the ship's oxygen supply. By now it has become so heavy that it drags the sub to the bottom. It is imperative to destroy it fast. Desperately, Nelson and Janus try choking it with carbon dioxide. First this makes it expand so rapidly that it crushes Janus.

Sound Bites:

Dr. Janus: "There's too much human misery. No reason today for allowing human beings to be born deformed. That's why this voyage is important; why it must be successful. You see, most of our work to date has been confirmed to the laboratory. We're going to learn so much more now; we're going to the very cradle of existence; we're going to obtain the basic materials of human life."

Crane: "Chip?" *Chip (woozy):* "Hi ya. Good morning there, Skipper, old buddy." *Crane:* "We're in practically the same spot we were in last night! You've been taking us around in circles! We'll never make it back to port in time now!" *Morton:* "Circles; we're going round in circles." *Crane: (to helmsman):* "Come to a bearing of three-four-eight degrees!" *Helmsman:* "Going in circles. Going round and round…" *Crane (interrupting):* "I want a bearing of three-five-eight degrees and I want it now! Keep it on that heading. You stray one fraction off course and you're going to draw brig time!" *Helmsman:* "Sure, Captain. Anything you say, Captain." *Crane (to Morton):* "Now, in words of one syllable – First, <u>how</u>? And then, <u>why</u>?" *Morton:* "Sure, anything my skipper says. My skipper knows I'll always tell my skipper anything…" *Crane (cuts him off):* "Now, you look here, we're a thousand miles off course! We've been going around in circles all night! Before I place you under arrest, I want some answers and I want them fast!" *Nelson (entering):* "What's wrong, Lee?" *Crane:* "I don't know. Look at them. They're either drunk or they've gone off the deep end!"

Assessment:

Voyage connoisseur Mike Bailey said, "This episode is reminiscent of Ivan Tors' *Magnetic Monster*, in which a minuscule bit of matter, the result of an experiment which gets out of hand, doubles in size every 12 hours. It's an interesting concept which plays on *Voyage* in fair 'B' movie style. And don't forget – there are some things that mankind just isn't meant to know!" (vttbots.com)

Ivan Tors wrote the screenplay for the 1953 film, *The Magnetic Monster*, which starred one of *Voyage to the Bottom of the Sea*'s first guest stars – Richard Carlson. In the story, a scientist bombards a new radioactive element called "serranium" with "alpha particles" for 200 hours, prompting it to grow geometrically, absorbing energy from the metallic objects surrounding it. The ticking clock in this situation is that within 24 hours, the serranium will have grown large enough to throw the Earth off its orbit.

Perhaps "Cradle of the Deep" writer Robert Hamner had seen *The Magnetic Monster*.

Despite the similarities to a sci-fi B-flick from eleven years earlier, "Cradle of the Deep" has many good ideas stuffed into its 50-minute run-time. Perhaps too many. The one thing that drags the whole show down – along with the sub – is the monster itself. It's rather silly-looking; you wonder why someone just doesn't pop it with a pin. Then there are the violent currents and the underwater earthquakes bouncing the Seaview from side-to-side; the scared-silly and mutinous junior officer (Seaman Clark, of course); and something we hadn't seen before – the Control Room crew seemingly stoned out of their heads ... on a little number called "nitrogen narcosis."

Yes, it's a high time on the old Seaview tonight.

Script:
Robert Hamner's treatment and 1st and 2nd draft teleplays: Dates unknown.
Mimeo Department's reformatted Shooting final teleplay: Date unknown.
William Welch's Rev. Shooting Final teleplay (blue paper): February 2, 1965.
Page revisions by William Welch or Al Gail (pink paper): February 5.
Page revisions by writing staff (beige paper): February 11.
Page revisions (gold paper): February 12.

"Cradle of the Deep" was Robert Hamner's fifth of six script assignments for *Voyage*. He said, "Irwin always came to me with his problem shows. He called me up: 'Bob, we've got a problem.' So, I went over to his office, and there were 20 guys sitting around this huge conference table. Irwin said, 'Bob, we have no money to shoot the next show.' I said, 'Well then, what are you guys sitting around here for? Go home.' 'No!' said Irwin. 'We've got to have a show. Can you write a story that takes place 100 percent on the submarine and doesn't need any new actors or sets?' I said, 'Well, you'll need a heavy.' 'No! We haven't got money for a heavy!' 'Okay. The Seaview's cruising in this deep trench off the African coast where life on Earth first began and they pick up something.' And Irwin's eyes began to pop. 'What do they pick up?' 'Well, they don't know what it is. It's something.' And I'm ad-libbing all of this. I didn't know where this was going. And Irwin said, 'Well, what does it do?' I said, 'It grows.' And Irwin looked disappointed. 'It just grows?' I said, 'Yeah, and, as it grows, it gets heavier.' 'It just gets heavier?' And I said, 'Well, uh... the weight increases geometrically, Irwin. The mass is so heavy that it's going to sink the submarine.' 'Yeah, but what does it *do* as it grows?' I said, 'It pulsates.' 'It just pulsates?' Irwin asked. 'It throbs.' Now, Irwin is getting into it, and he turned to his art director [Bill Creber]. 'We'll put some nylon tubes under the skin and light it up!' And that's how the blob show came about." (RH-SL92)

Within early versions of the script was dialogue that suggested man evolved from single-cell organisms. ABC, like the other networks of the time, was unwilling to stir the muddy waters of the debate on evolution. Hamner said,

"I liked that show in a strange way, [but] it opened up so many things that drove people crazy. It wasn't approved by the network. I told them, 'This is crazy! What's wrong with it?' They said, 'It's anti-Christian. It goes against the Bible.' I replied, 'This is based on scientific fact. It's Charles Darwin! I'm not making a brief for it.' And they said, 'Oh, yes you are! You're saying this is where life began, and we don't want to get into that.' It became a very big problem, but I finally wore them down and the show went on." (RH-SL92)

Production:
(Filmed February 4-12, 1965; 7 days)
(Budget: $112,141)

Even though Robert Hamner recalled Irwin Allen saying that there was no money to pay for a guest star, "Cradle of the Deep" would get one nonetheless.

John Anderson was paid $1,750 for a week's work, as Dr. Janus. Anderson was a well-regarded character actor in television and films. He had a recurring role in the 1960-61 series, *The Life and Legend of Wyatt Earp*, as Virgil Earp. He appeared in four episodes of *The Twilight Zone*, and was especially well-liked at *The Rifleman*, where he appeared in 11 episodes.

Paul Carr had just turned 31 and was advanced in rank on *Voyage* to junior officer. This was his fifth of six appearances as Bill Clark. He'd appear in a seventh episode, again as a crewman, but with a different name (Benson, in "Terror of Dinosaur Island").

John Anderson in "Nightmare," an episode of *The Outer Limits*. (United Artists, 1963)

This was the last episode that included Henry Kulky as Chief Curley Jones. The actor died from a heart attack on February 12, 1965 (during the weekend) while he was studying the script for his next *Voyage*. He was 53.

Filming began on Thursday, February 4, 1965 for the first of seven days on Stage B. During the production, on Monday, February 8, "The Buccaneer" had its only airing on ABC.

Above: John Anderson and Richard Basehart. Center: They finally threw overly-reactive Seaman Clark in the brig. Bottom: Chip Morton gets high on bad air.

John Anderson told interviewer Mark Phillips, "I enjoyed doing *Voyage*. Richard Basehart was one of my closest friends and a wonderful actor. The only problem was working with the silly blob in that episode. It was just sitting there on the floor, obviously made of plastic and red ink. Sometimes, what you are asked to believe is so either banal or bizarre that you have trouble with it. We had to believe that a pulsating piece of plastic was a sea monster of some kind. It was awful! We all had a hard time keeping a straight face. I looked at it and said, 'What a piece of crap you are! But I guess you're the best blob they could come up with, so let's get on with it.'" (JA-VTTBOTS)

Anderson tried to play it straight. He was surprised that Basehart was not as serious in his approach. Anderson said, "By noon of the

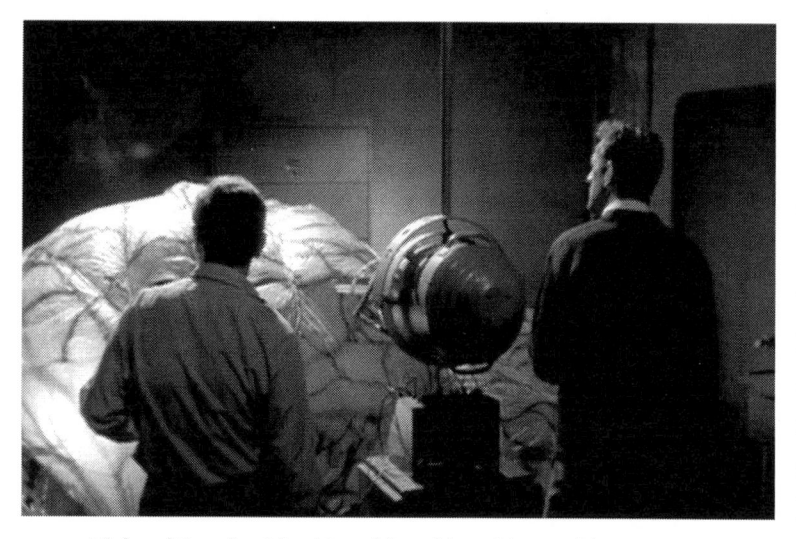

Richard Basehart had trouble taking this week's monster seriously. It was as scary as a half-inflated weather balloon.

fourth day, I noticed that Richard Basehart, who had suffered through 25 [sic] segments by this time, was poking fun at the lines and snickering over inside jokes. I was shocked that Basehart, who was a good friend, was engaging in such destructive behavior. After several hours of watching Dick indulge in this kid's shit, I decided to settle it. We went for lunch. I lit up my cigar and he had a drink. I said …. 'Dick, I have tremendous respect for you. You're one of the greatest living talents in the business. But do you have any idea how hard it is for me, as a guest star, to make this thinly drawn character work while you're making jokes about the script?' He looked at me very grimly. I wasn't out to hurt him. 'You're right, John,' he said. 'It's easy for me to kid the script, but it's got to stop.' He thanked me profusely and we went back to work. There was no more bullshit." (JA-SFTS)

The message stuck. Joe Tata, who appeared in three episodes of *Voyage* as well as working on Irwin Allen's other TV series, said, "Richard used to wear lifts in his boots, trying to be a little taller. One day I said to him, 'Man, if I had boots like those, I'd be a star!' The corners of Richard's eyes went up, like he was going to laugh, but he never did. He always wanted to laugh on that show but he couldn't let it out. Somebody had told him that as the show's star, he wasn't supposed to laugh. That was my interpretation." (JT-TVC99)

Release / Reaction:
(Only ABC broadcast: 3/1/65)

The Sound of Music was released this week, and immediately became the No. 1 film in America. "My Girl" by the Temptations was getting the most airplay on radio stations. The Beatles still had the best-selling record album across the country, with *Beatles '65*. Rink's Discount Department Stores were offering it in stereo for $3.47. But hold on – your neighborhood Thrifty Drugstore had it in stock for $2.83. While checking out, you could pick up the latest issue of *TV*

Guide. Donna Douglas, Irene Ryan, and Nancy Kulp, of *The Beverly Hillbillies*, had the cover, and you could buy it for 15 cents.

On March 1, 1965, "TV Scout," in the *Monessen Valley Independent*, among other newspapers, said:

> "Cradle of the Deep" is another science fiction tale. It's a suspenseful bit of nonsense concerning the Seaview's gallant attempt to find and stimulate "the beginning of life." Working on the theory that humans started from simple, one-celled protozoa, an energetic scientist (John Anderson) discovers a process to speed up the evolution, but unfortunately, not one to stop it.

Come first week of March, *Voyage* was holding in the Nielsen surveys, and had actually climbed one rung to No. 39. The ranking for its time slot was reported by A.C. Nielsen as follows:

A.C. Nielsen ratings report, March 1, 1965:	Rating:	Share:
7:30 – 8 p.m.:		
ABC: *Voyage to the Bottom of the Sea*	**20.7**	**31.8%**
CBS: *To Tell the Truth*	18.3	28.1%
NBC: *Karen*	16.9	24.9%
8 – 8:30 p.m.		
ABC: *Voyage to the Bottom of the Sea*	**21.2**	**30.8%**
CBS: *I've Got a Secret*	18.6	27.0%
NBC: *The Man from U.N.C.L.E.*	19.0	27.6%

On March 7, one week after "Cradle of the Deep" first aired on ABC, a syndicated newspaper story appearing in *The Fresno Bee The Republican* said:

> Richard Basehart and David Hedison, stars of 20th Century-Fox Television's *Voyage to the Bottom of the Sea*, seen Monday nights over ABC-TV, had a new experience the other day when they watched themselves in the Japanese version of their action-adventure series.
>
> *Voyage*, now sold in syndication around the world, including Japan, undoubtedly has one of the highest "world" popularity ratings of any television show yet devised. In the short time it has been on Japanese television, a country second only to the United States in volume of television sets and viewing audience, *Voyage* has risen to be one of the Far East's favorite shows.

The show, of course, is dubbed in Japanese for that country's consumption.

"And it certainly is interesting," Basehart offered after viewing the Japanese version of *Voyage*, "to see yourself on the screen talking like Sessue Hayakawa!"

Interesting, maybe. But a change in language couldn't make that monster any more believable. ABC did not give this one a summer repeat broadcast.

Farewell to the Chief – Henry Kulky, August 11, 1911 – February 12, 1965.

Episode 26: "The Exile"

(Prod. #7228; first aired Monday, March 15, 1965)
Written by William Read Woodfield
Directed by James Goldstone
Produced by Irwin Allen
Story Editor: William Welch; Associate Producer: Allan Balter
Assistant Story Editor: Al Gail
Also Starring Ed Asner
David Sheiner, Harry Davis, James Frawley, Jason Wingreen

From *Voyage* show files (Irwin Allen Papers Collection):

Mikhil Brynov, disposed Premier of an Iron Curtain country, escapes a firing squad and seeks asylum in the U.S. Nelson meets the tough, crafty, peasant-reared ex-dictator aboard a private yacht with orders to rendezvous with Seaview for the dash to freedom. But the yacht is sunk and Nelson finds himself cast adrift on a raft with Brynov and his closest associates. Now there begins a struggle for survival, both against the forces of nature and against the iron will of the crafty, ruthless, power-hungry man who still plans to return to his former position of absolute rule.

Sound Bites:

Nelson: "You murdered them!" *Brynov:* "Murdered? I saved our lives."
Nelson: "You killed three men." *Brynov:* "Sacrificed. So that the microfilms will

reach your country in time; so that your President will learn about surprise attack, and prevent. This is neither the time nor place for sentimentalities. Those men are on my conscience; not yours." *Nelson:* "Your conscience? What conscience? You've killed thousands of innocent men, women and children." *Brynov:* "I've only killed to free my country from tyrants; to rid it of traitors." *Nelson:* "No, Mr. Premiere. You've killed only to gain power."

Assessment:

Cult TV fan and *Voyage* enthusiast Mark Phillips was not enthusiastic over this one. "The old 'trapped in a lifeboat' routine, and it is stupefying. The emptier the lifeboat gets, the less interesting the drama becomes. Nelson and Brynov's battle for survival is an overblown endurance test for the viewer." (vttbots.com)

Voyage aficionado Mike Bailey differed: "In spite of the fact that the trapped-in-a-lifeboat formula is stultifying and the telling of it not particularly energized, it remains that this episode, typical of Season One, takes a moral position and tries to make a point (by exploring Brynov's ruthlessness). Not William Read Woodfield's best writing, which is to put it kindly." (vttbots.com)

Voyage tribute book authors William Anchors, Jr. and Frederick Barr were more impressed. "All the scenes in the raft between Nelson and Brynov were remarkable: the tyrant and bully versus the brave and resolute Nelson; a clash of philosophies of character, of basic good and evil, and of two indomitable men – only one [of whom] could survive in the end." They also cited the "good script" and "wonderful direction," but especially credited Ed Asner for "giving a bravura performance" and "the great Richard Basehart, who could invest even a slight smile and a wealth of meaning," for making this "one of the best of *Voyage*."

We'll lean toward Mike Bailey's appraisal – it's an entertaining hour, even if it can't hold an oar to Hitchcock's *Lifeboat*. But then, few directors could go that deep in the limitations of one tiny set. This story may be all on the surface, but it has its moments.

Script:
William Read Woodfield's writers contract for "The Survivors":
January 27, 1965.
Woodfield's story treatment and 1st and 2nd draft teleplays: Dates unknown.
Mimeo Department's reformatted Shooting Final teleplay: February 8.
Rev. Shooting Final teleplay, by Allan Balter, William Welch or Al Gail (beige paper): February 10.
Page revisions by writing staff (pink paper): February 12.
Page revisions (yellow paper): February 17.
Page revisions (dark green paper): February 18.

William Read Woodfield recalled, "Irwin would say, 'Billy, I need a new script. So I said, 'Okay, what about *Lifeboat*? And he would say, 'Good,' and I wrote it." (WRW-SL92)

Of course, Alfred Hitchcock's *Lifeboat* is absorbing storytelling, with sharply drawn characters and mounting suspense.

The working title of Woodfield's story was "The Survivors."

The representative of ABC's Continuity Acceptance Department wrote to Irwin Allen on February 10, 1965:

> General Caution: The uniforms, flags, emblems, newspapers, and other props and set dressing must in no way resemble, or indicate identification of any actual country. The cast also must not resemble any actual officials of any country.
>
> Page 1: The masthead should of course be a mock-up. If possible the date of 1973 or later should be prominent.
>
> Page 3: Brynov's spit must be a "dry" spit.
>
> Confirming phone conversation with Mr. [Allan] Balter, a different method of eliminating the firing squad should be considered. In any event, the action should be indicated rather than shown in detail. Can be approved only on film.
>
> Page 12: Mikhil's last line; substitute for "God".
>
> Page 26: Josip's first line; delete "idiot".
>
> Page 29: Do not show actual contact of piece of wood and sailor's head. This scene should not be excessively violent or drawn-out.
>
> Pages 37 & 38: As discussed, the action at the close of Act Two and the opening of Act Three should be telescoped [covered with long shots only]. It must not become gruesome or horrifying. Can be approved only on film.
>
> Page 54: Keep blood to a minimum on Nelson's wound.
>
> Pages 54 & 55: Lower position of gun to chest or neck area. Do not press against head.

When watching the Teaser, you'll see a fine example of "dry spit."

Production:
(Filmed February 15-23, 1965; 7 days)
(Budget: $123,636)

This was James Goldstone's fifth and final episode of *Voyage* (he had directed part of "Mutiny" without credit).

Edward Asner was paid $1,750 to play Brynov. The character's first name in the springboard had been Mikhil. This was changed to Aleksei, and Brynov's brother was then given the first name of Mikhil.

Asner was 34 and fairly early in his career, although with enough appearances on such series as *Studio One*, *The Untouchables*, and *Route 66* to get an "also starring" billing and a decent paycheck. To earn that money, Asner spent a couple days in the Green Tank.

Above: Ed Asner encountering the inconceivable in *The Outer Limits*. (United Artists, 1963)
Below: David Sheiner, adrift.

Over his ensuing career, Asner would win five Emmy Awards for playing Lou Grant (three for *The Mary Tyler Moore Show* and two for its spinoff series, *Lou Grant*), a sixth Emmy for *Rich Man, Poor Man*, and a seventh for *Roots*. His character here is very one-dimensional (blame the script). You can see Asner play a more interesting villain in "The Night of the Amnesiac," a 1968 episode of *The Wild, Wild West*, and watch him project true terror in "It Crawled Out of the Woodwork," a 1963 episode of *The Outer Limits*.

David Sheiner received $1,500 for playing Josip, Brynov's "trusted" officer, who saves him from the firing squad. He was 36.

In the late 1950s, Sheiner had the lead on Broadway in *Will Success Spoil Rock Hunter?*, which led to many guest-star roles in television, usually as villains and foreign military thugs. He appeared in six episodes of *Mission: Impossible*, five for *The Man from U.N.C.L.E.*, three for *The Six Million Dollar Man*, and was seen twice on *I Spy*, often playing characters like the one seen here. He'd return to *Voyage* for the 1966 episode, "Death Ship."

Harry Davis played Konstantin, Brynov's personal doctor. He was 58, and, among his many guest appearances on TV, including three episodes of *The Man from U.N.C.L.E.* and three for *Mission: Impossible*. Producers who liked David Sheiner seemed to like Davis as well, and, like Sheiner, Davis would be seen in another episode of *Voyage* – in fact, the very same episode – "Death Ship."

James Frawley played Semenev, who spills the beans about Brynov to Nelson, and takes a bullet in the back for doing so. He was 28, and had been seen in the two-part episode of *The Outer Limits*, "The Inheritors," which was directed by Goldstone. Frawley had been seen briefly in "The Price of Doom," and would return for a third *Voyage* – Season Two's "Killers of the Deep." But, as they say, what Frawley really wanted to do was direct … and produce. And this is where he left his mark in Hollywood. Frawley directed 28 episodes of *The Monkees* in 1966, '67 and '68. He won an Emmy for Best Comedy Direction for one – "Royal Flush" – and was nominated for a second – "The Devil and Peter Tork." He directed 12 episodes of *Cagney & Lacey*, six for *Columbo*, and 15 for *Judging*

Amy, which he also produced. Frawley was nominated for a Hugo Award for directing 1979's *The Muppet Movie*.

Jason Wingreen played Mikhil, Brynov's brother. He was 44 and in the middle of an acting career which would bring him roughly 200 TV and film appearances. He'd already been seen in three episodes of *The Twilight Zone*, and three for *The Outer Limits*. Wingreen would appear in four episodes of *The Man from U.N.C.L.E.* and two for its sister show, *The Girl from U.N.C.L.E.* He'd do two episodes of *The Invaders* and show up in a 1968 episode of *Star Trek* ("The Empath"). Wingreen is best known for playing Harry Snowden in 25 episodes of *All in the Family* and another 92 for its spinoff, *Archie Bunker's Place*. But this was his only acting job for Irwin Allen.

Paul Zastupnevich, the series wardrobe designer, as well as overworked assistant to Irwin Allen, makes a cameo as one of the survivors.

Voyage had fallen behind in its delivery of episodes to ABC. It was in danger of missing air dates, which would have both damaged Irwin Allen's relationship with the network and brought severe financial penalties. Something drastic had to be done to get the show ahead in its deliveries. It was decided that this episode and the next ("The Amphibians") would be filmed simultaneously.

This was quite an undertaking. First, the scripts for both episodes had to be sped through the polishing process. In order to "split" the cast for dual production, "The Exile" had to be written to remove Captain Crane and the crew of the Seaview from nearly all of it, allowing Richard Basehart to carry most of this story. At the same time, Admiral Nelson would be excised from most of "The Amphibians," centering that story on Captain Crane and the crew of the Seaview.

This reworking brought a second consideration – where the episodes would be shot. We'd see very little of the Seaview sets on Stage B in "The Exile," allowing "The Amphibians" to mostly be shot there. On the days when the Seaview sets were necessary for "The Exile," "The Amphibians" filmed on Stage 2, on the sets for the XP-1 underwater facility. The only regular cast member needed there – and only briefly – was David Hedison. The two filming units could stay out of one another's way ... provided they kept up with their own schedules.

Day 1: "Int. Yacht Stateroom," with Richard Basehart and Ed Asner (above); David Sheiner with Asner (center); and (below) James Frawley, Sheiner, Jason Wingreen, and Asner.

In addition, cinematographer Carl E. Guthrie would head the camera crew on "The Exile," while Winton Hoch would film "The Amphibians."

Also filming on the 20th Century-Fox lot were the feature films *Do Not Disturb* and *Fantastic Voyage*, as well as the television series *Valentine's Day, 12 O'Clock High, Daniel Boone*, and *Peyton Place*. Now two episodes of *Voyage to the Bottom of the Sea*, simultaneously. It was suddenly a very busy lot.

Filming began on Monday, February 15, 1965, on Fox Stage 4, for the "Int. Yacht Stateroom & Radio Hut." Although the cast was called to the set at 8 a.m., the camera didn't begin rolling until 10:15. Because of the late start, they continued filming until 8:05 p.m., covering 10 and two-eighths pages from the script. Director James Goldstone was working with D.P. Carl E. Guthrie, who always proved slower at lighting the set and pulling the trigger on the camera than Winton Hoch.

Meanwhile, work

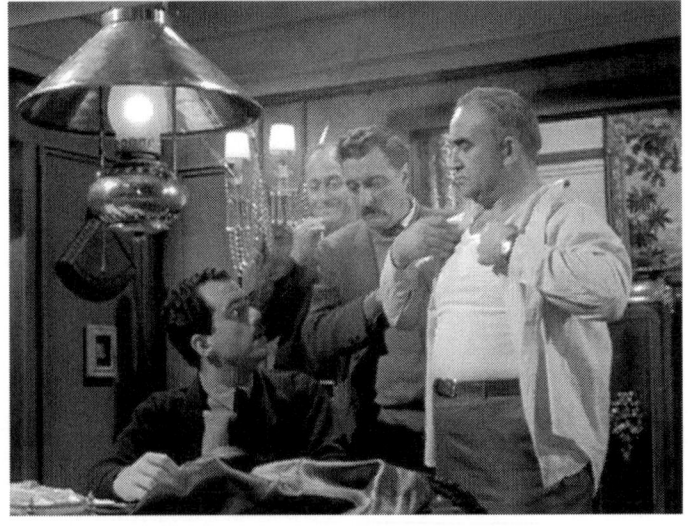

had begun on "The Amphibians," on Stage B with the Seaview sets. Felix Feist was directing there, and he had the ever-reliable Winton Hoch by his side. They commenced production at 8:25 a.m. The race was not only for the two filming units to stay in synch with one another, but to avoid overtime. Those involved with "The Amphibians" took their last shot of the day at 6:45 p.m. and made it home in time to see the broadcast of "The Human Computer" on local ABC affiliate KABC, Channel 7. James Goldstone and Carl Guthrie, working with Richard Basehart on "The Exile," would be later in getting home.

Tuesday and Wednesday were spent on Stage 11 for all the shots of the raft on the open sea. An indoor water tank was used for these sequences, with fog machines and night lighting obscuring the backgrounds. These were the shots in which many cast members had to go into the water.

There were four good reasons why this wasn't filmed outdoors in the Moat. First, the night scenes could be filmed here, even when it was sunny outdoors. Second, the sound was clean, whereas, if filmed on the Moat, most of the dialogue would have to be looped later. Third: The water could be kept warmer for the cast members. Lastly, it was easier to maintain and control the fog. The company filmed until 6:55 p.m. on each day.

James Goldstone said, "All of those guys [in the guest cast] were members of my stock company at the time. That was one of the first shows Ed Asner did after coming out here from Cincinnati. I used David Sheiner and Harry Davis in many other shows. I had worked with Jason Wingreen's kids, and Jimmy Frawley watched me direct some other things and later became a film director. The story was so serious and melodramatic, but the rehearsals were improvised and crazy. It was like the Yiddish Art Theater reborn. We shot on a water tank with six guys on a rubber raft, and they were very uncomfortable. We had fog blowing past and wind machines on them. I would say, 'Okay, guys, into the water. You first, David.' And they were sneezing, coughing, laughing and making sick jokes. Or somebody would yell, 'Get us a towel!' It was absurd." (JG-SLP94)

Thursday, the fourth day of production, was the only day spent filming on the series' home base, Stage B, for the scenes in the Seaview's Control Room, Missile Room, and Sickbay. They had to cover 10 and one-eighth pages from the script, and did so by 6:18 p.m.

On Friday, the company spent the day on Stage 11, again shooting on the raft, this time utilizing a process screen. For many of these scenes, no water was needed. The camera angled up, as the actors sat in the raft, with the sea projected on the screen behind them.

After dinner, and sunset, the company moved outdoors to film the "Ext. Courtyard" scene.

James Goldstone said, "Some of the lines in that show are wonderfully funny. Ed Asner's first line, 'Today you kill me! Tomorrow I kill you!' is hysterical. It belongs on [the pioneering comedy series] *Your Show of Shows*. But it comes off." (JG-SLP94)

A reader of current comic books would also have recognized the humor. In DC's *The Adventures of Bob Hope* #89, cover-dated November 1964, one Roman soldier says to another: "Flavius, I'll make you a deal! You slay me and I'll slay you!"

Above and center: Day 5, the first day of filming the raft against a process screen. Bottom image: After nightfall, the company continued filming at the "Ext. Courtyard" location.

Friday was a long day, beginning with a 6:30 a.m. call time for make-up and lighting crew, then an 8 a.m. call to the set, and not wrapping until 9:45 p.m. The idea was that everyone could sleep in on Saturday.

Monday, February 22, was the sixth day of production, and meant to be the last. It was another day on Stage 11 with the raft, and process shots to create the stormy sea around it. It was clear that director Goldstone would not finish, so filming was stopped at 7 p.m., and the next episode scheduled, "The Creature," was pushed back a day.

522

Meanwhile, work was wrapping up on "The Amphibians." Felix Feist and Winton Hoch had managed to shoot their episode in its allotted six-day schedule. "The Saboteur" aired this night on ABC.

Tuesday, February 23. It took a full seventh day to

Day 6 and 7: Two more full sessions filming the raft against the process screen.

finish "The Exile," with camera beginning its roll at 8:28 a.m. and Goldstone not completing the final shot until 6:55 p.m. Then James Goldstone exited the building, not to return. Decades later, after re-watching the episodes he directed for *Voyage*, Goldstone told interviewer Mark Phillips, "I was very pleased by the avoidance of hokum in the episodes, because the hokum traps in *Voyage* were manifold and infinite. They were pretty well done, and I have to give credit to Irwin Allen. ... If you had asked me a year ago what I thought of *Voyage*, I would have said, 'It was an eminently forgettable show.' Now, having looked at them again, I must say, they're pretty darn good!" (JG-SLP94)

Release / Reaction:
(ABC premiere broadcast: 3/15/65; network repeat airing: 8/9/65)

The Sound of Music had the No. 1 slot at the movie houses, and would continue to sit on top for the next four weeks. The soundtrack to *Goldfinger* was the fastest-selling record album in America, having displaced *Beatles '65*. But America was still experiencing Beatlemania. The Fab Four had the song getting the most radio airplay in the land, with "Eight Days a Week." Michael Landon,

Lorne Greene, Dan Blocker, and Pernell Roberts had the top-rated show on TV, *Bonanza*, and the cover of *TV Guide*.

On March 15, 1965, syndicated "TV Scout," in the *Edwardsville Intelligencer*, serving Edwardsville, Illinois, said:

> There's lots of adventure when Admiral Nelson (Richard Basehart) is cast on a raft with a hostile ex-premier in "The Exile." The big scene in this one is an at-sea explosion. Things become more murky when it's up to Nelson to command his crowded life raft and put up with his passenger, the sinister foreign politician (Edward Asner) who has orders to destroy the free world.

A.C. Nielsen ratings report, March 15, 1965:	Rating:	Share:
7:30 – 8 p.m.:		
ABC: *Voyage to the Bottom of the Sea*	**19.1**	**30.3%**
CBS: *To Tell the Truth*	17.6	27.9%
NBC: *Karen*	16.6	26.3%
8 – 8:30 p.m.		
ABC: *Voyage to the Bottom of the Sea*	19.0	27.0%
CBS: *I've Got a Secret*	17.2	24.4%
NBC: *The Man from U.N.C.L.E.*	**21.8**	**30.9%**

Voyage failed to attract a minimum of a 30% audience share during its second half-hour, losing to *The Man from U.N.C.L.E.* Irwin Allen wasn't worried. He already had his second-season pickup from ABC and a new time slot for the Fall, far away from the agents from U.N.C.L.E.

The morning after "The Exile" aired, Sandra Hinson wrote in her column for *The Orlando Sentinel*:

> *Voyage to the Bottom of the Sea* (ABC) last night had one of its most engrossing episodes to date.
>
> Richard Basehart survived the explosion at sea of a foreign dictator's yacht and found himself a helpless prisoner as ruthless dictator Edward Asner calmly killed off his former political cronies. When the struggle was reduced to only the two main characters, they faced almost unbelievable odds in their attempt to try to rendezvous with the Seaview as they fought out a storm and the heat of the day.

ABC and Irwin Allen liked this one too, and scheduled it for a summer repeat.

Episode 27: "The Amphibians"

(Prod. #7229; first aired Monday, March 8, 1965)
Written by Rik Vollaerts
Directed by Felix Feist
Produced by Irwin Allen
Story Editor: William Welch; Associate Producer: Joseph Gantman
Assistant Story Editor: Al Gail
Co-Starring Skip Homeier and Curt Conway

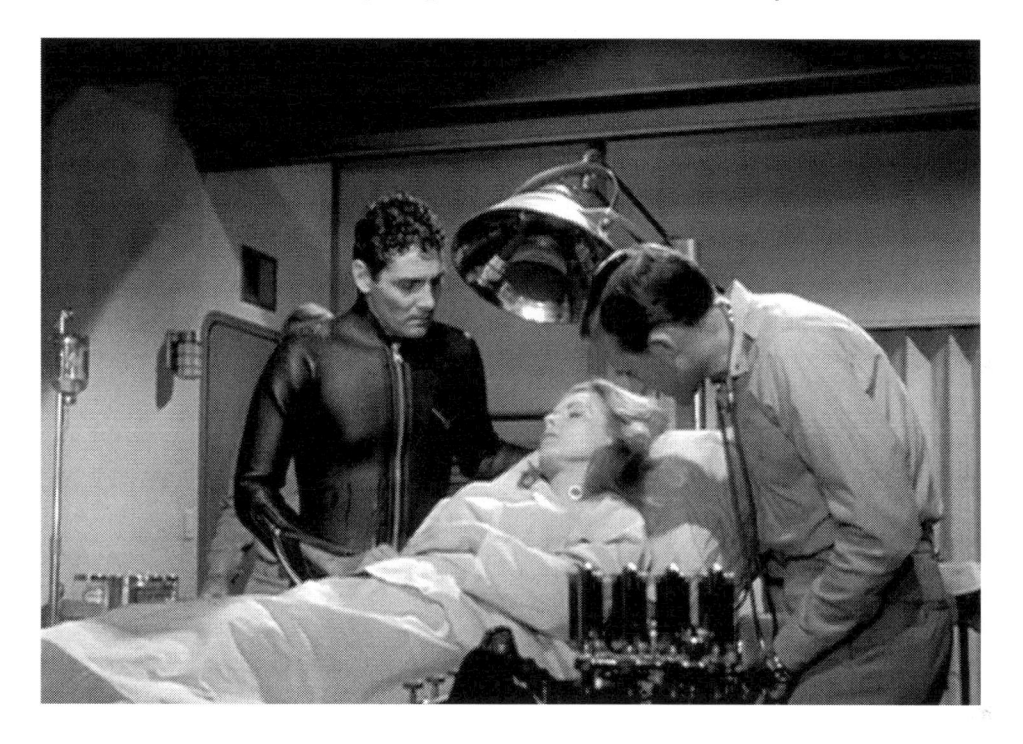

From the *Voyage* show files (Irwin Allen Papers Collection):

Two distinguished scientists have been experimenting with the conversion of air breathing animals into true amphibians. The Nelson Institute is cooperating, unaware that the men have taken a short cut and actually converted themselves into creatures which can breathe underwater. The operation, however, produces a marked change in their minds and they begin to kidnap skin divers, operate on them and change them into amphibians like themselves. When Crane and the Seaview discover the truth, there commences an underwater battle of wits between the men of the submarine and the weird amphibious creatures which used to be men.

Sound Bites:

Dr, Jenkins: "When are we going to stop playing games and let Admiral Nelson know what we've already done, instead of pleading with him to let us do it sometime in the future?" *Dr. Winslow:* "Because I'm not sure of what we've done. I don't know what side effects all these chemicals and medical changes in the human body will cause." *Jenkins:* "Well, do you feel any real difference?" *Winslow:* "No, but I've observed changes in you. You're not the same man you were when we entered the XP1 for the first time." *Jenkins:* "No, and neither are you. Doctor, you're an amphibian. And I might say I've done as expert a job on you as you did on me." *Winslow:* "I'm talking about the mind; the brain. Do the courses of injections change the nervous tissue?" *Jenkins:* "Well, you know it does. I'm more alert. My mind seems to have expanded; to have opened up."

Assessment:

Jenkins's belief that the injections have improved his alertness and expanded his mind is typical of many drug abusers. At this time – early 1965 – many individuals, including teachers and students in universities, and even movie stars, like Cary Grant, and self-acclaimed messiahs, such as Dr. Timothy Leary, were experimenting with LSD, convinced that it expanded their minds. Others warned, "Expand your mind, but don't blow it." Users of marijuana and cocaine also claimed that the narcotic enhanced their ability to think … or perhaps it merely enlarged their egos. This episode of *Voyage* makes a very "establishment" argument – that experimenting with drugs can mess you up. In this story's case, the Establishment was clearly correct!

It all makes for a thought-provoking and entertaining hour. And if you like a little titillation, the lovely, talented, and agile Zale Parry adds greatly to the episode. Her underwater acrobatics are first-rate, contributing both eye-pleasing and eerie moments to the story. This episode has something for everyone.

Script:
Rik Vollaerts's writers contract: January 28, 1965.
Vollaerts's treatment and 1st and 2nd draft teleplays: Approved on February 9.
Mimeo Department's reformatted Shooting Final teleplay (pale green paper): February 8.
Rev. Shooting Final teleplay, by William Welch or Al Gail (yellow paper): February 11.
Page revisions by writing staff (green paper): February 12.

This was the first of six *Voyage* scripts written by Rik Vollaerts. He was 45 and had been working in TV since 1950, with multiple assignments on *My Hero* (with 13 scripts), *I Led 3 Lives* (6 scripts), *Science Fiction Theatre* (4),

Whirlybirds (5), *Harbor Command* (6), *Highway Patrol* (12), *M Squad* (6), *The Deputy* (4) and *Lawman* (4). Most were half-hour shows produced on the quick-and-cheap by ZIV Productions, a company that wasn't looking to win any Emmys. Vollaerts, by his own résumé, was a TV hack. He would categorize himself and his material that way in a 1968 letter he wrote after finishing his sixth *Voyage*, sent to Gene Roddenberry at *Star Trek*:

> I would appreciate an opportunity to meet with you on two matters. One, to submit material for *Star Trek*, and two, to discuss with you my desire to get off the treadmill of writing hack material for TV and getting on the other side of the desk.

Vollaerts had heard that *Star Trek* had a staff position to fill, looking for a new story editor for its third season. He wanted the job, and told Roddenberry:

> One reason I persist in trying to write a script for *Star Trek* is a rather obvious one – [your series is] a damn sight better than most, even when it makes its bows to the network or the advertising agencies and lowers its standards a little. ... So raise a glass to ZIV and *Mr. District Attorney* and let's meet. I know talking to you will be helpful to me, and I might be helpful to you by delivering a damn solid *Star Trek*. (RV-ST68)

Vollaerts would not get the story editor job, but he did deliver a fairly solid script, "For the World Is Hollow and I Have Touched the Sky." But for now, he was working for Irwin Allen's "hack" machine.

Calvin Ward of ABC responded to Vollaerts' script on February 9, 1965:

> Page 6: The injection will as usual be off-camera or covered.
>
> Page 10: Winslow's third line: delete "mother's womb." ...
>
> Page 19: Morton's first line: delete "Good Lord in heaven."
>
> Page 57, Scene 86: Do not show the spear striking Jenkins; also, the spear must not "penetrate him clear through" as described. Can be approved only on film.

Of course, the injection was never shown. And both "mother's womb" and "Good Lord in heaven" were dropped. And, while the divers from the Seaview carried spear guns, they didn't use them. Instead, Jenkins would meet his match with an electrified field around the Seaview.

More from Calvin Ward:

> Page 63: Nelson's second line: Nelson might consider that breaking the law and violating scientific procedure are both equally bad, but he must not say that anything is worse than breaking the law.
>
> Page 64: A casual agreement between Nelson and the Sheriff about Winslow's mental responsibility is not enough. We must know that Winslow will pay the full penalty for the crimes before being permitted to return to his research.

The Sheriff was dropped, helping keep the budget in line. In his place, Nelson suggested to Dr. Winslow that the surgery that made him into an amphibian, and corrupted his thinking, and his morality, might be reversed. Winslow doubted that it could. And this prompted the closing line, from Nelson, that Winslow better pray that he is wrong.

One day later, and before even seeing the memo from ABC, Irwin Allen delivered his own notes on the same draft to Welch, Gail, and Gantman:

> P. 1, Sc. 4: Winslow's last speech, re: "The two of us, at the bottom of the sea." This line is negative and not proper to the events that follow. Would it be possible for Jenkins and Winslow to mention that they have been there 3 months at the time of the teaser. ...
>
> P. 10: Is it necessary to include the phrase "in his mother's womb" in Winslow's second speech? I question the advisability of stating the scientific theory of evolution of man as undisputed fact. Winslow could say, "According to scientific belief, etc.," as this statement might prove controversial. ...
>
> First Act has many repetitive lines between Winslow and Jenkins. There is virtually no action in this act.

The repetition remained. And no action was added. William Welch and Al Gail – the two story editors – chose to ignore Allen's comments. And, while it was not his job to make script changes, Joseph Gantman ignored this specific note from Allen as well. Tony Wilson often ignored Allen's notes over at *Lost in Space* as well.

ABC program director Lew Hunter commented, "While Irwin's associate producers and script editors always struck me as 'yes men,' they also really knew how to handle him. They all knew exactly the breaking point with him, and they would back off the minute that was coming up. They would meet with Irwin and say, 'Yeah, yeah, Irwin, that's great.' Then they would go ahead and do it their way. And Irwin wouldn't remember what he had asked for, and wouldn't know that he wasn't seeing what he had asked for." (LW-AI15)

But, in this instance, Allen was right about the preponderance of talk. The first act of "The Amphibians" is indeed redundant, with three separate dialogue scenes between Dr. Winslow and Dr. Jenkins. Each time they debate the same issue, with little new information. Welch and Gail should have harkened, in this case.

Production:
(Filmed February 15-22, 1965; 6 days)
(Budget: $120,807)

Felix Feist returned to direct, on his fifth of six assignments.

Skip Homeier had appeared in *Fixed Bayonets!*, which starred Richard Basehart. He was 34 here, and had been playing villains since a teen, when he made his film debut as a "Hitler Youth" who embraces Nazism in 1944's *Tomorrow the World*. Other notable menacing characters included 1950's *The Gunfighter* (as Gregory Peck's nemesis), 1954's *Cry Vengeance* (as an albino hitman), and 1956's *Stranger at My Door* (as a bank robber). Homeier got to play a good guy in his own series, as a police lieutenant – the title character in 1960's *Dan Raven*. But the actor made great Nazis, playing them again on *Combat!*, and even on *Star Trek* (1968's

Skip Homeier had a long string of villains in his film career, beginning with his first role, as a Nazi youth, seen here taking a knife to Betty Field, in *Tomorrow the World*.
(United Artists, 1944)

"Patterns of Force"). He was also good playing non-Nazi power mad nut-jobs, as he did in a second *Star Trek* episode (1969's "The Way to Eden"). And he played

Jekyll-and-Hyde type in the 1964 *The Outer Limits* episode, "The Expanding Human." *Voyage* tapped him to play a couple of more villains, in 1966's "The Day the World Ended" and 1968's "Attack!" You can see Homeier play comedy – and quite nicely – in the 1979 TV Movie, *The Wild, Wild West Revisited*.

For the role of Dr. Jenkins, Homeier was paid $1,000 to swim around in the Green Tank. The deal was based for a three-day commitment. He and Curt Conway were given equal "co-starring" billing.

Curt Conway played Dr. Winslow. He was 51, back in the day when 51 looked more like 61. He received more money than Homeier – $1,250 – and was needed for more days of production, appearing on the XP-1 set, as well as Stage B's Seaview set, where Homeier never set foot. Conway had appeared on *The Twilight Zone*, as Adolph Hitler, in the 1963 episode "He's Alive." He made two trips into the *Outer Limits*, and was about to begin appearing in 17 episodes of *Peyton Place* as Judge Jessup. Conway was pretty convincing as a judge, and sat behind the bench in episodes of *Dr. Kildare*, *Rawhide*, *Judd for the Defense*, *Cannon*, *The Odd Couple*, among other series, and in numerous movies.

Above: Curt Conway in an episode of *The Outer Limits*. (United Artists, 1964)
Below: Zale Parry with Lloyd Bridges in *Sea Hunt*. (Ziv Television, 1958-61)

Zale Parry was hired as the amphibian diver Angie Maxxon because of her stunning looks and underwater swimming ability. Her $600 salary didn't require any dialogue, although she did gasp a few times. In 1954 she'd set the woman's depth record of 209 feet (because she hit bottom). She had the cover of

Sports Illustrated on May 23, 1955, and made her screen debut in the 1954 TV series *Kingdom of the Sea,* which led to her appearing in seven episodes of *Sea Hunt,* usually as an underwater damsel-in-distress. Parry was an avid underwater photographer, and, in 1960, was the first woman president of the Underwater Photographic Society.

Parry praised this *Voyage* episode as the cutting edge of science. She told Mark Phillips, "The story was very up-to-date by presenting people with mechanical gills that oxygenated the breathing medium for underwater swimmers. I enjoyed doing the show. It was a very friendly and courteous cast and crew. The makeup of our mechanical gills were circular screens of bezel, attached to our throats by an adhesive. The only thing I didn't like about the show was they made my character mute!" (ZP-VTTBOTS)

There was no reason, as far as the story was concerned, for Angie to be mute. The surgery to turn one of us into one of them didn't rob Dr. Jenkins and Dr. Winslow of the ability to speak. Why, then, do their underlings never speak? And when Angie is on the Seaview, in sickbay, she does cry out – therefore, she has a voice. The answer was simple economy – a nonspeaking character was cheaper.

Frank Graham played the other amphibian swimmer. He too was silent.

As discussed earlier, *Voyage* had fallen behind on delivering episodes to ABC and was in danger of missing its air dates. For this reason, it was decided to film this episode simultaneously with "The Exile."

Filming began on Monday, February 15, 1965 with Felix Feist in the director's chair and Winton Hoch as Director of Photography, the same day that work started on "The Exile." While that episode filmed on Stage 4 with Richard Basehart and a group of guest players, Feist and Hoch had the bulk of the regular cast and the Seaview sets on Stage B.

Feist took his last shot of the day at 6:45 p.m., enabling David Hedison to get home in time to see the ABC premiere of "The Human Computer" at 7:30 p.m., an episode which focused on Captain Crane.

Day 2: Filming in the Missile Room with Dowdell and Basehart. Meanwhile (below), a Second Unit team filmed in the green tank with the divers. Zale Parry (below) also was filmed underwater off the coast of Long Beach.

Day 2: Tuesday, February 16. Feist split his company in two, filming with the Main Unit on Stage B, for scenes in the Seaview's Control Room and Missile Room. Meanwhile, a smaller Second Unit filmed in the Green Tank, with underwater sequences featuring Zale Parry and Frank Graham, as well as stunt doubles John Lamb, Paul Stader, George Robotham, Peter Peterson, and Peter Dixon. Stader was also director of the Second Unit, and Lamb ran the underwater camera (except when he was featured as a stunt double).

Despite utilizing professional divers and stuntmen, the underwater sequences were not always risk-free. When interviewed for *Science Fiction Television Series*, George Robotham recalled one such close call: "Paul Stader and I were in the water tank at Fox. We were playing Seaview divers snared by the net. We got totally entangled in the thing. We sank to the bottom, stuck. Our air was running low, and Paul and I exchanged looks of, 'Well, where do we go from here?' The special effects guy, Glen Galvin, finally hauled us up to the surface. It was a little on the life-threatening side!" (GR-SCTS2)

The Main Unit filmed until 6:20 p.m., while the Second Unit took their last shot at 7. "The Exile," meanwhile, was filming on Fox Stage 11, creating a rare situation when *Voyage* had three separate units filming on the lot on the same day.

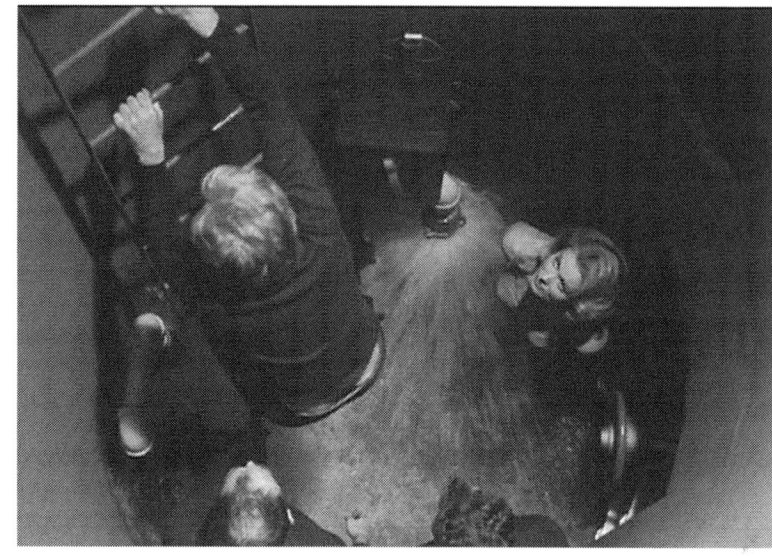

Day 3: Wednesday. Another day of running two separate units for this production (and a third for "The Exile"). Feist worked with Hoch and the regular cast on Stage B for "Int. Missile Room," "Int. Stern Escape Hatch Compartment" and "Int. Sick Bay," while Paul Stader and John Lamb filmed stunt sequences in the Green Tank.

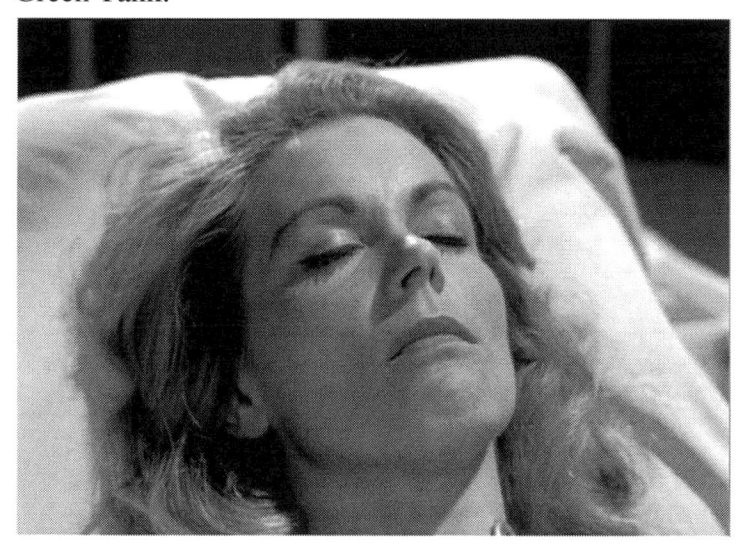

Day 3 included a look into the "Int. Stern Escape Hatch" and "Int. Sick Bay," with Zale Parry.

The shots from the "Int. Stern Escape Hatch Compartment" are especially impressive. We had never been given this inside look before, as the compartment fills with water and those within wait for the pressure to equalize so that the upper hatch can open.

"The Exile," meanwhile, needing only Richard Basehart and that episode's guest players, continued to film on Stage 11. Feist filmed "The Amphibians" until 8:05.

Day 4: Thursday. Again, Paul Stader and John Lamb led the Second Unit in the Green Tank, filming Zale Parry and Frank Graham swimming underwater without benefit of scuba gear. Reginald Parton doubled for David Hedison in the swimming sequences. Meanwhile, the Main Unit filmed on Stage 2 with the XP-1

533

Above: **Skip Homeier and Curt Conway had the "XP-1" Sea Lab set all to themselves, for Day 4 of the production. Below: Days 5 & 6 included other cast members on the Sea Lab sets.**

set (surgery and aquarium), needing only Skip Homeier and Curt Conway. Meanwhile, the unit assigned to "The Exile" had Basehart, Hedison, and the crew of the Seaview, on the Seaview sets on Stage B.

The Second Unit also did some filming off the coast of Catalina, in order to utilize Zale Parry. She told Terry Yermon of "Tele-Vues" in the Long Beach *Independent*: "It's the beauty of the ocean that attracts me. The kelp forests around channel islands off the Southern California coast are beyond description.."

Zale said that Florida and the Bahamas were popular locations for undersea filming because the water was clear and easier to work in. She added, "But the real under-sea excitement is in Southern California." (ZP-I65)

Day 5: Friday. Filming continued on Stage 2 and the XP-1 underwater facility set. Hedison joined Homeier and Conway on this day. The unit filming

"The Exile," meanwhile, took Richard Basehart and moved on to Stage 11, as well as some exterior shots on the Fox lot. Since it was Friday, and no one was needed for work the next day, "The Exile" filmed until 9:45 p.m. "The Amphibians" filmed until 8 p.m.

Day 6: Monday, February 22. Director Feist and cinematographer Hoch were able to get it all done, finishing their segment on this sixth day of production, with a third day of filming on Stage 2 with the XP-1 set, as well as close-up shots of Hedison in swimming gear, taken in the Green Tank. James Goldstone's unit was not as fortunate, filming "The Exile" on Stage 11 with Richard Basehart. It would need a seventh day of production, requiring that the next episode, "The Creature," would begin without Basehart's participation on Tuesday.

Days 5 & 6 on the XP-1 Sea Lab set.

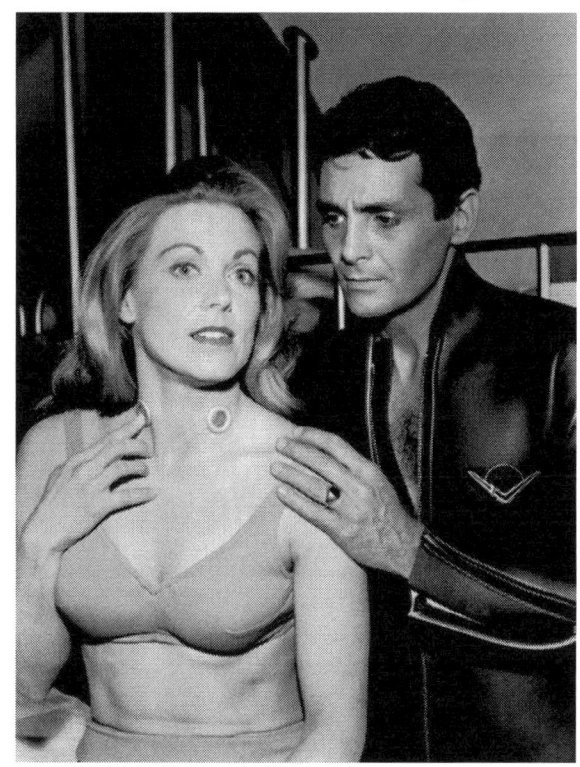

Photo caption in countless newspapers: "David Hedison discovers in Zale Parry, a young lady who has been scientifically converted into a creature who lives and breathes beneath the water, in 'The Amphibians,' on *Voyage to the Bottom of the Sea* tonight, at ____ on Ch. ___."

Release / Reaction:
(ABC premiere broadcast: 3/8/65;
network repeat airing: 8/2/65)

On the day that "The Amphibians" premiered on ABC, the first U.S. combat troops arrived in Vietnam, as 3,500 Marines landed at China Beach to defend the American air base at Da Nang. They were joining 23,000 American military "advisors" already there. Meanwhile, America thrilled to a

535

musical invasion. The Beatles had the top song on the radio, with "Eight Days a Week." Their most recent album, *Beatles '65*, however, had just been displaced from the No. 1 spot on *Billboard* by the soundtrack to *Mary Poppins*, featuring Julie Andrews. In addition, Andrews was in the current top film at the movie houses – *The Sound of Music*. She also graced the cover of *Life* magazine. But she didn't have the cover of *TV Guide*. That honor went to David Janssen, *The Fugitive*.

For a syndicated newspaper article profiling David Hedison, carried by *The North Adams Transcript* on August 14, 1965, entertainment correspondent Erskine Johnson wrote:

> It's one of the Hollywood imponderables that Hollywood keeps pondering – the fact that one of its handsomest young leading men never gets the girl. David Hedison is the man. Tall, dark and single, he is an obvious bet to set feminine hearts a-fluttering, and in his private life there is considerable amount of fluttering going on. But not in the scripts of ABC-TV's *Voyage to the Bottom of the Sea* in which he plays Cmdr. Crane. Girls, obviously, do not fit into life on an atomic-powered submarine.

Hedison told Johnson, "Sure, I'm frustrated. I keep mentioning the lack of pretty young things in the plot and the producer keeps promising a story with an Embassy party where I could wear a dinner jacket, a blonde on one hand and a martini in the other. But I'm still waiting."

Johnson wrote:

> There was a gleam in his eyes, he laughs, when he heard mention of a plot in which a foreign agent turns out to be a sexy blonde. Then he read the script. The show's fantasy minded writers had dreamed up a feminine Flipper, a girl who could breathe under water as the result of a throat operation which equipped her with gills. The plot has her busy on the outside of the submarine, trying to blow it up. Hedison felt like blowing up, too, when one of his fellow actors kidded him, "Well, you're finally getting a girl in the script. What are they going to title the show, 'Gill Meets Boy.'" (DH-NAT65)

Syndicated "TV Scout," in the March 8, 1965 edition of the *Monessen Valley Independent*, said:

> Here's another deep water science fiction mystery called "The Amphibians." Two scientists (Skip Homeier and Curt

Conway) discover a way to turn men into "fish," complete with gills. They experiment on themselves and cover up their secrets by wearing high turtle neck sweaters. All goes well until they become greedy and begin capturing scuba divers (including pretty Zale Parry) and equipping them with gills, too. The Seaview, in this wild adventure, enters the scene when their creatures became more foul than fish.

Steven Scheuer, for "TV Key," in other newspapers across America, was more interested in the feminine angle. He included a publicity photo sent out by ABC-TV and added:

> A beautiful girl has been scientifically converted into an underwater creature who lives and breathes beneath the waters.

One can only wonder if Scheuer noticed that Skip Homeier could also breathe underwater.

A.C. Nielsen ratings report, March 8, 1965:	Rating:	Share:
7:30 – 8 p.m.:		
ABC: *Voyage to the Bottom of the Sea*	21.4	31.2%
CBS: *To Tell the Truth*	18.8	27.4%
NBC: *Karen*	**19.1**	**37.9%**
8 – 8:30 p.m.		
ABC: *Voyage to the Bottom of the Sea*	21.0	29.4%
CBS: *I've Got a Secret*	19.3	27.0%
NBC: *The Man from U.N.C.L.E.*	**22.7**	**31.8%**

It had taken several months, but *The Man from U.N.C.L.E.* had finally surpassed *Voyage to the Bottom of the Sea* in Nielsen's ratings. On this night, while *Voyage* was swimming with amphibians, *The Man from U.N.C.L.E.* aired an episode concerned with mind control, like *Voyage*'s "The Saboteur" from a month before. In "The Brain Killer Affair," guest star Elsa Lanchester plays a mad scientist out to operate on the brain of Mr. Waverly, the boss of U.N.C.L.E. Her purpose? Turn him into a puppet under Thrush control.

Meanwhile, the rough draft of the ABC schedule for 1965-66 suggested a shift for Irwin Allen's sci-fi series ... from Monday to Sunday night, and from 7:30 p.m. to the earlier-than-primetime 7 p.m. slot. It might be considered a step down in prestige for the series, but, considering its young audience, perhaps just what *Voyage* needed.

Episode 28: "The Creature"

(Prod. #7230; first aired Monday, March 22, 1965)
Written by Rik Vollaerts
Directed by Sobey Martin
Produced by Irwin Allen
Story Editor: William Welch; Associate Producer: Joseph Gantman
Assistant Story Editor: Al Gail
Guest Star Leslie Nielsen

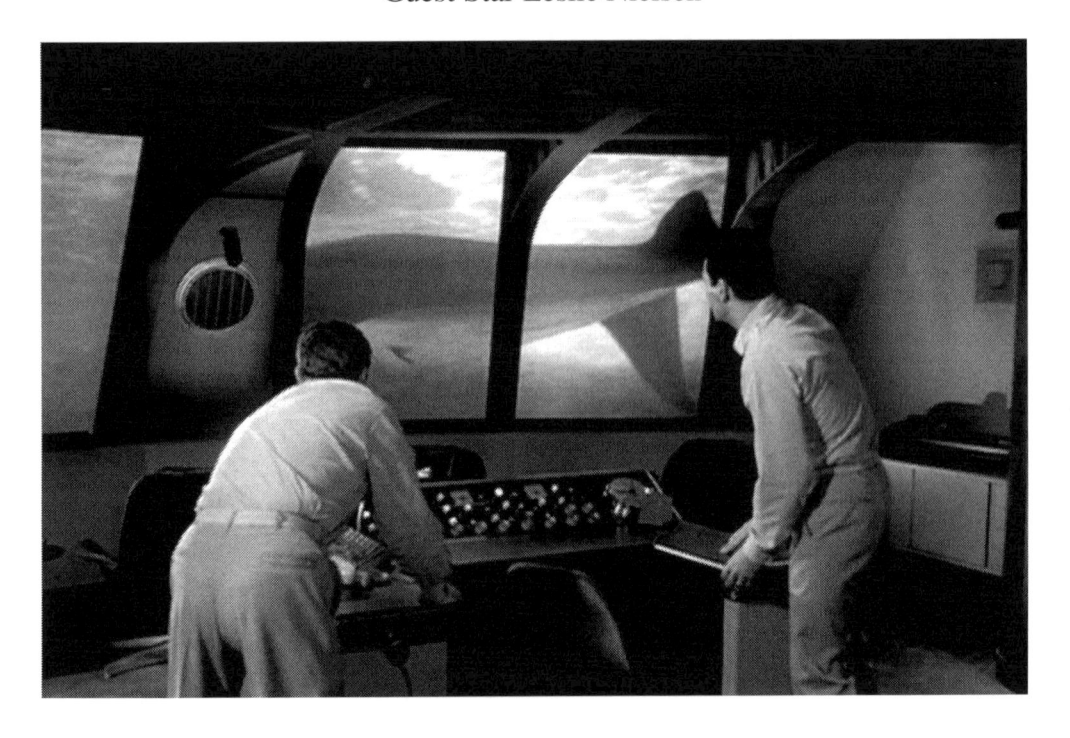

From the *Voyage* show files (Irwin Allen Papers Collection):

A gigantic Manta Ray emits supersonic cries which upset the electronic balance of a missile firing, causing a fatal blast. Seaview investigates, discovers the giant and finds itself in a battle to the death with the menacing creature.

Sound Bites:

Capt. Adams (as Nelson enters the lab ... followed by Crane): "Admiral. ... *(less welcoming)* ... Oh, you too, Captain. Come on in. ... *(to Nelson)* ... I've discovered the source of our sound. It originates with a herd of porpoises, as I suspected. Look, this is what we hear ... *(indicated oscillator)* ... the audible. ... *(indicating sonar)* ... This is what we don't hear – ultrasound." *Crewman's voice over intercom:* "This is sonar, Captain." *Crane:* "Yes." *Crewman's voice:* "The sound on our present bearing is a herd of porpoises. ... *(dryly)* ... We're following porpoises." *Crane (guarded irritation):* "I know. Hold bearing. Carry on. ... *(to*

Adams) ... How long are we going to stay on this course?" *Adams:* "Captain, I intend to investigate every source of sound in the area that could possibly go into the ultrasound range." *Crane (exchanges a subtle look of frustration with Nelson, then):* "Yes, Captain." *Nelson (after Crane exits):* "Adams, having us track a herd of porpoises seems to be a waste of our time ... and yours." *Adams:* "Well, we're not now, Admiral. We've tracked them long enough to rule them out. The intensity of the ultrasonic they produce is not strong enough." *Nelson:* "Well, why didn't you tell Captain Crane that? After all, he's commanding the ship." *Adams:* "As a bus driver is in command of a bus."

Assessment:

Nowadays, we're familiar with Leslie Nielsen as the poker-faced, mechanically melodramatic Lt. Frank Drebin in TV's *Police Squad!*, and three big-screen *Naked Gun* movies. With that great comic legacy in mind, you may find that some of the scenes in this episode provoke laughter. It's almost as if Nielsen, an excellent actor, were preparing an audition for the Zucker brothers. And that can't help but detract from the drama.

But in 1965, no one had imagined *Police Squad!* or *The Naked Gun*, or the Zucker's *Airplane!* movies, also featuring Nielsen. "The Creature" made for engaging TV fare.

There are traces of *Moby Dick*'s Captain Ahab, as Nielsen's Captain Wayne Adams obsesses over finding the creature which destroyed his command, and tarnished his reputation. Instead of a giant whale, we get a giant stingray. The concept of stingrays using ultrasound to fight back against man, while implausible, is nevertheless intriguing. And downright entertaining.

What makes "The Creature" a *Voyage* worth taking are the astonishing visual effects – beyond state of the art for their time. Just as the battle sequences between the big whale and the sub in "The Ghost of Moby Dick" were visually stunning, so are these, between the giant stingray and the Seaview. Set this episode's effects sequences against anything made during this period, for TV or films – you'd be hard-pressed to find special effects visuals that are as wondrous and effectively dramatic. Hats off to L.B. Abbott and his technical wizards.

Prepare yourself!

Script:

Rik Vollaerts's writers contract: February 9, 1965.
Vollaerts's treatment and 1st and 2nd draft teleplays: Dates unknown.
Mimeo Department's reformatted Shooting final reformatted teleplay: Date unknown.
Rev. Shooting Final teleplay, by William Welch or Al Gail (on yellow paper):
February 22.
Page revisions by writing staff (on blue paper): February 23.

Page revisions (on pink paper): February 26.
Page revisions (on gold paper): March 1.
Page revisions (on beige paper): March 2.

Come February 25, 1965, Irwin Allen was mortified by William Welch's Revised Shooting Final teleplay, from three days earlier. Problems which had been discussed during various meetings in Irwin Allen's office had not been properly addressed, and production for the episode had already begun – also two days earlier.

Among the four pages of single-spaced notes Irwin Allen wrote on February 25, 1965 to Joseph Gantman and William Welch:

> P. 2, Sc. 3: This scene's dialogue must be carefully checked for:
>
> 1. Countdown time is wrong.
> 2. Adams appears to be speaking to Station 8 in his 3rd speech, page 2 – yet he asks a second man (Speech 4) if he has heard anything from the tracking stations. This needs clarifying. Adams then says "Zero minus 2 minutes thirty seconds" – however his previous speeches 1 & 2, P. 2, are as follows: "Zero minus one minute and counting" and "Zero minus 50 sec." Something is wrong.
>
> Please check facts on sonar equipment, re: can sonar be recorded from above water as in scene on island. ...
>
> P. 3: If Scene 3 has not been shot yet – consider the possibility of having a man whose voice (and/or face) is heard and seen doing official countdown in background, as I cannot believe that the operation is so small as to preclude this most important position.
>
> Certainly someone other than Adams should say:
> "Zero minus 30 and counting"
> "Zero minus 20 and counting"
> "Zero minus 10 and counting"
> "9, 8, 7, 6, 5, 4, 3, 2, 1 – Explosion!"
> Audiences are too well acquainted with proper procedure from actual blastoffs to overlook it on a TV show.
>
> All men except Adams (who obviously survives) should be obviously buried in debris.

Allen was right, of course. The scene was rewritten and several additional cast members were added, along with all the new and flashy computer consoles made for the recent *Lost in Space* pilot. The explosion, with a wall bursting in and debris burying the men, was beautifully handled.

Allen's notes continued:

> ACT I, P. 4, Sc. 7: It should not be necessary for Seaview to be above water in order to search areas by means of radar – as Nelson explains. Nelson should refer to Adams as "Mr. Adams" or whatever his proper title is. Captain? Just plain Adams seems impolite at first hearing of his name.
>
> P. 4, Sc. 7... If Seaview is cruising on surface at beginning of Act I – someone should be topside to report that the area is clear before orders to dive are given. Or, telescope should be used, not radar alone. If radar alone is being used, then Seaview should be between 50 and 75 feet below sea level, which would be a less expensive shot (taken from stock).
>
> P. 5, Sc. 10: Talk of course 215 in relation to depth of 4000 ft., Page 6, is very confusing. Can this be clarified? ...
>
> P. 7, Sc. 13: Crane asks Adams "How long are we going to stay on this course?" Adams' answer is not really an answer to his question at all, yet Crane says, "Yes, sir." Yes, Sir, what? And why does he say "sir" when talking to Adams?
>
> P. 8, Sc. 13: Nelson's reply to Adams' last speech, Page 7 – seems to be an attempt to reprimand Adams who, (no matter how sarcastically his lines are read) has not said anything which calls for this type of dialogue. It seems to me this whole scene 13 needs a rewrite if it is to serve as a set-up for animosity between Adams and Crane and Nelson. If everyone was bitingly over-polite, it might help. But all dialogue should follow a logical course in order to make sense.
>
> Adams sounds like an idiot who doesn't know what he's doing because, without further investigation of the sound he's recording he says the porpoises weren't strong enough to produce the intensity of ultrasonics necessary to explode a missile. Nelson sounds like he's talking to a child instead of a scientist and Captain in the Navy.

> P. 10, Sc. 17: Morton says, "Not one living thing moving in the water out there!" This is quite a statement! How can he ascertain this from the TV screen?? Perhaps the TV scanner would be better to use.

The scenes were rewritten, and much improved. This memo illustrates that when Allen was focused on only one series, his notes could be very helpful. He may have had a tendency to resist probing his characters, and using clichés in dialogue to help the audience – especially a young audience – to quickly grasp the characterizations and situations. Nonetheless, he had a good sense for pacing, dramatics, and military formalities. Regarding the latter, is it surprising that Allen, who never served in the military, was so astute when it came to formalities between the ranks, and military jargon (especially in respect to submarines). Then again, Allen, a vivacious reader, absorbed information voraciously.

Joseph Gantman echoed many of Allen's thoughts in his own lengthy memo:

> 1. P. 4 – The reason for friction between Adams and Crane is silly. (Crane ordered a radar search of the surface before the submarine submerges). A possible reason for friction, which is only hinted at a couple of times in lines, is Adams' guilt or anger at being blamed for the death of his men.
> 2. P. 5-8 – These pages are difficult for me to follow just in terms of information, but especially in terms of character. Why is Nelson the tool of Adams (who isn't making much sense)? Nelson is working for the Navy who has said something about a "device." Why would he go chasing porpoises?
> 3. P. 14-15 – Scenes in laboratory (now between Adams, Nelson, Crane) could take place between Morton and Nelson. Then it would be Morton and Nelson who see the Manta while Crane and Adams are still out in the water trying to get back to the sub. This way the end of Act One would have two lives in jeopardy instead of just viewing the Manta at the window.
> 4. ...
> 5. P. 22 – The laboratory scene is just padding.
> 6. P. 23 – Control room – just padding. And the men don't know about the small manta's being aboard?
> 7. P. 24 – This laboratory scene as now written is mostly padding. The scene could be written with the

suspense of will the experiment work. Are they on the right track.
8. P. 26-27 – Why doesn't the Seaview destroy the giant manta or at least make the attempt. Research could be done with smaller ones. What was the Seaview's mission anyway?
9. P. 27-28 – Nelson-Crane scene. Unfortunately Nelson is taking a ridiculous position with no cause. What was the Seaview's mission anyway?
10. P. 28-29 – Nelson-Adams scene: Why doesn't Nelson heed his own words? <u>What was the Seaview's mission anyway</u>?
11. P. 29B – Is Adams <u>mad</u> by this time? The klaxon is sounding and he's talking to the baby manta. He's pretty far gone.
12. P. 31 – Adams should not stand by acquiescent while the baby manta is flushed out of the sub – And then go on and on about why it should not have been done. Let him put up some fight to stop it and let Nelson make a decision that it be done in spite of Adams.
13. ...
14. ...
15. P. 34 – Nelson is now interested in the manta ray, and Adams says "think about the missiles"???? Still no thought of destroying the giant manta. <u>What was the Seaview's mission</u>?
16. P. 39A – Doesn't Nelson or someone know by now that Adams is pretty far gone?
17. P. 40 – Crane-Nelson in the corridor is like an Abbot & Costello scene.
18. P. 47 – If Nelson is going to get a sudden idea from nowhere on connecting the "scramafram" to something else, and it works, what does this do to Adams' experiments and doesn't he react? (possible scene) Wouldn't it be better if Nelson can cleverly do something to stop Adams and this stops the Manta?
19. P. 52-55 – These four pages of dialogue we have had a few times by now. It holds up the show.
20. P. 62 – "Adams got carried away with his curiosity"??? What happened to any guilt feeling or anger Adams may have had about 20 dead men?

By the tone – and the questions – of Gantman's memo, one could easily get the impression that this was the first time he'd read the script – a script that was already being filmed. Of course, this was not possible. As the line producer,

Gantman would have had a hand in "breaking the script down," preparing it for production. Clearly, he had read it, if only to determine the production requirements. But it was only when writing this memo that he seemed to have actually paid attention to much of the dialogue. This was the assembly-line grind of episodic TV in the 1960s, with a standard full-season order comprising 32 hour-long episodes. By Episode 28 – which happened to be "The Creature" – things began to blur together. The first thing to go out the window was sometimes the interior logic of a story.

Production:
(Filmed February 23 through March 2, 1965; 6 days)
(Budget: $127,465)

Sobey Martin was hired to direct. It was his fifth episode.

Leslie Nielsen was paid $2,500 to guest star as Captain Wayne Adams. He was 38 and, at this time, already a star on television. He was the title character in "The Swamp Fox," a recurring series within a series, from 1959 through 1961 on *Walt Disney Presents*, and star of a weekly series of his own, as Lt. Price Adams in *The New Breed* (1961-62). Nielsen had third billing in *Forbidden Planet*, playing spaceship Commander Adams. He would go on to play John Bracken, the head of a motion-picture studio, in the 1970 Fox series *Bracken's World*, before returning to work for producer Irwin Allen again – as the Captain of the doomed S.S. Poseidon in 1972's *The Poseidon Adventure*. Nielsen found his true calling in comedy, with the *Airplane!* movies, then comedy superstardom as Detective Frank Drebin in the TV series *Police Squad!* and its big-screen *Naked Gun* movie series.

Leslie Nielsen as the Captain of the space cruiser in *Forbidden Planet*. (MGM, 1958)

Nigel McKeand sat in for the role of "Sonar" in this episode. He was a guest player on numerous TV shows in the 1960s, but aspired to be a writer and producer. He went on to be nominated for three Emmys for his scripts and production on the 1970s series, *Family*. He was also a busy writer for *The Waltons*. He told interviewer Mark Phillips, "It was a strange experience. Associate Producer Joseph Gantman asked me to audition. I knew nothing about the show and I wasn't a science fiction buff. My character didn't even have a name. He just sat there, looking at the sonar screen. My best line was usually, 'There is a monster dead ahead!' At the end of the day I'd collect my paycheck and leave. I knew some of the other actors on the show were unhappy; they wanted their roles expanded. That wasn't a frustration for me because I knew I was going to get out of acting. *Voyage* was popular but they ran out of steam with the monsters. [But] the cast was always a pleasure to work with." (NM-TVC99)

Filming began on Tuesday, February 23, 1965, for the first of six days on Stage B. Director Sobey Martin stayed on course, although dipping into overtime each day between 30 and 90 minutes. The longest day was the last. They actually

545

began filming at 7:28 a.m. in hopes of getting ahead, but were kept late anyway, with the last shot completed at 8 p.m.

On Thursday, the third day of production, a Second Unit team filmed for nine hours in the Green Tank while the Main Unit worked on Stage B, on the Control Room set. Preston Patterson handled the underwater camera for the Second Unit, while Carl Guthrie used a second camera, filming through the glass window. The men in the wetsuits were Paul Stader doubling for David Hedison, Mike Donovan for Richard Basehart, and Reg Parton for Leslie Nielsen. During the production, on Monday March 1, the *Voyage* episode "Cradle of the Deep" aired on ABC-TV.

While we have avoided pointing out bloopers in this book – we'll leave it to the internet to put focus on such trivia – there is one mishap on camera in this episode worth noting. In the lab which has been set up for Captain Adams onboard the Seaview, the baby mantra ray has been put in a tank for observation. In one scene during Act III, as Adams enters the room, we see the hand of a special-effects technician dip into the tank and drop a handful of tablets, which bubble as they dissolve. We don't mention this to draw attention to a flaw, but to illustrate one of the techniques used to create bubbles.

Release / Reaction:
(ABC premiere broadcast: 3/22/65; network repeat airing: 7/12/65)

While this episode was airing, Martin Luther King, Jr. was leading a march of 25,000 people from Selma to Montgomery, Alabama. And Gemini 3, the first U.S. two-man spaceflight, was launched. Another U.S. spacecraft, Ranger 9, which was unmanned, had been taking pictures of the lunar surface until its impact. The soundtrack to *Goldfinger* continued to be the best-selling album in America, and had made ... (dramatic pause) ... one million dollars. And "Stop! In the Name of Love," by the Supremes, was getting the most spins on U.S. radio-station turntables.

On March 22, 1965, syndicated "TV Scout," in Nashville's *The Tennessean*, among other newspaper, opined:

> "The Creature" on *Voyage to the Bottom of the Sea* is not the scaly monster you might expect from this series. In this well-thought-out and intelligent episode, the excitement is over some mysterious radiation that may have caused a missile to misfire. The sole survivor is a captain who didn't go down with his ship. As you might suspect, the public hates him for living and he has to enlist the Seaview on a mission to prove his innocence. Leslie Nielsen plays the controversial captain with conviction.

Steven Scheuer at "TV Key" (in Binghamton, New York's March 22nd *Press and Sun-Bulletin*, among other newspapers) didn't seem as impressed:

Leslie Nielsen gusts as a screwball missile captain who boards the Seaview to try to learn what mysterious ultra-sonic beam downed his missile. The culprit turns out to be a giant devilfish who's annoyed by man's ultra-sonic waves. Nelson has his hands full. Not only must he do something about the nasty fish, he has to contend with the missile captain who's obsessed with the idea of capturing it alive. Shades of King Kong, but with more inadvertent laughs.

Also on March 22, a debate over *Voyage* in Vince Leonard's column for Pennsylvania's *The Pittsburgh Press*. Leonard, getting his digs in against the series, had awarded David Hedison his "award" as "Worst New Actor."

As a TV critic, you might think Leonard knew that Hedison was not a new actor; that he'd had his own series a few years earlier, and starred in numerous movies. Hedison was also a fine actor. But, for what critics often lack in knowledge, they make up for in opinions.

"P.G.," of Upview Terrace, wrote in response:

> What exactly do you have against *Voyage to the Bottom of the Sea*? It seems that every time this show is mentioned in your column, you always hint in some fashion you dislike it. I think it is a fine show and a welcome change from doctor or western shows. I was glad to read where it was renewed for next year.

Leonard wasn't glad. And he wasn't hinting. The big bad wolf responded:

> Don't like the show, because it, except on rare occasions, is cliché-ridden, the actors look bored, and the younger ones seem to be without talent. Above all, it deals with ridiculous undertakings, handled in a straight fashion. That's unforgivable.

A.C. Nielsen ratings report, March 22, 1965:	Rating:	Share:
7:30 – 8 p.m.:		
ABC: *Voyage to the Bottom of the Sea*	**20.0**	**30.8%**
CBS: *To Tell the Truth*	19.8	30.5%
NBC: News special: "The Flight of Gemini 3"	14.0	21.6%
8 – 8:30 p.m.		
ABC: *Voyage to the Bottom of the Sea*	20.4	29.4%
CBS: *I've Got a Secret*	17.3	25.1%
NBC: *The Man from U.N.C.L.E.*	**22.8**	**33.1%**

The lead-in program for *The Man from U.N.C.L.E.* was changed this night, from the half-hour sitcom *Karen* to a news special, "The Flight of Gemini 3." *Voyage* was airing an episode that had an intriguing title for sci-fi fans and the young crowd – "The Creature." The results, according to A.C. Nielsen, put *Voyage* back above a 30% audience share (the safety zone for renewal). From 8 to 8:30 p.m. was a different story, as *U.N.C.L.E.* maintained its recent jump in popularity.

Episode 29: "The Enemies"

(Prod. #7231; first aired Monday, March 29, 1965)
Written by William Read Woodfield
Directed by Felix Feist
Produced by Irwin Allen
Story Editor: William Welch; Associate Producer: Allan Balter
Assistant Story Editor: Al Gail
Guest Star Henry Silva
Co-Starring Malachi Throne, Robert Sampson, Tom Skerritt

From the *Voyage* show files (Irwin Allen Papers Collection):

A scientific genius secludes himself on a remote island to experiment in behaviorist psychology, turning normally friendly creatures into mortal enemies. Nelson and Crane find themselves alone on the island at the mercy of the man who, with diabolical cleverness, maneuvers them into a position where they begin a desperate duel with each other for survival.

Sound Bites:

Dr. Shinera: "Admiral Nelson and Captain Crane are now entering the first phase of the test. They have been separated and have been placed in different cells. Alone in the dark loneliness, each man's thoughts turn to the other, perhaps each is blaming the other for his predicament." *General Tau:* "You can't frighten brave men by locking them up in a dark room." *Dr. Shinera:* "Darkness, absolute silence, complete isolation, and the knowledge that you are surrounded by hostile forces that control your destiny can frighten the bravest of men, General. But I don't want to frighten them; I only want to chip away a single layer of the veneer of civilization that covers the animal in each of us."

Assessment:

Mark Phillips thought this episode was "a definite classic." He pointed out: "The way the show opens, with the mental collapse of Captain Williams (unnerving with his staring, crazed expression) is gripping, as is Richardson's plaintive last cry as he grasps, too late, what is happening. Lots of shuddering moments – Nelson's observation that the island seems to be 'covered with slime,' the agonized dead bodies of the tiger cats locked in a death grip and treacherous pools of quicksand everywhere. The scene where a 'giant' General Tau confronts Nelson and Crane is a real, on-set 'special effect' that is stunning. … Henry Silva and Malachi Throne make an effective, evil duo." (vttbots.com)

David Hedison said, "I thought I did good work in several first season episodes when we had better writing. 'The Saboteur,' where I was brainwashed by the Chinese to kill Admiral Nelson; 'The Enemies' where I went mad and tried to kill the Admiral; 'Mutiny,' where Nelson went mad and I had to stop him. Hmmm. Do I sense a pattern here?" (DH-CFTV)

The pattern was as old as Cain vs Abel. And pitting two allies against each other still resonated. The stars were responsive, as were the producer and the audience. The never-fail plot device would be resurrected, often.

Another influence is behaviorism, which reached its most public notoriety with the "Skinner box." Named after American psychologist B.F. Skinner, this "operant conditioning chamber" would control the environment of a test animal to shape its actions. Sounds a lot like Shinera's "dark loneliness," doesn't it?

"The Enemies" is not only a top-notch thriller, but first rate science fiction, action/adventure.

Script:
William Read Woodfield's story treatment: February 15, 1965.
Woodfield's writers contract: February 17.
Woodfield's 1st and 2nd draft teleplays: Dates unknown.
Mimeo Department's reformatted Shooting Final teleplay (on pale green paper): March 1.
Page revisions by William Welch or Al Gail (blue paper): March 2.
Page revisions (pink paper): March 3.
Page revisions (dark green paper): March 4.

William Read Woodfield revealed that his sixth story got its start with the idea of the Ames Room – a distorted room designed in a trapezoidal shape and used to create an optical illusion, invented by American ophthalmologist Adelbert Ames, Jr. of the Dartmouth Eye Institute – served as the genesis of this story.

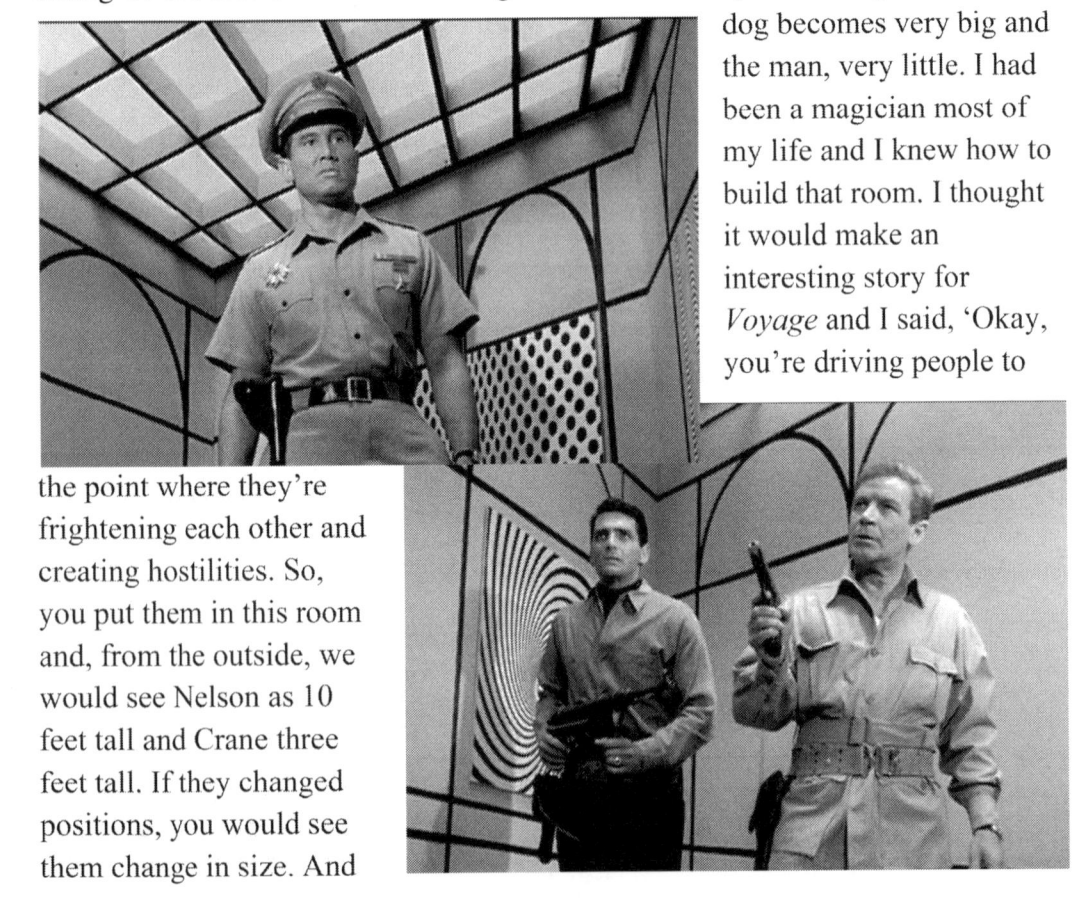

Woodfield said, "In psychology books, it's a room where you see a dog sitting on one side and a man standing on the other. They'll switch places and the dog becomes very big and the man, very little. I had been a magician most of my life and I knew how to build that room. I thought it would make an interesting story for *Voyage* and I said, 'Okay, you're driving people to the point where they're frightening each other and creating hostilities. So, you put them in this room and, from the outside, we would see Nelson as 10 feet tall and Crane three feet tall. If they changed positions, you would see them change in size. And that's how the story evolved.... Irwin said, 'I don't believe it. I'm the king of special effects. How would you build it?' So I told him, and he called up his art director, Bill Creber. I told Bill about my idea and he said, 'Yeah, that would work.' And Irwin said, 'You mean we wouldn't have to use any special effects?' And Bill said, 'I'll show you,' and he built a little model of the room with a periscope that looked into it; moved these little toys around inside, and they got bigger and bigger. Well, Irwin could not believe his eyes! Winnie Hoch, *Voyage*'s Academy Award-winning cameraman, looked through this thing and said, 'Well, if that's the way it looks in the model, that's the way it's gonna look in real life.' And that convinced Irwin. But it was a real room. There were no FX used in those scenes." (WRW-SFTS2)

The scene Woodfield described – in which Nelson would tower over Crane, contributing to the Captain's fear and hatred of him – never took place in the finished episode. Regardless, the concept of the Ames Room, and its distorted perspectives, set the various elements of this story into motion in Woodfield's mind.

In fact, Woodfield's first thoughts concerning the story were much different than what would be scripted. From February 15, 1965, he wrote:

> Seaview, while on a charting mission in the South Pacific, comes upon a small island where Nelson is astonished to find a former colleague living in complete seclusion. The man was a renowned behavior psychologist who passed from the academic scene after advancing his controversial theories of hate manipulation.
>
> The psychologist persuades Nelson and Crane to remain on the island to witness experiments he is conducting while Seaview proceeds on its charting mission.
>
> Once the submarine has departed, the man reveals that he will prove his theory by involving Crane and Nelson in a duel to the death. He realizes, of course, that before the two friends will turn on each other, they will attempt to join forces and kill him. However, he has taken steps to frustrate their every effort and to push them closer and closer toward the psychological trap he has set for them.
>
> Ultimately he is successful in pitting two friends against each other in a life and death struggle for survival.

This was the springboard. But Woodfield had the startling visual of the Ames room – and the miniature that Bill Creber built – to sell Irwin Allen on the concept ... as vague as that concept clearly was, based on the February 25th one-page tease.

Although not mentioned in the initial written pitch, the Ames Room itself is featured in the story, foreshadowing the mental conditioning (along with a generous dose of drugs) which would trigger Crane's homicidal feelings for Nelson.

Woodfield said, "As for the basic story, I had always wanted to do *The Most Dangerous Game*, and this General makes them play the most dangerous game." (WRW-SFTS2)

That one-page proposal showed potential for a take on *The Most Dangerous Game*, but the only concept carried over from Richard Connell's 1924 story and the 1932 film adaption (which was often remade) was one man's hunt for another ... on an island.

Production:
(Filmed March 3-11, 1965; 7 days)

This was director Felix Feist's sixth and final episode of *Voyage*. His direction is quite good, especially with the handling of the Ames Room. Losing him would be a loss for the series. But it wasn't only *Voyage* which lost Felix Feist. He would pass away a few months later, during *Voyage*'s summer hiatus, at age 55.

Henry Silva was 35 when given top guest-star billing, and $1,750 to go along with it, for playing General Tau. He had carved out a name for himself playing heavies in movies such as *The Bravados* (1958), *Ocean's 11* (1960), *The Manchurian Candidate* (1962), and *Johnny Cool* (1963). He had recently appeared in two episodes of *The Outer Limits*.

Above: Ten of *Ocean's 11*; Henry Silva is second from left.
(Warner Bros., 1960)

Malachi Throne, in his second appearance on *Voyage*, played Dr. Shinera, and was paid $850. Throne would be back to chew the scenery in "The Return of

Above: Malachi Throne with a new look for his second Voyage of the year. Below: Robert Sampson and Tom Skerritt.

Tom Skerritt was 31 when he received fourth billing, sharing the same title card as Throne and Sampson. He also received $300 for a single day's work. He was 30 and early in a career that would bring him co-starring billing in the 1970 big-screen version of *M*A*S*H*, *Alien*, and *The Dead Zone*, and starring roles on TV, such as

Blackbeard" on *Voyage*, as well as a pair of *Time Tunnel* episodes and one trip into the *Land of the Giants*. He said, "Oh God, I loved doing those shows. Irwin Allen just let me do any piece of shtick that I wanted. And I had them all. And I just loved them." (MT-AI11)

Robert Sampson was 32 when he received third billing, and $300 for one day's work, playing Captain Jim Williams. They grayed him up a bit at the temples to make him appear older, befitting a ship's captain. Sampson was a reliable actor who worked often in television. He had multiple turns on *Bonanza*, *Alfred Hitchcock Presents*, and *The Lawless Years*. He had a recurring role in the 1958-59 series *Steve Canyon*, and visited both *The Twilight Zone* ("Little Girl Lost") and *The Outer Limits* ("The Mutant").

Sheriff Jimmy Brock in *Picket Fences*, for which he won an Emmy. But first came one more job for Irwin Allen – "The Death Trap" episode of *The Time Tunnel*.

Day 1: Bon voyage to Derik Lewis (on the left, as Lt. O'Brien).
Also filmed this first day: The Teaser, in the *other* Control Room, with Robert Sampson and Tom Skerritt.

"The Enemies" was the eighth and final episode to feature Derrik Lewis, as Lt. O'Brien. Lewis's time on *Voyage* left him with great respect for the cast, and for its "General." He said, "I think Irwin was a genius. I've done a lot of producing in my life – I've produced concerts, theater, various events – and I know more than someone who has only acted, as to what it takes to put something together; to pull all the elements together and keep them there. So, I have admired and identified often in my life the great producers of our time – from David Merrick to Irwin Allen, and P.T. Barnum. It's just a breed all of its own. You can't go to college to learn how to be a producer; you have to do it from experience and learn little by little how to do this and that. The time it takes to put a piece together – you have to be on top of it, and deal with so many different elements, and problems, and be sure that nothing you're doing is going to result in you being sued. It's amazing. And I was very fortunate to be able to work on a series produced by Irwin, and observe what he was able to do. I'm a big fan of what he did; I found him very inspiring – awe-inspiring, in fact. And we were doing the special effects before CGI! It was real stuff – or real-looking stuff – with projections, and smoke, and miniatures, and all of that. Everybody was working together, because these are the type of things – when special effects are involved – are the things you don't want to have to do twice. And I don't remember very many times, if any, that we had to do that twice. Irwin Allen ran a tight ship." (DL-AI18)

Filming began Wednesday, March 3, on Stage B, for scenes in the Control Room and Missile Room. After calling the cast to the set at 8 a.m., Director Felix Feist took his first shot at 9, and wrapped for the day at 6:40 p.m. Thursday and Friday were spent filming at the Moat on the backlot, with "Ext. Jungle Corridor," "Ext. Cave Entrance," "Ext. Dense Hollow Berry Bushes," "Ext. Rocky Terrain & Cliff," "Ext. Island Beach" and "Ext. Quicksand Area."

Days 2 and 3: Filming alongside the Moat and in the adjoining jungle area of the backlot.

On Monday, March 8, the company began two days' work on Stage 2 for the "Int. Illusion Room" set, as well as "Ext. Cave Door," "Int. Cell," "Int. Tau's Laboratory," "Int. Nelson's Cell" and "Int. Crane's Cell." They filmed to 6:50 p.m., with "The Amphibians" airing 40 minutes later on ABC.

557

Wednesday, the sixth day of production, began at the outdoor Moat location for pickup shots, and this put Feist behind. He made it to Stage B by midday to shoot scenes in Captain Crane's quarters, then onto the Missile Room. At 6:45 p.m., they called it a night, informing director Sobey Martin that he would be getting a late start on his final episode of the season, "The Secret of the Loch." It couldn't begin on Thursday morning, as previously scheduled.

Thursday, March 11, was the seventh and final day of production. Feist filmed on Stage B from 8:10 a.m. until 2:05 p.m., finishing the scenes in the Missile Room, then returning to the Control Room for pickup shots. And then, finally, he handed the camera crew over to Sobey Martin to begin the thirtieth episode of the first season.

Day 4: Filming in the cave entrance alongside the Moat (you may recall seeing this same angle in "The Blizzard Makers," when Hedison, Kulky, and Monroe walked into a trap). Also filmed were the interiors in the illusion room (center). One last trip to the Missile Room (bottom image) on Day 7, and they were able to call it a week.

Release / Reaction:
(ABC premiere broadcast: 3/29/65; network repeat airing: 8/16/65)

Martin Luther

558

King, Jr. had the cover of *LIFE* magazine. Mary Tyler Moore and Dick Van Dyke of *The Dick Van Dyke Show* had the cover of *TV Guide*. Later in the week, America would meet a super-cool spy that was already the rage on television in England – Patrick McGoohan as John Drake – with the premiere of *Secret Agent*. CBS had tried to interest America with Drake once before, in 1961, with a 30-minute version called *Danger Man*. We didn't take notice then. We did now – both on TV and the radio, where the title song became a Top 10 hit for Johnny Rivers.

"Tele-Vues," by Terry Vernon, and included in the March 29, 1965 edition of the *Long Beach Press-Telegram*, spoiled the surprise of the perspective-room illusion:

> In mathematics, a trapezium is an irregular, four-sided figure in which no two sides are parallel. The producers of *Voyage to the Bottom of the Sea* will use a trapezium tonight. They call it an "illusion room." It is, actually, an optical illusion. If, for example, you were at one end of the room and another person entered from the opposite side, he would look to you like a giant. If he walked across the room and stood next to you, it would be evident that he was a normal size.

On the same day, "TV Key" previewed "The Enemies" in Mansfield, Ohio's *News Journal*:

> Despite a slow start, this adventure should hold the interest of series fans. The Seaview's mutual admiration society, Admiral Nelson and Captain Crane, become guinea pigs in an experiment involving a "hate" serum which turns friends into enemies.

Also on March 29, "TV Scout," in Pennsylvania's *Monessen Valley Independent*, said:

> Fans of David Hedison, who plays Commander Crane, will catch their breaths for a moment or two in "The Enemies." The slick young officer becomes the prisoner of foreign scientists who use drugs to turn him into an irascible foe of his admiral (Richard Basehart), who has also been subjected to the same bitter medicine. Lots of suspense here, with an able supporting cast of sinisters headed by Henry Silva and Malachi Throne.

Cleveland Amory reviewed this episode in *TV Guide*'s May 1, 1965 issue:

... Nelson and Crane are trying to track down "something that made two friends hate each other enough to kill." Well, sir, as sure as you're born, they take off to the sort of misty half-world this show loves – which is kind of a cross between *Wuthering Heights* and *Here Comes Mr. Jordan*, only it's all underwater – and in no time at all they're on an island. Here there is all sorts of skullduggery, including a general of the People's Republic and a mad scientist who's tired of testing his hate drug on animals and wants to start on people.

"Something," says Nelson, "is watching us." Well, something is, all right – and, you can believe this or not, it turns out to be the scientist's television cameras. ... But when the scientist turns them loose, the general of the People's Republic is worried. "I thought there was no place on the island they could hide from our cameras," he said inscrutably. "There isn't," replies the scientist, like the good network man he is. "Let our automatic tracker track them."

But the scientist has underrated his Nielsen – or, rather, Nelson. First the admiral stops Crane from eating berries so he won't get contaminated with the hate drug, and then he turns his attention to "the automatic camera with the self-activating transmitter." "If," he tells Crane, "we aim the two cameras directly at each other, the self-activating activator will lock and the automatic transmitter will automatically..." Well, if you think we're going to spoil the summer rerun of this gem for you, we're not.

A.C. Nielsen ratings report, March 29, 1965:	Rating:	Share:
7:30 – 8 p.m.:		
ABC: *Voyage to the Bottom of the Sea*	**19.9**	**29.5%**
CBS: *To Tell the Truth*	18.8	27.9%
NBC: *Karen*	18.7	27.7%
8 – 8:30 p.m.		
ABC: *Voyage to the Bottom of the Sea*	19.7	28.2%
CBS: *I've Got a Secret*	18.8	26.9%
NBC: *The Man from U.N.C.L.E.*	**22.6**	**32.3%**

Episode 30: "The Secret of the Loch"

(Prod. #7232; first aired Monday, April 5, 1965)
Written by Charles Bennett
Directed by Sobey Martin
Produced by Irwin Allen
Story Editor: William Welch; Associate Producer: Joseph Gantman
Assistant Story Editor: Al Gail
Guest Star Torin Thatcher
Hedley Mattingly, George Mitchell, John McLiam

ABC-TV press release (late March 1965):

The submarine Seaview follows a secret course beneath the ocean and through a huge natural conduit leading to the depths of Scotland's Loch Ness, on *Voyage to the Bottom of the Sea* ....

In "Secret of the Loch," Professor MacDougal claims he has witnessed the deaths of several men who were attacked by a monster from the loch. Because the professor has been working for the United States and British governments in a jointly-owned underwater laboratory in Loch Ness, Admiral Nelson and Commander Crane are sent to investigate the so-called "monster" incident.

Sound Bites:

Nelson: "Lee, how much do you know about Loch Ness?" *Crane:* "Well, not very much, except the old legend of a Loch Ness monster, and all of that." *Nelson (indicating picture):* "It's quite a place, about 30 miles long and about two miles wide. Parts of it are so deep they've never been found." *Crane (looking at picture):* "Looks pretty lonely." *Nelson:* "Yeah. Few places are lonelier. That's why the laboratory was built here. It was done top secretly. The laboratory's built 700 feet under the surface of the Loch." *Crane:* "That's going to a lot of trouble to insure privacy."

MacDougall: "I know you gentlemen were expecting to meet Dr. Carruthers. I've bad news for you. He died last night." *Nelson:* "Died?!" *MacDougall:* "Aye. Out there on the loch. The memory of it will be with me until my dying day ... *(deliberate dramatic pause)* ... I know you gentlemen will have difficulty in believing this, but have you ever heard of the Loch Ness monster?" *Crane:* "That's a legend." *MacDougall:* "Aye. Well then, it was a legend that killed him."

Assessment:

"The Secret of the Loch," like many first-season episodes of *Voyage to the Bottom of the Sea*, was made before the series truly found its course. It came before the series fell into the rut of dependence on a monster-of-the-week ... or on good friends Nelson and Crane becoming mortal enemies due to brainwashing, possession, or doppelgangers. This episode is not only unique but absorbing and nicely textured with interesting characters and good twists. The moody photography is aided by excellent black-and-white cinematography and a generous dose of a Scottish fog "thick as pea soup."

Alistair MacDougall is a curious character, thanks in part to effective writing, but also to a first-rate performance from Torin Thatcher. From their first meeting, Nelson and Crane aren't sure if he is to be trusted, and neither is the audience, yet we are never quite sure. His wit – again a combination of sharp writing and acting – slowly evolves as the story builds. Consider the following:

- When we first meet MacDougall, he is in a frenzied state; it almost seems he is putting on a show for the men in the tavern. Torin Thatcher seems to be laying it on a bit thick, crossing over into theatrical melodramatics. But what at first seems like hammy acting is actually an inspired choice from Thatcher – for McDougall is indeed putting on a performance, attempting to alarm the tavern patrons.

- Upon our next meeting, as MacDougall greets Nelson and Crane, he is calmer. Yet there is still something about him which raises suspicion. Note the deliberate dramatic pause he takes after divulging that Professor Crothers has died … and then revealing the cause of the death – the Loch Ness monster. He is even watching their reactions closely before deciding to continue. Something else: He tells Nelson and Crane that he will be guarded when questioned by the authorities about the death of Crothers … even if it means lying under oath. Why would he say this – what was he willing to lie about? Does this mean that everything he has been saying is a lie? And can we blame Nelson and Crane for not fully trusting a man who admits to them that he is prepared to lie under oath?
- Once on the Seaview, MacDougall is relaxed, poised, savoring every drop of the fine Scotch he is offered. This causes Nelson and Crane to lean toward trusting him. Liars and spies are usually careful not to drink, not to let their guard down. But MacDougall is so at ease, so seemingly candid in everything he says, that he comes across as genuine.
- When MacDougall reveals himself to Nelson and Crane in the observation nose, Thatcher has the character drop the Scottish accent and switch to one of a refined Englishman. It is such a subtle shift, but Thatcher – with the MacDougall character – has been subtle all along. And he has much to work with, from a script rich in Scottish and English dialogue and mannerisms, written by an Englishman – Charles Bennett.

Most authors who have studied and written about *Voyage to the Bottom of the Sea give* this episode high marks … although some were disappointed by one aspect.

Mark Phillips said, "What this episode lacks in action it makes up for in ambience – plenty of fog, dark forests, forbidding pools of black water and a frightening scene where Inspector Lester's boat is destroyed by the monster. The revelation that the creature is an enemy submarine is disappointing, especially given the low-grade appearance of the submarine." (vttbots.com)

Mike Bailey said: "Mood, mood, mood. The first 40 minutes of this are a delight. The revelation at the end about the enemy sub is a big letdown. How much more interesting it would have been for Seaview to go head to head with a real live plesiosaur, possibly the product of enemy experiments or something." (vttbots.com)

But hasn't *Voyage* already had enough exotic monsters? For many, it's refreshing that the "monster" turns out to be humans … behaving monstrously … in a submarine made to look like a sea creature. The fact that we see through the visual ruse the moment we get a good look of the sub is okay. The enemy altered the sub just enough to work under opportune conditions, with darkness, fog, and by human nature. They know that most people will see what they have been told to see … and let their fears get the better of them.

So go ahead and let your fears get the better of you. You may agree that "The Secret of the Loch" is a delight.

Script:
Charles Bennett's writers contract: January 4, 1965
Bennett's story treatment, approved on February 9.
Bennett's 1st and 2nd draft teleplays: Dates unknown.
Mimeo Department's reformatted Shooting Final teleplay (pale green paper): March 8.
Page revisions by William Welch or Al Gail (blue paper): March 10.
Page revisions (pink paper): March 11.
Page revisions (yellow paper): March 12.
Page revisions (gold paper): March 19.
Page revisions (beige paper): March 20.

This was Charles Bennett's first script for the series, though he could be considered a co-developer, since he co-wrote the *Voyage* feature film. Bennett, who a few years earlier had been writing screenplays for the likes of Alfred Hitchcock, now found himself slumming in the grist mills of the television industry. Without shame, he admitted, "I don't remember any of them. It's true! I only wrote those for the sake of the bloody money they paid me. The series was, for me, just something to fill up airtime. Once they paid me, I couldn't care less what happened to the scripts. …

Charles Bennett with the only other director/producer who hired him as often as Irwin Allen – Alfred Hitchcock.

"I thought the casting [of Basehart and Hedison] was rather ordinary TV casting, and, frankly, I didn't give a damn who they cast. Let me make something clear: I've enjoyed writing novels, plays and movies, but the only reason I wrote anything for TV was for the money. I've written more than 200 TV shows, but I loathe TV. I wish it had never been invented. I've enjoyed directing some of it, but TV writing is a tenth-rate form of writing." (CB-SL92)

Bennett didn't even bother to come up with an original idea for his first *Voyage*. He had already written a movie called *The Secret of the Loch*, which had been made and released in England during 1934. The story involved an eccentric Scottish professor who attempts to prove the existence of the Loch Ness Monster. Everyone thinks he's crazy, except for a young reporter, who stays close by, hoping to get a scoop on the story. Among the characters in the movie was one named Angus, the same name that shows up for a character in this *Voyage* episode. Bennett was clearly phoning his assignment in.

Too bad that Charles Bennett's disdain was so evident. It didn't seem to matter that perhaps as many as 20 million people would be watching the program he wrote ... admittedly only for the money.

On the upside, for someone with Bennett's literary pedigree, a lesser effort didn't necessarily mean a shabby product.

Regardless, Associate Producer Joseph Gantman wasn't quick to take to Bennett's work – at least, not based on the writer's first-draft script. Gantman wrote to Irwin Allen:

1. (Sc. 11-16) Audience already knows this information. So the headlines and radio are a dull and unnecessary way to get the Seaview & Co. involved in the story.
2. (Sc. 17-25) Long dull 10 pages of more exposition. All this for the introduction of MacDougall?

There is indeed a great deal of exposition dialogue in the early part of Act One, especially the scene in Nelson's cabin between the Admiral and Captain Crane. But Bennett had cut his teeth writing movie scripts in England, including those in collaboration with Alfred Hitchcock. The pacing of films was slower back then – deliberately so. None of this made the script bad; it just wasn't standard *Voyage to the Bottom of the Sea* with emphasis on action, action, and more action.

Others on Allen's team clearly liked this as a change in pace, and the trims made were minor.

Gantman continued:

3. (Sc. 29-31) This Act ending seems to me to be just thrown in for a curtain.
4. I suggest that LESTER (of the teaser) and MACDOUGALL be combined into one character. And that Act One begin with Nelson and Crane having no knowledge of the tragic incident of the monster – that they expect Dr. Carruthers to join them on the submarine to discuss the "project". When the boat

which was to bring Carruthers arrives, its passenger is LESTER MACDOUGALL. He informs them of Carruther's death.

Gantman was spot on here, and the changes were made. Lester and MacDougall were combined into one character, now named Alistair MacDougall. The name Lester was kept, but assigned to another character already in the script – the police inspector.

5. (Sc. 33) Act Two begins still marking time.
6. (Sc. 33) Of course Chip won't prompt Nelson on his geography.
7. (Sc 33) Why does Nelson, in the first place, and then so doggedly continue to seek information on MacDougall's background? Is he a suspicious character?
8. (Sc. 34-51) Nelson presumably came to Scotland in connection with the underwater early warning system, but all that is forgotten once he meets MacDougall. If there is a connection between what Nelson undertakes with MacDougall and his original mission it is so vague it escapes me.

The pacing in Act Two remained on the slow side for *Voyage to the Bottom of the Sea*, but it makes a nice change. There is certainly enough going on to hold the attention of most viewers … over the age of 20, anyway (back in the 1960s … perhaps more likely 40 today).

The other notes were addressed. Nelson questioned MacDougall less, and was less obvious concerning his suspicions. The reason for Seaview's visit to Loch Ness was also better explained and kept in the forefront of the story.

9. (Sc 35-48) DIGBY and his death seems to make no connection nor have any effect on the story. He is incidental and his death is incidental. Why is it important no one else hear Digby on the telephone? Why can't Nelson react to what he hears? As it is now I think the effect can be pretty funny.

Digby remained, but had a name change to Inspector Lester. And, while it may appear that Lester is incidental, removing him would have taken much out of the story. The character is utilized to instill some action into the script – the attempted murder of Nelson and Crane, and the attack on the Loch by the "monster," which destroys Lester's boat and helps to strengthen the idea that there may indeed be a monster. That second attack by the monster also raises the danger elements in the story for Seaview, and, even when we learn the truth behind the monster, we are fully aware of how merciless the adversaries can be. They will not hesitate to kill.

> 10. (Sc. 52-79) Getting to the Loch via the underground channel should be made more difficult, more hazardous, more suspenseful. It is made to seem pretty easy. Perhaps we could put divers out ahead of the sub to lead the way. What is MacDougall's reasoning in showing Nelson a channel to the Loch? – All this just to capture Nelson. In fact, why does MacDougall do all that he does? He says he already has all the information about the secret laboratory. He really doesn't make much sense.

These insightful notes from Gantman illustrate his importance to *Voyage*, and the great loss to the series when he – and fellow co-producer Allan Balter – exited. Changes were made to the script. The trip through the underwater caverns was indeed enhanced and made quite suspenseful. And MacDougall's motivations were clarified. It was an easy fix – he knew of the underwater lab, but needed the charts and other documents from Nelson to show its exact location and vulnerabilities.

> 11. (Sc. 93 to end) WHY doesn't the Seaview attack the "monster"? They have plenty of time and nothing to lose. The ruse with the mini-sub can't come off because all the time the audience will be saying, "Why don't they just shoot?" Because of all this, Nelson and Crane act and sound like idiots.
> 12. (Sc. 118) Why would MacDougall give his gun to Nelson?

The solutions: MacDougall sabotages the ship so that it cannot fire its torpedoes, and MacDougall never uses a gun – he has too much class, and confidence.
Lastly:

> 13. Much of the dialogue comes off as though the writer is ribbing us (a parody). This is probably Bennett's style, but it doesn't work for our people or our show.

Bennett had instilled a sense of humor into his script, using English wit to create suspense with comedy relief and elegant villains. This was trimmed, but much of the wit in the dialogue – especially concerning the character of MacDougall – survived the rewriting.

The notes Allen got from the network, after Charles Bennett performed his rewrite, arrived on March 10. Calvin Ward wrote, in full:

> Page 4: Please use your usual good taste on the appearance of the dead body. Keep blood to a minimum. The body should appear mangled. As usual can be approved only on film.
>
> Page 29: Please ascertain that "Cream of Drumadrochit" is not an actual brand name.
>
> Page 37: The shots of the monster's head lunging forward, etc., must not be overly frightening or horrifying. Can be approved only on film.
>
> Page 54: Nelson's last line; substitute for "crazy."

No doubt laughing all the way to the bank, script editor William Welch removed the offending term and made the other minor changes; then Irwin Allen and Joseph Gantman proceeded to production.

Production:
(Filmed March 11-19, 1965; 7 days)
(Budget: $126,414)

Sobey Martin returned to direct. His work, thanks to the good support of crisp writing, thoughtful acting, and moody cinematography, actually seems inspired.

Torin Thatcher was 59 when he played Alistair MacDougall, receiving $1,750 and top "Guest Star" billing. He was educated in England, at Bedford School and The Royal Academy of Dramatic Arts, explaining his

Torin Thatcher in *Jack the Giant Killer*.
(United Artists, 1962)

expert handling of British accents. Thatcher was well-known for playing villainous roles on the stage and in major motion pictures, from England during the 1930s and '40s, and from Hollywood, beginning in the 1950s. Perhaps you may recall him in 1958's *The 7th Voyage of Sinbad*, as the evil magician who shrinks the princess to the size of a Barbie doll. Irwin Allen was fond of Thatcher and brought him back, as "The Space Trader" in *Lost in Space*. He would also appear in one episode each for *The Time Tunnel* ("The Crack of Doom") and *Land of the Giants* ("Nightmare").

Hedley Mattingly was 49 when he played Inspector Lester, receiving $250 for one day's work. Like Thatcher, Mattingly was raised and educated in England, making him ideal for this episode. He too rated a "Guest Star" credit, having had a recurring role in the 1963-64 series, *The Travels of Jaimie McPheeters*, and soon to begin work on *Daktari*, in 78 episodes, as Officer Hedley.

Above: Hedley Mattingly (center) and the cast of *Daktari*, including Judy the Chimp (aka Debbie the Bloop from *Lost in Space*). (MGM Television, 1966-69)
Below: Filming began on the Seaview sets ... and, with this episode, we got a glimpse at the sub's blueprint.

George Mitchell played Angus, at a pay rate of $250 for one day's filming. He was 59 and had appeared in over 100 films and TV episodes, including a recurring role in the 1962-63 series, *Stoney Burke*, which also had *Voyage*'s Robert Dowdell as a regular.

John McLiam was 46 when he played Andrews, and also received $250 for one day in front of the camera. Like the others, he had a pedigree as a character actor in TV and films.

Series that brought McLiam back more than once included *The Twilight Zone*, *The Untouchables*, *The Fugitive*, and *Ben Casey*.

Paul Kremin, the boat skipper crossing the loch, was actually Paul Zastupnevich, the series' costume designer.

Filming began Thursday, March 11, 1965. It would take seven days to finish, with five of those on Stage B for the standard Seaview sets, and two days on Fox Stage 2, for "Ext. The Lochside," "Ext. Wayside Pub" and "Ext. Beside the Loch" on one day (Monday) and "Int. Wayside Pub" and "Int. Cabin of Launch" on Tuesday. The 20th Century-Fox craftsmen and film technicians did their usual excellent job at transforming the areas around the Moat into chilly, foggy Scotland, and the interior sets rich in the flavor of the location.

Another thing that plays authentic in these latter scenes is when Richard Basehart puts on a Scottish accent. You may recall that Basehart's first Broadway success was as a Scot in *The Hasty Heart*. He won acclaim for that role. The brief moment as he shows his talent for dialects in this episode helps you to appreciate why he won a 1945 New York Critic's Award.

"The Exile" aired on ABC during the production.

The last day of filming, the seventh day on this episode, was Friday, March 19, 1965, spent on Stage B for sequences in the ship's corridors, the Radio Hut, and, finally, Nelson's Cabin. They finished at 3:15 p.m., allowing "The Condemned" to begin filming.

The rough cut was screened for ABC on March 23, 1965. The Final Air Print was approved on March 29. The episode aired only a week later. That's how little lead time there was.

Release / Reaction:
(Only ABC broadcast: 4/5/65)

The soundtrack for *Mary Poppins* was the top-selling record album in America. "I'm Telling You Now," by Freddie and the Dreamers, was the song getting the most airplay on radio stations. In the movie houses, the top two contenders were both musicals – *The Sound of Music*, with Julie Andrews, and *Girl Happy*, with Elvis Presley.

As for "The Secret of the Loch," syndicated "TV Key Previews," in the April 5, 1964 edition of New York's *The Oneonta Star*, among other newspapers, said:

> A cloak and dagger mystery that should appeal to the youngsters. The Seaview is involved in a mission which takes the crew to the coast of Scotland where a superstition about a prehistoric sea monster serves the purpose of the enemy.

Also on April 5th, "TV Scout," in Pennsylvania's *Monessen Valley Independent*, said:

> Remember the old scary film, *Creature from the Black Lagoon*? Well, here's an updated version of the watery tale as the Seaview goes on a mission to find a monster in the lonely depths of Scotland's Loch Ness. It seems it has been gobbling up scientists left and right, much to the dismay of Torin Thatcher, professor of marine biology at the University of Edinburgh. There are some fine photographed underwater scenes, but don't be surprised if the "monster" doesn't turn out to be what you thought it was.

A.C. Nielsen ratings report, April 5, 1965:	Rating:	Share:
7:30 – 8 p.m.:		
ABC: ***Voyage to the Bottom of the Sea***	**21.4**	**34.6%**
CBS: *To Tell the Truth*	15.0	24.3%
NBC: *Karen*	16.4	26.4%
8 – 8:30 p.m.		
ABC: ***Voyage to the Bottom of the Sea***	**22.3**	**33.3%**
CBS: *I've Got a Secret*	16.4	24.5%
NBC: *The Man from U.N.C.L.E.*	20.9	31.2%

The ratings indicated that people were still interested in tales about the Loch Ness monster ... faked or not. But this episode was passed over for a repeat showing.

From the Mailbag:

Days after "The Secret of the Loch" aired on ABC, Steven H. Scheuer printed a letter in his syndicated "TV Key Mailbag" column, saying:

> Which of the two leading stars of *Voyage to the Bottom of the Sea* passed away recently? I heard something about one of them passing away, but I can't recall which one it was? – G.S., Memphis.

In a day before the internet, rumors like these were not easily confirmed for the average TV viewer. No doubt many hearts stopped for a moment until fans of the show could read Scheuer's response:

> The two leading stars, David Hedison and Richard Basehart, are hale and hearty. Character actor Henry

Kulky, who played one of the crew on the sub, passed away.

On April 8, 1965, the syndicated newspaper column "Ask TV Scout," found in the *Abilene Reporter-News*, printed the following letter from a reader:

> OFF LIMITS FOR SCIENCE FICTION? – Has *Outer Limits* been permanently discontinued? If so, do any of the three networks have plans for a similar series? – Dale Johnson, Greenshore, N.C.

Answer:

> Yes, ABC-TV took *Outer Limits* off the air, with no plans for its return. The only program similar to it is *Voyage to the Bottom of the Sea* on the same network. So far, there are two new science fiction series possible next season: *Star Trek* and *Lost in Space*.

By this time, Irwin Allen had produced the pilot film for *Lost in Space* and was awaiting word from CBS as to whether he would have a second hour-long sci-fi series on the air for the 1965-66 TV season. The first *Star Trek* pilot ("The Cage") had also been shot but rejected by NBC. A second pilot, "Where No Man Had Gone Before" would soon be ordered.

Episode 31: "The Condemned"

(Prod. #7218; first aired Monday, April 12, 1965)
Written by William Read Woodfield
Directed by Leonard Horn
Produced by Irwin Allen
Story Editor: William Welch; Associate Producer: Allan Balter
Assistant Story Editor: Al Gail
Guest Star J.D. Cannon
Co-Starring Arthur Franz and Alvy Moore

From the *Voyage* show files (Irwin Allen Papers Collection):

> An ambitious Admiral – Chief of the President's Inner Space Program – is rushing ahead with a project which actually needs further study. It is his plan to ionize the atmosphere of a sub to enable it to operate at a depth of 30,000 feet. Against Nelson's better judgment and over his objection, Seaview is chosen for the experiment. Once down at 30,000 feet, where the men move about almost in slow motion, they discover that the process is irreversible and they are doomed to spend the rest of their lives at the bottom of the sea.

This was the springboard. When the story was further developed, some important changes were made. The slow-motion gimmick was tossed out the porthole. As for the crew of the Seaview being doomed to spend the rest of their lives at the bottom of the sea, those lifespans would be, to borrow the 1651 words of English writer Thomas Hobbes, "solitary, poor, nasty, brutish and short."

Sound Bites:

Nelson: "Press conference? If this is his project, his test, he should be here. Who does he think he is?" *Crane:* "But we don't need him for any of these preliminary tests." *Nelson:* "That's not the point! He's a scientist conducting an important experiment. How the devil does he call a press conference before the experiment is even half through? His headline grabbing is a disgrace to the scientific community."

Nelson: "Lee, you're the only one familiar enough with the characteristics of this hull to detect trouble before it becomes critical. I'll be on the radio-telephone at all times. At the slightest hint of danger to the hull, you have the authority to abort this mission." *Adm. Falk:* "Only I have that authority, Admiral." *Nelson:* "One word from Captain Crane and I'll haul you up here faster than Hoff can shoot pictures. Is that clear enough?"

Assessment:

Mike Bailey ranked this one high, saying, "Another classic. Separately, director Leonard Horn and writer William Read Woodfield were at the top of the heap in *Voyage*'s Year-One stable of talent, and did their very best work in this season. United for this episode, they delivered the goods and then some. Dark mood, excellent set design and top-notch film cutting unite in effect." (vttbots.com)

Mark Phillips said: "When Nelson puts Admiral Falk on the spot, demanding to know who really created the experimental atmosphere, the tension is dynamite."

"The Condemned" is indeed a fine episode, but we have an issue with the characterization of Admiral Bentley Falk, both as written and as depicted by J.D. Cannon. The man is unlikable from the get-go and remains that way throughout the story. He has no redeeming qualities whatsoever. Worse, he is transparently rotten. He's too one-sided. Granted, one could argue that, in the end, Falk endangers his own life to make amends for the harm he has caused. But you could also argue that he is merely doing what he always does – wanting to get the credit, believing that he can survive the encounter with the giant undersea creature.

However, this episode pleases many fans, including the majority of the authorities on the series. It is a good episode, and you will probably like "The Condemned" too.

Script:
*William Read Woodfield's writers contract: March 3, 1965.
Woodfield's treatment and 1st and 2nd draft teleplays: Dates unknown.
Mimeo Department's reformatted Shooting Final teleplay: March 17.
Revised Shooting Final teleplay (by William Welch or Al Gail):
Date unknown.
2nd Rev. Shooting Final teleplay, by writing staff (pink paper): March 22.
Page revisions (blue paper): March 24.*

Although "The Condemned" carried the Production number 7218, it was not the eighteenth episode filmed. It was planned that way, but the tale was delayed to very nearly the end of the season. It finally went before camera as the 31st of 32 productions for the first season. No explanation for the delay was given in the *Voyage to the Bottom of the Sea* show files, or the various documents stored in the Irwin Allen Private Papers Collection. With most of the principle players – writers, director, producers, actors – now gone, we may never know why.

What we do know is that those involved with this episode have held it in high regard. David Hedison, discussing the writers and scripts for the first season, said, "I actually thought it was the best year – the first year in black & white. And William Reed Woodfield, with Allan Balter, were our best writers. They'd written a lot of shows in the first year, and the second year… and I was terribly impressed. No, *really*! I thought [the first season] was very well done; which makes me think that Irwin was right. I didn't laugh once; I didn't smile once, but I got caught up in the action." (DH-TCF07)

Production:
*(Filmed March 22-29, 1965; 6 days)
(Budget: $128,432)*

Twentieth Century-Fox was a busy lot at this time, with three features filming (*Our Man Flint, Fantastic Voyage,* and *Do Not Disturb*), and five series (*Valentine's Day, 12 O'Clock High, Daniel Boone,* and *Peyton Place,* as well as *Voyage*).

Leonard Horn returned to direct. This was his sixth episode, and he had proven one of the series' best directors, with "The Fear-Makers," "The Mist of Silence," "Submarine Sunk Here," and "The Sky Is Falling."

J.D. Cannon was 42 when given top guest-star billing, and $2,500 to go along with it, for playing Falk. He came from the stage before becoming a well-regarded guest performer on television. Prior to this, he had been featured in recurring roles as a doctor in *The Doctors and the Nurses*, and a district attorney in *The Defenders*, but would be best remembered for his Emmy-nominated role as Chief Peter Clifford in *McCloud* during the 1970s.

Arthur Franz was 44 and had co-star billing, and pay of $1,000, for

Above: Arthur Franz with Helena Carter, from *Invaders from Mars*. (20th Century-Fox, 1953)
Center: Alvy Moore, studio publicity photo, circa 1950s.
Bottom: J.D. Cannon, looking out from the Sick Bay Decompression Chamber, filmed on Day 1.

playing Dr. Archer, the true inventor of the atmospheric-mixing formula. He was a highly regarded character actor from television and films with 150 appearances, including *The Caine Mutiny*, *The Sands of Iwo Jima*, and *Invaders from Mars*. He had pulled submarine duty before, as Lt. Arnie Carlson in 1951's *Submarine Command*, which starred William Holden.

Alvy Moore was 43 and shared co-starring billing, receiving $750 for his role as Hoff. He had been a regular on the 1960-61 sitcom *Pete and Gladys*, as Howie, but is best known for playing Hank Kimball in 138 episodes of *Green Acres*.

Filming began Monday, March 22, 1965 for the first of six days on Stage B, for Int. Sick Bay and Decompression Chamber. They worked until 7 p.m., with the *Voyage* episode "The

Creature" premiering on ABC just 30 minutes later.

Tuesday saw more work in the Decompression Chamber, then the company moved on to the Seaview Control Room, then the "Missile Room + Winch + Test Hull." Work continued there on Wednesday and Thursday, then finished up in the Admiral's Quarters.

On Friday, they filmed in the "Int. Air Revitalization Room" and "Int. Test Hull." Horn worked until 8:30 p.m. Cast and crew had become used to Fridays running late; the producers rationalized this practice by maintaining that everyone could rest up over the weekend.

Monday, March 29 was the final day of production, with more scenes filmed in the Revitalization Room, then into the Observation Nose, utilizing process shots. In order to finish and not delay "The Traitor,"

Above: From Day 2, in the Control Room, with Hedison tuning in a picture of the two-headed seaweed monster at the bottom of the sea. Below: Later that day, filming in the "Missile Room + Winch + Test Hull," with Alvy Moore and J.D. Cannon.

the last episode of the season to film, director Horn worked until 9 p.m.

578

The best way to get through long days such as this on the set was humor. Ray Didsbury said, "David Hedison was one of the saving graces of *Voyage*. He had a wonderful sense of humor, and kept the cast and crew up. He was great with Richard, and not intimidated by Richard's acting reputation. He helped keep us sane during the terribly long hours we worked." (RD-FF01)

Days 5 & 6 in the Air Revitalization Room. Above: Hedison, Moore, Basehart, and Cannon. Center: Arthur Frank and J.D. Cannon. Bottom: From late Day 6, Int. Observation Nose, with Cannon, Basehart, and, on the process screen, the thing.

The standout *Voyage* episode "The Enemies" aired this night, and cleared the air 30 minutes *before* cast and crew of *Voyage* were even able to leave the studio.

ABC screened the rough cut of "The Condemned" on April 2, 1965. The Final Air Print was approved April 6, and the episode was televised six days after that. *Voyage* was so far behind, episodes were now being delivered less than a week before their air date.

579

Release / Reaction:
(ABC premiere broadcast: 4/12/65; network repeat airing: 8/23/65)

The three big movies playing across America during the week that "The Condemned" had its first broadcast were *In Harm's Way*, starring John Wayne, Kirk Douglas and Henry Fonda; *Girl Happy*, starring Elvis Presley; and *The Sound of Music*, starring Julie Andrews and Christopher Plummer. You could get a ticket to see any of them for about a buck. Matinees were usually 75 cents. Or you could stay home and watch *Voyage*, on a brand-new 1965 Admiral 23-inch black & white console TV, with maple cabinet, for $222.

On April 12, 1965, "TV Key," syndicated to numerous newspapers, including Arizona's *Tucson Daily Citizen*, said:

> Good actor J.D. Cannon plays a mad scientist who gets control of the Seaview and decides to experiment by diving her below the pressure limits. The pressure stabilizer system goes haywire, the mad scientist doesn't know how to get the ship back to the surface and the sub encounters a subterranean monster. And you think you've got troubles!

On the same day, syndicated "TV Scout," in Arizona's *The Phoenix Gazette*, said:

> *Voyage to the Bottom of the Sea* sinks deeper into its no-man's land of science fiction with "The Condemned." Just when you think the episode hinges on whether or not a

power-hungry admiral is going to get his comeuppance by his fellow man, up pops one of those "creatures" from the briny deep.

A.C. Nielsen ratings report, April 12, 1965:	Rating:	Share:
7:30 – 8 p.m.:		
ABC: *Voyage to the Bottom of the Sea*	16.4	27.3%
CBS: *To Tell the Truth*	**17.2**	**28.7%**
NBC: *Karen*	16.7	27.8%
8 – 8:30 p.m.		
ABC: *Voyage to the Bottom of the Sea*	16.5	24.4%
CBS: *I've Got a Secret*	19.6	29.0%
NBC: *The Man from U.N.C.L.E.*	**22.3**	**33.0%**

Voyage claimed second-place bragging rights for the 7:30 to 8 p.m. time period, but dropped to third position from 8 to 8:30, a victim of *The Man from U.N.C.L.E.*'s hip status with the teen set. "The Condemned" was the lowest-rated first-run episode of the first season.

Episode 32: "The Traitor"

(Prod. #7225; first aired Sunday, April 19, 1965)
Written by William Welch and Al Gail
Directed by Sobey Martin
Produced by Irwin Allen
Story Editor: William Welch: Associate Producer: Joseph Gantman
Assistant Story Editor: Al Gail
Guest Star George Sanders
Also Starring Michael Pate and Susan Flannery

From the *Voyage* show files (Irwin Allen Papers Collection):

A woman identified as the sister of Admiral Nelson is kidnapped on a tour of Paris and Nelson is apparently led by circumstances into betraying one of the top secrets of his country. Crane becomes increasingly suspicious of the Admiral's behavior and reluctantly concludes that his friend is a traitor.

Sound Bites:

General Fenton: "You know, this has been a most intriguing case for us. There was one school [of thought] which maintained that you were an individual of such integrity that nothing in the world would seduce you to betray your county's secrets." *Nelson:* "I'm flattered." *Fenton:* "Others of us maintain that you, like everyone else in the world, had a vulnerable spot. Now, the question is, have we found that spot?" *Nelson:* "I'm here." *Fenton:* "Quite. But you betray nothing by your presence beyond the deep concern for your sister's safety." *Nelson:* "And I don't intend to betray anything until I'm sure that my sister's alive and unharmed." *Fenton:* 'Well, come, Admiral, we can now go to a place where we can talk privately." *Nelson:* "Lead the way."

Assessment:

Mark Phillips said, "There is genuine mystery as Crane begins to suspect Nelson of selling out America's defense secrets to save his kidnapped sister. Unfortunately, much of the show's momentum is undercut by boring exposition. This is one of many episodes that has the *Star Trek* 'Red Shirt' syndrome, where unknown crewmen are killed off. Here, a shore party consisting of Crane, Morton, Kowalski and a nameless sailor (played by Dick Dial) battle General Fenton's forces. When the sailor is gunned down, no one laments his loss." (vttbots.com)

Mike Bailey's opinion: "Sanders is great as the sophisticated spy and the sets are fine – excellent ambience. This is certainly one of William Welch and Al Gail's best scripts. They were often guilty of writing in see-saw action that went nowhere or had no real relevance to the story, other than to take up minutes of screen time. But in this episode, the action works fairly well. Mark [Phillips] is right about the boring exposition, but compared to what came in some of the later-season shows, this one's a gem." (vttbots.com)

Script:
Al Gail's and William Welch's writers contract: March 25, 1965.
Gail's and Welch's treatment, and 1st and 2nd draft teleplays: Dates unknown.
Mimeo Department's reformatted Shooting Final teleplay: Date unknown.
Rev. Shooting Final teleplay, by William Welch or Al Gail (gold paper): March 26.
Page revisions (blue paper): April 1.

This was Associate Story Editor Al Gail's second script assignment following "The Buccaneer." His collaborator was again Story Editor William Welch. Besides these two scripts, Welch had also gotten a screen credit on "The Blizzard Makers," which he had given a substantial rewrite.

Calvin Ward, of the network's Continuity Acceptance Department, wrote to Irwin Allen on March 29:

> Page 1: The manhandling of the girl should not become too violent or brutal. Keep the blood in Scene 8 to a minimum. This sequence can be approved only on film.

To the credit of director Sobey Martin, the resisting woman got in some good swats with her purse, even managing to shove one of her attackers through a storefront's plate-glass window. The only people in the fight to get "manhandled" were the men! Regardless, it is a very realistic and frightening sequence, thanks to its direction, and Susan Flannery's performance.

> Page 7: Do not show actual contact of blackjack and man's skull in Scene G-20.
>
> Page 13: I assume the man in the trunk is alive. If not, his eyes of course must be closed.
>
> Page 40: Do not show actual contact of the Karate Chop on the base of the skull.

The chop, delivered from Nelson to Crane, was quick and sharp. And Hedison's acting, afterwards, conveyed that he had one hell of a shoulder and neck ache. ABC was right to express concern. In real life, a karate chop to the back of the neck can have lasting results; it's not something which can be quickly shrugged off, despite that depiction in movies and TV from this era. Just as likely, permanent paralysis could be the result.

> Page 53: Usual caution that this fight does not become excessively violent and brutal. Can be approved only on film.

It was approved; what's surprising is that ABC allowed the sequence to air without some serious cuts. What begins as a typical "TV fight" soon escalates to a stunning sequence. Colonel Hamid, a high-ranking security officer – and clearly a highly skilled commando – switches from punches to swift and alarmingly forceful kicks, slamming his foot to Nelson's midriff with lightning speed and precision. Nelson flies over his desk and crashes to the floor. The fight is remarkably energetic and brutal. When the bruised Nelson regains awareness, he wraps some ice in a towel, gingerly touches it to his facial wounds during his forthcoming dialogue scene with Crane. You can not only see the damage, but feel the pain.

Page 54: Keep blood to a minimum in all shots showing the knife in Hamid's back.

This warning was adhered to, and the knife is left protruding from the corpse, as it would so often happen in comedies such as *Get Smart*. Regardless, the violence of the fight between Nelson and Col. Hamid was surprisingly realistic – and shockingly vicious.

Production:
(Filmed March 30 through April 6, 1964; 6 days)
(Budget: $117,855)

Sobey Martin returned to direct his seventh episode.

George Sanders was given top guest-star billing and paid $2,500 to play General Fenton. He would later say about many of his acting jobs, "I don't ask questions. I just take their money and use it for things that really interest me."

Sanders' sardonic statements are legendary. He also said, "Acting is like roller-skating. Once you know how to do it, it is neither stimulating nor exciting."

Sanders often played cads, such as Jack Favell in Alfred Hitchcock's *Rebecca*. But he also had many lead roles. He was Simon Templar – "The Saint" – in the film series from the late 1930s and '40s, and Gay Lawrence (aka "The Falcon") from another 1940s film series. He won the Academy Award for Best Supporting Actor for his role in the 1950 film *All About Eve*.

People loved George Sanders, and others simply loved to hear his comments. When asked how he felt following his divorce from Zsa Zsa Gabor, Sanders said, "Like a squeezed lemon."

Sanders was 58 by the time he was taking guest-starring roles in TV episodes like this one. He said, "I never thought I'd make the grade. And, let's face it, I haven't."

Sanders was just as morose in 1972, when he committed suicide at the age of 65. He left a note that read, "Dear World, I am leaving because I am bored. I feel I have lived long enough. I am leaving you with your worries in this sweet cesspool. Good luck."

Michael Pate was billed as co-star and paid $850 for up to four days work, as Colonel Hamid. He was 43 and had appeared in hundreds of television shows and films, specializing in unsavory characters of all types.

Susan Flannery was also given co-starring status, although only paid $200 for one day's work. She was 24 and this was her second of three appearances on *Voyage*, always in different roles. She only had a handful of TV credits at this point in a long career that would eventually see her with recurring roles on daytime soaps and prime-time soaps such as *Dallas*. She worked for Irwin Allen again, in that third *Voyage*, plus an episode of *The Time Tunnel*, and his most famous 1970s disaster movie. Allen always saw Flannery as a promising newcomer, but he was premature in his prediction that she would be a star. Flannery did make the grade eventually, winning a Golden Globe as Most Promising Newcomer … in 1975 … for Allen's *The Towering Inferno*. She also won four daytime Emmy awards (one for *Days of Our Lives* and three for *The Bold and the Beautiful*).

Above: Michael Pate, circa 1950s.
Below: Susan Flannery, from the *Chicago Tribune*, in 1968.

Production began on Tuesday, March 30, 1965 for the first of four days on Stage B with all the usual Seaview sets.

On Monday, April 5, the company was filming on the studio's "French Street," with a 6:30 a.m. make-up call, a 7:30 set call for the crew, an 8 a.m. set call for the cast. "The Secret of the Loch" had its only network airing on this night, and yet the production crew, as well as some of the actors from the series, never had a chance to see it. The company was served sandwiches and hot soup at 7:30 p.m., then continued to film until 9:17 at night.

Actor Michael Pate, quoted in the book *Science Fiction Television Series*, said, "George Sanders was a charming, easy man to work with. He was one of the greatest actors of all time. I remember him murmuring through this role. It's a pity that he had to act in such shit as this episode in the twilight of his career." (MP-SCTS2)

The sixth day of production, the last for the season, was on Stage 2, for "Int. Warehouse Office," "Int. Warehouse" and "Ext. Sidewalk Café." It was another late night, with sandwiches and hot soup again served at 7:30, then back to work, finishing the last scene at 11:10 p.m.

ABC got to see the rough cut on April 9, 1965. The Final Air Print was approved on April 13 and rushed to the network, airing just six days later. If there had been a thirty-third episode made during the first season, it most likely would have been delivered late.

Above: Basehart and Sanders, between scenes. Center: Pate and Hedison, spying. Bottom: A bruised, scuffed, and swelling Admiral Nelson, after a most realistic and brutal fight scene.

Release / Reaction:
(Only ABC broadcast: 4/19/65)

The week that "The Traitor" had its only network airing, the New York World's Fair opened for the summer. "Game of Love," by Wayne Fontana & the Mindbenders, and "Mrs. Robinson, You've Got a Lovely Daughter," by Herman's Hermits, were the songs playing the most from transistor radios. Robert Vaughn and David McCallum, of *The Man from U.N.C.L.E.*, had the cover of *TV Guide*.

"The Condemned" was aired before the 38th Annual Academy Awards Broadcast on ABC. Bob Hope was the host. *My Fair Lady* won for Best Picture, as did its star, Rex Harrison (Best Actor). Julie Andrews won as Best Actress, for *Mary Poppins*.

On April 18, 1965, Bill Shenton, writing for Alabama's *Cullman Times*, said about "The Traitor":

> George Sanders continues to get around on TV these days, having a part on Monday's *Voyage to the Bottom of the Sea*. ... He portrays an enemy agent who helps pull off

a kidnapping which is supposed to make Commander Nelson tell the whereabouts of a secret missile site.

Syndicated "TV Scout," in California's *The Lima News* on April 19, said:

> *Voyage to the Bottom of the Sea* has a reasonably good adventure with "The Traitor." The episode is one of the more adult of the series. Guest star is George Sanders at his irascible, charming best playing a top-ranking security officer for a Western nations alliance who is drawn into the search for Admiral Nelson's (Richard Basehart) missing sister (Susan Flannery). It seems the young lady will be killed unless the admiral reveals the site of a missile base underneath the sea.

A.C. Nielsen ratings report, April 19, 1965:	Rating:	Share:
7:30 – 8 p.m.:		
ABC: *Voyage to the Bottom of the Sea*	**18.7**	**31.3%**
CBS: *To Tell the Truth*	17.1	28.6%
NBC: *Karen*	15.4	25.8%
8 – 8:30 p.m.		
ABC: *Voyage to the Bottom of the Sea*	18.1	28.5%
CBS: *I've Got a Secret*	16.6	26.2%
NBC: *The Man from U.N.C.L.E.*	**20.7**	**32.6%**

***

Cleveland Amory, resident critic for *TV Guide*, America's top-selling magazine, reviewed *Voyage* in the May 1, 1965 issue:

> We promise you we are going to resist the temptation to say this show is the bottom; because it isn't. Neither, however, is it, shall we say, high adventure. It's just middling. Your children will love it and, as often as not, *Voyage to the Bottom of the Sea*'s suspense will offer you escape. And these days, that's not too bad, television fare being what it is.
>
> The chief character is an admiral named Nelson. No kidding. Anyway, played by Richard Basehart, he is admirable. He plays it straight, and, considering the plots and dialog, that isn't easy. Captain Crane (David Hedison), on the other hand, is a less successful character

– possibly because, the way his role is written, he doesn't seem to have any.

To continue in Amory's vein, "we" must disagree. We found Crane to be an intriguing character – all that seriousness, and derring-do, and a sense of humor too. David Hedison brought him to life. And we must credit Hedison for Crane's sense of humor. It certainly wasn't on the page.

Cleveland Amory – whom we nevertheless admired – just hadn't seen enough episodes to know what we all knew. Captain Crane, and David Hedison, you're fine by us.

***

According to the June 2, 1965 issue of *Variety*, when tracking the performance of roughly 90 prime-time series from the September 1964 fall kickoff of the first-run season, through the middle of May 1965 (the start of summer repeats), *Voyage to the Bottom of the Sea* was a solid Top 40 contender. The top shows were ranked by A.C. Nielsen as follows:

1. *Bonanza* (NBC)
2. *Bewitched* (ABC)
3. *Gomer Pyle, U.S.M.C.* (CBS)
4. *The Andy Griffith Show* (CBS)
5. *The Fugitive* (ABC)
6. *The Red Skelton Show* (CBS)
7. *The Dick Van Dyke Show* (CBS)
8. *The Lucy Show* (CBS)
9. *Peyton Place II* (ABC)
10. *Combat!* (ABC)
11. *The Ed Sullivan Show* (CBS)
12. *The Beverly Hillbillies* (CBS)

13. *Walt Disney's Wonderful World of Color* (NBC)
14. *My Three Sons* (CBS)
15. *Petticoat Junction* (CBS)
16. *Branded* (ABC)
17. *The Munsters* (CBS)
18. *Peyton Place I* (ABC)
19. *The Jackie Gleason Show* (CBS)
20. *Gilligan's Island* (CBS)
21. *The Addams Family* (ABC)
22. *The Virginian* (NBC)
23. *My Favorite Martian* (CBS)
24. *Flipper* (NBC)
25. *I've Got a Secret* (CBS)
26. *The Patty Duke Show* (ABC)
27. *McHale's Navy* (ABC)
28. *Gunsmoke* (CBS)
29. *The Wednesday Night Movie* (NBC)
30. *The Lawrence Welk Show* (ABC)
31. *The Saturday Night Movie* (NBC)
32. ***Voyage to the Bottom of the Sea* (ABC)**
33. *Candid Camera* (CBS)
34. *No Time for Sergeants* (ABC)
35. *To Tell the Truth* (CBS)
36. *Perry Mason* (CBS)
37. *The Donna Reed Show* (ABC)
38. *Bob Hope's Chrysler Theatre* (NBC)
39. *Daniel Boone* (NBC)
40. *Ben Casey* (ABC)

***

When the Emmys were awarded this year, those who had worked on *Voyage* probably didn't have many expectations. None of the actors were nominated, nor were any writers, directors … or producers. But it must have been extremely gratifying for all when L.B. Abbott, their heavily burdened special effects supervisor, was awarded an Emmy for "Outstanding Individual Achievements in Entertainment - Special Photographic Effects."

Irwin Allen was now the producer of an Emmy-winning series. Imagine that.

9

Wrapping Season One

Staff changes and realignments were always part of the preparation for a new TV season.

With the end of production for the first season, Associate Producer Joseph Gantman departed in search of greener pastures. He wanted to work on a show where he could have a real say over the scripts being bought and developed. Gantman immediately found work at Arena Productions on the MGM lot, as an production associate on *The Man from U.N.C.L.E.* But Arena's and MGM's real desire was for Gantman to produce a half-hour comedy pilot called "Separate Lives," for CBS. When it failed to sell, Gantman moved to Desilu. He produced *Mission: Impossible* for the 1966-67 TV season. He won two Emmy Awards when *Mission* was selected Outstanding Dramatic Series in both 1967 and '68. While at *Mission*, Gantman lured two other members of the *Voyage* creative staff away from Irwin Allen. (More about them later.)

After two years with *Mission: Impossible*, Gantman moved over to *Hawaii Five-O* for its first season (1968-69), then one season producing *Young Dr. Kildare* (1972-73), and one with *Movin' On* (1974-75).

Voyage's other Associate Producer also stepped down. Allan Balter, however, didn't leave Irwin Allen's employ – at least not for another year. Instead, he switched to the work he preferred – screenwriting. In collaboration with William Read Woodfield, Balter had written the first-season episode, "The Saboteur," under the pseudonym George Reed. Now, as a team, Balter and Woodfield would write nine more scripts for the series (although two were not produced). They were also given a pair of *Lost in Space* script assignments, and one for *The Time Tunnel*.

Taking the place of Gantman and Balter as *Voyage*'s associate producer was Frank La Tourette. He had actually been among the ranks for a few months, as Season One wound down, although he wasn't given a screen credit. At this time, La Tourette served as an unofficial advisor to Irwin Allen.

It is curious that, as of this book's publication in 2018, there is very little information regarding La Tourette on the internet … or in reference books. And it's too bad, considering how well-regarded he was in broadcasting, and the many prestigious series he had a hand in making. It is also curious, once we know of La Tourette's background in television, that he would connect, and stay connected for several years, with Irwin Allen. During this time he worked on series which were in complete contrast to his previous efforts. For these reasons, La Tourette warrants more than a passing mention.

Born in 1914, Frank La Tourette studied philosophy and language at St. Thomas Seminary in Denver. He wasn't sure if he wanted to be a Catholic priest or a writer. He chose the latter, and, while still attending St. Thomas Seminary, he became a columnist for the *Denver Catholic Register*. In 1936, he began two year's study at Gregorian University in Rome, although at this time Italy was under the rule of Benito Mussolini and his National Fascist Party. La Tourette finished his studies and returned to the United States two years before Italy entered World War II as part of the Axis alliance with Nazi Germany.

Frank LaTourette (left) and James Mosher look at negative of caesarian section birth scene film they accuse Francis Cardinal Spellman of having cancelled from TV showing on *Medic*.
(United Press Telephoto, 1956)

Upon his return to Denver, La Tourette entered Register College of Journalism for two years of study. In 1941, he went to Hollywood, becoming a reporter for International News Service. He continued to write newspaper articles regarding the Catholic church and church matters, as well as branching out into mainstream reporting. During World War II, La Tourette worked in San Francisco's Office of War Information.

In 1945, with the end of the war, La Tourette became News Director at San Francisco radio station KGO, an ABC affiliate. By 1950, he assumed the title and responsibilities of Western Division News Director for the ABC radio network, a position he held until early 1954.

It was while at KGO that La Tourette hired James Moser, a writer for *The San Francisco Examiner*, to work evenings in the radio station's newsroom. But what Moser really wanted to do was write screenplays. Moser met Jack Webb, an announcer at the station, and the two collaborated on a new radio drama called *Dragnet*. When the series made the move to television in 1951, Moser went along as the head writer. Webb was the show's producer, director, and star. La Tourette had good reason to believe his association with both men had ended with their move to television. However, events would bring their professional orbits once more into conjunction.

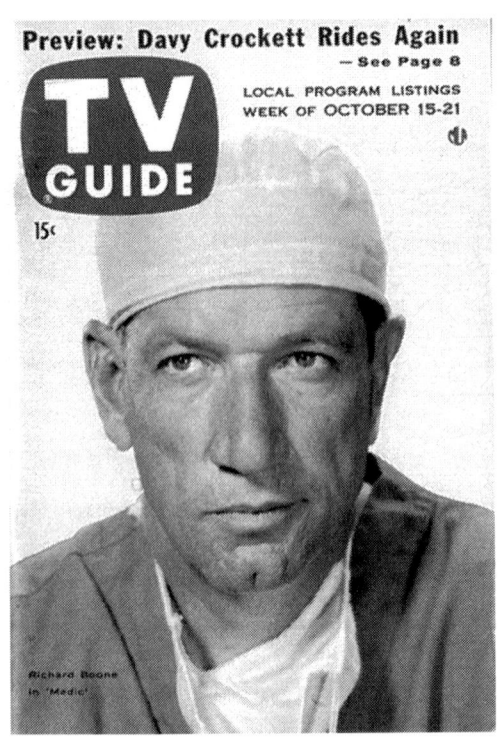

After writing 169 scripts for *Dragnet*, as well as half a dozen more for another Jack Webb series, *Pete Kelley's Blues*, Moser went out on his own. He had devised a TV property that, he felt, could do for hospital shows what the Emmy-winning *Dragnet* had done for police dramas – bring a sense of stark realism to television. Moser had someone in mind to serve as producer for the series – his old radio boss, Frank La Tourette.

Medic, which starred Richard Boone (later of *Have Gun – Will Travel*), premiered on NBC-TV in the fall of 1954, on Monday nights, from 9 to 9:30 p.m., opposite the most popular show on TV, CBS's *I Love Lucy*. Moser was creator and head writer; La Tourette was producer.

In its September 15, 1954 issue, *Variety* said:

> *Medic* is television at its creative and dramatic best. ... Employing a dramatic-documentary style, it's a model for television to aim at – factual and educational in content, but with dramatic kick that few shows in any media have ever rivaled. ...

Broadcasting, in its September 27th issue, concurred.

> NBC-TV can be well pleased with its new *Medic* series. Billed as a medical version of *Dragnet*, the show manages to put across the realistic note that made its predecessor famous while still permitting its characters full use of the English language. ...

Despite its aspirations, the show wasn't expected to do well in the ratings. NBC had yet to find a good rival for *Lucy*. But one night when CBS preempted the hit sitcom for President Eisenhower's election speech, *Medic* shot into the Top 10 in Trendix, as the third highest-rated program of the week. CBS rarely preempted *I Love Lucy* again. Regardless, *Medic* offered a refuge for those who didn't love Lucy – adult viewers more interested in serious drama than comedy.

In early December 1954, the Sylvania Television Awards singled out *Medic* with the grand award as "the most outstanding program on television." More awards soon came its way – including a couple of Emmys. The TV critics seemed to love *Medic*, when they noticed it.

A critic for *Broadcasting* magazine, in the trade's December 27, 1954 issue, reviewed the episode "Red Christmas."

> It takes calm nerves, a philosophical approach, if not a sedative, to view *The Medic* on NBC-TV. ... Last Monday's episode was appropriately labeled "Red Christmas," a word play on the story's bloody theme. Keeping within form, the program portrayed a saddened Christmas Eve through the jaundiced, cynical eye of a neuro-surgeon on duty at a hospital prepared for an annual influx of cut up cutups. ...
>
> The program, already tinseled with the Sylvania Award, carried through its morbid message format without a hitch. To those who like their Yuletide stories merry, spiritual, heartwarming, and even jolly, last Monday night's unhappy jolt was hard to take, with or without an anesthetic.

For "Flash of Darkness," an episode aired in early 1955, syndicated Hollywood columnist Emily Belser wrote:

> Producers of the television program, *The Medic*, have filmed a realistic show for Feb. 14 which is designed to picture just what would happen if an H-bomb fell on a big city. ...
>
> Frank La Tourette, the show's producer, says he hopes the vivid half-hour drama will help civil defense directors get an all-important message to the public. He added: "People everywhere should realize that if an attack does come, we are NOT ready for it, and something has got to be done to correct a very sad situation."
>
> La Tourette hopes the mock attack shown on the program will help wake up the populace to the need for further civil defense efforts.
>
> "We are trying to make things as realistic as possible," he said, pointing to battle scarred actors and the debris littering the set. ...

The somber mood of this latest *Medic* conjures up images of "Doomsday" on *Voyage to the Bottom of the Sea*. Coincidental? Perhaps not.

Reviewing "Flash of Darkness" for the February 21st issue of *Broadcasting*, a trade critic wrote:

> If only *Medic* would use a scalpel and not a meat cleaver on its viewers' sensibilities. Large, gory bunches of so-called "realism" still persist in botching up what otherwise, at times, could be standout film playlets in the highly-touted, medical documentary series. ...
>
> Aside from the questionable scenes, "Flash of Darkness" was a more noble effort from *The Medic*'s prescription pad. Whether it is just what the doctor ordered for our entertainment is a moot question, but some of the shockwave is certain to have reached the audience. ...

And there were more shockwaves forthcoming.

From mid-September 1955, for a United Press International wire story, Aline Mosby wrote:

> *Medic* is set to toss its most startling ailments at television viewers this season, with one controversial episode on sterility before the camera today. ... [T]his season's *Medic* will present shows on leprosy, teenage acne and even menopause. ...
>
> The idea for a sterility story, like many *Medic* plots, came from a real-life doctor. *Medic* not only bought the idea but hired the doctor, Edward Tyler, as technical advisor.
>
> "This is the first time a sterility story has been on TV," said the doctor as he stood on the set. "We will even show sperm, through a microscope, for the first time on TV."
>
> Another eye-opening show suggested by a viewer is one on "post partum psychosis." It deals with a mentally-ill woman who is tormented by a desire to kill her baby. ... One scene that will jolt the home audience shows the woman nearly throwing her baby into the stove.

La Tourette told Mosby, "[Jim] Moser and I think TV audiences are ready to learn as much as possible, and fan mail indicates the audience welcomes the realism. This season we'll send our cameras into hospitals for more operations.

The mail shows people want that. ... We've even discussed doing a story about homosexuality and how it was treated by a psychoanalyst." (FLT-BB55)

As for the subject of sterility, Jack Singer, a reviewer for *The Billboard* magazine, wrote:

> *Medic* added another feather in its public service cap this week by combining an absorbing drama with a message of hope for couples plagued by the problems of sterility. ... What particularly sets this head and shoulders above being a merely good dramatic show is that its basic theme is to provide information about what the medical profession can do and is doing to solve the physical problems of people.

Jim Mosby and Frank La Tourette continued to push the limits with *Medic*. The title of Aline Mosby's UPI column on March 9, 1956 was "Caesarian Birth Makes TV History on *Medic*." For the first time on TV, the birth of a baby would be shown, by Caesarean delivery. While the show was a dramatic fiction, the surgical procedure was real – filmed at Santa Monica Hospital.

"People fainted at the preview of that show," La Tourette told Mosby. "I never thought we'd get an actual birth on the air. We wanted to show the actual operation, but the network and even the doctors were against it. Finally we tried one operation. The viewers loved it. The reaction convinced doctors, and the network, that people want to see operations. So we have a rule now – our camera doesn't go into surgery without filming the actual operation. People feel they're cheated if you just show the nurses' faces. After all, *Climax*, or any dramatic show, does that. People lose faith in our program if we don't show more. ... These shows are educational. I'm letting my young children watch the Caesarian birth program. Oh, we'll never run out of diseases. We're signed for another season and this show could go on forever." (FLT-GBPG56)

La Tourette's enthusiasm was too optimistic.

The advance promotion for the episode resulted in its being pulled from broadcast. The Archdiocese of New York registered a complaint, and NBC buckled. La Tourette went public with his displeasure, blaming Cardinal Francis Spellman, of the Archdiocese. La Tourette and Jim Moser even sent a telegram to the Cardinal, calling his action "an unwarranted and very disappointing use of your high office." And then they shared that telegram with the press.

A short time later, despite having been assured renewal by both NBC and the series' sponsors, *Medic* got its pink slip.

On May 30, 1956, *Variety* reported:

> While it's true that NBC-TV had a wrestling match with the masterminds of *Medic* (notably producer Frank La Tourette and creator James Moser) stemming from a recent installment that was to include a Caesarian birth sequence which never got to the home screens, its dumping from the 9 p.m. Monday niche is apparently based on weightier considerations. One of these is realism, with *Medic* showing up a straggling 81st in the latest Nielsens. ...

The network and the show's sponsors had endured the low ratings because of the show's prestige. But that shine was quickly diminished when the show's producers took on the Catholic Church. In the mid-20th century, disagreement with a Catholic official was considered near-sacrilege by the public and the press – however hypocritical this reaction, when compared to the behavior of the finger-pointers.

During its two seasons, *Medic* was nominated for 13 Emmy Awards, winning two (both for cinematographer). The nominations included acknowledgments for star Richard Boone, and for writing, direction, and production (Best Dramatic Series, as well as Best Producer, for Frank La Tourette).

But the producer wasn't out of work for long. He and colleague Jim Moser wrote a highly acclaimed episode of *Schlitz Playhouse*. Then La Tourette went into the employ of old acquaintance Jack Webb for a few seasons as associate producer and story editor on *Dragnet*. Webb also had La Tourette produce a pair of pilot films for Mark VII Productions. The first, "Man on the Street," aired as a standalone under the title of "People." It didn't sell as a series, but the other, *The D.A.'s Man*, did. La Tourette served as producer.

At the end of the 1958-59 TV series, La Tourette left Mark VII to go to CBS. He took over production of its popular cop show, *The Lineup*, now expanded from 30 to 60 minutes. The reviews were mostly bad, with *Variety* saying that the hour-long version "dragged." The writer continued, "It's a shame that given more time, producer Frank La Tourette didn't use it to offer some insight into the violence that surrounds us."

The hour-long version was cancelled after 17 episodes. La Tourette was quickly reassigned to take over production of a pilot film called "Emergency Ward." It didn't sell, but the pilot aired in late December 1959.

One month later, La Tourette was assigned another pilot for CBS – "Turnpike." It never got on the road, but, by year's end, La Tourette was producing episodes for the documentary series called *Close Up!* Joan Crosby, of "TV Scout," wrote in her October 13, 1960 syndicated column:

> You'll get a surprising picture of Haiti on *Close-up!* tonight, as the new documentary series presents "Paradise in Chains." This is the Haiti tourists don't see – the people, suffering from poverty, malnutrition and fear, living under a dictatorship. Producer Frank La Tourette tells us he found the people "more afraid than they were in Italy under Mussolini. And I was there!" ... La Tourette says filming this was "cloak-and-dagger stuff," as he and his crew were constantly trailed by "government spies," and consequently filmed material they didn't want [in order] to throw them off the track. This is an unexpected side of Haiti and it could be a shocker.

By 1964, La Tourette began a new phase of his career, working as a consultant under William Self at 20th Century-Fox Television, while, at the same time, beginning a two-decade relationship with UCLA, where he would soon advance (in 1967) to serve as head of the university's Radio and Television Division. One of the shows for which Bill Self wanted La Tourette's assistance was *Voyage to the Bottom of the Sea*.

When you know this and take into account La Tourette's strong history in realistic drama, some of the choices seen in *Voyage*'s freshman year make more sense. Irwin Allen was into spectacle and escapism entertainment; La Tourette leaned more toward realism, and using TV not only to shock, but educate. Mix these two seemingly opposing agendas together and the stage was set for episodes such as "Hot Line," "Hail to the Chief," "Submarine Sunk Here," and "Doomsday."

Voyage to the Bottom of the Sea was a first-season hit, quickly renewed for a second term. Now Allen's *Lost in Space* was preparing to go into weekly production at 20th Century-Fox for CBS. ABC had expressed interest in a new Irwin Allen project called *The Time Tunnel*, which would in all likelihood go into series production the following year. Only one other producer in television during the 1960s had three hour-long series running consecutively – Quinn Martin. At this time, for the 1965-66 season, he had three – *The Fugitive*, *12 O'Clock High*, and *The F.B.I.*, all for ABC. By 1967, he would add a fourth, *The Invaders*, also for the alphabet network. With the upcoming challenges presented by multiple Irwin Allen series, Bill Self knew he needed Frank LaTourette, and he met no resistance from Allen.

In fact, Irwin Allen immediately took to Frank La Tourette, the former philosophy student who held a Bachelor's Degree in Journalism and a Masters in Literature. Allen, as you will recall, had only attended Junior College in New York City, with some night classes at Columbia University. While Allen, with an adopted Boston accent, was working his way up in the industry, he could only dream of having the confidence assured by prestigious college degrees. But now he had the benefit of those degrees – not framed on the wall, but standing at his side, in the person of La Tourette, Allen's new right-hand man.

La Tourette not only served *Voyage to the Bottom of the Sea* as associate producer for the 1965-66 TV season, but he was also an unofficial –although ever-present – consultant on the new *Lost in Space* series, as well as the new pilots and TV series produced by Allen throughout the remainder of the decade.

***

It should come as no surprise that *Voyage to the Bottom of the Sea* was nominated – and also won – only one Emmy award for its 1964-65 TV season. L.B. Abbott took home the trophy for Outstanding Achievement in Special Photographic Effects. He – representing himself, his team, and the series – was the only individual to even be nominated. Nothing else on television even came close to the awe-inspiring special effects of *Voyage*.

The Academy of Television Arts and Sciences was not in the habit of acknowledging science fiction with Emmy awards. Rod Serling had won two, for his writing on *The Twilight Zone*, and the series had been acknowledged with a one other Emmy, for Cinematography, and five other nominations, during an equal amount of years. Remarkably, *The Outer Limits* had been nominated only once, for its Art Direction and Scenic Design, but had never gotten a nod for its striking direction, make-up, and wardrobe. Not to mention some very fine performances by the likes of Nick Adams, Ed Asner, Robert Culp, Bruce Dern, Robert Duvall, Don Gordon, Steve Ihnat, Salome Jens, Martin Landau, David McCallum, Warren Oates, Philip Pine, Donald Pleasence, William Shatner, Warren Stevens, and many others. Now it was *Voyage*'s turn to get snubbed. Even William Hoch was ignored, with the Best Cinematographer nominations going instead to *Bonanza*, *The Man from U.N.C.L.E.*, and *Twelve O'Clock High*. The latter was the winner. Leonard Horn and James Goldstone weren't even mentioned for their work on *Voyage*. Instead, the directors of an episode of *Hallmark Hall of Fame* and the TV special *My Name Is Barbra* were given bragging rights with nominations, and Paul Bogart won for an episode of *The*

Defenders. And Richard Basehart and David Hedison weren't even honored with a nomination, despite making every moment of *Voyage* as dramatic, grim, and terrifying as an actor could hope to achieve. And, with some episodes, this had been a pretty tall order. David McCallum received a nomination for *The Man from U.N.C.L.E.*, as did Dean Jagger for *Mr. Novak*, Robert Coote for *The Rogues*, and Richard Crenna for *Slatery's People*, among others. Who won for best dramatic performance? Alfred Lunt for the TV special *The Magnificent Yankees*.

Regardless, *Voyage* had received the best rewards any freshman series could hope for – the cover of *TV Guide* (on June 19, 1965, as Season One repeated over ABC), and a network renewal.

Irwin Allen was now poised to return for his second year as a producer of ambitious science fiction television – with two ambitious hour-long series, a third in development, and ideas aplenty for more shows to come.

When we resume our story, in Volume 2, we'll complete the rest of the voyage, through all 78 color episodes – an extended three years of an overall adventure which would make *Voyage to the Bottom of the Sea* the longest-running of all Irwin Allen series.

There were many hurdles ahead – making the switch to color; finding the right formula to bring the series back to the top of the ratings during its time period; appeasing the network by delivering the type of stories ABC most wanted to see … while staying clear of the subjects they most frowned upon; and doing it all within budget and on schedule.

Many fans consider the next batch of episodes – Season Two – to be the finest of the entire series. We agree.

Stay tuned.

APPENDIX A
The Composers of *Voyage to the Bottom of the Sea*

The Human Touch:
The Craft and Art of TV Soundtracks in the 1960s

In the 1960s, American television audiences took background scores for granted. Music heightened the suspense, or warned that love scenes were beginning, so younger viewers could look elsewhere before the dreaded smooching started. Sometimes Baby Boomers received a musical education that was only appreciated much later. For many of us, our first exposure to Rossini's "William Tell Overture" was *The Lone Ranger*. How many people would recognize Gounod's "Funeral March of a Marionette" without Alfred Hitchcock?

In many ways the 1960s and 1970s were a Golden Age of TV music. Some TV scores of this era have been released on CD, such as *Battlestar Galactica*, *Star Trek*, NBC's U.N.C.L.E. series (*Man* and *Girl*), and those of a certain "master of disaster," Irwin Allen.

A well-established system had been developed to provide music for scripted programs. In the early days of the industry, bootlegged music from low-budget films had been rerecorded, parsed, and labeled. The still-running *The Adventures of Superman* (1952-1958) is one of the highest-profile shows to feature such canned, repackaged music. For "prestige" live programs, scores were written and performed during the broadcast.

By the 1960s and the prevalence of filmed, scripted series, production executives were assigned to supervise the music for a series. This involved contracting the composition and recording of original music to match the onscreen scenes. As with film music, the score was provided to sweeten the story, helping to set or enhance the characters or mood.

As with most Hollywood trades, the performers of music for television belonged to a union. The American Federation of Musicians maintains strict rules regarding their members' employment. In the 1960s, the AFM required a TV show's producer to buy a certain number of hours of studio recording time, per season. This figure was negotiated with an eye to several factors including the type of show, episode length, and so on.

In the early to mid-1960s, here's how a TV episode was typically scored: A TV show's producer or associate, along with the show's music supervisor, would select a composer. Most production departments built a list, over time, of music writers who were generally available, affordable, and dependable. Often a composer would have from one to two weeks, but no more, to produce a score.

When a final print of the episode was ready, the composer would view it with one or two executives, timing sequences and deciding which scenes should be scored. Notes would be made, with times figured to fractions of a second.

The composer was now dependent on these notes as to the mood, duration, dialog, and other elements of the story. Remember, these times were long before the luxuries of digital video and instant review. The scorer's job was to fill the allotted time with a musical background that would enhance, accompany, and emphasize – but not overwhelm. The score would then be recorded by ensembles of six to fifteen or more very talented session musicians, usually conducted by the composer.

The demands of budget and time prohibited full-fledged symphonic music for a television series. A large ensemble was simply too costly in time, fees, and the coordination of players. Not only that, most TV sets had a single three-to-five-inch speaker. Dense, complicated music would likely as not sound mushy or confused. Besides, background music was a poor cousin to dialogue and sound effects. Although much great music was created by music writers, who at their best achieved brilliance on a budget, the product was never meant to be compared to Brahms or Rachmaninoff.

Many screen composers succeeded despite the restrictions, earning lasting renown. For instance, Jerry Goldsmith was famous for not starting a project until it was mere days from coming due. However, he proved dependable, inventive, and adaptable. Successful TV tunesmiths of the 1960s and 1970s proved that creativity, innovation, and talent made up for any lack of "depth of field" in the ensembles.

After the music was written and recorded for any particular episode of a series, it was within the producer's rights to re-use it for one or more subsequent episodes, through "tracking." In pop music, "tracking" means "overdubbing." But in the television industry, the term means adding previously composed music to a new episode. While a cost-saving practice for the studios, tracking signified lost employment for AFM union members. (This topic is still a sore spot. As recently as 2015, the AFM was filing multiple lawsuits against studios, alleging unauthorized use of one film's music in another.)

In the 1960s, AFM rules allowed tracking, but limited any previously recorded music to the same broadcast season. A successful music editor was one who could successfully balance tracked episodes with the AFM's recording requirements for new music.

At times an episode would be partially tracked, with a few additional cues composed specially. Sometimes a show's contractually required recording time was fulfilled by recording "library cues" for later use, perhaps truncated to end with a "sting," or at a differing tempo.

Libraries of earlier cues and themes were sorted, cataloged, and laid into a varying percentage of series episodes. Music supervisors such as Wilbur Hatch at Desilu or Frank Anderson at MGM were wizards of the process. And, the legalities of music licensing required exact tallies be kept of all re-used music. The closing "composer" credits for a tracked episode were calculated from the percentage of music a composer's music occupied in the final cut.

These broad requirements and constrictions also applied, of course, to the TV series produced by Irwin Allen, including *Voyage to the Bottom of the Sea*.

The *Voyage* Composers

When it came to the television version of Irwin Allen's undersea epic, Paul Sawtell was drafted to compose the first episode's score. Along with Bert Shefter, Sawtell had composed the score for the 1961 *Voyage to the Bottom of the Sea* feature film. Sawtell's title theme appeared in every subsequent episode of *Voyage* – save one. The entire score for the Season Two opener, including opening and closing titles, was by Jerry Goldsmith.

Following, in alphabetical order, are necessarily brief notes about the credited composers for the series. These credits are as listed in the Internet Movie Database.

Alexander Courage (1919-2008) was a composer, conductor, and arranger for movies and TV. He's most widely known for his work laying the cornerstone of *Star Trek*'s musical edifice as composer for the two pilots, the opening theme, and for other episodes. Other well-known TV work was for such series as *Lost in Space*, *Daniel Boone*, and *The Waltons*. He composed the original score for *Superman IV: The Quest for Peace*, based on John Williams's original themes. He often arranged other composers' music for movies, including Williams and André Previn. As an arranger for Jerry Goldsmith, he provided (without credit) the "Captain's Log" arrangements of his own TV theme which was used in 1979's *Star Trek: The Motion Picture*.

First Season
The Fear-Makers (co-credit)
The Price of Doom (co-credit)
Second Season
The Cyborg
Leviathan
Third Season
The Lost Bomb
Fourth Season
Flaming Ice

Robert Drasnin (1927-2015) received an M.A. in Music from UCLA, and composed mostly for TV and film. *Voodoo*, his 1959 album, also featured a young John Williams as session pianist. He scored many notable shows in the 1960s, including *Hawaii Five-O*, *The Time Tunnel*, *Lost in Space*, *Mannix*, *The Twilight Zone*, *Mission: Impossible*, *The Wild, Wild West*, and *The Man from U.N.C.L.E.*, as well as *Voyage*. Some of Drasnin's work may be heard on soundtrack releases of *U.N.C.L.E.* and various Allen series.

Third Season
The Wax Men

Hugo Friedhofer (1901-1981), a native Californian, performed as a cellist before becoming an orchestrator for Fox and Warners. Among his more than 200 scores were his Oscar-winning music for 1946's *The Best Years of Our Lives*, and such films as *Lifeboat*, *Hondo*, *An Affair to Remember*, and *The Girl in the Red Velvet Swing*. His TV work included *I Spy*, *Barnaby Jones*, *Lancer*, and *The Over-the-Hill Gang*.

First Season
The Fear-Makers (co-credit)
The Mist of Silence
The Price of Doom (co-credit)
Turn Back the Clock

Harry Geller (1913-2008) was a jazz trumpeter and band leader as well as an arranger and composer. He also wrote music for such TV shows as *The Wild, Wild West*, *Judd for the Defense*, *Hawaii Five-O*, *Daniel Boone*, and *Gunsmoke*.

Fourth Season
The Deadly Dolls
Sealed Orders
Savage Jungle
The Death Clock

Irving Gertz (1915-2008) composed, sometimes without screen credit, for such well-known B-movies as *The Alligator People*, *The Incredible Shrinking Man*, and *It Came from Outer Space*. His TV work included *Peyton Place* and *Daniel Boone*.

Fourth Season
Attack!

Jerry Goldsmith (1929-2004) won an Oscar and five Emmys, but his single score for *Voyage* was the premiere of Season Two, and is not well-regarded by many fans. The music, including a new opening title theme, was never used again. Elsewhere, Goldsmith is lauded for his work on TV's *The Man from U.N.C.L.E.* and *The Waltons*; and various Star Trek films, as well as *Alien*, *Twilight Zone: The Movie*, *The Omen*, and many other motion pictures of all genres.

Second Season
Jonah and the Whale

Lennie Hayton (1908-1971) worked with Artie Shaw and Jimmy Dorsey before becoming music director for MGM in 1940. His musical arrangements won two Oscars, for *On the Town* and *Hello, Dolly!* Most of his work was for feature films; *Voyage* is the only series for which Hayton composed more than a single episode.

Second Season
... And Five of Us Are Left
The Silent Saboteurs
The Monster from Outer Space
The Phantom Strikes (co-credit)

Third Season
Werewolf
Night of Terror
The Death Watch

Fourth Season
Time Lock

Michael Hennagin (1936-1993) composed a few scores for television before leaving to become a classical composer and university professor. His later work included ballet scores and vocal music.

First Season
The Human Computer (co-credit)

Joseph Mullendore (1914-1990) composed in the 1950s and 1960s for stock-music libraries, film, and TV. Notable later work included *Star Trek*, *Burke's Law*, and *Honey West*, from which an LP of his music was released.

Fourth Season
The Return of Blackbeard

Nelson Riddle (1921-1985) composed and arranged for big bands and vocalists as well as TV, over a forty-year career beginning in the 1940s. Most famous for his iconic theme for the *Route 66* series, he also produced music from *Batman* and *Tarzan* to *The Man from U.N.C.L.E.* and *Newhart*.

Second Season
Escape from Venice

Paul Sawtell (1906-1971) was born in Poland and in 1923 immigrated to the United States, where he found work in theatres and radio as conductor and violinist. In the mid-1930s he found work in Hollywood as an arranger before becoming a music director at RKO. An early high mark was his score for the Sherlock Holmes film *Pearl of Death* (Universal, 1944). He then scored films for RKO and Universal, beginning with westerns and wreaking havoc on young American brains by scoring the 1950s horror and sci-fi films *It! The Terror from Beyond Space*, *The Fly*, and *Return of the Fly*. Beginning in 1959 he and Bert Shefter composed music for Irwin Allen's films *The Big Circus*, *The Lost World*, *The Big Show*, *Voyage to the Bottom of the Sea*, and *Five Weeks in a Balloon*. Besides his work for Allen, he was also music supervisor with Shefter for 68 episodes of *77 Sunset Strip* and 108 episodes of *Hawaiian Eye*.

First Season
Eleven Days to Zero
The City Beneath the Sea
The Village of Guilt
Hot Line
Submarine Sunk Here
Long Live the King
The Exile

Herman Stein (1915-2007) was a jazz composer as well as a writer for radio, TV, and film. Among his credits are *This Island Earth*, *The Monolith Monsters*, and music cues used in over 30 episodes of *Wagon Train*.

Second Season
The Phantom Strikes (co-credit)

Leith Stevens (1909-1970) was a Missouri-born conductor, composer, and music director. He served as music supervisor for such series as *Mannix*, *The Odd Couple*, and *Mission: Impossible*. His film scores include *When Worlds Collide*, *Destination Moon*, and *The War of the Worlds*. He composed for such varied TV shows as *Custer*, *Crusader Rabbit*, *Gunsmoke*, and *Climax!*

Second Season
Time Bomb
The Left-Handed Man
The X Factor
Third Season
Monster from the Inferno
Death from the Past
Fourth Season
A Time to Die
Blow Up
Terrible Leprechaun
Man-Beast

Morton Stevens (1929-1991), besides being music supervisor for shows such as *Gilligan's Island*, *Gunsmoke*, and *The Wild, Wild West*, also composed widely for other series, including his Emmy award-winning title music for *Hawaii Five-O*.

First Season
The Human Computer (co-credit)

The *Voyage* Music Staff

These professionals worked with composers and production staff to select and present the music used in the series.

Leonard A. Engel (1930-1988) was music editor for more than 60 films and TV series. Movie work included *The Boys from Brazil*, *The Towering Inferno*, and *The Secret of NIMH*. Among his many TV credits were *Peyton Place*, *Daniel Boone*, *Batman*, *Judd for the Defense*, and *The Green Hornet*.

Harry Eisen (1922-2001) was a music editor for over a dozen films in the 1950s and 1960s. He performed the same function for thirty-three episodes of *Voyage*.

Morrie McNaughton (dates unknown) performed as music editor for several TV series from the 1950s to the 1980s, including *Magnum, P.I.*, *Tales of the Gold Monkey*, and *The Rockford Files*.

Lionel Newman (1916-1989) worked more than forty years at Fox, composing, conducting, and performing musical supervision for many TV series, including *M*A*S*H*, *Julia*, *The Many Loves of Dobie Gillis*, and *Daniel Boone*.

He conducted scores for many films and was music supervisor for the original Star Wars trilogy – about 300 projects overall. He earned several Academy Award nominations for scoring, and shared an Oscar (with *Voyage* composer Lennie Hayton) for the music of *Hello, Dolly!*

First Season
Harry Eisen ... music editor
Leonard A. Engel ... supervising music editor
Lionel Newman ... music supervisor

Second Season
Harry Eisen ... music editor
Morrie McNaughton ... music editor
Leonard A. Engel ... supervising music editor
Lionel Newman ... music supervisor

Third Season
Leonard A. Engel ... supervising music editor
Morrie McNaughton ... music editor
Lionel Newman ... music supervisor

Fourth Season
Leonard A. Engel ... supervising music editor
Morrie McNaughton ... music editor
Lionel Newman ... music supervisor

Appendix B
Episode Quick Reference

Season One Production Order:

1	1-01	6008	9/14/64	Eleven Days to Zero (Nov. 18 – Dec 6, 1963; 12 days)
2	1-02	7202	11/02/64	The Village of Guilt (June 15 – 24, 1964, 7 ½ days)
3	1-03	7203	10/05/64	The Mist of Silence (June 24 – July 3, 1964; 7 days)
4	1-04	7204	9/21/64	The City Beneath the Sea (July 6 – 14, 1964; 7 days)
5	1-05	7205	10/26/64	Turn Back the Clock (July 15 – 22, 1964; 6 days)
6	1-06	7206	12/28/64	Hail to the Chief (July 23 – 31, 1964; 7 days)
7	1-07	7207	9/28/64	The Fear-Makers (August 3 – 10, 1964; 6 days)
8	1-08	7208	11/09/64	Hot Line (August 11 – 18, 1964; 6 days)
9	1-09	7209	10/19/64	The Sky Is Falling (August 20 – 28, 1964; 7 days)
10	1-10	7210	10/12/64	The Price of Doom (Aug. 31 – Sept. 8, 1964; 6 days)
11	1-11	7211	12/21/64	Long Live the King (September 9 – 16, 1964; 6 days)
12	1-12	7212	11/16/64	Submarine Sunk Here (September 17 – 25, 1964; 7 days)
13	1-13	7213	11/23/64	The Magnus Beam (October 8 – 16, 1964; 7 days)
14	1-14	7214	11/30/64	No Way Out (October 19 – 27, 1964; 7 days)
15	1-15	7215	12/07/64	The Blizzard Makers (Oct. 28 – Nov. 4, 1964; 6 days)
16	1-16	7216	12/14/64	The Ghost of Moby Dick (November 5 – 12, 1964; 6 days)
17	1-17	7217	01/18/65	Doomsday (Nov. 13 – 20 + Dec. 18; 6 ½ days)
18	1-18	7219	01/11/65	Mutiny (Nov. 23 – Dec. 1, 1964; 6 days)
19	1-19	7220	01/04/65	The Last Battle (December 2 – 9, 1964; 6 days)
20	1-20	7221	01/25/65	The Invaders (December 10 – 18, 1964; 7 days)
21	1-21	7223	01/01/65	The Indestructible Man (December 21 – 31, 1964; 7 ½ days)
22	1-22	7223	02/08/65	The Buccaneer

					(Dec. 31 - Jan. 13, 1965; 9 ½ days)
23	1-23	7224	02/15/65	The Human Computer	
					(January 13 – 25, 1965; 7 days)
24	1-24	7226	02/22/65	The Saboteur	
					(Jan. 26 – Feb. 3, 1965; 7 days)
25	1-25	7227	03/01/65	Cradle of the Deep	
					(February 4 – 12, 1965; 7 days)
26	1-26	7228	03/15/65	The Exile	
					(February 15 – 23, 1965; 7 days)
27.	1-27	7229	03/08/65	The Amphibians	
					(February 15 – 22, 1965; 6 days)
28	1-28	7230	03/22/65	The Creature	
					(Feb. 23 – March 3, 1965; 6 days)
29	1-29	7231	03/29/65	The Enemies	
					(March 3 – 11; 6 ½ days)
30	1-30	7232	04/05/65	The Secret of the Loch	
					(March 11 – 19; 7 days; 6 ½ days)
31	1-31	7218	04/12/65	The Condemned	
					(March 22 – 29, 1965; 6 days)
32	1-32	7225	04/19/65	The Traitor	
					(March 30 – April 6, 1965; 6 days)

Season One Broadcast Order:

1	1-01	6008	9/14/64	Eleven Days to Zero
2	1-04	7204	9/21/64	The City Beneath the Sea
3	1-07	7207	9/28/64	The Fear-Makers
4	1-03	7203	10/05/64	The Mist of Silence
5	1-10	7210	10/12/64	The Price of Doom
6	1-09	7209	10/19/64	The Sky Is Falling
7	1-05	7205	10/26/64	Turn Back the Clock
8	1-08	7202	11/02/64	The Village of Guilt
9	1-09	7208	11/09/64	Hot Line
10	1-10	7212	11/16/64	Submarine Sunk Here
11	1-11	7213	11/23/64	The Magnus Beam
12	1-12	7214	11/30/64	No Way Out
13	1-13	7215	12/07/64	The Blizzard Makers
14	1-14	7216	12/14/64	The Ghost of Moby Dick
15	1-15	7211	12/21/64	Long Live the King
16	1-16	7206	12/28/64	Hail to the Chief
17	1-17	7220	01/04/65	The Last Battle
18	1-18	7219	01/11/65	Mutiny
19	1-19	7217	01/18/65	Doomsday
20	1-20	7221	01/25/65	The Invaders
21	1-21	7223	02/01/65	The Indestructible Man
22	1-22	7223	02/08/65	The Buccaneer
23	1-23	7224	02/15/65	The Human Computer
24	1-24	7226	02/22/65	The Saboteur
25	1-25	7227	03/01/65	Cradle of the Deep
26	1-26	7229	03/08/65	The Amphibians
27	1-27	7228	03/15/65	The Exile

28	1-28	7230	03/22/65	The Creature
29	1-29	7231	03/29/65	The Enemies
30	1-30	7232	04/05/65	The Secret of the Loch
31	1-31	7218	04/12/65	The Condemned
32	1-32	7225	04/19/65	The Traitor
Repeat	-	-	04/26/65	(The Price of Doom)
Repeat	-	-	05/03/65	(The Sky Is Falling)
Pre-empted	-	-	05/10/65	(*"Saga of Western Man" special*)
Repeat	-	-	05/17/65	(Village of Guilt)
Repeat	-	-	05/24/65	(Submarine Sunk Here)
Repeat	-	-	05/31/65	(No Way Out)
Repeat	-	-	06/07/65	(The Ghost of Moby Dick)
Repeat	-	-	06/14/65	(The Invaders)
Repeat	-	-	06/21/65	(Mutiny)
Repeat	-	-	06/28/65	(Doomsday)
Repeat	-	-	07/05/65	(The Indestructible Man)
Repeat	-	-	07/12/65	(The Creature)
Repeat	-	-	07/19/65	(Hot Line)
Repeat	-	-	07/26/65	(The Saboteur)
Repeat	-	-	08/02/65	(The Amphibians)
Repeat	-	-	08/09/65	(The Exile)
Repeat	-	-	08/16/65	(The Enemies)
Repeat	-	-	08/23/65	(The Condemned)
Repeat	-	-	08/30/65	(The Fear-Makers)
Repeat	-	-	09/06.65	(The City Beneath the Sea)

Season Two Production Order:

33	2-01	8201	09/19/65	Jonah and the Whale
				(June 24-July 6, 1965; 7 days)
34	2-02	8202	10/03/65	... And Five of Us Are Left
				(July 8-15, 1965; 6 days)
35	2-03	8203	09/26/65	Time Bomb
				(July 16-23, 1965; 6 days)
36	2-04	8204	10/17//65	Escape from Venice
				(July 26-August 2, 1965; 6 days)
37	2-05	8205	10/10/65	The Cyborg
				(August 3-12, 1965; 7¾ days)
38	2-06	8206	10/31/65	The Deadliest Game
				(August 12-20, 1965; 6 days)
39	2-07	8207	10/24//65	The Left-Handed Man
				(August 23-30, 1965; 6 days)
40	2-08	8210	02/20/66	The Death Ship
				(August 31 – September 7; 5 days)
41	2-09	8209	11/28/65	The Silent Saboteurs
				(September 10 – 17, 1965; 6 days)
42	2-10	8211	11/07/65	Leviathan
				(September 20 – 28, 1965; 7 days)
43	2-11	8212	11/14/65	The Peacemaker
				(Sept. 29 – Oct. 6, 1965; 6 days)
44	2-12	8213	12/19/65	The Monster from Outer Space
				(Oct. 7 – 14 + Nov. 10 & 11, 1965; 7 days)
45	2-13	8214	12/05/65	The X-Factor
				(October 15 – 25, 1965; 6 ½ days)
46	2-14	8215	12/12/65	The Machines Strike Back
				(October 25 – Nov. 2, 1965; 6 ¼ days)
47	2-15	8216	01/02/66	Killers of the Deep
				(November 3 – 10, 1965; 5 ¾ days)
48	2-16	8217	12/26/65	Terror on Dinosaur Island
				(November 12 – 22, 1965; 6 ½ days)
49	2-17	8218	01/09/66	Deadly Creature Below!
				(Nov. 22 – 30 + Dec. 1 &2, 1965; 6 ½ days)
50	2-18	8219	01/16/66	The Phantom Strikes
				(December 3 – 14, 1965; 7 ½ days)
51	2-19	8220	01/23/66	The Sky's on Fire
				(December 16 – 27, 1965; 7 days)
52	2-20	8221	01/30/66	Graveyard of Fear
				(Dec. 27 – Jan. 5, 1966; 7 days)
53	2-21	8222	02/06/66	The Shape of Doom
				(January 5 – 12, 1966; 5 ½ days)
54	2-22	8223	02/13/66	Dead Men's Doubloons
				(January 13 – 21, 1966; 7 days)
55	2-23	8224	02/27/66	The Monster's Web
				(Jan. 24 – Feb. 3, 1966; 8 days)
56	2-24	8225	03/06/66	The Menfish
				(February 4 - 11, 1966; 6 days)
57	2-25	8226	03/13/66	The Mechanical Man

				(February 14 – 22, 1966; 6 ½ days)
58	2-26	8227	03/20/66	The Return of the Phantom
				(Feb. 22 – March 2, 1966; 8 days)

Season Two Broadcast Order:

33	2-01	8201	09/19/65	Jonah and the Whale
34	2-02	8203	09/26/65	Time Bomb
35	2-03	8202	10/03/65	... And Five of Us Are Left
36	2-04	8205	10/10/65	The Cyborg
37	2-05	8204	10/17/65	Escape from Venice
38	2-06	8207	10/24/65	The Left-Handed Man
39	2-07	8206	10/31/65	The Deadliest Game
40	2-08	8211	11/07/65	Leviathan
41	2-09	8212	11/14/65	The Peacemaker
42	2-10	8209	11/21/65	The Silent Saboteurs
Pre-empted			11/28/65	(*Dangerous Christmas of Red Riding Hood*)
43	2-11	8214	12/05/65	The X-Factor
44	2-12	8215	12/12/65	The Machines Strike Back
45	2-13	8213	12/19/65	The Monster from Outer Space
46	2-14	8217	12/26/65	Terror on Dinosaur Island
47	2-15	8216	01/02/66	Killers of the Deep
48	2-16	8218	01/09/66	Deadly Creature Below!
49	2-17	8219	01/16/66	The Phantom Strikes
50	2-18	8220	01/23/66	The Sky's On Fire
51	2-19	8221	01/30/66	Graveyard of Fear
52	2-20	8222	02/06/66	The Shape of Doom
53	2-21	8223	02/13/66	Dead Men's Doubloons
54	2-22	8210	02/20/66	The Death Ship
55	2-23	8224	02/27/66	The Monster's Web
56	2-24	8225	03/06/66	The Menfish
57	2-25	8226	03/13/66	The Mechanical Man
58	2-26	8227	03/20/66	The Return of the Phantom
Repeat	-		03/27/66	(The Cyborg)
Repeat	-	-	04/02/66	(Terror on Dinosaur Island)
Repeat	-	-	04/10/66	(Killers of the Deep)
Repeat	-	-	04/17/66	(Jonah and the Whale)
Repeat	-	-	04/24/66	(… And Five of Us Are Left)
Repeat	-	-	05/01/66	(The Monster from Outer Space)
Repeat	-	-	05/08/66	(The Death Ship)
Repeat	-	-	05/14/66	(Dead Men's Doubloons)
Repeat	-	-	05/22/66	(The Sky's on Fire)
Repeat	-	-	05/29/66	(The Deadliest Games)
Repeat	-	-	06/05/66	(The Machine Strikes Back)
Repeat	-	-	06/12/66	(The Peacemaker)
Pre-empted		-	06/19/66	(*U.S. Open sports special*)
Repeat	-	-	06/26/66	(Deadly Creature Below!)
Repeat	-	-	07/03/66	(The Mechanical Man)
Repeat	-	-	07/10/66	(The Left-Handed Man)
Repeat	-	-	07/17/66	(The Shape of Doom)
Repeat	-	-	07/24.66	(The X-Factor)

Repeat	-	-	07/31/66	(The Phantom Strikes)
Repeat	-	-	08/07/66	(The Menfish)
Repeat	-	-	08/14/66	(Leviathan)
Repeat	-	-	08/21/66	(Escape from Venice)
Repeat	-	-	08/28/66	(The Return of the Phantom)
Repeat	-	-	09/04/66	(Time Bomb)
Repeat	-	-	09/11/66	(Graveyard of Fear)

Season Three Production Order:

Monster from the Inferno	June 20-28, 1966 (7 days)
Werewolf	June 29-July 8, 1966 (7 days)
Day of Evil	July 11-18, 1966 (6 days)
Night of Terror	July 19-26, 1966 (6 days)
The Day the World Ended	July 27-August 3, 1966 (6 days)
The Terrible Toys	August 4-11, 1966 (6 days)
Deadly Waters	August 12-19, 1967 (6 days)
The Thing from Inner Space	August 22-29, 1966 (6 days)
The Death Watch	August 30-September 6, 1966 (5 days)
Deadly Invaders	September 7-14, 1966 (6 days)
The Lost Bomb	September 15-22, 1966 (6 days)
The Brand of the Beast	September 23-30, 1966 (7 days)
The Plant Monster	October 3-10, 1966 (6 days)
The Creature	October 11-18, 1966 (6 days)
The Haunted Submarine	October 19-25, 1966 (5 days)
The Death from the Past	October 26-November 3, 1966 (7 days)
The Heat Monster	November 4-11, 1966 (6½ days)
The Fossil Men	November 14-21, 1966 (6½ days)
The Mermaid	November 22-29, 1966 (5½ days)
The Mummy	November 30-December 6, 1966 (5 days)
Shadowman	December 7-15, 1966 (6 ¾ days)
No Escape from Death	December 16-23, 1966 (6 days)
Doomsday Island	December 27, 1966-January 4, 1967 (6 days)
The Wax Men	January 6-12, 1967 (5 days)
The Deadly Cloud	January 16-24, 1967 (6½ days)
Destroy Seaview	January 25-February 1, 1966 (6 days)

Season Three Broadcast Order:

59	3-01	9201	09/18/66	Monster from the Inferno
60	3-02	9202	09/25/66	Werewolf
61	3-03	9205	10/02/66	The Day the World Ended
62	3-04	9204	10/09/66	Night of Terror
63	3-05	9206	10/16/66	The Terrible Toys
64	3-06	9203	10/23/66	Day of Evil
65	3-07	9207	10/30/66	Deadly Waters
66	3-08	9208	11/06/66	Thing from Inner Space
67	3-09	9210	11/13/66	The Death Watch
68	3-10	9209	11/20/66	Deadly Invasion
69	3-11	9215	11/27/66	The Haunted Submarine
70	3-12	9212	12/04/66	The Plant Man
71	3-13	9211	12/11/66	The Lost Bomb
72	3-14	9213	12/18/66	The Brand of the Beast

12/25/66 *"The Dangerous Christmas of Red Riding Hood"* repeat

73	3-15	9214	01/01/67	The Creature
74	3-16	9216	01/08/67	Death from the Past
75	3-17	9217	01/15/67	The Heat Monster
76	3-18	9218	01/22/67	The Fossil Men
77	3-19	9219	01/29/67	The Mermaid
78	3-20	9220	02/05/67	The Mummy
79	3-21	9221	02/12/67	Shadowman
80	3-22	9222	02/19/67	No Escape from Death
81	3-23	9223	02/26/67	Doomsday Island
82	3-24	9224	03/05/67	The Wax Men
83	3-25	9225	03/12/67	Deadly Cloud
84	3-26	9226	03/19/67	Destroy Seaview
Pre-empted		-	03/26/67	(*The Robe* Sunday Night Movie)
Repeat	-	-	04/02/67	(The Terrible Toys)
Repeat	-	-	04/08/67	(Night of Terror)
Repeat	-	-	04/16/67	(The Plant Monster)
Pre-empted		-	04/23/67	(*Go!!!* variety special)
Repeat	-	-	05/01/67	(Werewolf)
Repeat	-	-	05/07/67	(Day of Evil)
Repeat	-	-	05/14/67	(The Thing from Inner Space)
Repeat	-	-	05/21/67	(The Heat Monster)
Repeat	-	-	05/28/67	(The Day the World Ended)
Repeat	-	-	06/04/67	(Deadly Invasion)
Repeat	-	-	06/11/67	(The Haunted Submarine)
Repeat	-	-	06/18/67	(The Monster from the Inferno)
Repeat	-	-	06/25/67	(Shadowman)
Repeat	-	-	07/02/67	(Deadly Waters)
Repeat	-	-	07/09/67	(The Creature)
Repeat	-	-	07/16/67	(Death from the Past)
Repeat	-	-	07/23/67	(The Deadly Cloud)
Repeat	-	-	07/30/67	(The Fossil Men)
Repeat	-	-	08/06/67	(The Mermaid)
Repeat	-	-	08/13/67	(The Mummy)
Repeat	-	-	08/20/67	(No Escape from Death)
Repeat	-	-	08/27/67	(Doomsday Island)
Repeat	-	-	09/03/67	(The Wax Men)
Pre-empted		-	09/10/67	("Africa" special)

Season Four Production Order:

1	4-06	1301	10/29/67	Man of Many Faces
2	4-08	1302	11/12/67	Time Lock
3	4-02	1303	10/01/67	The Deadly Dolls
4	4-01	1304	09/17/67	Fires of Death
5	4-03	1305	10/08/67	Cave of the Dead
6	4-05	1306	10/22/67	Sealed Orders
7	4-04	1307	10/15/67	Journey with Fear
8	4-07	1309	11/05/67	Fatal Cargo
9	4-09	1310	11/19/67	Rescue
10	4-10	1308	11/26/67	Terror
11	4-12	1313	12/10/67	Blow Up
12	4-13	1314	12/17/67	Deadly Amphibians
13	4-14	1316	12/31/67	The Return of Blackbeard
14	4-11	1317	12/03/67	A Time to Die
15	4-24	1318	03/17/68	Edge of Doom
16	4-17	1319	01/28/68	Nightmare
17	4-16	1320	01/21/68	The Lobster Man
18	4-15	1321	01/07/68	Terrible Leprechaun
19	4-18	1315	02/04/68	The Abominable Snowman
20	4-20	1323	02/18/68	Man-Beast
21	4-21	1322	02/25/68	Savage Jungle
22	4-19	1311	02/11/68	Secret of the Deep
23	4-22	1324	03/03/68	Flaming Ice
24	4-23	1325	03/10/68	Attack
25	4-26	1326	03/31/68	No Way Back
26	4-25	1312	03/24/68	The Death Clock

Season Four Broadcast Order:

85	4-01	1304	09/17/67	Fires of Death
Pre-empted			09/24/67	(*"Holiday On Ice"* special)
86	4-02	1303	10/01/67	The Deadly Dolls
87	4-03	1305	10/08/67	Cave of the Dead
88	4-04	1307	10/15/67	Journey with Fear
89	4-05	1306	10/22/67	Sealed Orders
90	4-06	1301	10/29/67	Man of Many Faces
91	4-07	1309	11/05/67	Fatal Cargo
92	4-08	1302	11/12/67	Time Lock
93	4-09	1310	11/19/67	Rescue
94	4-10	1308	11/26/67	Terror
95	4-11	1317	12/03/67	A Time to Die
96	4-12	1313	12/10/67	Blow Up
97	4-13	1314	12/17/67	Deadly Amphibians
Pre-emped			12/24/67	(*"Nativity Story"* Christmas special)
98	4-14	1316	12/31/67	The Return of Blackbeard
99	4-15	1321	01/07/68	Terrible Leprechaun
Pre-empted			01/14/68	(Bing Crosby golf special)
100	4-16	1320	01/21/68	The Lobster Man

101	4-17	1319	01/28/68	Nightmare
102	4-18	1315	02/04/68	The Abominable Snowman
103	4-19	1311	02/11/68	Secret of the Deep
104	4-20	1323	02/18/68	Man-Beast
105	4-21	1322	02/25/68	Savage Jungle
106	4-22	1324	03/03/68	Flaming Ice
107	4-23	1325	03/10/68	Attack
108	4-24	1318	03/17/68	Edge of Doom
109	4-25	1311	03/24/68	The Death Clock
110	4-26	1326	03/31/68	No Way Back
Repeat	-	-	04/07/68	(Fires of Death)
Repeat	-	-	04/14/68	(The Deadly Dolls)
Pre-empted		-	04/21/68	(*"Romp!"* entertainment special)
Repeat	-	-	04/28/68	(Cave of Death)
Repeat	-	-	05/05/68	(Journey with Fear)
Repeat	-	-	05/12/68	(Fatal Cargo)
Repeat	-	-	05/20/68	(Deadly Amphibians)
Repeat	-	-	05/26/68	(A Time to Die)
Repeat	-	-	06/02/68	(Man of Many Faces)
Repeat	-	-	06/09/68	(Secrets of the Deep)
Repeat	-	-	06/16/68	(Time Lock)
Repeat	-	-	06/23/68	(The Return of Blackbeard)
Repeat	-	-	06/30/68	(Terror)
Repeat	-	-	07/07/68	(Sealed Orders)
Repeat	-	-	07/14/68	(Blow Up)
Repeat	-	-	07/21/68	(Attack)
Repeat	-	-	07/28/68	(The Lobster Man)
Repeat	-	-	08/04/68	(Nightmare)
Repeat	-	-	08/11/68	(The Abominable Snowman)
Repeat	-	-	08/18/68	(Savage Jungle)
Repeat	-	-	08/25/68	(The Death Clock)
Repeat	-	-	09/01/68	(Flaming Ice)
Repeat	-	-	09/08/68	(Man-Beast)
Repeat	-	-	09/15/68	(Terrible Leprechaun)

Bibliography

Books:

Billboard Hot 100 Charts, edited by Joel Whitburn (Record Research, Inc., 1990)
Billboard Pop Album Charts, edited by Joel Whitburn (Record Research, Inc., 1993)
Complete Directory to Prime Time Network TV Shows, by Tim Brooks and Earle Marsh (Ballantine Books, May 1979)
Hitchcock's Partner in Suspense: The Life of Screenwriter Charles Bennett, by Charles Bennett (University Press of Kentucky, 2014)
Irwin Allen Scrapbook, Volume Two, Edited by William E. Anchors, Jr. (1992, Alpha Control Press)
Irwin Allen Television Productions, 1964-1970: A Critical History, by Jon Abbott (2006, McFarland & Company, Inc.)
Science Fiction Television Series, Volume 1, by Mark Phillips and Frank Garcia (1994, McFarland & Co.)
Science Fiction Television Series, Volume 2, by Mark Phillips and Frank Garcia (1996, McFarland & Co.)
Seaview: A 50th Anniversary Tribute to Voyage to the Bottom of the Sea, by William E. Anchors and Frederick Barr (2012, Alpha Control Press)
Seaview: The Making of Voyage to the Bottom of the Sea, by Tim Colliver (1992, Timothy L. Colliver)
Special Effects: Wire, Tape and Rubber Band Style, by L.B. Abbott (ASC Press, 1984)
Talks with the Dead, by William Welch (Pinnacle Books, 1975)

Websites:

CinemaRetro.com
Classicfilmtvcafe.com
Cultbox.co.uk
Diaboliquemagazine.com
Latimes.com
Mike'svoyagetothebottomofthesea.zone at vttbots.com
popcultureaddict.com
sci-fi-online.com

Newspaper & Magazine Articles:

Broadcasting, May 15, 1940, "Behind the Mike" – Irwin Allen is KMTR radio's publicity and promotion director, in addition to hosting *Hollywood Merry-Go-Round* six nights a week.
Los Angeles Times, September 13, 1940, "Your Radio Today," showing *Hollywood Merry-Go-Round* scheduled on KMTR at 9:45 p.m.
Los Angeles Times, September 13, 1940, "Your Radio Today," showing *Hollywood Merry-Go-Round*, identified as "Irwin Allen," scheduled on KMTR at 6 p.m.
The San Bernardino County Sun, January 2, 1942, "On Your Radio Dial for Today," showing *Hollywood Merry-Go-Round*, identified as "Irwin Allen," scheduled on KMTR at 6 p.m.
Los Angeles Times, July 31, 1942, "Your Radio Today," showing *Hollywood Merry-Go- Round*, identified as "Irwin Allen," scheduled on KMTR at 6 p.m.
Los Angeles Times, November 27, 1942, "Your Radio Today," showing *Hollywood Merry-Go-Round*, identified as "Irwin Allen," scheduled on KMTR at 6 p.m.
The Courier-Gazette (McKinney, Texas), February 13, 1943, Hollywood Feature Syndicates' "On the Set" column, by Irwin Allen.
Albuquerque Journal, March 21, 1943, Hollywood Feature Syndicates' "On the Set" column, by Irwin Allen.
Los Angeles Times, May 7, 1943, "Your Radio Today," showing *Hollywood Merry-Go-Round*, identified as "Irwin Allen," scheduled on KMTR at 5:30 p.m.
Daily Variety, November 10, 1943, Irwin Allen's radio work discussed in "First Lit Up Preem Since Jap Attack Set for Diary."
Daily Variety, February 2, 1944, "New Contracts," Irwin Allen's KMTR radio gossip show renewed for fifth year.
Los Angeles Times, March 24, 1944, "Your Radio Today," showing *Hollywood Merry-Go-Round*, identified as "Irwin Allen," scheduled on KMTR at 5:30 p.m.
Zanesville Times Recorder, February 13, 1945, "A Scot Who Was Never in Scotland."
Daily Variety, July 24, 1945, *The Hasty Heart* stage review.
Daily Variety, August 9, 1945, ad for new radio series, *Story of a Star*, with Irwin Allen, on KECA.
Los Angeles Times, September 27, 1945, "Your Radio Today," showing *Hollywood Merry-Go-Round*, identified as "Irwin Allen," scheduled on KMTR at 5:30 p.m.
Daily Variety, February 8, 1946, blurb concerning Irwin Allen initiating his association with the Orsatti Literary Agency.

Daily Variety, April 5, 1946, *She-Wolf of London* film review.
Los Angeles Times, June 11, 1946, "Your Radio Today," showing *Hollywood Merry-Go- Round*, identified as "Irwin Allen," scheduled on KLAC at 5:30 p.m.
Los Angeles Times, February 17, 1947, "Your Radio Today," showing *Hollywood Merry-Go-Round*, identified as "Irwin Allen," scheduled on KLAC at 5:15 p.m.
The Brooklyn Daily Eagle, June 2, 1947, "Richard Basehart, Hedgerow Actor, Now on the First Rung of Film Stardom," by Herbert Cohn.
Daily Variety, July 21, 1947, "Orsatti Agency to NY, London," identifying Allen's title as head of radio department and story editor.
Joplin Globe, November 19, 1947, "Jimmie Fidler in Hollywood."
Syracuse Herald-Journal, November 23, 1947, "New Broadway Star," by Jean Meegan.
Long Beach Independent, April 24, 1948, "Radio log," showing "Irwin Allen" scheduled at 5:30 p.m. on KLAC.
Daily Variety, May 3, 1948, "Allen Quits Orsatti for His Own Agency."
Daily Variety, September 13, 1948, "Hollywood Inside," reporting Allen's KLAC *Hollywood Merry-Go-Round* radio program going national.
Daily Variety, September 24, 1948, "Television Reviews: *Hollywood Merry-G-Round*."
Variety, September 28, 1948, TV review of *Hollywood Merry-Go-Round*, by "Frce."
The Evening News (Harrisburg, Pennsylvania), October 1, 1948, Hedda Hopper announces "It's Only Money," aka *Double Dynamite*, Irwin Allen's first movie as associate producer.
The San Bernardino County Sun, October 14, 1948, "On Your Radio Dial," showing "Irwin Allen" scheduled at 9 p.m. on KLAC-TV.
Daily Variety, October 15, 1948, "RKO Deal Brewing with Cummings."
Daily Variety, November 11, 1948, *He Walked by Night* film review.
The Independent Star (Indianapolis, Indiana), November 21, 1948, "Jane Russell Boom Comes After 8 Years of Big Pay, Few Films," by Sheilah Graham.
Daily Variety, November 22, 1948, "'Only Money' Getting Gun at RKO Today."
TELE-Views magazine, November 26, 1948. "Stars Are Coming Your Way!", by Albert H. Grogan.
Daily Variety, December 17, 1948, "Cummings' Canning 'Money' Under Sked."
Evening Journal. January 4, 1949, "Film Stars Coming Your Way in Effort to Boost Pictures," by Bob Thomas.
Cumberland Sunday Times, January 16, 1949, "Actor Son of Editor Hard to Interview, Columnist Finds," by Louella O. Parsons.
Variety, January 26, 1949, "Inside Stuff – Pictures," "It's Only Money" wrapping three days early.
Los Angeles Times, Feb. 27, 1949, "His Killer Roles Horrify Basehart," by Philip K. Scheuer.
Amarillo Daily News, March 8, 1949, "The Lyon's Den" by Leonard Lyon, reporting studios bidding on Leo Rosten's "A White Rose for Julie" screen story.
The Cincinnati Enquirer, April 20, 1949, "Edith Gwynn's Hollywood," concerning potential casting of Jane Russell in "A White Rose for Julie."
Daily Variety, April 25, 1949, ad for the *Irwin Allen Show* on KLAC-TV.
Daily Variety, May 6, 1949, "RKO Releasing 'Julie'."
Daly Variety, May 27, 1949, "Short Shots" – Arthur Ross hired to write screenplay for "A White Rose for Julie."
Daily Variety, July 21, 1949, "Short shots" – Charles Bennett now writing "A White Rose for Julie."
Los Angeles Times, August 9, 1949, *John Loves Mary* stage review, by Edwin Schallert.
Daily Variety, August 19, 1949, "On the Air Waves," Charles Bennett as guest on *Irwin Allen Show*.
Williamsport Sun-Gazette (Pennsylvania), September 2, 1949, "In Hollywood" by Erskine Johnson, concerning Ann Sheridan-RKO dispute.
Daily Variety, September 6, 1949, "Short Shots," Charles Bennett status, "White Rose for Julie."
Daily Variety, September 21, 1949, report that "A White Rose for Julie" in pre-production as "It's Only Money" is edited.
Lubbock Morning Avalanche, November 10, 1949, Louella O. Parsons' column – John Farrow to direct "A White Rose for Julie."
Daily Variety, November 14, 1949, "Farrow Megs 'Julie,'" due to start filming in late November.
Daily Variety, November 17, 1949, *Tension* film review.
The Brooklyn Daily Eagle, November 20, 1949, "Farrow Returns to RKO for 'Julie.'"
The Terre Haute Star (Indiana), November 22, 1949, UP wire story, "Star Ann Sheridan Sues RKO for $350,000."
Variety, November 23, 1949, *Tension* film review, by "Brog."
The Billboard, December 10, 1949, "Irwin Allen's *H'wood Party*" TV review.
Democrat and Chronicle (Rochester, New York), December 13, 1949, Louella O. Parsons column – Ann Sheridan reading "A White Rose for Julie," but still planning on suing RKO.
Variety, December 14, 1949, Howard Hughes wanting title "Where Danger Lives" for Laraine Day, Robert Ryan film.
Daily Variety, December 16, 1949, "Just for Variety," by Alta Durant – Jane Russell planned for "A White Rose for Julie."
The Cincinnati Enquirer, December 24, 1949, "Edith Gwynn's Hollywood," reporting that Ida Lupino was considered for female lead in "A White Rose for Julie," but lead would now go to Faith Domergue.
Daily Variety, December 27, 1949, "RKO Launching Steady Prod'n Program for the New Year," announcing "A White Rose for Julie," with Irving Cummings, Jr. and Irwin Allen set to produce.
Daily Variety, December 29, 1949, "Just for Variety," by Alta Durant, earmarking Barry Sullivan with Bob Mitchum for "A White Rose for Julie," with female lead still up in the air.
Daily Variety, January 6, 1950, "'Rose' Blooming" – set to roll following day, January 7th.
Daily Variety, January 9, 1950, "'Rose for Julie' Rolling Today at RKO."
Variety, January 11, 1950, The Paragon stage review, by "Klep."
Daily Variety, January 16, 1950, "Just for Variety," by Alta Durant, reporting "A White Rose for Julie" has a 40-day shooting schedule.
Daily Variety, January 26, 1950, "Hollywood Inside," reporting film crew for "White Rose for Julie," AKA *Where Danger*

Lives, appearing on new KLAC-TV program, *Irwin Allen's House Party*.
Dailey Variety, "Farrow Plucks 'Rose'" "A White Rose for Julie" wraps and starts post-production.
Daily Variety, March 15, 1950, "Hollywood Inside," regarding efficiency of production on "A White Rose for Julie" (AKA *Where Danger Lives*).
Daily Variety, March 17, 1950, "Short Shots" reporting title change for "A White Rose for Julie" to *Where Danger Lives*.
The Atchison Daily Globe (Kansas), March 19, 1950, "Jackie Akers in Hollywood," concerning Ann Sheridan not willing to star in "A White Rose for Julie."
Los Angeles Times, April 30, 1950, "Film to Shed Light on Mystery Woman," by Edwin Schallert.
Daily Variety, May 19, 1950, announcement of Allen resuming his TV talk show.
Independent Film Journal, June 1, 1950, *Where Danger Lives* film review.
Daily Variety, June 16, 1950, "TRADE SHOW: *Where Danger Lives*" film review.
Variety, June 21, 1950, TRADE SHOW: *Where Danger Lives* film review, by "Brog."
Los Angeles Times, August 13, 1950, "Star Under Wraps," by Louis Berg.
Daily Variety, October 25, 1950, reporting Groucho Marx to make "They Sell Elephants to Sailors" for Irwin Allen and Irving Cummings.
Daily Variety, November 15, 1950, "Just for Variety," by Mike Connolly, with update on "They Sell Elephants to Sailors," to be produced by Irwin Allen.
Variety, November 15, 1950, *Where Danger Lives* full-page ad.
Daily Variety, November 15, 1950, "Just for Variety" by Mike Connolly.
Los Angeles Times, November 17, 1950, *Where Danger Lives* film review, by Philip K. Scheuer.
Los Angeles Daily News, November 17, 1950, *Where Danger Lives* film review, by Darr Smith.
Hollywood Citizen-News, November 17, 1950, *Where Danger Lives* film review, by Lowell F. Redelings.
Los Angeles Examiner, November 17, 1950, *Where Danger Lives* film review, by Louella O. Parsons.
Variety, November 29, 1950, "Picture Grosses" for *Where Danger Lives*.
TIME, December 18, 1950, *Where Danger Lives* film review.
Cue magazine, January 6, 1951, *Where Danger Lives* film review, by Jessie Zunser.
The Brooklyn Daily Eagle, February 27, 1951, "Richard Basehart Plays *14 Hours* in the Same Spot."
The Cincinnati Enquirer, May 18, 1951, "Edith Gwynn's Hollywood," regarding Marie Wilson "leg-clot" delaying start of "They Sell Elephants to Sailors."
The Terre Haute Tribune, May 20, 1951, RKO press release for *Where Danger Lives*.
Variety, May 23, 1951, "House of Seven Gables" TV review.
Pottstown Mercury (Pennsylvania), June 12, 1951, Edith Gwynn's Hollywood," on recovery of Marie Wilson and plans to begin filming "They Sell Elephants to Sailors."
Los Angeles Daily News, June 23, 1951, Darr Smith column covering filming of *A Girl in Every Port*.
The Bridgeport Post (Connecticut), July 1, 1951, book review by Joe Wing of *The Sea Around Us*.
Independent Press-Telegram (Long Beach, California), July 22, 1951, book review by George Serviss of *The Sea Around Us*.
The Courier-Journal (Louisville, Kentucky), July 29, 1951, book review by John Clowes of *The Sea Around Us*.
The Palm Beach Post (Florida), July 29, 1951, "The Book Nook" on sales and reaction to *The Sea Around Us*.
Daily Variety, October 10, 1951, "Just for Variety" by Viola Swisher, reporting *The Sea Around Us* at top of non-fiction best-seller lists.
Variety, November 7, 1951, *Double Dynamite* film review, by "Brog."
Daily Variety, November 7, 1951, *Double Dynamite* film review.
Boxoffice, November 17, 1951, *Double Dynamite* film review.
Daily Variety, November 21, 1951, *Fixed Bayonets!* Film review.
TIME, November 26, 1951, *Double Dynamite* film review.
Los Angeles Times, December 2, 1951, "Radio Today," showing "Irwin Allen" scheduled on KLAC at 8:30 p.m.
The Salt Lake Tribune, December 19, 1951, RKO promotional piece for *Double Dynamite*.
Daily Variety, December 20, 1951, TRADE SHOW: *A Girl in Every Port* film review.
Hollywood Reporter, December 20, 1951, *A Girl in Every Port* film review.
Variety, December 13, 1950, "Must Not Forget Published Material for Films," reporting that RKO paid $20,000 for the screen rights for "They Sell Elephants to Sailors."
Pittsburgh Post-Gazette, December 25, 1951, review of *Double Dynamite*, by Harold V. Cohen.
The Cincinnati Enquirer, December 25, 1951, *Double Dynamite* review by E.B. Radcliffe.
The Pittsburgh Press, December 26, 1951, *Double Dynamite* review by Kasper Monahan.
The New York Times, December 26, 1951, *Double Dynamite* film review, by "H.H.T."
Variety, December 26, 1951, *A Girl in Every Port* film review, by "Brog."
Daily Variety, December 27, 1951, "RKO Fuses *Dynamite* with 85G Ad Budget."
Picturegoer, January 5, 1952, *Double Dynamite* review, by Alan Warwick.
Boxoffice, January 5, 1952, TRADE SCREENING: *A Girl in Every Port* film review.
Daily Variety, January 18, 1952, "Washington Hullabaloo" by Florence S. Lowe, reporting that Rachel Carson has said "a major studio has an option" on *The Sea Around Us*.
Daily Variety, January 25, 1952, reporting RKO is studio with option on *The Sea Around Us*.
Los Angeles Times, January 27, 1952, "Program Highlights," showing "Irwin Allen" scheduled on KLAC at 8:30 p.m.
Los Angeles Times, February 4, 1952, *Double Dynamite* review, by Philip K. Scheuer.
Los Angeles Daily News, February 4, 1952, *Double Dynamite* film review, by Howard McClay.
Los Angeles Mirror, February 4, 1952, *Double Dynamite* film review, by Fred W. Fox.
Variety, February 6, 1952, "Jan. Golden Dozen," with *Double Dynamite* at No. 5, and "National Boxoffice Survey" with movie at No. 6.
Cue magazine, February 16, 1952, *A Girl in Every Port* film review.
Beatrice Daily Sun, February 24, 1952, RKO press info for *Double Dynamite*.

Los Angeles Examiner, March 22, 1952, *A Girl in Every Port* review, by Kay Proctor.
Los Angeles Times, March 22, 1952, *A Girl in Every Port* film review, by John L. Scott.
TIME, February 25, 1952, *A Girl in Every Port* film review.
Variety, March 5, 1952, "National Boxoffice Survey," including *A Girl in Every Port*.
Joplin Globe, April 4, 1952, "Jimmie Fidler in Hollywood."
Daily Variety, April 7, 1952, "RKO Lot Personnel Cut to 375."
Valley Morning Star (Harlingen, Texas), April 11, 1952, Hedda Hopper reporting Bob Mitchum to do "Glacier Park" for Irwin Allen.
The Independent Record (Helena, Montana), May 7, 1951, "In Hollywood," by Erskine Johnson.
Daily Variety, May 14, 1952, "Short Shots" – Horace McCoy to write screenplay for Irwin Allen's production of "The Glacier Story."
The Holland Evening Sentinel, June 27, 1952, book review of *The Sea Around Us* by Arnold Mulder.
Daily Variety, July 25, 1952, "Just for Variety," by Sheilah Graham, reporting Bob Mitchum to head north for location filming of "The Glacier Story."
Los Angeles Times, October 30, 1952, Philip K. Scheuer reports that Irwin Allen has been working on *The Sea Around Us* for a year.
Boxoffice, November 8, 1952, "RKO's *The Sea Around Us* for December Release."
Variety, November 26, 1952, reporting Irwin Allen will premiere *The Sea Around Us* in Washington D.C. under sponsorship of National Geographic Society.
The Eugene Guard (Oregon), November 30, 1952, "Best Seller to Reach Screen" Irwin Allen hurriedly finished *Sea Around Us* and RKO to rush release in late December to qualify for Academy Award.
Daily Variety, December 17, 1952, "Manpower Problem Besets RKO Board in Revving Prod'n."
Los Angeles Times, December 2, 1951, "Radio Today," showing "Irwin Allen" scheduled on KLAC at 8:30 p.m.
Variety, December 31, 1952, "20 for RKO in '53, Tevlin Announces," including "Second Chance" to be co-produced by Irwin Allen.
Daily Variety, January 14, 1953, *The Sea Around Us* film review, by "Brog."
Boxoffice magazine, January 17, 1953, *The Sea Around Us* film review.
Daily Variety, January 19, 1953, two full-page ads with review blurbs for *The Sea Around Us*.
Daily News (Los Angeles), January 20, 1953, "Friends in *The Sea Around Us*," by David Bongard.
Daily Variety, January 28, 1953, "Chatter."
Daily Variety, January 29, 1953, "Chatter."
Lubbock Avalanche-Journal, February 15, 1953, UP wire story by Aline: "Scientists in 14 Countries Took Pictures for Hollywood Film, *The Sea Around Us*."
Franklin County Tribune, February 27, 1953, "*Claudia* At the Empress Starting Tuesday."
Variety, April 1, 1953, "*Bwana* in World Markets by Middle May Despite Print, Viewer Shortage."
Daily Variety, April 9, 1953, "Col's 3-D *Dark* Plenty Bright at B.O. on B'way."
Zanesville Times Recorder, April 18, 1953, "Illness Nearly Fatal to Wife of Zanesville-Born Actor."
United Press syndicated article, April 1953, "Award-Winning Film Sea Cost RKO Studio $200,000."
Los Angeles Times, July 3, 1953, *The Sea Around Us* film review.
The Cincinnati Enquirer, July 5, 1953, UP wire story: "Cast of Fish Wins Him Award for First Movie," by Vernon Scott.
Variety, July 15, 1953, "National Boxoffice Survey," including *The Sea Around Us*.
Daily Variety, July 17, 1953, title for "The Glacier Story" now changed to "Rangers of the North," with Vincent Price first star signed, and Lewis King directing.
Daily Variety, July 20, 1953, "Vincent Price Legit for 'Rangers'."
Los Angeles Times, July 20, 1953, Edwin Schallert report that Victor Mature, William Bendix, and Piper Laurie added to cast of "Rangers of the North."
The Pittsburgh Press, July 30, 1953, "Mature Given Ranger Role."
Daily Variety, August 4, 1953, location photography for "Rangers of the North" wraps after two weeks in Montana.
The Evening Standard (Uniontown, Pennsylvania), August 6, 1953, "Hollywood Roundup" by Jimmy Fidler; how Irwin Allen cast Victor Mature's son Mike in "Rangers of the North," aka *Dangerous Mission*; "the long and short" of Mature's hair and skirts.
Daily Variety, August 7, 1953, "Rangers of the North" leading film companies in shooting at national parks.
Daily Variety, August 13, 1953, "Hollywood Inside," reporting "Rangers of the North" reproducing glacier on RKO Stage 10.
The Corpus Christi Caller-Times (Texas), September 8, 1953, Victor Mature quote concerning kissing Piper Laurie, as heard by James Bacon.
The Indianapolis Star, October 8, 1953, review of *The Sea Around Us* by Barbara Wolfe.
The Cincinnati Enquirer, October 17, 1953, E.B. Radcliffe's film review of *The Sea Around Us*.
Daily Variety, December 7, 1953, reporting "Rangers of the North" receiving a second title change, to *Dangerous Mission*.
The Mason City Globe-Gazette, December 22, 1953, RKO press release for *The Sea Around Us*.
Daily Variety, January 13, 1954, "Allen, Wiesenthal Quit RKO."
Variety, February 10, 1954, "3-D Crowded Out of the Conversation."
Variety, February 24, 1954, *Dangerous Mission* film review.
Hollywood Reporter, February 24, 1954, *Dangerous Mission* film review by "M.L."
The Daily Inter Lake (Kalispell, Montana), February 25, 1954, "Great Falls First to See Glacier Film," with premiere of *Dangerous Mission* near Glacier National Park.
Boxoffice, February 27, 1954, *Dangerous Mission* film review.
Variety, March 3, 1954, "Irwin Allen's Own Co."
The Brooklyn Daily Eagle, March 6, 1954, film review by Jane Corby of *Dangerous Mission*.
Daily Variety, March 9, 1954, "Indie Haven."
New Yorker, March 13, 1954, *Dangerous Mission* film review, by John McCarten.

Los Angeles Times, March 17, 1954, *Dangerous Mission* review, by Edwin Schallert.
TIME, March 22, 1954, *Dangerous Mission* film review.
Variety, March 31, 1954, "National Boxoffice Survey," including *Dangerous Mission*.
Shamokin News-Dispatch, April 22, 1954, RKO press release for *Dangerous Mission*.
Filmindia, May 1954, *Dangerous Mission* film review.
Daily Variety, June 28, 1954, "Allen to Document *Animal* Lore for WB."
Daily Variety, September 2, 1954, "Irwin Allen Grooming *Animal* for WB Release."
Variety, September 8, 1954, reporting that Allen had checked in to the Warner Bros. lot.
Variety, September 15, 1954, review of *Medic* by "Chan."
Daily Variety, September 21, 1954, "Swink Leaves RKO; Joins Windsor Prod'ns."
Broadcasting, September 27, 1954, review of *Medic* (Frank La Tourette, producer).
Variety, November 17, 1954, "*Medic* in Top 10."
The Billboard, November 19, 1954, "Medic Gives Hope for Physically Ill."
Variety, December 6, 1954, "Great Talent Makes Great Pictures!"
Broadcasting, December 27, 1954, *Medic* "Red Christmas" review (Frank La Tourette, producer)
The Daily Times (New Philadelphia, Ohio), January 17, 1955, "Feb. 14 *Medic* TV Show to Picture Atomic Bomb Attack," by Emily Belser (Frank La Tourette, producer)
Daily Variety, January 20, 1955, "WB Lenses to Girdle Globe for Animal World Scenes."
The Corpus Christi Caller-Times, January 27, 1955, The Grand Prize stage review, by Mark Barron.
The New York Times, February 13, 1955, "From Primordial Ooze to Primates," by Oscar Godbout.
Broadcasting, February 21, 1955, *Medic* review (Frank La Tourette, producer)
Democrat and Chronicle (Rochester, New York), March 11, 1956, UPI wire story: "TV Medic Off; Spellman Blamed."
Albuquerque Journal, March 31, 1955, "Van Loon's *Story of Mankind* Is Purchased by Warners," by Louella O. Parsons.
Daily Variety, March 31, 1955, "WB to Film Van Loon's *The Story of Mankind*."
Pharos-Tribune (Logansport, Indiana), April 27, 1955, UP wire story: "Hollywood's Newest Stars Made Entirely of Rubber."
Daily Variety, July 29, 1955, "Can *Animal World* After 18 Mos. In Prod'n."
Picturegoer magazine, September 24, 1955, "Don't Misunderstand Me – Says Richard Basehart."
Los Angeles Times, January 18, 1956, "*Animal World* Producer Faces Big Human Issues."
Green Bay Press-Gazette (Wisconsin), March 9, 1956, "Caesarian Birth Makes TV History on *Medic*," by Aline Mosby.
Variety, March 16, 1956, "Nature Widens '7 Basic Plots'," by Fred Hift.
Los Angeles Times, March 21, 1956, "*Story of Mankind* Put on Full-Scale Footing," by Edwin Schallert.
Daily Variety, April 18, 1956, *The Animal World* film review, by "Whit."
The Hollywood Reporter, April 18, 1956, *The Animal World* review, by James Powers.
Daily Independent Journal, May 18, 1956, United Press wire story: "Science Goes to Hollywood."
Arizona Republic, May 27, 1956, "Irwin Allen Is Unusual As Director."
Daily Variety, May 29, 1956, "Chatter," reporting Allen's 28-day cross-country tour for *Animal World*.
Variety, May 30, 1956, "Why Was *Medic* Dumped?"
Cue magazine, June 2, 1956, *The Animal World* film review, by Jesse Zunser.
Poughkeepsie Journal, June 8, 1956, King Features Syndicate review of *The Animal World*, by Alice Hughes.
The Courier-Journal (Louisville, Kentucky), June 15, 1956, *The Animal World* review, by Boyd Martin.
Los Angeles Times, June 18, 1956, "*Animal World* Producer Faces Big Human Issue," by Edwin Schallert.
Los Angeles Times, June 21, 1956, *The Animal World* film review, by Edwin Schallert.
Los Angeles Mirror, June 21, 1956, review of *The Animal World*.
The Paris News, June 24, 1956, Warner Bros. press release for *The Animal Planet*.
Variety, June 27, 1956, "National Boxoffice Survey," including *The Animal World*.
Films in Review, June/July 1956, *The Animal World* film review.
Variety, July 4, 1956, "National Boxoffice Survey," including *The Animal World*.
Daily Variety, August 31, 1956, "On All Channels," by Dave Kaufman, reporting that Irwin Allen asked Greer Garson to play Queen Elizabeth in *The Story of Mankind*.
Arizona Republic, October 17, 1956, "Warner Plan to Make Film Epic of Van Loon's *Story of Mankind*," by Louella O. Parsons.
Albuquerque Journal, October 26, 1956, "More Cast Members Announced for Van Loon's *Story of Mankind*, by Louella O. Parsons.
Daily Variety, November 1, 1956, "Off-Type Casting," with Agnes Moorehead and Bette Davis up for roles in *The Story of Mankind*.
Daily Variety, November 6, 1956, "WB Story Parts for 3" – John Carradine, Melville Cooper, and Franklin Pangborn.
Los Angeles Times, November 9, 1956, "Groucho, Cesar Romero Aid Story of Mankind," by Philip K. Scheuer.
Daily Variety, November 9, 1956, reporting Dennis Hopper added to cast of *The Story of Mankind*. He would play Napoleon Bonaparte.
Daily Variety, November 12, 1956, "Mayo, Reg Gardiner In *Story of Mankind*."
Daily Variety, November 15, 1956, "Sheffield in *Story*."
Daily Variety, November 16, 1956, "Dexter, Marv Miller in WB *Story* Roles."
Los Angeles Times, November 18, 1956, "*Mankind* to Tour History of Humans in Three Hours," by Philip K. Scheuer.
Daily Variety, November 19, 1956, "Chico Marx to Play Monk, Harpo Sir Isaac Newton in *Story of Mankind*."
Moberly Monitor-Index, November 26, 1956, "Film Maker Maps Entire Story of Man," by Bob Thomas.
Daily Capital Journal (Salem, Oregon), December 3, 1956, UP wire story: "Ronald Colman Lured Back to Movies First Time in 7 Years [for *The Story of Mankind*]," by Aline Mosby.
Daily Variety, December 5, 1956, "Hitler in WB's *Story*," and "Assign Owen 72nd of 90 Speaking *Story* Roles."
Kalamazoo Gazette, December 9, 1956, "Stars in Sky Talk and *The Story of Mankind* Becomes Star-Studded Movie."
Daily Variety, December 14, 1956, "Handy Soles" for Francis X. Bushman in *The Story of Mankind*.

The Pittsburgh Press, December 16, 1956, "Vilest Villains Assembling for Forthcoming Movie," by Harold Heffernan.
The Franklin Evening Star (Indiana), December 29, 1956, "Producer is Attempting to Stage *Story of Mankind* in Three Hours," by Joan Hanauer.
Arizona Republic, December 30, 1956, "Marx Brothers Make Another Picture Together."
Daily Variety, January 21, 1957, *The Story of Mankind* wraps with Roman orgy scene to be shot on January 24th.
The Wisconsin Jewish Chronicle, March 1, 1957, "On the Screen," by Hubert C. Luft.
Daily Variety, March 4, 1957, "Just for Variety," by Army Archerd, reporting that Allen owns 25% of *The Story of Mankind*. And unlikely to renew Warners' pact.
New York Herald Tribune, March 10, 1957, "*Story of Mankind* Filmed as a Trial," by Thomas Wood.
Newsweek, May 6, 1957, "Movies: Everything, Then Some."
Daily Variety, May 22, 1957, "Just for Variety," by Army Archerd on preview of *The Story of Mankind*.
Daily Variety, June 27, 1957, "Allen Filming *Circus* in Todd-AO."
Variety, July 3, 1957, "Irwin Allen Doing a Todd with 62 Speaking Stars for *The Big Circus*."
Daily Variety, July 29, 1957, "Just for Variety" by Army Archerd, reporting Allen using clown to deliver copies of script for *The Big Circus*.
Daily Variety, August 27, 1957, "Irwin Allen Making *Big Circus* for Col."
Los Angeles Times, August 27, 1957, Irwin Allen Schedules *Big Circus*," by Philip K. Scheuer.
Los Angeles Times, September 15, 1957, "Basehart Back After 4 Years," by Hedda Hopper.
Daily Variety, September 18, 1957, *Time Limit* film review, by "Kap."
Daily Variety, October 3, 1957, "Wallace *Big* Plotter."
Daily Variety, October 8, 1957, "WB *Story* Wins A-Bomb Pix Race, Declares Allen."
Variety, October 9, 1957, "Irwin Allen's Slants on Stars and Trademark Value with Age."
Daily Variety, October 23, 1957, *The Story of Mankind* film review.
The Hollywood Reporter, October 23, 1957, *The Story of Mankind* film review, by James Powers.
The Independent Film Journal, October 26, 1957, *The Story of Mankind* film review.
Variety, November 6, 1957, "National Boxoffice Survey," with *The Story of Mankind*.
Cue magazine, November 9, 1957, *The Story of Mankind* film review, by Jesse Zunser.
Variety, November 13, 1957, "National Boxoffice Survey," with *The Story of Mankind*.
Los Angeles Mirror-News, November 14, 1957, *The Story of Mankind* film review, by Dick Williams.
Los Angeles Times, November 14, 1957, *The Story of Mankind* film review, by Philip K. Scheuer.
Los Angeles Examiner, November 14, 1957, *The Story of Mankind* film review, by S.A. Desick.
The Wisconsin Jewish Chronicle, November 15, 1957, review of *The Story of Mankind*, by Hubert C. Luft.
The New Yorker, November 16, 1957, *The Story of Mankind* film review.
The Bridgeport Post, November 17, 1957, Warner Bros. press release for *The Story of Mankind*.
Newsweek, November 18, 1957, *The Story of Mankind* film review.
Amarillo Globe-Times, December 18, 1957, review of *The Story of Mankind* by Bill McReynolds.
Variety, February 19, 1958, *Brothers Karamazov* film review, by "Pow."
The Marion Star (Ohio), May 20, 1958, "Radio and Television," by Marie Torre.
Daily Variety, September 8, 1958, "AA, Allen Dicker on *Circus* Deal."
Variety, December 10, 1958, "Allen's *Circus* Becomes Allied Artists Partnership."
Daily Variety, December 23, 1958, "*Circus* Rehearsals Set."
Daily Variety, January 2, 1959, "18-Acre Set Slated for Allen *Circus*.
The New York Times, January 11, 1959, "*Big Circus* Troupe Works to Equal Big Top's Authenticity and Color," by Thomas M. Pryor.
Daily Variety, February 12, 1959, Army Archerd reporting that Irwin Allen was giving *The Big Circus* director Joe Newsman plenty of "assistance," always on the set.
Los Angeles Times, February 27, 1959, "*The Big Circus* Set Magnificent," by Hedda Hopper.
Lebanon Daily News, March 4, 1959, "Stage for Filming *The Big Circus* Is Like Old Times," by Bob Thomas.
Anderson Daily Bulletin, April 20, 1959, Louella O. Parson's column, regarding David Nelson in *The Big Circus*.
Hollywood Reporter, May 26, 1959, "Irwin Allen Will Remake A. Conan Doyle's *Lost World* on $3 Million Budget in Todd-AO."
Variety, June 17, 1959, "No Titles Mentioned, But…" and "New York Sound Track."
Daily Variety, June 18, 1959, *Son of Robin Hood* film review.
The Troy Record, June 19, 1959, "TV Keynotes: David Hedison Knows All About Pavement," by Harvey Pack.
Daily Variety, June 24, 1959, "Just for Variety," by Army Archerd covering sneak peak at the Academy Theatre for *The Big Circus*.
Daily Variety, June 26, 1959, "Sound and Pictures," by Bob Chandler, and review of *The Big Circus* by "Ron."
Rocky Mountain News, June 30, 1959, "Producer 'Careful Shopper.'"
Daily Variety, June 30, 1959, "AA Circus to Get Saturation Bow in L.A. During August."
Denver Post, July 1, 1959, "Producer Allen Beats Drum for His Circus Extravaganza," by Larry Tajiri.
Variety, July 8, 1959, *The Big Circus* film review.
The New York Times, July 18, 1959, *The Big Circus* film review, by Bosley Crowther.
The Paris News, July 19, 1959, press release for *The Big Circus*.
The Lincoln Star (Nebraska), June 21, 1959, "Mrs. Groucho Says He's Funny."
Variety, July 22, 1959, "National Boxoffice Survey," including *The Big Circus*.
Democrat and Chronicle (Rochester, New York), July 30, 1959, *The Big Circus* film review by Brian Sullivan.
Daily Variety, July 31, 1959, "Irwin Allen Heads Up Circus Parade for Chicago Bow Bally."
TIME, August 3, 1959, *The Big Circus* film review.
The Corpus Christi Caller-Times, August 4, 1959, with syndicated *Chicago Daily News* story, "Advice to Would-Be Actresses: 'Stay Home,'" by Pat Dalton.
Los Angeles Times, August 6, 1959, *The Big Circus* film review, by Philip K. Scheuer.

Daily Variety, August 14, 1959, "Record Teleseries Productions Here Will Top 100 Next Week," by Larry Tubelle.
Daily Variety, October 1, 1959, "Irwin Allen Set to Film Lost World for 20th Release."
Daily Variety, October 6, 1959, *Five Fingers* TV review, by "Tube."
Variety, October 7, 1959, *Five Fingers* TV review, by "Trau."
Daily Variety, November 6, 1959, "Kiddin' Kids Takes More Coin These Days, Sez Irwin Allen," by Ron Silverman.
Variety, November 11, 1959, TV ratings, with *Five Fingers*.
New Castle News (Pennsylvania), December 1, 1959, UPI story, "David Hedison Battling for Perfection in Series," by Vernon Scott.
Variety, December 2, 1959, TV ratings, with *Five Fingers*.
Variety, December 23, 1959, TV ratings, with *Five Fingers*.
Anderson Herald, December 26, 1959, "Foreign Living Can Damage Star's Career."
The Times (Hammond, Indiana), March 22, 1960, "TV Keynotes: Richard Basehart Is a Jet-Age Actor," by Harvey Pack.
The Hollywood Reporter, July 1, 1960, *The Lost World* film review, by James Powers.
The Film Daily, July 1, 1960, *The Lost World* film review, by Mandel Herbstman.
Los Angeles Times, July 3, 1960, "Hedison Gets Star Billing," by Hedda Hopper.
Variety, July 6, 1960, "Better if Producer Directs, Too – Allen,' regarding *The Lost World*, and film review of *The Lost World*, by "Tube."
Motion Picture Herald, July 9, 1960, *The Lost World* film review.
Los Angeles Times, July 14, 1960, "*Lost World* Notable for Special Effects," by John L. Scott.
Hollywood Citizen-News, July 14, 1960, *The Lost World* review, by Lowell E. Redelings.
Los Angeles Mirror News, July 14, 1960, *The Lost World* review, by Margaret Harford.
Los Angeles Examiner, July 14, 1960, *The Lost World* film review, by Ruth Waterbury.
The New York Times, July 14, 1960, *The Lost World* film review, by A.H. Weiler.
Cue magazine, July 16, 1960, *The Lost World* film review.
TIME, July 18, 1960, *The Lost World* film review.
Variety, August 3, 1960, "National Boxoffice Survey," including *The Lost World*.
Arlington Heights Herald, August 4, 1960, review of *The Lost World* by Jim Phillips.
Variety, August 10, 1960, "National Boxoffice Survey," including *The Lost World*.
Variety, August 17, 1960, "National Boxoffice Survey," including *The Lost World*.
The Anniston Star, August 28, 1960, 20th Century-Fox press release for *The Lost World*.
Hollywood Reporter, October 5, 1960, "Irwin Allen Aims for Program of Features and TV at 20th."
Variety, October 5, 1960, *Adventures in Paradise* TV review, by "Bill."
Variety, October 12, 1960, "Irwin Allen in $9-Mil Program."
Lubbock Avalanche-Journal, November 1, 1960, Louella O. Parsons announced *Voyage to the Bottom of the Sea* as Allen's next movie for Fox.
Daily Variety, December 30, 1960, *How to Make a Man* stage review, by "Tew."
Tucson Daily Citizen, February 11, 1961, "He Came and Conquered," by Micheline Keating.
Daily Variety, April 10, 1961, "Reach *Bottom*; 20th Spends 860G on Special Effects."
Boxoffice, June 5, 1961, "Exhibitors to Meet Allen Promoting His *Voyage*."
Variety, June 7, 1961, "Irwin Allen's Road: Embassy vs. 20th."
The Evening Bulletin, June 13, 1961, "Director Must Rise Early for Today's Movies," by Rex Polier.
The Boston Globe, June 14, 1961, "Producer's Nightmare Science-Fiction Epic," by Kevin Kelly.
The Patriot Ledger, June 15, 1961, "*Bottom of Sea* Science Thriller," by Mabelle Fullerton.
Los Angeles Times, June 18, 1961, *Voyage to the Bottom of the Sea* film review, by Philip K. Scheuer.
The Charlotte News, June 21, 1961, "Pressure's On in Hollywood," by Brooks Yarborough.
Chicago American, June 21, 1961, "Irwin Allen Wooing Girl Movie Patrons," by Ann Masters.
Variety, June 21, 1961, "Allen's Round Figures; $250,000 for TV Plugs of 20th's *Bottom Sea*."
Christian Science Monitor, June 1961, "Technicolor Visions Mean Business to Irwin Allen," by Nora E. Taylor.
The Hollywood Reporter, June 23, 1961, *Voyage to the Bottom to the Sea* film review, by James Powers.
Motion Picture Herald, June 24, 1961, *Voyage to the Bottom of the Sea* film review.
Boxoffice magazine, June 26, 1961, *Voyage to the Bottom of the Sea* film review.
Los Angeles Mirror, July 27, 1961, *Voyage to the Bottom of the Sea* film review, by Dick Williams.
Los Angeles Times, June 28, 1961, "Irwin Allen Signs Multiple Film Deal."
Los Angeles Times, July 28, 1961, *Voyage to the Bottom of the Sea* film review, by John L. Scott.
Variety, June 28, 1961, *Voyage to the Bottom of the Sea* film review, by "Tube."
Motion Picture Limelight, June 29, 1961, *Voyage to the Bottom of the Sea* film review, by Jack Moffitt.
The Hollywood Diary, July 1, 1961, *Voyage to the Bottom of the Sea* film review, by Jonah M. Ruddy.
Variety, July 19, 1961, "National Boxoffice Survey," *Voyage to the Bottom of the Sea*.
The New York Times, July 20, 1961, *Voyage to the Bottom of the Sea* film review, by Howard Thompson.
TIME, July 21, 1961, *Voyage to the Bottom of the Sea* film review.
Variety, July 26, 1961, "National Boxoffice Survey," *Voyage to the Bottom of the Sea*.
Hollywood Citizen-News, July 27, 1961, *Voyage to the Bottom of the Sea* film review, by Lowell E. Redeling.
The Galveston Daily News, July 30, 1961, 20th Century-Fox press release for *Voyage to the Bottom of the Sea* feature film.
Variety, August 2, 1961, "National Boxoffice Survey," *Voyage to the Bottom of the Sea*.
Boxoffice, August 6, 1962, *Two Weeks in a Balloon* film review.
The Plain Speaker, August 4, 1961, "Hollywood Today!" by Erskine Johnson.
Variety, August 9, 1961, "National Boxoffice Survey," *Voyage to the Bottom of the Sea*.
Daily Variety, August 11, 1961, "*Bottom* Hits Top B.O."
Variety, August 16, 1961, *Marines, Let's Go* film review.
Variety, August 16, 1961, "National Boxoffice Survey," *Voyage to the Bottom of the Sea*.
Variety, August 23, 1961, "National Boxoffice Survey," *Voyage to the Bottom of the Sea*.

Variety, February 28, 1962, *Hitler* film review, by "Tube."
Daily Variety, March 22, 1962, "Bricken Talks Deal 'On Bitter' Fruit, Filming with 20th," mentioning *White Crocus* novel by Peter Packer.
The Post-Standard, March 22, 1962, *Hitler* film review.
Los Angeles Times, April 24, 1962, *Five Weeks in a Balloon* film review, by Margaret Harford.
Variety, May 2, 1962, "Status of the Telefilm Majors."
Corpus Christi Caller, June 3, 1962, "D-Day to Be Relived Today."
Bridgeport Post, June 18, 1962, *King Richard II* stage review.
Variety, June 20, 1962, *King Richard II* stage review, by "Hobe."
Daily Variety, July 24, 1962, "Allen's *Balloon* Campaign Follows *Voyage* Pattern."
The Hollywood Reporter, August 13, 1962, *Five Weeks in a Balloon* film review.
The Film Daily, August 14, 1962, *Five Weeks in a Balloon* film review.
Variety, August 15, 1962, *Five Weeks in a Balloon* film review, by "Tube."
Variety, August 15, 1962, "National Boxoffice Survey," with *Five Weeks in a Balloon*.
Cue, August 18, 1962, *Five Weeks in a Balloon* film review.
Variety, August 22, 1962, "National Boxoffice Survey," with *Five Weeks in a Balloon*.
Los Angeles Herald-Examiner, August 23, 1962, *Five Weeks in a Balloon* film review, by Harrison Carroll.
Hollywood Citizen-News, August 23, 1962, *Five Weeks in a Balloon* film review, by Hazel Flynn.
Variety, August 29, 1962, "National Boxoffice Survey," with *Five Weeks in a Balloon*.
TIME, August 31, 1962, *Five Weeks in a Balloon* film review.
Variety, September 5, 1962, "National Boxoffice Survey," with *Five Weeks in a Balloon*.
The Daily Herald (Provo, Utah), September 23, 1962, 20th Century-Fox press release for *Five Weeks in a Balloon*.
Boxoffice magazine, "October 15, 1962, "*Five Weeks in a Balloon* Wins Sept. Blue Ribbon Award," by Velma West Sykes.
Tucson Daily Citizen, June 25, 1963, "The Judge" TV review, by Leonard Hoffman.
Variety, August 21, 1963, "Irwin Allen, 20th in *Voyage* Series."
Daily Variety, September 23, 1963, "Just for Variety," by Army Archerd; Walter Pidgeon in TV *Voyage*.
Daily Variety, October 30, 1964, "*Voyage* Starts Nov. 18."
Daily Variety, November 11, 1963, "20th-TV Rolling 3 Pilots This Month."
Broadcasting, November 18, 1963, "20th Century-Fox Starts Work on Pilots."
Daily Variety, December 20, 1963, "5 Nations South of Border to Co-op with Lubin in Biopicturing Bolivar," mentioning Peter Packer novel *Love Thieves*.
Variety, April 15, 1964, "No Tint for 20th's *Bottom of the Sea*."
Daily Variety, May 5, 1964, "On All Channels: Irwin Allen 20-Year TVet," by Dave Kaufman.
Bristol Daily-Courier, May 30, 1964, "Actor Bets Future on New Series."
Los Angeles Times, June 28, 1964, "Fox Suddenly Jumps into the Series Picture," by Cecil Smith.
Abilene Reporter-News, July 7, 1964, "Submarine Rates as Scene-Stealer," by Erskine Johnson.
Daily Variety, July 9, 1964, "Light and Airy," by Jack Hellman, on Allen and *Voyage*.
The Indiana Gazette, August 14, 1964, AP article on filming the *Voyage* miniatures, by Cynthia Lowry.
Colorado Springs Gazette-Telegraph, September 5, 1964, 20th Century-Fox press release for *Voyage* episode "Turn Back the Clock."
Winnipeg Free Press, September 11, 1964, "Sea Adventure Set for CJAY."
Biddeford-Saco Journal, September 12, 1964, ABC press release for *Voyage* premiere episode "Eleven Days to Zero."
Tucson Daily Citizen, September 14, 1964, "TV Key" preview of "Eleven Days to Zero."
Lima News, September 14, 1964, "TV Scout" review of "Eleven Days to Zero."
Warren Times Mirror, September 15, 1964, review of "Eleven Days to Zero" by Cynthia Lowry.
The San Mateo Times, September 15, 1964, "TV Screening," by Bob Foster.
The Pittsburgh Press (Pennsylvania), September 15, 1964, Vince Leonard's review of "Eleven Days to Zero."
Orlando Evening Star (Florida), September 15, 1964, Bill Summer's review of "Eleven Days to Zero."
Variety, September 16, 1964, *Voyage to the Bottom of the Sea* TV review, by "Pit."
Daily Variety, September 16, 1964, *Voyage to the Bottom of the Sea* TV review, by "Daku."
The Progress-Index, September 17, 1964, "*Voyage* Actors Upstaged by Sub."
Arizona Republic, September 17, 1964, Washington Post Service: review of "Eleven Days to Zero," by Lawrence Laurent.
Long Beach Press-Telegram, September 21, 1964, "Tele-Vues" review of "Eleven Days to Zero," by Terry Vernon.
Lake Charles American Press, September 21, 1964, "TV Key" preview of *Voyage* episode "City Beneath the Sea."
San Antonio Express, September 21, 1964, "TV Scout" review of "City Beneath the Sea."
Monessen Valley Independent, September 28, 1964, "TV Scout" review of *Voyage* episode "The Fear-Makers."
The Daily Reporter, September 28, 1964, "TV Key" preview of "The Fear-Makers."
The Cincinnati Enquirer (Ohio), September 30, 1964, "*Voyage to the Bottom of the Sea* Sinking Fast," by James Devane.
Variety, September 30, 1964, National Arbitron ratings for September 28.
Cullman Times, October 4, 1964, "TV Tonight" preview of *Voyage*'s "The Mist of Silence."
Tucson Daily Citizen, October 5, 1964, "TV Key" preview of *Voyage* episode "The Mist of Silence."
San Antonio Express (Texas), October 5, 1964, "TV Scout" preview of "The Mist of Silence."
Broadcasting, October 5, 1964, Aribitron and Trendix ratings for September 28.
Broadcasting, October 12, 1964, TV ratings with *Voyage* at No. 16.
Doylestown Intelligencer, October 12, 1964, "TV Key" preview of "The Price of Doom."
The Times Record, October 17, 1964, "$1,000,000 Set Enjoyed in *Voyage*."
Cullman Times, October 18, 1964, *Voyage* episode "The Sky Is Falling" preview, by Bill Shelton.
Tucson Daily Citizen, October 19, 1964, "TV Key" preview of "The Sky Is Falling."
Monessen Valley Independent, October 19, 1964, "TV Scout" review of "The Sky Is Falling."
Broadcasting, October 5, 1964, Aribitron ratings for October 12.
The Raleigh Register Beckley Post-Herald, October 24, 1964, review of *Voyage* episode "Turn Back the Clock."

Waterloo Daily Courier, October 25, 1964, "TV Keynotes: High Adventure Series," by Charles Witbeck.
Monessen Valley Independent, October 26, 1964, "TV Key" preview of "Turn Back the Clock."
The Daily Reporter, October 26, 1964, "TV Previews" review of "Turn Back the Clock."
Broadcasting, October 26, 1964, Aribitron ratings for October 19.
The Indianapolis News (Indiana), October 27, 1964, "Seaview in a Lost World – That's New?" by Frank Wilson.
Orlando Evening Star (Florida), October 27, 1964, Bill Summers review of "Turn Back the Clock."
Variety, October 28, 1964, "Nielsen Top 50" ratings, with *Voyage to the Bottom of the Sea*.
News-Herald, November 2, 1964, preview of *Voyage* episode "The Village of Guilt."
Broadcasting, November 2, 1964, Aribitron ratings and TVQ score for October 26.
The Kansas City Times, November 7, 1964, "Letters" section, concerning *Voyage* episode "Turn Back the Clock" using sequences from *The Lost World*.
Broadcasting, November 9, 1964, Aribitron ratings for November 2.
Daily Variety, November 10, 1964, announcement that *Voyage* is picked up for full season.
TV Guide, November 14, 1964, "Letters" about *Voyage* taking footage from *The Lost World*.
The Delta Democrat-Times, November 15, 1965, UPI story: "TV Ratings Executioners."
Kokomo Tribune, November 15, 1964, "TV Key Previews" review of *Voyage* episode "Submarine Sunk Here."
Cullman Times, November 15, 1964, preview of "Submarine Sunk Here," by Bill Shelton.
Tucson Daily Currier, November 16, 1964, "TV Scout" review of "Submarine Sunk Here."
The Daily Intelligencer, November 16, 1964, "TV Preview" for "Submarine Sunk Here."
Broadcasting, November 16, 1964, Aribitron ratings for November 9, with *Voyage* at No. 40 in Top 50 shows.
Variety, November 18, 1964, "*Voyage* to Canada."
The North Adams Transcript, November 19, 1964, Erskine Johnson column, with a letter concerning *Voyage*'s "Turn Back the Clock" recycling from *The Lost World*.
Monessen Valley Independent, November 23, 1964, "TV Key Preview" review of *Voyage* episode "The Magnus Beam."
Variety, November 25, 1964, "20th's 5 New Shows Rack Up O'seas Sales" and "New Nielsen: Top 20."
Bakersfield Californian, November 28, 1964, "Fan Remembers Basehart in Role of Hitler."
The Post-Crescent, November 30, 1964, "TV Scout" review of "No Way Out."
Broadcasting, November 30, 1964, "TV ratings with *Voyage* at No. 17.
Courier Times, December 5, 1964, "Basehart Plays *Voyage* for Real," by Edgar Penton.
Hutchinson News, December 5, 1964, "Candid Capsules," Basehart on ratings.
The Post-Crescent, December 6, 1964, "Richard Basehart: TV's Favorite 'Admiral,'" by Edgar Penton.
The Pittsburgh Press (Pennsylvania), December 10, 1964, Vince Leonard's TV column, calling David Hedison the "Worst New Actor" of the season.
TV Guide, December 12, 1964, "Letters" section, "*Outer Limits* Out" and "Weekly Panic."
Cullman Times, December 13, 1964, preview of *Voyage* episode "Ghost of Moby Dick," by Bill Shelton.
The Times Herald (Port Huron, Michigan), December 14, 1964, "TV Scout" review of "Ghost of Moby Dick."
The Daily Reporter (Dover, Ohio), December 14, 1964, "TV Key" preview of "Ghost of Moby Dick."
Broadcasting, December 14, 1964, *Voyage* at No. 25 in Nielsen Top 40.
Daily Variety, December 16, 1964, "The Ghost of Moby Dick" review, by "Daku."
Winona Daily News, December 20, 1964, "TV Key" Mailbag.
The Post-Crescent, December 21, 1964, "TV Scout" review of "Long Live the King."
Monessen Valley Independent, December 28, 1964, "TV Key Preview" review of *Voyage* episode "Hail to the Chief."
Troy Record, December 28, 1964, "TV Time" review of "Hail to the Chief."
Broadcasting, December 28, 1964, "Entertainment: Goal and Glory of William Self."
Tucson Daily Citizen, January 4, 1965, "TV Key Previews" review of *Voyage* episode "The Last Battle."
Portsmouth Times, January 4, 1964, "*Bonanza* Tops List of TV's '10 Worst,'" by Hal Humphrey.
The Pittsburgh Press (Pennsylvania), January 4, 1965, "TV Scout" review of "The Last Battle."
The Bridgeport Post, January 7, 1965, "TV Key Mailbag."
The Fresno Bee The Republican, January 10, 1965, "*Voyage* Series Is British Hit."
The Post-Crescent, January 11, 1965, "TV Scout" preview of *Voyage* episode "Mutiny."
Zanesville Times Recorder, January 11, 1965, UPI review of "Mutiny."
Arizona Republic, January 11, 1965, "TV Key Preview" review of "Mutiny."
Idaho State Journal, January 12, 1965, AP story, "Monday Night TV Watchers Face Decision," by Cynthia Lowry.
Tucson Daily Citizen, January 18, 1965, "TV Key" review of *Voyage* episode "Doomsday."
The News-Palladium, January 19, 1965, "Hollywood Today!," by Dick Kleiner.
Bakersfield Californian, January 23, 1965, "Atom Sub Leads Fan Mail Race."
The Fresno Bee The Republican, January 24, 1965, "David Really Lives it Up."
Syracuse Post-Standard, January 25, 1965, "TV Key Previews" review of "The Invaders."
Abilene Reporter-News, January 25, 1966, "TV Scout" review of "The Invaders."
Tucson Daily Citizen, January 26, 1965, "TV Scout" review of "The Invaders."
TV Guide, January 30, 1965, "Down to the Sea in a Hollywood Moat."
Monessen Valley Independent, February 1, 1965, "TV Key Preview" review of *Voyage* episode "The Indestructible Man."
Redlands Daily Facts, February 1, 1965, "Show Beat," by Dick Kleiner.
San Antonio Express, February 8, 1965, "TV Scout" preview of *Voyage* episode "The Buccaneer."
Variety, February 10, 1965, "1965-66 Networks' Checkerboard (First Draft)," and "*Variety*-ARB Syndication Chart."
Charleston Gazette, February 15, 1965, "TV Key Previews" review of *Voyage* episode "The Human Computer."
The Post-Crescent, February 15, 1965, "TV Scout" review of "The Human Computer."
Variety, February 24, 1965, "1965-66 Networks' Checkerboard (Semi-Finals)."
Daily Variety, February 24, 1965, "Nets Neck 'n' Neck in Tightest Nielsen Competish Ever" and TV review of *Voyage* episode "The Saboteur," by "Daku."

Cullman Times, February 28, 1965, preview of *Voyage* episode "Cradle of the Deep," by Bill Shelton.
Monessen Valley Independent, March 1, 1965, "TV Key" review of "Cradle of the Deep."
The Fresno Bee The Republican, March 7, 1965, "*Voyage* Series Goes Over Big On Japan TV."
Monessen Valley Independent, March 8, 1965, "TV Scout" preview of *Voyage* episode "The Amphibians."
Independent (Long Beach, California), March 8, 1965, "Tele-Vues," by Terry Vernom, with interview of Zale Parry.
The Star Press (Muncie, Indiana), March 8, 1965, synopsis for this nights *The Man from U.N.C.L.E.*
Daily Variety, March 9, 1965, A.C. Nielsen report with *Voyage* at No. 39.
Variety, March 10, 1965, "It's Paley & Schneider & Dann: Troika Revamps CBS' Fall Sked."
Edwardsville Intelligencer, March 15, 1965, "TV Scout" review of *Voyage* episode "The Exile."
The Orlando Sentinel (Florida), March 16, 1965, Sandra Hinson's review of "The Exhile."
The Tennessean (Nashville, Tennessee), March 22, 1965, "TV Scout" review of *Voyage* episode "The Creature."
The Pittsburgh Press (Pennsylvania), March 22, 1965, Vince Leonard's TV column, with reader's letter defending *Voyage*.
Press and Sun-Bulletin (Binghamton, New York), March 22, 1965, "TV Key" preview of "The Creature."
Monessen Valley Independent, March 29, 1965, "TV Scout" preview of *Voyage* episode "The Enemies."
Mansfield News Journal, March 29, 1965, "TV Key" preview of "The Enemies."
Long Beach Press-Telegram, March 29, 1965, "Tele-Vues," by Terry Vernon.
Variety, March 31, 1965, "1965-66 Networks' Checkerboard."
Provo Daily Herald, April 5, 1965, *Voyage* episode "The Secret of the Loch" press release.
Oneonta Star, April 5, 1965, "TV Key" review of *Voyage* episode "The Secret of the Loch."
Monessen Valley Independent, April 5, 1965, "TV Scout" preview of "The Secret of the Loch."
Abilene Reporter-News, April 8, 1965, "Ask TV Scout" letters column about *Outer Limits* cancelled; *Voyage* is only sci-fi non network TV; but pilots have been filmed for *Lost in Space* and *Star Trek*.
The Bridgeport Post, April 7, 1965, "TV Key Mailbag."
Phoenix Gazette, April 12, 1965, "TV Scout" preview of *Voyage* episode "The Condemned."
Tucson Daily Citizen, April 12, 1965, "TV Key" preview of "The Condemned."
Cullman Times, April 18, 1965, preview for *Voyage* episode "The Traitor," by Bill Shenton.
Lima News, April 19, 1965, "TV Scout" preview of "The Traitor."
TV Guide, May 1, 1965, *Voyage* series review by Cleveland Amory.
Variety, May 13, 1964, "*Variety*-ARB Syndicated Chart."
The News-Herald, May 17, 1965, "TV Scout" preview of "The Village of Guilt."
Daily Variety, June 1, 1965, "On All Channels: Allen's 1997 *Space* Shot 1st Primetime Cliffhanger," by Dave Kaufman.
TV Guide, June 19, 1965, "Well, Of Course, It Isn't Exactly *Hamlet*…," by Marian Dern.
Los Angeles Times, July 4, 1965, "Smooth Sailing for David Hedison," by Aleene MacMinn.
The Post-Crescent, July 19, 1965, "TV Scout" preview of *Voyage* episode "Hot Line."
Abilene Reporter-News, July 26, 1965, "TV Scout" preview of *Voyage* episode "The Saboteur."
Variety, July 29, 1965, "The Season's Nielsen Wrap-up."
Quad-City Times (Davenport, Iowa), August 2, 1965, "TV Key" pix for "The Amphibians."
The Ogden Standard-Examiner (Ogden, Utah), August 2m 1965, "TV Revue and Prevue" for "The Amphibians."
Irwin Allen Sci Fi Journal, #13, 1981, "A Brief Interview with Del Monroe," by Joel Eisner.
Starlog, July 1986, "David Hedison: Submarine Hero," by Mike Clark.
Starlog, October 1990, "They Wrote Land of the Giants," by Mark Phillips, and "Misplaced Among the Stars," by Mike Clark.
LISFAN6, 1990, "Interview: Simon Wincelberg," by Flint Mitchell; "Interview: Robert Drasnin," by Flint Mitchell; "Interview: Gerald Fried," by Flint Mitchell; "Interview: Paul Zastupnevich," by Flint Mitchell.
Starlog, March 1992, "The Master of Disaster," by Mike Clark.
Starlog, June 1992, "Captain of Television," by Pat Jankiewicz.
Starlog, August 1992, "Giant Jellyfish & Time-Lost Dinosaurs," by Mark Phillips.
Starlog, September 1992, "Giant Jellyfish & Time-Lost Dinosaurs, Part 2," by Mark Phillips.
Starlog, October 1992, "Giant Jellyfish & Time-Lost Dinosaurs, Part 3," by Mark Phillips.
Starlog, February 1993, "Designing Man," by Mike Clark.
Starlog, May 1993, "Space Duty," by Tom Weaver.
Starlog, August 1993, "The Oldest Working Screenwriter Explains It All," by Tom Weaver.
Starlog, November 1993, "The Life of Riley," by Mark Phillips.
Starlog, April 1994, "The Man in the Bubble-Headed Mask," by Tom Weaver.
Starlog Platinum, 1994, "Voyages Long Past," by Mark Phillips.
TV Collector magazine, February 1999, "Do You Remember…" by Mark Phillips.
Filmfax, 2001, "Charting a *Voyage to the Bottom of the Sea*!, by Mark Phillips.
Starlog Yearbook, February 2003, "Man Down Under," by Mark Phillips.

Quote Index:

Abbott, L.B.	LBA-SE84. *Special Effects: Wire, Tape and Rubber Band Style*, by L.B. Abbott (ASC Press, 1984)
Allen, Irwin	IA-TV48. *TELE-Views* magazine, November 26, 1948. "Stars Are Coming Your Way!", by Albert H. Grogan.
Allen, Irwin	IA-DN53. *Daily News* (Los Angeles), January 20, 1953, "Friends in *The Sea Around Us*," by David Bongard.
Allen, Irwin	IA-UP53. United Press wire story: "Scientists in 14 Countries Took Pictures for Hollywood Film, *The Sea Around Us*", in *The Lubbock Avalanche-Journal*, February 15, 1953.
Allen, Irwin	IA-UP53-2. United Press syndicated article, April 1953, "Award-Winning Film Sea Cost RKO Studio $200,000."
Allen, Irwin	IA-CE53. *The Cincinnati Enquirer*, July 5, 1953, UP wire storey: "Cast of Fish Wins Him Award for First Movie," by Vernon Scott.
Allen, Irwin	IA-NYT55. *The New York Times*, February 13, 1955, "From Primordial Ooze to Primates," by Oscar Godbout.
Allen, Irwin	IA-V56. *Variety*, March 16, 1956, "Nature Widens '7 Basic Plots'," by Fred Hift.
Allen, Irwin	IA-LPT55. United Press wire story: "Hollywood's Newest Stars Made Entirely of Rubber," *The Logansport Pharos-Tribune*, April 27, 1955.
Allen, Irwin	IA-UP56. United Press wire story: "Science Goes to Hollywood," from *Daily Independent Journal*, May 18, 1956.
Allen, Irwin	IA-AR56. *Arizona Republic*, May 27, 1956, "Irwin Allen Is Unusual As Director."
Allen, Irwin	IA-LAT56. *Los Angeles Times*, June 18, 1956, "*Animal World* Producer Faces Big Human Issue," by Edwin Schallert.
Allen, Irwin	IA-KG56. *Kalamazoo Gazette*, December 9, 1956, "Stars in Sky Talk and *The Story of Mankind* Becomes Star-Studded Movie."
Allen, Irwin	IA-PP56. *The Pittsburgh Press*, December 16, 1956, "Vilest Villains Assembling for Forthcoming Movie," by Harold Heffernan.
Allen, Irwin	IA-FES56. *The Franklin Evening Star* (Indiana), December 29, 1956, "Producer is Attempting to Stage *Story of Mankind* in Three Hours," by Joan Hanauer.
Allen, Irwin	IA-NW57. *Newsweek*, May 6, 1957, "Movies: Everything, Then Some."
Allen, Irwin	IA-NWT59. *New York Times*, January 11, 1959, "*Big Circus* Troupe Works to Equal Big Top's Authenticity and Color," by Thomas M. Pryor.
Allen, Irwin	IA-ADB59. *Anderson Daily Bulletin*, April 20, 1959, Louella O. Parson's column, regarding David Nelson in *The Big Circus*.
Allen, Irwin	IA-RMN59. *Rocky Mountain News*, June 30, 1959, "Producer 'Careful Shopper.'"
Allen, Irwin	IA-DP59. *Denver Post*, July 1, 1959, "Producer Allen Beats Drum for His Circus Extravaganza," by Larry Tajiri.
Allen, Irwin	IA-CDN59. Chicago Daily News syndicated story in *The Corpus Christi Caller-Times*, August 4, 1959, "Advice to Would-Be Actresses: 'Stay Home,'" by Pat Dalton.
Allen, Irwin	IA-EB61. *The Evening Bulletin*, June 13, 1961, "Director Must Rise Early for Today's Movies," by Rex Polier.
Allen, Irwin	IA-BG61. *The Boston Globe*, June 14, 1961, "Producer's Nightmare Science-Fiction Epic," by Kevin Kelly.
Allen, Irwin	IA-QPL61. *Quincy Patriot Ledger*, June 15, 1961, "*Bottom of Sea* Science Thriller, by Mabelle Fullerton.
Allen, Irwin	IA-CN61. *The Charlotte News*, June 21, 1961, "Pressure's On in Hollywood," by Brooks Yarborough.
Allen, Irwin	IA-CA61. *Chicago American*, June 21, 1961, "Irwin Allen Wooing Girl Movie Patrons," by Ann Masters.
Allen, Irwin	IA-AJC61. *Atlanta Journal-Constitution*, June 1961, "Producer Irwin Allen – His Movies Are Potboilers, But He's Honest About Them," by Betty Carrollton.
Allen, Irwin	IA-CSM. *Christian Science Monitor*, June 1961, "Technicolor Visions Mean Business to Irwin Allen," by Nora E. Taylor.
Allen, Irwin	IA-EH62. Syndicated newspaper article by Elinor Hughes, 1962.
Allen, Irwin	IA-IAPC62. Irwin Allen Papers Collection belonging to Kevin Burns, 1962 file for *Five Weeks in a Balloon* – newspaper clippings.
Allen, Irwin	IA-DV64. *Daily Variety*, May 5, 1964, "On All Channels: Irwin Allen 20-Year TVet," by Dave Kaufman.
Allen, Irwin	IA-TR64. *The Times Record*, October 17, 1964, "$1,000,000 Set

	Enjoyed in *Voyage*."
Allen, Irwin	IA-WDC64. *Waterloo Daily Courier*, October 25, 1964, "TV Keynotes: High Adventure Series," by Charles Witbeck.
Allen, Irwin	IA-DV65. *Daily Variety*, June 1, 1965, "On All Channels: Allen's 1997 *Space* Shot 1st Primetime Cliffhanger," by Dave Kaufman.
Allen, Irwin	IA-NYJM65. *New York Journal American* TV Magazine, October 31, 1965, "*Lost in Space* Proud of its Scenic Tricks," by Frank Judge.
Allen, Irwin	IA-TVG65. *TV Guide*, June 19, 1965, "Well, Of Course, It Isn't Exactly Hamlet…," by Marian Dern.
Allen, Irwin	IA-KG67. *Kingston Gleaner*, January 22, 1967, "Monsters, Adventure on JBC-TV."
Allen, Irwin	IA-DMN68. *Dallas Morning News*, August 21, 1968, "Now It's Giants," by Bevo Baker.
Allen, Irwin	IA-HT69. *Hartford News*, April 2, 1969, "Producer Irwin Allen Follows in Footsteps of Jules Verne," by Allen M. Widem.
Allen, Irwin	IA-LISF1. *LISFAN ONE*, 1981, "An Interview with Jonathan Harris," by Jeff Blair; foreword by Flint Mitchell.
Allen, Irwin	IA-SL85. *Starlog*, November 1985, "Irwin Allen Remembers *Lost in Space*," interviewed by Mike Clark.
Allen, Irwin	IA-SL92. *Starlog*, March 1992, "The Master of Disaster," by Mike Clark.
Allen, Irwin	IA-TC09. Thunderchild.com, July 2009, "Underwater Adventures with the Crew of the Seaview," by Linda A. Delaney.
Allan, Michael	**MA-AI15. Author interview, 2015.**
Anderson, John	JA-VTTBOTS. "Memories of Watching *Voyage to the Bottom of the Sea*," by Mark Phillips and posted online at Mike's Voyage to the Bottom of the Sea Zone, at vttbots.com.
Anna-Lisa	AL-VTTBOTS. Mike'svoyagetothebottomofthesea.zone at vttbots.com, interviewed by Mark Phillips.
Ansara, Michael	MS-LISF. *Lost in Space Forever*, by Joel Eisner and/or Barry Magen (1992, Windsong Publishing, Inc.)
Basehart, Richard	RB-ZTR45. *Zanesville Times Recorder*, February 13, 1945, "A Scot Who Was Never in Scotland."
Basehart, Richard	RB-BDE47. *Brooklyn Daily Eagle*, June 2, 1947, "Richard Basehart, Hedgerow Actor, Now on the First Rung of Film Stardom," by Herbert Cohn.
Basehart, Richard	RB-CST49. *Cumberland Sunday Times*, January 16, 1949, "Actor Son of Editor Hard to Interview, Columnist Finds," by Louella O. Parsons.
Basehart, Richard	RB-LAT49. *Los Angeles Times*, February 27, 1949, "His Killer Roles Horrify Basehart," by Philip K. Scheuer.
Basehart, Richard	RB-PG55. *Picturegoer* magazine, September 24, 1955, "Don't Misunderstand Me – Says Richard Basehart."
Basehart, Richard	RB-JA56. 1956 syndicated article "I Hated Hollywood," by Jerry Asher.
Basehart, Richard	RB-LAT57. *Los Angeles Times*, September 15, 1957, "Basehart Back After 4 Years," by Hedda Hopper.
Basehart, Richard	RB-AH59. *Anderson Herald*, December 26, 1959, "Foreign Living Can Damage Star's Career."
Basehart, Richard	RB-HT-60. *The* [Hammond] *Times*, March 22, 1960, "TV Keynotes: Richard Basehart is a Jet-Age Actor," by Harvey Pack.
Basehart, Richard	RB-PS61. *The Plain Speaker*, August 4, 1961, "Hollywood Today!" by Erskine Johnson.
Basehart, Richard	RB-ARN64. *Abilene Reporter-News*, July 7, 1964, "Submarine Rates as Scene-Stealer," by Erskine Johnson.
Basehart, Richard	RB-PPI64. (Petersburg) *Progress-Index*, September 17, 1964, "*Voyage* Actors Upstaged by Sub."
Basehart, Richard	RB-TR64. *The Times Record*, October 17, 1964, "$1,000,000 Set Enjoyed in *Voyage*."
Basehart, Richard	RB-BC64. *Bakersfield Californian*, November 28, 1964, "Fan Remembers Basehart in Role of Hitler."
Basehart, Richard	RB-MS65. *The Minneapolis Star* (Minnesota), "Basehart Levels as Agent Squirms," by Forrest Powers.
Basehart, Richard	RB-LAT66. (Levittown) *Courier Times*, December 5, 1964, "Basehart Plays *Voyage* for Real," by Edgar Penton.

Basehart, Richard	RB-HN64. *Hutchinson News*, December 5, 1964, "Candid Capsules," Basehart on ratings.
Basehart, Richard	RB-FITM64. 1964 syndicated newspaper story "Face in the Mirror."
Basehart, Richard	RB-TVG65. *TV Guide*, June 19, 1965, "Well, Of Course, It Isn't Exactly Hamlet…," by Marian Dern.
Basehart, Richard	RB-HDM65. *Hagerstown Daily Mail*, October 9, 1965, "There, at the Bottom of the Sea, Is…"
Basehart, Richard	RB-GT65. *The Gettysburg Times*, November 13, 1965, "Basehart Pleased By Colorful Additions to *Voyage*," by Ruth Thompson.
Basehart, Richard	RB-AR65. *Arizona Republic*, December 9, 1965, "Basehart Doing TV Series Basically for Money," by Harold Stern.
Basehart, Richard	RB-LAT66. *Los Angeles Times*, January 23, 1966, "Basehart Changes Mind About TV," by Hedda Hopper.
Basehart, Richard	RB-GG66. *The Gaston Gazette*, March 13, 1966, "Profile: Richard Basehart," by Tom McIntyre.
Basehart, Richard	RB-OSE66. *Ogden Standard-Examiner*, October 30, 1966, "Acting Breeds Complexity, Star Asserts."
Basehart, Richard	RB-DS66. On set interview by Dick Strout, 1966.
Basehart, Richard	RB-IMDB. Quote section, internet movie data base.
Becker, Terry	TB-ARN67. *Abilene Reporter-News*, September 17, 1967, "Seaview's Chief to Produce Movie," by Stan Maays.
Becker, Terry	TB-AR67. *Arizona Republic*, July 2, 1967, "He Likes Series Role," by Harvey Pack.
Becker, Terry	TB-SFTS2. *Science Fiction Television Series*, Volume 2, by Mark Phillips and Frank Garcia (1996, McFarland & Co.)
Becker, Terry	TB-TVC99. *The TV Collector* magazine, February 1999, "Do You Remember…" by Mark Phillips.
Becker, Terry	TB-S50. *Seaview: A 50th Anniversary Tribute to Voyage to the Bottom of the Sea*, by William E. Anchors and Frederick Barr (2012, Alpha Control Press).
Becker, Terry	TB-SE98. Convention appearance, Sheffield, England, 1998, as printed in *Seaview: 50th Anniversary Tribute to Voyage to the Bottom of the Sea*, by William E. Anchors, Jr. and Frederick Barr (2012, Alpha Control Press)
Bennett, Charles	CB-SL92. *Starlog*, August 1992, "Giant Jellyfish & Time-Lost Dinosaurs," by Mark Phillips.
Bennett, Charles	CB-SL92. *Starlog*, October 1992, "Giant Jellyfish & Time-Lost Dinosaurs, Part 3," by Mark Phillips.
Bennett, Charles	CB-SL93. *Starlog*, August 1993, "The Oldest Working Screenwriter Explains It All," by Tom Weaver.
Bennett, Charles	CB-LISTTS96. *Lost in Space: The True Story*, by Ed Shifres (1996, Windsor House Publishing)
Bennett, Charles	CB-HPIS14. *Hitchcock's Partner in Suspense: The Life of Screenwriter Charles Bennett*, by Charles Bennett (University Press of Kentucky, 2014)
Binns, Edward	EB-NAT65. *North Adams Transcript*, August 21, 1965, "Wonderful Swimmer."
Bloomfield, Robert	RB-SL92. *Starlog*, October 1992, "Giant Jellyfish & Time-Lost Dinosaurs, Part 3," by Mark Phillips.
Brinkley, Don	DB-SL92. *Starlog*, September 1992, "Giant Jellyfish & Time-Lost Dinosaurs, Part 2," by Mark Phillips.
Brown, Jr., Arthur	AB-TVC99. *The TV Collector* magazine, February 1999, "Do You Remember…" by Mark Phillips.
Bull, Richard	RB-S50. *Seaview: A 50th Anniversary Tribute to Voyage to the Bottom of the Sea*, by William E. Anchors and Frederick Barr (2012, Alpha Control Press).
Caillou, Alan	AC-SL92. *Starlog*, September 1992, "Giant Jellyfish & Time-Lost Dinosaurs, Part 2," by Mark Phillips.
Carmel, Roger C.	**RCC-AI. Author interview, 1982.**
Clark, Mike	**MC-AI15. Author interview.**

Comi, Paul	PC-AI13. Author interview.
Culliton, Pat	PC-S50. *Seaview: A 50th Anniversary Tribute to Voyage to the Bottom of the Sea*, by William E. Anchors and Frederick Barr (2012, Alpha Control Press).
D'Agosta, Joe	**JDA-AI15. Author interview, 2015.**
Darrow, Henry	HD-VTTBOTS. Mark Phillips interview, posted online at Mike's Voyage to the Bottom of the Sea Zone.
Didsbury, Ray	RD-FF01. *Filmfax*, 2001, "Charting a Voyage to the Bottom of the Sea!, by Mark Phillips.
Didsbury, Ray	RD-S50. *Seaview: A 50th Anniversary Tribute to Voyage to the Bottom of the Sea*, by William E. Anchors and Frederick Barr (2012, Alpha Control Press).
Domergue, Faith	FD-LAT50. *Los Angeles Times*, April 30, 1950, "Film to Shed Light on Mystery Woman," by Edwin Schallert.
Dowdell, Robert	RD-JG68. *Joplin Globe*, February 11, 1968, "Life Aboard 'Seaview' Not Really Easy."
Drasnin, Robert	RD-LISF6. *LISFAN6*, 1990, "Interview: Robert Drasnin," by Flint Mitchell.
Brinkley, Don	DB-SL92. *Starlog*, September 1992, "Giant Jellyfish & Time-Lost Dinosaurs, Part 2," by Mark Phillips.
Eden, Barbara	**BE-AI15. Author interview, 2015.**
Ellis, Sydney	SE-SL92. *Starlog*, October 1992, "Giant Jellyfish & Time-Lost Dinosaurs, Part 3," by Mark Phillips.
Ellison, Harlan	**HE-AI13. Author's interview.**
Fried, Gerald	GF-LISF6. *LISFAN6*, 1990, "Interview: Gerald Fried," by Flint Mitchell.
Gail, Al	AG-SL92. *Starlog*, March 1992, "The Master of Disaster," by Mike Clark.
Gail, Al.	AG-SL92. *Starlog*, October 1992, "Giant Jellyfish & Time-Lost Dinosaurs, Part 3," by Mark Phillips.
Gail, Al	AG-KB95. Interview by Kevin Burns, 1995.
Gaynor, Jock	JG-SFTS2. *Science Fiction Television Series*, Volume 2, by Mark Phillips and Frank Garcia (1996, McFarland & Co.).
Goldstone, James	JG-SCTV. *Science Fiction Television Series*, by Mark Phillips and Frank Garcia (McFarland & Co., 1994)
Goldstone, James	JG-SLP94. *Starlog Platinum*, 1994, "Voyages Long Past," by Mark Phillips.
Goldstone, James	*Irwin Allen Television Productions, 1964-1970: A Critical History*, by Jon Abbott (2006, McFarland & Company, Inc.)
Goldstone, James	JG-VTTBOTS. "Memories of Watching *Voyage to the Bottom of the Sea*," by Mark Phillips and posted online at vttbots.com.
Hagen, Kevin	KH-LISF. *Lost in Space Forever*, by Joel Eisner and/or Barry Magen (1992, Windsong Publishing, Inc.)
Hamner, Robert	RH-SL92. *Starlog*, August 1992, "Giant Jellyfish & Time-Lost Dinosaurs, Part 2," by Mark Phillips.
Hamner, Robert	RH-SL92. *Starlog*, October 1992, "Giant Jellyfish & Time-Lost Dinosaurs, Part 3," by Mark Phillips.
Hamner, Robert	RH-SL95. *Starlog*, November, 1995, "Space Families Found, Part Two," interviewed by Mark Phillips.
Hamner, Robert	RH-LISF. *Lost in Space Forever*, by Joel Eisner and/or Barry Magen (1992, Windsong Publishing, Inc.)
Hamner, Robert	RH-VTTBOTS. Mike'svoyagetothebottomofthesea.zone at vttbots.com, interviewed by Mark Phillips.

Harris, Harry	HH-KB15. Interviewed by Kevin Burns, 1995.
Harron, Don	DH-VTTBOTS. "Memories of Watching *Voyage to the Bottom of the Sea*," by Mark Phillips and posted online at Mike's Voyage to the Bottom of the Sea Zone.
Harron, Donald	DH-TVC99. *The TV Collector* magazine, February 1999, "Do You Remember…" by Mark Phillips.
Hayes, Raphael	RH-SL92. *Starlog*, September 1992, "Giant Jellyfish & Time-Lost Dinosaurs, Part 2," by Mark Phillips.
Hedison, David	DG-TR59. *The Troy Record*, June 19, 1959, "TV Keynotes: David Hedison Knows All About Pavement," by Harvey Pack.
Hedison, David	DH-UPI59. *New Castle News*, December 1, 1959, UPI story, "David Hedison Battling for Perfection in Series," by Vernon Scott.
Hedison, David	DH-LAT60. *Los Angeles Times*, July 3, 1960, "Hedison Gets Star Billing," by Hedda Hopper.
Hedison, David	DH-BDC64. *Bristol Daily-Courier*, May 30, 1964, "Actor Bets Future on New Series."
Hedison, David	DH-LAT65. *Los Angeles Times*, July 4, 1965, "Smooth Sailing for David Hedison," by Aleene MacMinn.
Hedison, David	DH-TVG66. *TV Guide*, July 16, 1966, "Torpedoed by Success."
Hedison, David	DH-DV66. *Daily Variety*, August 3, 1966, "Beasts Not Beauts in *Sea*; Affair of Man-Girl Off," by Dave Kaufman.
Hedison, David	DH-DS66. On-set interview by Dick Strout, 1966.
Hedison, David	DH-AR67. *Arizona Republic*, October 1, 1967, "Seaview's Captain Still Misses Girl-type Stowaways on Show," by Richard K. Shull.
Hedison, David	DH-LN67. *Lima News*, November 26, 1967, David Hedison remarks to Joan Crosby.
Hedison, David	DH-SL86. *Starlog*, July 1986, "David Hedison: Submarine Hero," by Mike Clark.
Hedison, David	DH-AG93. Convention appearance, as presented in *Seaview: A 50th Anniversary Tribute to Voyage to the Bottom of the Sea*, by William E. Anchors and Frederick Barr (2012, Alpha Control Press).
Hedison, David	DH-SFTS2. *Science Fiction Television Series*, Volume 2, by Mark Phillips and Frank Garcia (1996, McFarland & Co.)
Hedison, David	DH-MB05. Interview with Michael Bailey, 2005.
Hedison, David	DH-TCF07. Twentieth Century Fox bts material, 2007 DVD set.
Hedison, David	DH-CR10. CinemaRetro.com, 2010, interview with Herb Shadrak.
Hedison, David	DH-LAT11. From latimes.com, July, 2011, 'David Hedison Looks Back on Periscope," by Susan King.
Hedison, David	DH-S50. *Seaview: A 50th Anniversary Tribute to Voyage to the Bottom of the Sea*, by William E. Anchors and Frederick Barr (2012, Alpha Control Press)
Hedison, David	DH-CB12. Cultbox.co.uk, "David Hedison, James Bond, *Voyage to the Bottom of the Sea*, by William Martin.
Hedison, David	DH-CFTV. ClassicFilmTVCafe.com, 2013. "David Hedison Talks with Café."
Hedison, David	DH-DM13. Diaboliquemagazine.com, 2013, interviewed by Harvey Chartrand.
Hedison, David	DH-VTTBOTS. Interviewed by Mark Phillips, posted by Mike'sVoyageToTheBottomOfTheSea.zone at vttbots.com.
Hedison, David	**DH-P17. Interviewed on behalf of Prometheus Entertainment for this project by Mike Clark, November 2017.**
Homeier, Skip	SH-WFT68. *Wichita Falls Times*, March 10, 1968, "Skip Started as Mean Brat."
Hughes, Howard	HH-DV52. *Daily Variety*, April 7, 1952, "RKO Lot Personnel Cut to 375."
Hunter, Lew	**LH-AI15. Author interview, 2015.**
Jolly, Stan	SJ-20th-67. 20th Century Fox Press Release, 1967.
Juran, Nathan	NJ-LISF. *Lost in Space Forever*, by Joel Eisner and/or Barry Magen (1992, Windsong Publishing, Inc.)
Landau, Richard	RL-SL92. *Starlog*, August 1992, "Giant Jellyfish & Time-Lost Dinosaurs," by Mark Phillips.

La Tourette, Frank	FLT-GBPG-56. *Green Bay Press-Gazette* (Wisconsin), March 9, 1956, "Caesarian Birth Makes TV History on *Medic*," by Aline Mosby.
La Tourette, Frank	FLT-DAC56. *Democrat and Chronicle* (Rochester, New York), March 11, 1956, UPI wire story: "TV Medic Off; Spellman Blamed."
La Tourette, Frank	FLT-MS58. *The Marion Star* (Ohio), May 20, 1958, "Radio and Television," by Marie Torre.
Leader, Tony	TL-LISF. *Lost in Space Forever*, by Joel Eisner and/or Barry Magen (1992, Windsong Publishing, Inc.)
Lewis, Derek	**DE-AI18. Author interview, January 2018.**
Lindsey, George	GL-SFTS2. *Science Fiction Television Series*, Volume 2, by Mark Phillips and Frank Garcia (1996, McFarland & Co.)
Lopez, Marco	ML-TVC99. *The TV Collector* magazine, February 1999, "Do You Remember…" by Mark Phillips.
Luna, BarBara	**BL-AI15. Author interview, 2015.**
Marlo, Steve	**SM-AI15. Author interview, 2015.**
Marx, Harpo	HM-AR56. *Arizona Republic*, December 30, 1956, "Marx Brothers Make Another Picture Together."
Mature, Victor	VM-ES53. *The Evening Standard* (Uniontown, Pennsylvania), August 6, 1953, "Hollywood Roundup" by Jimmy Fidler.
Mature, Victor	VM-CCCT53. *The Corpus Christi Caller-Times* (Texas), September 8, 1953, by James Bacon.
McGreevey, John	JM-SL92. *Starlog*, August 1992, "Giant Jellyfish & Time-Lost Dinosaurs," by Mark Phillips.
McKeand, Nigel	NM-TVC99. *The TV Collector* magazine, February 1999, "Do You Remember…" by Mark Phillips.
Melchior, Ib J.	IJM-LISTTS96. Interviewed by Scott Halper on TV program *Around the Mind Bend*, as printed in *Lost in Space: The True Story*, by Ed Shifres (1996, Windsor House Publishing).
Meriwether, Lee	**LM-AI15. Author interview, 2015.**
Merlin, Jan	JM-VTTBOTS. Mike'svoyagetothebottomofthesea.zone at vttbots.com, interviewed by Mark Phillips.
Meyer, Gerald	GR-SFTS2. *Science Fiction Television Series*, Volume 2, by Mark Phillips and Frank Garcia (1996, McFarland & Co.)
Meyer, Gerald	GM-VTTBOTS. Mike'svoyagetothebottomofthesea.zone at vttbots.com, interviewed by Mark Phillips.
Mintz, Robert	RM-VTTBOTS. Mike'svoyagetothebottomofthesea.zone at vttbots.com, interviewed by Mark Phillips.
Mohr, Gerald	GM-SHJ66. *Syracuse Herald-Journal*, December 11, 1966, "Mohr's 'Heavy'."
Monroe, Del	DM-IASFJ13-81. *Irwin Allen Sci Fi Journal*, #13, 1981, "A Brief Interview with Del Monroe," by Joel Eisner.
Monroe, Del	DM-SE98. Convention appearance, Sheffield, England, 1998, as printed in *Seaview: 50th Anniversary Tribute to Voyage to the Bottom of the Sea*, by William E. Anchors, Jr. and Frederick Barr (2012, Alpha Control Press)
Monroe, Del	DM-SLY03. *Starlog Yearbook*, February 2003, "Man Down Under," by Mark Phillips.
Moore, Thomas	TM-SFTS2. *Science Fiction Television Series*, Volume 2, by Mark Phillips and Frank Garcia (1996, McFarland & Co.)
Mullally, Donn	DM-SL92. *Starlog*, October 1992, "Giant Jellyfish & Time-Lost Dinosaurs, Part 3," by Mark Phillips.

Mumy, Bill	**BM-AI15. Author interview, 2015.**
Parry, Zale	ZP-I65. "Tele-Vues," by Terry Vernon, from *Independent* (Long Beach, California), March 8, 1965.
Parry, Zale	ZP-VTTBOTS. "Memories of Watching *Voyage to the Bottom of the Sea*," by Mark Phillips and posted online at vttbots.com.
Pate, Michael	MP-SFTS2. *Science Fiction Television Series*, Volume 2, by Mark Phillips and Frank Garcia (1996, McFarland & Co.)
Pate, Michael	MP-TVC99. *The TV Collector* magazine, February 1999, "Do You Remember…" by Mark Phillips.
Penn, Leo	LP-SL92. *Starlog*, June 1992, "Captain of Television," by Pat Jankiewicz.
Perry, Elizabeth	EP-VTTBOTS. Interview by Mark Phillips posted on Mike's Voyage to the Bottom of the Sea Zone at vttbots,com.
Pine, Phillip	PP-VTTBOTS. Interview by Mark Phillips posted on Mike's Voyage to the Bottom of the Sea Zone at vttbots,com.
Polito, Gene	GP-LISF5. *LISFAN5*, 1988, "Interview with Gene Polito," by Flint Mitchell.
Priest, Pat	PP-SFTS2. *Science Fiction Television Series*, Volume 2, by Mark Phillips and Frank Garcia (1996, McFarland & Co.)
Robbie, Seymour	SR-SL95. *Starlog*, "Space Families Found, Part Two," interviewed by Mark Phillips.
Robotham, George	GR-SFTS2. *Science Fiction Television Series*, Volume 2, by Mark Phillips and Frank Garcia (1996, McFarland & Co.)
Robotham, George	GR-TVC99. *The TV Collector* magazine, February 1999, "Do You Remember…" by Mark Phillips.
Roley, Sutton	SR-SL95. *Starlog*, November, 1995, "Space Families Found, Part Two," interviewed by Mark Phillips.
Roley, Sutton	SM-SFTS2. *Science Fiction Television Series*, Volume 2, by Mark Phillips and Frank Garcia (1996, McFarland & Co.)
Russell, Jane	JR-IS48. *The Independent Star* (Indianapolis, Indiana), November 21, 1948, "Jane Russell Boom Comes After 8 Years of Big Pay, Few Films," by Sheilah Graham.
Rush, Herman	**HR-AI15. Author interview, 2015.**
Scala, Gia	GS-TVG65. *TV Guide*, October 9, 1966, "While Strolling Through the Whale One Day…"
Self, William	WS-LAT64. *Los Angeles Times*, June 28, 1964, "Fox Suddenly Jumps into the Series Picture," by Cecil Smith.
Self, William	WS-B64. *Broadcasting*, December 28, 1964, "Entertainment: Goal and Glory of William Self."
Slade, Mark	MS-SFTS2. *Science Fiction Television Series*, Volume 2, by Mark Phillips and Frank Garcia (1996, McFarland & Co.)
Slade, Mark	MS-TVC. *The TV Collector* magazine, February 1999, "Do You Remember…" by Mark Phillips.
Slade, Mark	MS-VTTBOTS. Mark Phillips' interview posted at Mike'svoyagetothebottomofthesea.zone at vttbots.com.
Stark, Sheldon	SS-SL92. *Starlog*, August 1992, "Giant Jellyfish & Time-Lost Dinosaurs," by Mark Phillips.
Stark, Sheldon	SS-SFTS2. *Science Fiction Television Series*, Volume 2, by Mark Phillips and Frank Garcia (1996, McFarland & Co.)
Stewart, Larry	LS-LISF. *Lost in Space Forever*, by Joel Eisner and/or Barry Magen (1992, Windsong Publishing, Inc.)
Stewart, Larry	LS-SFTS2. *Science Fiction Television Series*, Volume 2, by Mark Phillips and Frank Garcia (1996, McFarland & Co.)

Stewart, Margaret	MS-SL95. *Starlog*, October 1995, "Space Family Lost, Part One," interviewed by Mark Phillips.
Stone, Ezra	ES-LISF5. *LISFAN5*, 1988, "Interview: Ezra Stone," by Flint Mitchell.
Stone, Ezra	ES-SL95. *Starlog*, "Space Families Found, Part Two," interviewed by Mark Phillips.
Swink, George	GS-LISF. *Lost in Space Forever*, by Joel Eisner and/or Barry Magen (1992, Windsong Publishing, Inc.)
Tait, Bobby	BT-HC65. *Hartford Courant* (Connecticut), October 3, 1965, "$15,000 'Quake on Voyage."
Tata, Joe E.	JT-SFTS2. *Science Fiction Television Series*, by Mark Phillips and Frank Garcia.
Tata, Joe E.	JT-LISF. *Lost in Space Forever*, by Joel Eisner and/or Barry Magen (1992, Windsong Publishing, Inc.)
Tata, Joe E.	JT-TVC99. *TV Collector* magazine, February 1999, "Do You Remember…" by Mark Phillips.
Throne, Malachi	**MT-AI. Author's interview, 2011.**
Throne, Malachi	MT-SL93. *Starlog*, May 1993, "Throne of Villainy," interviewed by Joel Eisner.
Throne, Malachi	*LISFAN8*, 1994, "Interview: Malachi Throne," by Flint Mitchell.
Turley, Jack	JT-SL90. *Starlog*, October 1990, "They Wrote for Giants," interviewed by Mark Phillips.
Turley, Jack	JT-LISF8. *LISFAN8*, 1994, "Interview: Jack Turley," by Flint Mitchell.
Vollaerts, Rik	RV-ST68. *Star Trek* show files, UCLA Special Collections, February 21, 1968.
Welch, William	WW-TWTD75. *Talks with the Dead*, by William Welch (Pinnacle Books, 1975)
Whiton, James	JW-VTTBOTS. Mike'svoyagetothebottomofthesea.zone at vttbots.com, interviewed by Mark Phillips.
Wickerman, Sven	SW-VTTBOTS. Mike'svoyagetothebottomofthesea.zone at vttbots.com, interviewed by Mark Phillips.
Wilber, Carey	CW-LIS25. *Lost in Space 25th Anniversary Tribute Book*, by James Van Hise (1990, Pioneer Books)
Wilson, Marie	MW-IR51. *The Independent Record* (Helena, Montana), May 7, 1951, "In Hollywood," by Erskine Johnson.
Wincelberg, Shimon	SW-LISF. *Lost in Space Forever*, by Joel Eisner and/or Barry Magen (1992, Windsong Publishing, Inc.)
Wincelberg, Shimon	SW-SL85. *Starlog*, November 1985, "Irwin Allen Remembers *Lost in Space*," interviewed by Mike Clark.
Wincelberg, Shimon	SW-SL90. *Starlog*, October 1990, "Misplaced Among the Stars," interviewed by Mike Clark.
Wincelberg, Shimon	SW-LISF6. *LISFAN6*, 1990, "Interview: Simon Wincelberg," by Flint Mitchell.
Wincelberg, Shimon	SW-SL95. *Starlog*, November, 1995, "Space Families Found, Part Two," interviewed by Mark Phillips.
Woodfield, Lili Glinski	LGW-LISF. *Lost in Space Forever*, by Joel Eisner and/or Barry Magen (1992, Windsong Publishing, Inc.)
Woodfield, William Read	WRW-SL92. *Starlog*, August 1992, "Giant Jellyfish & Time-Lost Dinosaurs," by Mark Phillips.
Woodfield, William Read	WRW-SL92-2. *Starlog*, August 1992, "Giant Jellyfish & Time-Lost Dinosaurs, Part 2," by Mark Phillips.
Woodfield, William Read	WRW-SFTS2. *Science Fiction Television Series*, Volume 2, by Mark Phillips and Frank Garcia (1996, McFarland & Co.)
Woodfield, William Read	WRW-LISF. *Lost in Space Forever*, by Joel Eisner and/or Barry Magen (1992, Windsong Publishing, Inc.)

Wright, Robert Vincent	RVW-SL92. *Starlog*, August 1992, "Giant Jellyfish & Time-Lost Dinosaurs, Part 2," by Mark Phillips.
Wright, Robert Vincent	RVW. *Science Fiction Television Series*, Volume 2, by Mark Phillips and Frank Garcia (1996, McFarland & Co.)
Wright, Robert Vincent	RVW. *Irwin Allen Television Productions, 1964-1970*.
York, Francine	**FY-AI.** **Author's interview, February 2015.**
Zastupnevich, Paul	PZ-WDN66. *The Winona Daily News*, April 10, 1966, "Monsters Figure in Ratings Battle," by Charles Witbeck.
Zastupnevich, Paul	PZ-LISF6. *LISFAN6*, 1990, "Interview: Paul Zastupnevich," by Flint Mitchell.
Zastupnevich, Paul	PZ-LISF. *Lost in Space Forever*, by Joel Eisner and/or Barry Magen (1992, Windsong Publishing, Inc.)
Zastupnevich, Paul	PZ-SL93. *Starlog*, February 1993, "Designing Man," by Mike Clark.
Zastupnevich, Paul	PZ-KB95. Interviewed by Kevin Burns, 1995.
Zastupnevich, Paul	PZ-S50. *Seaview: A 50th Anniversary Tribute to Voyage to the Bottom of the Sea*, by William E. Anchors and Frederick Barr (2012, Alpha Control Press).

Printed in Great Britain
by Amazon